NICHOLSON

River Thames & the Southern Waterways

WATERWAYS GUIDE 7

CONTENTS

Key to map pages	4
General information for waterways users	6
Environmental guidance for boaters	12
General guidance for paddlers using the inland waterways	14
Basingstoke Canal	17
Bridgwater & Taunton Canal	32
Grand Western Canal	41
Exeter Ship Canal	48
Kennet & Avon Canal	58
River Ouse	110
River Thames	126
Wey & Arun Junction Canal and Arun Navigation	202
Wey & Godalming Navigations	219
Index	229

Published by Nicholson
An imprint of HarperCollins Publishers
Westerhill Road, Bishopbriggs, Glasgow G64 2QT
www.harpercollins.co.uk

HarperCollins Publishers
Macken House, 39/40 Mayor Street Upper, Dublin 1, D01 C9W8, Ireland

River Thames Guide first published by Nicholson 1969
This edition first published by Nicholson and Ordnance Survey 1997
New edition published by Nicholson 2000, 2003, 2006, 2009, 2012, 2014, 2017, 2021, 2025

© HarperCollins Publishers Ltd 2025
Maps © Collins Bartholomew

Map data © OpenStreetMap contributors
Contains OS data © Crown copyright and database right (2025)
Contains Sustrans data © licenced under Open Government Licence

The representation in this publication of a road, track or path is no evidence of the existence of a right of way.

Researched and written by Jonathan Mosse.
All photos © Jonathan Mosse.

Front cover photo: Above Keynsham Lock on the Kennet & Avon, © Jonathan Mosse.

The publishers gratefully acknowledge the assistance given by Canal & River Trust and their staff in the preparation of this guide. Grateful thanks are also due to the Environment Agency, members of the Sustainable Boating Group of the Inland Waterways Association, Paddle UK, National Trails, and CAMRA representatives and branch members.

All rights reserved. No part of this publication may be reproduced, stored in a retrieval system, or transmitted, in any form or by any means, electronic, mechanical, photocopying, recording or otherwise without the prior permission in writing of the publisher and copyright owners.

Every care has been taken in the preparation of this guide. However, the Publisher accepts no responsibility whatsoever for any loss, damage, injury or inconvenience sustained or caused as a result of using this guide.

HarperCollins does not warrant that any website mentioned in this title will be provided uninterrupted, that any website will be error free, that defects will be corrected, or that the website or the server that makes it available are free of viruses or bugs. For full terms and conditions please refer to the site terms provided on the website.

A catalogue record for this book is available from the British Library.

Printed in Malaysia

ISBN 978-0-00-870992-1

10 9 8 7 6 5 4 3 2 1

This book contains FSC™ certified paper and other controlled sources to ensure responsible forest management.

For more information visit: www.harpercollins.co.uk/green

INTRODUCTION

Wending their quiet way through town and country, the inland navigations of Britain offer boaters, walkers and cyclists a unique insight into a fascinating, but once almost lost, world. When built this was the province of the boatmen and their families, who lived a mainly itinerant lifestyle: often colourful, to our eyes picturesque but, for them, remarkably harsh. Transporting the nation's goods during the late 1700s and early 1800s, negotiating locks, traversing aqueducts and passing through long narrow tunnels, canals were the arteries of trade during the initial part of the industrial revolution.

Then the railways came: the waterways were eclipsed in a remarkably short time by a faster and more flexible transport system, and a steady decline began. In a desperate fight for survival canal tolls were cut, crews toiled for longer hours and worked the boats with their whole family living aboard. Canal companies merged, totally uneconomic waterways were abandoned, some were modernised but it was all to no avail. Large scale commercial carrying on inland waterways had reached the finale of its short life.

At the end of World War II a few enthusiasts roamed this hidden world and harboured a vision of what it could become: a living transport museum which stretched the length and breadth of the country; a place where people could spend their leisure time and, on just a few of the wider waterways, a still modestly viable transport system.

The restoration struggle began and, from modest beginnings, Britain's inland waterways are now seen as an irreplaceable part of the fabric of the nation. Long-abandoned waterways, once seen as an eyesore and a danger, are recognised for the valuable contribution they make to our quality of life, and restoration schemes are integrating them back into the network. Let us hope that the country's network of inland waterways continues to be cherished and well-used, maintained and developed as we move through the 21st century.

If you would like to comment on any aspect of the guides, please write to Nicholson Waterways Guides, HarperCollins Publishers, Westerhill Road, Bishopbriggs, Glasgow G64 2QT or email nicholson@harpercollins.co.uk.

Also available from **www.collins.co.uk/nicholson** :

NICHOLSON
Waterways guides and map

1. **Grand Union, Oxford & the South East**
2. **Severn, Avon & Birmingham**
3. **Birmingham & the Heart of England**
4. **Four Counties & the Welsh Canals**
5. **North West & the Pennines**
6. **Nottingham, York & the North East**
8. **Norfolk Broads**

Inland Waterways Map of Great Britain

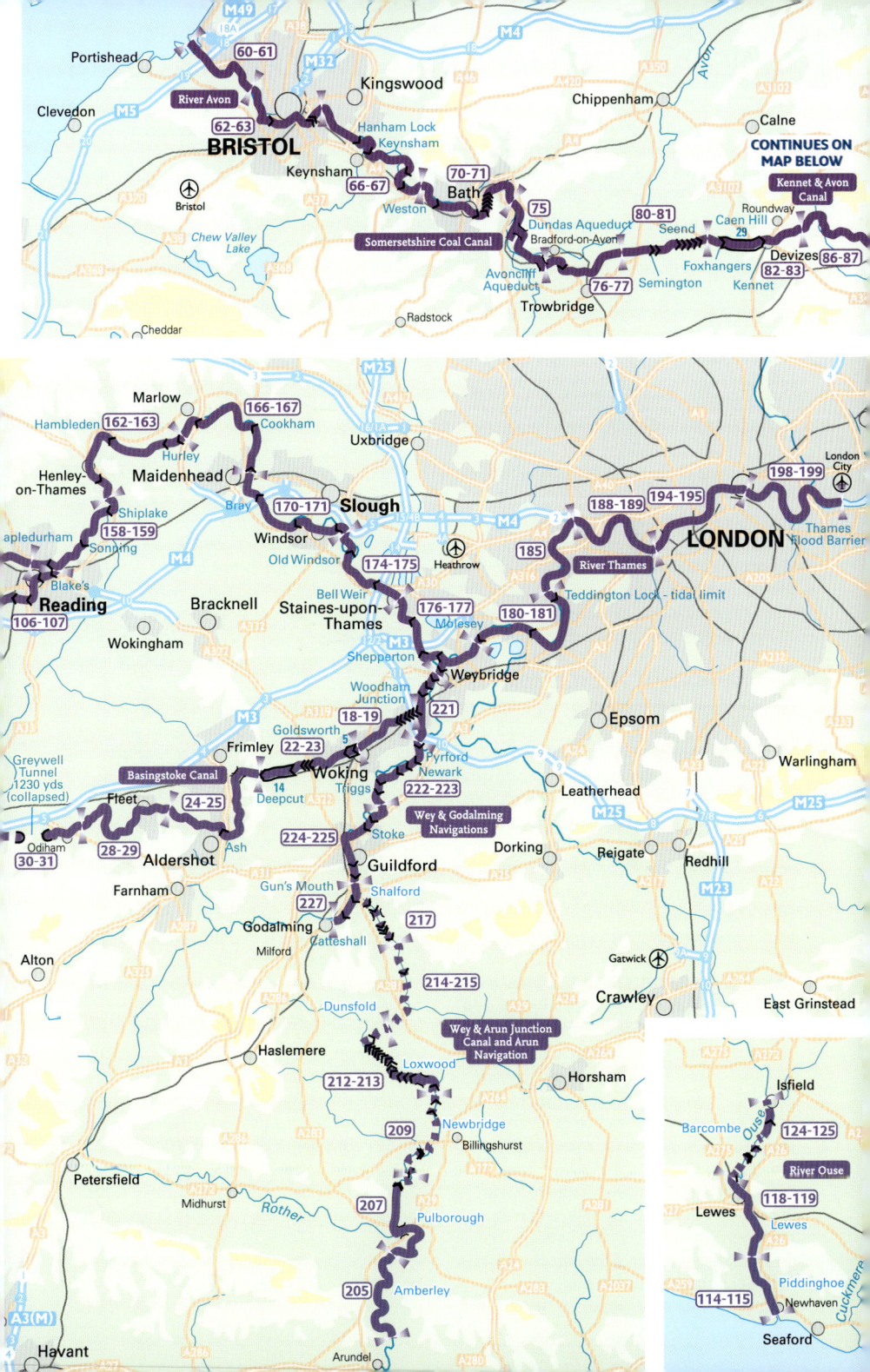

GENERAL INFORMATION FOR WATERWAYS USERS

Boaters, walkers, fishermen, cyclists and gongoozlers (on-lookers) all share in the enjoyment of our quite amazing waterway heritage. Canal & River Trust (CRT) and the Environment Agency, along with other navigation authorities, are empowered to develop, maintain and control this resource. A series of guides, codes, and regulations have come into existence over the years, evolving to match a burgeoning – and occasionally conflicting – demand. Set out in this section are key points as they relate to everyone wishing to enjoy the waterways.

The *Boater's Handbook* is available from all navigation authorities. It contains a complete range of safety information, boat-handling know-how, warning symbols and illustrations, and can be downloaded from www.canalrivertrust.org.uk/boating/go-boating/a-guide-to-boating/boaters-handbook. It is complimented by this excellent video: www.youtube.com/watch?v=lXn47JYXs44 and by www.canalrivertrust.org.uk/refresh/media/thumbnail/44024-waterway-code-for-boaters-anglers-and-unpowered-craft.pdf.

ENVIRONMENTALLY-FRIENDLY BOATING

Considerate and sustainable boating (*see* pages 12–13) usually go hand in hand. Enshrined within the byelaws of most navigation authorities is a requirement not to run your engine 20.00–08.00 so as not to disturb neighbouring boaters. This is not only inconsiderate, it is also damaging to the environment. Further details can be found at: www.waterways.org.uk/campaigns/sustainable-boating. In a similar vein it is worth noting that smoke control zones in towns and cities are gradually starting to apply to boat stoves.

CANAL & RIVER TRUST CUSTOMER SERVICES

The Customer Services Team is staffed *Mon-Fri 08.00-18.00 & Sat-Sun and B Hols 09.00-17.00*. The helpful staff will answer general enquiries and provide information about boat licensing, mooring, boating holidays and general activities on the waterways. They can be contacted on 0303 040 4040; customer.services@canalrivertrust.org.uk; Canal & River Trust, Head Office, National Waterways Museum, South Pier Road, Ellesmere Port CH65 4FW. Visit www.canalrivertrust.org.uk for up to date information on almost every aspect of the inland waterways from news and events to moorings.

Emergency Helpline Available from Canal & River Trust outside normal office hours on weekdays and throughout weekends. If lives or property are at risk or there is danger of serious environmental contamination then immediately contact 0800 47 999 47; www.canalrivertrust.org.uk/contact-us/contacting-us-in-an-emergency.

ENVIRONMENT AGENCY

The Environment Agency (EA) manages around 600 miles of the country's rivers, including the Thames and the River Medway. For general enquiries or to obtain a copy of the *Boater's Handbook*, contact EA Customer Services at PO Box 544, Rotherham S60 1BY (03708 506 506; enquiries@environment-agency.gov.uk), open Mon-Fri 08.00-18.00. To find out about their work nationally (or to download a copy of the *Handbook*) and for lots of other useful information, visit www.gov.uk/government/organisations/environment-agency.

The website www.visitthames.co.uk provides lots on information on boating, walking, fishing and events on the river.

Incident Hotline The EA maintain an Incident Hotline. To report damage or danger to the natural environment, damage to structures or water escaping, telephone 0800 80 70 60. For Floodline, telephone 0345 988 1188.

LICENSING – BOATS

The majority of the navigations covered in this book are controlled by CRT and the EA and are managed on a day-to-day basis by regional offices (details of these are in the introductions to each waterway). All craft using the inland waterways must be licensed and charges are based on the dimensions of the craft. In a few cases, these include reciprocal agreements with other waterway authorities (as indicated in the text). CRT and the EA offer an optional Gold Licence which covers unlimited navigation on the waterways of both authorities. Permits for permanent mooring on CRT waterways are issued by CRT.

Contact Canal & River Trust Boat Licensing Team on 0303 040 4040; www.canalrivertrust.org.uk/boating/licence-your-boat; Canal & River Trust Licensing Team, PO Box 162, Leeds LS9 1AX.

For the Thames and River Medway contact the Environment Agency as above.

BOAT SAFETY SCHEME

CRT and the EA operate the Boat Safety Scheme aimed at maintaining boat safety standards and featuring four-yearly testing, primarily intended to identify third party risks. A Boat Safety Scheme Certificate (for new boats, a Declaration of Conformity) is necessary to obtain a craft licence from all navigation authorities. CRT also requires proof of insurance for Third Party Liability for a minimum of £2,000,000 for powered boats. Contact details are: 0333 202 1000; www.boatsafetyscheme.org; Boat Safety Scheme, National Waterways Museum, South Pier Road, Ellesmere Port CH65 4FW. The website offers useful advice on preventing fires and avoiding carbon monoxide poisoning.

PADDLING

(see also pages 14–15)

All portable, unpowered craft such as canoes, kayaks, dinghies, rowing boats, paddleboards and even light inflatable craft require a license to access the majority of British waterways. A Paddle UK "waterway licence" provides the best value for money at less than 50% of the cost of individual licenses from the Canal and River Trust, the Environment Agency and the Broads Authority and gives access to over 5000 miles of inland waterways. A wide range of information is also available from Paddle UK (www.paddleuk.org.uk) and www.gopaddling.info is a useful source of launch points. More detailed, canal specific information is available from the Canal and River Trust at www.canalrivertrust.org.uk/things-to-do/canoeing-and-kayaking-near-me, while paddling in tunnels is covered at www.canalrivertrust.org.uk/things-to-do/canoeing-and-kayaking-near-me/canoeing-through-tunnels.

Know your **Paddlers Code**: there are three simple steps to follow for everyone to enjoy paddling and the countryside: Respect, Protect, Enjoy. Find out more at www.paddlerscode.info. For your personal safety observe the RNLI-backed campaign at www.gopaddling.info/safe-paddle-summer and if you want to meet like-minded paddlers, you could always join a club: www.gopaddling.info/find-paddling-clubs.

INVASIVE NON NATIVE SPECIES

Paddle UK, alongside inland waterways navigation authorities, is committed to protecting the environment, particularly when it comes to tackling invasive non-native species. The simple three-point code, common to all craft, is:

Check – check your boats, equipment and clothing for living organisms. Remove anything you find and leave it at the site.

Clean – clean everything thoroughly as soon as you can (using hot water if possible), paying attention to the inside of your boat and areas that are damp and hard to access.

Dry – drain water from every part of your boat and dry with a sponge or towel before leaving the site. Dry everything thoroughly for as long as possible. Some invasive plants and animals can survive for two weeks in damp conditions.

It is also usually a requirement that all boats that are transported from one area of the country to another follow the same procedure before re-launching.

TOWPATHS

Few, if any, artificial cuts or canals in this country are without an intact towpath accessible to the walker at least and the Thames is the only river in the country with a designated National Trail along its path from source to sea (for more information visit www.nationaltrail.co.uk). However, on some other river navigations, towpaths have on occasion fallen into disuse or, sometimes, been lost to erosion. The indication of a towpath in this guide does not necessarily imply a public right of way. Cyclists are asked to abide by the Towpath Code available at www.canalrivertrust.org.uk/things-to-do/cycling, which also details an excellent selection of rides. Horse riding, motorcycling and eScooters are forbidden on all towpaths. An excellent short video outlines the Towpath Code and explains the rationale behind it: www.youtube.com/watch?v=JBgElUNZPxg.

STOPPAGES

CRT and the EA both publish winter stoppage programmes which are sent out to all licence holders, boatyards and hire companies. Inevitably, emergencies occur necessitating the unexpected closure of a waterway, perhaps during the peak season. You can check for stoppages on individual waterways between specific dates on www.canalrivertrust.org.uk/notices/winter-stoppages, lockside noticeboards or by telephoning 0303 040 4040; for stoppages and river conditions on the Thames, visit www.gov.uk/guidance/river-thames-restrictions-and-closures.

NAVIGATION AUTHORITIES AND WATERWAYS SOCIETIES

Most inland navigations are managed by CRT or the EA, but there are several other navigation authorities. For details of these, contact the Association of Inland Navigation Authorities on 0844 335 1650 or visit www.aina.org.uk. The boater, conditioned perhaps by the uniformity of our national road network, should be sensitive to the need to observe different codes and operating practices.

The Canal & River Trust is a charity set up to care for England and Wales' legacy of 200-year-old waterways, holding them in trust for the nation forever, and is linked with an ombudsman. CRT has a comprehensive complaints procedure and a free explanatory leaflet is available from Customer Services. Problems and complaints should be addressed to the Regional Waterways Manager in the first instance. For more information, visit their website.

The EA is the national body, sponsored by the Department for Environment, Food and Rural Affairs, to manage the quality of air, land and water in England and Wales. For more information, visit www.gov.uk/government/organisations/department-for-environment-food-rural-affairs.

The Inland Waterways Association (IWA) campaigns for the use, maintenance and restoration of Britain's inland waterways, through branches all over the country. For more information, contact them on 01494 783453; iwa@waterways.org.uk; www.waterways.org.uk; The Inland Waterways Association, Unit 16B First Floor, Chiltern Court, Asheridge Road, Chesham HP5 2PX. Their website has a huge amount of information of interest to boaters, including comprehensive details of the many and varied waterways societies, together with an ever-expanding section devoted to all aspects of sustainable boating.

STARTING OUT

Extensive information and advice on booking a boating holiday is available from the Inland Waterways Association, www.visitthames.co.uk and www.canalrivertrust.org.uk/boat-holidays. Please book a waterway holiday from a licensed operator – this way you can be sure that you have proper insurance cover, service and support during your holiday. It is illegal for private boat owners to hire out their craft. If you are hiring a holiday craft for the first time, the boatyard will brief you thoroughly. Take notes, follow their instructions and do ask if there is anything you do not understand. *See* page 6 for books and videos.

MORE INFORMATION

An internet search will reveal many websites on the inland waterways. Those listed below are just a small sample:

Accessible Waterways Association (www.awa-uk.org.uk) is independent of all waterways authorities and has been set up to make the waterways more accessible for everyone.

National Community Boats Association is a national charity and training provider, supporting community boat projects and encouraging more people to access the inland waterways. Contact 07899 822113; www.national-cba.co.uk.

National Association of Boat Owners is dedicated to promoting the interests of private boaters on Britain's canals and rivers. Visit www.nabo.org.uk.

National Bargee Travellers Association seeks to represent the interests of itinerant, liveaboard boaters. Contact 0118 321 4128; www.bargee-traveller.org.uk.

www.canalplan.org.uk is an online journey-planner and gazetteer for the inland waterways.
www.canals.com is a valuable source of information for cruising the canals, with loads of links to canal and waterways related websites.

GENERAL CRUISING NOTES

Most canals and rivers are saucer shaped, being deepest at the middle. Few canals have more than 3-4ft of water and many have much less. Keep to the centre of the channel except on bends, where the deepest water is on the outside of the bend. When you meet another boat, keep to the right, slow down and aim to miss the approaching craft by a couple of yards. If you meet a loaded commercial boat keep right out of the way and be prepared to follow his instructions. Do not assume that you should pass on the right. If you meet a boat being towed from the bank, pass it on the outside. When overtaking, keep the other boat on your right side.

Some CRT and EA facilities are operated by pre-paid cards, obtainable from CRT and EA regional and local waterways offices, lock keepers and boatyards. Weekend visitors should purchase cards in advance. A handcuff/anti-vandal key is commonly used on locks where vandalism is a problem. A watermate/sanitary key opens sanitary stations, waterpoints and some bridges and locks. Both keys and pre-paid cards can be obtained via CRT Customer Service Centre.

Safety

Boating is a safe pastime. However, it makes sense to take simple safety precautions, particularly if you have children aboard.

- Never drink and drive a boat – it may travel slowly, but it weighs many tons.
- Be careful with naked flames and never leave the boat with the hob or oven lit. Familiarise yourself and your crew with the location and operation of the fire extinguishers.
- Never block ventilation grills. Boats are enclosed spaces and levels of carbon monoxide can build up from faulty appliances or just from using the cooker.
- Never operate portable generators inside a boat and ensure that you meet the relevant Boat Safety Scheme regulations when storing the fuel.
- Be careful along the bank and around locks. Slipping from the bank might only give you a cold-water soaking, but falling from the side of, or into a lock is more dangerous. Beware of slippery or rough ground.
- Remember that fingers and toes are precious! If a major collision is imminent, never try to fend off with your hands or feet; and always keep hands and arms inside the boat.
- Weil's disease is a particularly dangerous infection present in water which can attack the central nervous system and major organs. It is caused by bacteria entering the bloodstream through cuts and broken skin, and the eyes, nose and mouth. The flu-like symptoms occur two-four weeks after exposure. Always wash your hands thoroughly after contact with the water. Visit www.leptospirosis.org for details.

Speed

There is a general speed limit of 4 mph on most CRT canals and 5 mph on the Thames. There is no need to go any faster – the faster you go, the bigger a wave the boat creates: if your wash is breaking against the bank, causing large waves or throwing moored boats around, slow down. Slow down also when passing engineering works and anglers; when there is a lot of floating rubbish on the water (try to drift over obvious obstructions in neutral); when approaching blind corners, narrow bridges and junctions.

Mooring

Generally you may moor where you wish on CRT waterways, as long as you are *not causing an obstruction*. Do not moor in a winding hole or junction, the approaches to a lock or tunnel, or at a water point or sanitary station. On the Thames, generally you have a right to anchor for *24 hours* in one place provided no obstruction is caused, however you will need explicit permission from the land owner to moor. There are official mooring sites along the length of the river; those provided by the EA are free, the others you will need to pay for. Your boat should carry metal mooring stakes, and these should be driven firmly into the ground with a mallet if there are no mooring rings. Do not stretch mooring lines across the towpath and take account of anyone who may walk past. Always consider the security of your boat when there is no one aboard.
On tideways and commercial waterways it is advisable to moor only at recognised sites, and allow for any rise or fall of the tide.

Bridges

On narrow canals slow down well in advance and aim to miss one side (usually the towpath side) by about 9 inches. *Keep everyone inboard when passing under bridges and ensure there is nothing on the roof of the boat that will hit the bridge.* If a boat is coming the other way, the craft nearest to the bridge has priority. Take special care with moveable structures – the crew member operating the bridge should be strong and heavy enough to hold it steady as the boat passes through.

Tunnels

Again, ensure that everyone is inboard. Make sure the tunnel is clear before you enter, and use your headlight. Check the instruction boards by the entrance and be aware that you may be sharing the tunnel with canoeists and paddleboarders. Consult www.canalrivertrust.org.uk/things-to-do/canoeing-and-kayaking-near-me/canoeing-through-tunnels for further deails.

Fuel

Diesel can be purchased from most boatyards and some CRT depots. To comply with HMRC regulations you must declare an appropriate split between propulsion and heating so that the correct level of VAT can be applied. However, few boatyards stock petrol. Where a garage is listed under a town or village's facilities, petrol (and DERV) are available. Electric boat recharging points are gradually making an appearance around the inland waterways system but they are some way off from being a regular feature or operated via a standardised payment system.

Pump out
Self-operated pump out facilities are available at a number of locations on the waterways network. These facilities are provided by CRT and can be operated via an 18-unit prepayment card. CRT account holders can buy these from the online shop or they are available from canalside CRT waterway offices and some marinas, boatyards, shops or cafés. The cards provide for one pump out or 18 units of electricity. In some areas CRT are trialling standard credit card readers in place of the current pre-payment systems.

Boatyards
Hire fleets are usually turned around at a weekend, making this a bad time to call in for services.

VHF Radio
The IWA recommends that all pleasure craft navigating the larger waterways used by freight carrying vessels, or any tidal navigation, should carry marine-band VHF radio and have a qualified radio operator on board.

PLANNING A CRUISE
Don't try to go too far too fast. Go slowly, don't be too ambitious, and enjoy the experience. Mileages indicated on the maps are for guidance only. A *rough* calculation of time taken to cover the ground is the lock-miles system:

Add the number of *miles* to the number of *locks* on your proposed journey, and divide the resulting figure by four. This will give you an approximate guide to the number of *hours* your travel will take.

TIDAL WATERWAYS
The typical steel narrow boat found on the inland waterways is totally unsuitable for cruising on exposed tidal water. However, passage is possible in most estuaries if careful consideration is given to the key factors of weather conditions, tides, crew experience, the condition of the boat and its equipment and, perhaps of overriding importance, the need to take expert advice. In many cases it will be prudent to employ the skilled services of a local pilot. Within the text, where inland navigations connect with a tidal waterway, details are given of sources of advice and pilotage. It is also essential to inform your insurance company of your intention to navigate on tidal waterways as they may very well have special requirements or wish to levy an additional premium. This guide is to the inland waterways of Britain and therefore recognises that tideways – and especially estuaries – require a different approach and many additional skills. We do not hesitate to draw the boater's attention to the appropriate source material.

LOCKS AND THEIR USE
A lock is a simple and ingenious device for transporting your craft from one water level to another. When both sets of gates are closed it may be filled or emptied using gates, or ground paddles, at the top or bottom of the lock. These are operated with a windlass. On the Thames, the locks are manned *all year round, with longer hours from April to October*. You may operate the locks yourself *at any time*.

If a lock is empty, or 'set' for you, the crew open the gates and you drive the boat in. If the lock is full of water, the crew should check first to see if any boat is waiting or coming in the other direction. If a boat is in sight, you must let them through first: do not empty or 'turn' the lock against them. This is not only discourteous, and against the rules, but wastes precious water.

In the diagrams the *plan* shows how the gates point uphill, the water pressure forcing them together. Water is flooding into the lock through the underground culverts that are operated by the ground paddles: when the lock is 'full', the top gates (on the left of the drawing) can be opened. One may imagine a boat entering, the crew closing the gates and paddles after it.

In the *elevation*, the bottom paddles have been raised (opened) so that the lock empties. A boat will, of course, float down with the water. When the lock is 'empty' the bottom gates can be opened and the descending boat can leave.

Remember that when going *up* a lock, a boat should be tied up to prevent it being thrown about by the the rush of incoming water; but when going *down* a lock, a boat should never be tied up or it will be left high and dry.

At the lock interface between a canal and a river, signs are appearing to indicate the river height. They show four possible states. Red – danger. Yellow and falling. Yellow and rising. Green – no danger. The alternative to the signs is the coloured strip on the lock wall around water level. The signs give you extra information in the yellow band – as to whether the level is going up or down – and tell you about locations remote from where you are now.

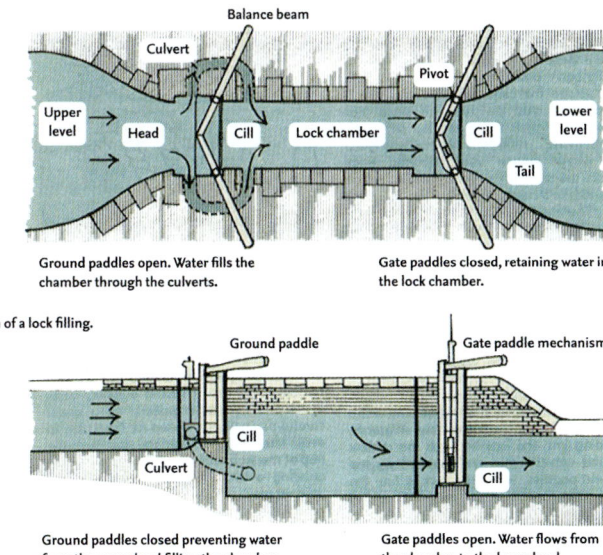

Ground paddles open. Water fills the chamber through the culverts.

Gate paddles closed, retaining water in the lock chamber.

A plan of a lock filling.

Ground paddles closed preventing water from the upper level filling the chamber.

Gate paddles open. Water flows from the chamber to the lower level.

An elevation of a lock emptying.

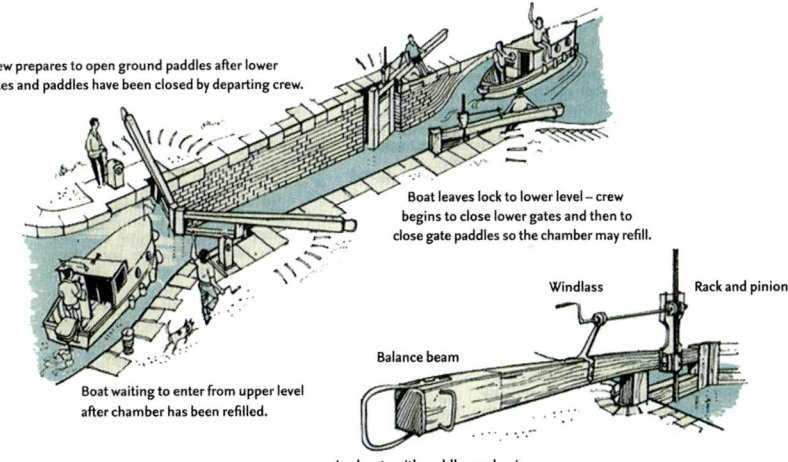

Crew prepares to open ground paddles after lower gates and paddles have been closed by departing crew.

Boat leaves lock to lower level – crew begins to close lower gates and then to close gate paddles so the chamber may refill.

Boat waiting to enter from upper level after chamber has been refilled.

Lock gate with paddle mechanism.

- Make safety your prime concern. *Keep a close eye on young children.*
- Always take your time, and do not leap about.
- Never open the paddles at one end without ensuring those at the other end are closed.
- Keep to the landward side of the balance beam when opening and closing gates. Whilst it may be necessary to put your back behind the balance beam to gain a better purchase when starting to close a gate, always move to the correct position as soon as possible.
- Never leave your windlass slotted onto the paddle spindle – it will be dangerous should anything slip.
- Keep your boat away from the top and bottom gates to prevent it getting caught on the gate or the lock cill.
- Never drop the paddles – always wind them down.
- Be wary of fierce *top gate* paddles, especially in wide locks. Operate them slowly, and close them if there is *any* adverse effect.
- Always follow the navigation authority's instructions, where given on notices or by their staff.

ENVIRONMENTAL GUIDANCE FOR BOATERS

The Problem

The principal emissions of concern are Carbon Dioxide (CO_2), because of its contribution to global warming, Nitrogen Oxides (NOx) and particulates less than 10 microns in diameter (PM10s) because of their damaging effect on the respiratory system. Sources include boat engines, wood-burning, solid fuel and oil stoves, together with central heating boilers.

Emissions from inland waterways boats are currently relatively small. The Inland Waterways Association's Sustainable Boating Group (SBG) estimates that boats on the UK's inland waterways account for about 0.05% of retail fuel sales in the UK, while the draft London Environment Strategy suggests that boats on the Thames contribute only about 1% of the total NOx and PM10s produced in the London area. However, these can still be significant, especially at the local level in residential areas, and will become more so as pollution from roads is reduced. The Canal & River Trust has noted that local authorities in Oxford, London and Bath & North East Somerset are particularly affected because of the high concentrations of residential boats and the geography of the areas.

Legislation

The Clean Air Act 1993 gives local authorities the power to make a 'smoke control order'. Properties falling under such an order are subject to restrictions on the emission of smoke from chimneys attached to buildings. This act was amended by the Environment Act 2021, which fundamentally changed how smoke control orders work and how the rules are enforced by local authorities.

Under the amended restrictions, it is unlawful to emit smoke from a property that falls under a smoke control order. Officers of the council can issue a financial penalty where they witness the emission of a 'significant quantity of smoke from a chimney', regardless of the appliance being used or the type of fuel burnt. Smokeless fuel should be used or timber/logs need to be burned in a DEFRA approved stove.

As well as a change to how smoke control orders work, there has been an alteration in their scope. Local authorities now have the discretion to extend the range of smoke control orders to include moored vessels, although emissions are still allowed from an engine used to move, or provide electric power to the vessel.

Propulsion

Most boats on inland waterways have diesel engines, which is not ideal from a pollution perspective. While newer designs of diesel engines are much cleaner in many respects than their predecessors, in particular exhibiting reduced PM10 and NOx emissions, they are often less fuel efficient and thus ultimately produce more CO_2.

Two simple behavioural changes can significantly reduce fuel use, and thus emissions (together with cost). Stopping engines and using ropes while locking and reducing cruising speed by about 10% can each give a reduction of about 30%, with the latter adding only four or five minutes per hour to cruising times after allowing for locking time.

Biodiesel is now legally required to be added to all mineral diesel at the rate of 7%, shown by the marking 'B7' on fuel pumps, a requirement currently met almost entirely by the addition of Fatty Acid Methyl Ester (FAME). While this represents a small step towards carbon neutrality and reducing other emissions, it causes problems in marine engines by producing sticky deposits and increasing the risk of 'diesel bug' by attracting water. Either can result in fuel system blockages and thus breakdowns.

Fortunately, a superior alternative is now available in the form of fully hydrogenated vegetable oil, retailed as 'HVO'. This is chemically fundamentally different to FAME so causes none of the latter's problems and, being much purer than mineral diesel, reduces particulate and NOx emissions significantly while also being about 90% Carbon neutral. Its use is approved by just about every current manufacturer of diesel engines worldwide and the SBG arranged a series of trials in a range of marine domestic appliances and older engines, including semi-diesels, all of which were successful. Unfortunately, conflicting Government subsidy and tax regimes mean that it is currently both expensive and difficult to obtain.

Alternatives to diesel are limited. Petrol and Liquefied Petroleum Gas (LPG) are less widely available, have safety issues and offer only modest environmental advantages, though the development of electric drive systems has now advanced to the point where they merit consideration. Battery-powered boats charged by shorelines are increasingly used by trip boat operators and one hire company has a number of boats using this type of system. However, other than on the River Thames, the number of charging points (except in marinas) is minimal and, as solar panels can provide only a contribution to the power needed for electric propulsion, a generator-based charging option is essential.

Two basic systems exist, often termed Serial and Parallel Hybrids, although the former isn't strictly a hybrid. In this a small generator charges a large battery bank, which then powers an electric drive motor. In the latter, a standard propulsion engine with a larger alternator charges a more modest battery bank while cruising; this then powers an electric drive motor for part of the time. Either can also take power from solar panels and/or landlines and either can support an electrical domestic system. The SBG has produced an *Introduction to Electric Boating* (www.waterways.org.uk/campaigns/sustainable-boating/electric-boats) in which these options are examined in more detail though, to summarise, the former system will prove more fuel efficient than the latter in most circumstances.

There are suggestions of more radical alternative fuels such as hydrogen, used either directly in modified spark-ignition engines or to produce electricity in fuel cells to power electric motors. In both cases water is the only emission. However, hydrogen presents comparable hazards to petrol and LPG and the production of the hydrogen currently available uses so much energy that its use as a fuel is arguably worse than using diesel, while less than a third of the energy used to make so-called 'Green' Hydrogen can ultimately be recovered for propulsion. Hydrogen is also very expensive. Fuel cells which will run on LPG exist and could be a low carbon stop-gap but are not, as yet, available in a form suitable for use in boats.

Electricity Generation

Engines are often run while boats are moored, to heat water and recharge batteries and/or power larger domestic appliances such as washing machines or ovens. It is generally regarded as anti-social to run engines, including generator engines, between 20:00-08:00 and many navigation authorities expressly forbid it. Even if not a legal requirement, care should always be taken to avoid making excessive noise or fumes, especially in residential areas. The need to run engines or generators can be reduced by installing solar panels and/or by using shorelines where possible. The IWA is encouraging the provision of more electric bollards.

However, it must be recognised that the running of propulsion engines while moored is a particularly polluting practice and should be avoided altogether if possible. Not only are the emissions not dispersed, as they are while a boat is moving, but a typical modern diesel engine will burn up to 2 litres of fuel to produce one domestic unit of electricity. A dedicated generator, by contrast, will produce up to 10 times that power from a similar volume of fuel. Buying a small generator will thus be a good move for anyone needing to charge frequently whilst moored.

Stoves

The regulations for Smoke Control Areas state that only smokeless fuels should be burned. The exception is that wood may be burned in an 'exempt' appliance that has been tested to ensure that it does not create smoke. You will find details at www.gov.uk/smoke-control-area-rules. Although these provisions may not currently be a legal requirement for boats, it is considered good practice to comply with them.

The Europe-wide programme *Ecodesign* came into force in the UK in 2022 with the aim of improving air quality. It is possible to buy stoves that meet this standard and bear the Stove Industry Alliance's 'Ecodesign Ready' label – although advice should be sought to make sure that stoves from this list are suitable for use in a boat. Similarly, the UK's wood fuel accreditation scheme *Woodsure* has launched a voluntary 'Ready to Burn' label to help consumers to choose wood that is dry and ready to burn. Burning wet or treated wood should always be avoided. Further guidance on reducing smoke from solid fuel stoves can be found at www.canalrivertrust.org.uk/enjoy-the-waterways/boating/go-boating/a-guide-to-boating/living-on-a-boat/heating-your-boat.

Diesel-fired stoves became popular as an alternative to solid fuel ones when diesel was very cheap. They emit little visible smoke but do still emit pollutants, the nature and quantity of which vary with how well the stove is set up. Keeping the burning pot and catalyser clean and ensuring a good air supply will minimise these.

Water Pollution

Hydrocarbons in oil and fuels can affect both human health and the aquatic environment. An iridescent sheen on the water and a characteristic smell are signs of spillages of oil, diesel or petrol. Sometimes these result from catastrophic spills, but more commonly they are the result of an accumulation of small, everyday events. Correct maintenance of engines will help to reduce emissions and oil leaks, and care should be taken when refuelling to keep fuel out of the water.

Discharges into the water from boat sinks and showers are another source of pollution. Environmentally friendly cleaning products and cosmetics are available and will help to reduce toxic chemicals and plastic micro-beads. Laboratory testing has repeatedly shown such cleaning products to be less effective than their mainstream competitors, although one has finally gained a 'Best Buy' award from the Consumers Association. Advice on green products and services for boaters is available from The Green Blue – www.thegreenblue.org.uk – an environmental programme created by the Royal Yachting Association and British Marine.

(This analysis has been prepared by the Inland Waterways Association's Sustainable Boating Group who are continuously updating and revising their research, so visit www.waterways.org.uk/campaigns/sustainable-boating to keep up to date with developments in this fast-moving area of contemporary boating.)

GENERAL GUIDANCE FOR PADDLERS USING THE INLAND WATERWAYS

As with all navigations, whether inland, coastal or deep sea, a variety of rules, regulations and customs have, over the centuries, been established to ensure safe and efficient operation. The canals and rivers of Britain are no exception and described below are those most likely to affect canoeists and paddleboarders.

1. Boats travel on the right and you would therefore overtake a slower vessel on its left (or port) side. Meeting a craft coming towards you, you should expect to pass left side to left side (or port to port). On rare occasions boats may need to pass right side to right side (or starboard to starboard) when, for instance, their size and/or weather conditions make manoeuvring difficult. This would also be the case where a loaded commercial vessel needs to stay in the deep water channel.

2. Infrastructure – whether locks, bridges, tunnels or aqueducts – can potentially pose hazards for unpowered craft.
    i) In most cases, locks will have to be portaged for which a small folding trolley is often a great help. When approaching the top of a lock, beware of the draw of a swollen by-wash stream pulling you sideways, possibly away from your intended landing point. This will be more pronounced on river navigations where the same draw will be caused by an adjacent weir, especially when the current is strong following rain and snow melt. River locks are always accompanied by their attendant weirs which will be protected by large orange buoys strung across the top of the structure by a stout cable stretching from bank to bank. Note that these have been designed to catch larger powered vessels rather that unpowered craft.
    ii) On most canals, bridges are pinch points through which there is usually only space for one craft to pass. Judge your timing carefully, bearing in mind that your relatively small profile may not always be visible to the helmsman of a long narrowboat until he or she has committed to the bridge hole, as the structure can curtail their forward vision until the last moment (especially on bends).
    iii) Tunnels are clearly marked as being either accessible to unpowered craft or to be portaged. Follow instructions clearly displayed on the large boards at the mouth of the tunnel, taking account of the timings in each direction that you will often find controlling craft access on narrow-beam canals. A bright, forward-facing light must be carried on each unpowered vessel.
    iv) Paddleboarders, in particular, may not want to paddle across high aqueducts, therefore an assessment from the towpath should first be made!

3. In order to maintain steerage and keep on course, powered boats have to achieve a certain minimum speed so are often unable to come safely to standstill to allow a paddler to pass in a constricted space. Note also that two vessels passing under way generate an area of low pressure along their adjacent hull sides which, in turn, can create a noticeable 'suck'.

4. A waterway describing itself as a 'Navigation' will generally be a mix of river and canal, with the canal length protected from a river section by a flood gate designed to be closed to prevent the canal flooding when the river flows are swollen and levels increased. During the normal river state the gates are left open and all vessels can navigate straight through. Once closed they operate as normal locks and, with care, powered craft can still proceed. A flood lock will be accompanied by red, yellow and green bands (supported by an adjacent interpretation board) painted at the tail of the lock giving essential information about water levels, which you will also find detailed as appropriate in this guide's Navigational Notes for each waterway. As a general rule meeting a closed flood lock after launching tells you that the river is either rising or falling but that paddling will be difficult as flow rates are increased, so don't portage around a closed flood lock unless you are used to paddling swollen rivers.

5. In the introduction to each navigation in this guide, waterways have been loosely categorised – according to their suitability for paddlers – from Category 1 through to Category 4. Paddlers encountering most of the navigations constructed as commercial waterways to accommodate vessels in access of 100ft, will find that embarking and disembarking from their craft will be difficult or impossible and as such they are listed Category 4. 'Keel-sized' locks on some of the north east waterways were built for commercial craft measuring 56 x 14ft and their scale is therefore a deal good more paddler-friendly and warrants a Category 3 rating. Category 2 is reserved for waterways that would normally be rated at Category 1 (narrow- and wide-beam canals, placid rivers, etc) but can include hazards such as sharing the bed of a river for a short section, weed growth or, in the case of a stand-alone river, become hazardous in times of flood.

Since the beginning of the new decade paddling, in all its forms, has really taken off on the inland waterways – until recently the almost exclusive domain of the diesel-powered boat. Full integration may still be a little way off but the fundamental needs of all owners and their craft are remarkably similar, and include mutual respect, safety, support (including everything from boatyards to sustenance) and, above all, courtesy.

There are plenty of ready-made paddling opportunities detailed in these pages but for those who want to make their own way, listed below are a few useful pointers:

1. To avoid the repetition of 'out and back' trips, a waterway 'ring' or a linear expedition has many attractions. Typically, a hire boater may well feel the same way and in a week might undertake, say, the Cheshire Ring, the Warwickshire Ring or the Black Country Ring. General guidance is available at www.canalrivertrust.org.uk/enjoy-the-waterways/boating where you will also find details of specific 'ring' cruises.

2. Under the **Pubs and Restaurants** headings you will find details of both Bed & Breakfast and camping listed alongside the availability of food and drink. There is also mention of fixed 'pods' and cottages under both this heading and, occasionally, under **Boatyards**. The latter may not yet be totally aware of the nascent demand for somewhere safe for paddlers to leave their craft, on completion of a one-way trip but a polite phone call and the offer of payment is more than likely to procure secure storage and, probably, use of their facilities.

3. All Canal & River Trust licence holders are entitled to a Watermate key (often, for reasons of history, referred to as a BW key) which gives them access to basic facilities such as toilets, showers, laundry and water. This will be useful for paddlers that are on camping trips and can be obtained from www.canalrivertrust.org.uk/enjoy-the-waterways/boating/go-boating/boat-services-and-directory/where-to-buy-keys-cards-and-more or from internet sites such as eBay. You may also need to buy smart cards to operate some of these facilities which can be obtained through the same website.

4. To keep abreast of extreme weather events and stoppages that may affect navigation, real-time information can be delivered to your smartphone by registering for those waterways that you are interested in at www.canalrivertrust.org.uk/media/original/39685-getting-your-smartphone-to-tell-you-about-stoppages-on-your-canal-or-river.pdf. This will include the closure (and re-opening) of flood locks.

Boats Moored at the Canal Centre, Mytchett

BASINGSTOKE CANAL

MAXIMUM DIMENSIONS
Length: 72'
Beam: 13'
Headroom: 5' 10"
Draught: 3'

MILEAGES
WOODHAM JUNCTION (River Wey) to:
Woodham Top Lock: 1 mile
Goldsworth Bottom Lock: 5 miles
Pirbright Bridge: 8 miles
Deepcut Top Lock: 10 miles
Mytchett: 13 miles
Ash Lock: 16 miles
Pondtail Bridges: 20 miles
Crookham Wharf: 23 miles
Barley Mow Bridge: 27 miles
Odiham Wharf: 29 miles
Limit of navigation: 30¾ miles
Greywell Tunnel: 31 miles
29 locks

LICENCES
All craft wishing to use the canal navigation require a licence issued by: Basingstoke Canal Authority Canal Centre, Mytchett Place Road
Mytchett
Surrey GU16 6DD
01252 370073
www.hants.gov.uk/thingstodo/basingstokecanal
In an emergency contact the Canal Duty Ranger on 07894 425588 (*24hr cover*).

Paddling: Category 1. *Although not a Canal & River Trust waterway, Paddle UK members are automatically licensed to paddle this canal. Non-members should contact the office.*

An Act of Parliament for the building of this canal was passed in 1778, and the navigation opened to Basingstoke in 1794. Intended as an artery to and from London, mainly for agricultural produce – timber, grain, fertilizers, chalk and malt – it was never a financial success. Built by the great canal contractor, John Pinkerton (who issued his own tokens or coins as payment to his navvies), it was originally estimated to cost £86,000. By 1796 £153,463 had been spent. Tonnages of goods carried averaged about 20,000 per annum, 10,700 tons below what was anticipated, and profit forecasts of £7,783 8s 4d proved wildly optimistic, the best figure achieved being £3,038 4s 2d in 1800.

The Napoleonic Wars, and the danger they brought to coastal shipping, benefited the Basingstoke Canal, which could transport goods bound for Portsmouth and Southampton in safety. But with the advent of peace, trade slumped – the canal managers commenting that 'some considerable injury must be sustained by the Canal'.

There was a minor boom in goods carried in 1839 to build the London & South Western Railway, but when this opened it was clear that the navigation had been instrumental in its own demise. Trade flourished for a while in 1854 with the building of the barracks at Aldershot, but this was short-lived. Plans for a revival by building a link canal from Basingstoke to the Kennet & Avon Canal at Newbury came to nothing, and the company went into liquidation in 1866. A dissolution order followed in 1878.

Purchased by new owners in 1896, and renamed the Woking, Aldershot & Basingstoke Canal, a considerable amount of money was spent on improvements, to link with the new brickworks at Up Nately, but all to no avail, and by 1904 it was once again offered for sale. In 1913, *Basingstoke*, the last narrowboat to almost reach Basingstoke, carried 5 tons of moulding sand. The canal was owned by A.J. Harmsworth between 1923 and 1947, and he did much to ensure its ultimate survival, despite the collapse of Greywell Tunnel in 1934. Munitions were transported on the canal during World War II, and the last commercial traffic, 50 tons of timber on *Gwendoline*, came to Woking in June 1949. In 1950 the canal was auctioned and sold to the Inland Waterways Association but due to insufficient funds being raised the canal was sold on to what was to become the New Basingstoke Canal Company. Now owned by the County Councils of Hampshire and Surrey, its restoration represents a magnificent achievement by both councils, the Surrey & Hampshire Canal Society and the IWA.

Woking

The Basingstoke Canal leaves the River Wey Navigation at Woodham Junction, near a large electricity sub-station and overshadowed by the M25 motorway. Its course is immediately lined with a fine mixture of mature trees, a feature which is to persist throughout most of its route, isolating the canal from much of its surroundings. The pump house, which back pumps water on the Woodham flight of six locks, and alleviates a long-standing water supply problem, is passed before you reach the peaceful, almost secret, houseboat world which still exists between Locks 1 and 3. There is easy access to *shops, a bank, restaurants and pubs* from Lock 2 – walk south west into West Byfleet; and to the south of Chobham Road Bridge. Above Woodham Top Lock the waterway maintains its seclusion, with the large private gardens of a smart residential area backing onto the canal. Horsell Common provides more open views before Woking is reached, where the last commercial traffic on the canal was a load of timber in 1949. The navigation passes through an area of extensive new development with busy roads, and tower blocks to the south.

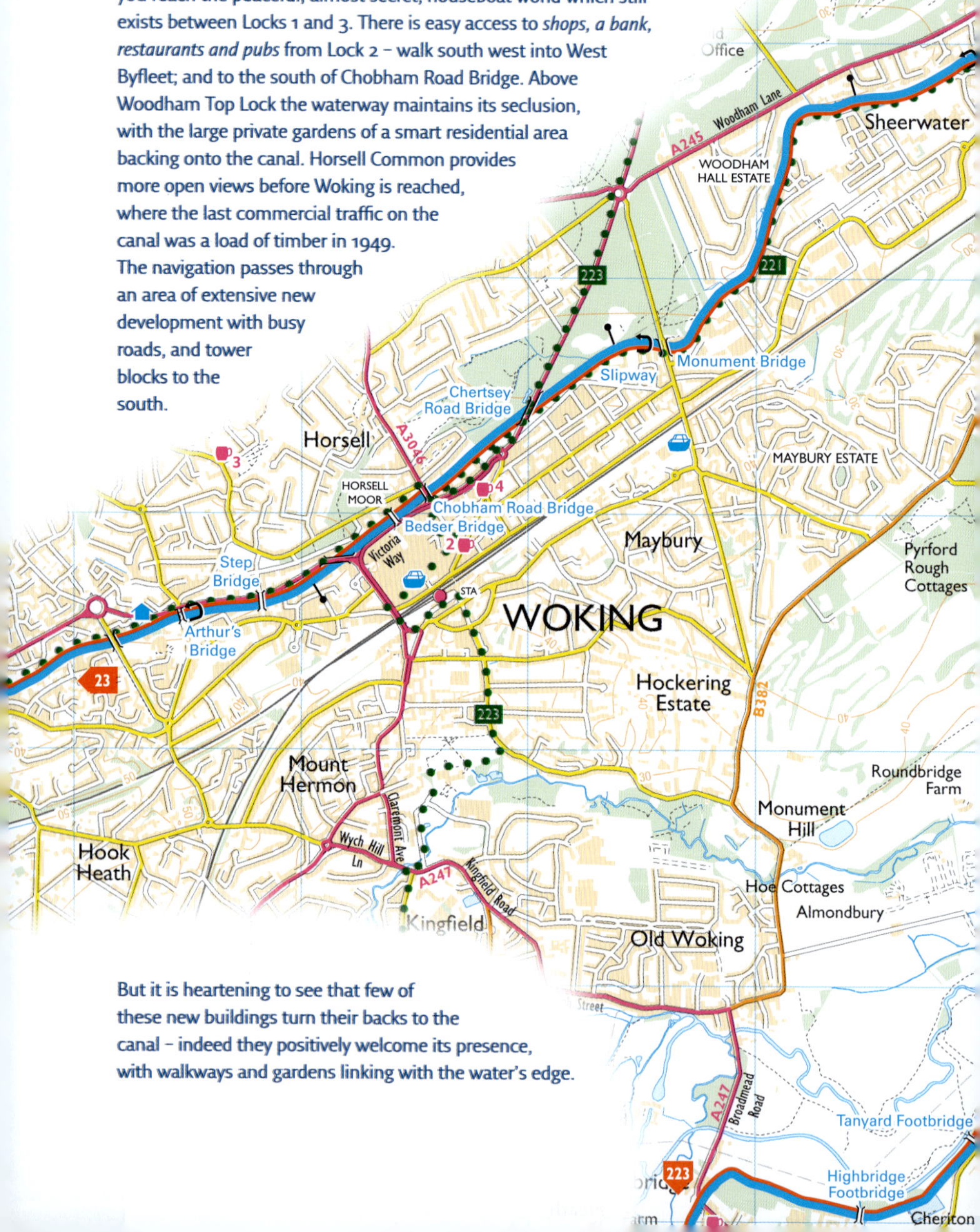

But it is heartening to see that few of these new buildings turn their backs to the canal – indeed they positively welcome its presence, with walkways and gardens linking with the water's edge.

Basingstoke Canal — Woking

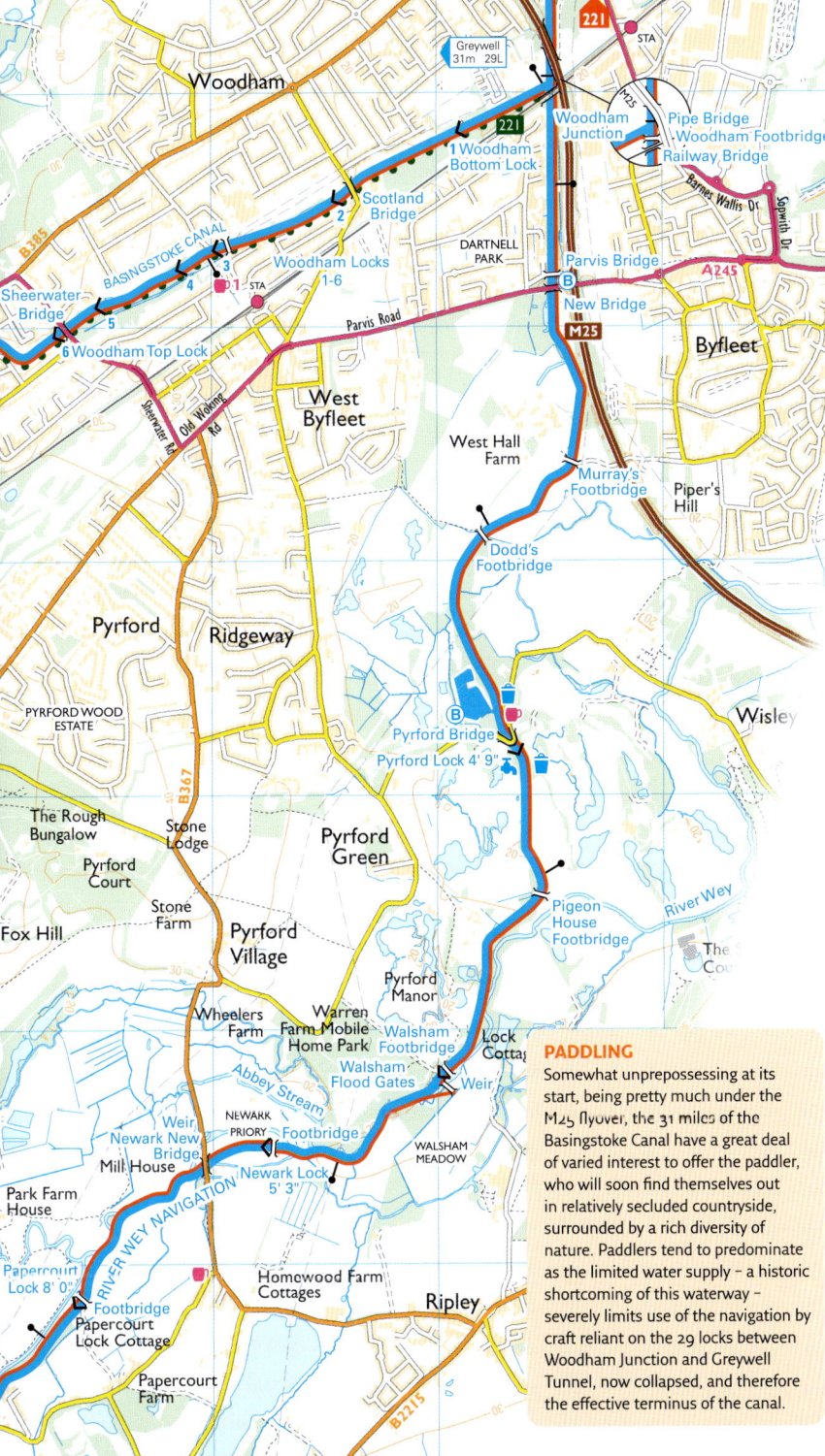

PADDLING

Somewhat unprepossessing at its start, being pretty much under the M25 flyover, the 31 miles of the Basingstoke Canal have a great deal of varied interest to offer the paddler, who will soon find themselves out in relatively secluded countryside, surrounded by a rich diversity of nature. Paddlers tend to predominate as the limited water supply – a historic shortcoming of this waterway – severely limits use of the navigation by craft reliant on the 29 locks between Woodham Junction and Greywell Tunnel, now collapsed, and therefore the effective terminus of the canal.

19

NAVIGATIONAL NOTES

1. Facilities for boaters are fairly limited on the Basingstoke Canal. There is water available at Mytchett; Ash Lock; Barley Mow; Bridge Barn pub, Woking and Odiham (CRT Watermate key required for all sites) together with pump-out facilities at Mytchett and Galleon Marine, Odiham.
2. Slipways are available at Barley Mow Bridge, Winchfield, Farnborough Road Aldershot, and Potters Pub, Mytchett (restricted hours only). Charge.
3. Dry dock facilities are available at Frimley Lock 28 and can be booked through the Canal Centre, Mytchett.
4. Lock flights are opened by appointment between the hours set out in the table which can be accessed from www.hants.gov.uk/thingstodo/countryparks/basingstokecanal/onthewater/narrowboats. To book a passage telephone 01252 370073 by 15.00 on the working day before you intend to go through. Boats need to clear Thames Lock on the River Wey by 5pm (2pm in Winter) the day before the planned entry onto the Basingstoke Canal. Any boats arriving after the locking times will have to wait until the next day. *Between Oct-Mar* the office is *closed at weekends* so you must call the office *before 15.00 on Friday* if you wish to access the canal *over the weekend*.

BOAT TRIPS

Woking Recreational Boating for the Handicapped offer free trips for small groups aboard **Maggie G**, a boat specially designed for wheelchair users. Trips operate from Woking. For further details telephone 01483 760566. From *Easter-Sep*, trips are offered to disadvantaged community groups aboard **River Wey** which is also wheelchair accessible. The boat is operated by the Surrey Care Trust who work with volunteers and offenders on Community Punishment Orders, carrying out conservation work along the canal. Contact 01483 426990/07973 for more information. Details of further boating opportunities on the canal can be found at www.hants.gov.uk/thingstodo/countryparks/basingstokecanal/onthewater/boathire.

● Woking

Surrey. All shops and services. Surrey's largest town, built around the railway, which came here in 1838. The original village, Old Woking, lies 2 miles to the south. Development carries on apace, making dormitory homes for the thousands of commuters who rush up to the city daily. It is, however, worth walking south from Monument Bridge, and taking the third turning on the right, Oriental Road, to see the Shah Jehan Mosque, built in 1889 and reminiscent of the Taj Mahal in India with its onion-shaped dome. Built by the enormously rich Begum Shah Jehan, ruler of Bhopal State in India, its design, by W. I. Chambers, is honest and dignified. A P&O captain was employed to take bearings to ensure an exact orientation towards Mecca.

Brooklands Museum Brooklands Road, Weybridge KT13 0SL (01932 857381; www. brooklandsmuseum.com). Assembled within what remains of the Brooklands race track, the world's first purpose-built motor racing circuit, constructed by wealthy landowner Hugh Locke King in 1907. Its heyday was in the 1920s and 30s, when records were being set by the likes of Malcolm Campbell and John Cobb, driving vehicles with evocative names, such as the Delage, Bentley and Bugatti. It became very fashionable, and was known as the Ascot of Motorsport. It was also an aerodrome and an aircraft factory, and it was here that A. V. Roe made the first flight in a British aeroplane. The Sopwith Pup and Camel were developed here, and later the Hawker Hurricane and the Vickers Wellington were built here – the only Wellington that saw war time service, salvaged in 1985 from Loch Ness and restored, is on display. The outbreak of war in 1939 brought an end to racing, and aircraft production ceased in 1987. Now you can walk on part of the legendary circuit, and see historic racing cars and aircraft, including a *Concorde*, in the museum. The clubhouse is a listed building. You can also visit the Raleigh Cycle Exhibition, a reminder that cycle races were also held at Brooklands. Shop. Special events are staged throughout the year. Telephone for *opening times. Closed Xmas*. Charge.

Elmbridge Museum Civic Centre, Esher KT10 9SD (01932 474911; www..elmbridgemuseum.org.uk). A collection established in 1909 and refurbished in 1996, covering local and social history and featuring items relating to Oatlands Palace, near Weybridge, which was built by Henry VIII in 1537. Also finds from a Romano-British bathhouse near Cobham. Visit website or telephone for *opening times*. Free. Buses or train from Weybridge.

New Victoria Theatre Peacocks Centre, Woking GU21 6GQ (Box office 0333 009 6690; www.atgtickets.com/venues/new-victoria-theatre). Situated in the Peacocks Arts & Entertainments Centre and providing a 1300-seat venue for drama, musicals, opera and ballet. Also big-screen cinemas, bars, cafés and restaurants.

Woking Leisure Centre and Pool in the Park Woking Park, Kingfield Road GU22 9BA (01483 771122; www.freedom-leisure.co.uk/centres/woking-leisure-centre). Three swimming pools and a cafeteria. The leisure centre includes aerobics, gym, health suite, squash, badminton, children's activities, a multisensory suite and a 1930s Wurlitzer organ, restaurant and bar.

Woking Visitor Information Centre Crown House, Crown Square, Woking GU21 6HR (01483 720103; www.woking.org.uk/info/1308/#google_vignette).

- **Woodham**
Surrey. All shops and services. A typical commuter conurbation of dull, closely packed houses, only pretty in the more expensive areas, where large, spacious houses and gardens nestle among trees. Definitely at its best and most characterful by the canal.

- **Horsell**
Surrey. Indistinguishable from Woking (*see page 20*), although if you look hard enough, you will find a few original cottages.

UPS AND DOWNS ON THE BASINGSTOKE

The Basingstoke Canal was at one time often portrayed as a restoration failure, but this was borne entirely out of a misconception. At the outset the objective of the two county councils involved was to create a 32-mile, linear country park for the benefit of a wide variety of potential users, of which boaters were to be but one (albeit significant) group.

Two barge movements a day was the average traffic when the waterway was opened and water supply was always constrained by an undertaking not to tap existing watercourses, jealously guarded by millers and landowners alike. Apart from springs and rainwater run-off – plentiful during the winter months – the only other water source is limited to two pumped supplies: one at Woking and a second at Frimley, lifting storm water from a drainage sump on the trackbed of the mainline railway.

A pumping station, installed at the bottom of Woodham Locks, serves to stop water losses to the River Wey, and maintains the level in the pound above the flight. Springs work on more or less a six month cycle so a good time to visit the canal is between February and mid June when water supplies should be at their maximum. It has aptly been described as a sleepy backwater of a canal and navigating it is more akin to boating in the 1950s: locks fill slowly and require care, and the waterway itself is not to be rushed along. Herein lies its real charm and to appreciate it – together with the abundant wildlife and SSSIs – visitors must understand its constraints, together with the way in which it has successfully fulfilled all the aims of its restorers and delighted one-and-a-half million diverse visitors annually.

Greywell Tunnel (collapsed) 1230yds

WALKING AND CYCLING
The towpath is in excellent condition throughout the entire length of the navigation, including the disused section west of Greywell Tunnel as far as Penny Bridge. The short section across Greywell Hill, however, may be uneven and overgrown. The towpath is well used by walkers and cyclists alike and in conjunction with the numerous British Rail stations, situated at regular intervals close to the canal, it is fairly easy to plan excursions without having to double back.

Pubs and Restaurants (pages 18-19)

There are plenty of pubs and restaurants in Woking and West Byfleet but only one is adjacent to the canal.

1 The Station 2 Station Road, West Byfleet KT14 6DR (01932 336353; www.thestationwestbyfleet.co.uk). Family-run pub, restaurant and hotel serving a wide range of home-made food *Mon-Thu L and E & Fri-Sun 12.00-21.30 (Sun 17.00)* together with real ales and interesting bottled beers. Large outdoor seating area; children and dogs welcome. Sports TV and Wi-Fi. Quiz Wed. B&B. *Open daily 12.00-23.00 (Sat-Sun 23.30).*

2 O'Neill's Crown Square, Woking GU21 6HR (01483 728304; www.oneills.co.uk/national-search/south-east/woking). A typical example of the O'Neill's pub chain with wooden furniture and wall panelling throughout. Food available *daily 12.00-21.00.* Dog- and child-friendly (*until 20.00*). Weekend live music, sports TV and Wi-Fi. *Open 11.00-23.00 (Thu 01.00 & Fri-Sat 02.00).*

3 The Red Lion 123 High Street, Horsell GU21 4SS (01483 768497; www.redlionhorsell.co.uk). Popular dining pub with a large garden that welcomes children (*until 19.00*) and well-behaved dogs. Real ale. Occasional music and real fires. A wide-ranging menu is served *Mon-Sat 12.00-21.00 (Fri-Sat 21.30)* and *Sun 12.00-20.00. Open Mon-Sat 10.00-22.30 (Fri-Sat 23.00) & Sun 10.00-22.00.*

4 The Herbert Wells 51-57 Chertsey Road, Woking GU21 5AJ (01483 722818; www.jdwetherspoon.com/pubs/all-pubs/england/surrey/the-herbert-wells-woking). Popular, town centre Wetherspoon's pub serving inexpensive real ales. Children welcome if dining. Wi-Fi. Food available *08.00-22.00. Open 08.00-00.00 (Fri-Sat 01.00).*

Brookwood

Woking is gradually left behind as the canal rises through the five St John's Locks (where back-pumping is now installed) to Kiln Bridge, where there are good *moorings* above the bridge. Here there is easy access to *shops, takeaways, a chemist, fish & chips, cafés, a launderette and a butcher*. The railway, which accompanies the canal to Frimley Green, comes very close at Knaphill, and is then replaced by the trees of Brookwood Lye. Houseboats moored here, by Hermitage Bridge, add a picturesque touch. Brookwood Locks are pleasantly situated and once again the trees reappear. An old overgrown pill box still guards Pirbright Bridge – beyond the bridge is the first of the Deepcut, or Frimley, flight of locks. The canal now climbs steadily up the 14 locks in a superb, tree-lined, setting. Even the vast

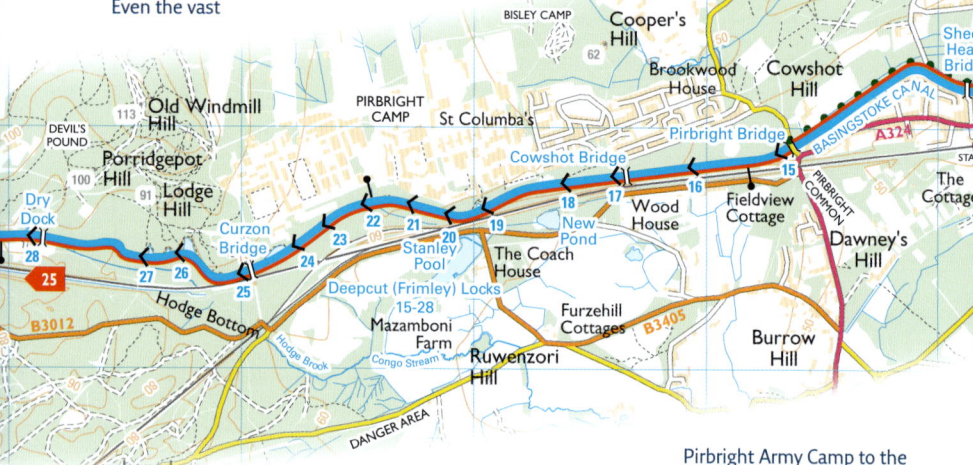

Pirbright Army Camp to the north hardly intrudes, although you may hear the odd burst of practice gunfire. Between many of the locks there are wide pools – check the depth of these carefully if you dare to stray off the direct course (not recommended). Each of the locks has a footbridge, and a ladder in the chamber, but not all have an easy means of landing below the bottom gates, so it is a good idea for a member of the crew to walk ahead to open the gates while ascending. Above the top lock is a dry dock, rebuilt in 1984, and available for hire. (see Navigational Note 3, page 20). The building here was once a workshop and forge.

● **St John's**
Surrey. PO, stores, butcher, fish & chips, chemist, launderette. Swallowed up by Woking, the area around Kiln Bridge somehow, against all odds, manages to retain the feel of a village centre. Notice the well-restored building topped by a clock tower, right by the bridge.

● **Knaphill**
Surrey. Basically a large Victorian village around the barracks and the site of the gaunt Brookwood Mental Hospital, a mid 19th-C asylum which was once entirely self-sufficient, generating its own electricity and running its own farm in the grounds. To the west is Bisley, famous for its annual rifle shooting competitions.

● **Brookwood**
Surrey. PO, stores, takeaways, fish & chips, off-licence, station. Most shops are just west of Brookwood Locks. **Brookwood Cemetery** Four miles west of Woking GU24 0BL (01344 891041; www.tbcs.org.uk). Superbly landscaped expanse of heathland covering 2,400 acres, to the south of Brookwood Station, where mature trees and eccentric mausoleums coexist harmoniously. Founded by the London Necropolis Company in 1854, when the numbers of dead Londoners were becoming increasingly difficult to accommodate, it was once served by a railway – indeed one of the station buildings still survives. There is a military cemetery in the south west corner, where British and American soldiers are buried.

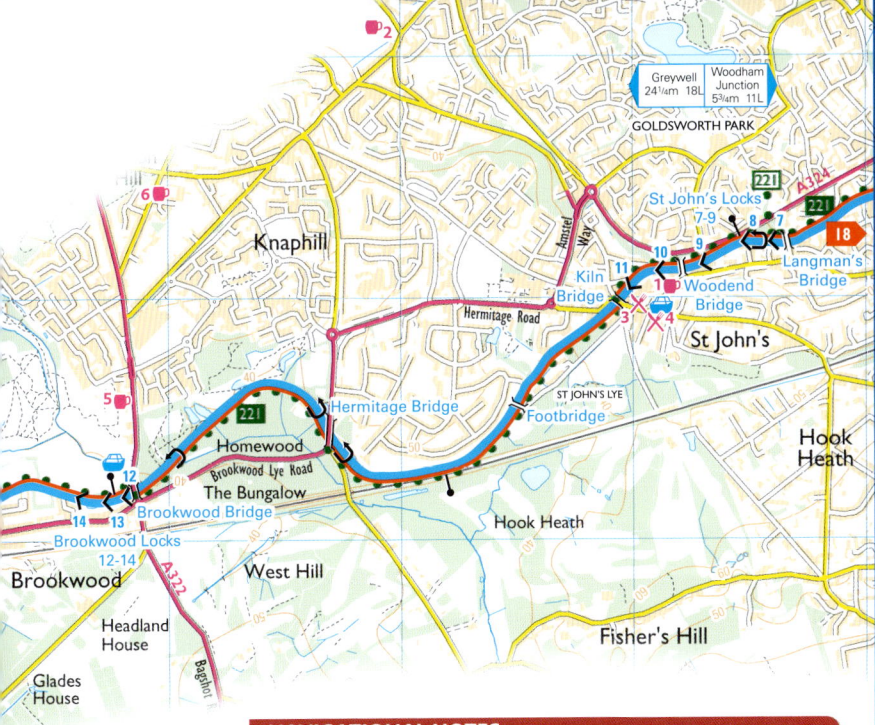

NAVIGATIONAL NOTES

1 Do not stray from the direct course of the canal without first checking the depth. Many of the wide pools are quite shallow.

Pubs and Restaurants

1 The Rowbarge 39 St John's Road, St John's GU21 7SA (01483 761618; www.rowbarge.co.uk). Friendly, village-style pub and restaurant serving appetising food *Wed-Thu L and E & Fri-Sun 12.00-21.00 (Sun 17.00)*. Real ales, real fires and Wi-Fi. Family-friendly, large garden. *Open Wed-Sat 11.30-22.00 (Fri-Sat 00.00) & Sun 11.30-21.00*.

2 The Royal Oak Anchor Hill, Knaphill GU21 2JH (01483 473330; www.facebook.com/theroyaloakwoking). Traditional 17th C village local serving an excellent range of well-kept real ales and real cider. Highly-thought of food available *Wed-Fri L and E (not Wed L) & Sat-Sun 12.00-20.00 (Sun 15.15)*. Dog- and child-friendly *(until 21.00)* large garden. Traditional pub games, newspapers, real fires, sports TV and Wi-Fi. *Open Mon-Sat 12.00-22.00 (Fri-Sat 23.00) & Sun 12.00-21.00*.

3 Tiang Restaurant 1 St Johns Road, St John's, Woking GU21 7SE (01483 726290; www.facebook.com/TiangRestaurant). Beside Kiln Bridge. Smart, friendly restaurant serving a variety of Oriental cuisine. *Open Thu-Sun L and E; Mon & Wed E*. Takeaway service.

4 The Village 3 St Johns Road, St John's, Woking GU21 7SE (01483 722822, www.thevillagewoking.uk). Excellent Indian food available *daily 17.00-22.00*.

5 The Nags Head Bagshot Road, Knaphill, Woking GU21 2RP (01483 474602; www.thenagsheadinnwoking.co.uk). North of Brookwood Bridge. Attractive and welcoming pub. Real ale. Food available *daily 12.00-22.00 (Sun 21.30)*. Dog- and family-friendly, large garden. *Open 12.00-23.00 (Sun 21.30)*.

6 The Garibaldi 134 High Street, Knaphill, Woking GU21 2QH (01483 473374; www.thegaribaldiknaphill.co.uk). Ten minute walk north along Bagshot Road. A traditional pub, describing itself as a 'pub for the village', rather than a village pub. Home-cooked food prepared from local ingredients available *L and E (not Mon L or Sun E)*. Dog- and child-friendly, large garden. *Occasional* live music and Wi-Fi. *Open Mon-Thu 17.30-23.00; Wed-Sat 12.00-23.00 (Fri-Sat 00.00) & Sun 12.00-22.30*.

Mytchett

Having climbed 90ft, the navigation now enters the dramatic Deepcut cutting, 1,000yds long and up to 70ft deep. Lined with large, mature, deciduous trees, it is pleasantly shady and remote. Beyond Wharfenden Lake, now part of a country club, and the supposedly lead-lined aqueduct over the railway, the canal turns sharply south towards Mytchett, with woods and heathland rising to the east. Mytchett Lake, owned by the army and renowned amongst anglers for the size of its pike, adjoins the canal, but is closed to navigation. The canal continues south, enclosed by the railway and thick woods on one side, and leafy gardens on the other. Just beyond the railway bridge at Ash Vale is the corrugated iron boathouse, dated 1896, where 15 barges were built between 1918 and 1935, and repairs were undertaken until 1947. There is a *takeaway* and a *stores* here (by the *station*) as well as a *café*, *chemist*, *an off-licence* and easy access to the *shops*. Great Bottom Flash, which contains the sunken remains of *Basingstoke*, the last narrowboat to almost reach Basingstoke, is surrounded by trees. It was here that Samuel F. Cody came to test his early seaplanes, prior to World War I. It is now a Danger Area, used by the army. Large houses with gardens landscaped to the water's edge face a busy road at Ash Vale before the navigation resumes its general westerly course. There is a *post office, chemist and fish & chips* together with a good range of *shops* and *takeaways* in the local shopping centre at Ash Wharf Bridge. It then crosses Spring Lake on an embankment and the Blackwater Valley Road on an aqueduct, leaving Surrey and entering Hampshire. There are good *moorings* above Ash Lock, opposite the Canal Depot *(slipway)*. The reappearance of army property – barrack blocks behind high wire fences – announces the approach to Aldershot. The canal has now climbed 195ft since leaving Woodham Junction. Queen's Avenue Bridge is notable for its modestly ornate iron balustrades, bringing a little light relief from the army camps which now completely enclose the waterway. Beyond Eelmoor Bridge, the canal widens at Eelmoor Flash, a Site of Special Scientific Interest (SSSI) due to its exceptional dragonfly population.

The canal continues its westward course eventually to reveal the low buildings of Farnborough airfield, which still hosts the world-famous Farnborough Air Show.

> **WALKING AND CYCLING**
> There are excellent waymarked trails for walkers in Lakeside Park (*see* page 26).

NAVIGATIONAL NOTES

1. Do not stray from the direct course of the canal without first checking the depth. Many of the wide pools are quite shallow.
2. Wharf Bridge is very low – 5ft 10in – so keep to the non-towpath side for maximum headroom.

Boatyards

Basingstoke Canal Authority Canal Centre Mytchett Place Road, Mytchett GU16 6DD (01252 370073; www.basingstoke-canal.co.uk). Pump out, long-term mooring, camping and caravan park, tearooms, slipway (nearby), dry dock, toilets, showers, gift shop, children's play area. Canoe, pedalo and rowing boat hire.

Frimley Lodge Park Sturt Road, Frimley Green GU16 6HY (01276 707100; www.facebook.com/frimleylodgepark). Playing fields, café, pitch & putt, play areas together with miniature railway, canalside and woodland walks. *Closes at dusk.*

Basingstoke Canal Visitor Centre Mytchett Place Road, Mytchett GU16 6DD (01252 370073; www.basingstoke-canal.co.uk). Overlooking the canal, also the location of the boating facilities. Picnic and play area, information centre, gift shop, tearoom and campsite. The information centre contains a detailed map, historical references, interactive lock model and a replica barge cabin. *Open Apr-Sep, Tue-Sun 10.30-16.45 and Oct-Mar, Tue-Fri 10.30-16.00 (Fri 15.45). Boat booking times Apr-Sep, Mon-Sun 09.00-16.45 and Oct-Mar, Mon-Fri 09.00-16.45 (Fri 15.45).*

- **Ash and Ash Vale**
Surrey. PO, stores, takeaways, chemist, fish & chips, station. Villages which are now enclosed by the sprawl of Aldershot. St Peter's Church, Ash, is early medieval and retains a Norman window, a finely detailed south door, c.1200 and a 17th-C wooden font.

Museum of Military Medicine Keogh Barracks, Ash Vale, Aldershot GU12 5RQ (01252 523176; www.museumofmilitarymedicine.org.uk/visit). Tells of the contribution the Army Medical Services have made in the history of medicine, nursing, dentistry and veterinary science. Shop. Free. *Open Mon-Fri 09.30-15.30.*

Lakeside Park Lakeside Road, Ash Vale GU12 5AA (01252 331353; www.guildford.gov.uk/lakeside). Access by foot from Blackwater Valley Path, between the canal and Lakeside Road Railway Bridge. Gravel extraction during the 1950s created the fine landscape of lakes and woods we see today. Remnants of the original field system still remain, and common spotted and bee orchids flower annually. Dragonflies are prolific during the summer months. On warm evenings bats can be seen. Network of footpaths and children's natural play area.

- **Farnborough**
Hants. All services (but they are some distance north of the canal). A name synonymous with the famous biennial air show (*see* below), Farnborough is now just a northerly extension of Aldershot, the original village having been engulfed by light industry, housing and the military. Almost 2 miles north of Wharf Bridge is St Peter's Church, dating from around 1200, with a wooden porch and weatherboarded tower. A short walk further north of this is Farnborough Hill, the former home of the Empress Eugenie, wife of Napoleon III of France, from the time of her exile to England in 1871 until her death in 1920. The building is now a convent school but is occasionally open to the public. The Empress built an extravagantly French mausoleum for her husband, her son and herself in 1871, as well as an abbey, known as St Michael's, now occupied by English Benedictine monks.

Farnborough Airport Farnborough. This aerodrome was set up in 1905 as His Majesty's Balloon Factory. The American showman, Samuel Cody, and a Red Indian friend, made the first powered flight in Britain at Laffan's Plain, Farnborough, in 1908, when Cody was Chief Kiting Instructor at the Balloon School here. Cody died in an air crash in 1913. During the two World Wars extensive research into developing military aircraft was carried out at the airfield. Much of the design and development work on *Concorde* was executed here. The world-famous Farnborough Air Show is held here biennially in *July*, and attracts over 200,000 visitors with its static exhibitions and dramatic flying displays. Considering the orientation of the main runway, you should get a good view from the canal.

- **Aldershot**
Hants. All services (but they are some distance south of the canal). In 1854 the army bought 10,000 acres of heathland surrounding the rural hamlet of Aldershot, bringing in building materials on the Basingstoke Canal and descending upon the area in force. It has never been the same since. In spite of a great deal of redevelopment it is still, for the most part, an uninspiring place, with the military being all pervasive. What is left of the original village, and it is not much, is to the south east of the station. The spectacular biennial army display has become a free one-day celebration of Armed Forces Day.

Aldershot Military Museum Queen's Avenue, Aldershot GU11 2JL (01252 314598; www.hampshireculture.org.uk/aldershot-military-museum). North of Queen's Avenue Bridge. The story of Aldershot Military Town and the civil towns of Aldershot, Farnborough and Cove, housed in the only surviving brick-built barrack blocks left in Aldershot. Visitors can learn about daily life for both soldier and civilian since 1854. *Open Wed-Fri 10.00-17.00, Sat-Sun 11.00-16.00.* Shop. Charge.

Royal Army Physical Training Corps Museum Army School of Physical Training, Queen's Avenue, Aldershot GU11 2LB (01252 787852; www.raptcmuseum.co.uk). Records, equipment, medals and history of the corps. *Open Mon-Fri 09.00-16.00.* Free.

Princes Hall Princes Way, Aldershot GU11 1NX (01252 329155; www.princeshall.com). Theatre, concerts and other events.

West End Centre 48 Queens Road, Aldershot GU11 3JD (01252 330040; www.westendcentre.co.uk). Licensed bar, comedy, music, jazz, theatre, classes in pottery and art, and other events.

Tourist Information Centre Princes Hall, Princes Way, Aldershot GU11 1NX (01252 320968; www.visit-hampshire.co.uk/visitor-information/aldershot-visitor-information-centre-p80141). *Open Mon-Fri 10.00-17.30, Sat 10.00-15.00 (closed Sun & B Hols).*

BOAT TRIPS
Nb Rosebud operates chartered cruises from the Canal Centre which include a 2½ hr evening cruise, an all day cruise and a picnic cruise to (and through) Ash Lock. Telephone 01252 370073 for availability.

PADDLING
Paddle UK, in the form of their Go Paddling website: www.gopaddling.info/canals/basingstoke-canal has plenty of information on the Basingstoke Canal as well as an interactive map to search for routes for your next paddle. Pedalos, canoes, kayaks and rowing boats are available to hire at the Canal Visitor Centre Mytchett Place Road, Mytchett, Camberley GU16 6DD (01252 370073; www.hants.gov.uk/thingstodo/basingstokecanal) *from Easter to the end of Sep*. You can make bookings and pay at reception or over the phone.

There are three canoe clubs operating on the Canal:
- The Basingstoke & Deane Canoe Club (07874 831362; www.badpaddlers.org) 11 Highlands Road, Andover SP10 2PX
- The Basingstoke Canal Canoe Club (01252 370073; www.hants.gov.uk/thingstodo/basingstokecanal) Mytchett Place Road, Mytchett, Camberley GU16 6DD
- The Blackwater Valley Canoe Club (www.bvcc.org.uk) based at Aldershot.

Further Reading: *The Paddle Guide to the Basingstoke Canal* by Fiona Shipp is also available to purchase from the Basingstoke Canal online shop – www.basingstoke-canal.org.uk/product/paddle-guide-to-the-basingstoke-canal). The first part of the guide contains information about the canal and its facilities and general advice to paddlers, while the second half has 10 suggested trips on the canal listing distances, facilities and points of interest.

Pubs and Restaurants (pages 24-25)

1 The King's Head Old Guildford Road, Frimley Green, Camberley GU16 6NR (01252 835431; www.harvester.co.uk/restaurants/southeast/thekingsheadcamberley). A chain restaurant with a large garden. Food is available *11.30-22.00 (Breakfast Fri-Sun 09.00)*. Family-friendly. Wi-Fi. *Open 11.30-22.00 (Fri-Sun 09.00)*.

2 The Rose & Thistle 1 Sturt Road, Frimley Green GU16 6HT (01252 834942; www.theroseandthistlefrimleygreen.co.uk). West of the King's Head overlooking the village green. Real ale, good choice of wine and Belgian beers. Food is available *daily 12.00-23.00 (Sun 22.00)*. Dog- and child-friendly *(until 21.00)*, garden. Quiz *Wed*. Traditional pub games, real fires and Wi-Fi. *Open Mon-Sat 12.00-23.00 (Fri-Sat 00.00) & Sun 12.00-22.00*.

3 The Old Wheatsheaf 205 Frimley Green Road, Frimley Green GU16 6LA (01252 835074; www.theoldwheatsheaf.co.uk). South of the Rose & Thistle along A321. Traditional village local with panelled alcoves. Real ale. Home-made food and à la carte restaurant *Tue-Sat L and E & Sun 12.00-18.00*. Outside patio area and Wi-Fi. *Open Tue-Sat L and E & Sun 12.00-20.00*.

4 Canal Centre Tearooms Canal Centre, Mychett Place Road, Mychett GU16 6DD (01252 669000). Friendly, welcoming establishment. Inexpensive and enticing array of home-baked cakes and light meals. Tea, coffee, soft drinks and ice creams. Garden with children's play area. *Open Tue-Sun 09.30-15.00*.

5 Miners Arms 2 Mytchett Road, Mytchett GU16 6EZ (01252 516701; www.facebook.com/minersarmsmytchett). Large, single-room pub, with a predominantly local clientele, playing host to a tandoori restaurant, *open daily 17.30-23.00 (Sat 23.30)* which also offers a takeaway service. Dog- and family-friendly, garden. Traditional pub games, sports TV and Wi-Fi. *Open Mon-Fri 15.00-23.00 & Sat-Sun 12.00-00.00*.

6 The Swan 2 Hutton Road, Ash Vale, Aldershot GU12 5HA (01252 325212; www.facebook.com/SwanAshVale). Large pub with garden overlooking the canal serving real ale. Food available *Mon-Fri 11.30-21.00 (Sat-Sun 09.30)*. Weekend brunch. Dog- and child-friendly, garden. Real fires and Wi-Fi. *Open Mon-Fri 11.00-23.00 & Sat-Sun 09.30-23.00 (Sun 22.30)*.

7 Spice of India 2 Wharf Road, Ash Vale, Aldershot GU12 5AZ (01252 313638/325163; www.spiceofindiaash.com). By Ash Wharf Bridge. Locally recommended Indian restaurant with friendly service and generous portions. *Open daily 17.30-23.00*. Takeaway and delivery service.

Crookham

The course of the navigation is now rural and isolated and, notwithstanding all the military presence, approaches Fleet in a richly wooded cutting through Pyestock Hill. There is an excellent licensed *supermarket* selling fresh meat and vegetables as well as the usual things – this marks the eastern extremity of Fleet. Houses and gardens back on to the canal and generally seem to appreciate it being there. A canoe slalom course is marked out (slow down and take care) and there are some moored craft. *Shops* are close at hand to the north west of Reading Road South Bridge. Between Chequers and Double Bridges old World War II anti-tank barriers still stand by the waterway, and pill-box defences can be seen gently crumbling away in the undergrowth.

- **Fleet**
  Hants. All services. Useful for its shops and services, but little else of interest.
- **Church Crookham**
  Hants. PO, stores, chemist, baker, takeaways, fish & chips. Home to the only commercially successful tobacco plantation in Britain, abandoned in 1938, now the site of a garden centre. Best approached from Coxheath Road Bridge or Malt House Bridge.
- **Crookham Village**
  Hants. Takeaway. Offering a more rural setting than its ecclesiastical namesake.
- **Dogmersfield**
  Hants. A well-preserved village with pretty thatched and timbered houses.
- **Winchfield**
  Hants. Walk north from Barley Mow Bridge to see the church of St Mary, a Norman building dating from c.1170. There are three original windows in the tower, and boldly decorated doorways.

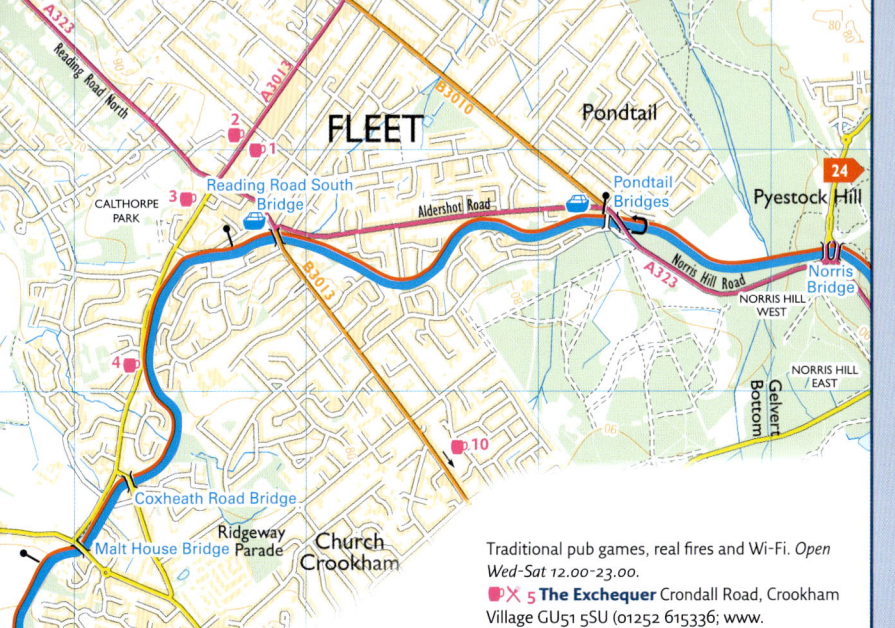

Basingstoke Canal

Crookham

Pubs and Restaurants

1 Propaganda Music Centre 317-321 Fleet Road, Fleet GU51 3BU (01252 620198; www.musiccanteen.co.uk). Formerly the Hogs Head. Now described as having a casual, fun and relaxing approach to food and drink with excellent service in stylish surroundings. Large variety of lager and ciders, cocktails, soft drinks and coffee. Inexpensive, pizza-based food available *all day*. Live music *Wed-Thu*; DJ *Fri-Sat*. Relatively quiet *during the day*. Open *Tue-Sat 16.00-00.00 (Fri-Sat 02.30)*.

2 The Emporium 271 Fleet Road, Fleet GU51 3QW (01252 816797; www.facebook.com/EmporiumFleet). Trendy, young persons' pub, described as an Ale Café. Real ale. Interesting selection of snacks and bar meals *daily 10.00-21.00*. Garden and patio seating. Dog- and family-friendly, traditional pub games, sports TV and Wi-Fi. Open *Mon-Sat 12.00-23.00 (Fri-Sat 01.00) & Sun 12.00-22.00*.

3 The Oat Sheaf 2 Crookham Road, Fleet GU51 5DR (01252 819508; www.theoatsheaf.co.uk). Primarily a dining pub, refurbished with modern decor, serving real ale with food available *daily 12.00-22.00 (Sun 21.00)*. Dog- and family-friendly, garden. Real fires and Wi-Fi. Open *11.00-23.00 (Sun 22.00)*.

4 The Fox & Hounds 71 Crookham Road, Church Crookham GU51 5NP (01252 663686; www.foxandhoundscc.co.uk). Friendly pub with large canalside garden. Real ale. Homemade, freshly prepared meals *Wed-Fri L and E & Sat-Sun 12.00-20.30 (Sun 18.00)*. Dog- and family-friendly, garden. Traditional pub games, real fires and Wi-Fi. Open *Wed-Sat 12.00-23.00*.

5 The Exchequer Crondall Road, Crookham Village GU51 5SU (01252 615336; www.exchequercrookham.co.uk). North of Crookham Wharf. Described as a 21st-century local and majoring on food. Good selection of real ales and a wide range of food available *Mon-Fri 12.00-21.30 & Sat-Sun 09.00-21.30 (Sun 20.00)*. Dog- and family-friendly, garden. Real fires and Wi-Fi. Open *Mon-Fri 11.00-22.00 (Fri 23.00) & Sat-Sun 09.00-23.00 (Sun 21.00)*.

6 The Spice Merchant The Street, Crookham Village GU51 5SJ (01252 621126; www.spicemerchantcrookhamvillage.com). Beamy old village pub doubling up as the purveyor of Thai and South East Asian cuisine. Real ales and food available *Mon-Fri L and E & Sat-Sun 12.00-21.30 (Sun 20.30)*. Dog- and child-friendly, large garden and play area. Traditional pub games and Wi-Fi. Open *daily 12.00-22.30 (Fri-Sat 23.30)*.

7 The Queen's Head Pilcot Lane, Dogmersfield RG27 8SY (01252 613531; www.queensheadpub.co.uk). Fine 17th-C country pub, where Catherine of Aragon met Arthur, Henry VIII's brother. Real ale. Extensive range of meals *Tue-Fri L and E & Sat-Sun 12.00-21.30 (Sun 18.30)*. Patio, large garden and Wi-Fi. Open *Tue-Thu L and E & Fri-Sun 12.00-23.00 (Sun 21.00)*.

8 The Barley Mow The Hurst, Winchfield RG27 8DE (01252 617490; www.barley-mow.com). Large country pub, with an intriguing central fireplace. Meals *Wed-Sun L and E (not Sun E)*. Real ale. Traditional pub games, real fires and Wi-Fi. Open *Wed-Fri L and E & Sat-Sun 12.00-22.00 (Sun 15.30)*.

Try also: **9 The Wyvern** 75 Aldershot Road, Church Crookham, Fleet GU52 8JY (01252 624772; www.thewyvernpub.co.uk) and **10 The Tweseldown** Beacon Hill Road, Church Crookham, Fleet GU52 8DY (01252 266657; www.thetweseldown.co.uk).

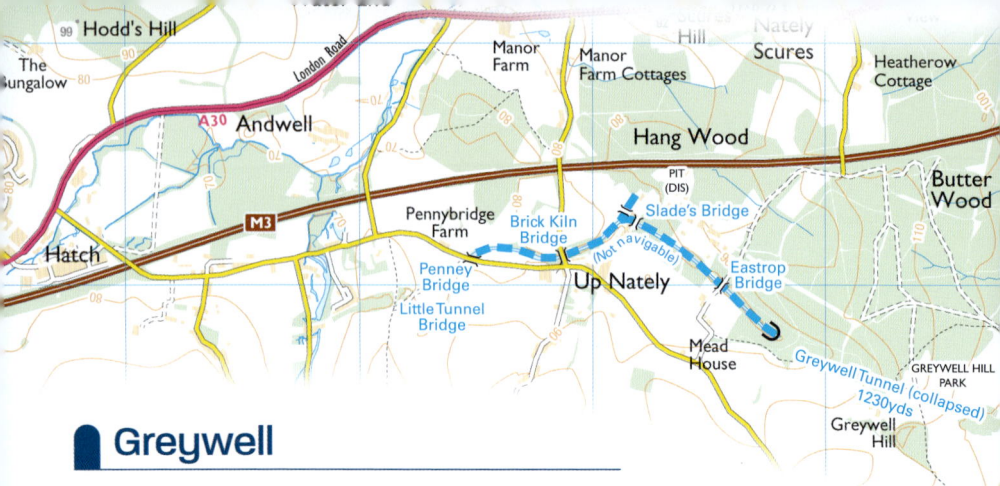

Greywell

At Colt Hill Bridge there is a wharf, a boatyard and good *moorings*.
The course of the canal now becomes more open as it makes its approach to Greywell Tunnel. The few houses and gardens of North Warnborough are followed by a mechanised lift bridge, beyond which is the limit of navigation for cruisers, by Odiham Castle. The last commercial boat reached Odiham in 1916. It is then just a short walk to the eastern portal of the collapsed Greywell Tunnel (1,230yds), passing the remains of Lock 30. This was built to raise the water level above here by 12ins, to give increased draught and aid navigation. A footpath leads over the tunnel portal to Greywell village, and the Fox & Goose pub. It is possible to follow rough paths over Greywell Hill to see what remains of the western entrance to the tunnel and a short isolated stretch of the canal passing the village of Up Nately. Greywell Tunnel is well known for its colony of some 12,500 bats, including the largest known colony of Natterer's bats in the UK.

NAVIGATIONAL NOTES

1. The mechanised lift bridge at North Warnborough is operated with a Watermate key.
2. The limit of navigation is a few yards beyond Odiham Castle. Do not attempt to take your boat any further than this. *Turn here.*

BOAT TRIPS

John Pinkerton II This is a 50-seater boat operated by the Surrey & Hampshire Canal Society for public trips and private charter. Telephone 07305 340547 or visit www.basingstoke-canal.org.uk/take-a-cruise-on-the-john-pinkerton-ii for details.
The Accessible Boating Association operate two boats (*Dawn* and *Madam Butterfly*) for self-steer hiring or skippered trips. Both craft have been especially designed to provide facilities for disabled passengers. Bookings and further details on 07934 926683; or visit www.accessibleboating.org.uk.

WALKING AND CYCLING

The path over Greywell Hill connects with other footpaths through Butter Wood. You can, if you wish, make a circular route back to Warnborough Green, where there are a couple of pubs.

Boatyards

Ⓑ**Galleon Marine** Colt Hill Bridge, Odiham RG29 1AL (01256 703691; www.galleonmarine.co.uk). Pump out, gas, narrowboat hire, day hire craft, overnight mooring (by arrangement), winter storage, slipway, used boat sales, chandlery, books, maps and gifts, ice cream. Hire of rowing boats, canoes, kayaks and punts by the hour, or longer. Picnic area. *Open Thu-Tue 11.00-17.00.*

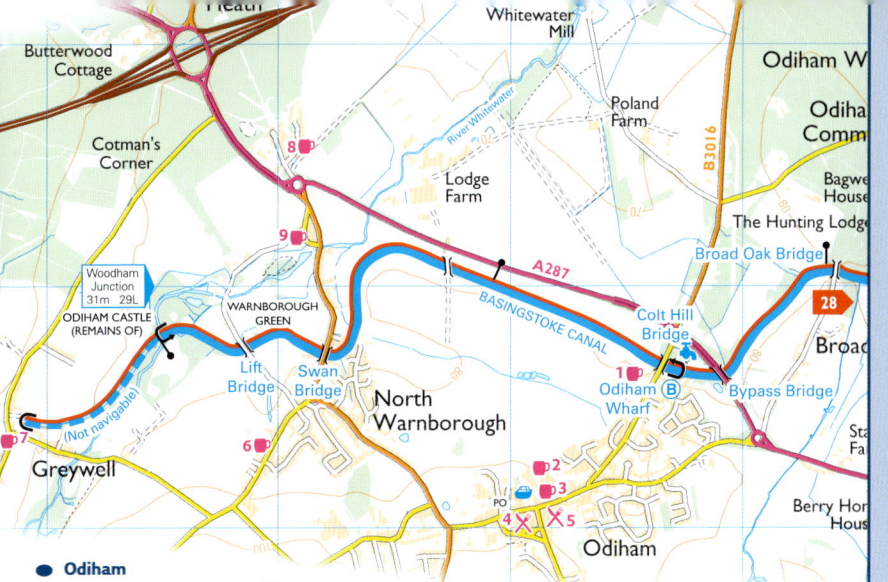

Basingstoke Canal — Greywell

- **Odiham**
Hants. PO, stores, chemist, off-licence, takeaways, garage. It is a pleasant walk up the road from Colt Hill Bridge, past May's Model Cottages (1862) and a pub to the broad High Street, rich with 17th- and 18th-C buildings.

- **North Warnborough**
Hants. Garage. A group of attractive houses, some thatched and dating from the 15th C. There is no church, the village being virtually an extension of Odiham.

- **Odiham (King John's) Castle** RG29 1HQ. Dating from 1207, this picturesque pile of flint is all that remains of the only octagonal keep in England, a three-storeyed building used by King John as a stopping place between Windsor and Winchester.

- **Greywell**
Hants. A village of charming red-brick houses around the pub and tunnel entrance.

Pubs and Restaurants

1 The Waterwitch Colt Hill Bridge, London Road, Odiham RG29 1AL (01256 702778; www.chefandbrewer.com/pubs/hampshire/waterwitch). Comfortable beamed pub with rustic bar decorated with canal artefacts. Vast waterside garden. Real ale together with food available *daily 11.30-21.00 (Fri-Sun 09.30)*. Family-friendly. *Open 11.00-23.00 (Fri-Sun 09.30)*.

2 The Red Lion 102 High Street, Odiham RG29 1LP (01256 701145; www.redlionodiham.co.uk/ourfoodanddrink). Originally a 17th-C ale house, now greatly refurbished, this cosy pub dispenses real ale and fresh local Hampshire fare *Mon Thu L and E & Fri-Sun 12.00-21.00 (Sun 20.00)*. Family-friendly, Wi-Fi. B&B. *Open daily 11.00-23.00 (Sun 22.00)*.

3 Bel & The Dragon at The George 100-102 High Street, Odiham RG29 1LP (01256 702696; www.belandthedragon-odiham.co.uk). Handsome 16th-C hotel with a Georgian façade. Inside are beams and an Elizabethan fireplace taken from Old Basing House. Food available *Mon-Sat L and E & Sun 12.00-21.00*. Breakfast served *08.00-12.00*. B&B. *Open Sun-Thu 11.00-23.00 (Sun 22.30) & Fri-Sat 11.00-23.30 (Sat 10.30)*.

4 La Creperie 101 High Street, Odiham RG29 1LA (01256 541720; www.facebook.com/lacreperieinodiham). Odiham's hidden gem serving coffee and tasty French dishes including crêpes and galettes. Children welcome. *Open Tue-Sat 10.00-17.00*.

5 El Castello 83 High Street, Odiham RG29 1LB (01256 704281; www.elcastello-odiham.co.uk). Friendly, attentive staff. An ideal place for informal eating. Children welcome. *Open daily 10.30-22.00 (Sun 21.30)*. Takeaway service.

6 The Anchor Inn The Street, North Warnborough RG29 1BE (01256 702740). Cheerful 18th-C village pub. Real ale. Inexpensive meals *Sun L & Tue-Wed E*. Children and dogs welcome, garden. Traditional pub games, newspapers, real fires and Wi-Fi. *Open Mon-Fri 17.00-23.00 (Mon 17.30) & Sat-Sun 12.00-23.00 (Sun 20.00)*.

7 The Fox & Goose The Street, Greywell RG29 1BY (01256 702062; www.facebook.com/foxandgoosegreywell). Comfortable 16th-C country pub with two open fires. Real ale. Meals, including game in season, *11.00-23.00*. Large garden; dog- and child-friendly. Traditional pub games, real fires and sports TV. *Open Mon-Sat 11.00-23.00 (Mon-Tue 22.00) Sun 12.00-21.00*.

Try also: **8 The Derby Inn** RG29 1HD (01256 279022; www.thederbyinn.co.uk) and **9 The Mill House** RG29 1ET (01256 702953; www.brunningandprice.co.uk/millhouse).

BRIDGWATER & TAUNTON CANAL

MAXIMUM DIMENSIONS
Length: 51' 10"
Beam: 10'
Headroom: 7' 1"
Draught: 2' 6"

MANAGER
0303 040 4040
enquiries.walessouthwest@canalrivertrust.org.uk

MILEAGE
TAUNTON Firepool Lock to:
Creech St Michael: 3 miles
Durston: 6 miles
North Newton: 8 miles
BRIDGWATER DOCK: 14 miles

6 locks

Paddling: Category 1

The Bridgwater & Taunton Canal represents a small part of a far more ambitious scheme, the Bristol & Taunton Canal Navigation, for which Rennie gave a quotation in 1811 of no less than £429,990. This was to be part of a ship canal from Bristol to Exeter where it would join up with the long-established Exeter Ship Canal. However, although this sum was forthcoming, very little work seems to have been undertaken and instead, in 1824, an Act of Parliament was obtained to 'abridge, vary, extend and improve the Bristol & Taunton Canal Navigation', which resulted in the much briefer line between the River Parrett at Huntworth (just south of Bridgwater) and Taunton being adopted. The ship canal scheme was abandoned. Although the total cost of the canal on its opening was £71,000, toll receipts in the early days averaged £7,000 per year; most of this, however, was drawn from traffic passing to and from the Chard and Grand Western canals which the Bridgwater & Taunton Canal joined at Creech St Michael and Taunton respectively.

The size of the locks was unorthodox at 54'x 13' with a theoretical draught of 3' 0", which meant a normal craft load of 22 tons. The distance as originally constituted from Firepool Lock, Taunton, to Huntworth was 13½ miles. Prior to the building of the Bridgwater & Taunton Canal, there already existed a navigation of sorts on the rivers Parrett and Tone (i.e. an alternative route between Taunton and Bridgwater). This route suffered from drought in summer and floods in winter and so was not particularly reliable; but it was good enough to cause the shareholders of the Bridgwater & Taunton Canal great embarrassment and they were forced to purchase the river navigation in 1832, five years after their own opening.

In 1837 a further Act was obtained authorising the extension from Huntworth to Bridgwater and the building of the dock and its entrance lock from the River Parrett. This led to the curious anomaly of there being two sets of milestones in close juxtaposition. At the time of its jubilant opening on 25 March 1841, this extension had cost fully £175,000, leaving the proprietors badly out of pocket when the whole waterway and dock complex was sold to the Bristol and Exeter Railway Company for £64,000 in 1866. When control of the waterway eventually passed to the Great Western Railway, little attempt was made to maintain commercial traffic and the last barge tolls were collected in 1907.

In 1940, at the behest of the War Office, the Bridgwater & Taunton Canal, like the Kennet & Avon, was turned into a line of defence against the possibility of enemy invasion and pill boxes were erected at strategic points along it. The bridges were fixed and strengthened to carry military vehicles.

Little interest was shown in the waterway after nationalisation in 1947, although the Bridgwater Docks continued to operate under the Railway Executive of the British Transport Commission. In 1958 the Bowes Committee Report on waterways put the canal into category 'C', i.e. suitable for redevelopment, and various surveys were carried out, seemingly without any concrete results. The canal passed to the British Waterways Board (as was) in 1963 but Bridgwater Docks remained in Railways Board ownership. In the meantime the south western branch of the Inland Waterways Association had begun to consider the canal in terms of restoration and in 1965 the Bridgwater & Taunton Canal Restoration Group was formed. A year later this group became the Somerset Inland Waterways Society, which was formed to work towards restoration of the canal for amenity purposes. A subsequent arrangement negotiated by BWB allowed for the extraction of 3 million gallons of water a day from the canal, to provide much needed revenue. Eventually a partnership between Somerset County Council and British Waterways, encouraged by the West Country branch of the Inland Waterways Association, saw full restoration of the navigation and it was opened throughout in 1994. Bridgwater Docks have been developed into a marina, surrounded by new housing, shops and a pub.

PADDLING

Craft can be hired from the Somerset Boat Centre (see **Boat Trips** on page 37) and full details about paddling this detached waterway are available at www.gopaddling.info/canals/bridgwater-and-taunton-canal). With just six locks to portage, this 14-mile canal is not too taxing and has the added – and very novel – attraction of Pip Youngman's Space Walk, where a model of our solar system has been set out along the towpath, each planet built to scale. A recent addition has been Halley's Comet in anticipation of its reappearance in July 2061. The South Somerset Astronomical Society aims to move the marker, representing the comet, along the canal charting its progress through the Solar System as it heads back towards our skies: a unique 38-year project commenced in December 2023!

Unique Paddle-gear, the Ball and Chain forming a counterweight to aid operation

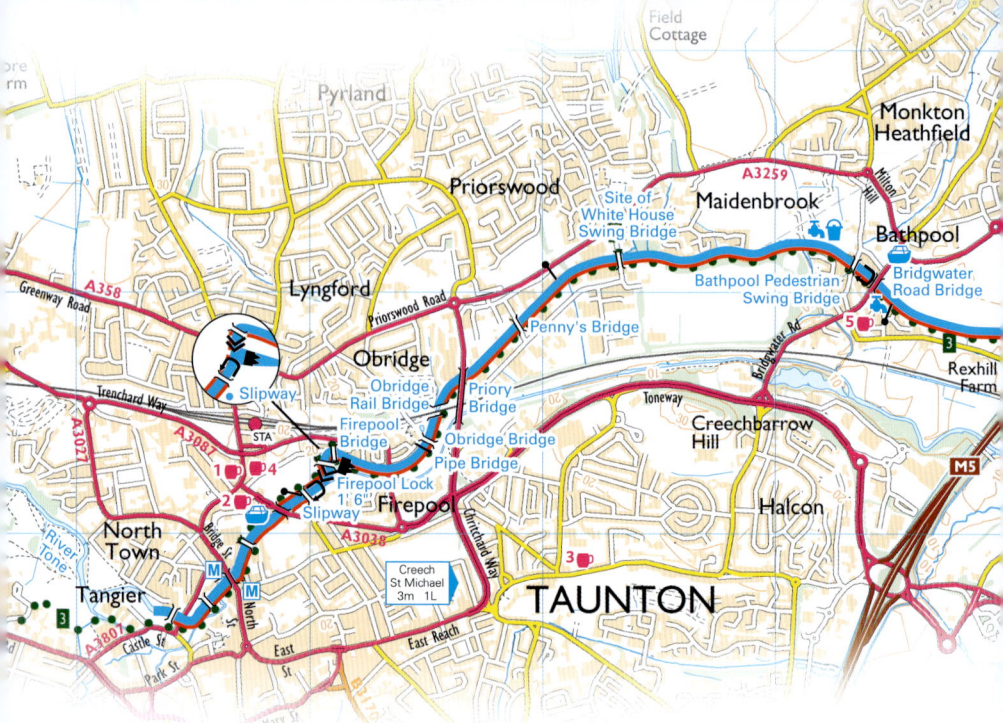

Taunton

The Bridgwater & Taunton Canal runs through attractive rolling scenery, typical of rural Somerset. It starts at Firepool Lock, at a junction with the River Tone. In the 18th- and 19th-C the Tone, which passes through Taunton before meeting the canal, was navigable from Taunton to its junction with the River Parrett. Firepool Lock, pleasantly situated beside the Tone weir, is the first stage of the canal's north easterly journey towards Bridgwater and the estuary of the Parrett. The lock is reached from Taunton by following signs to the cattle market, or by crossing the footbridge over the Tone from the town's Firepool district, on the river's south bank. The canal curves past the railway station, passing under the main Bristol to Exeter line, which follows it closely to Bridgwater. The tall railway warehouse is built on the site of the old junction with the Grand Western Canal. Taunton is quickly left behind as the waterway continues through flat pasture land to Bathpool, where the towpath runs briefly through the churchyard of a small corrugated iron church. Bathpool Swing Bridge used to be the first obstacle to restoring the navigation east of Taunton, being one of the structures fixed closed during the invasion scare of 1940, when the War Office destroyed the swinging mechanisms on all the navigation's swing bridges. Today it operates as a pedestrian bridge only. Contrary to popular opinion, this measure was not so much to prevent navigation by German forces, as to create lines of defence along natural barriers. The Bridgwater & Taunton, like the Kennet & Avon and Basingstoke Canals, was hastily turned into a fortified line of resistance. Leaving Bathpool the country becomes hilly and more wooded and a modern housing estate accompanies the canal into Creech St Michael. Before the village is the site of the junction with the Chard Canal. There is little to be seen of the junction itself but to the south the long embankment crossing the Tone flood plain is still visible.

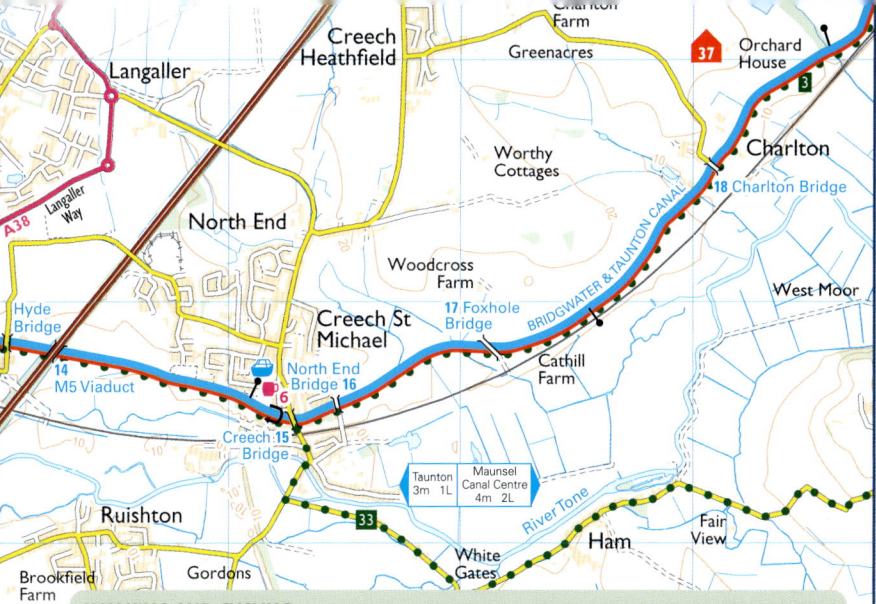

Bridgwater & Taunton Canal

Taunton

WALKING AND CYCLING

This detached and often isolated waterway, just 14½ miles in length, is ideal for walking and cycling. Railway stations at each end make one-way trips possible and well sign-posted car parks along its entire length mean that 'bite-sized' chunks can be tackled by the less energetic. The Somerset Space Walk adds a unique dimension to the experience (*see page 37 for details*). In Taunton there are walkers' trails (available from the TIC) covering the town's heritage and its wealth of non-conformist chapels. For the cyclist, a range of trail guides take one further afield on a variety of interesting quests. The towpath forms part of the West Country Way, National Cycle Network Route 3, from Padstow to Bristol. Route 33 links Taunton to the South Coast Route 2 at Axminster and Seaton. The South Somerset Cycle Ride is a waymarked route around the byways of South Somerset, centred on Taunton.

NAVIGATIONAL NOTES

1. When using the locks please leave bottom gates open after use.
2. Do not tamper with the settings of the paddle gear.
3. Report any problems to CRT on 0303 040 4040 or telephone the emergency helpline on 0800 47 999 47.
4. Slipways for the use of visiting trail boaters are located at: Bridgwater YMCA HQ (01278 726000) and at TA1 1AS approximately 300yds south west of Firepool Lock, on the river's south bank.
5. Boat licenses may be obtained from CRT. Contact CRT Customer Services on 0303 040 4040; enquiries.walessouthwest@canalrivertrust.org.uk or visit www.canalrivertrust.org.uk/enjoy-the-waterways/boating/buy-your-boat-licence.
6. Beware of reduced headroom at the following bridges: O'Bridge, Whites, Dairy and Huntworth.

- **Bathpool**
  Somerset. A straggling village, running into the outskirts of Taunton, much improved by severe traffic calming measures.
- **Creech St Michael**
  Somerset. PO, stores, off-licence. Although now surrounded by modern housing, the old part of the village still survives. The largely 13th-C church is a sturdy and attractive building; inside there are fine waggon roofs.
- **Chard Canal**
  The Chard Canal was one of the last to be built in England and was one of the shortest-lived of all navigations. Work began in 1835 and the 13½ mile line to Chard from Creech St Michael on the Bridgwater & Taunton Canal was opened in 1842. The canal included three tunnels, two major aqueducts, two locks and four inclined planes. It suffered from immediate railway competition and never made any money. Bought by the Bristol and Exeter Railway Company in 1867, it closed down the next year. It is possible to follow the line of the canal on foot, although there are few rights of way that correspond with its original bed.

● **Taunton**

Somerset. All services. Taunton has long been a rich agricultural market town and an important point on the old trunk route to the West Country. The skyline is dominated by the towers of the churches of St Mary Magdalene and St James. The first, rebuilt in 1862, is 163ft high; its ornamental splendour rather dwarfs the double aisled church. In Middle Street there is an octagonal 18th-C Methodist chapel. Wesley preached here when it was opened. The centre of the town contains an interesting mixture of buildings; 15th-C municipal buildings, the 18th-C Market House, the Victorian Shire Hall and the 20th-C County Hall. Remains of the medieval town can be seen, including fragments of the 13th-C priory.

Brewhouse Theatre and Arts Centre Coal Orchard, Taunton TA1 1JL (01823 283244; www.brewhouse.co.uk). Entertainment including folk, comedy, classical music, dance and drama. Box office *open Mon-Fri 10.00-16.00.*

Chapels in Taunton It was observed in the 17th C that Taunton was 'the vineyard of the Lord of Hosts and the inhabitants his precious plants'. A trail around the town's chapels has been laid out and a leaflet is available from the TIC in Paul Street, where non-conformity was founded in 1662. Less local trails are also available from the TIC and depict such oddities as Towers & Hunkypunks and Bench Ends & Pulpits.

ND Cycles 3A Roman Road, Taunton TA1 2BD (01823 365917; www.ndcycles.co.uk). *Open Mon-Sat 09.00-17.30 (Sat 16.00).*

The Museum of Somerset Taunton Castle, Castle Green, Taunton TA1 4AA (01823 255088; www.swheritage.org.uk/museum-of-somerset). Many galleries to explore and objects to discover, including the Frome Hoard, the second largest collection of Roman coins discovered in Britain. Shop and café. *Open Tue-Sat 10.00-17.00 and B Hol Mon. Free.*

Somerset Cricket Museum 7 Priory Avenue, Taunton TA1 1XX (01823 275893; www.somersetcricketmuseum.co.uk). Memorabilia from the Somerset County Cricket Club, bat-making demonstrations, cricket shop, refreshments. *Telephone for opening times. Donations.*

Tacchi-Morris Arts Centre School Road, Taunton TA2 8PD (01823 414141; www.tacchi-morris.com). Theatre venue offering a range of shows, workshops and classes for adults and children. Box office *open Mon & Wed-Fri 10.00-16.00 and Tue 10.00-12.00 & 17.00-19.00.*

Tourist Information Centre Taunton Library, Paul Street, Taunton TA1 3XZ (01823 336344; www.visitsomerset.co.uk/taunton/things-to-do). *Available during library opening hours.*

Pubs and Restaurants (pages 34-35)

🍺 1 **The Plough Inn** 75 Station Road, Taunton TA1 1PB (01823 324404; www.facebook.com/theploughtaunton). Real ales and local ciders. Bar snacks are available *Tue-Wed E; Thu L and E & Fri-Sun 12.00-21.00 (Sun 16.00).* Dog- and child-friendly, garden. *Occasional* live music. Traditional pub games, real fires and Wi-Fi. *Open Mon-Wed 15.00-23.00; Thu 10.00-00.00 & Fri-Sun 10.00-02.00 (Sun 23.00).*

🍺✕ 2 **The Crown & Sceptre** 74-76 Station Road, Taunton TA1 1NX (01823 284398; www.facebook.com/profile.php?id=100047161189540). Large, welcoming town pub serving real ale. Beer garden, dog-friendly. Traditional pub games, live music *Fri-Sat* and Wi-Fi. B&B. *Open daily 12.00-23.00.*

🍺 3 **The Rose Inn** Hamilton Road, Taunton TA1 2EL (01823 275571). Traditional, brick-built pub serving real ale. Family friendly. Traditional pub games, sports TV and Wi-Fi. B&B. *Open Mon-Sat 12.00-23.00 (Sat 11.00) & Sun 11.00-22.30.*

🍺 4 **The Ale House** 78 Station Road, Taunton TA1 1PD (01823 617408; www.thealehousetaunton.pub). Once The Cricketers Arms, and close to the station, this popular hostelry serves a good selection of real ales, together with food (including breakfast) *10.00-20.30 (Sun 17.30)* and offers live music *at the weekend*. Dogs welcome, outside seating. Traditional pub games and sports TV. *Open daily 10.00-23.00 (Fri-Sat 01.00).*

🍺✕ 5 **The Bathpool Inn** 102 Bridgwater Road, Taunton TA2 8BE (01823 335258; www.vintageinn.co.uk/restaurants/south-west/thebathpoolinntaunton#/). Low beamed, comfortable family pub. Real ales. Food available *12.00-22.00 (Sun 21.30).* Real fires and Wi-Fi. B&B. *Open 11.00-23.00 (Sun 22.30).*

🍺 6 **The Bell Inn** St Michael's Road, Creech St Michael, Taunton TA3 5DP (01823 444566; www.facebook.com/thebellinncreech). Village local, family-friendly pub. Real ales. Dogs welcome. Fully enclosed garden. *Regular* live music. *Open Wed-Thu 17.00-22.30 (Thu 23.30) & Fri-Sun 12.00-23.30 (Sun 20.00).*

North Newton

This section is typical of the quiet agricultural nature of the whole canal. The canal is slightly raised above the land on a low embankment, with views to the north across farmland and to the south across the low-lying flood plain of the River Tone. The canal leaves the river to the south, passing through marsh and moorland. Several small agricultural hamlets flank the waterway. At Durston, where the CRT maintenance yard is located, the busy A361 crosses. Beyond, the canal reaches the first lock which starts the descent to Bridgwater. The paddle gear is quite unique, composed of ball-shaped weights and chains to form a counter-balance mechanism.

North Newton

Somerset. An irregular farming village. The eccentric-looking church was rebuilt first in the 17th C and then again in the late 19th. Nothing remains of the original Saxon church, where the Alfred Jewel was found in 1693. This Saxon ornament, the oldest surviving Crown jewel, is now displayed in the Ashmolean Museum, Oxford.

Somerset Boat Centre Maidenhead Moorings, Higher Maunsel Lock, North Newton TA7 0DQ (07508 959996/07946 580050; www.somersetboatcentre.co.uk). The proprietors are a fund of information about the canal. Events include music, canal art painting demonstrations and art and photographic exhibitions and charity fundraisers. Food kiosk *open Thu-Sun 10.30-16.30*. Toilets (including disabled) and showers (Watermate key holders only). See Pubs and Restaurants for more details.

Somerset Space Walk
The brainchild of Pip Youngman, this unique portrayal of our Solar System has been set out to scale along the towpath using one scale for both the planets and the distances between them. There are no figures to conjure with, just the experience of a journey through space as you walk, cycle or boat the waterway.

BOAT TRIPS
Somerset Boat Centre
Maiden Mead Moorings, Higher Maunsel Lock, North Newton TA7 0DQ (07508 959996/07946 580050; www.somersetboatcentre.co.uk). Canoes, kayaks, rowing boats, paddle boards and self-drive motor boats for hire. *Nb Summersun* is available for charter and operates themed cruises. RYA Training Centre. *Open Thu-Sun 09.00-21.00.*

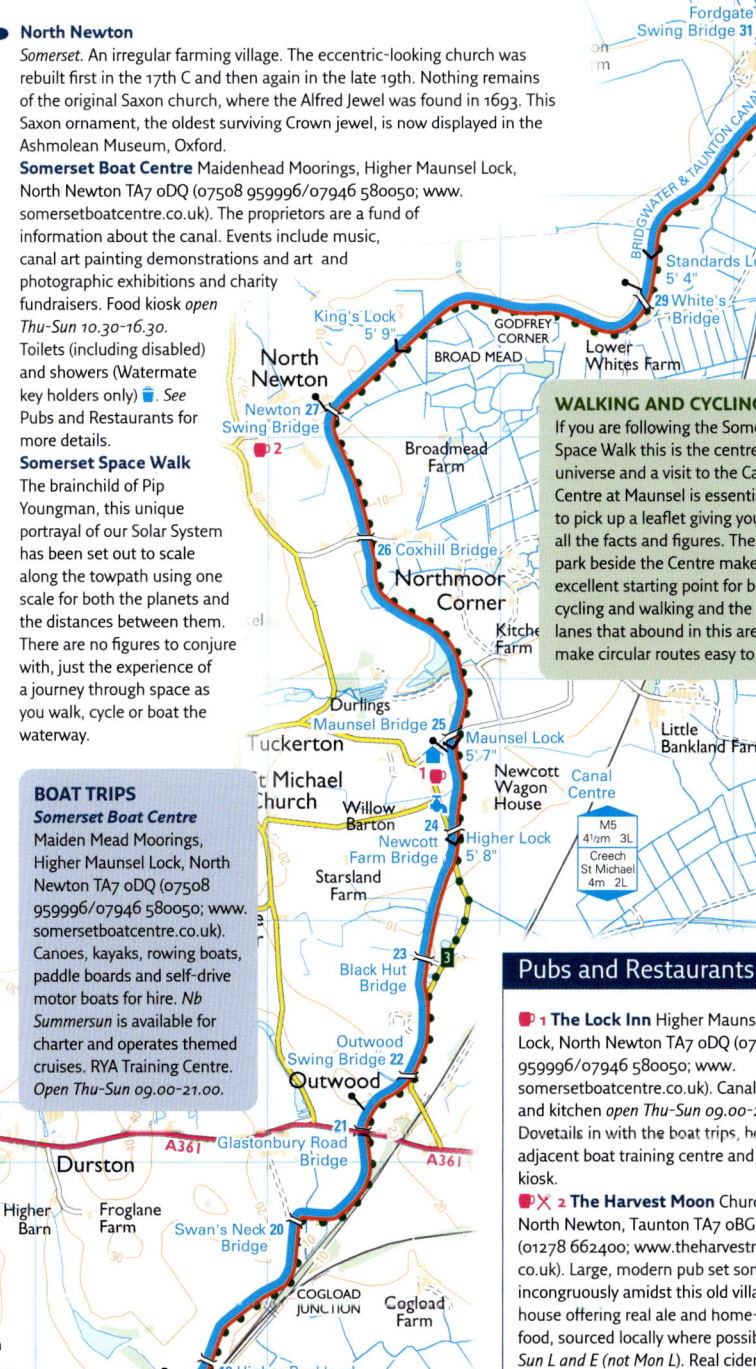

WALKING AND CYCLING
If you are following the Somerset Space Walk this is the centre of the universe and a visit to the Canal Centre at Maunsel is essential to pick up a leaflet giving you all the facts and figures. The car park beside the Centre makes an excellent starting point for both cycling and walking and the quiet lanes that abound in this area make circular routes easy to devise.

Pubs and Restaurants

1 The Lock Inn Higher Maunsel Lock, North Newton TA7 0DQ (07508 959996/07946 580050; www.somersetboatcentre.co.uk). Canalside bar and kitchen *open Thu-Sun 09.00-21.00*. Dovetails in with the boat trips, boat hire, adjacent boat training centre and food kiosk.

2 The Harvest Moon Church Road, North Newton, Taunton TA7 0BG (01278 662400; www.theharvestmoon.co.uk). Large, modern pub set somewhat incongruously amidst this old village. Free house offering real ale and home-made food, sourced locally where possible *Mon-Sun L and E (not Mon L)*. Real cider. Family-friendly. Skittle alley. Traditional pub games, real fires and sports TV. *Open Mon-Thu L and E (not Mon L) & Fri-Sun 12.00-23.00 (Sun 22.30).*

Bridgwater

Following the contours of the land, the waterway continues northwards towards Bridgwater. To the west, low hills rise gradually away from the canal; to the east low-lying farm and marsh land separates the navigation from the River Parrett. This tidal river, a vital drain for the whole area, swings ever nearer to the canal as it approaches Bridgwater. To the east the railway line stays close to the navigation until just before Bridgwater, when it turns away to pass east of the town. The course of the waterway is quiet and isolated. There are no villages near the canal, although there is easy access for Fordgate and Huntworth. Standard's Lock drops the navigation to the Bridgwater level. Nearing the town civilisation returns with a vengeance as traffic roars overhead on the M5 viaduct. After the motorway the towpath crosses to the west and the canal enters Bridgwater. South of Taunton Road Bridge there is a useful *parade of shops, including a post office, fish & chips, launderette, stores (open daily 06.00-23.00) takeaways and a toilet*, while to the north there is a large *supermarket* and a *garage*. The waterway passes through the town in a cutting, swinging in a wide arc to the west before turning back to the docks and the junction with the Parrett estuary. Access to the town is easy from the many bridges. The canal enters the dock through a stop lock which passes it into the large inner basin, laid out marina-fashion with floating pontoons. The original bonded warehouse is converted into flats *(and a pub)* and the availability of the extensive moorings here is currently open to doubt. The smaller outer basin is entered through a twin-bascular lift bridge and then a ship lock and a canal lock used to allow access to the River Parrett and thus the sea. The river locks have been blocked off with concrete barriers and so the Bridgwater & Taunton Canal remains just that: an isolated navigation linking its two eponymous towns and nothing else.

- **Bridgwater**
Somerset. All services. Bridgwater is an old market town straddling the River Parrett. Formerly the town was an important centre for the cloth trade, which encouraged development of the port from the Middle Ages onwards. The old quay, despite redevelopment, still has an attractive 18th-C flavour. It suffered severely during the Civil War and, in an artillery bombardment in July 1645, lost the greater part of its commercial and domestic buildings, many of which were of timber-frame construction. Elsewhere in the town are signs of 18th-C wealth: the handsome houses in Castle Street, built c.1725, were sponsored by James Bridges, first Duke of Chandos. Little of the medieval town survives. The 13th-C castle was destroyed by the Roundheads as a reprisal for the town's resistance. The watergate, on the west quay, is the only remaining relic of the castle and has a wall 12ft thick. Glass-making briefly flourished in the town when, in 1725, James Bridges built the 125ft Chandos Glass Cone. The venture failed within nine years and the cone, built from rubble from the derelict castle, was converted first to brick making and then to tile manufacture, only closing down during World War II.
Battle of Sedgemoor, 6 July 1685 When Charles II died, he was succeeded by his brother, James II, unpopular due to his Catholic faith. The Duke of Monmouth, an illegitimate son of Charles II, declared himself king in 1685 in Bridgwater. He landed at Lyme with a few supporters and soon raised an army 4000 strong, including 800 horsemen under Lord Grey. They moved to Bridgwater, while a Royalist army commanded by Lord Feversham and John Churchill (later the Duke of Marlborough) camped near Westonzoyland, 3 miles east of the town. Monmouth decided on a night attack but lost the element of surprise when caught crossing the Langmoor Rhine, one of the many drainage ditches in the area. A fierce battle broke out in which the artillery played a dominant part. Grey's cavalry tried to outflank Feversham but were prevented by the Bussex Rhine, another deep ditch. Although firing continued all night, Monmouth's cause was already lost. The leaders of the rebellion escaped for a while but the ill-armed rebel army was rounded up, many to be transported or executed on the orders of Judge Jeffreys. To find the site of the battle take the A372 east from Bridgwater; turn left in Westonzoyland. There are signs to the Sedgemoor Memorial Stone.
Blake Museum 5 Blake Street, Bridgwater TA6 3NB (01278 456127; www.bridgwatermuseum.org.uk). Robert Blake was born in Bridgwater in 1598 and represented the town as a Member of Parliament. After a distinguished army career he was appointed by Cromwell as one of his first Generals at Sea and went on to destroy the Dutch fleet in a battle of 1653 and to achieve a resounding victory over the Spaniards in 1657. He is recognised as one of the major influences in establishing the reputation of the Navy – later to become the Royal Navy. The museum houses a collection of Blake memorabilia; depicts the drama of the Monmouth Rebellion and the humour of an 18th-C artist; and presents a fascinating selection of local history and archaeology. Shop. *Open Wed-Sat 10.00-16.00. Donations.*

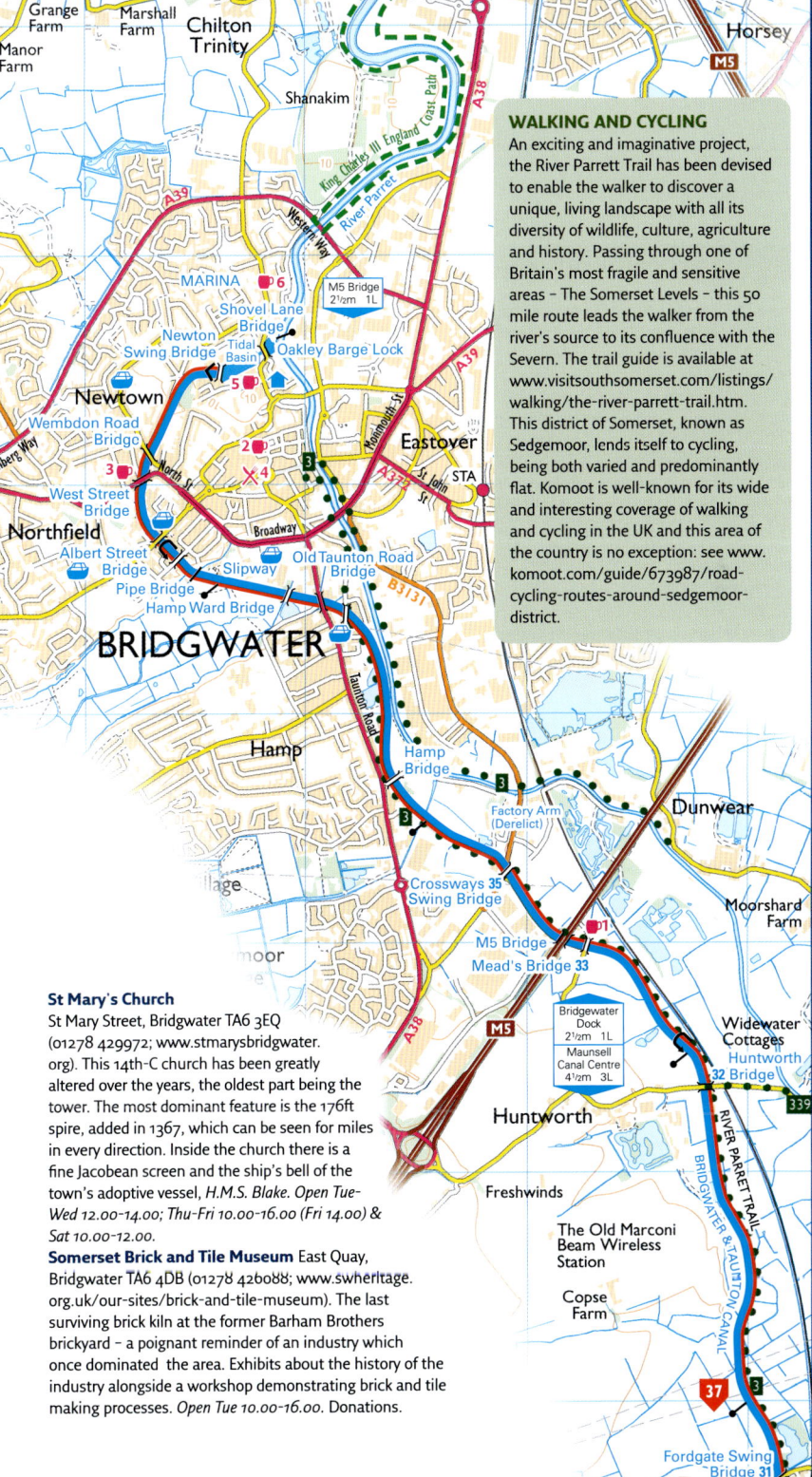

Bridgwater & Taunton Canal

Bridgwater

WALKING AND CYCLING

An exciting and imaginative project, the River Parrett Trail has been devised to enable the walker to discover a unique, living landscape with all its diversity of wildlife, culture, agriculture and history. Passing through one of Britain's most fragile and sensitive areas – The Somerset Levels – this 50 mile route leads the walker from the river's source to its confluence with the Severn. The trail guide is available at www.visitsouthsomerset.com/listings/walking/the-river-parrett-trail.htm. This district of Somerset, known as Sedgemoor, lends itself to cycling, being both varied and predominantly flat. Komoot is well-known for its wide and interesting coverage of walking and cycling in the UK and this area of the country is no exception: see www.komoot.com/guide/673987/road-cycling-routes-around-sedgemoor-district.

St Mary's Church St Mary Street, Bridgwater TA6 3EQ (01278 429972; www.stmarysbridgwater.org). This 14th-C church has been greatly altered over the years, the oldest part being the tower. The most dominant feature is the 176ft spire, added in 1367, which can be seen for miles in every direction. Inside the church there is a fine Jacobean screen and the ship's bell of the town's adoptive vessel, *H.M.S. Blake*. *Open Tue-Wed 12.00-14.00; Thu-Fri 10.00-16.00 (Fri 14.00) & Sat 10.00-12.00.*

Somerset Brick and Tile Museum East Quay, Bridgwater TA6 4DB (01278 426088; www.swheritage.org.uk/our-sites/brick-and-tile-museum). The last surviving brick kiln at the former Barham Brothers brickyard – a poignant reminder of an industry which once dominated the area. Exhibits about the history of the industry alongside a workshop demonstrating brick and tile making processes. *Open Tue 10.00-16.00. Donations.*

Westonzoyland Pumping Station Museum of Steam Power and Land Drainage Hoopers Lane, Westonzoyland, Bridgwater TA7 0LS (01278 691595; www.wzlet.org). A display of pumping engines, both static and in steam, housed in old pumping station buildings dating from the 1830s. Even without steam there is plenty to enjoy, including a Crossley engine, a Lister and a waterwheel. *Open* as a static display *Sun 13.00-17.00*. In steam *first Sun of the month and B Hols (except Xmas and Boxing day)*. Shop and tearoom. Charge.

Pubs and Restaurants (page 39)

🍺✕ **1 The Boat & Anchor** Meads Crossing, Huntworth, Bridgwater TA7 0AQ (01278 662473; www.theboatandanchor.co.uk). Six separate cottages, now all knocked into one. Home-cooked food *L and E daily*. Real ales and *Sunday* carvery. Children welcome. Canalside garden and orangery. Wi-Fi and B&B. *Open daily 12.00-23.00.*

🍺✕ **2 The Artichoke** 6 Clare Street, Bridgwater TA6 3EN (01278 238978; www.artichokegastropub.co.uk). Relaxing, laid back gastropub serving cocktails and food *daily 17.30-22.00 & Sun 11.00-14.30*. Large courtyard garden. Wi-Fi. *Open daily 17.30-23.30 & Sun 11.00-15.00.*

🍺 **3 The Malt Shovel** 2 Wembdon Road, Bridgwater TA6 7DN (01278 444905; www.greeneking-pubs.co.uk/pubs/somerset/malt-shovel). Lively pub near the river and town centre, dispensing real ale and food *daily 12.00-21.00*. Quiz *Mon* and live entertainment *Fri* (with much going on in between). Garden, family-friendly. Traditional pub games, sports TV and Wi-Fi. *Open daily 11.00-23.00.*

✕ 🍷 **4 Old Vicarage Hotel and Restaurant** 45-51 St Mary Street, Bridgwater TA6 3EQ (01278 458891; www.theoldvicaragebridgwater.com). Charming old establishment opposite the church serving fresh, locally grown food *Mon-Thu E & Fri-Sun L and E (not Sun E)*. Booking advisable. Bar *open Mon-Thu E & Fri-Sun L and E.*

🍺✕ **5 The Admiral's Landing** Admiral's Court, The Marina, Bridgwater TA6 3EX (01278 422515; www.facebook.com/AdmiralsLandingPub). Real ale and food served *L and E (not Sun E)* in an old warehouse. Children welcome. Dockside seating. Traditional pub games, newspapers, sports TV and Wi-Fi. *Open 11.00-23.00 (Sun 12.00).*

🍺 **6 The British Flag** 77-83 Chilton Street, Bridgwater TA6 3HX (01278 422537). Real ales. Children and dogs welcome. Large enclosed garden. Traditional pub games and sports TV. Live music *Sat*. B&B. *Open Mon-Thu L and E (not Mon L) & Fri-Sun 12.00-00.00.*

Horse-drawn Trip Boat on the Grand Western Canal

GRAND WESTERN CANAL

MAXIMUM DIMENSIONS

As there are no locks on this navigation the following measurements refer to the overall canal dimensions.

Length: Unlimited
Width: 40' except Waytown Tunnel: 12'
Draught: 4'
Headroom: 7' 3"

Realistically boats with a beam greater than 7' should not try to navigate throughout this waterway: Dudley Weatherley Jubilee Bridge being the constraining structure.

Permits are required for all boat use and are available from the Tiverton Canal Co., Mid-Devon Moorings and the Best-One Convenience Store, Canal Hill, Tiverton (see page 41), Minnows Touring Park (see page 44) and Holcombe Rogus Village Shop (approximately ½ mile east of Waytown Tunnel). Permits may also be bought in person from the Canal Ranger Service:

The Moorings, Canal Hill,
Tiverton, Devon
EH16 4HX
01884 254072; gwcanal@devon.gov.uk;
www.devon.gov.uk/grandwesterncanal.

MILEAGE

Tiverton to:
Halberton: 4½ miles
Sampford Peverell: 6½ miles
Ayshford: 7½ miles
Lowdwells: 11¼ miles

Paddling: Category 1. *Visiting paddlers must purchase a licence, obtainable from a variety of outlets detailed at www.devon.gov.uk/grandwesterncanal/thingstodo/boating*

Originally conceived as part of a proposal to link the English and Bristol Channels, the Grand Western Canal was to run from Taunton to Exeter, with branches to Tiverton and Cullompton. Subsequently an expanded scheme was floated to include a canal from Bristol to Taunton, linking in with the Kennet & Avon, to give a through navigation from London to Exeter. After much delay and conflicting advice from many engineers, including William Jessop and John Rennie, work started in 1810, on an 11-mile section which included the Tiverton branch and a small portion of the main line from Lowdwells to Burlescombe. This was completed four years later at a cost – for an entirely lock-free length – of £224,505; more than the original estimate for the entire canal. During the course of construction it had been decided to lower the planned level at Holcombe, necessitating an additional 16ft cutting, thereby setting the Tiverton branch on the summit level as a lock-free, contour canal. This was largely responsible for the considerable escalation in cost but subsequently proved beneficial to the large tonnages of limestone transported into Tiverton.

After another delay, work started on the main line in 1827. The section from Taunton to the Tiverton branch was finally opened in 1838 and included seven vertical lifts and one inclined plane: the site of the incline, at Wellisford, ½ a mile north of Thorne St Margaret, can still be seen. The construction of the lifts and the inclined plane was in the hands of James Green who, at the time, was engaged in enlarging the Exeter Canal and building a terminal basin in the city. However, his work on this navigation was less than satisfactory, and he was eventually replaced by Captain John Twisden, Royal Navy retired. The canal was never completed to Exeter. It was a financial disaster, suffering from its over-ambitious engineering, together with railway competition almost from its opening day. The canal was leased to the Great Western Railway in 1854, and they gradually absorbed most of the canal traffic. The predictable pattern of minimal maintenance, coupled with an inevitable decline ensued and the main line was closed in 1867. It has largely disappeared.

However, the trade in limestone persisted and boats continued to ply between Burlescombe and Tiverton until 1924, when a major leak developed, severing the navigation into two separate sections. At this point the canal was finally abandoned as a commercial carrying enterprise.

Some 50 years later, in a joint venture with Mid Devon District Council, Devon County Council purchased the waterway and set about restoration. Today it offers an attractive, linear country park, well patronised by boaters, walkers, anglers and cyclists alike.

> **PADDLING**
> This is another detached waterway where motorised craft do not predominate and the paddler and oarsman can have the upper hand. Just bear the following in mind:
> 1. Do not launch a boat or navigate without a permit. *See* www.devon.gov.uk/grandwesterncanal/thingstodo/boating
> 2. Trailed boats may be launched at Boehill Bridge slipway and cars and trailers stored by arrangement with Minnows Touring Park. *See* Boatyards page 46. Please note that that there is no parking at the slipway.
> Excellent guidance is available, as always, at www.gopaddling.info/canals/grand-western-canal.

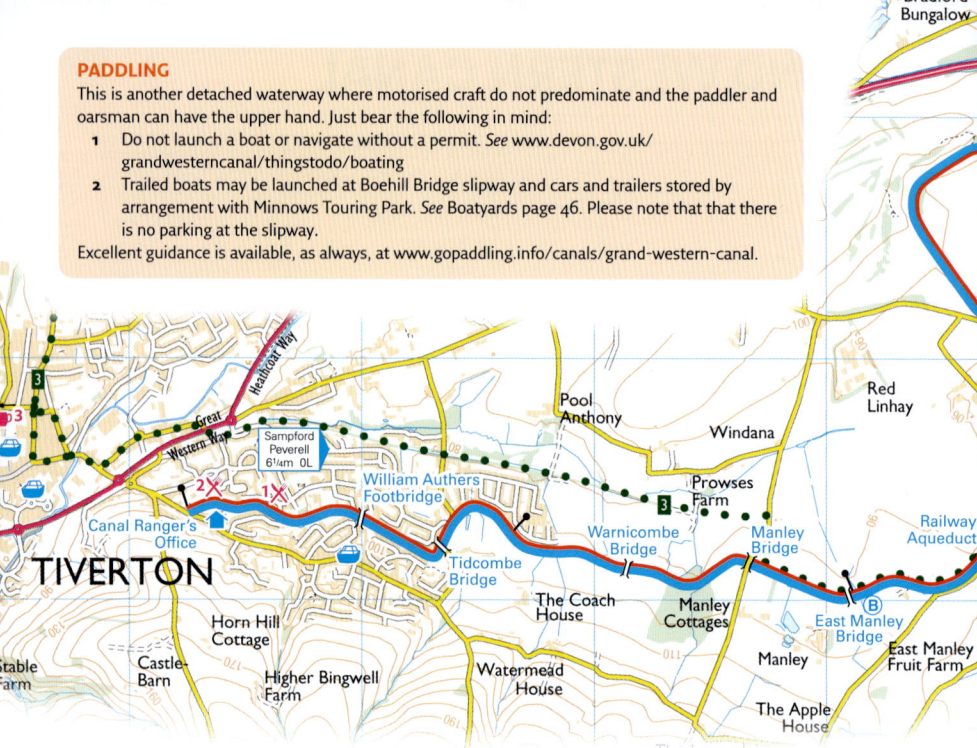

Tiverton

The canal occupies an elevated position above Tiverton and is set some way out of the town. The terminal basin is cut into the hill on the south side while to the north, limekilns form a sturdy embankment, squatting solidly beside the towpath. Positioned thus, they serve the function of retaining wall and are also ergonomically placed for direct loading from arriving tub boats. These were towed in chains of three, carrying the waterway's dominant cargo of limestone and coal; the former being burnt in the kilns to produce a soil conditioner-cum-fertiliser for the local acid soils. Nearby is a pretty thatched cottage, now a *tearoom* but originally the lime-burner's dwelling. Heading west out of the basin, the waterway soon wanders beyond Tiverton's suburbs before bending sharply to the north under Tidcombe Bridge. Here it skirts Tidcombe Hall, originally called Rectory House and once the home of the Bishop of Exeter. In 1810 the then incumbent refused to allow the navigation to come any nearer to the house than 100yds, hence its exaggerated course at this point. At Manley Bridge the canal passes East Manley Farm, which is mentioned in the Domesday Book. More recently it was home to the Victorian Jesuit priest, Gerard Manley Hopkins. Following the road round to the north, the waterway crosses an aqueduct 40ft above the disused trackbed of the old Tiverton Junction to Tiverton line. It consists of a cast iron trough, supported by brick-encased cast iron arches, the structure being wide enough to span the original broad gauge line. At Crownhill Bridge the towpath changes over to the east side of the navigation where it remains, almost to Lowdwells. Tiverton Road Bridge heralds an old wharf, now a car park; another sharp bend and mile marker number three. Alongside the road bridge is the lift bridge, Dudley Weatherley Jubilee Bridge. It is named for a well-known local artist and canal restoration campaigner who sadly died in 2004, aged 92. The combination for the bridge is given to boaters when they purchase their permit. The next mile of the canal bed, running over badly fissured rock, was a constant source of leakage during the waterway's commercial usage and has now been sealed with an artificial membrane. Beyond, the navigation comes suddenly upon a delightful side

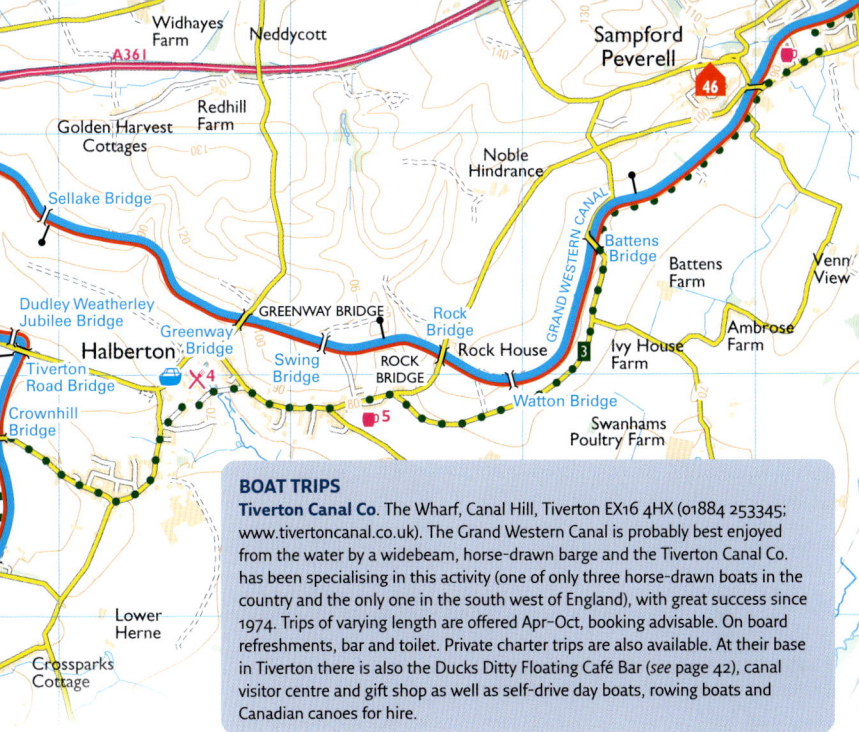

Grand Western Canal — Tiverton

BOAT TRIPS

Tiverton Canal Co. The Wharf, Canal Hill, Tiverton EX16 4HX (01884 253345; www.tivertoncanal.co.uk). The Grand Western Canal is probably best enjoyed from the water by a widebeam, horse-drawn barge and the Tiverton Canal Co. has been specialising in this activity (one of only three horse-drawn boats in the country and the only one in the south west of England), with great success since 1974. Trips of varying length are offered Apr–Oct, booking advisable. On board refreshments, bar and toilet. Private charter trips are also available. At their base in Tiverton there is also the Ducks Ditty Floating Café Bar (*see page 42*), canal visitor centre and gift shop as well as self-drive day boats, rowing boats and Canadian canoes for hire.

cutting. Then Greenway Bridge is approached, providing the best access to Halberton village (cycle hire here). Crossing another diminutive valley, the canal runs through old sandstone quarries; these were the source of much of the material used to build the attractive bridges seen throughout the navigation. Standing beside Rock Bridge is an intriguing house built for Captain John Twisden, who completed the main line of the canal to Taunton. Complete with Doric columns and somewhat eccentric detailing, Rock House is thought to have been constructed to a design of the Captain's. Leading out of the cutting, the waterway now heads for Sampford Peverell. There are fine views to the east over the Blackdown Hills.

Boatyards

Ⓑ **Mid Devon Moorings** Orchard Farm, East Manley, Tiverton EX16 4NJ (01884 252178/07749 001631; www.middevonhireboats.co.uk) 🚽🚿⛽D Boat sales, narrowboat moorings (short- and long-term), on-site car park, BBQ area, gas, fuel and trailer storage, boat-handling tuition. *Open Mon-Sat 09.00-17.00.*

● **Tiverton**

Devon. All services (station at Tiverton Parkway 5 miles away). The town grew up on a narrow spit of land between the Rivers Exe and Lowman; its name derived from Twyford, meaning two fords. The oldest part of the settlement is probably around the castle and church and the main street pattern, as seen today, would have developed beside the Exe bridge in the 14th C. By the beginning of the 13th C the town was recorded as having a market and three fairs. Throughout the Middle Ages it quietly prospered, its wealth based on the local cloth trade, becoming one of the key centres in the county by the 16th C. Few buildings from before this time remain due to a series of disastrous fires spanning a period 1598–1731, after which legislation was enacted decreeing that all roofs were to be of a tile, slate or lead construction. Surviving houses from the 18th and 19th C testify to the town's wealth and the Industrial Revolution was heralded by the arrival of John Heathcoat's lace factory in the town. This arrested the decline that was setting into other cloth towns in the area and brought Tiverton renewed prosperity. In the 100 years between 1790 and 1891, the population more than doubled as Heathcoat's new bobbin net lace machine placed the town at the forefront of the country's lace production. He had attempted to install this machine in a factory in Loughborough, in 1816, whereupon it was destroyed by a mob from Nottingham. His response was to move to Tiverton where, with a few skilled workers recruited from the Midlands, he established production in a closed cloth- weaving factory. Here, for the first time, water power was harnessed to lace-making machinery. Heathcoat went on to become a significant benefactor to the town, providing housing and community facilities.

Knightshayes Court Bolham, Tiverton EX16 7RQ (01884 257281; www.nationaltrust.org.uk/visit/devon/knightshayes). A house designed by William Burges combining medieval romanticism with lavish Victorian decoration in a series of rich interiors. The well-known garden features rare shrubs, fine specimen trees, a water lily pond and topiary. Woodland walks. Shop and plant centre. Licensed restaurant. For *opening times*, which are seasonal, visit the website.

Mid Devon Bus Information Traveline (0345 155 1004; www.traveldevon.info/bus).

Pannier Market Market Square, Off Fore Street, Tiverton EX16 6NH (01884 243351; www.tivertonmarket.com). Friendly local market operating *Mon-Tue & Thu-Sat 08.30-16.00.*

Tiverton Castle Park Hill, Near Tiverton EX16 6RP (01884 255200; www.tivertoncastle.com). Originally built in 1106 by Richard de Redvers, later the home of the Courtnays and besieged by Fairfax in 1645 during the Civil War. It fell to him after a chance shot hit a drawbridge chain. It was subsequently modernised by a rich Tiverton merchant, Peter West, although the early gatehouse remains one of its most striking features. Walled, kitchen and woodland gardens. *Usually open Thu & Sun 14.30-17.30 but check before visiting.*

Tiverton Museum of Mid Devon Life Beck's Square, Tiverton EX16 6PJ (01884 256295; www. tivertonmuseum.org.uk). Reputed to contain the largest social history collection in the south west, housed in a listed building that was once the National School. The collection is displayed in a variety of galleries on a site covering half an acre. *Open Tue-Sat 10.00-16.00.* Charge.

Pubs and Restaurants (pages 42-43)

✕ **1 The Canal Tearooms and Gardens** Grand Western Canal, Tiverton EX16 4HX (01884 252291; www.canaltearooms.co.uk). Once the lime-burner's dwelling, this 18th-C thatched cottage serves cream teas, home-made cakes, coffee and light lunches. Covered seating area and canalside gardens. *Open daily Apr-Sep 10.30-17.00.*

✕ ♀ **2 The Duck's Ditty Floating Café Bar** The Wharf, Canal Hill, Tiverton EX16 4HX (01884 253345; www.tivertoncanal.co.uk/floating-cafe-bar). Teas, coffees, soft drinks, real ales, wines and cider. Also sweet and savoury snacks. *See website for seasonal opening times.*

🍺✕ **3 The Racehorse** Wellbrook Street, Tiverton EX16 5JW (01884 252696). Busy local serving real ales, food *Wed-Sun 12.00-19.00 (Sun 15.30)* and a *Sun* Carvery. Children and dogs welcome; garden. Traditional pub games, *regular* live music, sports TV and Wi-Fi. *Open Mon-Thu 13.00-23.00 (Mon 22.00) Fri 13.00-00.00 & Sat-Sun 11.00-01.00 (Sun 22.00).*

✕ **4 The Swans Neck Café** Halberton Court Farm Shop, Halberton, Tiverton EX16 7AW (01884 829543; www.halbertoncourtfarmshop.co.uk/swansneckcafe). Leave the canal at Greenway Bridge and walk downhill towards the village of Halberton, turning right at the foot of the hill. A bright, airy, welcoming establishment serving a wide range of home-made delights including breakfasts, lunches, delicious cakes and afternoon teas. Child- and dog-friendly. *Open Mon-Sat 09.00-16.00.* Farm shop adjacent selling wide range of fresh produce including meat. Also PYO.

🍺✕ **5 The Hickory Inn** 93 High Street, Halberton, Tiverton EX16 7AG (01884 798338; www.thehickoryinn.co.uk). Transformed, and now a welcoming village hostelry with an appetising selection of home-cooked food available *when open*, together with real cider. Dog- and family-friendly; garden. Traditional pub games, *monthly* live music and newspapers. Real fires, sports TV and Wi-Fi. *Open Mon-Thu 17.00-23.00 (Thu 12.00) & Fri-Sun 12.00-00.00 (Sun 21.00).*

WALKING AND CYCLING

National Cycle Network Route 3, otherwise known as The West Country Way, makes use of the towpath throughout. Whilst the route can be entirely off-road (by remaining on the towpath) the official route diverts through villages along the way. It links in with the 1-mile Tiverton Parkway Station to Grand Western Canal route, a combination of off- and on-road tracks. It also connects with the 3-mile Tiverton Parkway to Culm Valley route. Other connected (or nearby) routes include the Exe Valley Cycle Route, Lowman Valley Cycle Route and eight routes in the Blackdown Hills. Detailed leaflets (charge) are available from local TICs. An interesting and varied range of walking and cycling routes for Mid-Devon can be viewed at www.visitmiddevon.co.uk/walking-routes, while Komoot also detail an excellent selection of walking opportunities: www.komoot.com/guide/673118/hiking-in-mid-devon.

Burlescombe

The village of Sampford Peverell was bisected by the newly-dug canal with the loss of several buildings and the re-alignment of the main road. It also cut through land belonging to the old Rectory and, in 1841, a new Rectory was constructed by the Canal Company in Regency Gothic style with stone mullioned windows, as recompense. This was again replaced in 1993 by a modern building. An attractive skew brick bridge crosses the waterway in the village centre, close to the old wharf situated on the north bank. Beyond Buckland Bridge there is an example of a syphon culvert, not uncommon on this navigation, which carries a stream beneath the canal bed. Where an intersecting water course 'crosses' a canal at a similar level, the more usual culvert is unworkable and the water has to be dropped vertically to a point below the canal bed. It is then led up the other side, via a curved masonry tube, to resume its course across the adjoining fields; the water being effectively syphoned under the navigation. On the offside, just beyond Boehill Bridge, lies the overgrown 'Engineers Clay Pit': in past times a source of the clay puddle material used to seal the canal bed against leaks. At Ayshford, one of the waterway's architectural gems appears in the form of Ayshford Court and Chapel. The rendered front of the house conceals a medieval manor, dating from the 17th C, complete with two-bay hall and evidence of its central open fire witnessed by the smoke-blackened ridge purlin supported on jointed cruck trusses. On the chimney stack is the inscription 'Built 1607, restored 1910'. The adjoining chapel is a small, freestanding, Perpendicular construction complete with tiny pierced quatrefoils, set into its side walls. The plain roof is topped with a pleasing, simple belfry. The building was restored in 1847 and contains some striking Victorian stained glass. The navigation continues, bounded by open countryside but with higher ground beyond. Soon the main Bristol to Exeter railway line is approached and the waterway bends sharply to the north. This marks the point at which it was originally intended that the Tiverton branch would meet the main line. It was to have continued southwards to meet the River Exe at Topsham, running down the Clyst valley and with a branch to Cullompton. Ahead is the tramway bridge that used to lead from the limestone quarries at Westleigh to the main line railway, now swinging away to the east. In the bed of the canal, just before Fenacre Bridge, there was a spring which provided a feed for the canal; two others remain, in the vicinity of Whipcott and near Waytown Tunnel. The discovery of these natural water sources, when plans were modified and the navigation was 'dropped' into a 16ft deep cutting, eliminated the need to construct storage reservoirs in the Lowdwells area. It also did away with the proposed locks on the Tiverton branch, making it the contour canal we see today. Beyond Whipcott Bridge is a quarry which, during the early 20th C, was an important source of roadstone for the area, the material being regularly transported along the waterway to wharves at Tiverton Road Bridge and Halberton. There are also limekilns in the area so that limestone could be burnt for local use. At Waytown Tunnel the towpath crosses on the south portal and ducks into the trees. A length of chain attached to an iron ring was the means of propulsion through the tunnel and probably an improvement on the alternative of legging. The navigation terminates at Lowdswell lock, beside the restored lock keeper's cottage, from whence it would have continued to the first lift, crossing the nearby lane on an aqueduct.

Pubs and Restaurants

🍺✕ **1 The Globe Inn** 14-16 Lower Town, Sampford Peverell, Tiverton EX16 7BJ (01884 821214; www.the-globeinn.co.uk). Traditional country pub with two comfortable bars and a restaurant serving an appetising range of home-made food *L and E daily. Breakfast can be booked 08.00-11.00.* Bar and restaurant menus and a range of real ales. Beer garden and children's play area. Dogs welcome. Canalside seating and moorings. Real cider. Traditional pub games, newspapers, real fires and Wi-Fi. Cycle Hire – see Walking and Cycling page 47. *Open 11.00-00.00.*

🍺✕ **2 Redwoods Inn** Lowman Cross, Tiverton EX16 7DP (01884 820148; www.facebook.com/RedwoodsInn). Free house dating from the 17th C serving real ale and home-cooked food daily *L and E (not Mon L).* Family-friendly, garden. Traditional pub games and real fires. *Open Mon-Sun L and E (not Mon L).*

🍺 **3 The Globe Inn** Ham Hill, Appley TA21 0HJ (01823 673147; www.facebook.com/globeinnappley). Grade II listed building of cob construction, featured in the CAMRA Historic Interiors guide, dispensing real ale, real cider and food *Wed-Sat E & Sun 12.00-16.00.* Family-friendly, garden and play area. Traditional pub games and real fires. Holiday cottage to let. *Open Wed-Sat 11.00-23.00 & Sun 12.00-16.00.*

✕ **4 Little Tuberfield Farm Shop** Tiverton Parkway Way, Sampford Peverell EX16 7EH (01884 820908/07588 837353; www.coombefarmwoods.co.uk/wp-content/uploads/2010/06/little%20turberfield%20farm%20shop.pdf). Locally produced meat, poultry and vegetables. Homemade sausages and burgers. Freshly baked pies and pasties together with soft drinks. *Open Tue-Fri 08.00-17.00 (Fri 17.30) & Sat 08.00-15.30.*

✕ **5 Tiverton Parkway Golf Centre** Sampford Peverell, Tiverton EX16 7EH (01884 820825). Teas, coffee, snacks and ice creams are available at this golf driving range on the lane leading to Tiverton Parkway Station.

● **Halberton**
Devon. *Stores, farm shop, café.* A village strung out along the Tiverton road, set a little way away from the canal, containing a mix of old and new housing. See www.halbertoncourtfarmshop.co.uk for shop and café opening times.

● **Sampford Peverell**
Devon. *PO, stores, off-licence, farm shop, station (1 mile away).* A village of character ranged around the canal which clearly led to the demolition of some properties and a diversion to the approach from Tiverton. The church was founded in the 13th C by Sir Hugh Peverell, with later work on the tower and nave and the addition of the porch and south aisle in 1498. Restored in Victorian times, there remains a Norman font and a 17th-C brass. The *PO* is located in the village store.

● **Holcombe Rogus**
Devon. *PO, garage.* Very much the focus of the village, Holcombe Court is a rebuilt medieval manor house constructed by Sir Roger Bluett in the early part of the 16th century, making it one of the grandest Tudor houses in Devon. Today it is generally considered to be the finest house of that period still surviving in the county. Although not open to the public, a good view of the main south elevation, with its four-storey entrance porch, can be seen from the gateway. The grounds are beautifully landscaped and include a fine walled garden. The *post office is at the garage and is open Tue & Thu 09.00-11.00.*

● **Westleigh**
Devon. A quarry village.

Boatyards

ⓑ **Minnows Touring Park** Sampford Peverell, Tiverton EX16 7EN (01884 821770; www.minnowstouringpark.co.uk). 🚿♿ Gas. Boating and fishing permits, parking for cars and trailers.

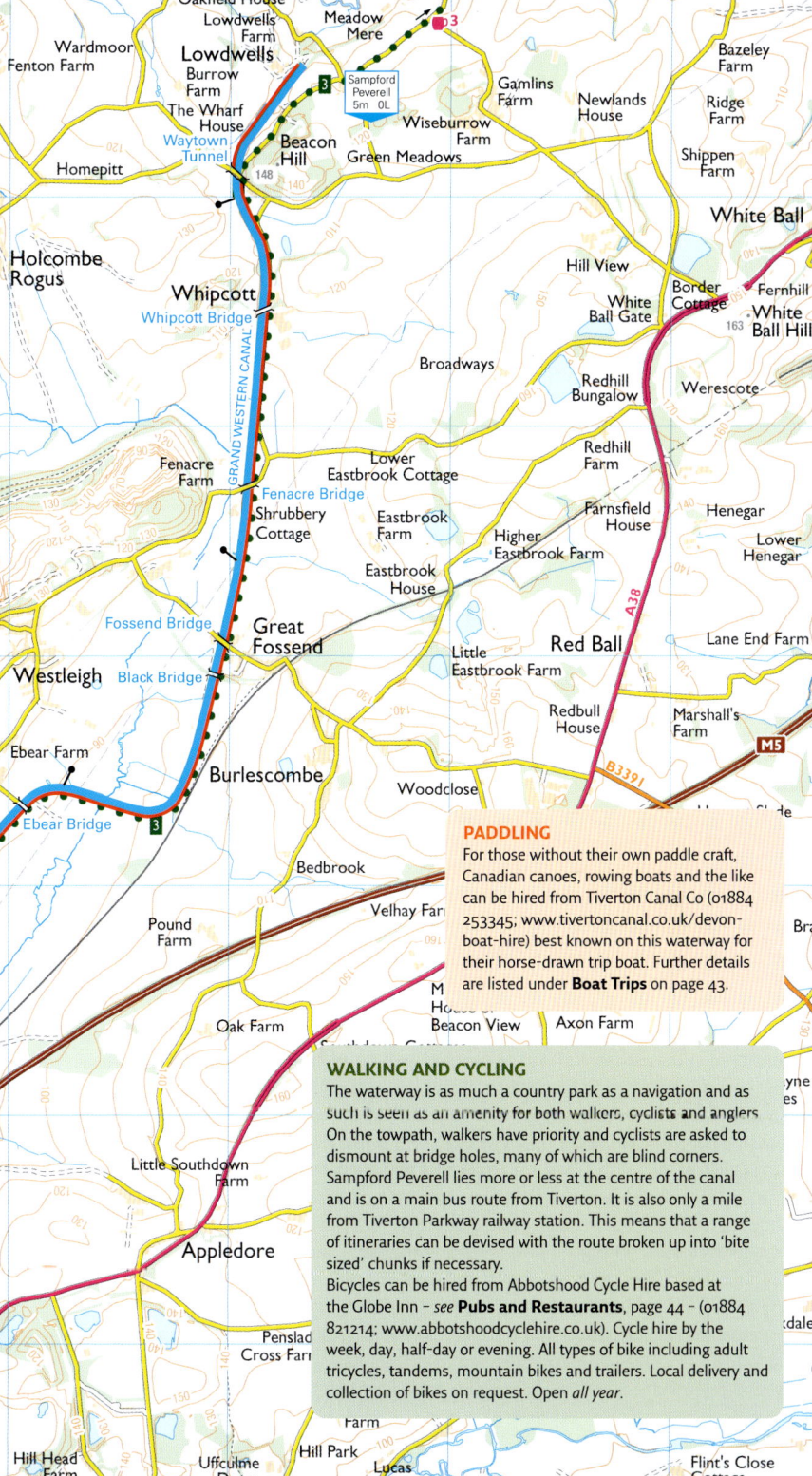

Grand Western Canal — Burlescombe

PADDLING

For those without their own paddle craft, Canadian canoes, rowing boats and the like can be hired from Tiverton Canal Co (01884 253345; www.tivertoncanal.co.uk/devon-boat-hire) best known on this waterway for their horse-drawn trip boat. Further details are listed under **Boat Trips** on page 43.

WALKING AND CYCLING

The waterway is as much a country park as a navigation and as such is seen as an amenity for both walkers, cyclists and anglers. On the towpath, walkers have priority and cyclists are asked to dismount at bridge holes, many of which are blind corners. Sampford Peverell lies more or less at the centre of the canal and is on a main bus route from Tiverton. It is also only a mile from Tiverton Parkway railway station. This means that a range of itineraries can be devised with the route broken up into 'bite sized' chunks if necessary.

Bicycles can be hired from Abbotshood Cycle Hire based at the Globe Inn – see **Pubs and Restaurants**, page 44 – (01884 821214; www.abbotshoodcyclehire.co.uk). Cycle hire by the week, day, half-day or evening. All types of bike including adult tricycles, tandems, mountain bikes and trailers. Local delivery and collection of bikes on request. Open *all year*.

EXETER SHIP CANAL

MAXIMUM DIMENSIONS
Length: 122'
Beam: 26' 3"
Headroom: 32' 9"
Draught: 9' 9"

MANAGER
01392 265791; www.exeter.gov.uk/leisure-and-culture/sport-and-leisure/exeter-port-authority/visitor-berths-on-the-exeter-canal)

Operating Authority
Exeter City Council
River and Canal Office
Haven Road
Exeter EX2 8DU

MILEAGE
Turf Lock to:
Topsham Lock (closed): 1½ miles
Double Locks: 3½ miles
Kings Arms: 4½ miles
Exeter St David's Station: 6½ miles

Locks: 2

Paddling: Category 1. *Licence covered by Paddling UK membership.*

The Exe estuary is up to 1½ miles wide, although it narrows considerably between Exmouth and Dawlish Warren. Its deep water channel can be tortuous and it has proved difficult for shipping since vessels first traded to Topsham and Exeter. Seaborne trade with the city was further constrained by the construction of a weir – by Isabella de Fortibus, Countess of Devon – during the reign of Edward I. This was built above Topsham and ensured that all craft had to unload downstream of the city until an Inquisition, held in 1290, decreed that a 30ft gap be formed in the obstruction. Thirty years later the Earl of Devon, whose successors went on to establish a thriving quay at Topsham, blocked the hole and all goods to Exeter passed through the town, attracting considerable shipping dues in the process.

Towards the middle of 16th C, Exeter Corporation obtained an Act of Parliament to remove what were now three weirs across the river and in 1539 unsuccessfully attempted to remove a series of shoals which had built up in the river and estuary. Passage into the city remained all but impossible so John Trew, of Glamorgan, was engaged to dig a canal, parallel to the river on its west bank. This opened in 1566, at a cost of £5000. For this he received £225 and a percentage of the tolls. This original navigation ran from just below the city walls to a connection with the Exe at Matford Brook, and shipping still had to pass Topsham, attracting dues, despite the quays not being used. The navigation was 16ft wide, 3ft deep and enabled vessels to carry 16 tons. It is reputed to be the first navigation constructed in this country with pound locks; three in total, with guillotine gates. Boats loaded direct from sea-going craft anchored in the estuary but had to contend with an awkward entrance into the canal that was only possible at high tide. Silting in both the estuary and the canal remained an additional problem, as did opposition from quay owners in Topsham who still collected dues from passing barges. This was temporarily overcome when Exeter Corporation bought the Topsham Quay lease, but this was not renewed when it expired in 1614.

After the Civil War the waterway was in poor condition, suffering water shortages from unauthorised mill abstraction, silting and continuing rivalry with Topsham. In 1676 the Corporation decided on improvements, dredging the canal and extending it south by half a mile thereby eliminating one mile of awkward river navigation. They built a larger entrance lock and an adjoining transhipment basin able to handle 60-ton craft.

Exeter was becoming an increasingly prosperous city, its wealth founded on the cloth-making industry and again it found the need to enlarge its waterway. In 1698, the Corporation put in hand a scheme to improve the navigation but the engineer in charge absconded with the city funds, leaving an unnavigable canal and the Corporation to complete the task on its own. Completed in 1701, the enlarged waterway measured 50ft wide, 10ft deep and could carry coasters up to 150 tons. The three old locks were removed and replaced by Double Locks, and flood gates were installed at King's Arms. However, it was still approached up a narrow, winding side channel and was only accessible to larger vessels on spring tides.

In the first part of 18th C an average of 310 craft used the canal per year; by the end of the century this had risen to 448. Notwithstanding this modest increase, the decision was taken in 1825 to further improve and extend the canal and under the direction of James Green, work commenced. He had previously dredged and straightened the navigation and his new strategy was a two mile extension to Turf; raised banks to allow passage by vessels of 14ft draught and the construction of a deep-water basin in Exeter. The old entrance lock was blocked up and as a result of representations from Topsham, a new side lock opposite the port was built in 1829. The total cost was £113,355, more than a fifth being absorbed by Turf Lock which was built on piles driven through clay and bog to the underlying bedrock. Although silting continued to be a problem, the largest ship recorded as using the improved navigation was of 350 tons, drawing 13ft 6ins. The new basin, measuring 900 x 120ft, came into its own – handling paper, leather, wheat, oats and manganese.

In the 1840s steam-driven vessels appeared on the canal but because their speed exceeded the 5 mph limit and their wash threatened the banks, they were prohibited from using their own power and had to be towed by horses. This unpopular move was a turning point for the navigation and the tonnage handled began to decline, as shipping unloaded at nearby coastal ports for onward carriage by rail. In the first half of 20th C traffic stabilised but then steadily dropped off with a single sludge tanker the only vessel finally left. With an end to the estuarine dumping of raw sewerage, this tanker is now no longer visible from the elevated section of the M5, berthed beside the city's sewerage works. Today Exeter is working hard to exploit the leisure potential of the navigation and her once commercially vibrant and historic quays.

WALKING AND CYCLING
To make the most of this section you will need to use a combination of bike/hike on the canal towpath, ferry and train. It is straightforward to start at Dawlish Warren or Starcross and travel north – you can then bike or hike all the way to Exeter St David's.
From here you can either retrace your journey to Topsham lock and then use the ferry over to Topsham and catch the train to Lympstone, or you can catch a train from Exeter St David's to Lympstone. In March 2008, the first part of the Exeter to Exmouth cycleway was opened from Lympstone to Exmouth. From Exmouth catch the ferry over the river to Starcross (see page 50) to complete your route. Alternatively you can start at Exeter St David's, Exmouth, Lympstone or Topsham, which all have car parks.
At the Countess Weir Road Bridges National Cycle Route 2 – The South Coast Route – joins the Ship Canal and follows it into Exeter on the east bank. Plans are in hand to extend southwards, along the estuary, but routing through the SSSI may take some time to finalise.
In Exmouth there is the Exmouth to Budleigh Salterton Cyclepath along the old railway line; a quiet and almost level route. For the keen off-roader there is the challenging terrain of Woodbury Common. Details of both these possibilities can be obtained from Knobblies Bike Hire (see page 50), who will also help you plan a route.
Running south from Exeter, along the estuary and around Torbay, is the South West Coast Path, a challenging walk that can be followed all the way to Lands End.
The 40-mile East Devon Way starts at Lympstone and runs to the county border at Lyme Regis. There are four circular linking paths that tie in with it and further details can be found at www.eastdevonway.org.uk/walk-route.
Cycle hire is also available near Topsham Quay from Route 2 Bike Shop, 4 Amity Place, Topsham EX3 0JE (01392 879160; www.route2bikes.co.uk) *open Mon-Sat 09.00-17.00.*

Powderham

At Starcross the road is set somewhat below the level of the railway track, separating it from the Exe estuary. Motorists are thus initially greeted with a view of grubby carriage bogies as trains race backwards and forwards to and from the West Country. The railway is very much a central feature of the village, as it was here that Brunel built a pumping station to create vacuum for his ill-fated atmospheric railway. The Italianate building survives today and now houses the local yacht club. The route north closely follows the trackbed, which from the road interrupts views out across the river into east Devon, 1½ miles away at this point. The ferry operates from a pier in the village and is accessible by crossing the railway. Soon a minor road leaves the main A379 and walkers and cyclists can proceed in relative peace, broken only by the passing trains: a mix of the new Class 800 derivatives and a regular procession of local, stopping DMUs. Pre-Beeching there were two routes into Cornwall; a more northerly one via Okehampton and this route, perched precariously on the sea wall, prone to the vagaries of foul weather and high tide. The most spectacular section, to the south of Dawlish, is also the most vulnerable, and services can be interrupted during storms. Hopefully, the recent £30 million upgrade, following serious damage during the winter storms of 2014, will prevent future devastation. Powerham Castle nestles, immediately to the west on raised ground, looking out across the estuary. It is passed not long before the route leaves the road for good, crossing over the railway to join the foreshore. After a mile Turf Lock and its attendant and very isolated hotel are approached: this is the beginning of the Exeter Ship Canal. It is an excellent spot to linger, to enjoy the views and the wildlife and to wonder at this unusual location (more solitary in winter than in summer). The railway finally diverges from the towpath and makes a beeline for the distant suburbs of Exeter, to ultimately follow the river to St David's as it loops round the city's western boundary. The path leads through Exminster Marshes, an SSSI and nature reserve administered by the RSPB; home to geese, curlew and widgeon in winter and lapwings, redshank and warblers in summer. River and canal run now in close partnership, only separated (in varying degrees according to the state of the tide) by mudflats as walker and cyclist approach Topsham which is spread out along the river's east bank.

Walkers setting out from Exminster are confronted by a mix of track, road, footpath and foreshore and are accompanied throughout by the bustling, single-track railway line. Views across the estuary are at all times uninterrupted and the sea and mudflats, in a continuous state of flux, can be constantly enjoyed. Cockle Sand provides a rich feeding ground for a variety of birds and the area is important for its abundance of eel grass, a favourite food of the Brent goose.

PADDLING
Three Exeter-based companies offering canoe, kayak and paddleboard hire, plus tuition are:
- Saddles & Paddles (01392 424241; www.sadpad.com/paddlesports-hire.html)
- Kayak Hub (07788 957223; www.kayakhub-exeter.co.uk)
- AS Watersports (01392 219600; www.aswatersports.co.uk)

They will not necessarily limit you to the canal as sea canoeing tuition and trips are also on offer.
The Exe Estuary Management Partnership (*see* also **Walking and Cycling** on page 56) offer a series of river and canal, canoe and kayak loops, while GoPaddling completes the picture at www.gopaddling.info/canals/exeter-ship-canal.

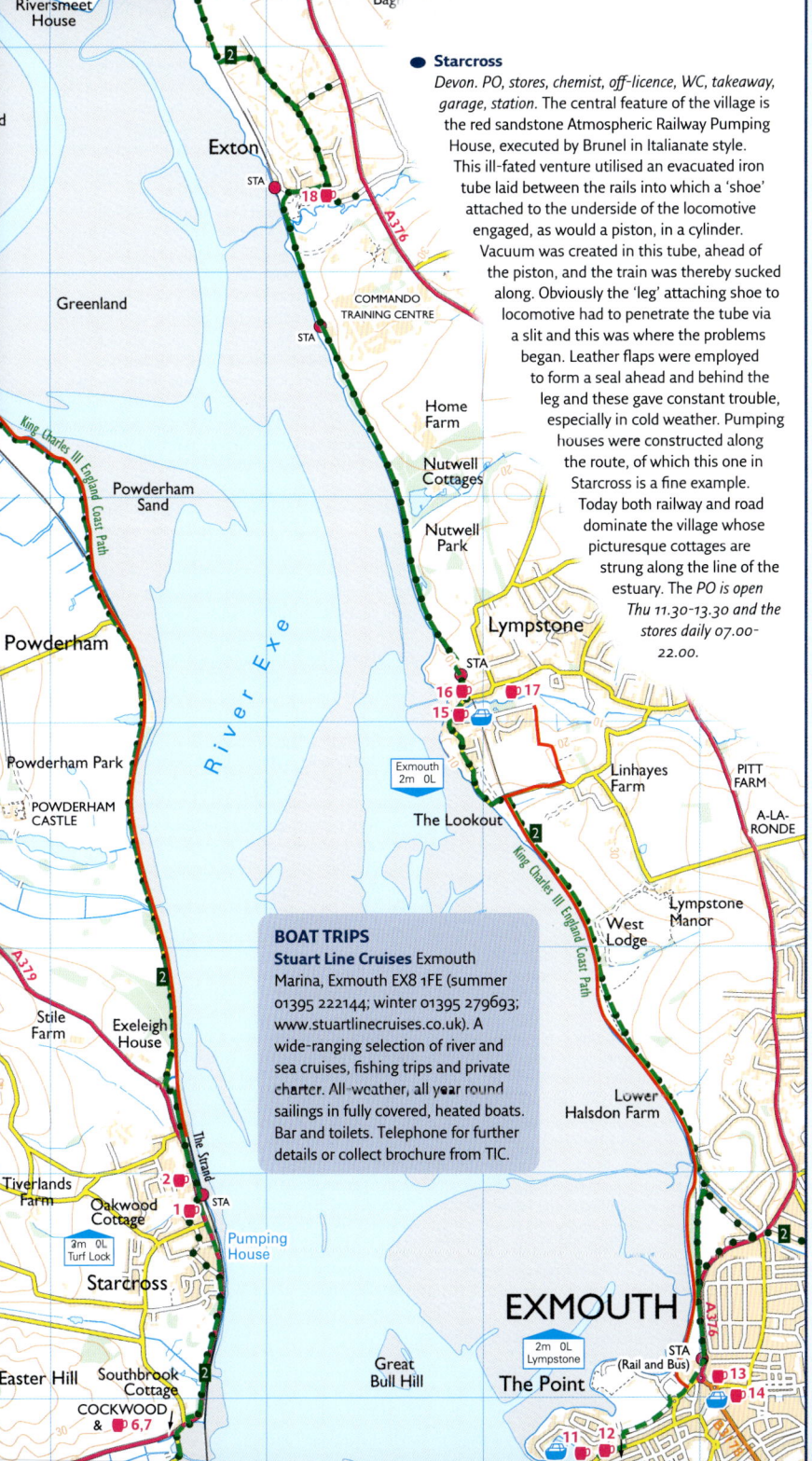

Exeter Ship Canal — Powderham

Starcross

Devon. PO, stores, chemist, off-licence, WC, takeaway, garage, station. The central feature of the village is the red sandstone Atmospheric Railway Pumping House, executed by Brunel in Italianate style. This ill-fated venture utilised an evacuated iron tube laid between the rails into which a 'shoe' attached to the underside of the locomotive engaged, as would a piston, in a cylinder. Vacuum was created in this tube, ahead of the piston, and the train was thereby sucked along. Obviously the 'leg' attaching shoe to locomotive had to penetrate the tube via a slit and this was where the problems began. Leather flaps were employed to form a seal ahead and behind the leg and these gave constant trouble, especially in cold weather. Pumping houses were constructed along the route, of which this one in Starcross is a fine example. Today both railway and road dominate the village whose picturesque cottages are strung along the line of the estuary. The *PO* is open Thu 11.30-13.30 and the stores daily 07.00-22.00.

BOAT TRIPS
Stuart Line Cruises Exmouth Marina, Exmouth EX8 1FE (summer 01395 222144; winter 01395 279693; www.stuartlinecruises.co.uk). A wide-ranging selection of river and sea cruises, fishing trips and private charter. All-weather, all year round sailings in fully covered, heated boats. Bar and toilets. Telephone for further details or collect brochure from TIC.

Starcross – Exmouth Ferry Starcross, EX6 8PR (07934 461672/07779 157280; www.facebook.com/StarcrossExmouthFerry). Operates *Apr–Oct* from the pier beside the Atmospheric Railway Pumping House. *First crossing 10.00 and thence hourly, on the hour. Last crossing 16.10 (mid-May – mid-Sep 17.10).* Also various cruises. Cycles carried.
See Exmouth for return crossing details and visit www.exe-estuary.org/visitor-information/activites/cruises-ferries for the bigger estuarine picture.

- **Kenton**
Devon. PO, farm shop. Set a little way off from the estuary, the village provides the access point for Powderham Castle. It is a pretty village, especially the streets behind the main road, with a striking Perpendicular church. The ashlar tower is 120ft high; there are elaborate porches and carvings, and the mullions are in Beer stone. In contrast, the remaining stonework is red sandstone, much patched with grey and white. The pulpit is 15th-C and there is considerable Victorian restoration. Opposite stands a charming row of late 19th-C almshouses.
Powderham Castle Kenton EX6 8JQ (01626 890243; www.powderham.co.uk). Medieval castle with beautiful gardens and grounds, miniature steam railway, children's secret garden and fort, picnic area. Tea room, farm shop and plant centre. Castle and grounds *open Apr–Oct, Sun-Fri 10.00-16.00. Last guided tour 1 hour before closing.* Charge. Sometimes closed for private functions: telephone in advance of visit.

- **Cockwood**
Devon. Estuary village, 1 mile south of Starcross. Well worth a diversion to the pubs here.

- **Exminster**
Devon. PO, stores, chemist, off-licence. Again a little way from the navigation. The old village centre is now almost totally submerged in prolific dormitory housing for Exeter. *Stores open daily 07.00-22.00.*

- **Exmouth**
Devon. All services. Exmouth probably first attracted attention when the Danes landed in 1001; the town became of consequence by the beginning of 13th C, by which time a castle had been built to guard the entrance to its sheltered harbour. During the Civil War it was alternately held by Parliamentarians and Royalists, finally falling to the former in March 1646. After a lengthy period of decline, the benefit of its balmy sea air, together with the sheltering hills to the east, was finally recognised and Exmouth became a celebrated seaside resort in Victorian times. The town developed in an irregular pattern with fine Georgian housing on Beacon Hill overlooking the sea and later building occupying the flat ground, at the base of the Beacon and facing the estuary. Further change was initiated by the Hon. Mark Rolle, during the second half of the 19th C, in an attempt to capitalise on the town's popularity – in its heyday it vied with Torquay in its importance as a seaside destination – but this has produced little of architectural importance. The docks were constructed on the south west point in 1867 and proved to be financially unsuccessful. Notwithstanding, they were rebuilt in 1882 and today, somewhat incongruously, have been developed into a marina, totally encased with upmarket 'New England' style housing.
A la Ronde *NT.* Summer Lane, Exmouth EX8 5BD (01395 265514; www.nationaltrust.org.uk/a-la-ronde). Sixteen-sided cottage built in 1798 by Miss Jane Parmiter and her cousin, Mary Parmiter. It was inspired by San Vitale in Ravenna, which they visited as part of their ten year Grand Tour. Built of stone, with lozenge-shaped windows, the central hall – from which rooms radiate – is top-lit by a lantern roof. The gallery is reached by a narrow, grotto-like, shell-lined staircase. The tiled roof was originally thatched. Coffee, teas and light lunches. Shop. *Open Mar-Oct 10.30-17.30.* Charge. Timed tickets operate during busy periods.
Bicton Park Botanical Gardens East Budleigh, Budleigh Salterton EX9 7BJ (01395 568465; www.bictongardens.co.uk). Sixty acres of beautiful gardens, a magnificent 19th-C palm house, an arboretum and a house of shells. An indoor exhibition hall packed with nostalgic delights for all ages. Miniature train, nature trail and children's play areas. Restaurant, shop and plant centre. *Open summer 10.00-17.00 and winter 10.00-16.30. Closed Xmas day and boxing day.* Charge.
Knobblies Bike Hire 107 Exeter Road, Exmouth EX8 1QE (01395 270182; www.knobbliesbikes.co.uk). Adult, children and toddler cycle hire. Repairs, spares and free safety checks. Good advice on local cycle routes. *Open Mon-Fri 09.00-17.30.*
World of Country Life Sandy Bay, Exmouth EX8 5BY (01395 274533; www.worldofcountrylife.co.uk). Hall of transport, exhibition hall, pets centre and children's play areas, falconry centre, adventure playground, quad bikes. *Open daily mid Mar- Oct, 10.00-17.00.* Shop.
Tourist Information Centre 45A The Strand, Exmouth EX8 1AL (01395 830550; www.visitexmouth.org). *Open Mon-Sat 10.00-12.30 & 13.30-16.00.*

- **Lympstone**
Devon. PO, stores, off-licence, station. A charming village set out around the inlet. Winding, narrow cobbled streets, little more than passages, tightly flanked by irregular rows of cottages, rambling down to the water. The village is best approached on foot or by train.
Peters Tower Lympstone. Delightful red and yellow brick-built clock tower, with a short spire, erected in 1885 by W.H. Peters in memory of his wife. The clock was designed to face seawards to tell the fishermen the time of the tides. There are two stone limekilns nearby.

- **Exton**
Devon. Station. Just a few houses, sandwiched between the river and main road, lining the estuary and with splendid views. The Royal Marines Commando Training Centre, complete with its own railway station, lies a little way to the south. The excellent pub is well worth a visit, justifying a break in the train journey!

Pubs and Restaurants (pages 50–51)

🍺✕ **1 The Driftwood Inn** The Strand, Starcross, Dawlish EX6 8PR (01626 890412; www.facebook.com/thegalleonstarcross). Reputedly the ghost of a child can be heard bouncing a ball along the landing, whilst bottles are knocked off shelves in the bar by a more mature, female spirit. Food *L and E (not Mon-Wed L)*. Real ale. Children welcome. Patio garden. B&B. *Open daily 11.00-23.00 (Sat 00.00).*

🍺✕ **2 The Atmospheric Railway Inn** The Strand, Starcross, Dawlish EX6 8PA (01626 906290; www.facebook.com/atmosphericrailwayinn). A striking inn sign, although somewhat strangely depicting a train hauled by a steam locomotive. Real ales, real cider and food available *Wed-Sun all day (not Sun E)*. Dog- and child-friendly, garden. Real fires, sports TV and Wi-Fi. *Open Wed-Sun 12.00-22.00 (Sun 17.00).*

🍺 **3 The Ley Arms** Kenn EX6 7UW (01392 832341; www.theleyarmskenn.co.uk). Archetypal thatched pub, dating from 12th C, serving real ale, real cider and appetising food *Mon-Fri L and E & Sat-Sun 12.00-21.00 (Sun 20.00)*. Dog- and family-friendly, garden. Camping nearby. *Open Mon-Sat 11.00-23.00 & Sun 12.00-22.30.*

✕♀ **4 Chi Restaurant & Bar** Fore Street, Kenton, Dawlish EX6 8LD (01626 890213; www.chi-restaurant.co.uk). Fine oriental cuisine and fresh seafood served *L and E* in this restaurant with several dining rooms, a landscaped garden and comfortable, modern hotel rooms. Takeaway service. B&B. Dining room *open Fri-Sat 17.30*. Takeaway and delivery *Thu-Sat from 17.30.*

✕♀ **5 Rodean Restaurant** The Triangle, Kenton, Dawlish EX6 8LS (01626 890195; www.rodeanrestaurant.co.uk). Attractive, village-centre restaurant serving a tasty range of British cuisine, prepared from local produce. À la carte and house menus available *Thu-Sat E & Sun L*. Telephone for opening times *out of season*.

🍺✕ **6 The Anchor Inn** Church Road, Cockwood, Starcross EX6 8RA (01626 890203; www.anchorinncockwood.com). Overlooking the old harbour, this charming inn is over 465 years old and is reputedly haunted by a friendly ghost and his dog. À la carte restaurant and bar snacks, fish dishes a speciality: *daily 12.00-19.00*. Real ale and real cider. Dog- and child-friendly, outside seating. Traditional pub games, newspapers, real fires. *Open Mon-Sat 11.00-23.00 & Sun 11.30-22.30.*

🍺✕ **7 The Ship Inn** Cockwood, Starcross EX6 8NU (01626 890373; www.shipinncockwood.co.uk). Open fires, real ales, homemade meals available *Mon-Sat L and E*. Dog- and family friendly, garden. Traditional pub games, newspapers, sports TV and Wi-Fi. *Open Mon-Sat 11.00-23.00 & Sun 12.00-22.30.*

🍺 **8 The Turf Hotel** Exminster, Exeter EX6 8EE (01392 575200; www.the-turf.com). Only accessible by boat, bike or on foot, this establishment enjoys a unique position in the Exe estuary at the entrance to the Ship Canal. Real ales together with food served *daily 12.00-17.00 (last orders 16.00)*. B&B. *Open 10.00-17.00.*

🍺✕ **9 The Swan's Nest** Station Road, Exminster, Exeter EX6 8DZ (01392 832371; www.palmersbrewery.com/pubs/swans-nest). Elton John's 1941 Wurlitzer occupies pride of place in this large pub-cum-restaurant with an extensive menu serving traditional English food *daily 09.00-21.00 (Sun 20.00)*. Real ales and real cider. Dog- and child-friendly, garden. Wi-Fi. *Open 12.00-22.00.*

🍺✕ **10 The Stowey Arms** Main Road, Exminster, Exeter EX6 8AT (01392 824970; www.stoweyarmsexminster.co.uk). Comfortable establishment created from a terrace of three cottages, originally belonging to the Stowey Estate. Food available *Thu-Sat E & Sun L*. Real ale. Family-friendly, garden and patio. *Open Tue-Sat 16.00-23.00 (Sat 12.00) & Sun 14.00-22.00.*

🍺 **11 The Beach** Victoria Road, Exmouth EX8 1DR (01395 272090; www.facebook.com/beachpubexmouth). Overlooking the harbour and the estuary. Real ales and food available *daily L and E*. No children under fourteen. Dogs welcome. Patio seating. Live bands *Fri*. *Open Sun-Thu 12.00-23.00 & Fri-Sat 12.00-00.00 (Sat 11.00).*

🍺 **12 The Grove** The Esplanade, Exmouth EX8 1BJ (01395 272101; www.groveexmouth.com). Overlooking the seafront, large garden at the front of the pub. Homemade food served *Mon-Fri L and E & Sat-Sun 12.00-21.30 (Sun 21.00)*. Dog- and family-friendly. *Open Mon-Sat 11.00-23.00 & Sun 12.00-22.30.*

🍺 **13 The Strand** 1 The Parade, Exmouth EX8 1RS (07971 174466). A long, low establishment with wooden panelling and floors and a friendly, local trade. Dog-friendly, garden. Traditional pub games, sports TV and Wi-Fi. *Open Mon-Sat 11.00-23.00 (Fri-Sat 00.00) & Sun 12.00-22.30.*

🍺 **14 The Powder Monkey** 2–2A The Parade, Exmouth EX8 1RJ (01395 280090; www.jdwetherspoon.com/pubs/all-pubs/england/devon/the-powder-monkey-exmouth). Busy, town pub dispensing an ambitious range of real ales, including at least two from local breweries at any time. Real cider. Patio seating, real fires and Wi-Fi. *Open 08.00-00.00 (Fri-Sat 01.00)* and food available *08.00-22.00*.

🍺✕ **15 The Globe Inn** The Strand, Lympstone, Exmouth EX8 5EY (01395 263166). This pub offers open fires. A previous landlady fell down the stairs to her death, and is reputed to be still in residence. A reputation for excellent food, majoring on fresh, locally caught fish served *Thu-Sun 12.00-21.00 (Sun 19.00)* together with a fine selection of real ales. Child- and dog-friendly; outside seating. Traditional pub games, newspapers, real fires and Wi-Fi. B&B. *Open 12.00-22.00 (Sun 19.00).*

🍺✕ **16 The Swan Inn** The Strand, Lympstone, Exmouth EX8 5ET (01395 272644; www.theswaninn-lympstone.co.uk). Traditional, friendly village local serving bistro-style food *daily L and E*. Real cider and real ales. Children and dogs welcome, patio seating. Newspapers, real fires and Wi-Fi. *Open Mon-Thu L and E & Fri-Sun 12.00-22.00 (Sun 19.00).*

🍺✕ **17 The Redwing Bar & Dining** Church Road, Lympstone, Exmouth EX8 5JT (01395 222156; www.redwingbar-dining.co.uk). Cosy pub/restaurant serving real ale and fresh food *Mon-Sat L and E & Sun 12.00-18.00*, locally sourced and cooked to order. Dog- and child-friendly, garden. *Open Mon-Sat 12.00-22.00 (Fri-Sat 23.00) & Sun 12.00-21.00.*

🍺✕ **18 The Puffing Billy Inn** Station Road, Exton, Exeter EX3 0TR (01392 877888; www.thepuffingbilly.co.uk). Excellent food in spacious modern surroundings. Friendly, courteous and attentive staff. Meals available *Mon-Fri L and E and all day Sat-Sun*. Real ales. Dog- and child-friendly, garden. Wi-Fi. *Open Mon-Sat 09.00-22.00 (Sat 23.00) & Sun 09.00-18.00.*

Exeter

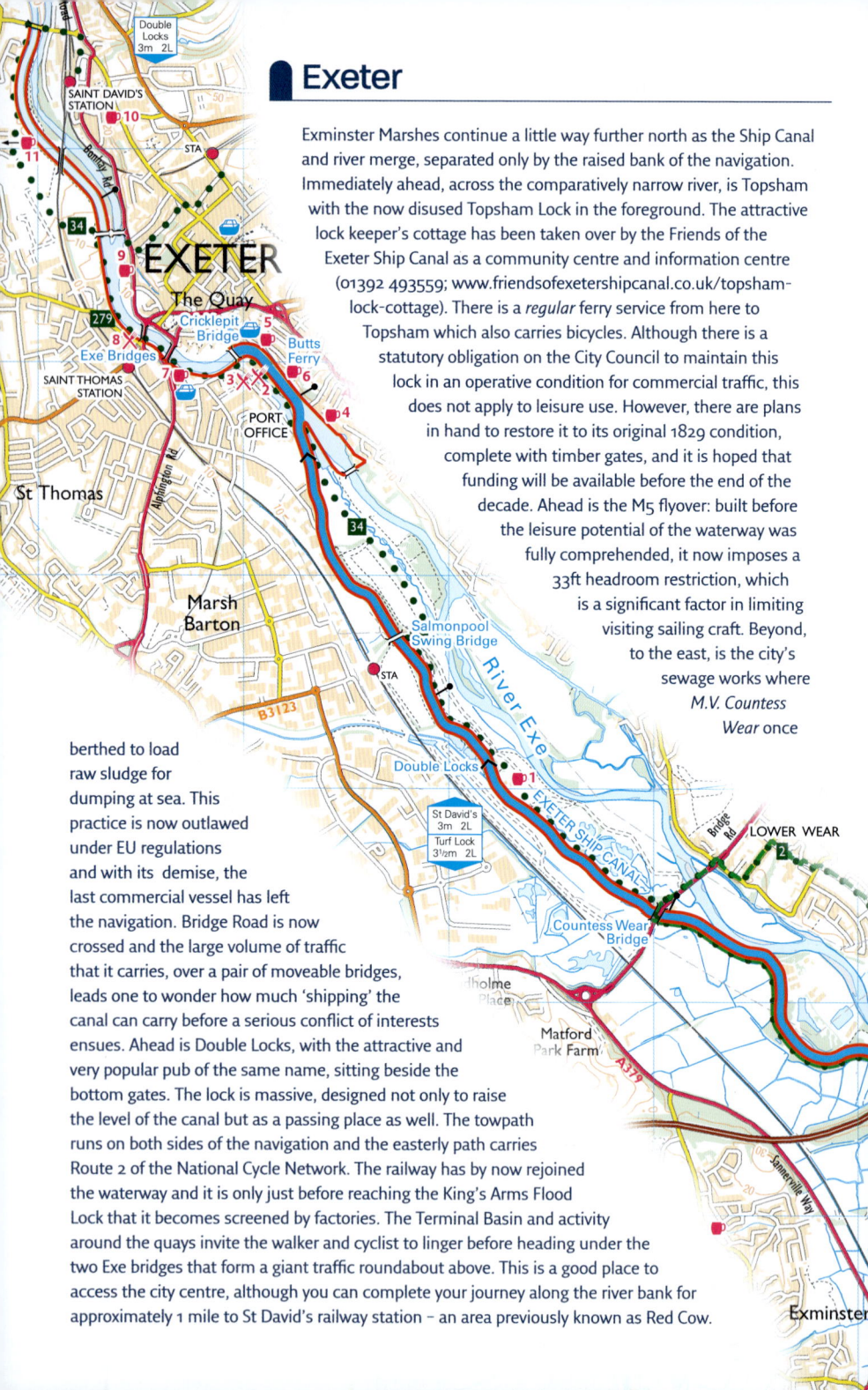

Exminster Marshes continue a little way further north as the Ship Canal and river merge, separated only by the raised bank of the navigation. Immediately ahead, across the comparatively narrow river, is Topsham with the now disused Topsham Lock in the foreground. The attractive lock keeper's cottage has been taken over by the Friends of the Exeter Ship Canal as a community centre and information centre (01392 493559; www.friendsofexetershipcanal.co.uk/topsham-lock-cottage). There is a *regular* ferry service from here to Topsham which also carries bicycles. Although there is a statutory obligation on the City Council to maintain this lock in an operative condition for commercial traffic, this does not apply to leisure use. However, there are plans in hand to restore it to its original 1829 condition, complete with timber gates, and it is hoped that funding will be available before the end of the decade. Ahead is the M5 flyover: built before the leisure potential of the waterway was fully comprehended, it now imposes a 33ft headroom restriction, which is a significant factor in limiting visiting sailing craft. Beyond, to the east, is the city's sewage works where *M.V. Countess Wear* once berthed to load raw sludge for dumping at sea. This practice is now outlawed under EU regulations and with its demise, the last commercial vessel has left the navigation. Bridge Road is now crossed and the large volume of traffic that it carries, over a pair of moveable bridges, leads one to wonder how much 'shipping' the canal can carry before a serious conflict of interests ensues. Ahead is Double Locks, with the attractive and very popular pub of the same name, sitting beside the bottom gates. The lock is massive, designed not only to raise the level of the canal but as a passing place as well. The towpath runs on both sides of the navigation and the easterly path carries Route 2 of the National Cycle Network. The railway has by now rejoined the waterway and it is only just before reaching the King's Arms Flood Lock that it becomes screened by factories. The Terminal Basin and activity around the quays invite the walker and cyclist to linger before heading under the two Exe bridges that form a giant traffic roundabout above. This is a good place to access the city centre, although you can complete your journey along the river bank for approximately 1 mile to St David's railway station – an area previously known as Red Cow.

Topsham

Devon. All services. Delightfully unspoilt, it is not hard to imagine the Topsham of 500 years ago when, as a port and centre for ship building, it was more important than Exeter. Its unique architectural heritage, with shops and housing dating from as early as the 14th C, can be enjoyed on foot. Take a stroll along The Strand to view some exquisite examples of 17th- and 18th-C merchant housing, with their characteristic Dutch gables. The nearby Goat Walk is equally charming; with its tiny beach it has been a walking and meeting place over many centuries. In spite of the bustle brought on by the tourist season, the locals remain tolerant, friendly and hospitable. There is a heated, open-air pool and a small museum.

Topsham Ferry Boat Ferry Road, Topsham EX3 0JJ – Trout's Boatyard (07801 203338; www.topshamturfferry.com). Plying between Ferry Road Causeway, Topsham and Turf Lock on the Ship Canal, carrying pedestrians, dogs and cycles. Operates *Mon-Fri late May-mid Sep & weekends Easter and Apr-Sep.* Private charter available. Also *winter* bird watching trips.

Exeter

Devon. All services. Early records for the city mention the construction of a fort, between AD55 and AD60, as headquarters for the 2nd Augustan Legion and located at the centre of the present city, overlooking the lowest possible crossing of the Exe. It was surrounded by a timber and earth rampart and a ditch; the foundation was exposed during an excavation in 1971, but was subsequently covered over again. The burgeoning Roman town took over much of the plan area of the fortress and spread beyond to be enclosed by a stone wall in the 2nd C. This is the basis of the present city wall which has been extensively rebuilt over the years. Urban life continued to flourish through the following centuries, with the withdrawal of the Roman garrison and the building of a monastery at which St Boniface was educated in the 7th C. The present High Street follows the line of the Roman main road and the four main medieval gates are sited on Roman gateways. Exeter was occupied by the Danes in AD877 when the chief religious establishment was St Mary Major, which survived in its Victorian form, in the cathedral close, into the 1970s. The city became a See in 1050 and the Norman cathedral was built in the 12th C; later to be much remodelled in medieval times. From the 15th C onwards, Exeter was the chief cloth marketing town in the south west and by the 17th C had become one of the richest cities in England. It was a significant port, although imports greatly outweighed exports and it was prey to serious and sustained competition from Topsham, downstream on the Exe estuary. However, the eventual confirmation of its customs rights over the entire estuary during the 17th C, together with the relative success of the canal, restored much of its prosperity and resulted in the construction of the delightful Custom House and development of the City Quays. Over the 19th C the population almost trebled, aided by the appearance of the railway in 1844. Some 130 years later, the arrival of the M5 was a further improvement in the city's communication links with the rest of the country and a variety of light industries thrive. Exeter lost much of its rich architectural heritage during the pernicious bombings of the 1942 air raids and this has been replaced, in varying degrees, by insensitive redevelopment dating from the 1950s.

Barnfield Theatre Barnfield Road, Exeter EX1 1SN (01392 270891; www.exeternorthcott.co.uk/get-creative/barnfield-theatre). Mix of amateur and professional theatre, dance and music. Coffee, snacks and bar.

Custom House Visitor Centre Exeter Quay, Exeter, Devon EX2 4AN (01392 271611; www.visitexeter.com/things-to-do/custom-house-visitor-centre-p136293). Source of walking and cycling leaflets and times for the Topsham Ferry Boat. Also bookings for a range of accommodation in the area, from hotels to camping barns. *Open Apr-Oct daily 10.00-17.00 & Nov-Mar Thu-Sun 11.00-16.00.*

Devon Wildlife Trust Cricklepit Mill, Commercial Road, Exeter EX2 4AB (01392 279244; www.devonwildlifetrust.org). The trust cares for some 40 nature reserves around the county, totalling more than 3,000 acres in all. Most are *open to the public at all times*. The Old Sludge Beds lie between the Ship Canal and the Exe, just upstream from the M5 flyover, and are maintained as an area of reed bed which is home to a wide variety of wetland birds. There are two further reserves within reach of Exmouth.

Exeter Cathedral Cathedral Close, Exeter EX1 1HS (01392 255573; www.exeter-cathedral.org.uk). Although completed in the 14th C by Bishop Grandisson, the two Norman transept towers date

BOAT TRIPS

Boat trips aboard *Kingsley*, locally built in Teignmouth in 1926 by T. Bulley & Son and a registered historic vessel. Trips available *Apr, May and Sep, weekends and B Hols; Jun-Aug, daily*. Also private hire and events. The company also operate Butt's Ferry from Exeter quay (07984 368442; www.facebook.com/exetercruises).

from the building's foundation. It was extensively remodelled by Bishop Bronescombe in the 13th C and the pepperpot roofs replaced the traditional Norman pyramids during further work in the 15th C. There is much original glass in the late 14thC east window and Sir Gilbert Scott's canopied choir stalls incorporate the oldest set of misericords that survive complete; they were carved 1260–80. The bishop's throne, carved from oak in 1312, is quite exquisite. Shop and café. *Open Mon-Sat 09.00-17.00 & Sun 11.30-16.00.* Donations.

Royal Albert Memorial Museum & Art Gallery Queen Street, Exeter EX4 3RX (01392 265858; www.rammuseum.org.uk). Extensively enhanced and refurbished during 2011. A wealth of interesting items in a Victorian treasure house. Exhibitions include world cultures, local history and archaeology, exotic birds and butterflies, glassware and West Country silver, clocks and watches. Temporary visiting art exhibitions alongside a rotating permanent collection. Workshops and activities for children and adults throughout the year. Shop and licensed café. *Open Tue-Sun 10.00-17.00 (Tue 10.30).* Free.

Exeter Picture House 51 Bartholomew Street West, Exeter EX4 3AJ (0871 902 5730; www.picturehouses.co.uk/cinema/exeter_picturehouse). Award-winning, purpose-built, two-screen cinema showing the best in contemporary film. Bar, coffee and tea.

Killerton House Broadclyst, Exeter EX5 3LE (01392 881345; www.nationaltrust.org.uk/visit/devon/killerton). Elegant 18th-C house containing treasures from the renowned Killerton dress collection, revealing the secrets of a woman's wardrobe in days gone by. Large hillside garden, Victorian rock garden, ice house and woodland walks. Gift shop, plant centre and licensed restaurant. House open *Feb-Dec at varying times. Garden open daily throughout year, 10.00-19.00.* Charge. Seven miles north of Exeter.

Exeter Northcott Theatre Stocker Road, Exeter EX4 4QB (01392 726363; www.exeternorthcott.co.uk). Venue for professional visiting theatre companies and the theatre's resident company. Backstage tours, theatre talks and visiting musicians. Restaurant serving tea, coffee and light meals. Licensed bar.

Phoenix Arts Centre Bradninch Place, Gandy Street, Exeter EX4 3LS (01392 667080; www.exeterphoenix.org.uk). High calibre, eclectic mix of varied material on offer, including galleries, workshops and courses. Excellent café and bar. Worth a visit just to see the automaton phoenix in action as the hour strikes.

Exeter Quay Striking example of an inland port that has developed over the ages to reflect the city's prosperity, founded on the production of serge cloth. Today it is given over solely to leisure use but this does nothing to detract from the wealth and diversity of the buildings, some dating back to the late 17th C. The Custom House, completed in 1681, was designed by Richard Allen and enabled Exeter to re-establish its dominance as a port over its long-time rival, Topsham, situated downstream in the tidal estuary. The building is brick-fronted, with two storeys and five bays and white painted stone quoins. The stairhall, together with some of the downstairs rooms, have superb plasterwork ceilings and the staircase incorporates bulbous, urn-shaped balusters. The warehouses north of the Custom House date from a similar period; cut into the cliffs, they provided a bonded stores. The two five-storey warehouses fronting the cliffs date from 1835, and the open fish market is also 19th-C. It incorporated a King's Beam, used for weighing dutiable goods. There are also two further warehouses nearby, built in the late 19th C, and used for storing wine. Further west, Cricklepit Mill (which gives its name to the nearby pedestrian bridge) dates from the end of the 17th C and encloses a large waterwheel. It was variously used for fulling, grist production and malting. On the other side of the water, set beside the basin constructed by James Green in 1830, is a large warehouse from the same period. The Quay House Interpretation Centre displays models, artefacts and pictures relating to the historic dock area, together with an audio-visual history of Exeter.

Rail Travel (National Rail Enquiries 08457 484950; www.nationalrail.co.uk). Exeter is served by five railway lines and has eight railway stations, two of which are on the mainline. On the east side of the Exe services run from both Exeter St David's and Exeter Central, having originated in Barnstaple. The run north is well worthwhile as an extension to activities around the estuary. On the west side of the Exe stopping services depart from both Exeter stations (many also stop at Exeter St Thomas) and may have originated from Bristol or South Wales. A few are from Exmouth. For cyclists, advanced bookings are essential on some services, usually the long distance routes. The *Cycling by Train* leaflet can be downloaded from the website.

Saddles & Paddles 4 King's Wharf, The Quay, Exeter EX2 4AN (01392 424241; www.sadpad.com). Bike and canoe hire on the quayside. Sales, spares and repairs. Canoeing group nights out. *Open 09.00-18.00. Closed Wed Nov-Apr.*

WALKING AND CYCLING

Riverside Valley Park 15 West Grove Road, Exeter EX2 4LU (www.devonwildlifetrust.org/nature-reserves/riverside-valley-park). One mile down river from Exeter Quay, sandwiched between the River Exe and the Exeter Ship Canal, this is an area of over 100 acres offering a selection of walks and 'back to nature' close to the pulsating heart of the city. The website details a selection of cycling trails and walks and you can park close to the Double Locks Pub – *see page 57*. Otherwise in the absence of locally prepared walking and cycling information, Komoot invariably comes up with the goods and local routes are accessible at www.komoot.com/guide/673087/cycling-in-north-devon. For opportunities further afield, visit www.visitexeter.com/inspire-me/blog/read/2020/06/10-wonderful-walks-in-exeter-b365. The Exe Estuary Management Partnership (01392 382236; www.exe-estuary.org) is also a useful source of information. For cycle hire contact Route 2 Bike Shop (01392 879160; www.route2topsham.co.uk/cycling). *See also* **Walking and Cycling** on page 49.

Pubs and Restaurants (pages 54-55)

🍺 **1 Double Locks** Canal Banks, Marsh Barton, Exeter EX2 6LT (01392 256947; www.doublelocks.com). A popular family pub overlooking the canal and serving food *daily 11.00-20.00*, together with a selection of real ales. Dogs welcome. Lockside seating. Open fires and *regular* events and live music. *Open Mon-Sat 11.00-22.00 & Sun 10.30-21.00.*

🍺 **2 Topsham Brewery & Taproom** Haven Road, Exeter EX2 8GR (01392 275196; www.facebook.com/topshambrewery). Beside the brewery in an attractive, historic stone building, this hostelry serves its own real ales on gravity. Real cider. Dog-friendly, garden. *Open Mon-Thu 16.00-23.00 & Fri-Sun 12.00-00.00 (Sun 22.00).*

✕ ♀ **3 Venezia Italian Restaurant** 61 Waterside, The Quay, Exeter EX2 8GY (01392 423688; www.venezia-exeter.com). Ristorante and café bar beside the quay. Traditional Italian menu, pizzas and Italian-style snacks *all day*. Hot and cold drinks. Children welcome. Quayside seating. *Regular* dance classes. *Open Mon-Thu 09.00-23.00 & Fri-Sun 00.00.*

🍺✕ **4 The Port Royal** Weirfield Path, Exeter EX2 4DR (01392 272360; www.theportroyal.co.uk). Reputed to be the longest pub in Exeter, its low ceilings serve only to substantiate this claim. It incorporates the old boathouse and serves an à la carte menu and bar snacks *Wed-Sat L and E & Sun 12.00-18.00* together with real ales. Dog- and child-friendly, patio seating. Traditional pub games and Wi-Fi. *Open Wed-Sun 10.00-23.00 (Sun and Wed 21.00).*

🍺 **5 The Prospect Inn** The Quay, Exeter EX2 4AN (01392 273152; www.heavitreebrewery.co.uk/pubs/the-prospect-inn/). Set in an attractive old building with exposed beams, panelled walls and multi-level seating areas, this establishment serves food *Tue-Sun 12.00-21.00*, together with real ales and real cider. Family-friendly, garden. Wi-Fi. *Open daily 12.00-23.00 (Sun 22.30).*

🍺✕ **6 On the Waterfront** 4-9 The Quay, Exeter EX2 4AP (01392 210590; www.waterfrontexeter.co.uk). Occupying the bottom floor of a converted warehouse with vaulted brick ceilings, this establishment serves meals *11.00-21.00 (Fri-Sat 21.30)*. Dog- and family-friendly, patio. Takeaway service. *Open daily 11.00-22.30 (Fri-Sat 23.30).*

🍺 **7 The Malt House** 7 Haven Road, Haven Bank, Exeter EX2 8BP (01392 490555; www.harvester.co.uk/restaurants/southwest/themalthouseexeter). Old riverside malthouse, tastefully restored with exposed brickwork and lots of beams. Alongside a range of old malting paraphernalia it serves food *all day*. *Open 11.30-21.00 (Sun 09.00).*

✕ **8 Exe Bridge Café** 180 Cowick Street, Exeter EX4 1AA (07791 099407). Excellent and inexpensive home-cooked café meals. Children welcome, friendly service. *Open daily 08.30-16.00.*

🍺✕ **9 The Mill on the Exe** Bonhay Road, Exeter EX4 3AB (01392 214464; www.millontheexe.co.uk). Converted paper mill. Real ales and an extensive international selection of food in atmospheric surroundings. Dogs welcome. Upstairs river balcony overlooking the weir and downstairs garden contribute towards making this a unique building. Wi-Fi. *Open 10.30-23.00 daily* and food available *daily 12.00-21.00.*

🍺 **10 The Imperial** New North Road, Exeter EX4 4AH (01392 434050; www.jdwetherspoon.com/pubs/all-pubs/england/devon/the-imperial-exeter). This pub makes use of all the downstairs rooms in a Georgian country house which is now a grade II listed structure. It includes a stunning orangery, the roof supported on cast-iron bow trusses and possibly originally built by Brunel on a site at Streatham Hall. Popular with the nearby university, it dispenses an ever changing array of real ales and a range of snacks and light meals *08.00-23.00*. Children welcome, garden. Newspapers and Wi-Fi. *Open 08.00-00.00 (Fri-Sat 01.00).*

🍺✕ **11 The Thatched House Inn** Exwick Road, Exeter EX4 2BQ (01392 272920; www.thatchedhouse.net). Close to the river and dating from the 17th C, this welcoming thatched hostelry serves food made from local ingredients *Tue-Thu 17.00-21.00 (Tue 20.30); Fri-Sat 12.30-21.00 & Sun 12.30-14.30 (Sun carvery only)* together with real ales and real cider. Quiz *Wed*. Dog- and family-friendly, patio. Traditional pub games, real fires and Wi-Fi. *Open Tue-Thu 17.00-22.30 (Tue 21.30) & Fri-Sun 12.30-23.00 (Sun 18.30).*

✕ **12 Route 2** 1-2 Monmouth Hill, Topsham, Exeter EX3 0JQ (01392 875085; www.route2topsham.co.uk). Formerly the Steam Packet and now transformed into a licensed eco-cafe, which has cycle hire and repair next door and attractive apartments to rent. *Open daily 08.00-17.00.*

🍺✕ **13 The Lighter Inn** The Quay, Topsham, Exeter EX3 0HZ (01392 875439; www.lighterinn.co.uk). Once the custom house, now dispensing real ales and an appetising selection of food *daily 12.00-21.00*. Children and dogs welcome. Quayside seating and Wi-Fi. *Open 11.00-23.00 (Sun 22.30).*

✕ ♀ **14 The Galley Restaurant** 41 Fore Street, Topsham EX3 0HU (01392 876078; www.facebook.com/thegalleytopsham). Wherever possible only local, organic and seasonal produce is used in the preparation of a range of appetising food served *Tue-Sat, L and E* in this charming, scruffy-chic restaurant. Booking recommended. Children welcome.

🍺✕ **15 The Passage House Inn** Ferry Road, Topsham, Exeter EX3 0JN (01392 873653; www.passagehouseinntopsham.co.uk). One of the oldest pubs in Topham. Fresh fish is a speciality. Good collection of real ales. Food served *daily 12.00-21.00*. Riverside seating next to the ferry. Dog- and family-friendly, quayside seating. Wi-Fi. *Open daily 10.00-22.00 (Sun 12.00).*

Try also: 🍺✕ **16 The Globe Hotel** 34 Fore St, Topsham, Exeter EX3 0HR (01392 873471; www.theglobetopsham.co.uk).

KENNET & AVON CANAL

MAXIMUM DIMENSIONS
Avonmouth to Bristol Harbour
Length: 325'
Beam: 50'
Draught: 18'
Air Draught: 90'

Bristol Harbour to Hanham Lock
Length: 80'
Beam: 18'
Draught: 6' 3"
Air Draught: 10' 3"

DOCK MASTER
0117 927 3633

Hanham Lock to Bath
Length: 75'
Beam: 16'
Headroom: 8' 9"

Bath to Newbury
Length: 70'
Beam: 13' 6"
Headroom: 8'
or
Length: 72'
Beam: 7'
Headroom: 7'

Newbury to Reading
Length: 70'
Beam: 14'
Headroom: 7' 8"

MANAGER
0303 040 4040
enquiries.walessouthwest@canalrivertrust.org.uk

MILEAGE
AVONMOUTH entrance to Severn Estuary to:
Bristol Docks: 7¾ miles
HANHAM Lock (start of tidal section): 14¼ miles
Bath, junction with River Avon: 25½ miles
Dundas Aqueduct: 30¾ miles
Bradford on Avon: 35¼ miles
Devizes Top Lock: 47¼ miles
Pewsey Wharf: 59¼ miles
Crofton Top Lock: 65¾ miles
Hungerford: 73¼ miles
Kintbury: 76¼ miles
Newbury Lock: 82¼ miles
Aldermaston Wharf: 90¾ miles
Tyle Mill Lock: 92¾ miles
READING: 100¾ miles

Locks: 104

Paddling: Category 1. Although below Hanham Lock the Avon is mildly tidal making the stretch into Bristol Floating Harbour Category 2. You will also need to purchase a licence for this stretch from the harbour office – see Navigational Note 1 on page 63 for contact details. West of Bristol the navigation becomes the province of the sea-going paddler.

The Kennet & Avon Canal is one of the most splendid lengths of artificial waterway in Britain, a fitting memorial to the canal age as a whole. It is a broad canal, cutting across southern England from Reading to Bristol (shown in this guide from Avonmouth to Reading). Its generous dimensions and handsome architecture blend well with the rolling downs and open plains that it passes through, and are a good reminder of the instinctive feeling for scale that characterised most 18th- and early 19th-C civil engineering.

The canal was built in three sections. The first two were river navigations, the Kennet from Reading to Newbury, and the Avon from Bath to Bristol, both being canalised. Among early 18th-C river navigations the Kennet was one of the most ambitious, owing to the steep fall of the river. Between Reading and Newbury 20 locks were necessary in almost as many miles, as the difference in level is 138ft. John Hore was the engineer for the Kennet Navigation, which was built between 1718 and 1723 and included 11 miles of new cut. Subsequently Hore was in charge of the Bristol Avon Navigation, carried out between 1725 and 1727. These river navigations were interesting in many ways, often because of the varied nature of the country they passed through. The steep-sided Avon Gorge meant that a fast-flowing river had to be brought under control. Elsewhere the engineering was unusual: for example the turf-sided locks on the Kennet, now partially replaced with brick structures.

For the third stage, a canal from Newbury to Bath was authorised in 1794. Rennie was appointed engineer, and after a long struggle the canal was opened in 1810, completing a through route from London to Bristol. The canal is 57 miles long, and included 79 broad locks, a summit level at Savernake 452ft above sea level and one short tunnel, also at Savernake. Rennie was both engineer and architect, anticipating the role played by Brunel in the creation of the Great Western Railway; in some ways his architecture is the more noteworthy aspect of his work. The architectural quality of the whole canal is exceptional, from the straightforward stone bridges to the magnificent neo-classical aqueducts at Avoncliffe and Limpley Stoke. Rennie's solution to the anticipated water supply problems on the top pound was to build a 4312yd tunnel, thereby providing a reservoir 15 miles long. The company called in William Jessop to offer a second – and hopefully cheaper solution – and it was he who suggested a shorter tunnel in conjunction with a steam pumping engine. This resulted in a saving of £41,000 and a completion date two years earlier. In some places the canal bed was built over porous rock, and so leaked constantly, necessitating further regular pumping.

Nevertheless, the canal as a whole was a striking achievement. West of Devizes the waterway descends Caen Hill in a straight flight of 16 locks. In total 29 locks are navigated within 2 miles of Devizes. The many swing bridges were designed to run on ball bearings, one of the first applications of the principle. The bold entry of the canal into Bath, a sweeping descent round the south of the city, is a firm expression of the belief that major engineering works should contribute to the landscape, whether urban or rural, instead of imposing themselves upon it as so often happens nowadays.

Later the Kennet & Avon Canal Company took over the two river navigations, thus gaining control of the whole through route. However traffic was never as heavy as the promoters had expected, and so the canal declined steadily throughout the 19th C. It suffered from early railway competition as the Great Western Railway duplicated its route, and was eventually bought by that railway company. Maintenance standards slipped, and this, combined with a rapidly declining traffic, meant that navigation was difficult in places by the end of World War I. The last regular traffic left the canal in the 1930s, but still it remained open, and the last through passage was made in 1951 by *nb Queen*, with the West Country artist P. Ballance on board. Subsequently the canal was closed, and for a long time its future was in jeopardy. However, great interest in the canal had resulted in the formation of a Canal Association shortly after World War II, to fight for restoration. In 1962 the Kennet & Avon Canal Trust was formed out of the Association, and practical steps towards restoration were under way. Using volunteers to raise funds from all sources, and with steadily increasing inputs from what was then British Waterways, the trust has catalysed the reopening of the entire navigation as a through route from Reading to Bristol.

NAVIGATIONAL NOTES

1. Do not navigate in tidal waters without up-to-date charts, tide tables, an anchor suitable for the conditions and all the other essential safety equipment, carriage of which may be mandatory. It is your responsibility to ensure that your craft is suitable and well maintained for the safety of everybody aboard. Seek expert advice if in any doubt. Inland waterways craft do navigate the Severn Estuary to Sharpness (and vice-versa) but this is not recommended without charts, calm weather conditions and adequate local knowledge. Pilots are available if required. Gloucester Harbour Trustees (01453 811913; www.gloucesterharbourtrustees.org.uk) is the Statutory Harbour Authority for this part of the estuary and publishes regularly-updated safety, weather and tidal information for leisure users on its website Pilotage for leisure craft may be arranged directly through Gloucester Pilots' Partnership 07774 226143 during normal working hours. Helpful information is provided on the pilots' website www.gloucesterpilots.co.uk. See also *Nicholson Waterways Guide 2: Severn, Avon & Birmingham*.

2. Note that most insurance policies covering inland craft do not include cover for tidal waters for which there are often special requirements to be met and usually an additional charge. Contact your insurance company before planning your trip below Hanham Lock.

3. Bristol City Council publish the comprehensive *Bristol Harbour Information for Boat Owners*, visit www.bristol.gov.uk/documents/information-for-boaters.pdf. This covers everything from locking procedures into the floating harbour through to details relating to exiting the feeder canal at Netham Lock. There is also information relating to use of the Floating Harbour and its environs available at www.bristol.gov.uk/streets-travel/bristol-harbour.

Avonmouth

The Severn Estuary, with its two dramatic road crossings, must be well known to all who travel the motorway system into Wales and the West Country. Equally well known is its extreme range of tides – giving rise to the Severn Bore – which in the world record books come third, surpassed only by those in the Bay of Fundy (bordered by Nova Scotia and New Brunswick) and in Ungava Bay, Quebec. The inland boater is, therefore, only likely to venture along the River Avon between Bristol and Avonmouth and thence out onto the Severn when making passage north to Sharpness on the Gloucester & Sharpness Canal (or of course, in reverse). This provides a means, for the intrepid navigator, to access the non-tidal river beyond Gloucester, avoiding a lengthy easterly detour. It is not something that will be undertaken lightly as the Navigational Notes make only too clear. For every boater who passes under the elevated section of the M5 at Avonmouth there will, no doubt, be hundreds of thousands of walkers and cyclists anxious to enjoy the beauties of the Avon Gorge from a slightly less exciting (though equally dramatic) vantage point. From Pill, on the south bank of the river, there is a combined cycleway and pedestrian path running the 5 miles to Bristol's Floating Harbour, so-called to differentiate it from its predecessor, a series of mud berths along the old course of The Avon through the city. On the north bank, the busy A4 heads for the city accompanied for some of the way by the Severn Beach railway line which terminates close to the Second Severn Crossing. Running through Pill and close companion to the cycleway is another, newly re-opened, freight line connecting Bristol to the docks at Portishead. Beyond Pill the river bends north, around a steep promontory as the gorge begins to close in from both sides. Initially the sides are rocky and free from trees and walkers and cyclists alike have uninterrupted views across the river to Shirehampton Park on the north bank. Then the river curls round to head in an almost southerly direction past a disused quarry and the old Roman settlement of Abona. Soon the bare rock becomes cloaked by the dense foliage of Leigh Woods. Further quarries are followed by The Avon Gorge Nature Reserve and then path and river head for the graceful Clifton Suspension Bridge.

WALKING AND CYCLING

Bristol is the home of Sustrans whose vision spawned the National Cycle Network, and it would be very surprising indeed if the cyclist was not well catered for in this area. The Pill Riverside Path runs from the Harbour, along Cumberland Road to follow the river through to Pill. There is also a linking route into Leigh Woods and to Ashton. Further west the cycleway crosses the river by way of the M5 bridge and connects (at both ends) with the Avon Cycleway; an 85-mile signposted route along a mixture of traffic-free paths and quiet lanes around Bristol. The routes mentioned are, of course, available to both walker and cyclist alike. On the north bank of the river, in Shirehampton Park, there are excellent walks, offering spectacular open views to the south, along the river and beyond. A city cycling guide is available at www.cycle.travel/city/bristol/map and you can visit the Better by Bike website (www.betterbybike.info/), for comprehensive cycling information about Bristol, Bath, North Somerset and South Gloucestershire: you can download free cycle maps or order paper copies.

Kennet & Avon Canal — Avonmouth

- **Easton-in-Gordano**
Somerset. Garage. Largely a dormitory village for Bristol running into, and indistinguishable from, its neighbour, Pill. The western end, around the Kings Arms, is the more interesting part.

- **Pill**
Somerset. PO, stores, off-licence, takeaway, chemist, station. A continuation of Easton-in-Gordano, only with some shops. Beyond the Railway Inn there are views across the River Avon.

- **Avonmouth Dock**
In the 19th C, with the construction of increasingly larger ships such as the *SS Great Britain* in 1843, it was recognised that there was a need for an expansion of the deep-water docking facilities in the Port of Bristol. The more far-sighted realised that in order to compete with other large British ports (with their own seaboard) a new facility had to be built at the mouth of the Avon and not as an extension to the City Docks. Whilst this radical concept amounted to heresy in the eyes of many prosperous Bristol merchants, the construction of Avonmouth Dock was commenced in 1868 and completed in 1877.

- **Portishead Dock**
This was opened in 1879, covering an area of 76 acres, largely to make up for the deficiencies in size and lock capacity of Avonmouth Dock on the other side of the river mouth. Again absorbed by Bristol Docks Committee in 1884 to make one unified port, it too soon proved itself woefully inadequate in the face of rapidly increasing shipping tonnage.

- **Royal Edward Dock**
Opened by Edward VII in 1908 and interconnected with Avonmouth Dock, the Royal Edward Dock had an entrance lock measuring 875' x 100' thereby allowing the revitalised dock complex the chance to again become competitive.

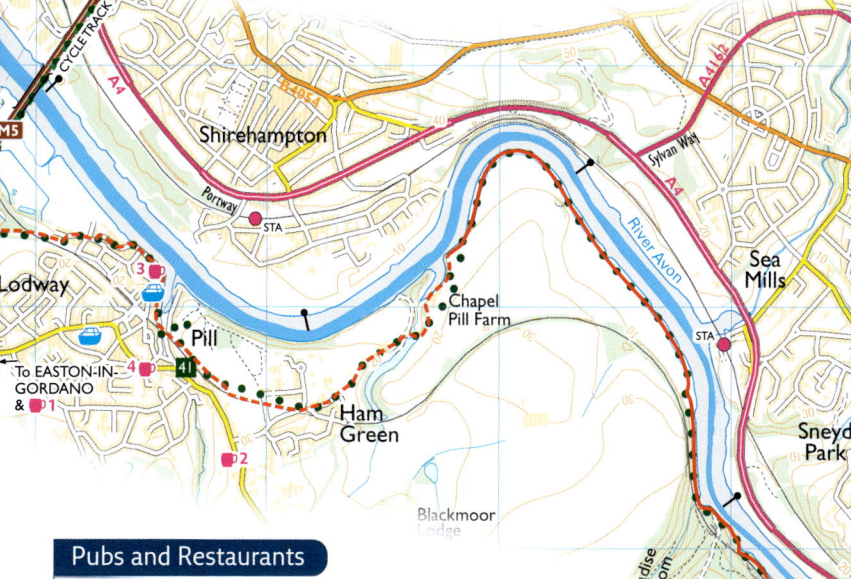

Pubs and Restaurants

🍺 1 **The Kings Arms** 12 St Georges Hill, Easton-in-Gordano BS20 0PS (01275 372208). At the west end of the village. Cheerful, village local serving real ales, traditional cider and traditional home-cooked pub food *L and E (not Sun E)*. Breakfast *from 10.00*. Dog- and child-friendly, beer garden. Skittle alley and pool, real fires, sports TV and Wi-Fi. *Open Sun-Thu 10.00-23.30 (Sun 12.00) & Fri-Sat 10.00-00.30 (Sat 10.30).*

🍺✕ 2 **The Anchor** 60 Ham Green, Pill BS20 0HB (01275 372253). A large open-plan pub with two dining areas and a pleasant garden serving real ales. Food available *L and E (not Sun E)*. Family-friendly. Wi-Fi. *Open Mon-Sat 12.00-23.00 (Fri-Sat 00.00) & Sun 11.00-22.00.*

🍺 3 **The Duke of Cornwall** Pump Square, Pill BS20 0BG (01275 371529). Sport-orientated pub, with a skittle alley, serving real ale. Dog- and child-friendly *(until 20.00)*. Traditional pub games, sports TV and Wi-Fi. *Open Mon-Thu 16.00-00.00 & Fri-Sun 12.00-01.00 (Fri 14.00).*

🍺 4 **The Kings Head** 3 Heywood Road, Pill BS20 0HT (01275 372423) A traditional two bar village pub serving real ale. Dog-friendly, outside seating. Traditional pub games, sports TV and Wi-Fi. *Open Mon-Fri 16.00-23.00 (Fri 00.30) & Sat-Sun 12.00-00.30 (Sun 22.30).*

Bristol

River and cycleway now pass under the spectacular shadow of the Clifton Suspension Bridge, poised some 230ft above. This 700ft-long crossing into the elevated Clifton district of Bristol is breathtaking in both its concept and execution. Designed by Brunel, when he was only 23, it was not in fact completed until 1864, nearly five years after his death. Half a mile eastwards the navigation reaches the Entrance Lock and divides. The northerly channel leads into the Floating Harbour through the Entrance Lock, Cumberland Basin and Junction Lock while the river skirts round to the south, along an artificial cut constructed in 1804 when the harbour was built.

Boatyards

Bristol Marina Hanover Place, Bristol BS1 6UH (0117 921 3198; www.bristolmarina.co.uk). Overnight mooring, long-term mooring, slipway, gas, boat repairs, wet dock, DIY facilities, telephone, toilets, showers, laundrette, chandlery. Free Wi-Fi.

Force 4 Chandlery Albion Dockyard, Hanover Place, Bristol BS1 6XT (0117 926 8396; www.force4.co.uk). Chandlery, books and charts. *Open Mon-Sat 08.30-17.30.*

Underfall Boatyard Cumberland Road, Bristol BS1 6XG (0117 929 3250; www.underfallboatyard.co.uk). Winter storage, slipway, boat building, facilities for large vessels to 180 tonnes, all boatyard trades available on site. The Underfall Boat Yard is owned and managed by the Underfall Trust. All income from tenants is put back into maintaining the historic yard and buildings. *Open Tue-Sun 10.00-17.00.*

BOAT TRIPS

Bristol Ferry Boats 44 The Grove, Bristol BS1 4RB (0117 927 3416; www.bristolferry.com). The company operates their distinctive yellow and blue round-trip waterbus services on the historic harbour *every day. (See web site for summer and winter timetables).* A selection of boats, each with an individual character, plying the harbour. Also available for private charter and public trips *throughout the year.*

Bristol Packet Boat Wapping Wharf, Gas Ferry Road, Bristol BS1 6UN 0117 926 8157; www.bristolpacket.co.uk). Award-winning cruises around the Floating Harbour and up and down the River Avon. Also available for private parties. Telephone or visit the website for timetables. *Open daily 09.30-17.00.*

Number Seven Boat Trips nb *Excalibur*, Welshback, Bristol BS1 4SB (0117 929 3659/07976 554024; www.numbersevenboattrips.com). Operators of the distinctive 'animal' boats running Floating Harbour ferry services and excursions from all points between Avonmouth and Bath running all the year round. Telephone or visit the website for timetables.

Waverley Excursions (0141 243 2224; www.waverleyexcursions.co.uk). *Waverley* operates an exciting and varied selection of trips departing from a host of locations including up and down the Bristol Channel. Telephone or visit the website for a timetable.

There is a pleasing combination of old and new quays – some dating back to the 13th C – and a contrasting selection of bridges all adding variety to what is now an entirely leisure- orientated dock complex. In the main harbour, before Redcliffe Bascule Bridge is reached, the navigation passes the 'Mud Dock', which dates from 1625 and provided a soft mud berth for shipping when the quays were still subject to the tidal fluctuations of the two rivers. It is now the site of a café and cycle hire centre. There is also an interesting district heating installation adjacent to the Floating Harbour utilising a heat pump and water from the tidal Avon. Turning through a right-angled bend, the waterway now makes a beeline for Netham Lock (0117 977 6590) in concert with a busy main road along its south bank. On the apex of the bend is the site of Totterdown Basin and Old Totterdown Lock, which once provided an access into the tidal Avon. This has now become a wildlife area. For those using the Avon Walkway leave the river path on the bend to the east of Temple Meads and join Feeder Road alongside the canal to complete the walk/ride to Netham Bailey Bridge as the river path is closed between these points due to bank erosion.

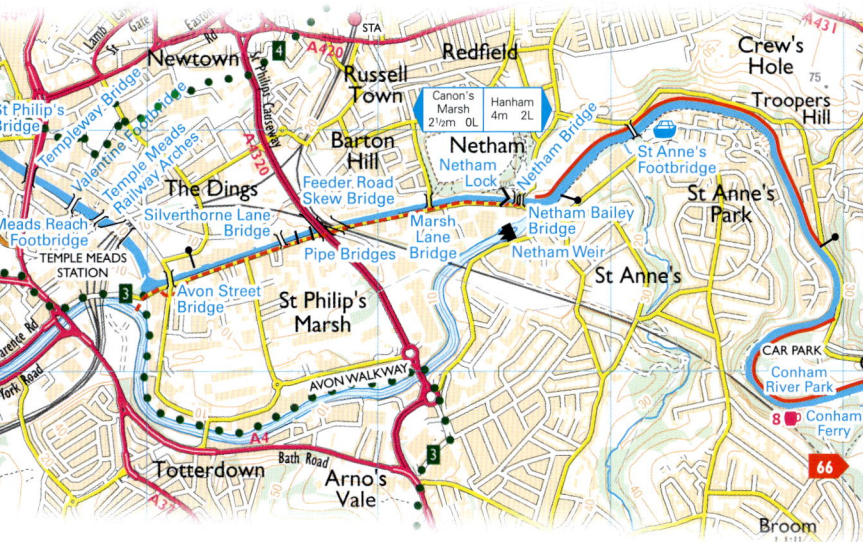

NAVIGATIONAL NOTES

1. Below Hanham Lock the river comes under the jurisdiction of Bristol City Council to whom a licence fee is payable. Visitors may purchase a licence – the cost of which is based on length of stay and length of craft – from the lock keeper at Netham Lock or from the Harbour Office (0117 903 1484; www.bristol.gov.uk/page/arrival-and-departure-bristol-harbour) Underfall Yard, Cumberland Road, Bristol – located at the western end of the Floating Harbour.
2. Visitor moorings are available in the Floating Harbour and are allocated by the Harbour Master (0117 903 1484; www.bristol.gov.uk/streets-travel/bristol-harbour). All moorings are controlled by the Harbour Office, please note there are no suitable overnight moorings between Netham and Hanham Locks.
3. To contact bridge operators for a bridge swing within the Floating Harbour telephone 0117 929 9338 or the Harbour Master as above.
4. When navigating under Redcliffe Bridge do not use east and west arches. For Bristol Bridge use centre of arches and do not use east arch.

● **Bristol**
Bristol. Daily markets. All services. Bristol grew up on the confluence of the Rivers Avon and Frome and was one of two cities prominent at the end of the Saxon period; the other being Norwich. It was probably established in the late 10th C beside a bridge over the Avon from which it derived the name Bridge-Stow: the place of the bridge. It developed on an easily defended site between the Avon and its tributary, the River Frome and initially built up trading links with South Wales and Ireland. By the 14th C Bristol had outgrown the small Saxon burgh of its origins and additional walls were built to enclose the newly populated areas to the south of the Avon. However, still left outside the walls were the church of St Mary Redcliffe, the Monastery of St Augustine, as well as three major friaries. The monastery and cathedral were by now one and the same. As a port Bristol was dominant along the coasts of the Severn Estuary and its local trade extended from Ireland to the Midlands where goods were transhipped into barges at Bewdley. That Bristol prospered as a port throughout the medieval period is somewhat surprising, given its location up the severely tidal River Avon and its unsatisfactory mud berthing arrangements. Yet it went on to dominate a burgeoning world trade as is witnessed by its rich legacy of Renaissance buildings – from brick classical merchants' town houses to country houses and suburban villas – and to embark on the Industrial Revolution second only to Liverpool as Britain's major transatlantic port. As a pivotal part of the slave trade, Bristol imported tobacco, timber, rum, cotton and sugar and together with its human cargoes, exported finished cotton goods, glass, brassware and soap. Its decline as a port, in the face of increasingly successful competition from Liverpool, lay as much in the Lancashire port's advantageous relationship to the expanding canal network, as to Bristol's position up a difficult tidal river in the face of the increasing size of 19th-C shipping. Today Bristol has an immense water-bound leisure facility in place of its once proud docks; home to a wealth of activity, maritime and otherwise. As a contemporary city, its prosperity is founded upon a range of financial institutions from insurance to banking; on the aerospace industry and on high technology electronic research and production.

Bristol Cathedral College Green, Bristol BS1 5TJ (0117 926 4879; www.bristol-cathedral.co.uk). Major example of a 'hall' church, one of the finest in the world; the nave, choir and aisles are all of the same height. Founded in the middle of the 12th C as the Abbey of St Augustine, the Chapter House and Abbey Gatehouse clearly remain to be seen. In 1539 the Abbey was closed and the unfinished nave demolished. However in 1868 the architect G. E. Street drew up plans to complete the nave founded on the original pillar bases. Book shop and coffee shop.

Bristol Zoo Project Blackhorse Hill, Easter Compton BS10 7TP (0117 428 5300; www.bristolzoo.org.uk). They breed endangered species, aim to raise awareness of the threat to a wide range of habitats, and support conservation projects worldwide. Pizzeria, café and picnic areas. *Open daily 10.00-16.00.* Charge. Buses 1, 2, 12 and T7 from the city centre.

City Museum & Art Gallery Queen's Road, Bristol BS8 1RL (0117 922 3571; www.bristolmuseums.org.uk/bristol-museum-and-art-gallery). Temporary exhibitions, fascinating objects and artworks from all over the world. Family activities and workshops. Shop and café. *Open Tue-Sun 10.00-17.00.* Free.

Clifton Suspension Bridge Visitor Centre Leigh Woods, Bristol BS8 3PA (0117 974 4664; www.cliftonbridge.org.uk). This potent symbol of the City of Bristol, from a design by I. K. Brunel, led a chequered career from its inception in 1754 to final completion in 1864. The centre explains all the ups and downs of the structure with the aid of models and interactive exhibitions. Photographic archive. *Open daily 10.00-17.00* Free guided tours *Easter-Oct, Sat-Sun 15.00* from the toll booth at the Clifton end of the bridge. Shop and coffee kiosk. Charge.

Floating Harbour (www.bristolfloatingharbour.org.uk). Towards the end of the 18th C Bristol's importance as a port started to slip, largely on account of the large rise and fall in the tides and the difficulties encountered by ships berthing on the river mud, placing considerable stress on a vessel's hull. In 1802 William Jessop was invited to submit plans for a 'floating harbour'. Work began in 1804 and was completed some five years later. For a while the port thrived but was always handicapped by its position up the river. The last steamships used the docks in the 1950s. Today the harbour is primarily a focus for recreational activity with a walking trail and a wealth of interpretation boards describing the harbour and its history.

Georgian House Museum 7 Great George Street, Bristol BS1 5RR (0117 921 1362; www.bristolmuseums.org.uk/georgian-house-museum). An 18th-C West India merchant's house furnished in the style of the period and owned by John Piny, a sugar trader who owned both land and slaves in the Caribbean. Currently engaged in honest conversations around the complex histories behind their objects, archives and spaces. *Open Sat-Tue 11.00-16.00.* Free.

M Shed Princes Wharf, Wapping Road, Bristol BS1 4RN (0117 352 6600; www.bristolmuseums.org.uk/m-shed). Exciting and innovative new museum telling the story of Bristol. Three galleries, train, boat and crane rides and lots of exhibitions and events. Café and shop. *Open Tue-Sun 10.00-17.00.* Free.

St George's Bristol Great George Street, off Park Street, Bristol BS1 5RR (0117 929 4929; www.stgeorgesbristol.co.uk). Music to suit all tastes in marvellously acoustic surroundings. Bar and gallery in beautifully restored crypt area. Café bar.

St Mary Redcliffe Redcliffe Parade West, Bristol BS1 6SP (0117 929 1487/0117 231 0060; www.stmaryredcliffe.co.uk). Described by Elizabeth I as 'The fairest, goodliest and most famous Parish Church in England'. Free lunchtime recitals. *Open Mon-Sat 08.00-17.00 & Sun 12.00-16.30*. Donations.
SS Great Britain Great Western Dockyard, Gas Ferry Road, Bristol BS1 6TY (0117 926 0680; www.ssgreatbritain.org). Sea travel took a great leap forward when the famous Victorian engineer Isambard Kingdom Brunel applied his skills to the construction of an iron, steam-driven passenger ship capable of maintaining a schedule on voyages to America and the antipodes. *Open Tue-Sun 10.00-17.00*. Charge.
Watershed 1 Canon's Road, Harbourside, Bristol BS1 5TX (0117 927 5100; www.watershed.co.uk). Bristol's arts centre with a wide mix of entertainment that is well up to expectation. Café/bar.
Tourist Information Centre The Galleries, Ground Floor, Bristol BS1 3XD (0117 239 7685; www.walkinbristol.com/tourist-information-centre). *Open daily 10.00-17.00*.

WALKING AND CYCLING

The Avon Walkway-cum-Cycleway can be seen as the spinal route following the River from Pill to Bath and thence to Limpley Stoke and beyond. As such it forms the basis for a series of superb expeditions which can be linked into the extensive collection of routes radiating out from the Bristol City centre, accessed from the Floating Harbour, just north of St Augustine's Reach. This also provides a direct link to the Bristol & Bath Railway Path which in turn interconnects with the Avon Cycleway – *see* previous notes for further details. Any permutation can provide circular routes with widely contrasting scenery. Many combinations are both flat and traffic-free. LifeCycleUk, a charity that promotes cycling throughout the former Avon area, can be contacted for a range of free maps and detailed route advice (0117 353 4580; www.lifecycleuk.org.uk). Bicycles are available for hire from Blackboy Hill Cycles, 180 Whiteladies Road, Clifton, Bristol BS8 2XU (0117 973 1420; www.black-boy-cycles.co.uk) who are *open Mon-Fri 09.00-17.30 & Sat 09.30-17.00*. *See* page 60 for more information.

Pubs and Restaurants (pages 62-63)

There are a wide range of pubs, bars, cafes, clubs and eating houses thronging the Floating Harbour. These represent a small selection of them.

1 The Pump House Merchants Road, Hotwells, Bristol BS8 4PZ (0117 927 2229; www.the-pumphouse.com). Old pumping station supplying water to the docks, turned chapel, turned slaughterhouse. Pub offering real ale, and an à la carte menu alongside traditional pub favourites. Food available *L and E (not Sun E)*. Large gin selection. Family-friendly, dockside patio seating. *Open daily 10.30 until late*.

2 Arnolfini Café Bar 16 Narrow Quay, St Augustine's Reach, Bristol BS1 4QA (0117 440 9741; www.arnolfini.org.uk/cafe-bar). Situated within the well-known art gallery. Superb quality and value food served *10.00-15.00 & Fri-Sat 17.00-21.00* in comfortably relaxed surroundings. Everyone welcome. Quayside location. Wi-Fi. *Open daily 09.00-17.00 (Fri-Sat 22.00)*.

3 Harbour House The Grove, Harbourside, Bristol BS1 4RB (0117 925 1212; www.hhbristol.com). Set in a 19th-C transit shed, this restaurant and bar serves a wide range of food – seasonal and local wherever possible, from an *all-day* menu – together with cocktails and local bottled beers. Sun roast. Dog-friendly. *Open daily 12.00-23.00 (Sun 22.00)*.

4 Under the Stars Narrow Quay, Harbourside, Bristol (0117 929 8392; www.underthestarsbar.co.uk). Tapas, pizza, drinks and cocktails in this friendly, though somewhat quirky, setting afloat. *Open daily 12.00-22.00 (Sun 17.00)*. Food available *L and E (not Sun E)*.

5 Riverstation The Grove Harbourside, Bristol BS1 4RB (0117 914 4434; www.riverstation.co.uk). This is an old river police building, right in the heart of Bristol's dockside, with excellent views out over the Floating Harbour serving breakfast, brunch, lunch and dinner *daily 10.00-21.30*. There are two floors of modern European dining, consisting of a first floor restaurant and a waterside bar/kitchen. *Open Mon-Fri 11.00-23.00 & Sat-Sun 10.00-23.00 (Sun 20.00)*.

6 Nova Scotia 1 Nova Scotia Place, Hotwells, Bristol BS1 6XJ (07794 781189; www.facebook.com/novascotiabristol/). This traditional old-style hostelry, established over 200 years ago, remains popular with families, young professionals, visitors and local workers alike. Real ales and food available *L and E (not Sun E)*. Dog-friendly, dockside seating. *Open Mon-Sat 11.00-23.00 & Sun 12.00-22.30*.

7 The Ostrich Inn Lower Guinea Street, Redcliffe, Bristol BS1 6TJ (0117 927 3776; www.butcombe.com/the-ostrich-pub-bristol). Traditional pub with a picturesque harbour-side setting, serving real ale and a wide range of appetising food available *daily 12.00-21.00*. Dog- and family-friendly, outside seating. Wi-Fi. *Open Mon-Sat 11.00-23.00 & Sun 12.00-22.00*.

8 Beeses Riverside Bar & Tea Garden Wyndham Crescent, Bristol BS4 4SX (0117 977 7412; www.beeses.co.uk). Waterside café set in the wooded Avon Valley serving buffet food, teas and barbecues. Bar with real ales. Mooring, large garden, children and dogs welcome. Ferry service from towpath. Food available *Fri-Sun and B Hols L and E (not Sun and B Hol E)*. *Open Apr-Oct, times vary*.

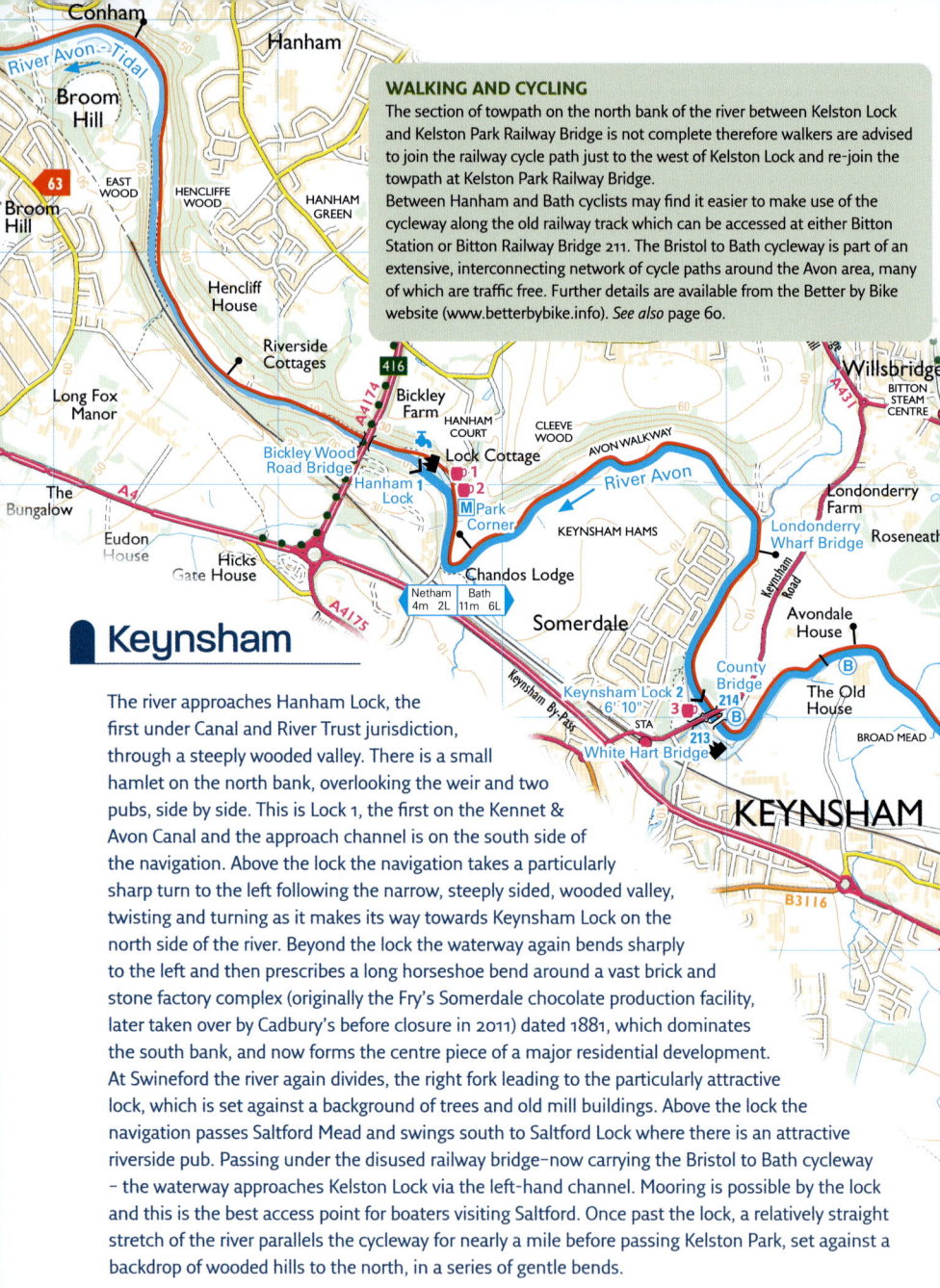

WALKING AND CYCLING

The section of towpath on the north bank of the river between Kelston Lock and Kelston Park Railway Bridge is not complete therefore walkers are advised to join the railway cycle path just to the west of Kelston Lock and re-join the towpath at Kelston Park Railway Bridge.

Between Hanham and Bath cyclists may find it easier to make use of the cycleway along the old railway track which can be accessed at either Bitton Station or Bitton Railway Bridge 211. The Bristol to Bath cycleway is part of an extensive, interconnecting network of cycle paths around the Avon area, many of which are traffic free. Further details are available from the Better by Bike website (www.betterbybike.info). *See also page 60.*

Keynsham

The river approaches Hanham Lock, the first under Canal and River Trust jurisdiction, through a steeply wooded valley. There is a small hamlet on the north bank, overlooking the weir and two pubs, side by side. This is Lock 1, the first on the Kennet & Avon Canal and the approach channel is on the south side of the navigation. Above the lock the navigation takes a particularly sharp turn to the left following the narrow, steeply sided, wooded valley, twisting and turning as it makes its way towards Keynsham Lock on the north side of the river. Beyond the lock the waterway again bends sharply to the left and then prescribes a long horseshoe bend around a vast brick and stone factory complex (originally the Fry's Somerdale chocolate production facility, later taken over by Cadbury's before closure in 2011) dated 1881, which dominates the south bank, and now forms the centre piece of a major residential development. At Swineford the river again divides, the right fork leading to the particularly attractive lock, which is set against a background of trees and old mill buildings. Above the lock the navigation passes Saltford Mead and swings south to Saltford Lock where there is an attractive riverside pub. Passing under the disused railway bridge—now carrying the Bristol to Bath cycleway – the waterway approaches Kelston Lock via the left-hand channel. Mooring is possible by the lock and this is the best access point for boaters visiting Saltford. Once past the lock, a relatively straight stretch of the river parallels the cycleway for nearly a mile before passing Kelston Park, set against a backdrop of wooded hills to the north, in a series of gentle bends.

● **Keynsham**

Somerset. All services. Keynsham has grown steadily along the Bristol road, and so is now a vast shapeless suburb. However, the centre still retains a feeling of independence, and has many traces of Keynsham's past.

● **Bitton**

Somerset. Stores, off-licence, farm shop. Although a main road village, Bitton's heart survives intact south of the road. Here is a fine group formed by the church, the grange and the 18th-C vicarage, all built around the churchyard. The church has a long Saxon nave with Norman details, a 14th-C chancel, and a magnificently decorative late 14th-C tower.

Avon Valley Railway Bitton Station, Bath Road, Bitton, Bristol BS30 6HD (0117 932 5538; www.avonvalleyrailway.org). Short length of preserved steam railway offering steam trips *Apr–Oct, Sat & Sun; Jun–Jul also Wed, plus many days during school holidays and special events at other times of the year*. The railway is operated by an enthusiastic bunch of dedicated volunteers and plans are in hand to progressively extend the line to the outskirts of Bath. *See* the excellent website for more information. Cream teas, snacks and light refreshments. The site is *open daily except Christmas day*.

● **Swineford**
Somerset. Although bisected by the A431, the settlement by the river is still attractive. The old mill buildings constructed in 1840 overlook the long weir.

● **Saltford**
Somerset. Stores, chemist, takeaways, off-licence, fish & chips, garage (distant). Although Saltford has been developed as a large-scale dormitory suburb, the older parts by the river are still pretty and secluded. Stores *open daily 06.00–23.00*.

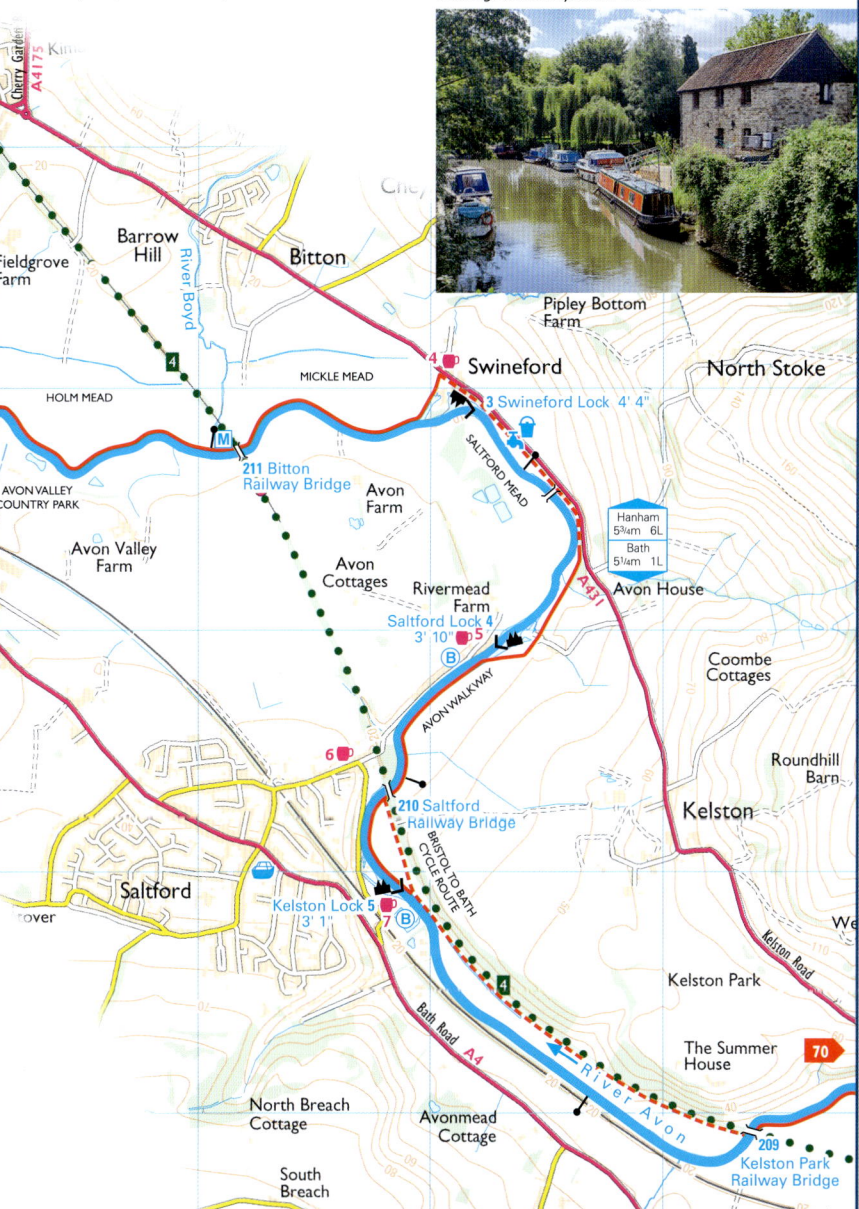

Moorings above Keynsham Lock

NAVIGATIONAL NOTES

1. The River Avon is usually only tidal to Hanham, however high spring tides can reach as far as Keynsham Lock.
2. Upstream craft should give way to downstream craft on fast-flowing sections of the river.
3. Downstream craft should approach the bend at Keynsham with caution and sound their horn to warn craft leaving Portavon Marina of their approach. Approach the lock cut entrance with care as it can be obscured by trees.
4. Visitor moorings are very limited on the river below Bath so boaters should plan their itinerary accordingly.
5. Bath Locks are padlocked when the river is in spate so at times of high water levels boaters should not embark on a journey upstream without first ensuring that they can leave the navigation for the safe haven of the canal.
6. See also Navigational Note 1 on page 59.

Pubs and Restaurants (pages 66-67)

1 **The Chequers** Ferry Road, Hanham BS15 3NU (0117 329 1711; www.thechequershanhammills.co.uk). Re-furbished, light airy and well appointed, riverside pub serving real ales. Fresh seasonal British menu served *daily 12.00-21.30 (Fri-Sat 22.00)*. Children and dogs welcome. Riverside garden and patio. Moorings for patrons. Wi-Fi. *Open 11.00-23.00 (Sun 22.30)*.

2 **The Old Lock and Weir** Ferry Road, Hanham BS15 3NU (0117 967 3793; www.oldlockandweir.com). Riverside pub serving real ales and food *Mon-Fri L and E & Sat-Sun 12.00-18.00 (Sun 16.00)*. Dog- and family-friendly, garden and heated patio. Sports TV and Wi-Fi. *Overnight* moorings for customers. *Occasional* live music. *Open Mon-Sat 11.30-23.00 & Sun 11.00-22.30*.

3 **The Lock Keeper** Keynsham Lock, Keynsham BS31 2DD (0117 986 2383; www.lockkeeperbristol.com). Unpredictable flood waters forced many a crew to stay the night at the Lock Keeper. Real ales and food available *daily 12.00-21.00 (Sun 20.00)*. Dog- and family-friendly, garden. *Occasional* live music. Traditional pub games and Wi-Fi. *Open Mon-Sat 11.00-00.00 & Sun 12.00-22.30*.

4 **The Swan** Bath Road, Swineford BS30 6LN (0117 932 3101; www.swanswineford.co.uk). 200-year-old stone-built cottage pub which has a modern face and a traditional heart. Real ales on offer, drawn from the 'wood'. Home-cooked food available *daily 12.00-21.00 (Sun 18.00)*. Dog- and family-friendly, garden. Newspapers, real fires and Wi-Fi. *Open 12.00-23.00 (Fri-Sat 00.00)*.

5 **The Jolly Sailor** Mead Lane, Saltford BS31 3ER (01225 873002; www.facebook.com/JollySaltford). A popular pub dating back to 1726. Real ale and locally-sourced food available *Thu-Mon 12.00-21.00 (Sun 20.00)*. Riverside garden. Quiz *Thu* and *weekend* live music. Real fires. *Open Thu-Mon 11.00-23.00*.

6 **The Bird in Hand** High Street, Saltford BS31 3EJ (01225 873335; www.birdinhandsaltford.co.uk). A beautifully kept village local offering locally brewed real ales and superb country views. Good food is served *daily 12.00-21.00 (Sun 20.00)*. Dog- and family-friendly, garden. Large conservatory and terrace. Newspapers, sports TV and Wi-Fi. *Open 11.00-23.00 (Sun 22.30)*.

7 **The Riverside Inn** The Shallows, Saltford BS31 3EZ (01225 873600; www.riversidesaltford.co.uk). Refurbished bar and restaurant overlooking the river. Real ales. A wide range of food served *daily 12.00-20.00 (Sun 18.00)*. Dog- and child-friendly, outside seating. Traditional pub games, sports TV and Wi-Fi. B&B. *Open 08.00-22.00 (Sun 18.00)*.

Boatyards

Ⓑ **Portavon Waterside & Marina** Keynsham Road, Keynsham BS31 2DD (01225 424301; www.bwml.co.uk). Overnight mooring, long-term mooring, winter storage, slipway, boat sales and repairs, engine sales and repairs (including outboards), toilets, showers, CCTV, Wi-Fi. *24hr emergency call out*.

Ⓑ **Bristol Boats Ltd** Sheppards Boatyard, Mead Lane, Saltford BS31 3ER (01225 872032; www.bristolboatsltd.co.uk). Near Saltford Lock. Gas, long-term mooring, slipway, gantry, boat sales and repairs, outboard engine sales and repairs, chandlery, toilets, boat building. *Open 09.30-16.30 but closed Tue & Sun*.

Ⓑ **Saltford Marina** The Shallows, Saltford BS31 3EZ (01225 872226; www.saltfordmarina.co.uk) family-run marina beside Kelston Lock. Overnight and long-term mooring. Restaurant and bar.

Ⓑ **R.L.L. Boats** Unit 1 Broadmead Industrial Estate, Broadmead Lane, Bristol BS31 1ST (0117 986 9860; www.rllboats.co.uk). Boat building-narrow and wide-beam, repairs and modifications, hardstanding, painting, crane, DIY facilities. *Open Mon-Fri 07.00-17.00 (Fri 06.00) & Sat 08.00-12.00*.

 Bath

The river, on passing Kelston Park, prepares to leave its wide, wandering course and the pastures flanking both banks in favour of the urban sprawl of Bath. It soon passes under the elegant single stone arch of New Bridge carrying the A4 and again ducks through another disused railway bridge, now the Bristol to Bath cycleway. The main line from London to South Wales closely follows the south bank, vanishing at one point into a tunnel. Soon the River Avon approaches the industrial suburbs of Bath and enters a wooded section. Ahead is Weston Lock and the lock cut is the northern channel. Beyond the lock the navigation meanders into the city in long, gentle curves flanked by roads, the railway and areas of light industry. There are several footbridges across the river and the cycleway makes two further crossings. There are good moorings east of Churchill Road bridges, convenient for a *supermarket*. The canal joins the Avon immediately below Bath Bottom Lock No 7 in the middle of the industrial quarter of the city. The railway station is opposite the junction of canal and river and the fine Georgian city surrounds the unnavigable river to the north and east. The junction (and moorings to the north) are the best points of access for Bath as a whole. The Widcombe flight of six locks lifts the waterway swiftly above the city. There was once a seventh lock in the flight but locks 8 and 9 were merged as part of a road building scheme, making one new lock with a fall of over 19ft. This now vies with Tuel Deep Lock, on the Rochdale Canal, for deepest lock on the navigable waterways system. Above the flight the navigation enters a cutting and passes through an ornamental tunnel that carries housing and Cleveland House, the old canal company's headquarters. Beyond the tunnel another cutting carries the waterway past two pretty cast iron bridges, both dated 1800 and houses seem almost to hang out over the water. There is another tunnel with fine Adamesque portals as the canal leaves the confines of Sydney Gardens and passes the last of the Georgian buildings lining its banks. There are useful *parades of shops* both to the south of the Widcombe Flight and to the west of Bridge 188. The navigation makes a magnificent exit from the city, cut into the hill, sweeping round to the south to join the river as they begin to follow the same route towards Bathampton providing extensive views of Bath's Georgian terraces. The canal continues on a straight course, closely flanked by the railway, which is in a cutting below and then passes through Bathampton, on a low embankment above the school and church. Following the course of the River Avon the waterway swings sharply to the south, towards Bathford church on the opposite side of the valley, leaving behind the groups of houses that heralded the suburbs of Bath.

WALKING AND CYCLING
The towpath between Bath and Devizes is in good condition. The remainder of the towpath varies in surface; generally good through urban areas, rural sections are dependent on weather conditions. Eastern sections bordering the river navigation can become very overgrown in the height of the summer. It is a very popular long distance route for walkers and cyclists alike and the latter are asked to exercise care and to give way to people on foot. The Bristol & Bath Railway Path and the riverside walk give direct, safe access into the centre of Bath. East of Bath the National Cycle Network Route 4 follows the towpath to Devizes. This also forms part of the Bath 2 Tunnels Circuit, NCN 244, which can be accessed from the canal towpath in Bath. Bikes can be hired from Bath Narrowboats, Sydney Wharf (see page 72). A round trip from Sydney wharf – following the Two Tunnels route to their base at Brass Knocker Wharf and returning along the canal towpath – forms a round trip of 13 miles. An audio trail has been installed on the Widcombe Lock Flight in Bath providing an interesting, historical insight into the area.

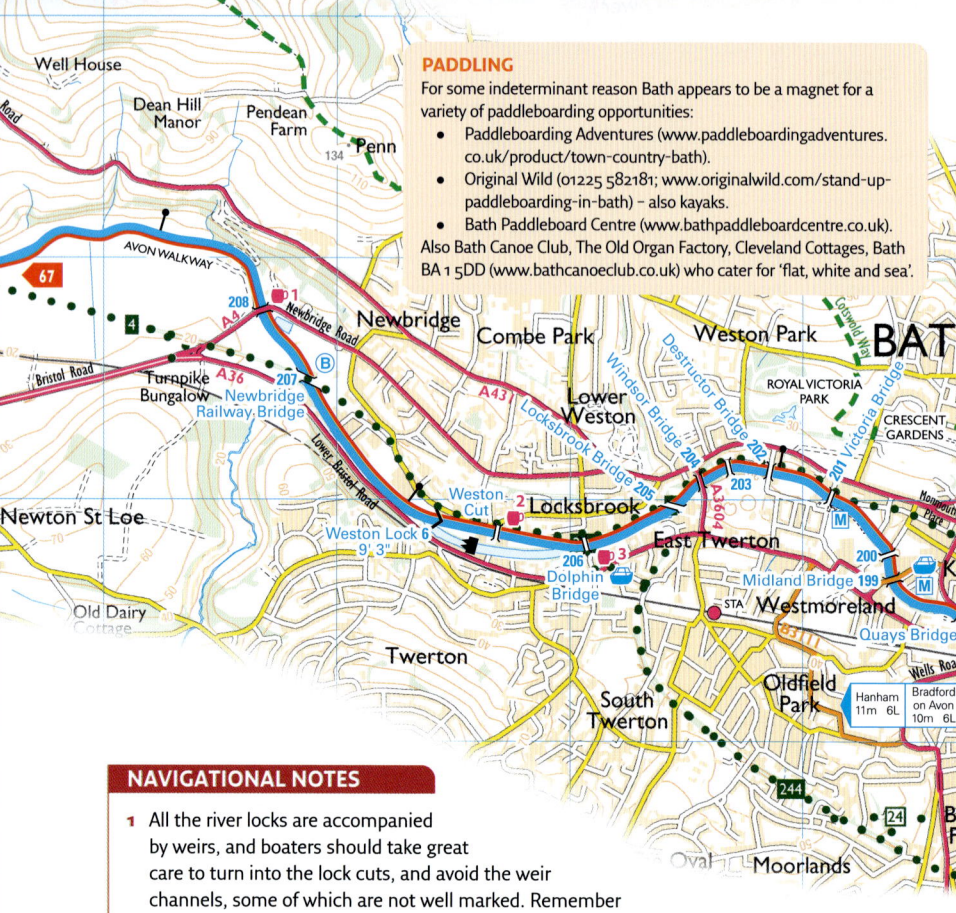

PADDLING

For some indeterminant reason Bath appears to be a magnet for a variety of paddleboarding opportunities:
- Paddleboarding Adventures (www.paddleboardingadventures.co.uk/product/town-country-bath).
- Original Wild (01225 582181; www.originalwild.com/stand-up-paddleboarding-in-bath) – also kayaks.
- Bath Paddleboard Centre (www.bathpaddleboardcentre.co.uk). Also Bath Canoe Club, The Old Organ Factory, Cleveland Cottages, Bath BA1 5DD (www.bathcanoeclub.co.uk) who cater for 'flat, white and sea'.

NAVIGATIONAL NOTES

1. All the river locks are accompanied by weirs, and boaters should take great care to turn into the lock cuts, and avoid the weir channels, some of which are not well marked. Remember that a river always has a current, and is liable to change in speed and level of flow. When mooring, allow enough slack on lines. Do not moor in lock cuts or near weirs. All pleasure boats should moor up at night, and show a white light whilst on the river navigation. The locks are not manned. Remember that boats should always be held by ropes while the locks are being operated, as there is a strong flow in these large locks.
2. Do not moor in the Widcombe Lock flight as the levels of intermediate pounds are subject to considerable fluctuations.
3. See also Navigational Notes on page 68.

BOAT TRIPS

✕ ♀ **Bath Boating Station** Forester Road, Bathwick, Bath BA2 6QE (01225 312900; www.bathboating.co.uk). A unique surviving Victorian boating station with a licensed restaurant. Traditional skiffs, punts and canoes, for hire by the hour or the day. Free instruction for those new to punting. *Open Apr-Sep, Wed-Sun 10.00-17.30* for boating. Restaurant (01225 428844; www.bathwickboatman.com) *open Wed-Sun L and E (not Sun E)*. Reservations essential. No dogs. Picnic area. Self-catering accommodation also available.

Bath Narrowboats Sydney Wharf, Bathwick Hill, Bath BA2 4EL (01225 447276; www.bath-narrowboats.co.uk). **John Rennie** 48-seater restaurant boat available for private charter. On-board catering with a wide selection of menus. Dayboat, canoe and bike hire. Holiday boat hire and all the usual wharf services. *Open all year 09.00-1700 (except Xmas and New Year)*. See also Boatyards page 72.

Pulteney Cruisers Bridge Street, Bath BA2 4AT (01225 312900/07810 837787; www.pulteneycruisers.com) long-established boat tour operator running boat trips between Pulteney Weir and Bathampton. *Operating Apr-Oct 10.00-17.45*.

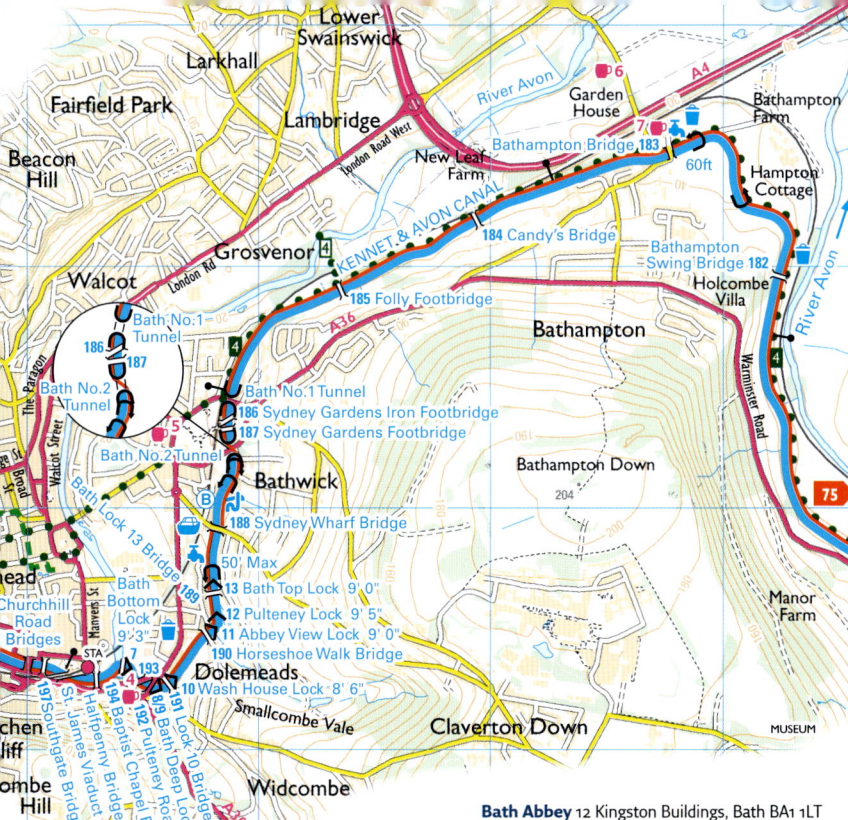

Bath

Somerset. All services. Bath was first developed by the Romans as a spa town and resort because of its natural warm springs. They started the trend of bathing and taking the waters which survives today. There are extensive Roman remains to be seen in the city, not least the baths themselves. The city grew further during the medieval period, when it was a centre of the wool trade; the fine abbey dates from this time. But the true splendour of Bath is the 18th-C development, when the city grew as a resort and watering place that was frequented by all levels of English society, from royalty downwards. Despite heavy bombing in World War II, Bath is still a magnificent memorial to the 18th C and Neo-classicism generally. The terraces that adorn the steep northern slope of the Avon valley contain some of the best Georgian architecture in Britain. Much of the city was designed by John Wood the Younger, who was responsible for the great sweeping Royal Crescent. Other architects included Thomas Baldwin, who built the Guildhall, 1766–75, and the Pump Room, 1789–99, and Robert Adam, whose Pulteney Bridge carries terraces of shops across the Avon. Bath is best seen on foot, for its glories and riches are far too numerous to list. Visitors should not fail to try the waters, which gush continuously from a fountain outside the Pump Room.

Bath Abbey 12 Kingston Buildings, Bath BA1 1LT (01225 422462; www.bathabbey.org). Set in an attractive piazza, the abbey is a pleasingly uniform Perpendicular building, founded in 1499. Twin towers crown the west front, decorated with carved angels ascending and descending ladders. Inside, the abbey is justly famous for its fan vaulting, which covers the whole roof of the building but is not all of the same date. Inside also is a wealth of memorials of all periods, an interesting indication of the vast range of people who, over the ages, have come to die in Bath. Shop and Discovery Centre. In addition to services, the Abbey is *open Mon-Sat 10.00–17.15 (Sat 17.45) & Sun 13.15–14.15 and 16.30–18.00.* Donations.

Holburne Museum Great Pulteney Street, Bath BA2 4DB (01225 388569; www.holburne.org). Housed in a recently restored 18th-C Palladian building that was designed as part of the Sydney pleasure gardens, and a spectacular modern extension. The remarkably varied collection includes silver, ceramics, 18th-C paintings and furniture, 20th-C art and craft work. Lots for families and children of all ages. *Open Mon-Sat 10.00–17.00, Sun and B hols 11.00–17.00.* Garden; café. Free (charge for temporary exhibitions).

Jane Austen Centre 40 Gay Street, Bath BA1 2NT (01225 443000; www.janeausten.co.uk). Enjoy the pleasure of Bath as Jane Austen knew it. A Georgian town house in the heart of the city where the visitor can find out more about the importance of Bath in her life and work. *Open daily 09.45–17.30.* Charge. Tearooms (free access).

Fashion Museum 27 Northgate Street, Bath BA1 1AJ (01225 477789; www.fashionmuseum.co.uk). Display of fashion from the 17th C to the present day; one of the largest collections of costume in the world. Currently re-locating so *visit website for opening details*. Charge.

Postal Museum 27 Northgate Street, Bath BA1 1AJ (01225 460333; www.bathpostalmuseum.org.uk/about-bath-postal-museum). The place from which the first postage stamp was sent on 2 May 1840. The history of the postal service and the development of the written word. *Open daily 11.00-17.00 (Sun 14.00)*. Charge.

Roman Baths Museum Abbey Churchyard, Bath BA1 1LZ (01225 477785; www.romanbaths.co.uk). The great bath buildings with their dependent temple were the centre of Roman Bath. Much of these survive, incorporated into the 18th-C Pump Room. The museum, attached to the bath buildings, contains finds excavated from the site. Shop. *Open daily but times are seasonal* so visit website for details. Charge.

1 Royal Crescent Bath BA1 2LR (01225 428126; www.no1royalcrescent.org.uk). The first house of this magnificent crescent built by John Wood the Younger between 1767-74. Complete with original furniture and fittings. *Open Tue-Sat 10.00-17.30 and Mon in Aug. Last admission 16.30*. Charge.

Thermae Bath Spa Hetling Pump Room, Hot Bath Street, Bath BA1 1SJ (01225 331234; www.thermaebathspa.com). Five historic buildings plus a contemporary addition by Nicholas Grimshaw & Partners allow all-year bathing in natural thermal waters. Full range of spa treatments and therapies, plus views from a roof-top pool! Wellness suite and café. *Open daily 09.00-21.30*. Charge.

Victoria Art Gallery Bridge Street, Bath BA2 4AT (01225 477233; www.victoriagal.org.uk). Collection of 18th-C and modern paintings, prints and ceramics. Visiting exhibitions. Shop. *Open Tue-Sun 10.30-17.00 & B Hol Mon*. Charge.

Tourist Information Centre Abbey Chambers, Abbey Churchyard, Bath BA1 1LY (0906 711 2000; www.visitbath.co.uk). *Open Mon-Sat 09.30-17.30 & Sun 10.00-16.00*.

● **Bathampton**
Somerset. PO, tel, stores, chemist. The centre of the village surrounds the canal and is still compact and undeveloped, but new housing around the edges has turned it into a suburb of Bath. The church is mostly 19th-C.

Pubs and Restaurants (pages 70-71)

Bath is well-endowed with distinguished restaurants, lively wine bars and excellent pubs. The following is a selection of pubs close to the canal.

🍺✕ **1 The Boathouse** Newbridge, Bath BA1 3NB (01225 482584; www.boathouse-bath.co.uk). Large pub serving real ales and food *daily 12.00-21.00 (Sun 20.00)* together with breakfast *08.00-10.00*. Real ale. Family-friendly, riverside garden. Wi-Fi. B&B. *Open 08.00-23.00 (Sun 22.00)*.

🍺 **2 The Locksbrook Inn** 103 Locksbrook Road, Bath BA1 3EN (01225 427119; www.thelocksbrookinn.com). On the Weston Cut. Real ales, coffee, brunch, lunch, evening meals and grazing in between: food available *08.30-21.30 (Sun 20.00)*. Dog- and family-friendly, riverside seating. Real fires and Wi-Fi. *Open Mon-Sat 08.30-23.00 (Fri-Sat 00.00) & Sun 08.30-22.30*.

🍺 **3 The Golden Fleece** 1-3 Avon Buildings, Lower Bristol Road, Bath BA2 1ES (01225 442195; www.facebook.com/TheGoldenFleece). One-bar local 50yds south of the river, serving a selection of real ales and a real cider. Traditional pub games and sports TV. B&B. *Open daily 12.00-00.00 (Sun 23.30)*.

🍺 **4 The Ram** 20 Claverton Buildings, Widcombe, Bath BA2 4LD (01225 426456; www.facebook.com/TheRamPub). Pleasant, traditional pub, serving real ales and incorporating the Widcombe Deli Café which serves *breakfast and brunch* in a myriad of different forms. Dog-friendly. Quiz *Sun*. Regular live music and events. Wi-Fi. *Open 08.30-23.30 (Sun 22.00)*. May close early on Sun in winter.

🍺 **5 The Pulteney Arms** 37 Daniel Street, Bath BA2 6ND (01225 463923; www.thepulteneyarms.co.uk). Open since 1792, and featuring the cat symbol from the Pulteney coat of arms, this popular hostelry dispenses real ale, real cider and highly-thought-of food *Wed-Sat L and E & Sun 12.00-17.00*. Dog- and child-friendly *(until 21.00)* courtyard seating. Quiz *Wed*. Traditional pub games and Wi-Fi. *Open Wed-Sat 12.00-00.00 (Wed 23.00) & Sun 12.00-22.30*.

🍺✕ **6 Bathampton Mill** Mill Lane, Bathampton BA2 6TS (01225 469758; www.thebathamptonmill.co.uk). Food and real ales available at the bar *all day* and in the restaurant *L and E: Mon-Fri and all day Sat and Sun*. Garden with play area and attractive riverside terrace. Moorings. Wi-Fi. *Open daily 11.00-23.00 (Sun 22.30)*.

🍺 **7 The George Inn** Mill Lane, Bathampton, Bath BA2 6TR (01225 425079; www.chefandbrewer.com/pubs/somerset/george-inn). Family pub with canalside garden and children's play area. Real ales. Extensive range of freshly prepared food available *daily 11.30-21.00 (Fri-Sun 09.30)* including breakfast *Fri-Sun*. Dog-friendly. Real fires and Wi-Fi. *Open Mon-Thu 11.00-23.00 & Fri-Sun 09.30-23.00 (Sun 22.30)*.

Boatyards

ⓑ **Bath Marina and Caravan Pak** Brass Mill Lane, Bath BA1 3JT (01225 424301; www.aquavista.com/find-a-marina/bath-waterside-marina-and-caravan-park). ⛽ D Gas, pump out, slipway, long-term mooring, toilets, showers, laundry, Wi-Fi, CCTV, *24hr emergency call out*.

ⓑ **Bath Narrowboats** Sydney Wharf, Bathwick Hill, Bath BA2 4EL (01225 447276; www.bath-narrowboats.co.uk). ⛽🔧D Pump out, narrowboat hire, day boat hire, gas, engine sales, boat repairs, chandlery, books, maps, gifts, boat sales, solid fuel, RYA training. *Emergency call out*. See also Boat Trips page 70.

Claverton

Open country continues, allowing views across the valley to Bathford church and Warleigh Manor. The navigation follows the contours of the land as it leaves Bath, maintaining the level of the nine mile pound that runs from Bath Top Lock to Bradford. The waterway approaches a thickly wooded stretch passing Claverton to the west. Although the village flanks the canal it is all but hidden by the folds of the land. Access is easy and both the village and Claverton Manor are worth a visit. Claverton Pumping Station houses a water-powered pump which lifts water from the Avon to feed the canal. The pump was restored by the Kennet and Avon Canal Trust, with help from engineering students from Bath University. Now a side-cutting takes the canal towards Dundas Aqueduct preceded by the turnover bridge and a basin complete with a small wharf and crane standing over the water. Here is the junction with The Somerset Coal Canal which, until its closure in 1904, ran south from the Kennet & Avon Canal towards Paulton. At the wharf the waterway turns suddenly onto the aqueduct – perhaps the best-known feature of the Kennet & Avon Canal – which carries it across the railway and the Avon valley to the east side. Passing the village of Limpley Stoke, scattered over the valley side, the navigation runs through thick woods clinging to steep banks until the countryside again opens out on the approach to Avoncliff Aqueduct.

Boatyards

Ⓑ **Bath Narrowboats** Brassknocker Wharf, Monkton Combe BA2 7JD (01225 722292 www.bath-narrowboats.co.uk). At the end of the Somersetshire Coal Canal, where boats up to 60ft can turn, BUT do not bring your boat in without first walking along the main road to the office to check if space is available. 🚻 DE Pump out, gas, electric, day-hire craft (including canoes), long-term mooring, dry dock, boat sales and repairs, dry dock, wet dock, cycle hire, historical display of Somerset Coal Canal, café, toilets. Store 200yds from Dundas Wharf selling groceries, off licence, sweets, ice creams and drinks.

- **Claverton**

Somerset. Although devoid of all facilities, Claverton is well worth a visit. It is a manorial village of stone houses, surrounding the 17th-C farm, and in early days was clearly dependent upon Claverton Manor. The main road misses the village, increasing the peace and seclusion.

American Museum & Gardens Claverton Manor, Bath BA2 7BD (01225 460503; www.americanmuseum.org). The manor was built in 1820 by Sir Jeffry Wyatville in the Greek revival style. It now houses a museum of American decorative arts from the late 17th C to the mid 19th C and offers 125 acres of gardens. Café. Gardens *open Tue-Sun 10.00-17.00 and House 11.00-16.00*. Charge

Claverton Pumping Station Ferry Lane, Claverton BA2 7BH (01225 483001; www.claverton.org). The waterwheel pump at Claverton is the only one of its kind on British canals. Designed by John Rennie, the pump was built to feed the 9 mile Bradford-Bath pound, and started operating in 1813. The two undershot breast wheels, each 15ft in diameter and 11ft wide, then powered the pumping machinery until a major breakdown in 1952 prompted its closure, and replacement by a temporary diesel pump. The original machinery has now been restored, and pumping weekends are organised. Electric pumps now do the day-to-day work, raising water from the Avon 47ft below. The Pumping Station is run by Kennet & Avon Canal Trust volunteers. *Open Apr-Oct, 10.00-17.00 on second Sun and second Tue of each month*. Pump operates on *Sat*. Charge.

- **Limpley Stoke**

Wilts. Built on the side of the valley overlooking the river, Limpley Stoke is a quiet village, a residential outpost of Bath. The little church includes work of all periods, from Norman to the 20th C: inside is a collection of carved coffin lids.

Dundas Aqueduct Built in 1804, this three-arch classical stone aqueduct is justifiably one of the most well-known features of the canal, and stands as a fitting monument to the architectural and engineering skill of John Rennie. It is necessary to leave the canal and walk down into the valley below to appreciate the beauty of the aqueduct, and to see it in the context of the narrow Avon valley into which it fits so well. The aqueduct was named in honour of the first chairman of the Kennet and Avon Canal Company and is widely regarded as Rennie's finest architectural work. The structure was relined in the early 1980s with reinforced concrete.

Somersetshire Coal Canal Opened in 1805, this narrow canal was sponsored by the Somerset Coal owners, who wanted a more efficient means of moving their coal to Bath, Bristol and the rest of England. Originally surveyed by Rennie in 1793, the canal was to run from Limpley Stoke to Paulton, with a branch to Radstock. There were steep gradients to overcome at Midford and Combe Hay, and these plagued the canal throughout its life. The Radstock Arm was never completed and tramroads were built over the difficult stretches. The main line was completed throughout, but not before some remarkable solutions to the problems of the Combe Hay gradient had been tried out. First there was Robert Weldon's caisson lock; a watertight caisson, large enough to hold a narrowboat and crew, was pulled up and down an 88ft-deep water-filled cistern by means of a rack and pinion. This terrifying device was soon replaced by an inclined plane, which in turn was replaced by a conventional flight of locks. Once open, the canal carried a large tonnage of coal throughout the 19th C: it served 30 collieries more directly than the railway. However, by the end of the century the inevitable competition was taking away the traffic, which finally stopped in 1898. The canal was officially abandoned in 1904. The first ¼ mile has been restored and is used by a boatyard, and for moorings. A stop lock at the entrance restricts its use to craft of 7ft beam only. It's western end is now the scene of enthusiastic restoration.

● **Freshford**
Somerset. PO, stores, off-licence, station. Although not on the canal, Freshford is well worth the ½ mile walk south from Limpley Stoke. It is a particularly attractive village, set on the side of the steep hill that flanks the confluence of the rivers Avon and Frome. At the top of the hill is the church, and terraces of handsome stone houses fall away in both directions, filling the valley below, and crowding the narrow streets. At the bottom of the hill is the river, crossed by the medieval bridge. The hills around were a rich source of Bath stone, limestone and fuller's earth and in the early 19th C the village was involved with the production of broad cloth in its extensive factory. Ruins of an old hermitage and friary, possibly connected with Hinton Abbey, were excavated locally, as were the remains of a Roman encampment. The *PO is in the stores and open Tue & Fri 09.00-12.45.*

Pubs and Restaurants

🍺✖ 1 **Angelfish Restaurant/Café** Brassknocker Basin, Monkton Combe BA2 7JD (01225 723483; www.facebook.com/TheAngelfishRestaurant). Generous portions of appetising, home-made food served in an attractive setting with a distinctly continental feel. Tea, coffee, home-made cakes, filled baguettes and crêpes, hot meals, drinks and ice creams. Family orientated. Café *open daily all year 10.00-17.00*. Also opens for functions and pre-booked groups. *Regular* events.

🍺 2 **Wheelwrights Arms** Church Lane, Monkton Combe BA2 7HB (01225 722287; www.wheelwrightsarmsbath.com). Popular historic village pub, ¾-mile walk, close to the course of the Somerset Coal Canal. Real ales. *Temporary reduced opening* with service limited to *weekends* and no food. See website for details. Family-friendly. Newspapers, Real fires and Wi-fi. B&B. *Open Fri 17.00-22.00 & Sat-Sun 12.00-21.00 (Sun 17.00).*

🍺 3 **The Inn at Freshford** The Hill, Freshford BA2 7WG (01225 722250; www.theinnatfreshford.com). It is well worth the walk to this splendid, traditional pub overlooking the river. Real ales. Bar meals available *Wed-Sun 12.00-21.00 (Sun 17.00)*. Dog- and family-friendly, garden. Real fires and Wi-Fi. *Open Wed-Sat 11.00-22.00 & Sun 12.00-18.00.*

✖ 4 **The Galleries Café** Freshford Lane, Freshford, Bath BA2 7UR (01225 723249; www.galleriesshop.co.uk). Fresh, local, seasonal food with a great range of salads, tarts, soups and cakes, all made on the premises or locally, served in an atmosphere that is friendly, informal and welcoming. *Open Mon-Fri 08.45-15.00 & Sat-Sun 09.00-12.30.*

🍺 5 **The Seven Stars** Bradford Rd, Winsley BA15 2LQ (01225 722204; www.sevenstarswinsley.co.uk). Footpath from Winsley Bridge 174. Traditional old village hostelry, parts dating back to 18th C, dispensing real ale and highly-regarded food *Mon-Fri L and E & Sat-Sun 12.00-21.00 (Sun 17.00)* – booking recommended. Dog- and family-friendly, garden. *Regular* live music. Camping nearby. Wi-Fi. *Open Mon-Thu L and E; Fri-Sat 12.00-23.00 (Sat 09.00) & Sun 12.00-20.00.*

Dundas Wharf and Aqueduct

Kennet & Avon Canal — Claverton

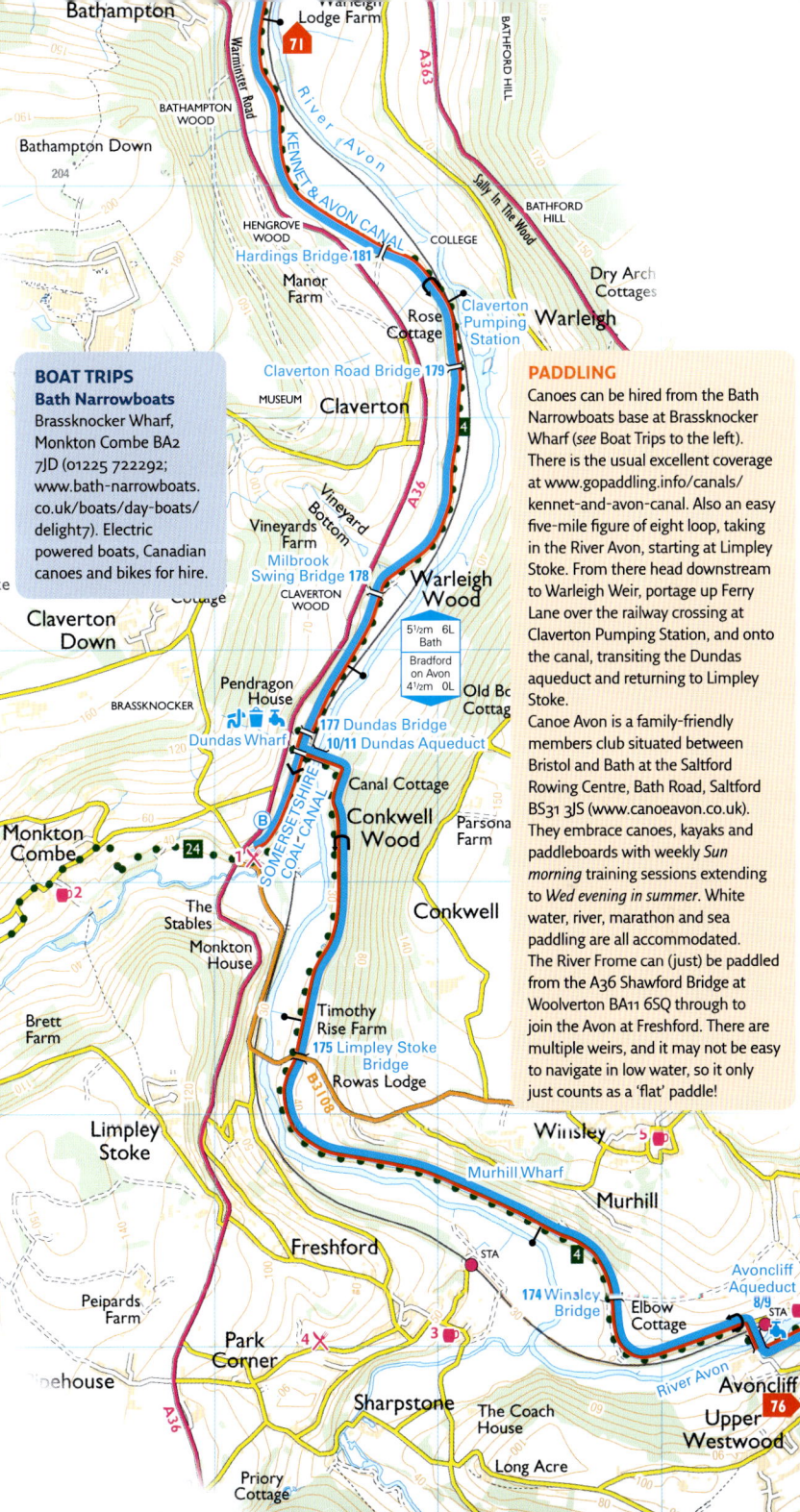

BOAT TRIPS
Bath Narrowboats
Brassknocker Wharf, Monkton Combe BA2 7JD (01225 722292; www.bath-narrowboats.co.uk/boats/day-boats/delight7). Electric powered boats, Canadian canoes and bikes for hire.

PADDLING
Canoes can be hired from the Bath Narrowboats base at Brassknocker Wharf (see Boat Trips to the left). There is the usual excellent coverage at www.gopaddling.info/canals/kennet-and-avon-canal. Also an easy five-mile figure of eight loop, taking in the River Avon, starting at Limpley Stoke. From there head downstream to Warleigh Weir, portage up Ferry Lane over the railway crossing at Claverton Pumping Station, and onto the canal, transiting the Dundas aqueduct and returning to Limpley Stoke.

Canoe Avon is a family-friendly members club situated between Bristol and Bath at the Saltford Rowing Centre, Bath Road, Saltford BS31 3JS (www.canoeavon.co.uk). They embrace canoes, kayaks and paddleboards with weekly *Sun morning* training sessions extending to *Wed evening in summer*. White water, river, marathon and sea paddling are all accommodated. The River Frome can (just) be paddled from the A36 Shawford Bridge at Woolverton BA11 6SQ through to join the Avon at Freshford. There are multiple weirs, and it may not be easy to navigate in low water, so it only just counts as a 'flat' paddle!

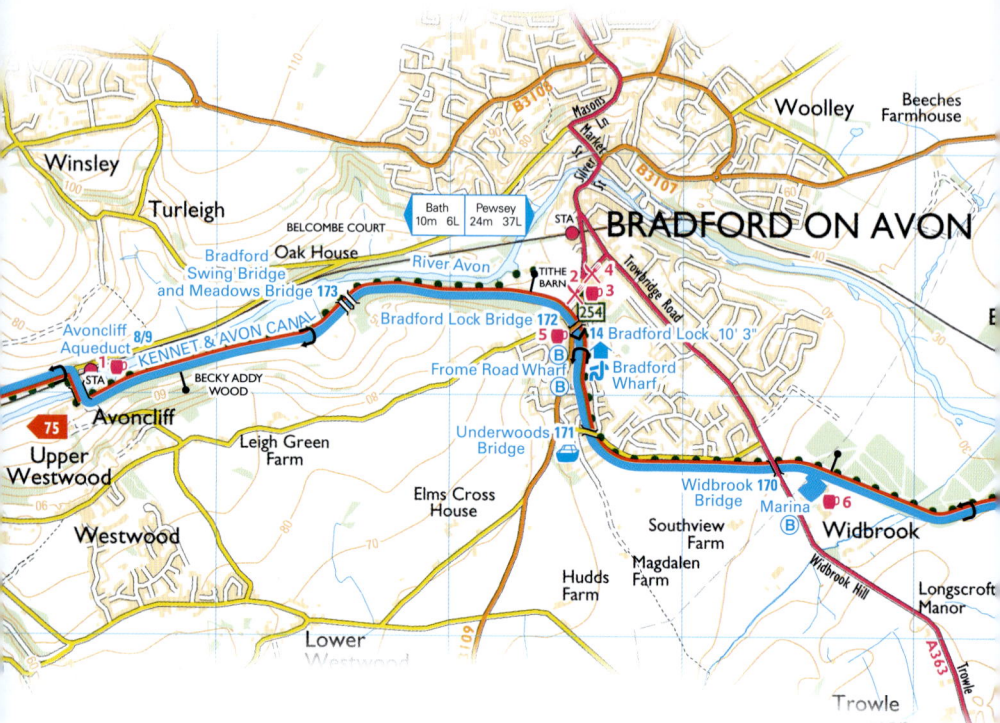

Bradford on Avon

At the aqueduct the towpath crosses under the canal to the north side and the thick woods give the canal user a feeling of total seclusion. Avoncliff makes a worthwhile stop with its tearoom and pub overlooking the river and the elegant stone arches (recently restored) of Rennie's fine aqueduct. Towards Bradford, the Avon rushes along beside the towpath and beyond it the railway appears and disappears among the trees on the far side of the valley, whilst the waterway pursues its more sedate course. Cyclists appear with great frequency since this is part of the Wiltshire Cycleway route. The town is approached through beautiful woods leading to the Tithe Barn, beyond which there are fine views of Bradford spread out above the river. Above the lock and Bradford Basin, the navigation skirts an extensive residential area and is set slightly below the surrounding area, burrowing out towards open countryside again. River and canal make their separate departures from the town to converge again with the canal high above in a side cutting, initially shielded by trees. Then fine views northwards open out over the Avon valley as the waterway crosses first the River Biss, followed by the railway on two, splendid stone aqueducts. The classical arch over the river is particularly handsome; it is necessary to walk down the side of the embankment to see it properly. To the west of Hilperton, the canal passes the grounds of Wyke House, whose Jacobean-style towers stand among the trees. Passing the boatyard and large marina basin the navigation curves around Hilperton; although the main part of the village is a mile to the south. Here is a convenient *pub, post office, garage, off-licence and a store* beside Bridge 166. Beyond, the countryside opens out into the wide Avon valley as the canal makes a beeline for Devizes and the Caen Hill Lock Flight.

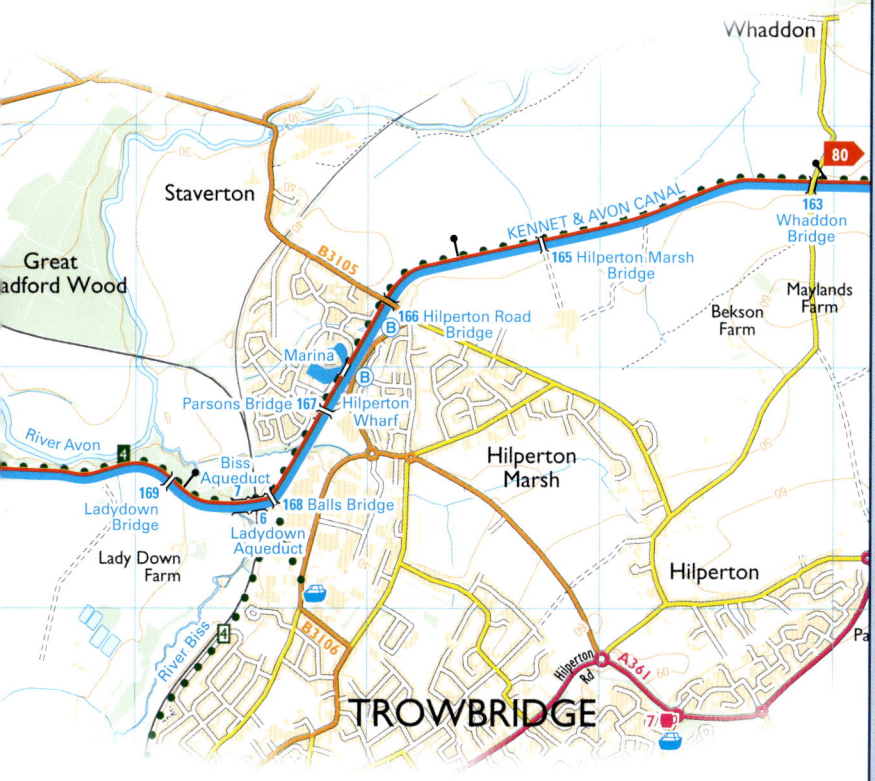

WALKING AND CYCLING
Bradford on Avon is an excellent place for the cyclist to access the towpath with level rides towards Bath and bikes for hire at TT Cycles, Units 6-8 Elm Cross Business Park, Bradford on Avon BA15 2AY (01225 867187; www.ttcycles.co.uk). *Open Mon-Sun 09.00-18.00 (Sun 17.30).*

Boatyards

ⓑ **Bradford Wharf Services** Upper Wharf, Frome Road, Bradford on Avon BA15 2EA (07975 799994/07538 595729; www.bradfordwharf.co.uk/coal-boat). Gas, solid fuel, drydock, fabrication, boat building, marine servicing, coal boat.

ⓑ **Wiltshire Narrowboats** Bradford, Frome Road, Bradford on Avon BA15 2EA (01225 863987/07561 096679; www.wiltshire-narrowboats.co.uk). D Pump out, gas, coal, narrowboat hire, day boat hire, dry dock, chandlery, maps, books and gifts. Agents for Black Prince Boats.

ⓑ **Sally Boats** Bradford on Avon Marina, Trowbridge Road, Bradford on Avon BA15 1UD (01225 864923; www.sallynarrowboats.co.uk). Gas, narrowboat hire, dry dock, DIY facilities, laundry service, hull blacking, day boat hire.

ⓑ **Bradford on Avon Marina** Trowbridge Road, Bradford on Avon BA15 1UD (01225 864562/07973 435177). D Pump out, gas, overnight and long-term mooring, narrowboat hire, slipway, cranage facilities, brokerage *open Wed-Sat 09.00-16.00*.

ⓑ **Hilperton Marina** Hammond Way, Trowbridge BA14 8RS (01225 765243; www.hilpertonmarina.com). D Pump out, gas, narrowboat hire, overnight mooring, long-term mooring, chandlery (on-line), books, maps, boat sales, solid fuel, toilets, crane (22 ton), slipway, engineering, brokerage, Gas Safe engineer. *Open daily 08.30-17.00*.

ⓑ **The Boatyard** 5 Hammond Way, Hilperton Marsh, Trowbridge BA14 8RS (01225 710017/07790 017418; www.ukboatyard.com). D Pump out, gas, chandlery, dry dock, solid fuel, boat sales, servicing, moorings, boat building, engineering and Gas Safe engineer.

BOAT TRIPS

Barbara Mclellan 53-seat widebeam boat operated by Kennet & Avon Canal Trust volunteers from Bradford Lock. 1½ hour public trips *Easter–Oct*. Disabled access by lift. Private charter with facilities for meals available. Telephone 01380 721279 or visit www.katrust.org.uk for information. Also welcoming tea garden (Wharf Cottage, 15 Frome Road BA15 1LE) beside the lock, selling teas, snacks, gifts, etc. *Open Easter–Oct daily, 10.00–16.00.*

- **Avoncliff**

Wilts. Station. A hamlet clustered in the woods beside the canal. Originally it was a centre of weaving, and many traces of the old industry can be seen: weavers' cottages, and the old mills on the Avon, which falls noisily over a weir at this point. At one time the mills were used for flocking, a process which involved the breaking up of old woollen material to make stuffing for mattresses and chairs. The hamlet is dominated by Rennie's aqueduct, built in 1804 to take the canal across the valley to the north side. A classical stone structure, it suffered from casual repair work and patching in brick when owned by the Great Western Railways, due mainly to the inferior nature of the stone from which it was constructed. Thankfully it has been extensively and skillfully restored.

- **Bradford on Avon**

Wilts. All services. Set in the steeply wooded Avon valley, Bradford is one of the beauty spots of Wiltshire, and one of the highlights of the canal. Rather like a miniature Bath, the town is composed of fine stone terraces rising sharply away from the river, which cuts through the centre of the town. Until the 19th C it was a prosperous centre for weaving, but a depression killed the industry and drove most of the workers away. At the time that the canal was built Bradford had no less than 30 water-powered cloth factories and some of these buildings still survive. Bradford is rich in architectural treasures from the Saxon period to the 19th C, while the abundance of fine 18th-C houses make the exploration of the town a positive pleasure. The centre is very compact, and so the walk down the hill from the canal wharf lays most of it open to inspection, including the town bridge, Holy Trinity Church, the Victorian town hall and the fine Gothic Revival factory that dominates the riverside. There is also a swimming pool near the canal.

Bradford Upper Wharf BA15 2EA. The canal wharf is particularly attractive. There is a small dock with some of the original buildings still standing, plenty of mooring space, and an old canal pub beside the lock. The lock here was built to raise the canal to the same level as the Wilts and Berks Canal which joins the canal at Semington.

Kennet & Avon Canal Trust Wharf Cottage, Bradford Lock, Bradford on Avon BA15 1LE (www.katrust.org.uk). Canal shop and exhibition, range of books, souvenirs, gifts, light refreshments and boat trips at weekends. Tea garden. *Open daily Easter–Oct 09.30–16.00.*

Great Tithe Barn Bradford on Avon BA15 2EF (www.english-heritage.org.uk). Standing below the canal embankment, this great stone building is one of the finest tithe barns in England. It was built in the 14th C by the Abbess of Shaftesbury. Its cathedral-like structure (168ft long) is broken by two porches, with massive doors that open to reveal the beamed roof. The barn is part of Barton Farm, a medieval farm which was part of the monastic estate of Shaftesbury Abbey. The Granary and Cow Byres now house craft shops and galleries. Barn *open 10.30–16.00.*

Holy Trinity Church Church Street, Bradford on Avon BA15 1LN (01225 864444; www.htboa.org). Basically a 12th-C building with additions dating from over the next three centuries. Inside are some medieval wall paintings, and fine 18th-C monuments. Many of the names that appear relate to the woollen industry.

Saxon Church of St Lawrence Mount Pleasant, Bradford on Avon BA15 1SJ (01225 308081; www.saxonchurch.org.uk). Founded in AD705, this tiny church was enlarged in the 10th C. Since then it has survived essentially unchanged, having been at various times a school, a cottage and a slaughterhouse. The true origins and purpose of the building were only rediscovered in the 19th C, and so it remains one of the best-preserved Saxon churches in England. *Open daily 10.00–18.00 (Oct–Mar 16.00).* Donations.

Town Bridge Bradford on Avon. The nine-arched bridge is unusual in having a chapel in the middle, one of only four still surviving in Britain. Parts of the bridge, including the chapel, are medieval, but much dates from a 17th-C rebuilding. During the 17th and 18th C the chapel fell out of use, and was turned into a small prison, serving as the town lock up.

Westwood Manor Lower Westwood BA15 2AF (01225 863374; www.nationaltrust.org.uk/visit/wiltshire/westwood-manor). One mile south west of Bradford. This 15th-C stone manor house contains original Jacobean plaster and woodwork, although much was lost when the manor became a farm in the 18th C. Skilful restoration by the National Trust has returned the manor to its former glory. *Opening times are seasonal* so visit the website for details. Charge.

Tourist Information Centre Kingston House Office, Kingston Road, Bradford on Avon BA15 1ES (01225 864240; www.bradfordonavontowncouncil.gov.uk/tourist-information-centre). *Open Mon-Fri 09.00–16.00.*

- **Staverton**

Wilts. The village lies to the north of the canal, spreading down to the bank of the Avon. A small isolated part of the Avon is navigable here, and is used by a few pleasure boats. In the village are terraces of weavers' cottages, a sign of what was once the staple trade of the area.

- **Hilperton**

Wilts. PO, stores, chemist, fish & chips, takeaway, off-licence, garage. A scattered village that stretches away from the settlement by the canal wharf. The Jacobean mansion, Wyke House actually built in 1865, is a replica of the original and lies to the west of the village, while the *PO, stores, chemist, etc* is some way to the south east. The somewhat closer supermarket is *open Mon–Sat 08.00–21.00 & Sun 10.00–16.00.*

Pubs and Restaurants (pages 76-77)

🍺✕ **1 The Cross Guns** 159-160 Avoncliff, Bradford on Avon BA15 2HB (01225 862335; www.crossgunsavoncliff.com). One of the most attractive pubs on the navigation with its low ceilings, stone walls and flagged floors. The terraced gardens are busy in summer with people enjoying this beautiful setting in a wooded valley. Real ale and real cider. Food *L and E*. Dog- and family-friendly. Traditional pub games, real fires and Wi-Fi. Camping. *Open Mon-Thu 12.00-20.00 & Fri-Sun 11.00-22.00 (Sun 19.00).*

✕ **2 The Lock Inn Café** 48 Frome Road, Bradford on Avon BA15 1LE (01225 868068; www.thelockinn.co.uk). A unique establishment whose proprietors openly admit to scant portion control; welcome (amongst others) 'kids, cats and dogs, muddy boots, scaffolders, bankers, plumbers (when they turn up) and old age travellers', whilst justifiably claiming to be 'suppliers of happiness and laughter'. Excellent, appetising and inexpensive food for all the family, served in the café including death-defying boatmen's breakfasts *daily 08.45-18.00* (earlier *outside school holidays*) and a tantalising restaurant menu *L and E*. Only moaners and unruly parents are banned! Canoe hire.

🍺 **3 The Canal Tavern** 49 Frome Road, Lower Wharf, Bradford on Avon BA15 1LE (01225 866100; www.canaltavern.co.uk). It was outside the back door of this friendly pub that the first sod for the commencement of the canal was cut. The pub continues to benefit from its trade with an attractive terrace overlooking the navigation. Real ale. Home-made food served *Mon-Tue 12.00-21.00 (Mon 17.00) & Wed-Sun 10.00-20.00 (Sun 15.00)*. Also breakfasts. Dog- and Child-friendly, outside seating. Wi-Fi. *Open daily 09.00-00.00 (Mon 17.00).*

🍺✕ **4 The Maharaja** 12 Frome Road, Bradford on Avon BA15 1LE (01225 866424). Across the road from the Canal Tavern. Authentic Indian food served by friendly, attentive staff. Takeaway. *Open Wed-Mon 18.00-22.30.*

🍺✕ **5 The Barge Inn** 17 Frome Road, Bradford on Avon BA15 2EA (01225 863403; www.thebargeinn.org). Comfortable one-bar pub. Good choice of real ales and wine list. Attractive eating area, Food served *08.00-21.15 daily*. Children and dogs welcome. Canalside garden. Real fires and Wi-Fi. B&B. *Open 08.00-23.00.*

🍺 **6 The Boathouse Pub** Bradford on Avon Marina, Bradford on Avon BA15 1UD (01225 309318; www.boathouse.pub). Overlooking the marina, this establishment serves real ales and food *L and E*. Children's play area. Dog-friendly. Garden and patio. Wi-Fi. *Open Wed-Sun 12.00-21.00.*

🍺✕ **7 The Red Admiral** Hackett Place, Hilperton BA14 7GW (01225 767400; www.redadmiralpub.co.uk). A new-build, family establishment, serving a large estate and dispensing real ale and inexpensive food *all day*. Family-friendly, outside seating. Wi-Fi. *Open Mon-Sat 11.00-23.00 (Sat 23.30) & Sun 11.00-22.30.*

Bradford Lock 14, Bradford on Avon

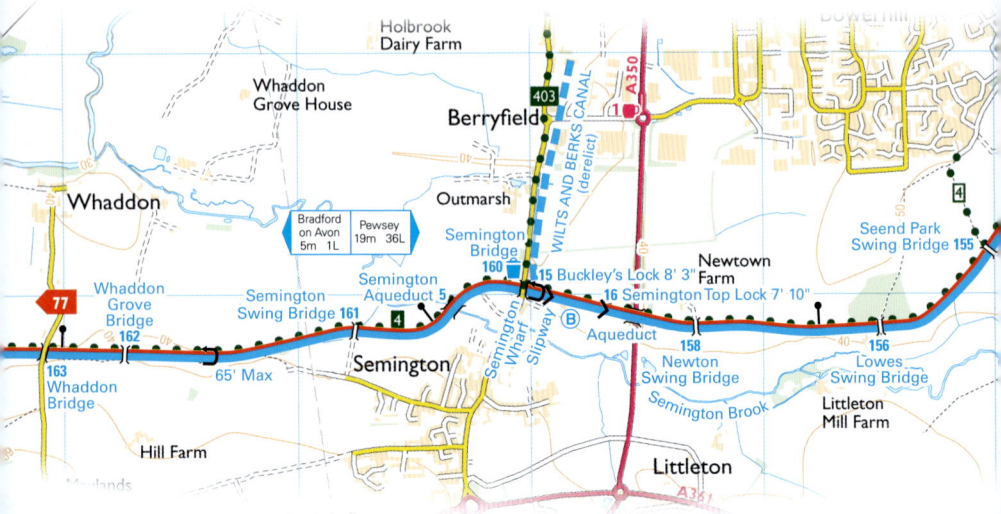

Seend Cleeve

The two Semington Locks continue the ascent towards Devizes with an attractive lock house by Lock 15. Just before the lock the canal is crossed by the A350; this is the best access point for Semington. A close examination of the north bank, just after the bridge, will reveal a bricked-up side bridge; this marks the site of the junction with the long abandoned Wiltshire & Berkshire Canal, now under active restoration (www.wbct.org.uk) which used to join the Thames at Abingdon. The navigation continues its easterly course, maintaining a fairly straight line through open country before reaching the five Seend Locks. Beside the third lock there is a pub and a lane leading to Seend Cleeve village, although the best access is from bridge 152 below Seend Top Lock. The hills to the south climb steeply up to the village of Seend and to the north flat pasture land stretches away as the canal, passing two swing bridges, turns through Sells Green in a low cutting that hides most of the village.

Boatyards

ⓑSemington Dry Dock Lock House, 545 Canal Bridge, Semington BA14 6JT (01380 870654; www.semingtondock.co.uk). Between locks 15 and 16, offering practical facilities for all aspects of canal boat maintenance and repair, 2 covered dry docks, wet dock, slipway, boat storage, DIY facilities. *Open Mon-Fri 08.00-17.00.*

ⓑWilderness Boats Cross Roads, Semington BA14 6JH (01380 870141/07973 815920; www.wildernessboats.co.uk). Wilderness Boat sales, repairs and deliveries. Outboard servicing, sales and repairs.

● **Semington**
Wilts. Semington is a pretty village. There are several large, handsome houses with fine gardens, some dating from the 18th C. The little stone church, crowned with a bellcote, is at the end of a lane to the west of the village.

● **The Wiltshire & Berkshire Canal**
Opened in 1810, the canal wound in a meandering course for 51 miles between Semington on the Kennet & Avon Canal and Abingdon on the River Thames. A branch was opened in 1819 from Swindon to connect with Latton on the Thames & Severn Canal. Although the carriage of Somerset coal was the inspiration for the canal, its eventual role was agricultural. Profits were never high, partly because the wandering line of the canal and its 45 locks made travel very slow, and so it suffered early from railway competition. By the 1870s, moves were

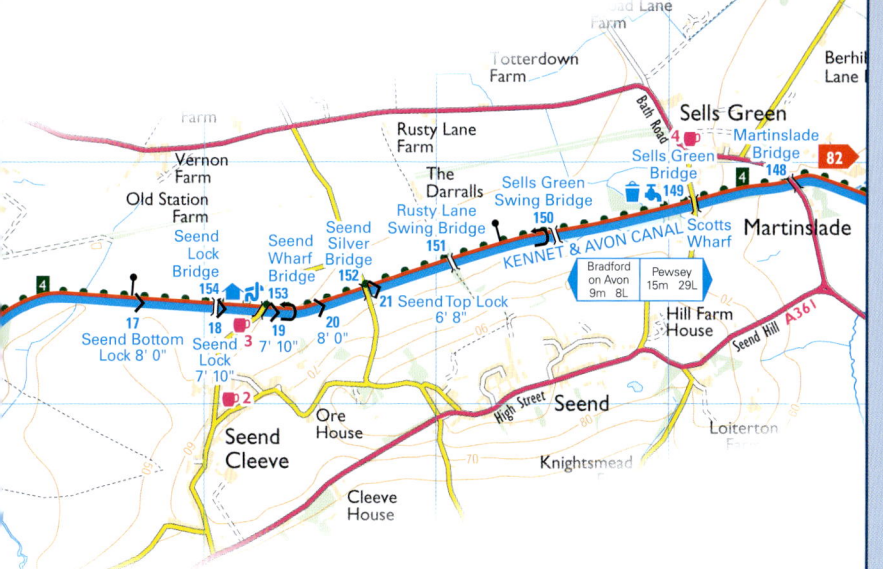

Kennet & Avon Canal

Seend Cleeve

afoot to close the canal, and, despite various efforts to give it a new lease of life, the situation had become hopeless by the turn of the century. Traffic finally stopped in 1906, and the canal was formally abandoned in 1914. In 1977 the Wilts & Berks Amenity Group (www.wbct.org.uk) was formed with the aim of preserving both the main line of the canal and the northern branch to Latton. Twenty years later its avowed aim is to restore the waterway to form a navigable link between the Kennet & Avon Canal, the Thames at Abingdon and either the Thames or the Thames & Severn Canal at Cricklade. A new junction, Jubilee Junction has been formed at Abingdon because the original junction was unusable. Funded by the IWA in its Jubilee year.

- **Seend Cleeve**
Wilts. An agricultural village built on the steep slopes of the hills that overlook the canal.

- **Seend**
Wilts. PO, stores. Although the main road cuts the village in half, Seend is still attractive. Elegant 18th-C houses flank the road, and conceal the lane that leads to the battlemented Perpendicular church.

- **Sells Green**
Wilts. A scattered main road village, the houses doing their best to hide from the traffic behind decorative gardens.

Pubs and Restaurants

- **1 The Milk Churn** Commerce Way, Melksham SN12 6AD (01225 706496; www.themilkchurn.co.uk). The walls adorned with pictures of the local dairy industry, this recently built pub serves real ale and food *daily 12.00-21.00*. Also breakfast. Dog- and family-friendly, play area and patio. Newspapers and Wi-Fi. *Open 08.00-23.00 (Sun 22.30).*

- **2 The Brewery Inn** Seend Cleeve SN12 6PX (01380 828463; www.facebook.com/breweryinnseend). A genuine, unadulterated village local with a strong community focus. Real ale and appetising home-made food served *L and E (not Sun E)*. Dog- and family-friendly, large garden with covered areas. *Regular* events. Traditional pub games, newspapers, real fires and Wi-Fi. *Open Mon-Sat 12.00-22.00 (Fri-Sat 23.00) & Sun 12.00-21.00.*

- **3 The Barge Inn** Seend Cleeve SN12 6QB (01380 828230; www.facebook.com/bargeinn). An extensive and extremely popular pub occupying the former wharf house and stables, dating back to 1805. The house was once the home of the Wiltshire Giant, Fred Kempster, who reached the inconvenient height of 8ft 2ins. Real ales and food available *Fri-Mon L and E & Tue-Thu 11.00-23.00*. Dog- and child-friendly, garden and outdoor covered areas. Traditional pub games, newspapers, real fires and Wi-Fi. Camping and mooring. *Open daily 10.30-22.00 (Fri-Sat 23.00).*

- **4 The Three Magpies** Sells Green, Seend, Melksham SN12 6RN (01380 828389; www.threemagpies.co.uk). A comfortable pub, with converted stables housing the restaurant. Real ale. Food available *Mon-Thu 12.00-19.00 (Wed-Thu 20.00) Fri-Sat 12.00-20.30 & Sun L and E*. Dog- and family-friendly, garden and play area. Traditional pub games, newspapers, real fires and Wi-Fi. Camping. *Open Mon-Tue 12.00-21.00; Wed-Sat 11.00-22.00 (Fri-Sat 22.30) & Sun 11.00-21.00.*

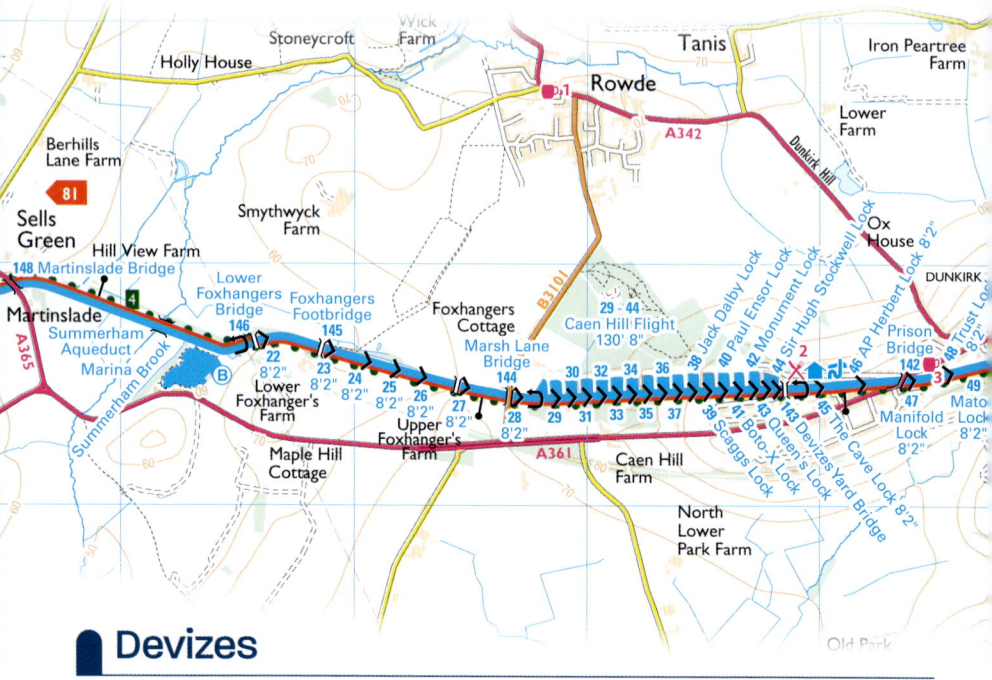

Devizes

At Lower Foxhangers the waterway swings left, under the turnover bridge, and enters Lock 22, the first of 7 locks with conventional pounds that precede the Caen Hill Flight proper. Immediately beyond Marsh Lane Bridge, carrying the B3101 to Rowde, the 16-lock Caen Hill section begins; wide lock follows wide lock up the hill, each with an enormous side pound. These were designed to hold sufficient water while permitting the locks to be close together to follow the slope. The scale of the whole flight is most impressive. The towpath is in very good condition and the whole area is obviously used for recreation by visitors and the people of Devizes alike. To the south the busy A361 accompanies the canal up the hill but it is out of sight for most of the way. Above Lock 44 you will find the CRT welcome boat *Admiral*, an excellent source of local information, leaflets and guides. Beyond here the remaining locks are spaced out and finish at the generous stone bridge, with its separate towpath arch, that leads the navigation into Devizes Wharf, where the Kennet and Avon Canal Trust has a museum and tearooms in a converted warehouse. Twenty-nine locks have been negotiated in just 2¼ miles. The wharf is also the home of a theatre and trip boat operation. The waterway now enters a long, wooded cutting, spanned by several very elegant large stone bridges (some listed as ancient monuments) all of which offer easy access to the town. Houses appear, their gardens overlooking the cutting or running down to the water's edge. Soon the navigation passes the marina and moves out into the more remote landscape of the Wiltshire Wolds.

NAVIGATIONAL NOTES

Operating times for the Caen Hill Flight (locks 29–44) are *Apr- mid-Sep 08.00-14.00 (clear locks by 17.00).* The lock keeper remains on duty until you have cleared the flight. There is strictly no mooring between Locks 44 and 29.

BOAT TRIPS

Kenavon Venture Couch Lane, Devizes SN10 1EB (01380 721279; www.katrust.org.uk/our-boats/kenavon-venture-bookings). Wide-beam boat operating from the Wharf at Devizes *Apr-Oct* and on themed trips for most of the year. Details from the website. Available for private charter.
White Horse Boats The Wharf, Devizes SN10 1EB (01672 810634; www.whitehorsenarrowboats.co.uk) are based at Devizes Wharf and operate narrowboats for self-drive hire for day trips, weekends, short breaks or by the week.

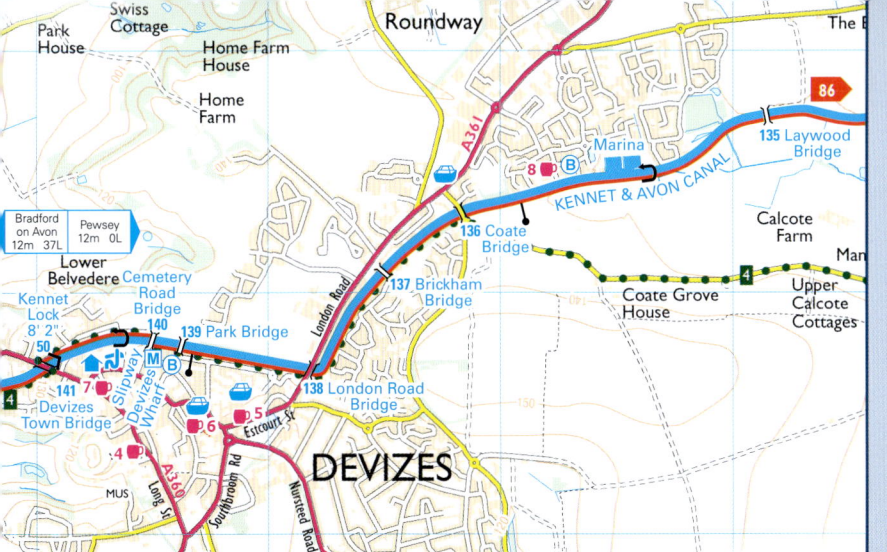

WALKING AND CYCLING

The National Cycle Network route 4 joins the towpath at Devizes before heading west to South Wales via Bath. Detailed information covering the entire Cycle Network from Sustrans (0300 303 2604; www.sustrans.org.uk/national-cycle-network) open *Mon-Fri 09.00-17.00*. Wiltshire County Council runs Wiltshire Connect (01225 712900; www.connectingwiltshire.co.uk/getting-around/bus/wiltshire-connect) using smart technology to operate a demand-responsive bus service in the Marlborough – Pewsey area of the county, which can be useful for walkers. There is a helpful cycle shop – Bikes 'n' Boards – at 121 Southbroom Road, Devizes SN10 1LY (01380 729621; www.facebook.com/BikesnBoards) *open 10.00-17.00 (closed Wed and Sun)*.

Pubs and Restaurants

There are many good pubs and restaurants in Devizes. The following are simply a convenient selection.

1 The George & Dragon High Street, Rowde, near Devizes SN10 2PN (01380 723053; www.thegeorgeanddragonrowde.co.uk). This pub is held in high esteem for its award-winning food, all freshly cooked to order, Served *L and E (not Sun E)*. Real ales. Dog-friendly, garden. Real fires and Wi-Fi. B&B. *Open daily 12.00-23.00*.

2 Caen Hill Café The Locks, Devizes, SN10 1QR (01380 724880). Beside Lock 44. Local ice creams, tea, cream teas, coffee, home-made cakes, pasties and sandwiches. *Open daily, Summer 10.00-17.00 & Winter 10.30-16.30 – weather dependant*.

3 The Black Horse Bath Road, Devizes SN10 2AU (01380 723930). Well placed to refresh those exhausted by the locks. Real ale and food *L and E*. Traditional pub games. Garden. *Open daily 11.00-23.00 (Fri-Sat 00.00)*.

4 The Lamb 20 St John's Street, Devizes SN10 1BT (01380 725426; www.wadworth.co.uk/find-a-pub/lamb-inn-devizes). Old-fashioned local drinking house dispensing real ale. Traditional pub games and enclosed courtyard. Dog-friendly. Real fires. *Open Mon-Sat 11.00-00.00 (Fri-Sat 01.00) & Sun 12.00-00.00*.

5 The British Lion 9 Estcourt Street, Devizes SN10 1LQ (01380 720665; www.britishliondevizes.co.uk). Traditional, good value, down-to-earth local, attracting a mix of customers of all ages who appreciate real ale, real cider and good conversation. Garden. Newspapers and Wi-Fi. *Open Mon-Wed 14.00-22.00 & Thu-Sun 12.00-23.00 (Sun 22.00)*.

6 The White Bear 33 Monday Market Street, Devizes SN10 1DN (01380 727588; www.whitebeardevizes.co.uk). Real ale and real cider served in a popular town local together with food *Tue-Sun L and E (not Tue L or Sun E)*. Dog-friendly. Real fires and Wi-Fi. B&B. *Open Tue-Sun 12.00-23.00 (Sun 20.00)*.

7 The Black Swan Inn 25-26 Market Place, Devizes SN10 1JQ (01380 727777; www.blackswandevizes.co.uk). Attractive, Grade II listed, town-centre hostelry, dating from 18th C, serving real ale and food *L and E*. Well-behaved children and dogs welcome. B&B. *Open Mon-Sat 12.00-22.00 (Fri-Sat 23.00) & Sun 12.00-21.00*.

8 The Hourglass Horton Avenue, Devizes SN10 2RH (01380 727313). Modern bar-restaurant, serving traditional pub meals *Mon-Sat L and E & Sun 12.00-19.30*, together with real ale. Large canalside terrace. Wi-Fi. *Open Mon-Sat 11.00-23.00 (Fri-Sat 00.00) and Sun 11.00-22.00*.

Boatyards

ⒷCaen Hill Marina Lower Foxhangers, Rowde, Devizes SN10 1SS (01380 827062; www.caenhillmarina.com). 🚻🚰♿DE Pump out, gas, solid fuel, short-term moorings, long-term moorings, launderette, toilets, showers, Wi-Fi. *Open Mon-Fri 09.00-17.30 & Sat-Sun 09.00-14.00 (Sun 12.00).*

ⒷFoxhangers Lower Foxhangers, Devizes SN10 1SS (01380 828254; www.foxhangers.co.uk). Gas, narrowboat hire, long-term moorings, engine sales and repairs, boat building, boat hire, chandlery, camping, self-catering holidays. *Open Mon-Fri 08.00-17.30 & Sat 09.00-17.00 in season.*

ⒷWhite Horse Boats The Wharf, Devizes SN10 1EB (01672 810634; www.whitehorsenarrowboats.co.uk). Telephone, toilets, hire boats – short and long-term.

ⒷDevizes Marina Horton Avenue, Devizes SN10 2RH (01380 725300; www.devizesmarina.com). 🚻♿ Pump out, gas, overnight mooring, long-term mooring, slipway, boat sales and repairs, boat painting, boat building and fitting out, engineering, slipway, solid fuel, chandlery, books, maps and gifts, toilets. *Open Mon-Sat 09.00-17.00.*

● **Devizes**

Wilts. PO, stores, banks, butcher, bakers, ironmonger, chemist, off-licence, takeaways, fish & chips, cinema, garage. Despite the effects of traffic, Devizes still retains the atmosphere of an old country market town. Originally the town grew up around the castle, but as this lost its significance the large marketplace became the focal point. In the early 19th C Devizes held the largest corn market in the west of England and was also a centre for the selling of hops, cattle, horses and cloth, there being many manufacturers of wool and silk in the area. The lower floor of the town hall was the site of the cheese market. Handsome 18th-C buildings now command the square, while the market cross records the sad story of Ruth Pierce. Elsewhere there are timbered buildings from the 16th C. The two fine churches, one built for the castle and the other for the parish, dominate the town. Only the mount and related earthworks survive of the original Norman castle; the present building is an extravagant Victorian folly. The town's own brewery, Wadworth, in Northgate Street, fills the air with the aroma of malt and hops. Wadworth still deliver their beer around the town by horse and dray. Stores *open Mon-Sat 06.00-23.00 & Sun 07.00-19.30*.

Battle of Roundway Down, 13 July 1643 Devizes was held by a Royalist army that had already tested the Roundhead forces, who were tired, dispirited and short of supplies after their defeat at Lansdown Hill, near Bath. A Royalist cavalry charge took the Roundheads by surprise, and most of the confused and battle-weary Roundheads were killed or captured. The battlefield, off the A361 north east of Devizes, is still largely intact, and can easily be explored on foot. Mock battles are re-enacted here.

Devizes to Westminster Canoe Race The toughest and longest canoe race in the world takes place *every Easter*. The course, from Park Road Bridge, Devizes, to County Hall Steps, Westminster, includes 54 miles of the Kennet & Avon, and 71 miles of the Thames, the last 17 of which are tidal. There are 77 locks. The race grew from a background of local rivalry in Pewsey and Devizes to find the quickest way to the sea by boat; in 1948 the target was 100 hours. In 1950 the first regular annual race over the course took place; three years later the junior class was introduced. Anyone may enter the race, but they would have difficulty in beating the highly trained army and navy teams.

Wiltshire Museum 41 Long Street, Devizes SN10 1NS (01380 727369; www.wiltshiremuseum.org.uk). One of the finest prehistoric collections in Europe including finds from the Neolithic, Bronze and Iron Age sites in Wiltshire, the most famous being the Stourhead collection of relics excavated from burial mounds on Salisbury Plain. There are also Roman exhibits. *Open Mon-Sat 10.00-17.00 (Thu-Sat 16.00).* Charge.

Kennet & Avon Canal Trust Canal Centre, Couch Lane, Devizes SN10 1EB (01380 721279; www.katrust.co.uk). The Trust's headquarters with an award-winning museum tracing the history of the canal by interactive video and exhibitions. Small charge. *Open Tue-Wed and when volunteers available 10.00-15.00.* Charge. Meeting room and well-stocked shop with large selection of canal books, souvenirs, maps and videos. Canal Information Centre *Mon-Thu 10.00-15.00.*

St John's Church SN10 1NS. Built by Bishop Roger of Sarum, who was also responsible for the castle, this 12th-C church with its massive crossing tower is still largely original. There are 15th-C and 19th-C additions, but they do not affect the Norman feeling of the whole.

St Mary's Church Dating from the same time as St John's, this church was more extensively rebuilt in the 15th C; plenty of Norman work still survives, however.

Wadworth Tap & Shop 41 Northgate Street, Devizes, SN10 1JN (01380 732277; www.wadworth.co.uk/brewery-tap-shop). Interactive brewing process exhibition, working cooper, shire horses, brewery tours, tastings, shop. Telephone or visit website for times and details.

Wharf Theatre The Wharf, Couch Street, Devizes SN10 1EB (0333 616 3366; www.wharftheatre.co.uk). Small, ambient canalside theatre hosting a variety of performances throughout the year. Telephone or visit Devizes Library (see below) for further details.

Devizes Library and Community Hub (01380 826190; www.facebook.com/DevizesLibrary). Tourist information and Wharf Theatre bookings apart from the more obvious functions. *Open at 09.30 Mon-Sat, closes at 19.00 on Mon and Thu; 17.00 on Tue and Fri; 12.30 on Wed & 16.00 on Sat.*

All Cannings

At Horton Bridge, where there is a convenient canalside *pub*, the waterway leaves another short cutting and the tower of Bishop Canning church comes into view, half hidden by trees: a footpath from the swing bridge is the quickest way into the village. The rolling hills climb fairly steeply to the north, while the pasture falls away to the south. Beyond Horton, the lock-free pound now extends eastwards all the way to Wootton Rivers. Following the contour of the land, it swings in a series of wide arcs past All Cannings, curling around the Knoll, a major feature of the landscape to the north. Several villages are near the navigation, all visible and easily accessible from the many bridges but none actually approach the waterside. Their interests lie rather in the rich agricultural lands that flank the canal. The waterway continues to meander through the open countryside, roughly following a contour line to maintain its level. Its progress is marked by a series of shallow cuttings and low embankments. The navigation passes the delightfully named Honeystreet with its *pub*, *boatyard* and canalside *café* and *shop*. Beyond the village, to the north, can be seen the white horse cut into the hill in 1812, a copy of the one at Cherhill. Approaching Woodborough Hill, the tower of Alton Priors church comes into view as the long pound continues eastwards. To the south the land falls away while to the north the hills take on an almost sculptural quality as evidence of ancient terracing can be seen.

- **Bishops Cannings**
Wilts. Apart from one or two old cottages, the main feature of this village is the very grand church. This cruciform building, with its central tower and spire, is almost entirely Early English in style; its magnificence is unexpected in so small a village. Traces of the earlier Norman building survive. Inside is a 17th-C penitential seat, surmounted by a giant hand painted on the wall with suitable inscriptions about sin and death.

PADDLING
Somewhat west of here, it is worth considering the upper reaches of the Wiltshire Avon which, anyone following the length of this navigation, will have met in Bath and points west. The upper limit of navigation for paddlers is generally considered to be Malmesbury and it can be followed all the way down into Bath, via Bradford on Avon. Bradford offers an opportunity to connect between river and canal as does Limpley Stoke to the west of the town – *see* Paddling page 75. It should be just possible (under favourable conditions) to also connect just downstream of the River Biss junction using the footpath up through Widbrook Wood (www.wiltshirewildlife.org/widbrook). The Malmsbury to Bath stretch of the Frome is classed as Grade 1-2. The River Biss is kayakable for approximately 4½ miles when there is plenty of water about, but hazards include small weirs, fallen trees and, in the Trowbridge area, supermarket trolleys!

Caen Hill Locks (see page 82)

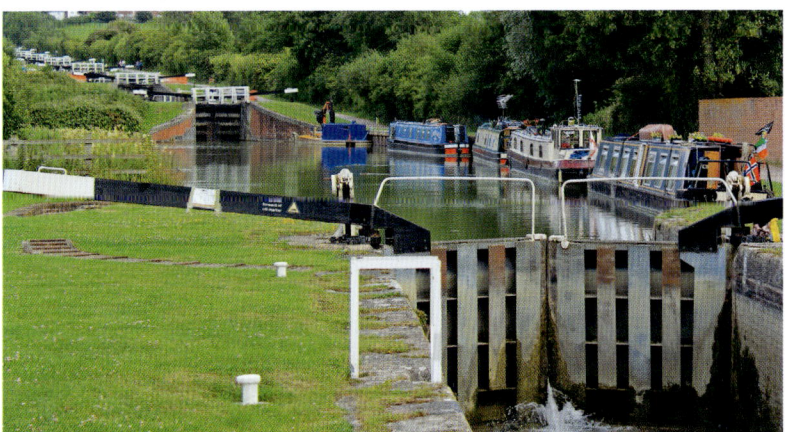

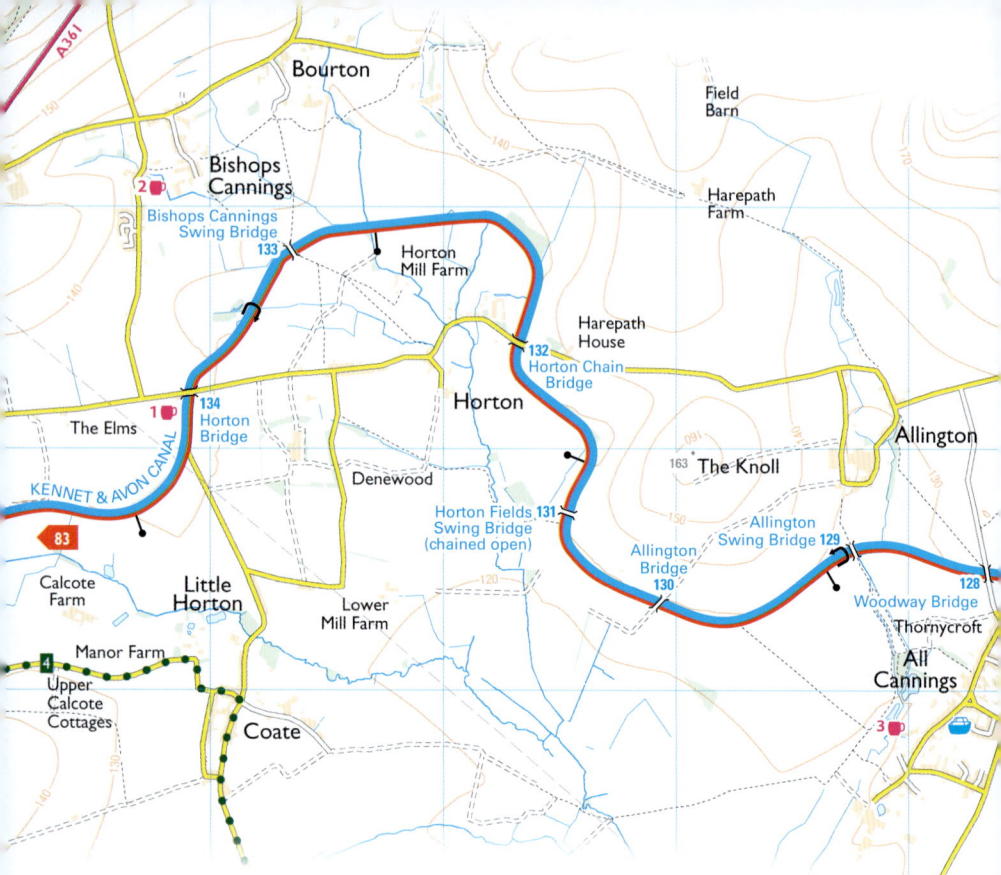

- **Allington**
  Wilts. A small agricultural village with picturesque cottages scattered around a Victorian church. East of the village is All Cannings Cross, a large Iron Age settlement.
- **All Cannings**
  Wilts. An attractive village built around a square, with houses of all periods. To the south there is a large green, overlooked by the church with its tall central tower. There is a useful *shop* selling food, beer, wine and newspapers. *Open Mon–Thu 07.30–13.00 and 15.00–21.00, Sat 09.00–16.00, Sun 09.00–12.00.*
- **Stanton St Bernard**
  Wilts. Built in a curve of the hills, the village has one main street, flanked by pretty gardens. The best building is the 19th-C manor, which incorporates relics of an earlier house. The battlemented church is Victorian.
- **Alton Priors**
  Wilts. Approached along a footpath from Alton Barnes churchyard, the isolated church is the best feature of this scattered hamlet. This pretty Perpendicular building with its wide, well-lit nave contains a most interesting monument: a big box tomb is surmounted with a large engraved Dutch brass plate, dated 1590, rich in extravagant symbolism. To the east of the village the Ridgeway runs southwards towards Salisbury; this Bronze Age drover's road swings north east along the downs for 50 miles, finally joining the Thames valley at Streatley.
- **Alton Barnes**
  Wilts. The village runs along the road northwards from Honey Street. The best part is clustered around the church. Fine farm buildings and an 18th-C rectory are half hidden among the trees. The church is essentially Anglo Saxon, but has been heavily restored; everything is in miniature, the tiny gallery, pulpit and pews emphasising the compact scale of the whole building.
- **Honeystreet**
  Wilts. Farm shop. A traditional canalside village. At the wharf the old mill buildings have been developed into a range of businesses including a shop selling fair trade and Indian-style goods, a farm shop, café and the Crop Circle Visitor Centre (www.cropcircleaccess.com) *open daily 11.00-17.00*.

Boatyards

ⓑ **Moonraker Canalboats** The Old Builders Wharf, Honeystreet SN9 5PS (01672 733017; www.moonboats.co.uk). D Pump out, gas, solid fuel, long- and short-term moorings, narrowboat and day boat hire. *Open Apr-Oct, Wed and Thu only 10.00-17.00. Winter by appointment.*

ⓑ✗ **Honeystreet Boats** Honeystreet Mill, Honeystreet SN9 5PS (01672 851166; www.honeystreetboats.co.uk). Narrowboat and day boat hire. Excellent café.

Pubs and Restaurants

🍺 1 **The Bridge Inn** Horton Road, Devizes SN10 2JS (01380 860273; www.thebridgeinnhorton.com). Attractive, welcoming pub with mellow brick interior. Real ales and food available in the bar and restaurant *L and E daily. Sunday roasts 12.00-17.00.* Children's menu. Dogs and children welcome. Canalside garden and patio. Moorings. *Open daily 11.00-23.00 (Sun 18.00).*

🍺 2 **The Crown Inn** Chandlers Lane, Bishops Cannings SN10 2JZ (01380 860218; www.crownbishopscannings.co.uk). Friendly village pub serving real ale. Traditional pub meals *L and E Wed-Sat and Sun L.* Children welcome. Spacious garden and small campsite. *Open L & E Wed-Sat; Sun 12.00-16.00.*

🍺✗ 3 **The Kings Arms** Pub Lane, All Cannings SN10 3PA (01380 860328; www.kingsarmsallcannings.co.uk). Comfortable and charming village pub, serving a good selection of real ale, and good value, home-made bar food *Tue-Sun L and E (not Sun E).* Dog-friendly, large garden. Traditional pub games and real fires. *Open Mon-Fri L and E (not Mon L) & Sat-Sun 12.00-23.00.*

🍺 4 **The Barge Inn** Honeystreet, Pewsey SN9 5PS (01672 851222; www.the-barge-inn.com). An imposing canalside pub which was once a slaughterhouse, a bakehouse, a brewery and a grocers; now functioning as a community pub. Real ale and food served *L and E (not Sun E).* Dog- and family-friendly, garden. *Sat* music. Real fires and Wi-Fi. Camping. *Open Mon 11.00-22.30 & Tue-Sun 11.00-23.00 (Fri-Sat 00.00).*

✗ 5 **The Honeystreet Mill Café** Honeystreet Mill, Honeystreet SN9 5PS (01672 851853; www.honeystreetmill.co.uk). Charming canalside tea gardens, nestled in the Pewsey Vale (with views of the white horse) offering freshly made cakes, tasty sandwiches, homemade scones, tea, coffee and daily specials, together with the opportunity to indulge in a hearty breakfast served until *11.30.* Also a farm shop. *Open daily 09.00-17.00.*

Pewsey

The canal skirts Woodborough Hill giving views to the south over open countryside to the village of Woodborough itself. The equally dominant Picked Hill now fills the north bank, giving a good view of the field terracing that is a relic of Celtic and medieval cultivation. Further east, the waterway passes through the elaborately decorated Lady's Bridge and enters the tranquil, wooded Wide Water. In 1793 this stretch was owned by Lady Susannah Wroughton who objected to the canal cutting through her land. She was appeased by £500, the building of a highly ornate bridge (dated 1808 and attributed to Rennie) and the landscaping of the marshy area around it.

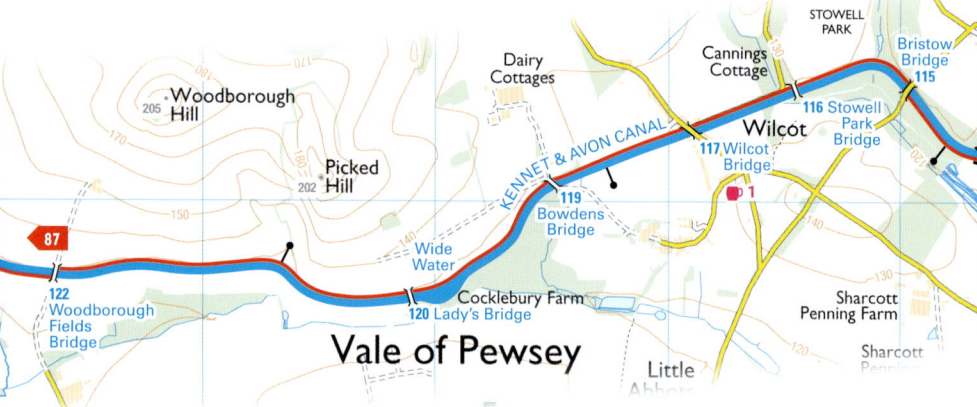

Beyond, a straight stretch leads to the first cottages of Wilcot; the rest of the village is to the south. Woods lead the waterway past Stowell Park, whose landscaped grounds extend to the north. The house, built early in the 19th C, can be seen clearly from the canal. Closer to the navigation is a selection of delightful estate cottages built in the picturesque style. A miniature suspension bridge, the only surviving example of its kind, carries a private footpath from the park across the canal which now approaches Pewsey Wharf in a low, wooded cutting. The waterway passes well outside the town which fills the Vale to the south. Pewsey Wharf is 1 mile from the town centre and so has developed as a separate canalside settlement, with a *pub*, cottages and warehouse buildings. To the north, hills descend to the water's edge and to the south the land opens out, giving fine views over the Vale of Pewsey. The 15-mile-long pound continues east, now accompanied by the railway, passing New Mill – a small hamlet to the south of the canal – where there is still evidence of a small wharf.

- **Wilcot**
  Wilts. A pretty village scattered round the green; there are several thatched houses, and a converted village school with a prominent bell. Parts of the church date from the 12th C, but it was mostly rebuilt in 1876 after a fire. An important event in the village is the annual carnival dating back to 1898. Lasting for two weeks it *commences on the third Sat in Sep* – drawing large crowds – and there are events every evening thereafter.

- **Pewsey**
  Wilts. All services. The little town is set compactly in the Vale of Pewsey. At its centre is a fine statue of King Alfred, erected in 1911, from where all the roads radiate. There is the usual mixture of buildings; but while many are attractive, none are noteworthy. The church is mostly 13th- and 15th-C, but parts of the nave are late Norman: the altar rails were made from timbers of the *San Josef*, captured by Nelson in 1797. The immaculate railway station harks back to the former days of GWR supremacy and is a joy to patronise. There is a useful cycle shop, Pewsey Velo, 16 High Street, Pewsey SN9 5AQ (01672 562264; www.facebook.com/pewseyvelo) *open Mon-Fri 10.00-18.00 (Fri 20.00) & Sat 10.00-17.00*.

- **New Mill**
  Wilts. A pretty hamlet scattered below the canal. The mill that gave it its name is now a house, with a fine garden.

WALKING AND CYCLING

The Pewsey Vale is an absolute gem for anyone who enjoys a country walk with spectacular views, beautiful countryside and plenty of history. Ideas of where to go and what to see can be downloaded from www.visitpewseyvale.co.uk. For the 77-mile Pewsey Vale Circular Walk visit www.visitpewseyvale.co.uk/pewsey-vale-circular-walk.

Pubs and Restaurants

🍺✕ **1 The Golden Swan** Wilcot, Pewsey SN9 5NN (01672 562289; www.thegoldenswan.co.uk). A one-handed ghost is said to haunt this pub, which stands beyond the green at the far end of the village. However, in the flesh, there is an affable landlord and friendly locals together with real ale and home-made bar meals served *daily L and E (except Tue)*. Dog- and child-friendly, garden. Traditional pub games, open fires, sports TV and Wi-Fi. Camping. *Open Mon-Fri L and E & Sat-Sun 12.00-23.00 (closed Tue).*

🍺 **2 The Crown Inn** 60 Wilcot Road, Pewsey (01672 562653; www.facebook.com/crownpewsey). This is a serious (and very welcoming) real ale pub with its own micro brewery. Additional ales from local micro breweries (together with ciders and perrys) are also available. Dogs and children welcome. Garden and play area. Food available *Fri E & Sun L. Thu* live music. Traditional pub games, real fires and Wi-Fi. *Open Mon-Thu 16.00-22.00 (Thu 12.00) & Fri-Sun 12.00-23.30 (Sun 18.00).*

✕ **3 The Little Lunch Box Café** 14 High Street, Pewsey SN9 5AQ. (01672 564901; www.facebook.com/Thelittlelunchbox2019). Great range of food, breakfast, lunches, teas and sandwiches. Eat in or takeaway. Children welcome. *Open Mon-Fri 08.00-16.00 & Sat 09.00-15.00.*

🍺✕ **4 The Waterfront** Pewsey Wharf, Marlborough Road, Pewsey SN9 5NU (01672 564020; www.facebook.com/Thewaterf). Upstairs bar (above a bistro) in the old Pewsey Wharf building serving real ale and food (from the Bistro) *Thu-Sun L and E (not Sun E)*. Dog- and family-friendly, canalside seating. Traditional pub games, real fires, sports TV and Wi-Fi. Mooring and slipway. W and pump out. *Open Mon L; Wed-Fri L and E & Sat-Sun 12.00-23.00 (Sun 21.00).*

🍺 **5 The Royal Oak** 35 North Street, Pewsey SN9 5ES (01672 563426; www.theroyaloakpewsey.co.uk). An 18th-C hostelry in the town centre, dispensing real ale, real cider and food *daily L*. Dog-friendly, garden. Traditional pub games, real fires and sports TV. *Open Tue-Thu L and E & Fri-Sun 12.30-22.30 (Sun 18.00).*

🍺 **6 The Shed Alehouse** 20 North Street, Pewsey SN9 5EX (07769 812643; www.theshedalehouse.com). A quirky, cosy and friendly small bar serving a selection of real ales and ciders from micro breweries. Child-friendly *until 19.00*. Traditional pub games. *Open Wed-Thu 17.00-21.00; Fri-Sat 16.00-21.30 (Sat 14.00) & Sun 13.00-16.30.*

Pewsey Wharf

Burbage Wharf

The charming, predominantly thatched, village of Wootton Rivers lies beside the eponymous bottom lock, stretching away to the north. The third lock is in the middle of Brimslade Farm, whose attractive tile-hung buildings date from the 17th C; while Wootton Top Lock sits beside a pretty cottage and garden. Above, the short summit pound leads the waterway through pasture and arable land and, as the ground rises steeply on both banks, it prepares itself for the short Bruce Tunnel. Immediately before the high brick bridge, carrying the A346, lies Burbage Wharf; several of the original brick canal buildings still stand, attractively converted to domestic use, and a restored wooden wharf crane hangs, beside the water. This was originally built at the Newark Works in Bath and is a reminder of crane-maker Stothert & Pitt's glory days by the Avon. Woods line the approach to the tunnel's western portal, hiding the railway, which is on the south bank before crossing over the tunnel. To the north are the extensive parklands of Tottenham House and Savernake Forest itself. The towpath, passing under the railway, climbs over the top of the tunnel and descends steeply to the navigation, still secluded in a deep, wooded cutting.

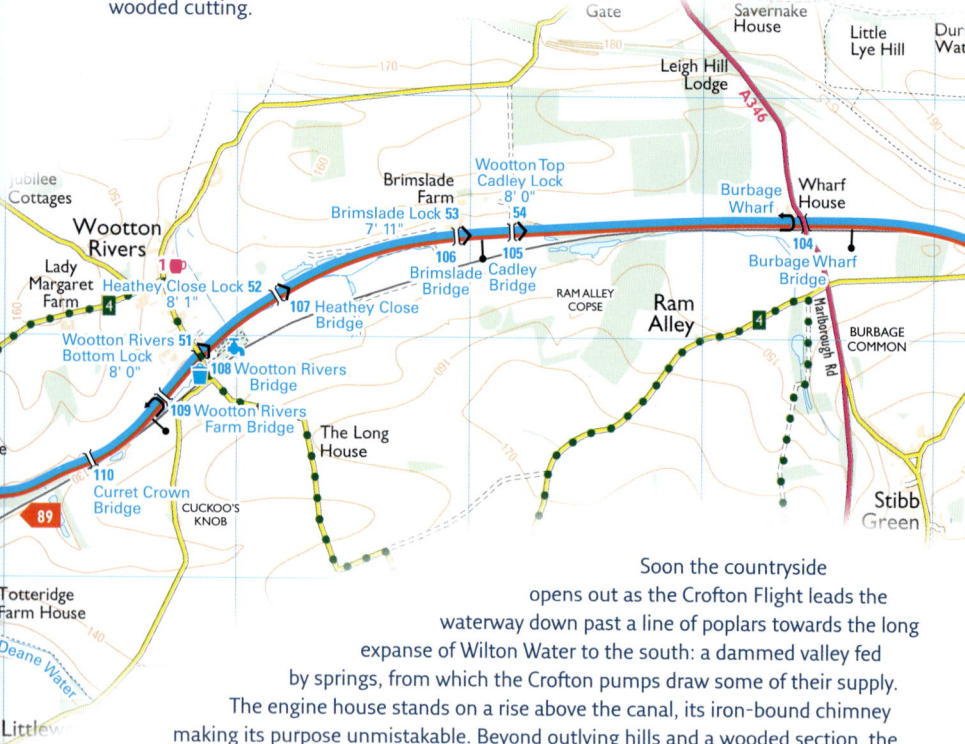

Soon the countryside opens out as the Crofton Flight leads the waterway down past a line of poplars towards the long expanse of Wilton Water to the south: a dammed valley fed by springs, from which the Crofton pumps draw some of their supply. The engine house stands on a rise above the canal, its iron-bound chimney making its purpose unmistakable. Beyond outlying hills and a wooded section, the navigation descends towards Great Bedwyn, passing the church at the final lock before the wharf and village are reached.

Boatyards

Ⓑ **Cruise England Ltd** Burbage Wharf, Burbage, Marlborough SN9 3BJ (01672 733017; www.cruise-england.co.uk). Luxury narrow- and wide-beam boat hire.

- **Wootton Rivers**

Wilts. A particularly pretty village composed almost entirely of timber-framed, thatched houses, climbing gently up the hill away from the waterway. The church has an unusual clock, its face having letters in place of numbers. Inside, its mechanism is equally eccentric, being assembled from a bizarre collection of cast-off agricultural implements.

- **Crofton**

Wilts. The scattered village is dominated by the brick pumping station with its separate chimney. It houses two 19th-C steam engines, one built in 1812 by Boulton and Watt, the oldest original working beam engine in the world still performing its original duties, the other in 1845 by Harvey's of Hayle, Cornwall. Both have been restored, and are steamed on several *weekends* in the year. The pumping station, engines and café are open *Easter-Oct, daily 10.30–16.30.* On steam weekends, the Old Forge Bar serving real ales and cider is also open. For details of steaming weekends, telephone 01672 870300; www.croftonbeamengines.org.

Bruce Tunnel Named in honour of Thomas Bruce, Earl of Ailesbury. 502yds with the remains of the chains on the walls, which were used to pull boats through.

- **Wilton**

Wilts. A compact village at the southern end of Wilton Water, with a pretty duck pond in the centre.
Wilton Windmill Wilton Hill, Wilton SN8 3SW (07712 010501; www.wiltonwindmill.co.uk). 1 mile south of the canal, along the footpath at Lock 60. *Open Easter-Sep, Sun and B hols 14.00–17.00.* Also *regular* events outside these times – *see website for details.*

Pubs and Restaurants

- **1 The Royal Oak** Wootton Rivers SN8 4NQ (01672 810322; www.facebook.com/royal.oak1). An attractive 16th-C pub in the main street, serving real ale and a good choice of wines. Extensive range of home-cooked meals, prepared with fresh local ingredients, available *Tue-Sat L and E & Sun 12.00–18.00.* Dog-friendly, garden. Traditional pub games, real fires and Wi-Fi. *Open Tue-Fri L and E & Sat-Sun 12.00–23.00 (Sun 21.00).*

- **2 The Swan** Wilton, Marlborough SN8 3SS (01672 870274; www.theswanwilton.co.uk). ½ mile south east of Lock 60, along a footpath running beside Wilton Water. Friendly establishment in a 1920s building that replaces the original 1724 pub, now a private dwelling. Real ale and real cider, together with appetising home-cooked food *daily L and E (not Sun E).* Dog- and family-friendly, garden. Real fires and Wi-Fi. Takeaway service *L and E (not Sun E). Open Mon-Fri L and E & Sat-Sun 12.00–23.00 (Sun 22.30).*

Froxfield

Great Bedwyn is ranged over the hillside to the north of the waterway, newer houses spilling downwards towards the canal and railway station. The navigation leaves the village, accompanied by the infant River Dunn and approaches Little Bedwyn in a shallow side-cutting. To the north is a hill fort, overlooking ridges that break up the farmland. The village is cut in half by the navigation and the railway. In the centre the lock continues the descent towards Hungerford. The spire of the village church is a prominent feature as is the Berks and Wilts main railway line that keeps constant

BOAT TRIPS

Kennet & Avon Canal Trust 1½ hour trips from Hungerford Wharf (RG17 0EQ) on *Rose of Hungerford*, Apr–Oct at weekends, Weds and on B Hol afternoons. Also longer *4-hour* trips to Froxfield on *summer evenings*. Available for private charter, up to 50 persons. Details from 01380 721279; www.katrust.org.uk/our-boats/the-rose-of-hungerford-bookings.

The Bruce Trust PO Box 21, Hungerford, Berks RG17 9YY (07789 727493; www.brucetrust.org.uk) operates four beautifully fitted-out wide-beam boats on the Kennet & Avon for disabled, disadvantaged and elderly people. For further details regarding availability telephone 01380 721279 or visit www.bruceboats.katrust.org.uk.

companion with the waterway for some considerable distance. Three locks carry the canal past Froxfield which lies to the north, flanked by the A4; the best access is from bridge 90. This was rebuilt in 1972 during a road improvement scheme using traditional methods and materials, even down to the correct colour of brick. To the west of the River Dunn Aqueduct the railway crosses the waterway and remains on the south bank through Hungerford. The roar of the frequent GWR Hitachi 800 Series trains to and from the West Country is the only interruption to the natural peace and solitude of the canal. Crossing a tree-lined embankment, beside the river, the navigation approaches the common land of Hungerford Marsh via Cobblers Lock. Water meadows and pasture, rich in buttercups, meet the water, which seems to form more of a river than a canal. On the outskirts of the town the 19th-C church is passed to the south as the waterway descends to the old wharf, flanked by an original stone warehouse. The handsome bridge gives easy access to the centre of the town set out along a wide, main street. Beyond, the waterway once again strikes off through open meadows, closely paralleled by the clear, sparkling waters of the River Kennet.

NAVIGATIONAL NOTES

1. Hungerford Marsh Swing Bridge is over Hungerford Marsh Lock. Boats over 30ft long (approx) will have to swing it clear before using the lock.
2. In spite of its benign appearance the River Kennet can make a considerable impact on the navigation when in spate. In such conditions the boater should consider carefully his own capabilities and those of his craft before proceeding east beyond Hungerford (or west beyond Reading). Hazards to be particularly aware of are: **a)** Strong pulls at the top of all draw-off weirs – look out for signs. **b)** Powerful side currents at the bottom of locks and lock cuts. **c)** Speed of craft downstream necessitated by need to maintain steerage in fast currents. **d)** Craft heading upstream, often obscured by the many blind bends on the navigation. **e)** Difficulty setting down and picking up crew at locks and moveable bridges – plan all such manoeuvres well ahead.
3. Many of the winding holes marked between Hungerford and Reading are at points where the river and lock cuts diverge and therefore should NOT be used to turn a boat when the river is flowing strongly as they lead directly to weirs.
4. Top paddles between Hungerford and Reading are a mixture of ground and gate paddles. The gate paddles can be particularly fierce, especially in the deeper locks. Secure your boat well back in the lock chamber and open gate paddles with great care.

- **Great Bedwyn**

Wilts. PO, stores, off-licence, station. The main street climbs gently away from the canal and the railway. It is wide, with generous grass verges; attractive houses of all periods line the street. At the top are the pubs. The large church, with its well-balanced crossing tower, is mostly 12th- and 13th-C; inside are some interesting monuments. Relics from the old Bedwyn Stone Museum adorn the façade of the village shop. These are from a collection of stonework of all types, not without humour, and show the work of seven generations of stonemasons. There are statues, tombstones, casts, amusing plaques and even the fossilised footprint of a dinosaur. Stores *open Mon-Sat 07.00-20.00 (Sat 08.00) & Sun 08.30-14.00.*

- **Little Bedwyn**

Wilts. Divided by the canal, the village falls into two distinct parts. North is the estate village, pretty 19th-C terraces of patterned brick running eastwards to the church, half hidden among ancient yew trees. To the south is the older farming village, handsome 18th-C buildings climbing the hill away from the canal.

- **Froxfield**

Wilts. The village is ranged along the A4, which has obviously affected its development. The main feature of the village is the Somerset Hospital, a range of almshouses founded by the Duchess of Somerset in 1694, extended in 1775 and again in 1813. Facing onto the road, the hospital is built round a courtyard, which is entered by a Gothic-style gateway, part of the 1813 extension.

- **Littlecote** 1½ miles north of Froxfield. A Tudor building of the 16th C. Littlecote is the most important brick mansion in Wiltshire with its notable Great Hall, Armoury and Long Gallery. The formal front overlooks the gardens that run down to the Kennet. Not open to the public.

- **Hungerford**

Berks. *All services.* Hungerford is built along the A338, which runs through the town southwards from the junction with the A4. The pleasant 18th- and 19th-C buildings are set back from the road, giving the spacious feeling of a traditional market town. None of the buildings are remarkable, but many are individually pretty. Note the decorative ironwork of the house by the canal bridge. The manor was given to John of Gaunt in 1366, and any monarch passing through the town is given a red rose, the Lancastrian emblem, as a token rent.

Hocktide Ceremonies On the *second Tuesday after Easter*, 99 Hungerford commoners (those living within the original borough who have the rights of the common and the fishing) are called to the town hall by the blowing of a horn. Two Tuttmen are appointed, who have to visit the houses of the commoners to collect a 'head penny' from the men and a kiss from the women: they give oranges in return. All new commoners are then shod by having a nail driven into their shoes. This ceremony dates from medieval times.

WALKING AND CYCLING
Great Bedwyn is a good, central point to access the Ridgeway Walk.

Little Bedwyn Lock

Pubs and Restaurants (pages 92-93)

🍺✕ **1 The Three Tuns** 1 High Street, Great Bedwyn SN8 3NU (01672 870280). This cosy, award-winning hostelry offers real ales and home-made food (sourced locally wherever possible) *Tue-Thu L and E & Fri-Sun 12.00-20.30 (Sun 14.30)*. Dog- and family-friendly, garden. Traditional pub games, newspapers, real fires and Wi-Fi. *Open Tue-Thu L and E; Fri-Sat 11.30-23.00 & Sun 12.00-19.00.*

✕ **2 Wendy's Community Café & Juice Bar** Farm Lane, Great Bedwyn SN8 3LU (07901 668302). Eclectic and quirky, friendly and welcoming, offering a varied menu of hot and cold food for all tastes. Teas, coffees and juice. Vegans catered for. Dog and child-friendly. *Open Wed-Sun 10.00-15.00.*

🍺✕ **3 The Pelican** Bath Road, Froxfield SN8 3JY (01488 682479; www.pelicaninn.co.uk). Country pub set in an area of outstanding natural beauty, two minutes' walk from the canal. Real ales and food available *Mon-Sat L and E & Sun 12.00-18.00*. Large country garden with lake and river. Dog- and family-friendly. Wi-Fi. B&B. *Open daily 12.00-22.00 (Sun 21.00).*

🍺✕ **4 The Bear Hotel** 41 Charnham Street, Hungerford RG17 0EL (01488 682512; www.facebook.com/TheBearHotel). Hotel with a 13th-C restaurant serving modern dishes *L and E*. Real ales. Visited by several illustrious visitors over the centuries – including Elizabeth I, Henry VIII and Samuel Pepys – this hotel has, today, a very relaxed atmosphere together with charming courtyard and riverside seating. Also an original Parliamentary clock used to time the mail coaches. Garden. *Open daily 11.00-23.00 (Sun 12.00).*

🍺 **5 The John of Gaunt Inn** 21 Bridge Street, Hungerford RG17 0EG (01488 683535; www.john-o-gaunt-hungerford.co.uk). 16th-C pub north of the canal, serving real ale brewed in the microbrewery at their sister pub and bar meals *Mon-Fri L and E & Sat-Sun 12.00-21.00 (Sun 20.00)*. Wide range of real ciders. Dog- and child-friendly, award-winning garden. Traditional pub games, real fires and Wi-Fi. *Open daily 12.00-23.00 (Sun 22.30).*

🍺 **6 The Plume** 113 High Street, Hungerford RG17 0NB (01488 682154; www.facebook.com/theplumehungerford). Real ale and food served *Tue-Sun L and E (not Tue-Wed L or Sun E)*. Dog- and family-friendly, courtyard. Traditional pub games and Wi-Fi. *Open Tue-Sun 12.00-23.00 (Sun 19.00).*

🍺 **7 The Three Swans Hotel** 117 High Street, Hungerford RG17 0LZ (01488 682721; www.threeswanshotel.co.uk). Real ale and real cider served in this comfortable hotel together with food *L and E*, morning coffee and afternoon tea *14.00-18.00*. Dog- and child-friendly, garden. Wi-Fi. B&B. *Open daily 10.00-00.00.*

🍺 **8 The Railway Tavern** Station Road, Hungerford RG17 0DY (01488 683100; www.facebook.com/TheRailywayTavern). 200 yds south of Station Road footbridge. Real ale. Garden. Traditional pub games and sports TV. *Open daily 12.00-21.00 (Fri-Sat 23.00).*

🍺 **9 The Borough Arms** 77 High Street, Hungerford RG17 0NA (01488 683233; www.borougharms.co.uk). Large, sports-oriented establishment dispensing real ale and good cheer. Dog- and family-friendly, garden. Traditional pub games, real fires, sports TV and Wi-Fi. *Regular events. Open daily 12.00-23.00 (Fri-Sat 00.00).*

PADDLING

For most people the overall remoteness, peace, quiet and extended open views are reason enough to be content with paddling this section of the Kennet & Avon Canal. It is a rural idyll punctuated by a series of small hamlets with alluring names. Few have anything these days for the consumer to engage with apart from some charming hostelries. This section is for quiet contemplation and rumination on a different type and pace of paddling, examples of which are depicted at www.gopaddling.info/places-to-paddle-in-surrey-and-berkshire).

CLOSE(ISH) ENCOUNTERS

Hungerford commoners, anxious to exercise their piscatorial rights (*see* Hocktide Ceremonies, opposite), should be grateful to have been spared the experience of one Alfred Burtoo. This 78-year-old fisherman, whilst casually casting into the nearby Basingstoke Canal one night, was disturbed by the arrival of two figures in green overalls, 4 feet tall, wearing helmets with smoked visors. After pausing for several seconds they beckoned him to follow them, which he did. 'I was curious,' explained Alfred, 'They showed no sign of hostility and at 78, what had I to lose?' He was led along the towpath to a large oval object – 40-50 feet wide – and upon ascending some steps found himself inside an octagonal room. Here he stood until a voice instructed him to stand under an amber light fixed to the cabin wall. He was asked his age and, after a further pause, the voice bade him depart, stating: 'You are too old and infirm for our purpose'.

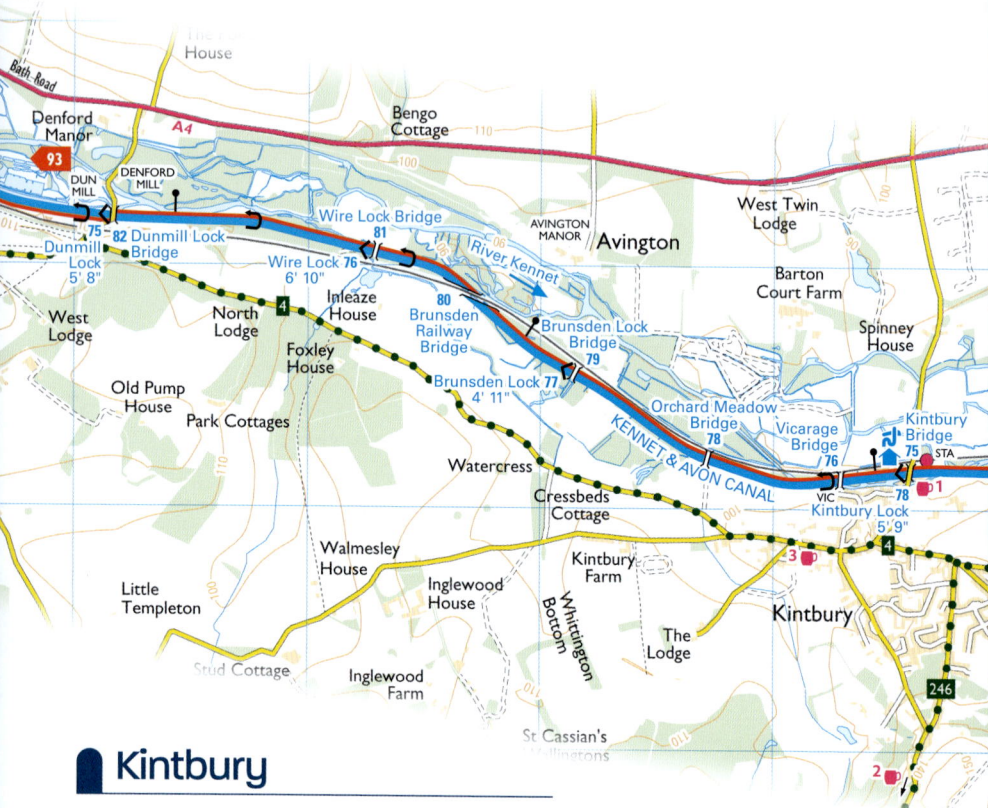

Kintbury

Pretty woods keep company with the waterway to the south as it leaves Hungerford, while to the north river and canal run side by side through water meadows and Common Portdown, an attractive common area, separated only by a narrow ridge carrying the towpath. As the diminutive River Kennet accompanies the canal past Dunmill Lock, the towpath turns over to the north bank. From the bridge there is a good view of Denford Mill. Locks 76 and 77 carry the navigation past Avington, with its Norman church visible among the trees. The railway and the River Kennet are constantly present as the waterway heads towards Kintbury through open countryside, passing the Victorian Gothic vicarage. The canal enters the village beside the railway station and the Dundas Arms, which overlooks the lock. The centre of Kintbury is up on the hill to the south of the lock. Leaving the wharf, the navigation steadily descends the locks towards Newbury, making this a particularly attractive stretch. Wooded, rolling hills flank the waterway to the south as it passes through Drewett's, Copse and Hamstead Locks and into the delightful landscape of Hamstead Park.

● **Avington**
Berks. The village is best approached along the footpath running north then west from Bridge 76, or the more adventurous can go directly across the water meadows, crossing the Kennet on a small footbridge. The church is still wholly Norman, and contains a variety of original work; the chancel arch, the corbels and the font are particularly interesting.

● **Kintbury**
Berks. PO, stores, off-licence, baker, station. A quiet village with attractive buildings by the canal, including a watermill and canalside pub. The church is originally 13th-C, but was restored in 1859; the railway lends excitement, and noise, to the situation.

NAVIGATIONAL NOTES

Allow for river current when winding and when approaching Copse Lock, especially after heavy rain.

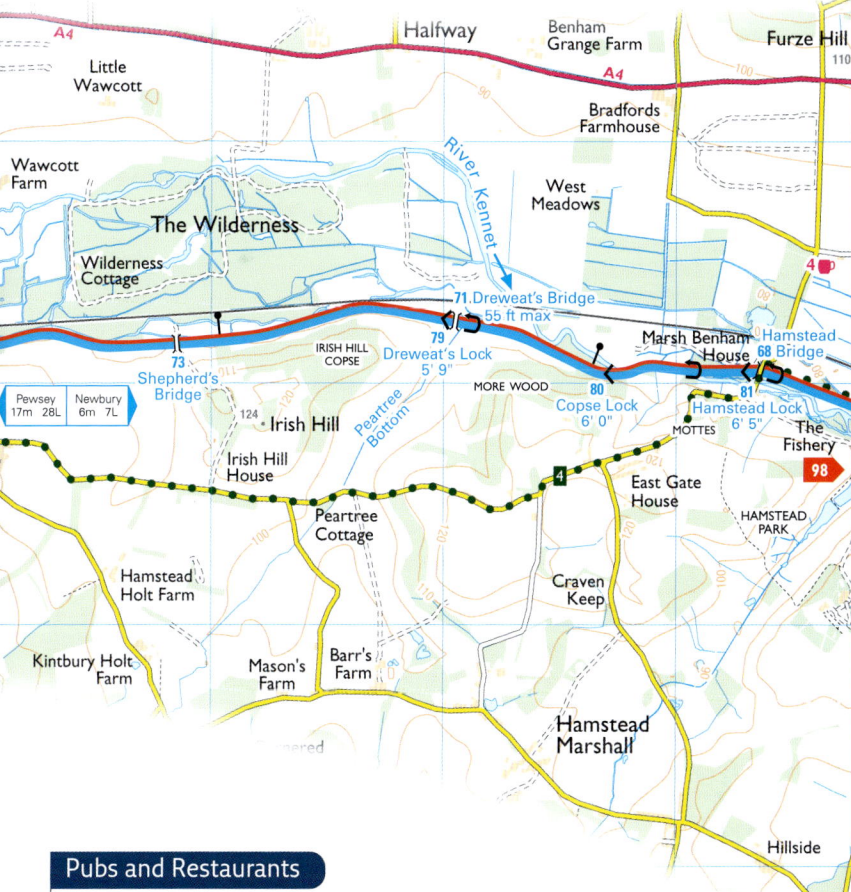

Pubs and Restaurants

🍺❌ **1 The Dundas Arms** 53 Station Road, Kintbury RG17 9UT (01488 658263; www.dundasarms.co.uk). The River Kennet and the canal flow on either side of this pub, which was named after the Lord Dundas who opened the canal in 1810. Real ale and real cider. Excellent menu and wine cellar: food available *Mon-Fri 07.30-11.00 (breakfast) L and E & Sat-Sun 08.00-21.00 (Sun 20.00)*. Dog- and family-friendly, canalside garden. Real fires and Wi-Fi. B&B. *Open Mon-Fri 07.30-10.30 (Fri 23.00) & Sat-Sun 08.00-23.00 (Sun 22.00)*.

🍺❌ **2 The Crown & Garter** Inkpen Common, Inkpen RG17 9QR (01488 668325; www.crownandgarter.co.uk). Former coaching inn now serving real ale and excellent food *L and E (not Sun E)* together with breakfast *08.00-10.00* and a coffee shop *08.30-16.00*. Real ale and real cider. Family-friendly, garden. Real fires. B&B. Camping. *Open Mon-Sat 08.00-22.00 (Fri-Sat 23.00) & Sun 08.00-19.00*.

🍺❌ **3 The Blue Ball** High Street, Kintbury RG17 9TJ (01488 608126; www.thetasteofthai.co.uk/the-blue-ball-kintbury). Friendly village pub dispensing real ale and authentic Thai cuisine *Thu-Fri L and E & Sat-Sun 12.00-2.30*. Family-friendly, garden. Traditional pub games. *Open Mon-Wed 17.00-23.00 & Thu-Sun 12.00-23.00 (Sun 22.00)*.

🍺 **4 The Red House** Marsh Benham RG20 8LY (01635 582017; www.theredhousepub.co.uk). Charming pub-cum-restaurant in a thatched estate village near Benham Park. Once the local bakery it now dispenses real ales. Expensive, though appetising menu served in bar and restaurant *Mon-Thu L and E & Fri-Sun 12.00-21.00*. Attractive conservatory and gardens. Newspapers and real fires. Camping. *Open daily 12.00-21.00 (Thu 09.00)*.

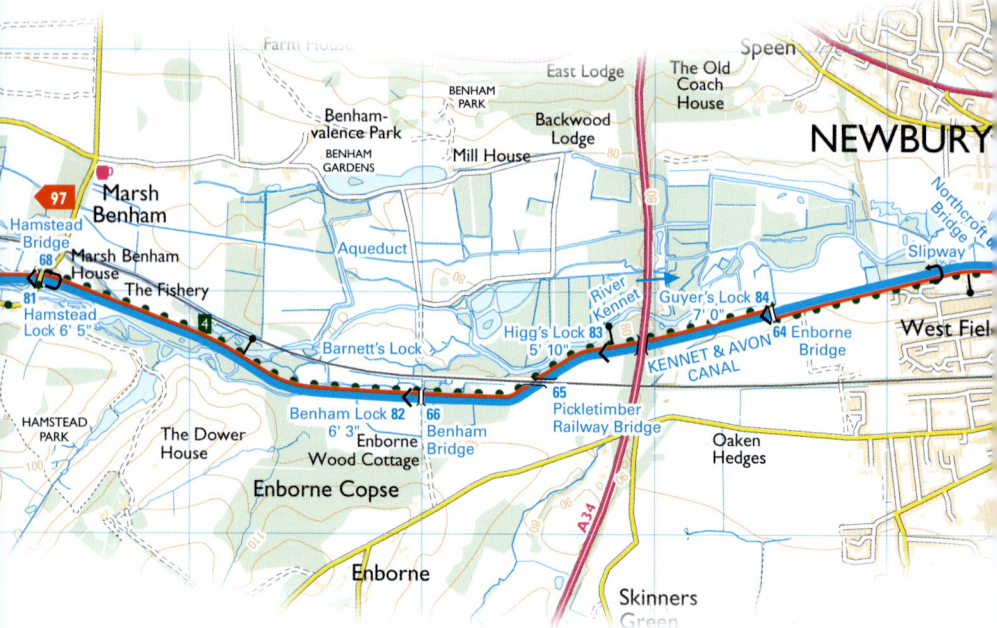

BOAT TRIPS

Nb Jubilee The Wharf, Newbury RG14 5AS (01380 721279; www.katrust.org.uk/our-boats/jubilee). Operated by the Kennet & Avon Canal Trust volunteers. Public and private charter trips from Newbury Wharf. Available *Thu, Sat, Sun and BH Mon at 12.00 and 14.00*. Licensed bar and toilet. Visit website for further details.

Newbury

West of Newbury the waterway again passes through extensive water meadows as the wooded hills open out to the south revealing a stretch of the controversial bypass. Above Newbury Lock is the delightful, quiet West Mills area, where rows of terraced houses face the navigation and there are extensive moorings. The river cuts right through the town and the town makes the most of it. Below the lock, where the channel gets narrower and faster, is a splendid stone balustraded bridge followed, after 500yds, by a park and an extensive wharf area opposite. This used to be the terminus of the Kennet Navigation from Reading, before the Kennet and Avon Canal Company extended it to link up with the Avon at Bath. There is also a collection of old warehouses and a stone building used by the K & A Canal Trust as an *information centre*, *tearooms* and *shop*. The waterway leaves Newbury Wharf under a handsome new road bridge.

NAVIGATIONAL NOTES

1. Below Newbury lock there are strong cross-flows from both sides of the navigation when the river levels are raised. Upstream boaters should prepare the lock ahead of the craft.
2. In times of fresh water there are strong flows in the narrow section below Newbury bridge and progress upstream can be very slow. Downstream craft should keep a very careful lookout.

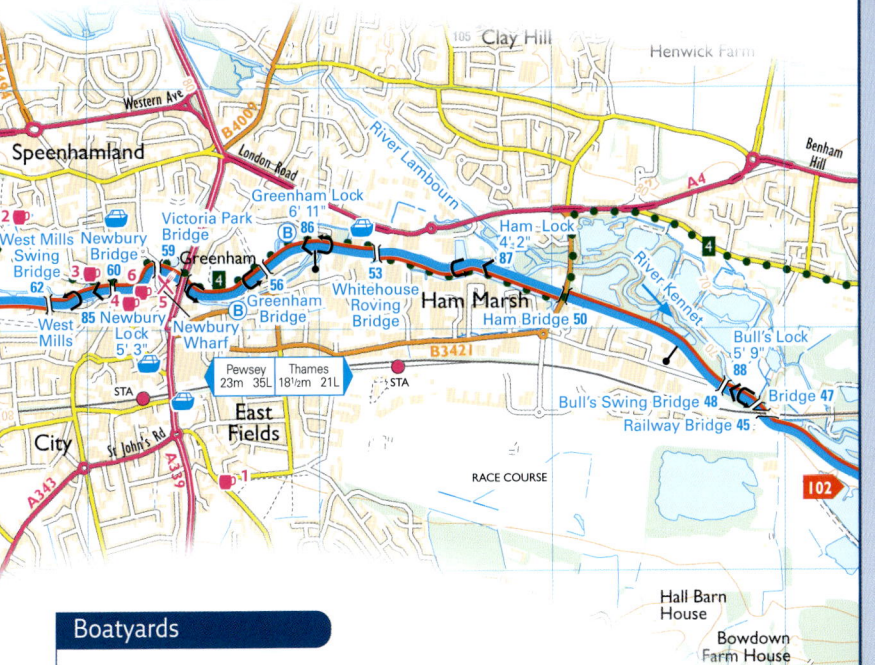

Boatyards

Ⓑ**Greenham Lock Marina** Greenham Lock Cottage, Ampere Road, Newbury RG14 5SN (01635 42943; www.greenhamlockmarina.co.uk). 🚽⛽🧺 Pump out, gas, long-term mooring, toilet, laundry.

ⒷThe Dry Dock Company Ampere Road, Newbury RG14 5SN (07799 640644; www.facebook.com/TheDryDockCompany). Dry dock, DIY facilities. *Open Mon-Sat 08.00-17.00.*

ⒷNewbury Marina Mill Lane, Newbury RG14 5SG (07584 566197; www.newburymarina.com). ⛽ D Pump out, gas, long and short term moorings, chandlery, solid fuel, toilets, CCTV. *Open Mon-Sat 09.00-15.00 (Apr-Sep 17.00).*

● Newbury
Berks. All services. Newbury developed in the Middle Ages as a cloth town of considerable wealth, its stature indicated by the size of the church. Although the cloth trade has long vanished, the town has managed to retain much of its period charm. It is a busy shopping centre, and the shop fronts in the main streets have buried many 17th- and 18th-C houses. Elsewhere in the town the 18th C is well in evidence, especially in the West Mills area. There are fine almshouses, and a pretty ornamental stone bridge over the navigation. There are also signs of the agricultural importance of Newbury: the 19th-C Italianate Corn Exchange, for example (*see across*).

1st Battle of Newbury, 20 Sep 1643 Site of Wash Farm off A343. 1¾ miles south of Guyer's Lock. The Royalists were defeated by the Parliamentarians in one of the bloodiest onslaughts of the Civil War. Guyer's and Higg's Locks are named after troop commanders in the battle.

2nd Battle of Newbury, 28 Oct 1644 Donnington Castle, Donnington. 1½ miles north of Newbury Lock off the A34. The Royalists were in possession of Donnington Castle when the Parliamentarians attacked. Charles' army withdrew to Oxford, but a week later they returned and relieved the castle.

Corn Exchange Market Place, Newbury RG14 5BD (01635 522733; www.cornexchange.org.uk/whats-on). The Corn Exchange offers an extensive range of arts activities – film, theatre, dance, music, comedy and children's events. *Open Tue-Sat 10.00-19.00 (Tue 17.00) & Sun 11.00-17.00.*

The Teashop by the Canal, Kennet & Avon Canal Trust, The Wharf, Newbury RG14 5AS (01635 522609; www.teashopbythecanal.co.uk). Canal shop and exhibition. Books, gifts, souvenirs, maps and information. Picnic area, tea, coffee, light refreshments. A place for a chat and the opportunity to find out more about the canal in Newbury. *Open daily 09.30-16.30.*

Crane beside the Navigation in Newbury

Newbury Fair Northcroft Lane, Northcroft, Newbury RG14 5BT. Leave canal at Kennet Bridge. Annual Michaelmas fair held since 1215, on the *Wed following 11 Oct*.

Newbury Buses (01635 33855; www.reading-buses.co.uk/newbury-district). Network of local urban and rural services.

Newbury Racecourse Newbury RG14 7NZ (01635 40015; www.newbury-racecourse.co.uk). *Midweek and weekend racing*. Flat racing *Apr–Sep* and National Hunt Racing *Oct–Mar*. Charge.

Round Barrow Cemetery Wash Common RG14 6PZ (www.historicengland.org.uk/listing/the-list/list-entry/1012811). Near the site of the 1st Battle of Newbury in 1643. Memorial stones to the victims surmount the two smaller mounds.

St Nicolas Church West Mills, Newbury RG14 5HG (01635 47018; www.st-nics.org). Borders the canal on the south bank. A large Perpendicular church, built *c*.1500 at the height of Newbury's prosperity as a wool town. Its 17th-C pulpit is most unusual. *Open Mon-Fri 10.00-15.00 & Sun 10.00-11.30 and 18.00-19.30.* Donations.

St Nicholas School Enborne Road, Newbury RG14 6AH. By Butterfield, 1859.

Watermill Theatre & Restaurant Bagnor, near Newbury RG20 8AE (01635 46044/45834; www.watermill.org.uk). Enterprising theatre, set in an idyllic location, staging a variety of drama, music and musicals, including world premieres. Also licensed restaurant serving snacks and meals for *2 hours before* performances. Box office *open Tue-Sat 13.00-18.00 and Mon on performance days*.

The Living Rainforest Hampstead Norreys, Thatcham, near Newbury RG18 0TN (01635 202444; www.livingrainforest.org). The opportunity to experience the beauty of rainforest plant life under glass. Three climates featuring different plant species and rainforest creatures. Outside play area, shop and café. *Open daily 09.30-15.30*. Charge.

Hamstead Park Old Lane, Hampstead Marshall RG20 0JA (www.berkshiregardenstrust.org/hamstead-park). A very fine park and gardens bordered by the canal. There used to be a castle here and several interesting buildings adjoin the church on the side of the hill. There is an old watermill by the lock. The hamlet of Hamstead Marshall lies to the south, 1½ miles from Hamstead Lock.

Tourist Information Centre The Town Hall, Market Place, Newbury RG14 5AA (01635 30267; www.visitnewbury.org.uk).

Pubs and Restaurants (pages 98-99)

🍺 **1 The Plough on the Green** The Folly, Newbury RG14 7HY (01635 45207; www.ploughonthegreenpub.co.uk). Comfy family-oriented pub. Real ales and food served *daily 12.00-21.00 (Sun 19.00)*. Dog- and family-friendly, garden. Wi-Fi. *Open Mon-Sat 12.00-23.00 (Fri-Sat 00.00) & Sun 12.00-22.30*.

🍺 **2 The Lion** 39 West Street, Newbury RG14 1BD (01635 528468; www.facebook.com/thelionatnewbury). Alcoved areas in the bar give this pub a cosy atmosphere, set off by the wooden floor. Real ale and real cider. Quiz *Thu*. Dog- and family-friendly, patio seating. Traditional pub games, sports TV and Wi-Fi. *Open daily 12.00-23.00 (Fri-Sat 00.00)*.

🍺 **3 The Lock Stock & Barrel** 104 Northbrook Street, Newbury RG14 1AA (01635 580550; www.lockstockandbarrelnewbury.co.uk). Real ale served in a spacious, riverside pub with an attractive terrace. Food available *daily 12.00-20.00 (Sun-Mon 17.00)*. Regular live music. Dog- and child-friendly *(until 21.00)* garden. Dog biscuits and blankets provided. Sports TV and Wi-Fi. *Open Mon-Sat 12.00-23.00 (Fri-Sat 00.00) & Sun 12.00-22.30*.

🍺 **4 The Old Waggon & Horses** 26 Market Place, Newbury RG14 5AG (01635 35081; www.craftunionpubs.com/old-waggon-and-horses-newbury) This pleasant pub has a comfortable terrace with moorings overlooking the river. Real ale. Traditional pub games, sports TV and Wi-Fi. *Open daily 11.00-23.00 (Thu 02.00 and Fri-Sat 03.00)*.

✗ **5 The Teashop by the Canal** The Stone Building, The Wharf, Newbury RG14 5AS (01635 522609; www.teashopbythecanal.co.uk). An old fashioned delight offering teas, coffees, light meals, cakes, sandwiches, ice creams and canal gifts in a relaxed friendly atmosphere. *Open daily 09.00-16.30*.

🍺✗ **6 The Slug & Lettuce** 1-3 Wharf Street, Newbury RG14 5AN (01635 569895; www.facebook.com/Slugandlettuce.Newbury). This spacious building, next to the canal – once the local auction rooms – is now part of a national chain, serving food *daily 12.00-21.00*. Dog- and family-friendly, outside seating. *Open Sat-Thu 12.00-22.00 (Wed-Thu 23.00) & Fri-Sat 12.00-00.00 (Sat 01.00)*.

BOAT TRIPS

Kennet Horse Boat Co. 1 Holt Road, Kintbury RG17 9UY (01488 658866; www.kennet-horse-boat.co.uk). Trips from Kintbury on the horse-drawn and motor barge. *Two hour* public trips *mid Apr–Sep* on the motor barge **Avon** from Newbury Wharf. Also *2 hour* trips from Kintbury on the horse-drawn barge **Kennet Valley**, of varying durations, operating *daily from Easter–Sep*. Tea, coffee, bar and catering facilities on board. Private charter. Telephone for further details. Booking advisable. Also day boat hire available aboard **nb Cygnet** and the opportunity to rent a dog-friendly shepherds hut.

Aldermaston Lift Bridge

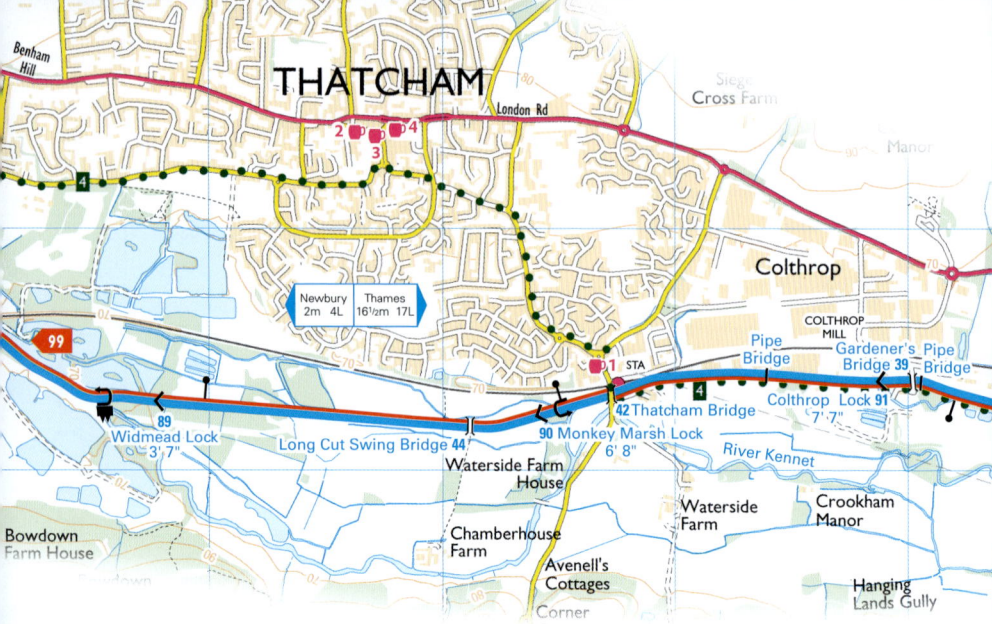

Thatcham

Beyond Bull's Lock and the railway bridge the canal now runs very straight through isolated water meadows towards Thatcham. The village itself is a mile to the north west but the station is conveniently close beside the navigation. This section of the waterway probably best serves to illustrate the wide variety of restoration work jointly undertaken by a consortium made up of county and district councils, job creation programmes, the then British Waterways and the Kennet and Avon Canal Trust, who have been at the forefront of fund raising for more than 30 years. For example, Heale's Lock to the east and Bull's Lock to the west have both been rebuilt with consortium labour, while Widmead Lock was reconstructed to a very high standard by outside contractors at a cost in excess of £385,000. The many swing bridges have either been totally rebuilt or, in some cases, replaced by a high-level structure: Colthrop Bridge being privately funded. Old Monkey Marsh Lock, one of only two remaining examples of a turf-sided lock, has been listed as an ancient monument by Historic England. It is now restored with iron-piling to two feet above low-water level, turf-lined banks sloping to the top of the lock, together with a timber framework to delineate the actual lock chamber when full. The lock should be left empty after use.

● **Thatcham**
Berks. All services. The main square of this rapidly expanding village, now almost a suburb of Newbury, is all but dominated by sprawling housing development. Set back from the A4, it manages to retain some peace which carries over into the nearby cluster of older buildings grouped at the east end of the pretty Victorian church and churchyard.

Nature Discovery Centre Muddy Lane, Lower Way, Thatcham RG19 3FU (01635 874381; www.bbowt.org.uk). North of Widmead Lock. A centre for the study of the unique lake and reed bed habitats of the area, rare moths and large Reed and Sedge Warbler populations. A multi-activity base where children (and adults) can make their own discoveries and have the chance to get a bird's eye view of the world. Shop, café, outdoor play and picnic areas. Toilets. *Open Tue-Sun 10.00-17.30. Donations.*

• **Woolhampton**
Berks. Station. A village on the A4 that owes its existence to the days of mail coaches on the old Bath road. There is a good mixture of buildings in the main street, including several pubs and hotels. Up on the hill to the north of the village are the Victorian church, the Georgian buildings of Woolhampton Park and Douai Abbey and School, the latter a fine group of 19th-C buildings with more recent additions.

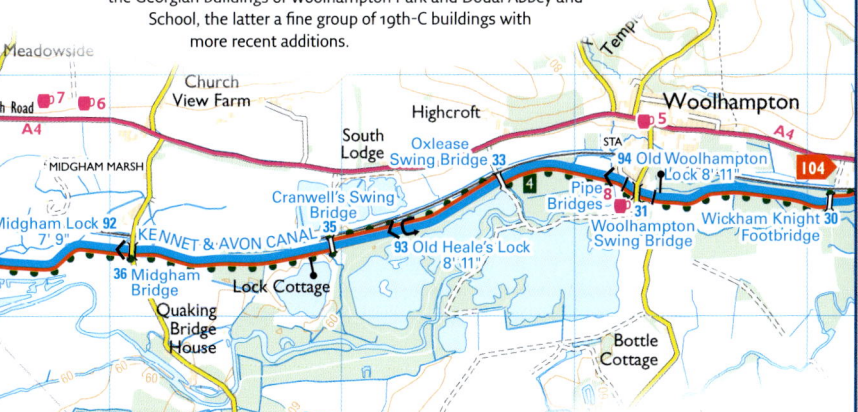

NAVIGATIONAL NOTES

Woolhampton Lock The current below the lock can cause problems, so take care! When approaching **upstream** set the lock before swinging the bridge, head into the current, turning into the lock at the last moment. When coming **downstream** swing the bridge before leaving the tail of the lock and aim straight for the skewed bridge. **Ensure that the bridge is fully open.**

Pubs and Restaurants

1 The Swan Station Road, Thatcham RG19 4QL (01635 862084; www.swanpubthatcham.co.uk). Food *L and E*. Real ales. Outside seating. Children and dogs welcome. B&B. *Open 11.30-23.00 (Sat-Sun 12.00-00.00).*

2 The Crickets 24 High Street, Thatcham RG19 3JD (01635 862113; www.facebook.com/cricketsph). Real ales are served in a pub that takes sport very seriously: a cricket and a football team are based at this establishment. No children or dogs. Garden and sports TV. *Open Mon-Thu 11.00-23.00 & Fri-Sun 11.00-01.00 (Sun 00.00).*

3 The White Hart 2 High Street, Thatcham RG19 3JD (01635 863251; www.facebook.com/Whitehartthatcham). Old coaching inn, dating back more than 350 years. Real ales. Food served *L and E*. Dog- and child-friendly, patio. Quiz *Mon* and live music *Sat*. Real fires. B&B. *Open daily 12.00-23.00 (Fri-Sat 00.00).*

4 The Kings Head 59 The Broadway, Thatcham RG19 3HP (01189 304 2655). Reputedly, it was here that Britain's first mail coach changed horses in 1724. Today this community pub serves real ale and food *L and E*. Dog- and family-friendly, outside seating. Traditional pub games and sports TV. *Open daily 12.00-23.00 (Fri-Sat 00.00).*

5 The Angel Inn Bath Road, Woolhampton RG7 5RT (0118 971 3827; www.angelwoolhampton.co.uk). An imposing ivy-clad building in the centre of the village. Award-winning restaurant *L and E*. Dog-friendly, garden. Real fires, sports TV and Wi-Fi. *Open daily 12.00-23.00.*

6 The Coach and Horses Bath Road, Midgham RG7 5UX (0118 971 3384; www.facebook.com/TheCoachandHorsesMidgham). A traditional pub and restaurant, serving a wide range of food to suit all tastes. Food available *Mon-Sun L and E (not Sun E)*. Family-friendly, garden. Real Fires. *Open Tue-Sat 11.30-22.00 (Sat 22.15) & Sun 12.00-18.00.*

7 The Berkshire Arms Bath Road, Midgham, RG7 5UX (0118 467 7617; www.chefandbrewer.com/pubs/berkshire/berkshire-arms). A rustic, former farmhouse, dating back to the 18th C, serving traditional pub food including *Sunday roasts*, classic seasonal specials, fine wine and real ales. Food *daily 07.00-21.00 (Sat-Sun 08.00)* and real ale. Family-friendly, garden. Wi-Fi. B&B. *Open 07.00-23.00 (Sun 22.30).*

8 The Rowbarge Station Road, Woolhampton RG7 5SH (0118 971 2213; www.brunningandprice.co.uk/rowbarge). Popular canalside pub offering both restaurant and bar food *daily 12.00-21.00*. Real ale and real cider. Dog- and family-friendly, large riverside garden. Newspapers, real fires and Wi-Fi. Mooring. *Open 11.30-23.00 (Sun 22.30).*

Aldermaston

At Aldermaston Wharf there is a mechanically operated lift bridge carrying a busy road into the Village. There is also ample car parking for the attractive canal-side *tearooms, shop* and *Information Centre* (0118 971 2868; www.kennetandavonaldermaston.co.uk) which are open all the year round. The navigation remains close to the railway and A4 which have both shared its course for many miles. The canal heads north east, constantly joining and rejoining the River Kennet. The moorings at Tyle Mill are administered, together with many others on this waterway, by CRT: telephone 0303 040 4040 for further details. Beyond Tyle Mill are a series of gravel pits, excavated since 1960, which offer an undisturbed habitat for all forms of wildlife. The nature reserves of Cumber Lake to the north and Woolwich Green Lake to the south can both be reached by a short walk from Sulhamstead Lock. A pleasant, tree-lined straight cut takes the navigation through wooded fields towards Sulhamstead. Further woods and pasture land lead to Theale Swing Bridge; the village is 3/4 mile to the north. Fortunately, since the completion of the M4, this bridge has reverted to carrying relatively infrequent road vehicles, so the passage of a boat no longer causes a major traffic hold-up.

Boatyards

Ⓑ**Froud's Bridge Marina** Froud's Lane, Aldermaston RG7 4LH (0118 971 4508/07529 247751; www.froudsbridgemarina.co.uk). 🏠🎁⛽DE Pump out, gas, overnight mooring, long-term mooring, winter storage, boat sales, toilets, showers, chandlery, books, maps, gifts, solid fuel, engineering, floating dry dock, paint dock, Wi-Fi, CCTV. *Open daily 09.00-17.00.*

Ⓑ**ABC Leisure** Aldermaston Wharf, Padworth, Reading RG7 4JS (0118 971 4123; www.aldermastonwharf.com). 🏠🎁 ⛽DE Pump out, gas, narrowboat hire, solid fuel, cranage facilities, hard standing, DIY facilities, short and long term mooring, shop, chandlery, books, maps and gifts, boat sales and repairs, engine sales and repairs. *Open daily 08.30-17.00.*

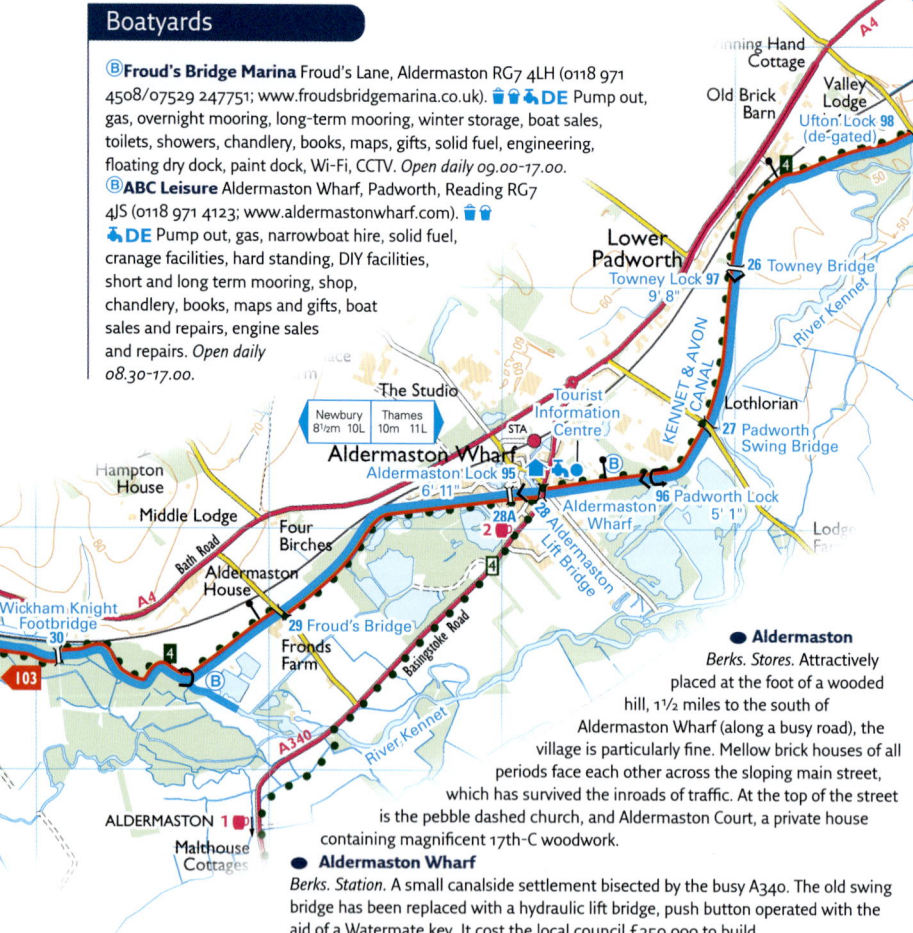

● **Aldermaston**
Berks. Stores. Attractively placed at the foot of a wooded hill, 1½ miles to the south of Aldermaston Wharf (along a busy road), the village is particularly fine. Mellow brick houses of all periods face each other across the sloping main street, which has survived the inroads of traffic. At the top of the street is the pebble dashed church, and Aldermaston Court, a private house containing magnificent 17th-C woodwork.

● **Aldermaston Wharf**
Berks. Station. A small canalside settlement bisected by the busy A340. The old swing bridge has been replaced with a hydraulic lift bridge, push button operated with the aid of a Watermate key. It cost the local council £250,000 to build.

Kennet & Avon Canal
Aldermaston

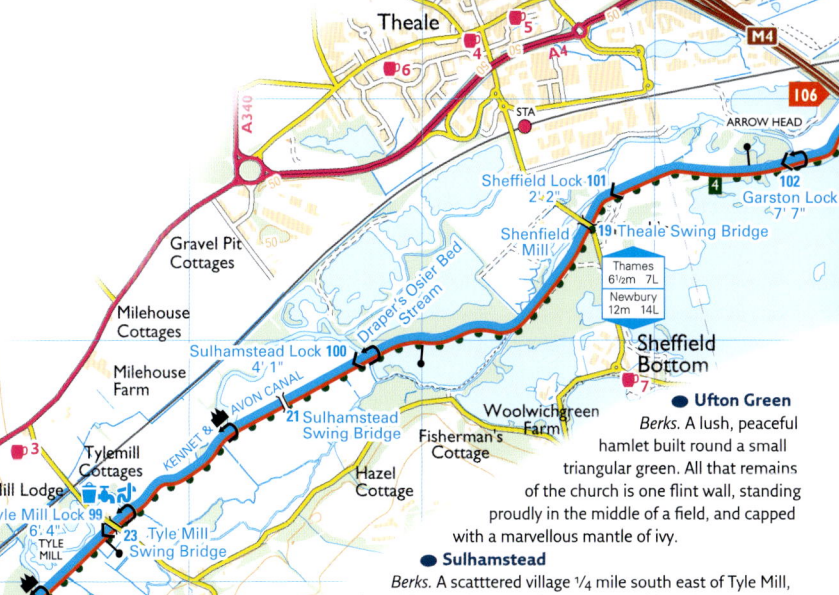

Ufton Green
Berks. A lush, peaceful hamlet built round a small triangular green. All that remains of the church is one flint wall, standing proudly in the middle of a field, and capped with a marvellous mantle of ivy.

Sulhamstead
Berks. A scatttered village ¼ mile south east of Tyle Mill, but with no real centre. There are several large houses standing in their own grounds; the most impressive is Folly Farm, built by Lutyens in 1906 in a William and Mary style. In 1912 Lutyens extended the house, this time using a Tudor style. The mixture of the two periods is most successful. The house is private.

Theale
Berks. PO, stores, chemist, takeaways, off-licence, garage, station. ¾ mile north of swing bridge. Although largely a Reading suburb, Theale has been given a new lease of life by the opening of the bypass and the M4 motorway. The main street is now quiet and relatively traffic free, and the Georgian terraces can be enjoyed. The large church with its tall tower is interesting. It was designed by E.W. Garbett and built 1820-32 in a style based entirely on Salisbury Cathedral. Theale station is half way between the town and Theale swing bridge. *Stores open daily 06.00-22.00.*

Pubs and Restaurants

▶✕ **1 The Hind's Head** Wasing Lane, Aldermaston RG7 4LX (0118 971 2194; www.hindsheadaldermaston.co.uk) An imposing Grade II listed building which faces up the main street. Formerly the Congreve Arms, until it changed hands following the devastation of a great fire. Real ale. Breakfast *Mon-Fri 07.00-11.00; Sat-Sun 08.00-10.00 (Sun 09.30)* & food *daily L and E (not Sun E)*. Dog- and family-friendly, impressive garden. Quiz *Thu*. Real fires and Wi-Fi. B&B. *Open Mon-Sat 07.00-23.00 (Sat 08.00) & Sun 08.00-21.00.*

▶✕ **2 The Butt Inn** Aldermaston Wharf, Station Road, Aldermaston RG7 4LA (0118 996 4216; www.thebuttinn.com). Charming old hostelry dispensing real ale and appetising food *daily 12.00-21.00 (Sun 17.00)*. Family-friendly, garden. Wi-Fi. B&B. *Open 12.00-23.00 (Sun 22.30).*

▶✕ **3 The Spring Inn** Bath Road, Sulhamstead RG7 5HP (0118 930 3440; www.thespringinn.co.uk). Pub/restaurant serving real ale, bar meals and à la carte menu. Food available *Mon-Fri L and E & Sat-Sun 12.00-21.00 (Sun 20.00)* together with afternoon tea *daily*. Dog- and family-friendly, garden. Wi-Fi. *Open 11.00-23.00 (Sun 22.30).*

▶ **4 The Crown Inn** 2 Church Street, Theale RG7 5BT (0118 930 2333; www.thecrowninntheale.co.uk). A characterful, community pub dispensing real ale and food *Tue-Sun L and E (not Sun E)*. Dog- and family-friendly, garden with covered area. Traditional pub games, sports TV and Wi-Fi. *Open Mon-Sat 11.00-23.30 & Sun 12.00-22.00.*

▶ **5 The Falcon** 31 High Street, Theale RG7 5AH (0118 930 2523). Grade II listed 18th-C pub, sporting several friendly ghosts who appear to bar staff and customers alike from time to time. Real ales. Dog- and child-friendly *(until 20.30)* beer garden. Traditional pub games, real fires, sports TV and Wi-Fi. B&B. *Open Mon-Thu 14.00-23.00 & Fri-Sun 12.00-23.00 (Sun 22.30).*

▶ **6 The Volunteer** 65 Church Street, Theale RG7 5BX (0118 930 2917; www.thevolunteertheale.co.uk). Large, friendly pub serving real ales and appetising food *Mon-Sat L and E (not Sat E) & Sun 12.00-17.00*. Dog- and family-friendly, attractive garden. Traditional pub games, real fires and sports TV. *Open Mon-Sat 12.00-23.00 (Fri-Sat 00.00) & Sun 12.00-22.00.*

▶✕ **7 The Fox & Hounds** Sheffield Bottom, Station Road, Theale, RG7 4BE (0118 930 2295; www.butcombe.com/the-fox-hounds-berkshire). 200-year old traditional rural pub dispensing real ale and food *daily 12.00-21.00 (Sun 19.00)*. Quiz *Sun*. Dog- and family-friendly, garden. Real fires and Wi-Fi. *Open 11.30-23.00 (Fri-Sat 23.30).*

Reading

The M4 motorway and the railway inevitably affect the peace and quiet of this section, although almost to the outskirts of Reading the gravel pits bring a degree of serenity. The Kennet winds through water meadows, the straight stretches marking the canal sections. Continuing east, the navigation passes Burghfield Bridge, a handsome stone arch. The river gradually approaches the town, descending Fobney Lock and passing through Fobney Meadow, before beginning to wriggle its way through the outskirts. At County Lock the navigation passes over a low weir which at times of fresh water can become quite ferocious. Rows of riverside cottages and a surprising variety of bridges decorate the Kennet in Reading, High Bridge being the most central access point. The river cuts across the middle of the town and so access to all facilities is easy. However, the waterway through Reading is narrow, shallow and fast flowing, being a river navigation; also there are several sharp blind bends (now reduced as a result of the Oracle Development, *see* page 108).
This section is controlled by traffic lights – boaters should not proceed until a green light is displayed. A variety of new developments complement the river's passage through this part of the town.

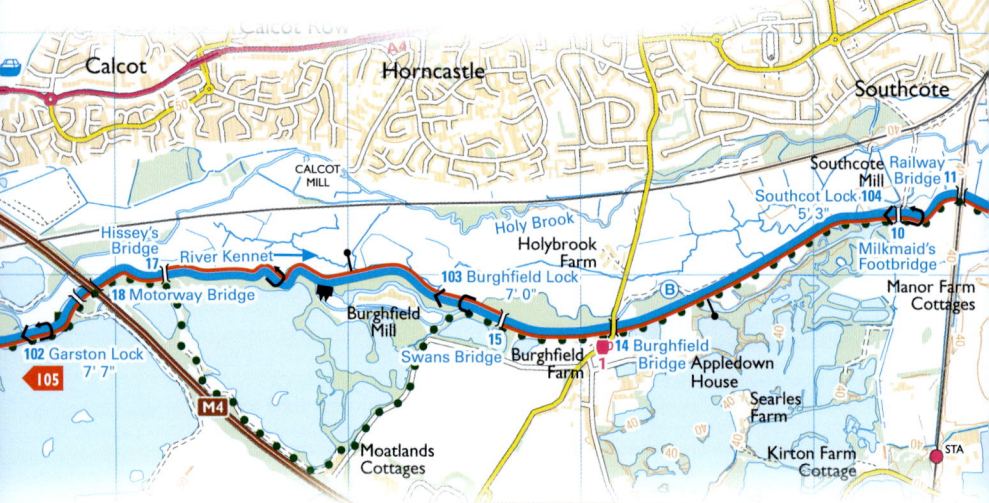

The Kennet leads north east out of the centre of Reading, passing Blake's Lock, the only lock maintained by the Environment Agency that is not actually on the Thames which was once marked by a prominent gasometer and the main railway, which runs parallel with the south bank of the river.

> **WALKING AND CYCLING**
> The towpath varies, generally good through urban areas, weather dependent in rural areas. Sections bordering the river navigation can become very overgrown in the height of the summer. It is becoming a popular long distance route for walkers and cyclists alike and the latter are asked to exercise care and give way to people on foot.

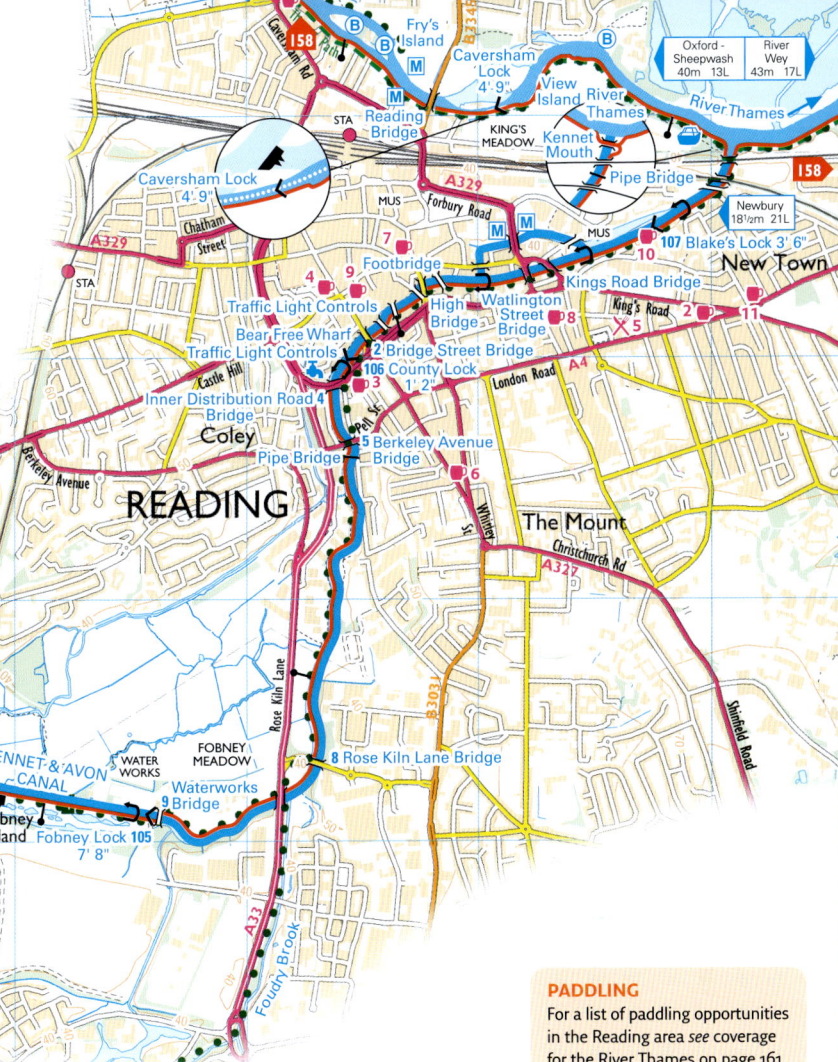

Kennet & Avon Canal — Reading

PADDLING

For a list of paddling opportunities in the Reading area *see* coverage for the River Thames on page 161.

NAVIGATIONAL NOTES

1. *See* Navigational notes on page 70 before heading west from Reading.
2. **Fobney Lock** – care should be taken when using the landing stage below the lock as a strong weir stream flows at right angles.
3. To operate County Lock 106 it is advisable to first moor under the Inner Distribution Road Bridge, on the east side, to drop off crew to set the lock. Once prepared, power into the lock to avoid being swept to the west side of the river, towards the weir and away from the lock entrance.
4. River Thames licences are obtainable from the Environment Agency (*see* page 110).
5. For up-to-date information on lock closures, the Thames winter works programme and flood conditions, visit www.gov.uk/guidance/river-thames-current-river-conditions.

The River Kennet running through the Oracle Shopping Centre in Reading

● **Reading**
Berks. All services. The town lies at the extremity of the Berkshire Downs and the Chiltern Hills, where the Thames becomes a major river. It is the Victorian architecture that makes this town interesting, as the university buildings are not to everyone's taste. Since completion of the Oracle Development, in the centre of Reading, the towpath along the Kennet is continuous from the Thames throughout the town.
Abbey Ruins Abbey Street, Reading RG1 3BA (0118 937 3400; www.readingmuseum.org.uk/your-visit/abbey-quarter/abbey-ruins). Fragmentary remains of this 12th-C abbey built by Henry I lie on the edge of Forbury Park. The 13th-C gatehouse, altered by Scott in 1869, still stands. *Open dawn to dusk.* Free.
Reading Gaol Forbury Road, Reading RG1 3JD (0118 937 3400; www.readingmuseum.org.uk/blog/very-short-history-reading-gaol). Designed by by Scott and Moffatt in 1842–44 in the Scottish Baronial style. Oscar Wilde wrote *De Profundis* while imprisoned here.
Reading Museum The Town Hall, Blagrave Street, Reading RG1 1QH (0118 937 3400; www.readingmuseum.org.uk). Features *The Story of Reading*, tracing the town's development from a Saxon settlement on the River Kennet to the present day. Special features include a reconstructed section of the abbey and the Oracle gates entrance to the 17th-C workhouse. In the upper gallery is a full 230ft sweep of Britain's Bayeux Tapestry, Reading's faithful replica of the 11th-C original. *Open Tue-Sat 10.00-16.00 (Sat 17.00).* Donations.
Museum of English Rural Life University of Reading, Redlands Road, Reading RG1 5EX (0118 378 8660; https://merl.reading.ac.uk). All aspects of rural life in England as it was lived around 150 to 175 years ago, before the invention of the tractor. *Open Tue-Sun 09.00-17.00 (Sat-Sun 10.00).* Free.

Riverside Museum Blakes Lock, off Kenavon Drive, Reading RG1 3DH (0118 939 9800; www.readingmuseum.org.uk). Attractive museum in the city's old sewerage pumping station, originally constructed in 1873 when the disposal of local sewerage was described as being 'very imperfect and unsatisfactory; injurious to public health'. Today the museum explores the story of Reading's two rivers and displays a gipsy caravan constructed on the banks of the Kennet. The old turbine house offers panoramic views out over the river. *Open Apr-Sep daily 10.00-18.00. Free.*

South Street Arts Centre 21 South Street, Reading RG1 4QU (0118 960 6060; www.facebook.com/southstreetarts). A wide-ranging programme of music (all types) workshops and drama in a lively arts centre.

The Hexagon Queen's Walk, Reading RG1 7UA (0118 960 6060; www.whatsonreading.com/hexagon). Mainstream theatre, pantomime, films, shows and art exhibitions.

Reading Buses (0118 959 4000; www.readingbuses.co.uk). Information on urban and rural services. *Available Mon-Fri 09.00-17.00.*

Tourist Information Visit www.visit-reading.com/visitor-info/tourist-information.

Pubs and Restaurants (pages 106-107)

1 The Cunning Man Burghfield Road, Burghfield Bridge RG30 3RB (0118 959 8067; www.facebook.com/cunningmanburghfield). Country pub and restaurant with large canalside garden serving real ale and food *Mon-Fri 12.00-22.00 & Sat-Sun 09.00-22.00 (Sun 21.30)*. Dog- and family-friendly. Quiz *Thu*. Real fires and Wi-Fi. *Open Mon-Fri 11.30-23.00 & Sat-Sun 09.00-23.00 (Sun 22.30).*

2 The Hope and Bear 151-153 London Road, Reading RG1 5DE (0118 935 4095; www.hopeandbearreading.co.uk). Thriving gastropub serving real ale, real cider and food *daily 12.00-22.00 (Sun 21.00)*. Dog- and child-friendly, garden. Live music *Fri*. Traditional pub games, real fires, sports TV and Wi-Fi. *Open 12.00-23.00 (Fri-Sat 00.00).*

3 The Hook & Tackle (Namaste Kitchen) Kategrove Lane, Reading RG1 2ND (0118 950 5221; www.hookandtacklereading.pub.co.uk). Situated below the noise from Reading's overzealous flirtation with the motor car, this pub offers sanctuary, together with a selection of real ales. Majoring on Nepalese food served *daily 11.00-22.00*. Regular live music. Family-friendly. Traditional pub games, newspapers and Wi-Fi. *Open 11.00-23.00.*

4 The Sweeney & Todd 10 Castle Street (off St Mary's Butts), Reading RG1 7RD (0118 958 6466; www.sweeneyandtodd.co.uk). Something of a local institution - a pub integrated with a pie shop and dispensing real ale. Excellent, inexpensive food *Tue-Sat 12.00-20.30 (Tue 16.00)*. Family-friendly. *Open Tue-Sat 12.00-20.30 (Tue 16.00).*

5 Piwnica Restaurant 81 London Road, Reading RG1 5BY (0118 958 9908/07831 851434; www.piwnica.co.uk). Welcoming, family-run establishment offering a tasty trip through a selection of appetising Polish cooking, exploring a wide range of national dishes. Children welcome. Their website is a wee gem of a scene-setter! Takeaway service. *Open Thu-Sun 12.00-22.00.*

6 The Hop Leaf 163-165 Southampton Street, Reading RG1 2QZ (0118 931 4700; www.hopback.co.uk). Thriving town local, serving a selection of their own real ales and real cider. Dog- and child-friendly *(until 19.00)* outside seating. Traditional pub games, sports TV and Wi-Fi. *Open Mon-Thu 16.00-23.00 & Fri-Sun 12.00-00.30 (Sun 23.00).*

7 The Alehouse 2 Broad Street, Reading RG1 2BH (0118 950 8119). Untouched old-school atmosphere with bare boards, alcove booths, real ales real ciders, perries and mead. Dog- and family-friendly. Traditional pub games and sports TV. *Open Mon-Sat 11.00-23.00 (Fri 00.00) & Sun 12.00-22.30.*

8 The Retreat 8 St John's Street, Reading RG1 4EH (0118 957 2130; www.theretreat.pub). Known for its fiercely-fought pickled onion competition and *regular* live music, this pub serves real ales and a good selection of bottled beers and ciders. You can take your own food. Family-friendly. Traditional pub games, newspapers and sports TV. *Open Mon-Sat 12.00-23.00 (Fri-Sat 23.30) & Sun 12.00-22.30.*

9 Zerodegrees 9 Bridge Street, Reading RG1 2LR (0118 959 7959; www.zerodegrees.co.uk). Constructed around a micro brewery, this open plan pub serves a range of their own real ales together with pizzas from a wood-fired oven and food that compliments their beer, available *daily 12.00-22.00*. Customers can sit on comfy sofas and imbibe the aromas emanating from the shiny brewing vessels, admiring the exposed beams and ducting. Dog- and family-friendly, outside seating. Live music *Fri*. Wi-Fi. *Open 12.00-00.00 (Sun 23.30).*

10 The Fisherman's Cottage 224 Kennet Side, Reading RG1 3DW (07925 336269; https://thefishermanscottagepubreading.co.uk). Gastropub serving Mediterranean and Asian selections, alongside traditional pub favourites - *Tue-Sun 12.00-22.00 (Sun 19.00)* - together with real ale. Dog- and child-friendly *(until 20.00)* outside seating. Regular live music. Quiz *Tue*. Traditional pub games, real fires and Wi-Fi. *Open Tue-Thu 12.00-23.00 (Tue 16.00) & Fri-Sun 12.00-00.00 (Sun 22.00).*

11 Up The Junction 231 London Road, Reading RG1 3NY (0118 926 0544; www.facebook.com/UptheJunctionRDG). Makes a lot of noise for a small place but its 3 am licence offers bottled beer drinking into the *wee small hours*. Live music *Wed*. Sports TV and Wi-Fi. *Open Mon-Sat 17.00-02.00 (Fri-Sat 03.00).*

RIVER OUSE

MAXIMUM DIMENSIONS
Newhaven to Hamsey Weir
Length: unlimited
Beam: 10' (16' to Lewes)
Draught: 3' (low tide)
Headroom: 8' (Lewes Railway Bridge)

MILEAGE
Newhaven Harbour Mouth to:
Newhaven Swing Bridge: 1 mile
Piddinghoe: 2½ miles
Southease Swing Bridge: 4¼ miles
Lewes Bridge: 8 miles
Lewes Corporation Bridge & Phoenix Wharf: 8¼ miles
Hamsey Lock (site of): 9½ miles

NAVIGATION AUTHORITIES
Newhaven Port & Properties Ltd
East Quay
Newhaven
BN9 0BN
01273 616070
admin@newhavenport.com

Environment Agency
National Customer Contact Centre
PO Box 544
Rotherham
S60 1BY
03708 506 506
enquiries@environment-agency.gov.uk

Paddling: No licence required. Category 1 above Barcombe Mills. Category 2 (and above) on the tidal section below Barcombe Mills, south to the sea. *Below Lewes landing can be difficult (see Navigational Notes on page 120) and flows can run at 7 - 8 knots.*

By the close of the 18th C, with the country in the throes of canal mania, several local Sussex businessmen looked at ways in which they might invest to improve the efficiency of river transport along the Ouse. For centuries boats had navigated the eight and a half-mile tidal stretch of the river, while its tortuous course above Lewes had proved totally unsuitable for reliable water-borne traffic.

In 1787 William Jessop was invited to produce a survey with a view to extending navigation up to Slaugham and between 1790 and 1814 several Acts were passed to promote traffic on the upper stretches of the river.

The 1790 Act saw the formation of a company of proprietors and work was commenced. Progress was slow and inevitably costs soon escalated above the initial estimates, the work finally being completed around 22 years later. By then it was possible to reach Balcombe, some 22 miles and 19 locks above Lewes.

As an extremely rural navigation, traffic was primarily limited to lime, chalk and manure (the former from the heavy Wealden hinterland) together with aggregates for road construction and coal for domestic use and lime burning.

At its most successful there were over 50 barges on the navigation, almost half of them trading above Lewes. However, the waterway was never a great commercial success due to the management being lax, maintenance poor and a somewhat lackadaisical attitude to collecting tolls.

There was a relatively brief flurry of industrial activity at Isfield, with the establishment of a paper mill and expansion of the corn mill, to the point where a population of over 40 souls was recorded, but by 1855 the former had closed down and the workers' cottages sold off, later to be demolished. Other paper mills operated at Lewes, Sharpsbridge and Lindfield. Inevitable railway competition in the area brought decline from the middle of the 19th C onwards, something that reduced tolls was unable to combat. By 1868 there was no trade above Lewes and locks began their slow, mouldering decay into the obscurity we find today. However, until the 1950s Thames barges traded regularly to cement works in Lewes.

The river is now managed by the Environment Agency as a source of drinking water, a conduit for treated sewerage and for drainage of the local area. The remains of most of the old locks are still visible and the Sussex Ouse Restoration Trust (www.sxouse.org.uk/V2018/index.php) are actively looking after the navigation's interests.

With the exception of easily-portaged small craft, there is little water-borne activity on the river above Lewes today, but the Sussex Ouse Valley provides one of the most stunning long-distance walks in the south of England and, wherever possible, follows the course of the river from infancy to tidal toreador.

WALKING AND CYCLING

The Sussex Ouse Valley Way is a long-distance walk which represents by far the best means of sampling the splendid scenery that flanks this outstandingly beautiful Sussex waterway. Riparian rights have long ago superseded those inferred by navigation and the needs of the ambling horse, so it is no longer possible to follow the river bank at every stage. However, an excellent guide, penned by Terry Owen & Peter Anderson (second edition published 2012 by Per-Rambulations, www.per-rambulations.co.uk) ensures that the walker is led seamlessly along the entire 42-mile route from Lower Beeding to Seaford: an extent well beyond the scope of this guide.

The tidal stretch of waterway running Newhaven to Lewes – one suited to cycling and walking – is covered by the Egret's Way (www.egretsway.org.uk/route). This is still a work in progress as some of the land is proving difficult to acquire, particularly in the Piddinghoe area. To avoid stretches of the busy, narrow minor road, the path makes a couple of excursions west of the river to avoid these obstructions, whilst keeping pedestrians and cyclists to the confines of quiet country lanes. The scenery more than compensates for the additional mileage incurred!

To help with the planning of walking routes in the wider area, it is well-worth turning up in person at the Tourist Information Centres in either Seaford or Lewes: both are a fund of information. A virtual visit by the walker to Walking in the South Downs (www.southdowns.gov.uk/get-active/south-downs-walks) to Sussex Downs Walks (www.eastdeanvillage.org.uk/walks.html) to the Long Man's Walking Guide to Sussex (www.longmaninn.co.uk/products/20-sussex-walks) or to Walking Britain (www.walkingbritain.co.uk/South-Downs-walks) will be equally well rewarded. The starting point for the cyclist, as always, is www.sustrans.org.uk for information on the National Cycle Network, while for off-road routes, bridleways and the like – covered by printed leaflets, books and maps – visit www.eastsussex.gov.uk/leisure-tourism/discover-east-sussex/walks-east-sussex-map and www.southdowns.gov.uk/get-active/by-bike-horseback/cycling. For guided outdoor activities in the area contact So Sussex (07739 050816; www.sosussex.co.uk). Cycle hire is available from Sussex Bike Hire (07732 202208; www.sussexbikehire.com) *open daily 09.00-17.00* amongst others.

The stretch of cliffs running Brighton to Newhaven go to make up a 414-acre biological and geological SSSI while the span Peacehaven Cliffs to Newhaven's Castle Hill is an important fossil site. This can be accessed by walking down the steep Bastion Steps BN10 8LT or via a ramp at the west end BN10 7RS. The ancient village of Telscombe lies approximately 3 miles inland from the cliffs at Peacehaven but has no metalled road access. It can be approached on foot or by bicycle across the bridleways of Telscombe Tye BN2 8DY – an area of common land running north from the A259. With a population of no more than 50 inhabitants, its picturesque buildings nestle beside its 10th-C St Lawrence's church BN7 3HZ. There are no pubs or shops.

For cycle rides in the Peacehaven area see the *South Downs Cycle Rides* leaflet published by South Downs National Park (01730 814810; www.southdowns.gov.uk/wp-content/uploads/2016/02/South-Downs-Leaflet-Peacehaven-cycle-rides.pdf).

NAVIGATIONAL NOTES

1. It is possible to navigate from Newhaven to Lewes on the tide and small craft that can be portaged may, with difficulty, be able to continue up river above the double locks at Barcombe.
2. The river is tidal and navigable at high water to Lewes Bridge but this is for experienced, sea-going boaters only as at half-tide, in the area of Southease Swing Bridge, the stream runs at 7 – 8 knots.
3. High water at Lewes is approximately one hour after high water Newhaven, which is about two minutes after high water Dover.
4. Spring tides can rise by as much as 10' 0".

Piddinghoe

Industry and general port movement make the journey north out of Newhaven interesting, adding colour, bustle and varied activity. On the east bank is the ferry port and usually a ship loading scrap metal or other materials for recycling. The western bank is generally more domestically urban, with the marina and town dominating. This is followed by the swing bridge, the artificial Denton Island, another marina and the futuristic recycling works that struggled against considerable local opposition ahead of its final construction. Soon the navigation leaves the town behind, striking a fairly determined course for Piddinghoe and the open countryside. The colourful sails of the dinghies zig zagging across the sailing lake, framed by a bend in the river, provide further interest and activity before the squat outline of Southease Swing Bridge comes into view. This is the area where private ownership of the river's west bank requires a diversion and, rather than risk the traffic of the narrow (and extraordinarily busy) minor road, it is wise to follow the waymarked Sussex Ouse Valley Way.

- **Seaford**

Sussex. PO, stores, takeaways, fish & chips, chemist, off-licence, baker, butcher, library, garage, cinema, station. A port of some importance in the Middle Ages, Seaford fell into decline due to repeated raids by French pirates and sedimentation from coastal erosion. In medieval times its fortunes revived when it became one of the south coast Cinque Ports, although the French continued with their incendiary attacks. The 16th C saw the inhabitants gain considerable notoriety and the nickname 'cormorants' owing to their enthusiastic looting of ships wrecked in the bay, some reputed to have been lured to their doom by false lights placed on the cliffs. The 19th C, with the coming of the railway, saw the town's fortunes in the ascendency in its rôle as a seaside destination and, more recently, a dormitory town for Eastbourne, Brighton and London.

Crypt Gallery 23 Church Street, Seaford BN25 1HD (www.facebook.com/CryptGallerySeaford). Gallery set in what is reputed to be a medieval merchants wine cellar. Flint gallery, undercroft and front room providing an exciting space to host international and local artists and makers. Also used as a performance space. *Open daily 10.00-17.00.*

The Barn Theatre Saxon Lane, Seaford BN25 1QL (01323 492240; www.seafordcinema.org and www.seafordmusicaltheatre.org). Home to local theatricals and meeting a demand for local cinema. Worth patronising to see a show or film during your visit.

Crouch Gardens East Street, Seaford BN25 1PX. Peaceful walled garden and open space on the site of the former medieval market.

Mr Cycles 26 Clinton Place, Seaford BN25 1NP (01323 893130; www.mrcycles.co.uk). The home of good, old-fashioned service, spares and repairs, together with advice on where to cycle in the surrounding area. *Open 09.00-17.30 but closed Wed, Sun & B Hols.*

Seaford Museum Martello Tower 74, The Esplanade, Seaford BN25 1JH (01323 898222; www.seafordmuseum.co.uk). Completed in 1810, and built to keep Napoleon out, this was one of several Martello towers constructed on the south coast between Aldeburgh and Eastbourne. Redundant even before completion, the fortification went on to see active service in both World Wars as an observation tower and machine gun post. Surprisingly large inside, the tower was remodelled in 2018 to provide a visitor experience and house a range of displays and exhibits from Seaford's long history as a significant Cinque Port. Memories and reminiscences well catered for! *Open Sat-Sun & Wed 11.00-16.00.* Charge.

Tide Mills Marine Parade, Seaford BN25 2QR. Site of a tide mill driven by water impounded in a brackish lagoon. The mill complex, destroyed in 1900, included a windmill and parts of the building together with the mill race are still visible. There was also a sizeable settlement here which was condemned as unfit for habitation in 1936 and abandoned three years later. Today this is one of the few beaches in the area free from development and therefore popular with wild swimmers.

Tourist Information Centre 37 Church Street, Seaford BN25 1HG (01323 897426; www.staylewes.org). *Open Mon-Fri 09.00-16.00.*

Travel: by train 0845 748 4950; www.nationalrail.co.uk; by car ferry service via DFDS Ferries on the Newhaven – Dieppe route 0871 574 7235; www.dfds.com/en; www.nationalexpress.com/en and the local bus network Compass Travel 01903 264077; www.compass-travel.co.uk. Further information is available from the excellent Tourist Information Centres in the area.

- **Denton**

Sussex. Stores, takeaways, chemist, off-licence, fish & chips, butcher, baker, garage, station (Newhaven Town). Together with Mount Pleasant on the eastern slope of the Downs, Denton is largely a residential area of Newhaven, one that gives its name to the man-made island in the middle of Newhaven Harbour, now an industrial estate. Once connected to the mainland by a toll bridge, villagers were exempt from paying tolls.

- **Newhaven**

Sussex. All services. The River Ouse used to run parallel to the shore behind a shingle bar, meeting the sea close to Seaford. However, a combination of storms in the 16th C and a man-made cut broke

Pubs and Restaurants (pages 114–115)

🍺❌ **1 The Wellington** 33 Steyne Road, Seaford BN25 1HT (01323 899517; www.facebook.com/wellingtonhotelseaford). Sitting on the former quayside of the historic Cinque Port, this substantial pub now dispenses real ale and food *Mon-Thu E & Fri-Sun L and E (not Sun E)*. Dog- and family-friendly, beach close by. Quiz *Wed* and live music *Fri*. Real fires, sports TV and Wi-Fi. *Open daily 12.00-23.00 (Sun 20.00).*

🍺 **2 The Steamworks** Cafe Unit, Seaford Station, Station Approach, Seaford BN25 2AR (01323 895541; www.facebook.com/SteamworksSeaford). Café bar at the station serving a range of local real ales and a selection of ciders. Bar snacks available. Dog- and child-friendly, platform seating. *Open Mon-Fri 18.00-23.00 (Fri 00.00) & Sat-Sun 09.00-00.00 (Sun 22.00).*

🍺 **3 The Old Boot Inn** 16 South Street, Seaford BN25 1PE (01323 895454; www.facebook.com/theoldbootinnseaford). Large pub, close to the church, serving an excellent selection of real ales and a real cider. Food is available *L and E*. Dog- and family-friendly, outside seating. Wi-Fi. *Open Mon-Sat 10.00-23.00 (Fri-Sat 00.00) & Sun 11.00-22.30.*

🍺 **4 Cinque Ports** 49 High Street, Seaford BN25 1PP (01323 892106; www.cinqueportspub.com). Friendly, locals' town pub with somewhat eclectic furniture, dispensing real ale and authentic Thai food *Wed-Sun E*. Dog-friendly. Traditional pub games, real fires and sports TV. *Open daily 11.00-00.00 (Sun 23.30).*

🍺❌ **5 The Flying Fish** Denton Road, Denton, Newhaven BN9 0QB (01273 515440; www.flyingfishdenton.co.uk). Popular, 17th-C whitewashed inn, tucked away in this village extension of Newhaven, serving real ale and food *Wed-Mon 12.00-21.00 (Sun 20.00)*. Its cosy interior attracts walkers, cyclists and French tourists alike, some lingering *overnight* in the adjoining cottage. Dog-friendly, large secluded garden. *Regular* live music and real fires. *Open Wed-Mon 12.00-23.00 (Sun 22.00).*

🍺 **6 The Hampden Arms** Heighton Road, South Heighton BN9 0JJ (01273 514529; www.facebook.com/HampdenArmsSouthHeighton). Friendly local pub serving real ale, real cider and food *Wed-Sun L*. Garden, live music *Fri*, real fires, darts and pool table. *Open Sun-Tue 16.00-22.30 (Sun 12.00) & Wed-Sat 12.00-23.00 (Fri-Sat 23.30).*

🍺 **7 The Hope Inn** West Pier, Newhaven BN9 9DN (01273 515389; www.revivedinns.co.uk/thehope). Close to Newhaven Fort, with a balcony overlooking the harbour entrance, this pub serves real ale, real cider and food *Mon-Fri L and E & Sat-Sun 12.00-21.00 (Sun 20.00)*. Dog- and family-friendly, outside seating. Traditional pub games, real fires and Wi-Fi. *Open 11.00-23.00 (Sun 22.00).*

through the bar at its western end, creating a new river mouth close to the village then called Meeching (or Myching). Part of the former channel of the river remains as a brackish lagoon, the stored water once driving a tide mill. Longshore drift continued to threaten this new, more westerly channel, until the construction of a breakwater under the Ouse Navigation Act of 1790, finally established a 'new haven'. The present breakwater was constructed in 1890. There is a Iron Age fort on Castle Hill and also evidence of later Saxon activity in the area. Today the town is a significant Channel ferry port with freight and passenger ferries operated by DFDS Seaways using 19,000 gross tonne Ro-Ro vessels running to Dieppe. The port is also well-sited to service the 400-megawatt Rampion Wind Farm commissioned in April 2018.

Ho Chi Minh Memorial West Quay, Newhaven BN9 9GG. Born on 18th May 1890, the former Vietnamese Communist leader worked as a pastry chef on the Newhaven-Dieppe ferry in the years following WWI.

Newhaven Fort Fort Road, Newhaven BN19 9DS (01323 517622; www.newhavenfort.org.uk). Victorian fortification with substantial ramparts and a vast network of tunnels and subterranean passages. Range of military artefacts on display and the chance to see a realistic air raid recreation in the Blitz Bomb Shelter beside the Home Front exhibition. The young at heart can run, climb and swing their way around the activity playground. 1940s-themed tearoom. Changing programme of activities for children and special events for the whole family. Also, the opportunity to uncover the truth behind Newhaven's Iron Age fort. Gift shop. *Open daily mid-Feb-Oct, 10.00-17.00. Last admission 16.00. Charge.*

Newhaven Museum Paradise Park Avis Road, Newhaven BN9 0DH (01273 517603/07831 900130; www.newhavenhistoricalsociety.org.uk/visiting-the-museum). Combining Planet Earth Museum, Paradise Gardens, Plant Houses, a heritage trail and a play zone. The Plant Houses reside under a full-scale replica of the Iguanondon fossil found in the Sussex Weald in 1834 and is zoned to include desert, Mediterranean and Australian flora and fauna. An oriental-style garden features Koi carp. Paradise gardens are Newhaven's hidden gem and feature lakes, waterfalls and fountains teaming with fish. The Sussex History Trail meanders through the gardens. Also, a dinosaur safari embraces the sights and sounds of prehistoric times and features an exciting collection of life-sized creatures. An indoor play area and tree top walkways vie with soft play for the under-fives. Plant centre and coffee shop. *Open Fri-Sat & Tue-Wed 11.00-16.00. Charge.*

St Michael's Church Church Hill, Newhaven BN9 9LY (01273 515251; www.stmichaelsnewhaven.com). The early to mid-12th C apse and axial tower remain from the original Meeching church while the remainder, after earlier reconstruction, dates from 1854 and has timber arcades.

Pubs and Restaurants

🍺 **8 The Peacehaven** 295 South Coast Road, Peacehaven BN10 7HX (01273 589332). A chain family-friendly pizza and carvery establishment serving real ale and food *daily 11.00-21.30 (Sat-Sun 11.30)*. Wi-Fi. *Open 08.00-22.00*.

🍺 **9 The White Hart** 17 High Street, Newhaven BN9 9PD (01273 611808; www.whitehartnewhaven.co.uk). Sports-themed, historic pub in the centre of the town, serving real ale and food *Tue-Sun 12.00-20.00 (Sun 17.00)*. Dog-friendly. *Regular* live music, traditional pub games, sports TV and Wi-Fi. *Open Sun-Thu 12.00-23.00 (Sun 22.30) & Fri-Sat 12.00-00.00 (Sat 11.00)*.

🍺✕ **10 The Ark** West Quay, Newhaven BN9 9BP (01273 517808; www.facebook.com/ArkNewhavenSussex). Known for its good-value food, this riverside pub dispenses real ale, a good continental wine selection and sustenance *daily 12.00-22.00*. Family-friendly and outside seating. Traditional pub games and Wi-Fi. *Open 11.00-23.00 (Fri-Sat 00.00)*.

✕🍷 **11 Padella D'oro Restaurant** 12 Bridge Street, Newhaven BN9 9PJ (01273 516334; www.padelladoro.co.uk). Family-run restaurant, offering welcoming friendly service in a relaxed atmosphere, serving all the Italian favourites. Children welcome. Takeaway service. *Open Tue-Sat 17.00-23.00*.

🍺 **12 The Prince of Wales** 49 South Road, Newhaven BN9 9QL (01273 513364). Traditional two-roomed pub with a delightful tiled exterior, run by the same couple for over 20 years, serving real ale. No machines. Traditional pub games and quiet conversation. *Open daily 11.00-23.00*.

✕🍷 **13 Luna Rossa Italian Restaurant** Unit 1 Villandry, West Quay, Newhaven BN9 9GB (01273 515600; www.facebook.com/LunaRossaItalianRestaurant/?locale=en_GB). Traditional Italian cooking with a seafood slant. Children welcome, outside seating. Takeaway service. *Open Tue-Fri 09.00-14.45 and 17.00-21.00 & Sat-Sun 09.00-21.00 (Sun 18.30)*.

🍺 **14 The Avenue Kitchen & Tap** 174 South Coast Road, Peacehaven BN10 8JH (01273 587744; www.theavenuepeacehaven.com). A simple, modern venue, dispensing local and international real ale and no-nonsense café-style food *Wed-Fri 16.00-21.30 (Fri 22.00) & Sat-Sun 13.00-22.00 (Sun 21.30)*.

● **Peacehaven**

Sussex. PO, stores, takeaways, off-licence, chemist, library, garage. Sited at the point where the Greenwich meridian crosses the south coast, the town was established by entrepreneur Charles Neville in 1916, who had purchased land in Piddinghoe and then set up a company to develop it. Initially called Anzac-on-Sea, following a competition to choose the name, Neville renamed it in 1917. First conceived as a place for returning WWI veterans to set up home, the town was laid out in American-style, grid fashion: 'Avenues' running north to south and 'Roads' east to west, with no 'Streets'. Land was cheap and consequently working-class families bought plots in pursuit of fresh sea air and a simple life. By 1924 there were 3,000 people living in Peacehaven in a motley collection of semi-permanent buildings, ranging from former army huts to redundant railway carriages. Some still remain, now clad with concrete blocks but the oblong shape is the giveaway! Eventually the local authority elevated what was becoming a shanty town by providing electricity and running water, together with tarmac roads. Gracie Fields bought a house in Peacehaven overlooking the sea, while the pebble beach can be accessed by stairway and a concrete driveway.

Cormorant Sculpture by Local Artist Christian Funnell

River Ouse — Piddinghoe

- **Piddinghoe**
Sussex. PO box, Farm shop. Sitting beside the tidal Ouse and embracing a sailing lake, it is hardly surprising that Piddinghoe – known also as Pydynghowe in 14th C – was once recognised as an important centre for smuggling. It is home to the last remaining bottle kiln in Sussex and has one of only three Norman churches in the river valley with a round tower. It also had a quarry and a whiting works which relied heavily on the river for coal deliveries.

- **Southease**
Sussex. PO box, station. Home of the second Norman church with a round tower, this is the only river crossing between Newhaven and Lewes. The 1791 Lower Ouse Improvement Act required the ferry to be replaced by a bridge and a wooden cantilever structure was built, replaced by the current swinging design – with wrought iron, bow-string trusses – in 1879. Overhauled in 2010, the bridge has not been operated since 1967, although the turntable is still in place. The operating mechanism, however, is not. It gained Grade II listed building status in 2009. There is a slipway just upstream on the west bank and a Youth Hostel ¼ mile east of the station.

- **Rodmell**
Sussex. PO box. There has been a habitation here since the Norman Conquest, the parish church of St Peter dating back to Saxon times. This is a quintessentially, timeless English village as witnessed by traces of both early Iron Age and Romano-British settlements within its boundaries. Another, more ancient site, can be found on Heathy Brow where tumuli and field-banks abound. Leonard and Virginia Woolf lived in the village at Monk's House for 21 years.

Breaky Bottom Vineyard White Way, Rodmell, Lewes BN7 3EX (01273 476427; www.breakybottom.co.uk). Undeniably one of the most successful vineyards in Britain, Breaky Bottom sits in a beautiful secluded fold in the Sussex Downs, wonderfully remote. Peter Hall planted the award-winning vineyard in 1974, seeing the potential offered by a climate similar to that of Champagne and the Loire. This was at a time when modern plant science was developing early-ripening varieties, and demand was emerging for clean, elegant cool-climate wines. Visits welcome by appointment only. Access to Breaky Bottom is by a 1½-mile track over the Downs.

Monk's House National Trust The Street, Rodmell, Lewes BN7 3HF (01273 474760; www.nationaltrust.org.uk/monkshouse). Leonard and Virginia Woolf's 16th-C country retreat, this weather-boarded cottage – chosen for the 'shape and fertility and wildness of the garden' – was home to the couple from 1919 until Leonard's death in 1969. Still full of their favourite things, the house appears as if they have just stepped out for a walk. Telephone or visit the website *for opening times.* Charge.

- **Kingston**
Sussex. PO box. A picturesque mixture of cottages and larger farmhouses grouped around St Pancras Church and the village pound. It was instrumental in the establishment of nearby Sussex University, with orchard land deployed in the construction of family houses in the early 1960s. Known locally as 'The Estate', it features a new village green with generous provision for sporting pastimes, including the traditional Sussex game of Stoolball.

Ashcombe Windmill Kingston, Lewes BN7 3JT (www.sussexmillsgroup.org.uk/ashcombe.htm). The original mill, completed in 1828, was thought to have been designed by Samuel Medhurst of Lewes. It blew down in a storm in 1916. In 2007 the Sussex Mills Group obtained planning permission for its replacement, built on a steel frame, traditionally clad and designed to generate sufficient electricity to power three dwellings. It can also grind corn and is a cleverly constructed habitation in its own right.

Lewes

The river mooches towards Lewes, at times uncertain which side of the valley floor it wants to occupy. The valley itself is spacious, with Downs in the distance on its western extremity, and gentle rolling wold-like country to the east. Drawing closer to Lewes, the valley closes in with steep, chalky scarps rising almost vertically, forming an eastern flank wall, pressing the river in towards the town. Somnolent cows and grazing sheep populate the water meadows paralleling the waterway's erratic course, which is hemmed in by raised flood banks, intersected from time to time by small tributaries, stagnant lagoons and drainage ditches. Additional colour and movement are provided by the Southern Railways' trains ambling their way to the coast and back.

● **Firle**
Sussex. PO, stores, off-licence, farm shop, station (distant at Glynde). Abutting the edge of the South Downs and steeped in history, Firle (or Ferla as it was once known – meaning overgrown with oak) is mentioned in the Domesday Book. The original manor house, now supplanted by Firle Place, dating from 14th C, was occupied by the Levett family who were founders of the Sussex iron industry, rectors, royal courtiers, educators and knights. In the early 20th C, the village was a stronghold of the Bloomsbury Group and numbered Vanessa and Quentin Bell, Katherine Mansfield and John Maynard Keynes amongst its inhabitants.
Charleston House Firle, Lewes BN8 6LL (01323 811626; www.charleston.org.uk). In 1916, on Virginia Woolf's recommendation, the painters Vanessa Bell and Duncan Grant, his friend and lover David Garnett, and Vanessa Bell's two sons, Julian aged 8 and Quentin aged 6, along with Henry the dog, moved to Charleston, an ordinary farmhouse in East Sussex. Dating from the late 16th C and altered in the nineteenth century, it had previously been used as a boarding house. It was to be occupied and brought to life by the family and their friends for the next 64 years. Reinvented as the Bloomsbury Home of Art and Ideas, visitors today have the opportunity to explore the house and garden and enjoy the galleries, shop and Café. *Open Wed-Sun 10.00-17.00.* Charge.

Firle Place The Street, Firle, Lewes BN8 6NS (01273 977364; www.firle.com/firle-place). Firle Place has been the home of the Gage family for over 500 years. With a celebrated collection of old master paintings, porcelain and furniture, Firle Place is well worth a visit to enjoy both the house and the gardens. Tearoom and open-air cinema. Telephone or visit the website *for opening times.* Charge.
Glyndebourne Opera House
Glyndebourne, Lewes BN8 5UU (01273 815000; www.glyndebourne.com). Home of opera and tasked with 'the promotion of aesthetic education and the cultivation and improvement of public taste in music opera or the other arts.' Box office *open Mon-Fri 10.00-17.00.* Also bookable tours – see website.
Middle Farm Firle, Lewes BN8 6LJ (01323 811411; www.middlefarm.com). An open farm welcoming visitors; delicatessen and butchery; farm shop; gift shop; plant sales and tearoom. *Open daily 09.30-17.00.* Charge for the open farm.

● **Ringmer**
Sussex. PO, stores, chemist, fish & chips, off-licence, takeaway, baker, butcher. Infamous for the detonation of the whole stock of the display fireworks held at the Festival Fireworks Factory on 3rd December 2006, in which two members of the Sussex Fire Service died. Pictures showed a large fireball at the centre of the blaze and rockets continued to detonate five hours after the initial blasts. Stores *open daily 06.00-22.00 (Sun 07.00).*

Pubs and Restaurants (pages 118-119)

🍺✕ **1 The Abergavenny Arms** Newhaven Road, Rodmell BN7 3EZ (01273 041396; www.abergavennyarms.com). Part dating from the Norman Conquest, with beams reputed to have come from Spanish Armada shipwrecks, this traditional hostelry serves appetising local food cooked to order *daily 12.00-20.30 (Sun 20.00)* and real ales. Dog- and child-friendly, garden. Traditional pub games, newspapers, real fires and Wi-Fi. *Open 12.00-22.00 (Fri-Sat 22.30).*

🍺 **2 The Ram Inn** The Street, Firle BN8 6NS (01273 858222; www.raminn.co.uk). The local court house until well into the 19th C, this vibrant village pub is popular with locals, walkers and visitors alike, dispensing real ale, real cider and excellent home-cooked food – including breakfast – *daily 09.00-21.30 (booking recommended).* Dog- and family-friendly, garden. Traditional pub games, real fires and Wi-Fi. Camping nearby. B&B. *Open 09.00-23.00.*

✕ **3 Ringmer Café & Grill** 58 Springett Avenue, Ringmer BN8 5QX (01273 933770; www.caferingmer.co.uk). Family-run café serving appetising breakfasts, light lunches and tea, coffee and cakes. Everything from baguettes to burgers, including kebabs and wholesome salads. Takeaway service. *Open Tue-Sat 08.00-16.00; Fri-Sat 17.00-21.30 & Sun 09.00-15.00.*

Lewes

Sussex. All services. Situated on the Greenwich meridian and occupying a gap carved through the South Downs by the River Ouse, this is a town steeped in history which today provides everything an urban dweller could wish for. Built on a hill, with stunning vistas across the Downs, liberally populated with buildings dating back to medieval times, bisected by a charming river once the focus for trade in the area, this town is surely unrivalled in Britain. Archaeological evidence suggests local prehistoric dwellings, while artefacts uncovered in the area point to Roman occupation. An Anglo-Saxon charter of 961 AD first attests to the town's name, while the Norman invasion saw William de Warenne rewarded for his local pugnacity with a gift of land embracing the Ouse from the coast to the Surrey border. He rebuilt the castle and with his wife, Gundred, founded the Priory of St Pancras. Warring forces of Simon de Montfort and Henry III fought the Battle of Lewes in 1264 and de Montfort's victorious army once again had the castle rebuilt. The construction of Newhaven removed the town's not insignificant status as a South Coast port, which was to some extent compensated for by the arrival of a second railway in 1847. Harvey's Brewery, founded in 1790, is a significant employer and its rustic 1880, neo-Gothic buildings stretching along the east bank of the river, provide an attractive backdrop to the town's waterfront.

Anne of Cleeves House, Museum & Gardens
52 Southover High Street, Lewes BN7 1JA (01273 474610; www.sussexpast.co.uk/attraction/anne-of-cleeves-house). The house was given to Anne as part of her divorce settlement from Henry VIII and is an excellent example of a late medieval hall house, dating from 14th C with 16th- and 17th-C additions, and rooms furnished in contemporary style. The attractive gardens are inspired by Tudor planting schemes. Café and gift shop. *Open Tue-Sun 10.00-16.00. Charge.*

Chalk Gallery 4 North Street, Lewes BN7 2PA (01273 474477; www.chalkgallerylewes.co.uk). Features a changing and diverse group of artists working in a variety of media, styles and techniques. One of several high quality galleries – which includes St Anne's Galleries (07860 728220; www.stannesgalleries.com) – within the town. *Open Wed-Sun 10.00-16.00.*

The Cycle Shack 53 Cliffe High Street, Lewes BN7 2AN (01273 479688; www.cycleshack.co.uk). Useful for repairs and spares. *Open Mon-Sat 09.00-17.30 & Sun 10.00-16.00.*

The Depot Pinwell Road, Lewes BN7 2JS (01273 525354; www.lewesdepot.org). Stylish, independent arts venue which includes a three-screen cinema together with a café, bar and restaurant. Also, exhibitions and events. *Open daily 10.00-22.00 (box office 11.00-21.30).*

Landport Bottom Lewes BN7 1QF (www.lewes-eastbourne.gov.uk/article/1461/Landport-Bottom-Nature-Reserve). A large Downland site on the edge of Lewes with panoramic views across the town and South Downs. It was the site of the Battle of Lewes in 1264 and contains significant Bronze Age burial mounds. Lewes Old Race Course borders the site to the west, while the National Trust Blackcap site (BN7 3QN) lies a few hundred yards to the north. The chalk grassland is a nationally scarce habitat, home to rare plants, butterflies and animals.

Lewes Castle & Museum of Sussex Archaeology 169 High Street, Lewes BN7 1YE (01273 486290; www.sussexpast.co.uk/attraction/lewes-castle). Built by William de Warenne shortly after the Norman invasion in 1066, it is one of the earliest examples of a medieval castle. From the top of the fortification there are stunning panoramic views across the Sussex countryside, while the museum is home to a rich collection of artefacts dating from pre-history through to medieval times, including both the Roman and Anglo-Saxon periods. Exhibitions, talks, tours and workshops, together with a model of the town as it would have appeared in the late 19th C. *Open Tue-Sun 10.00-17.00. Charge.*

Needlemakers West Street, Lewes BN7 2NZ (020 7700 4114; www.needlemakers.co.uk). Once used as a factory producing needles during WWI, it is now jammed full of boutique and specialist shops, set over three uneven floors in this historic landmark building, together with a variety of eateries. *Open Mon-Sat 10.00-17.00 & Sun 11.00-16.00.*

Pells Pool Brook Street, Lewes BN7 2BA (01273 472334; www.pellspool.org.uk). Spring-fed, this public lido is the oldest documented freshwater outdor public swimming pool in the country. Picnics are welcome and cakes, ice creams, tea and cold drinks are available. Open daily in the summer months with restricted opening outwith. *Open Mon-Fri 07.00-20.00 & Sat-Sun 08.00-19.00. Charge.*

The Priory of St Pancras Cockshut Road, Southover, Lewes BN7 1HP (www.lewespriory.org.uk). Following in the footsteps of medieval monks, a visit provides the opportunity to discover the secrets of the 11th-C Priory ruins, now revealed after major restoration. A peaceful and tranquil site with an excellent interpretation trail. *Open and free access all year round.*

Tourist Information Centre 6 High Street, Lewes BN7 2AD (01273 483448; www.visitlewes.co.uk/information/tourist-information-centres). This first class, friendly information centre is *open Mon-Fri 09.00-17.00. Closed B Hols.*

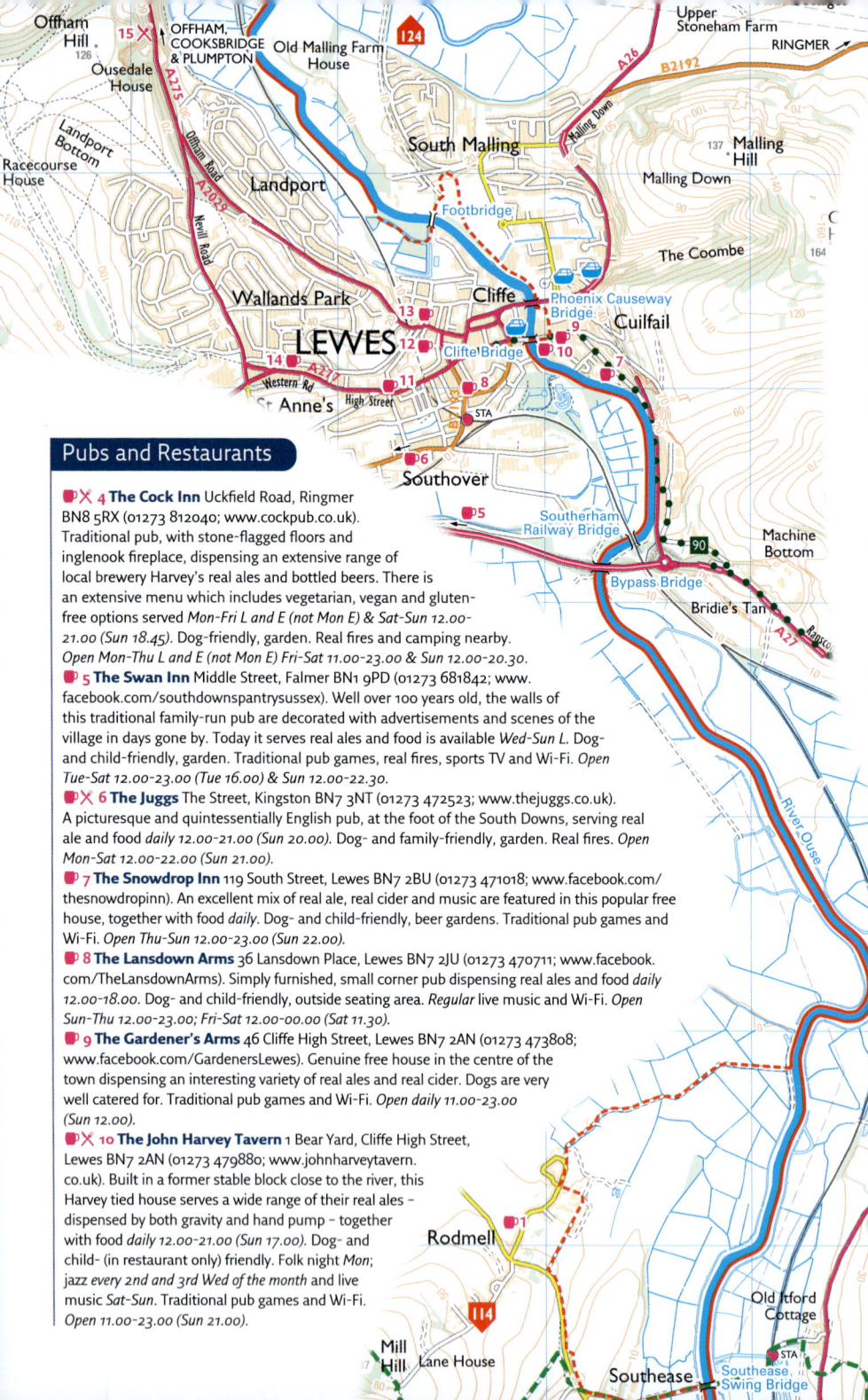

Pubs and Restaurants

🍺✕ **4 The Cock Inn** Uckfield Road, Ringmer BN8 5RX (01273 812040; www.cockpub.co.uk). Traditional pub, with stone-flagged floors and inglenook fireplace, dispensing an extensive range of local brewery Harvey's real ales and bottled beers. There is an extensive menu which includes vegetarian, vegan and gluten-free options served *Mon-Fri L and E (not Mon E) & Sat-Sun 12.00-21.00 (Sun 18.45)*. Dog-friendly, garden. Real fires and camping nearby. *Open Mon-Thu L and E (not Mon E) Fri-Sat 11.00-23.00 & Sun 12.00-20.30*.

🍺 **5 The Swan Inn** Middle Street, Falmer BN1 9PD (01273 681842; www.facebook.com/southdownspantrysussex). Well over 100 years old, the walls of this traditional family-run pub are decorated with advertisements and scenes of the village in days gone by. Today it serves real ales and food is available *Wed-Sun L*. Dog- and child-friendly, garden. Traditional pub games, real fires, sports TV and Wi-Fi. *Open Tue-Sat 12.00-23.00 (Tue 16.00) & Sun 12.00-22.30*.

🍺✕ **6 The Juggs** The Street, Kingston BN7 3NT (01273 472523; www.thejuggs.co.uk). A picturesque and quintessentially English pub, at the foot of the South Downs, serving real ale and food *daily 12.00-21.00 (Sun 20.00)*. Dog- and family-friendly, garden. Real fires. *Open Mon-Sat 12.00-22.00 (Sun 21.00)*.

🍺 **7 The Snowdrop Inn** 119 South Street, Lewes BN7 2BU (01273 471018; www.facebook.com/thesnowdropinn). An excellent mix of real ale, real cider and music are featured in this popular free house, together with food *daily*. Dog- and child-friendly, beer gardens. Traditional pub games and Wi-Fi. *Open Thu-Sun 12.00-23.00 (Sun 22.00)*.

🍺 **8 The Lansdown Arms** 36 Lansdown Place, Lewes BN7 2JU (01273 470711; www.facebook.com/TheLansdownArms). Simply furnished, small corner pub dispensing real ales and food *daily 12.00-18.00*. Dog- and child-friendly, outside seating area. *Regular* live music and Wi-Fi. *Open Sun-Thu 12.00-23.00; Fri-Sat 12.00-00.00 (Sat 11.30)*.

🍺 **9 The Gardener's Arms** 46 Cliffe High Street, Lewes BN7 2AN (01273 473808; www.facebook.com/GardenersLewes). Genuine free house in the centre of the town dispensing an interesting variety of real ales and real cider. Dogs are very well catered for. Traditional pub games and Wi-Fi. *Open daily 11.00-23.00 (Sun 12.00)*.

🍺✕ **10 The John Harvey Tavern** 1 Bear Yard, Cliffe High Street, Lewes BN7 2AN (01273 479880; www.johnharveytavern.co.uk). Built in a former stable block close to the river, this Harvey tied house serves a wide range of their real ales – dispensed by both gravity and hand pump – together with food *daily 12.00-21.00 (Sun 17.00)*. Dog- and child- (in restaurant only) friendly. Folk night *Mon*; jazz *every 2nd and 3rd Wed of the month* and live music *Sat-Sun*. Traditional pub games and Wi-Fi. *Open 11.00-23.00 (Sun 21.00)*.

DWYLE FLUNKING

Also known as dwile flonking, this arcane pub sport appears to have originated in East Anglia several decades ago, although its more fanatical proponents claim antecedents extending as far back as 16th C as depicted in a Brueghel the Elder painting of that time. Either way, it has clearly become a firm favourite at the Lewes Arms (who maintain that the rules of the game are impenetrable and the result is always contested) where it is played four to five times a year.

According to the Friends of the Lewes Arms, approximate rules (now enshrined in Wikipedia) are as follows: A dull-witted person is chosen as the 'jobanowl' (referee) and the two teams decide who flunks first by tossing a sugar beet. The game begins when the jobanowl shouts "Here y'go t'gither!"

The non-flunking team joins hands and dances in a circle around a member of the flunking team, a practice known as 'girting'. The flunker dips his dwile-tipped 'driveller' (a 1–2 ft long hazel stick) into a bucket of beer, then spins around in the opposite direction to the girters and flunks (flings) his dwyle (floor cloth) at them.

If the dwyle misses completely it is known as a 'swadge'. When this happens, the flunker must drink the contents of an ale-filled 'gazunder' (chamber pot) before the wet dwile has passed from hand to hand along the line of now non-girting girters, chanting the ceremonial mantra of "pot pot pot".

A full game comprises two 'snurds', each snurd being one team taking a turn at girting. The jobanowl adds interest and difficulty to the game by randomly switching the direction of rotation and will levy drinking penalties on any player found not taking the game seriously enough.

Points are awarded as follows:

+3 for a wanton: a direct hit on a girter's head

+2 for a morther: a body hit

+1 for a ripper: a leg hit

Minus 1 per sober person at the end of the game when the team with the most points wins, and will be awarded a ceremonial pewter gazunder.

St Peter's Church Hamsey Lewes BN8 5TB (www.friendsofhamsey.org). The church stands on what is effectively an island formed by a loop in the River Ouse to the south east and the cut above Hamsey Lock to the north west. Prior to the Black Death, Hamsey was a significant Saxon habitation where on at least one occasion King Ethelstan (925-940 AD) held court. In 1348 the inhabitants abandoned the village, establishing Offham and other nearby settlements. It is believed there was also a manor house in Hamsey, borne out by foundations unearthed in the churchyard. The basic structure of the church is Norman with an extended chancel, porch and the massive square tower added in 15th C. The building escaped Victorian 'meddling' as it was decided to build a new church in Offham, also dedicated to St Peter. Plans to demolish the existing structure were fortunately forgotten and today (still without heat, light or running water) it is designated a Chapel-of-Ease, used for services during the summer and a carol service in *December*.

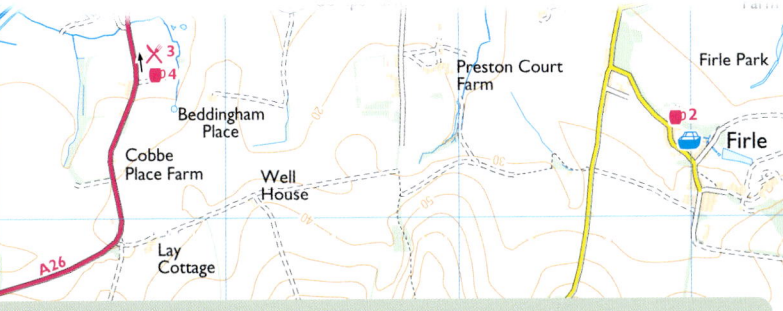

WALKING AND CYCLING

The Tourist Information Centre on the High Street in Lewes makes an excellent starting point for any boot- or bike-based expedition in the area. Detailed leaflets include *Lewes Walks – Towns & Downs* (a walking map of Lewes town with routes to and from the South Downs Way) and *The Priory History Trail*, a circular walk from the town centre, through the Priory Park, visiting historic sites and artefacts associated with Lewes Priory, to name but two.

The South Downs National Park Authority publish a wide range of first-class cycling guides and interpretation leaflets covering the surrounding area ranging from Car Free Holidays & Days Out to Cycle Rides Near Lewes (01730 814810; www.southdowns.gov.uk) and including a mountain bike guide to the South Downs Way. Guides are also available on View Ranger, an outdoor discovery app.

BOAT TRIPS

Ouse Cruises 130 South Street, Lewes, BN7 2BS (www.ousecruises.com) offers exclusive trips for small parties aboard *Lady Helen*. Visit the website for further details.

PADDLING

The river above Lewes is best explored by small portable craft and **The Kayak Coach** 10 Falmer Gardens, Brighton BN2 6NE (07796 203870; www.thekayakcoach.com/experiences-river-trips) offers excellent opportunities with everything provided. Telephone or visit website for further details. As always an excellent source of detailed information can be found at: www.gopaddling.info/rivers/river-ouse-in-sussex/.

- Small portable craft can be launched immediately north of the Harvey's Brewery site in Lewes (BN7 2RD) and close to the road bridge crossing the river at Barcombe Mills (BN8 5BP).
- There are slipways at **Lewes Rowing Club** 120 South Street, Lewes BN7 2BS (secretary@lewesrowingclub.org.uk) but the club requires membership or payment for private use.
- There is a substantial slipway immediately north of Southease Swing Bridge on the west bank (contact the Environment Agency page 110).
- Boatyards on Denton Island, Newhaven operate slipways on both the east (01273 514907; www.newhaventown.co.uk/Organisation/Meeching_Boats) and west banks (01273 515987; www.peterleonardmarine.co.uk) of the island.

WALKING AND CYCLING

Once again the South Downs National Park (01730; 814810; www.southdowns.gov.uk) stars in providing interpretation to the fascinating, early industrial area around Hamsey, for both the walker and, to a lesser extent, the cyclist. Heritage Walks Around Hamsey, a Footpath Map of Hamsey Parish and Hamsey Heritage are but three gems in this field.

Pubs and Restaurants (pages 118-119)

🍺 **11 The Brewers Arms** 91 High Street, Lewes BN7 1XN (01273 475524; www.thebrewersarmslewes.com). Two-bar, family-run, free house dispensing real ales, real cider and food (including traditional breakfasts) *daily 12.00-20.00 (Sat 10.00)*. Dog-friendly, garden. Traditional pub games and Wi-Fi. *Open daily 12.00-22.30 (Sat 10.00).*

🍺 **12 The Lewes Arms** 1 Mount Place, Lewes BN7 1YH (01273 473152; www.lewesarms.co.uk). Home to the world pea-throwing championships, dwyle flunking (*see page 119*), spaniel racing and other outlandish events, this popular town-centre, heritage pub dispenses real ales and real food *Wed-Sun 12.00-22.00 (Sun 21.00)*. Dog- and child-friendly, patio garden. *Regular* live music. Traditional pub games, newspapers, real fires and Wi-Fi. *Open daily 12.00-23.00.*

🍺 **13 The Elephant & Castle** White Hill, Lewes BN7 2DJ (01273 473797). Affectionately known as the 'Ellie', this community pub – home to a *regular Sat* folk club and one of the famous Lewes Bonfire societies – serves real ales and food prepared from locally-sourced ingredients *Tue-Fri E & Sat-Sun 12.00-19.30 (Sun 16.00)*. Outside patio seating. Traditional pub games, real fires, sports TV and Wi-Fi. *Open Mon-Thu 15.00-22.30 & Fri-Sun 12.00-23.00 (Sun 22.00).*

🍺 **14 The Black Horse** 55 Western Road, Lewes BN7 1RS (01273 473653; www.theblackhorselewes.co.uk). A traditional, bay-windowed, community pub, serving a wide-range of real ales and food (including vegan options) *Tue-Sun 12.00-21.00 (Sun 17.00)*. Dog- and family-friendly, garden. Traditional pub games, real fires and Wi-Fi. *Open Mon-Sat 12.00-23.00 (Fri-Sat 23.30) & Sun 12.00-22.30.*

✕♀ **15 Curry Cottage** 275 Offham Road, Lewes BN7 3QF (01273 471124; www.currycottage-lewes.co.uk). Well-known locally for its freshly prepared, authentic Indian cuisine and excellent service, this restaurant offers the opportunity to sample all the popular culinary choices from the sub-continent, together with a takeaway service. *Open Wed-Mon 17.00-22.30.*

River Ouse

Lewes

- **Offham** (see page 124)
  Sussex. PO box, farm shop. Site of a once-busy chalk pit that loaded barges on the nearby Ouse via a funicular railway designed by William Jessop in 1809. Reputed to be the first railway in southern England, this loading system was so efficient that it remained in full-time use until 1870. Visit www.hamseyheritage.org.uk for more information.

- **Plumpton**
  Sussex. PO box. Home of Plumpton Agricultural College. A mile or so to the north of the village, Plumpton Green offers a *PO and stores* together with a *railway station*.
  Ditchling Museum of Art + Craft Craft Lodge Hill Lane, Ditchling BN6 8SP (01273 844744; www.ditchlingmuseumartcraft.org.uk). The site was originally established in 1985 by sisters Hilary and Joanna Bourne as somewhere to display their collection of local artworks. A £2.3 million Heritage Lottery Fund grant in 2012, supported by other donors, funded the construction of the present award-winning buildings, which set the collection of work by local designers – Eric Gill, printer Hilary Pepler and Edward Johnston, designer of the London Underground font – against the backdrop of the village where it was created. Shop and café. *Open Wed-Sun 10.30-17.00. Charge.*

- **Cooksbridge**
  Sussex. PO box, station. The village is home to the world-famous orchid grower, McBeans (01273 400228; www.mcbeansorchids.com/contact-us). Together with Offham, it forms part of the old parish of Hamsey.

Harvey's Brewery, on the East Bank of the River Ouse in Lewes

Barcombe

North of Lewes the river continues stoically on, adopting an altogether more placid course, less driven by tides. The west bank is favoured as much by walkers as by ruminating cattle and the inland boater will feel comfortable with the more familiar reeds and rushes that fringe the waterway. This stretch of the navigation is equally popular with canoeists, kayakers and paddleboarders as it rapidly takes on a narrow, twisting, tortuous rural aspect heading into deepest Sussex countryside. The straight, artificial cut at Hamsey bypasses several fluvial contortions but the lock is now derelict and the channel severely overgrown by trees. The lovely Hamsey Old Church sits proud on a mound looking down on the river, timeless, without equal anywhere in the neighbourhood. Barcombe, its varied selection of mills enshrined only in a variant of its name, is the limit of easily portaged navigation (and also the normal tidal limit of the river) but the adventurous will probably want to press on to the Anchor Inn and the village of Isfield further upstream. Here the Sussex Ouse Restoration Trust (www.sort.org.uk/V2018/index.php) have been active in partially restoring the lock and their extensive website provides an excellent introduction to the navigation, past and present.

Pubs and Restaurants (pages 124-125)

🍺✕ 1 **The Blacksmiths Arms** London Road, Offham, Lewes BN7 3QD (01273 472971; www.theblacksmithsarms-offham.co.uk). Originally a blacksmith's shop and forge, converted to a pub well over a hundred years ago, and now dispensing real ale and food *Wed-Sat L and E & Sun 12.00-18.00*. Garden and real fires in winter. B&B. *Open Mon-Sat 12.00-22.00 (Fri-Sat 23.00) & Sun 12.00-18.00*.

🍺✕ 2 **The Half Moon** Ditchling Road, Plumpton BN7 3AF (01273 890253; www.thehalfmoonplumpton.co.uk). Known for its high quality, locally produced food available *Mon-Sat L and E & Sun 12.00-18.00*. Dog- and child-friendly, garden. Traditional pub games and real fires. Camping nearby. *Open daily 12.00-22.30 (Sun 20.00)*.

🍺✕ 3 **The Rainbow Pub & Carvery** Resting Oak Hill, Cooksbridge BN8 4SS (01273 400134; www.revivedinns.co.uk/the-rainbow). With a cosy, warm and inviting atmosphere, this pub dispenses real ale and excellent food *Wed-Sat L and E & Sun 12.00-17.00*. Garden and real fires. *Open Wed-Sun 12.00-23.00*.

🍺 4 **The Five Bells** East Grinstead Road, Chailey Green BN8 4DA (01825 278328; www.facebook.com/thefivebellschaileygreen). Brass wall lanterns, a timber-fronted bar complete with carved moulded pilasters, together with pictures reputed to have been signed by Picasso, make up an eclectic interior mix of features in this pub dispensing real ales and food *Mon-Fri L and E & Sat-Sun 12.00-21.00 (Sun 20.00)*. Live music *Fri*. Family-friendly, garden. Real fires. *Open 11.00-23.00 (Sun 21.00)*.

🍺 5 **The Crown Inn** 22 Church Road, Newick BN8 4JX (01825 723293; www.thecrownatnewick.co.uk). An old coaching inn, once situated on the King's Highway, but now serving real ale, real cider and food *Wed-Sat L and E (not Wed L or Sun E)*. Dog- and child-friendly, garden. Traditional pub games, *regular* live music, newspapers, sports TV and Wi-Fi. *Open Mon-Fri 15.30-23.00 & Sat-Sun 12.00-23.00*.

🍺✕ 6 **The Bull on the Green** The Green, Newick BN8 4LA (01825 722743; www.bullnewick.co.uk). Country pub with accommodation serving real ale and appetising food *Mon-Fri L and E & Sat-Sun 12.00-21.00*. Secluded outdoor courtyard seating. Real fires and Wi-Fi. B&B. *Open daily 11.00-22.00 (Thu-Sat 23.00)*.

🍺✕ 7 **The Royal Oak** 1 Church Road, Newick BN8 4JU (01825 722506; www.royaloaknewick.co.uk). Sitting on the quiet side of the village green, this weather-boarded local serves real ale and food *Wed-Sun L and E (not Sun E)*. Outside seating. Traditional pub games and real fires. *Open daily 12.00-23.00 (Sun 21.30)*.

🍺✕ 8 **Anchor Inn** Anchor Lane, Barcombe BN8 5EA (01273 400414; www.anchorinnandboating.co.uk). Built in 1790, this beautifully located pub has always played an important part in the river and today serves real ale and food *L and E*. Family-friendly, large garden. B&B. Camping nearby at Boathouse Farm (07593 193476; www.boathousefarm.co.uk). Boats for hire at the pub. Helicopter trips (0203 988 7660; www.a2bhelicharters.co.uk). Pub *open 11.00-23.00*.

🍺 9 **Laughing Fish** Station Road, Isfield TN22 5XB (01825 750349; www.facebook.com/laughingfishisfield). Sitting beside the preserved Lavender Line and once the Station Hotel, this welcoming hostelry serves real ales, real cider and excellent food *Mon-Sat L and E (not Mon E) & Sun 12.00-19.00*. Dog- and family-friendly, children's play area and garden. Traditional pub games, real fires and Wi-Fi. Camping nearby. *Open Mon-Thu 12.00-22.00 (Mon 19.30) & Fri-Sun 11.00-00.00 (Sun 22.00)*.

🍺 10 **The Halfway House** Rose Hill, Isfield TN22 5UG (01825 750382; www.halfwayhouseisfield.co.uk). Nestling in the Sussex countryside, this traditional village pub serves Harvey's ales and home-cooked food made from locally sourced ingredients *Wed-Sun L and E (not Sun E)*. Dog- and family-friendly, garden. *Open Mon-Tue 15.00-20.30 & Wed-Sun 12.00-23.00 (Sun 20.30)*.

- **Barcombe**
Sussex. PO box. Site of an Iron Age roundhouse and a Roman settlement, it has been neighbouring Barcombe Mills that proved to be the more popular destination for tourists before the Second World War, set on visiting the Mills and its pub/restaurant. There have been a variety of mills on the site, dating back to Roman times, including flour, oil and button mills, the last mill being built in 1870. Sadly, that last iteration burnt down in 1939.

- **Barcombe Cross**
Sussex. PO, stores, off-licence. Confusingly, Barcombe Cross is known as Barcombe in the local area and is signposted accordingly. The habitation came into being when villagers were evacuated here during the outbreak of the Black Death. Kim Sears, wife of tennis star Andy Murray, was born in the village. Stores *open daily 07.00-19.00 (Sun 14.00).*

- **Isfield**
Sussex. PO box, butcher, farm shops. Situated at the confluence of the River Uck and the River Ouse, Isfield was an early fording point on the Roman road between London and Lewes. In Saxon times a Motte and Bailey fortification was constructed to guard the ford and both a paper mill and a large flour mill made use of the river's power. The well-known herbalist Nicholas Culpeper grew up in the village, while the area has also been heavily involved in the Wealden brick-making and iron industries since 15th C.
St Margaret Church of Antioch Church Lane, Isfield TN22 5XR (01825 764889; www.churchoftheholycrossuckfield.co.uk/stmargaretofantiochisfield.htm). With the coming of the railway the village gradually moved closer to the station leaving the church and medieval manor house standing alone. The base of the tower is thought to date from late 12th C while the nave is probably 13th C and the chancel and south chapel 14th C. The upper part of the tower, together with the north aisle were built in 19th C.
The Lavender Line Isfield Station, Uckfield TN22 5XB (01825 750515/07518 764445; www.lavender-line.co.uk). This friendly, preserved railway offers both steam and diesel days with trains departing from Platform 2 *between 11.00 and 16.30 at half-hourly intervals.* Driver experience is available *Apr-May* aboard one of the railway's two 'Thumper' units. Picnic area. Telephone or visit website for further details.

- **Newick**
Sussex. PO, stores, off-licence, chemist, takeaways, bakery. Situated midway between Haywards Heath and Uckfield, the village boasts a spacious village green surrounded by houses and shops of a variety of ages and appealing styles. Newick is a typical rural community and its tannery, laundry, two breweries, tailor's shop, dame school, charity school, bakery and jam factory all existed within living memory. The smithy, complete with chestnut tree, overlooked the Green and Village Pond until some thirty years ago.
Bluebell Railway Sheffield Park Station TH22 3QL (01825 720800; www.bluebell-railway.com). Running through 11 miles of beautiful Sussex countryside, the Bluebell Line was one of the first preserved steam railways in the country and consequently has a fine collection of locomotives and rolling stock. Linking East Grinstead and Sheffield Park, services re-commenced in August 1960 and this excellent family day out now offers the chance to learn about the history and science of a bygone industrial age via hands-on, interactive exhibitions. SteamWorks and museum. Café, shop and picnic site. *Open Wed-Sun 09.30-17.00 (Sat-Sun 17.30).*

- **Chailey Green**
Sussex. PO box. Protected within a conservation area, the village lies on heavy clay which is responsible for the predominance of brick and tile in the construction of its buildings. Parts of the Grade II* listed St Peter's Church are thought to date from 13th C, while several other buildings in the village go back to 17th C. A notable type of brick within the conservation area are the vitrified headers: glazed bricks which became fashionable in the Georgian period.
Chailey Windmill & Museum of Local Artefacts Mill Lane, North Chailey, Lewes BN8 4EG (01825 723519; www.chaileyparishcouncil.gov.uk/amenities/chailey-windmill-museum-of-local-artefacts). The windmill is a Grade II listed Smock Mill standing in a position said to mark the centre of the county of Sussex. Although the site was originally occupied by a post mill, this was replaced by the current building in 1864 which had previously worked as Hammingden Mill at West Hoathly and at Newhaven, arriving in its present location by bullock cart. It suffered severe damage in a gale on 5th January 1928 and was restored October 1933. Exhibiting items of local interest and village life. *Open Apr-Sep last Sun in month 15.00-17.00 and by special arrangement.* Charge.

- **Uckfield**
Sussex. PO, stores, off-licence, fish & chips, chemist, butcher, DIY, hardware, cinema, library, garage, station. Developed as a stopping-off point on the pilgrimage route between Lewes, Chichester and Canterbury, Uckfield also expanded around the natural bridging point of the river: 15th-C Bridge Cottage being the oldest house in the town and now a museum. In and around the town many buildings, now clad in brick and tile, are of timber-frame construction and have fallen prey to the Georgian habit of adorning and disguising what would then have been considered their much humbler composition. The town is situated on the southern boundary of the High Weald Area of Outstanding Natural Beauty (AONB), with Ashdown Forest nearby, while the River Uck meanders through the lower part of the town. Uckfield has existed since 12th C but evidence has been found of nomadic Stone Age tribes that wandered the locality around 9000 BC. The Saxons arrived to give the settlement its name Uckfield: Ucca's open land. Stores *open Mon-Sat 06.00-00.00 & Sun 10.00-16.00.*

Pubs and Restaurants

🍺 **11 The Peacock Inn** Shortbridge Road, Piltdown TN22 3XA (01825 762463; www.peacock-inn.co.uk). Traditional, historic country pub dispensing real ale and food *Mon-Sat L and E & Sun 12.00-21.00. Garden. Open Mon-Sat 11.00-22.30 (Fri-Sat 23.00) & Sun 11.00-19.30.*

✕🍷 **12 The Thai Terre Restaurant** 97-99 High Street, Uckfield TN22 1RJ (01825 761005; www.thaiterre.co.uk). Highly thought of food, based on traditional Thai recipes, with more than a passing nod to the locally-sourced fresh fish and seafood. The contemporary interior is adorned with original Thai artwork and sculpture. Friendly, attentive staff. Takeaway service. *Open Tue-Sun L and E (not Tue L).*

🍺 **13 The Alma Arms** 65 Framfield Road, Uckfield TN22 5AJ (01825 762232; www.almaarmsuckfield.co.uk). Named after the Crimean War Battle of the Alma, which was fought on 20th September 1854, this multi-roomed pub now serves real ale. Dog- and family-friendly, garden. Quiz *Thu*. Traditional pub games and Wi-Fi. *Open daily 12.00-23.00 (Sun 22.30).*

✕🍷 **14 Amira's Kitchen** Loxfield Chambers, Grange Road, Uckfield TN22 1QU (01825 764411; www.amiraskitchen.co.uk). A Bangladeshi and Indian restaurant, serving what they claim to be a unique selection of speciality dishes, incorporating traditional Indian techniques and ingredients. Takeaway and delivery service. *Open Mon-Sun 17.30-22.00 (Fri-Sat 22.30).*

🍺✕ **15 The Highlands Inn** Eastbourne Road, Ridgewood, Uckfield TN22 5SP (01825 762989; www.highlandsinn.co.uk). Large, roadside pub serving real ale and food *Mon-Sat L and E & Sun 12.00-18.00*. Family-friendly, garden and children's play area. Traditional pub games, real fires, sports TV and Wi-Fi. *Open daily 11.00-23.00 (Fri-Sat 00.00) & Sun 22.30.*

🍺 **16 The Pig & Butcher** Coopers Row, Five Ash Down, Uckfield TN22 3AN (01825 732191). Acquired by Harvey's in 2008, this spacious local dispenses real ale and food *Wed-Sun L and E (not Sun E)*. Family-friendly, garden. Real fires. *Open 12.00-23.00 (Sun 22.00).*

🍺✕ **17 The Hare & Hounds** The Street, Framfield, Uckfield TN22 5NJ (01825 890118; www.hareandhounds.net). Friendly village local, part-dating from 1428, heavily-beamed and with an inglenook fireplace, dispensing real ale, real cider and food *Tue-Sat L and E (not Sun E)*. Dog- and family-friendly, garden and play area. Real fires and Wi-Fi. *Open Tue-Sat 12.00-22.00 (Fri-Sat 23.00) & Sun 12.00-18.00.*

Bridge Cottage Heritage Centre High Street, Uckfield TN22 1AZ (01825 760734; www.bridgecottageuckfield.co.uk). Set in a medieval Wealden Hall House, built in 1436, today the building plays host to a variety of local history and community events. *Open Mon & Thu-Fri 09.15-14.30. Free.*

Farmers' Market Luxfords Car Park, Uckfield TN22 1AL. *1st Sat of the month, 09.00-12.30.*

Sheffield Park and Garden Sheffield Park TN22 3QX (01825 790231; www.nationaltrust.org.uk/sheffieldpark). Once the hunting ground of kings, successive gardeners from Lancelot 'Capability' Brown, through to the upwardly mobile Earls of Sheffield, have left their mark on the 300-acre park, woodland and gardens. Shop, tearoom and picnic area. *Open daily 10.00-17.00; parkland dawn to dusk. Charge.*

The Picture House Cinema & Restaurant 184 High Street, Uckfield TN22 1AS (01825 764909; www.picturehouseuckfield.com). Featuring new releases, classics, theatre performances, theme nights and National Theatre and Royal Opera cultural screenings. Theatre and cinema meal deals. Restaurant *open daily from 10.00*; box office *10.00-21.00 (Sun 13.00)*.

The Piltdown Man Memorial Barkham Lane, Uckfield TN22 3XE (www.nhm.ac.uk/our-science/departments-and-staff/library-and-archives/collections/piltdown-man.html) The so-called discovery of the Piltdown Man was a 1912 paleoanthropological fraud in which Charles Dawson, an amateur archaeologist, claimed to have discovered the 'missing link' between

River Ouse — Barcombe

BOAT TRIPS
During summer months, the **Anchor Inn** (see page 122) hires rowing boats from the pub, offering the opportunity to explore the river upstream, for approximately three miles, as far as the Fish Ladder Falls below Isfield Place, Isfield.

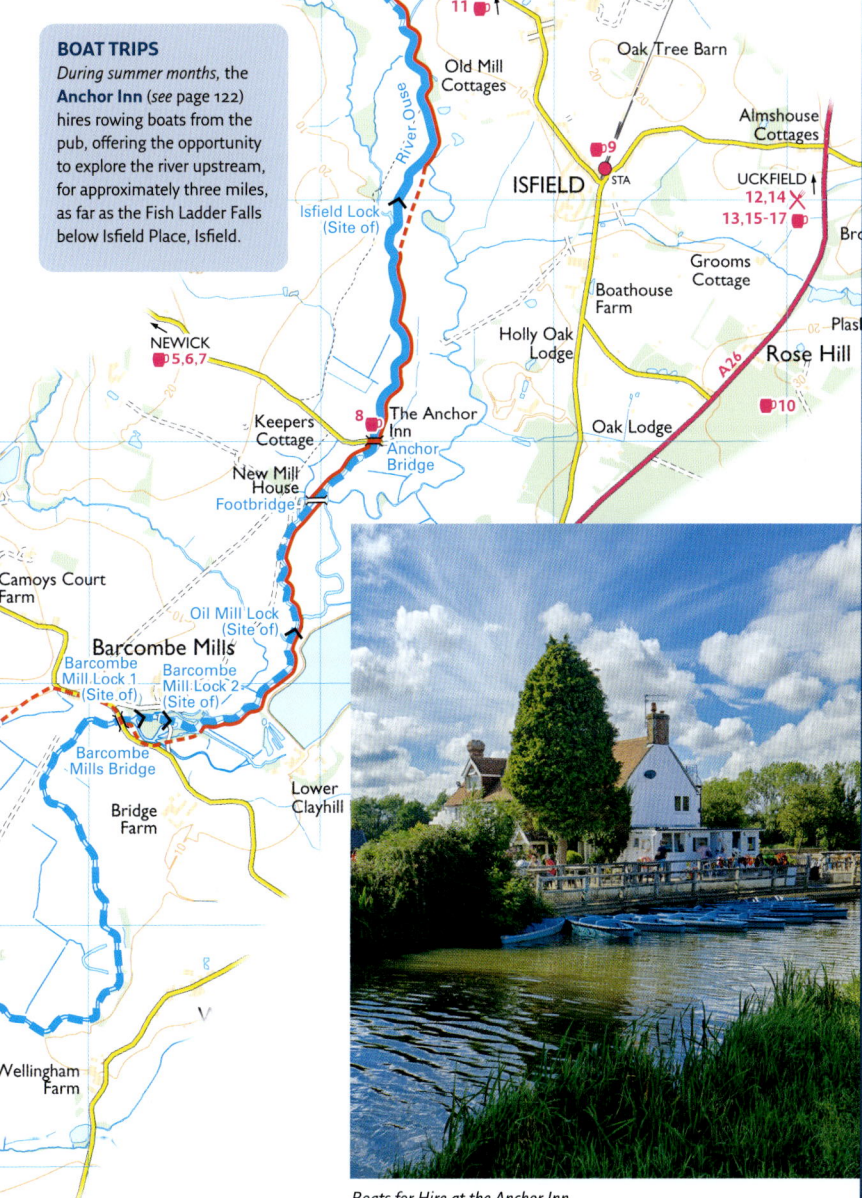

Boats for Hire at the Anchor Inn

ape and human. The find was only definitively established as a hoax in 1953. The Natural History Museum hold many documents and photographs relating to the Piltdown Man.

Uckfield Leisure Centre Downsview Crescent, Uckfield TN22 1UB (01825 761160; www.freedom-leisure.co.uk/centres/uckfield-leisure-centre). Typical mixed-use facility with pool, gym, sports pitches and hall. Café. *Open Mon-Fri 06.00-21.30 & Sat-Sun 08.00-16.30.* Charge.

Wilderness Wood Main Road, Hadlow Down, Uckfield TN22 4HJ (01825 830509; www.wildernesswood.org). 62 acres of chestnut coppice with stands of beech, Scots pine, douglas, cedar and giant Sequoia run by a community of individuals to form a home, workshop, design studio and ceremony space alongside a camping field, bunk-house, shelters and a shepherd's hut. Also, Lucy's Little Forest School (07469 789489; www.lucyslittleforestschool.com). Refreshments. *Open daily 09.00-17.00.* Donations.

RIVER THAMES

FROM INGLESHAM TO TEDDINGTON:
The Environment Agency
03708 506 506
enquiries@environment-agency.gov.uk

Before you set out on the river your boat must be registered with the Environment Agency and be displaying a current licence.

Short-period registrations are available for boats visiting the River Thames. These can be purchased at many of the locks as you come onto the river, or in advance. Contact the Environment Agency on 03708 506 506 for further details or download an application form at www.gov.uk/government/collections/river-thames-boat-registration-and-application-forms.

River Thames and Connecting Waterways: Cruising Guide is a useful publication for all river users. You can download a copy of this cruising guide at www.gov.uk/government/publications/river-thames-and-connecting-waterways-cruising-guide.
Boats must comply with the *Boat Safety Scheme*. Telephone 0333 202 1000 or visit www.boatsafetyscheme.org for more information.

Water points Most lockside water points have no hose connectors and are therefore suitable for containers only. Further information is available in the *River Thames and Connecting Waterways: Cruising Guide* detailed above.

Electric recharging Locks which have recharging points are indicated on the maps. Arrive before 16.00 to arrange use, or telephone ahead. A mooring charge is made.

Pollution If you notice any pollution, notify the relevant Waterway Office (numbers below), a lock keeper or call 0800 80 70 60.

Speed Limit This is 8 kilometres per hour (approx 5 miles per hour), the same as a brisk walking pace, or slower if your wash could cause damage to the riverbank or small craft.

Moorings The Environment Agency is the major provider of short stay visitor moorings on the non-tidal Thames. Full information on location, availability, fees and payment is available from the GOV.UK website. (www.gov.uk/guidance/river-thames-locks-and-facilities-for-boaters#short-stay-mooring)

BELOW TEDDINGTON:
Port of London Authority
London River House
Royal Pier Road
Gravesend
Kent DA12 2BG
01474 562200; www.pla.co.uk

All river users are governed by the *Port of London River Bye-laws*. The Port of London Authority (PLA) issues *River Thames Recreational Users Guide*.
Copies of both documents can be obtained by telephoning the above number or downloaded from the website.
All river movements on the tidal section of the river covered by this guide are under the control of London VTS who can be contacted by telephone on 020 8855 0315 and VHF channel 14.

All vessels over 45ft (13.7 metres) must carry VHF radio and boat owners are reminded that they should hold an appropriate licence to operate such equipment. The only exception to this rule is for narrow boats over 45ft in transit between Teddington and Limehouse.

MAXIMUM DIMENSIONS
Lechlade-on-Thames – Oxford (Folly Bridge)
Length: 100' 0"
Beam: 13' 2"

Oxford – Reading Bridge
Length: 109' 10"
Beam: 16' 5"

Reading Bridge – Windsor Bridge
Length: 121' 5"
Beam: 16' 5"

Windsor -Teddington
Length: 173' 10"
Beam: 19' 8"

MILEAGES:
INGLESHAM Junction with the Thames & Severn Canal to:
Lechlade-on-Thames: ½ mile
Newbridge: 17½ miles
Kings Lock *Junction with Duke's Cut, Oxford Canal*: 27½ miles
Oxford *Junction with Oxford Canal (Isis Lock)*: 30½ miles
Abingdon Lock: 39½ miles
Wallingford Bridge: 53½ miles
Reading *Junction with Kennet & Avon Canal*: 70½ miles
Marlow Lock: 87½ miles
Windsor Bridge: 100½ miles
Shepperton *Junction with River Wey*: 114 miles
Teddington Lock: 125½ miles
Brentford *Junction with Grand Union Canal*: 130½ miles
Limehouse Basin *Junction with Regent's Canal and River Lee*: 146½ miles

Paddling: Category 1 and 2 to Teddington, depending on river flows. *Below Teddington the river is tidal and very busy in Central London and paddlers should consult www.pla.co.uk/tideway-code, in conjunction with the guidance referenced above.*

River Thames

Introduction

The Thames enjoys a special place in the hearts and minds of the English. Stretching for 215 miles from west to east and flowing past the seat of government, it links the Cotswolds, in the centre of the country, with the nation's bustling capital city. Its importance was recognised by the Romans, who built Watling Street, the Fosse Way, Ermine Street and the Icknield Way to cross the river. When the Romans left, London's population declined, and its significance diminished. It was not until the 15th C that the capital began to grow into a great trading centre, eventually becoming the largest port in the world. Goods were shipped inland from the capital – carried up-river by horse-drawn or sailing barges.

Weirs were built on the river, often in places where they hindered navigation, to power mills, and these caused constant disputes between millers and the barge men. Some weirs, known as flash locks, had movable sections to allow barges to pass through. But even then the barge men would have to wait for the fierce rush of water to subside before passing the weir, or be pulled upstream by winch. Then they would have to wait on the far side for the depth of water to build up again. Legislation tried unsuccessfully to control the building of weirs, and so allow the river to fulfil its important role as a highway, but navigation did not begin to improve until pound locks were introduced on the Thames, one of the first being built at Swift Ditch, near Abingdon, around 1620. By the end of the 18th C the Thames had been linked to the main canal network, thereby affording access to many other parts of England. However, the importance of the river as a transport artery began to diminish with the expansion of the railways.

The Thames once also supplied food, and trout and salmon could be caught readily. The latter were indeed so common they were eaten by the poor. The river was also thick with eels. These would swim up the river in such numbers that they could be caught with sieves and buckets, and were made into a form of cake.

But as the population of London grew, the amount of waste grew with it, and began to accumulate in the streets. Gradually various schemes were devised to channel this into rivers which discharged into the Thames, and these water-courses were then covered, becoming known as 'the lost rivers of London'. At this time there were still fish in the river, but from the early 19th C increasing industrial pollution drove all the salmon and eels from the lower Thames, and there were outbreaks of cholera amongst the population of London. The year 1858 was known as 'The Great Stink'. The Commission of Sewers was established in 1847, and gradually the clean-up began. Recently a vigorous campaign has restored the quality of the water: salmon have returned and amateur fishermen are now a common sight right through central London.

In the 17th and 18th C Frost Fairs were held in London whenever the river froze. There were stalls, performing bears, fairground amusements and ox roasting on the ice. The last fair was held in 1814 – the removal of the old London Bridge, which had the effect of a dam, and the building of the embankments in the 19th C, narrowed the river, and deepened and speeded the flow of water, so that it is now no longer possible for the tidal river to freeze over. Since the early 19th C the river has become the scene of regattas in summer, that at Henley-on-Thames being an international event.

Many Londoners are now aware that their city is sinking at the rate of about twelve inches every 100 years. As long ago as 1236 the river flooded the Palace of Westminster; in 1928 central London was flooded with the loss of 14 lives; and the disastrous surge tide of 1953 left 300 dead along the east coast and Thames estuary. To protect London from this threat the magnificent Thames Flood Barrier was built at Woolwich. Movable barriers can be raised from the river bed to hold back the tide – the four main gates having a span of 200ft and the strength to withstand a load of more than 9000 metric tons. The stainless steel shells housing the machinery are built on hardwood ribs, their design reminiscent of the Sydney Opera House.

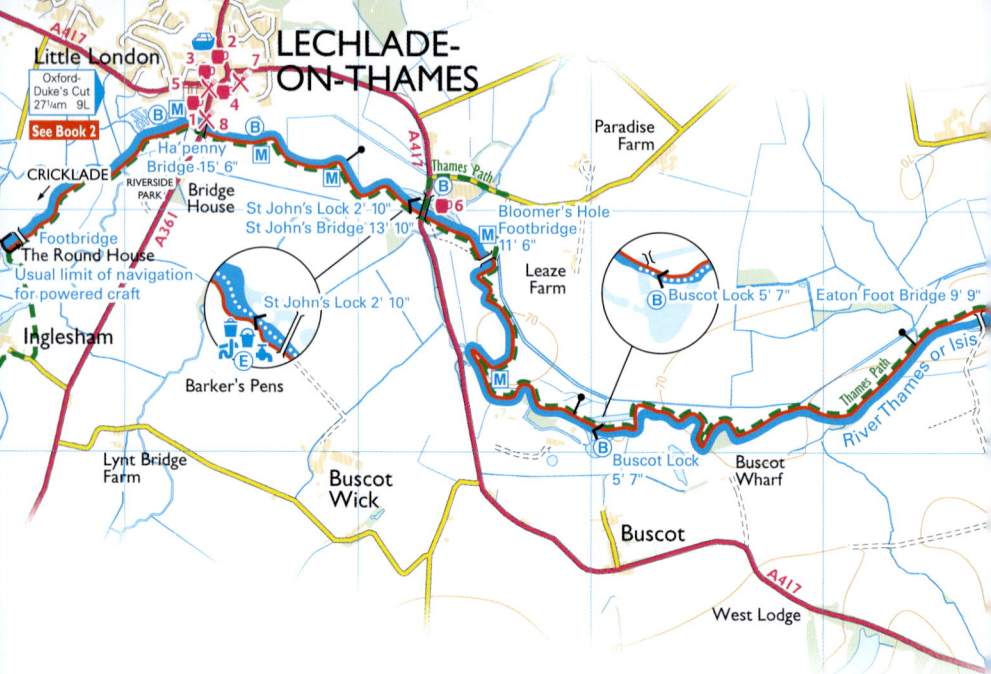

Lechlade-on-Thames

The navigable Thames begins at the Round House, at the junction with the presently unnavigable Thames & Severn Canal (see *Nicholson Waterways Guide 2: Severn, Avon & Birmingham*) near Inglesham – an attractive group of buildings by the river's edge. Moored craft and all the activities of a riverside park are present as the Thames passes Lechlade-on-Thames, flowing under Ha'penny Bridge, so named because a toll was once taken. The church at Lechlade-on-Thames can be seen for miles around – its tall spire always visible as the river meanders to St John's Lock, the highest on the Thames. Note the modern lock house, the quaint miniature buildings in the lock gardens, and the statue of Father Thames, which once marked the river's source at Thames Head, north of Kemble, Gloucestershire. Below the lock the Thames passes under Bloomers Hole Footbridge, the final link in the Thames Path from London to Lechlade-on-Thames. The river's course then becomes quite extravagant – at one point even doubling back before passing the church and beautiful rectory at Buscot. Beyond Buscot Lock the river is once again in open country, delightfully rural and lonely. The church at Eaton Hastings is by the river and provides interest before reaching Grafton Lock, a remote outpost. A very isolated and rural stretch of river then follows, meandering through meadowland and having little contact with civilisation.

NAVIGATIONAL NOTES

The normal limit of navigation for powered craft on the Thames is usually at the junction with the Thames & Severn Canal, marked by the Round House below Inglesham. Here a full-length narrowboat can wind, taking care to avoid the sandbank on the south side. Those not familiar with the river are urged to proceed no further, even though the right of navigation extends to Cricklade, and craft drawing 2ft 6in may be able to proceed as far as 3 miles above Lechlade-on-Thames when there is plenty of water in the river. The Thames & Severn Canal is currently undergoing restoration.

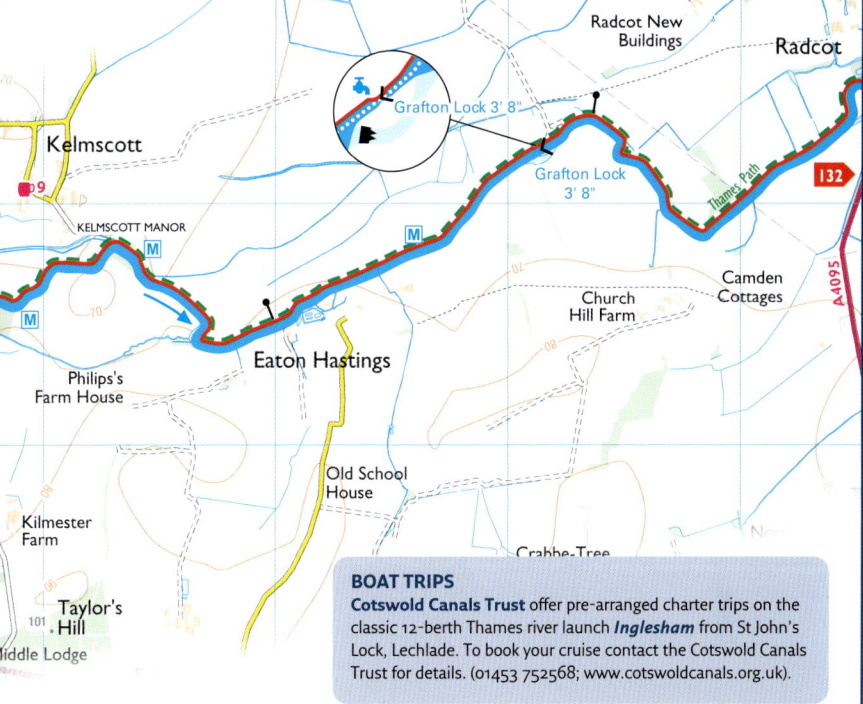

River Thames — Lechlade-on-Thames

BOAT TRIPS
Cotswold Canals Trust offer pre-arranged charter trips on the classic 12-berth Thames river launch *Inglesham* from St John's Lock, Lechlade. To book your cruise contact the Cotswold Canals Trust for details. (01453 752568; www.cotswoldcanals.org.uk).

PADDLING
For small craft, the Thames is navigable to Cricklade, 11 miles above Lechlade which is where powered craft will usually turn. While the main problem is likely to be fallen trees, fast flows over shallow sections, or through constrictions such as Hannington Bridge, can be a problem depending on river conditions. It will be paddleboarders that are more likely to have to trim trees to make progress but all are welcome at the riverside Red Lion in Castle Eaton (01285 706533; www.theredlioncastleeaton.co.uk) – proud to be the first pub on the Thames – to enjoy a pint or more.
This will give paddlers a feel for the Cricklade to Lechlade section: www.youtube.com/watch?v=ACdQTZF6FHc while those heading to the capital can seek inspiration from www.achievableadventure.com/adventures/canoeing-the-length-of-the-thames.

WALKING AND CYCLING
Walking the River begins with the start of the Thames Path at Kemble and full details, including sections available to cyclists, can be downloaded at www.nationaltrail.co.uk/ThamesPath. The path is in good shape throughout the length of the river to London. The ambitious could also look towards the west and follow the Thames & Severn Way detailed in *Nicholson Waterways Guide 2: Severn, Avon & Birmingham*. This will take you via Cricklade, the Cotswold Water Park, Cirencester, Stroud's Golden Valley all the way to Gloucester and the River Severn. The Upper Thames Path is not a metalled path suitable for the majority of cyclists. However, a suggested route marked on the map with a dotted red line, using quiet lanes wherever possible, aims to follow the River Thames as closely as possible. (*See also* Walking and Cycling page 135).

Boatyards

ⒷLechlade Marina Ltd Downington, Lechlade GL7 3DL (07889 070623; www.lechlademarina.co.uk). 🚰🚿 E. Pump out at St John's Lock, long-term mooring, occasional short-term mooring, winter storage, slipway, toilets, showers. *Open Mon-Fri 08.00-17.00 & Sat-Sun 10.00-16.00.*

ⒷCotswold Boat Hire Buscot Mill, Brandy Island, Buscot SN7 8DA (01793 354079/07947 993784). Moorings, long- and short-term boat hire, day boats, boat sales. *Open Apr-Sep daily 08.00-20.00.*

The Lechlade Waterside

- **Inglesham**

Wilts. A marvellous architectural group around the church. Although of late Saxon origin, the present building is largely 13th-C. William Morris was responsible for the remarkably original state of the building – he loved it and saved it from 19th-C restoration. There are the remains of a rare painted 13th-C reredos, box pews, and an ancient carving of the Mother and Child. The adjoining farm was once the priory. On the north bank the Inglesham Round House is a notable landmark. It once belonged to the lock keeper on the presently unnavigable Thames & Severn Canal, which joins the river at this point.

Thames & Severn Canal Stretching almost 29 miles between Inglesham and Wallbridge, Stroud, where it joins the Stroudwater Canal and, in turn, the Goucester & Sharpness Canal. This trade link was initially closed to navigation in 1893, but remedial works were carried out and it re-opened. Taken over by Gloucestershire CC in 1901, the last laden boat crossed the summit level in 1911 and its abandonment was finally confirmed by Act of Parliament in 1933. This heavily locked canal rises to 300ft above sea level, where the Sapperton Tunnel burrows under the Cotswolds for 3808yds. Now undergoing active restoration, it is hoped that it will eventually form part of a Cotswold Ring, linking with the Gloucester & Sharpness, River Avon, Stratford-on-Avon, Grand Union, Oxford and Thames. For more information visit www.cotswoldcanals.co.uk.

- **Lechlade-on-Thames**

Glos. PO, *stores, chemist, bakery, fish & chips, takeaways, off-licence.* A golden grey market town dominating the river in all directions and best seen from St John's Bridge, with the tall spire of the Perpendicular wool church rising above the surrounding cluster of buildings. Shelley's Walk leads from the river to the church, where his *Stanzas in a Summer Churchyard* is quoted on a plaque in the churchyard wall. Shelley, Peacock, Mary Godwin and Charles Clairmont stayed in Lechlade-on-Thames in 1815, after rowing from Windsor. *Stores open daily 06.30-22.00.*

Bloomers Hole Footbridge Completing the Thames Path National Trail, this bridge, although built of steel, is clad with timber. It was lowered into place by a Chinook helicopter from RAF Brize Norton.

Little Faringdon Mill GL7 3Q. One mile outside Lechlade-on-Thames on the A361 to Burford. A perfect 18th-C mill in its original state, with a farm and outbuildings. Private.

- **Buscot**

Oxon. A small village off the A417, notable for the very beautiful Queen Anne rectory (private) which stands on the riverside by the church, itself unremarkable apart from its Burne-Jones windows. The National Trust owns a small picnic site by the weir pool. Public Toilets & Tearooms.

Buscot Old Parsonage Buscot, Faringdon SN7 8DQ (01793 763303; www.nationaltrust.org.uk/visit/oxfordshire-buckinghamshire-berkshire/buscot-old-parsonage). A Cotswold stone building of 1703 on the river bank. *Opening times vary* so visit website for details.

Buscot Park Faringdon SN7 8BU (01367 240932; www.buscot-park.com). Built about 1780 in the Adam style by Edward Loveden Townsend, with a park and gardens laid out by Harold Peto. In 1859 the estate was aquired by Robert Tertius Campbell, and he embarked upon a scheme to make it one of the most advanced farms of its time. His major crop was sugar beet, and he installed 6 miles of railway track to aid harvesting. He also built a distillery on Brandy Island (*see* Buscot Wharf), a gasworks and concrete farm buildings. However these works exhausted his resources, and he became bankrupt. Fine furniture and The Faringdon Collection of Paintings, including works by Rembrandt and Murillo were later bought by Sir Alexander Henderson, First Lord Faringdon. The Second Lord Faringdon continued collecting, and restored much of the original character to the house. The Italianate Water Garden was created by Harold Peto during the 20th C. Tearoom and small shop. *Open times and dates are seasonal.* Visit website for further details. Charge.

Buscot Wharf Little trace remains of the wharf from which brandy was shipped to France. The short arm was known as Buscot Pill.

Tourist Information Centre The Pump House, 5 Market Place, Faringdon SN7 7HL (01367 240281; www.faringdontowncouncil.gov.uk/information-centre). *Open Mon-Fri 09.00-16.00 & Sat 09.30-13.00.*

● **Kelmscott**
Oxon. A pristine village of elegant grey stone houses, firmly entrenched against development. The quiet 15th-C church has a strong medieval atmosphere.

Kelmscott Manor Kelmscott, Lechlade-on-Thames GL7 3HJ (01367 252486; https://kelmscottmanor.org.uk). A beautiful house behind high walls, built in 1570, and added to in 1665. It became the summer home of William Morris from 1871 until his death in 1896, and he adored it, saying it had 'quaint garrets amongst great timbers of the roof, where of old times the tillers and herdsmen slept'. He shared it with Dante Gabriel Rossetti until 1874. William Morris was buried in the churchyard at Kelmscott after his death in Hammersmith; his tomb is the work of Philip Webb. Shop and tearoom (with Wi-Fi). *Open Apr-Oct, Thu-Sat 10.30-17.00.* Timed tickets. Charge.

● **Eaton Hastings**
Oxon. Quite inaccessible from the river. The 13th-C church is well situated by the water – the rest of the village is a mile away.

Pubs and Restaurants (pages 128-129)

🍺✕ **1 The Riverside** Park End Wharf, Lechlade-on-Thames GL7 3AQ (01367 252534; www.riverside-lechlade.com). Sitting amidst a pleasant mix of boats and antiques beside Ha'penny Bridge, this pub dispenses real ale, real cider and food *L and E*. Family friendly and riverside terrace. Traditional pub games. Camping. B&B. *Open Mon-Thu 10.00-22.00 & Fri-Sun 09.00-23.00 (Sun 22.00).*

🍺✕ **2 The Swan Inn** 7 Burford Street, Lechlade-on-Thames GL7 3AP (01367 253571; www.swaninnlechlade.co.uk). Cosy and peaceful stone-built pub, the oldest in Lechlade-on-Thames. Real ale, real cider and food *served L and E (not Sun E).* Family-friendly, garden. Real fires. Camping nearby. B&B. *Open daily 12.00-22.00 (Fri-Sat 23.00).*

🍺 **3 The Crown Inn** High Street, Lechlade-on-Thames GL7 3AE (01367 252198). Popular 16th-C coaching inn serving real ale. *Regular* live music. Dog-friendly, garden. Traditional pub games, real fires and Wi-Fi. Camping nearby. B&B *Open daily 12.00-23.00.*

🍺 **4 The New Inn Hotel** The Market Square, Lechlade-on-Thames GL7 3AB (01367 252296; www.newinnhotel.com). Attractive Georgian pub by the church, dispensing real ale and food *daily L and E.* Family-friendly, large garden. Traditional pub games and real fires. Camping nearby. B&B. *Open 11.00-23.00.*

✕ **5 Sourdough Revolution Bakery** 2 High Street, Lechlade Oxon GL7 3AE (01367 253122; www.sourdoughrevolution.co.uk/lechlade-shop). Artisan food shop, bakery and café serving lunch and takeaways. *Open daily 08.30-14.30 (Wed 17.30 and Fri 15.30).*

🍺 **6 The Trout Inn** St John's Bridge, Faringdon Road, Lechlade-on-Thames GL7 3HA (01367 252313; www.thetroutinn.com). A justly famous 13th-C Cotswold stone pub, with plenty of wood panelling, low beams and stuffed fish. Real ale. Tasty home-made meals available daily L and E. Family-friendly, large riverside garden bordering the weir stream. The focus for many events and festivals throughout the year. Traditional pub games and real fires. Camping nearby. *Open 11.00-23.00 (Sun 12.00).*

✕ **7 Lynwood & Co Café** Market Place, Lechlade-on-Thames GL7 3AD (01367 253707; www.lynwoodandco.com). Seasonal menu, specialist coffee, light lunches, cakes and pastries. All food sourced locally. *Open Mon-Sat 08.00-16.00 & Sun 8.00-15.00.*

✕ **8 The Tea Chest** Park End Wharf, Lechlade-on-Thames GL7 3AQ (01367 253015). A welcoming café, situated beside the Thames, serving platters, soup, toasties, light lunches and homemade cakes. Wood burning stove; children and dogs welcome. *Open Mon-Sat 09.00-18.00 & Sun 10.00-16.30.*

🍺✕ **9 The Plough at Kelmscott** Kelmscott GL7 3HG (01367 253543; www.theploughinnkelmscott.com). A fine 16th-C restaurant and bar with flagstone floors, serving real ale. Restaurant, with à la carte menu served *Wed-Sun L and E (not Sun E).* Bar meals *all day.* Dog- and child-friendly, garden. Traditional pub games, real fires and Wi-Fi. *Open Mon-Tue 15.00-18.00 & Wed-Sun 12.00-23.00 (Sun 18.00).*

Tadpole

A very isolated, rural stretch of river, meandering through meadowland and having little contact with civilisation. The river divides at Radcot where two fine bridges, the ever popular Swan Hotel and a large *picnic area* opposite are always busy with visitors on summer afternoons. Caravans line the north bank as once more the Thames enters open meadowland around Radcot Lock and then meanders on to the splendid Rushey Lock, with its charming house and fine garden, and the handsome 18th-C Tadpole Bridge. Then again the Thames enters lonely country, passing to the south of Chimney. It is about as far away from it all as you can get on the river.

PADDLING
Cotswold Canoe Hire, Park End Wharf, Lechlade GL7 3AQ offer canoes, kayaks and paddleboards for hire (01367 252303; www.cotswoldcanoehire.co.uk) together with all necessary equipment for a day on the river. Ultimate Canoe and Kayak (01432 264807; www.ultimate-canoeandkayak.co.uk/canoe-hire-lechlade) offer a similar service but without paddleboards and, where necessary, over extended periods (with accommodation) covering the whole river.

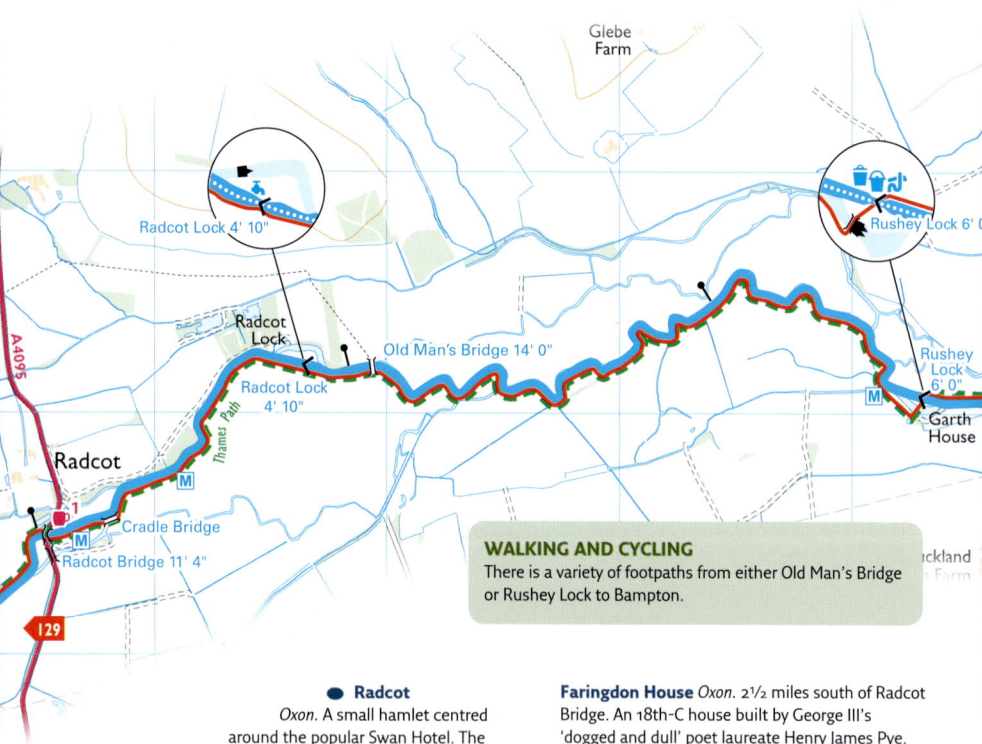

WALKING AND CYCLING
There is a variety of footpaths from either Old Man's Bridge or Rushey Lock to Bampton.

● **Radcot**
Oxon. A small hamlet centred around the popular Swan Hotel. The triple-arched 13th-C bridge is the oldest surviving on the Thames. The single-arched bridge spanning the navigation channel, an artificial cut, was built later, in 1787. The old bridge, made of Taynton stone, was the scene of a Civil War skirmish, when Prince Rupert's Royalist cavalry pounced on Cromwell's men, marching to an attack on Faringdon. Upstream caravans line the north bank – to the south picnics and tents sprawl across the meadow during the summer.

Faringdon House *Oxon*. 2½ miles south of Radcot Bridge. An 18th-C house built by George III's 'dogged and dull' poet laureate Henry James Pye. The surrounding parkland is reputedly haunted by a headless Hampden Pye, an earlier member of the family who was decapitated at sea. His story is recalled in *The Ingoldsby Legends*, 1840. The folly on Faringdon Hill, an octagonal Gothic lantern, was built by the artist and author Lord Berners in 1935.

● **Bampton**
Oxon. PO, *stores, chemist, off-licence, takeaway, bakery*. An attractive greystone town 2 miles from the river, easily approached by a variety of footpaths

Pubs and Restaurants

🍺✕ **1 Ye Olde Swan** Radcot Road, Radcot OX18 2SX (01367 810220; www.yeoldeswan.co.uk). Comfortable and friendly old inn of great character, beside what was once a wharf. Real ale. Meals available *daily L and E (not Sun E)*. Family-friendly, riverside garden. Traditional pub games and real fires. Camping and glamping. Mooring. *Open Sun-Tue 11.00-20.00 & Wed-Sat 11.00-21.00 (Fri-Sat 22.30)*.

🍺✕ **2 The Trout at Tadpole Bridge** Buckland Marsh, Faringdon SN7 8RF (01367 870382; www. butcombe.com/the-trout-at-tadpole-bridge-oxfordshire). Fine traditional riverside pub serving real ale, along with a restaurant menu *daily L and E*. Bar meals available *throughout the day* and breakfast *from 08.00*. Dog- and family-friendly, riverside garden, real fires and Wi-Fi. *Open 08.00-23.00 (Sun 22.00)*.

🍺 **3 The Horseshoe** Bridge Street, Bampton OX18 2HA (01993 200046). Unassuming village local just off the main square dispensing real ale. Dog-friendly, garden. Newspapers, sports TV and Wi-Fi. *Open Mon-Fri 15.00-23.00 (Fri 13.00) & Sat-Sun 12.00-00.00 (Sun 23.00)*.

✕ **4 Bampton Coffee House** Temple Market Square, Bampton OX18 2JH (01993 850929). All day breakfasts, paninis and jacket potatoes, freshly made sandwiches and baguettes, coffees, teas and pastries and a variety of light meals and snacks. *Open Mon-Sat 08.00-16.00*.

🍺 **5 Morris Clown** High Street, Bampton OX18 2JW (01993 850217). Fine 12th-C pub serving real ale. Dog- and family-friendly, garden. Traditional pub games, real fires, sports TV and Wi-Fi. *Open Mon-Sat 17.00-23.00 (Sat 15.00) & Sun 14.00-23.00*.

🍺 **6 The Talbot Hotel** Market Square, Bampton OX18 2JJ (01993 850326). Small, low-ceilinged, Grade II listed stone hotel – reputed to be haunted by a former staff member – now dispensing real ale. Dog- and family-friendly, garden. Traditional pub games, sports TV and Wi-Fi. B&B. *Open Mon-Thu 15.00-23.00 & Fri-Sun 12.00-00.00 (Sun 23.00)*.

🍺 **7 The Red Lion** The Square, Aston OX18 2DL (01993 850491; www.facebook.com/p/The-Red-Lion-Aston-100076386366011/). An archetypal, friendly village local dispensing real ale and serving food *Wed-Sun L and E (not Sun E)*. Dog- and family-friendly, outside seating. Traditional pub games and sports TV. *Open Tue-Fri 16.00-22.30 (Fri 23.30) & Sat-Sun 12.00-23.30 (Sun 21.00)*.

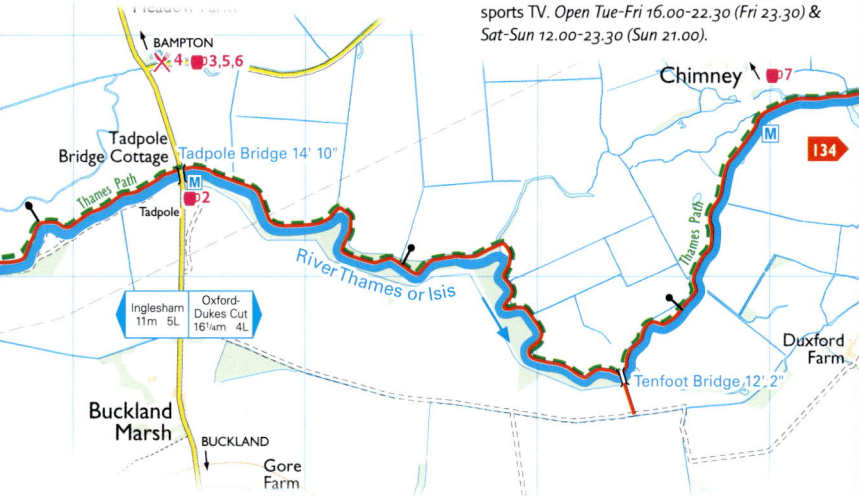

or by road north from Tadpole. It has a timeless appearance in that much of the new development is built from the same materials as, and often in a style similar to, the old. The result is both unusual and pleasing. The church, largely 13th- and 14th-C, has a slightly uneasy octagonal spire. Beside the church is the old grammar school, founded in 1653. At one time the town was called Bampton in the Bush – a description dating from before the 18th C when no roads served the community. Morris dancing is reputed to have originated here. Stores *open daily 07.00-22.00*.

● **Buckland**
Oxon. About a mile south of Tadpole Bridge. A village intimately connected with Buckland House, and best approached from the river, as there is a fine view over the Thames Valley.
Buckland House Built in 1757 by Wood of Bath, it is one of the most imposing 18th-C homes in Oxfordshire, although the wings were added in 1910. There is a Gothic stable in the park. Private.

Newbridge

The navigation channel passes through a tree-lined cut to Shifford Lock, the last lock to be built on the Thames, in 1898. Again the countryside is flat, glimpsed here and there over the steep river banks which are in places heavily overgrown. Electricity pylons do little to improve the scene. Welcome relief appears at Newbridge, with a fine *pub* on each side of the handsome old bridge. The nearest village is Standlake, a mile to the north. As the hills close in from the east the countryside gradually loses much of the bleakness of the upper reaches and the villages come a little closer. There are attractive woods below Northmoor Lock, and Bablock Hythe, with another riverside *pub*, is soon reached. To the north, the grassy banks of the vast Farmoor Reservoir, much loved by anglers, come down to the river's edge.

- **Shifford**
Oxon. A church and a few houses surrounded by lush pastureland are all that remain of what was once an important town. Alfred held a meeting of the English Parliament here in AD890. The church is situated in the middle of a field less than quarter of a mile from the river.

- **Hinton Waldrist and Longworth**
Oxon. Two pleasant straggling villages up on a ridge overlooking the valley. Longworth church contains a good example of Arts and Crafts stained glass by Heywood Sumner, 1906. The Old Rectory, Longworth, was the birthplace of Dr John Fell, 1625–86, who participated in the early development of the Oxford University Press, especially with regard to printing types; and also Richard Doddridge Blackmore, 1825–1900, author of *Lorna Doone* (1869), who spent only the first four months of his life here – sadly his mother died shortly after his birth.

- **Newbridge**
Oxon. A fine 13th-C stone bridge with pointed arches, one of the oldest on the river. The River Windrush joins the Thames here.

- **Northmoor**
Oxon. The 13th-C church contains a restored bell loft, dated 1701. Behind the church is a Tudor rectory. Northmoor Lock is the only remaining example of a paddle and rymer weir on the Thames, once the most common form of water control on the river. It's continued use is somewhat contentious, as its detractors maintain that it provides a less reliable means of flood prevention than its more modern cousins. However, agreement as to its suitability for the job appears to be on the point of being reached so, hopefully, an important piece of living history will be retained on the river. For more information visit www.manorfarmappleton.co.uk/local-facilities-attractions/northmoor-lock-weir/camping-supplies

- **Appleton**
Oxon. PO, stores, off-licence. A meandering thatch and stone village, with new development to the west. Appleton Manor, situated beside a splendid weather-boarded barn and gateway, was built at the end of the 12th C. An astonishing amount remains, including a fine doorway. The community shop and Post Office, stocks a wide range of produce and is *open Mon-Fri 07.00-18.00 & Sat-Sun 08.00-13.00 (Sun 12.00)*. The PO *opens Mon & Thu 09.00-13.00*.

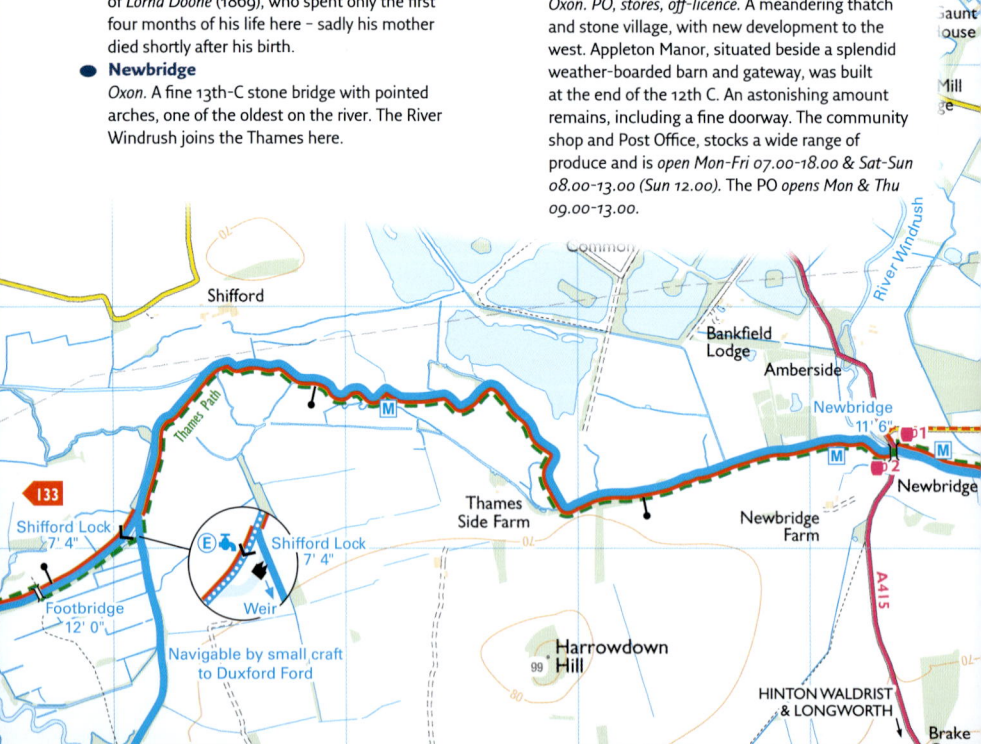

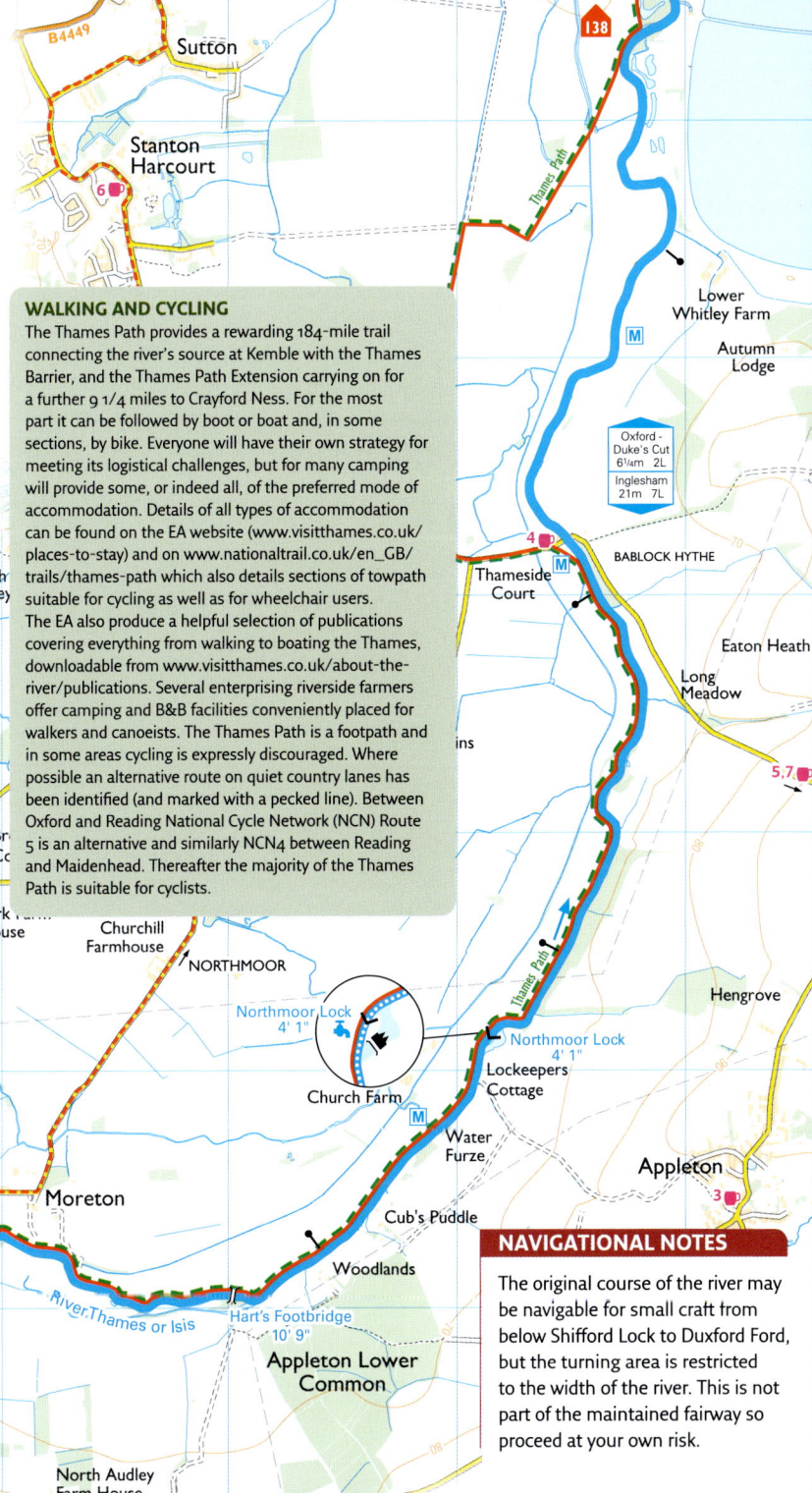

WALKING AND CYCLING

The Thames Path provides a rewarding 184-mile trail connecting the river's source at Kemble with the Thames Barrier, and the Thames Path Extension carrying on for a further 9 1/4 miles to Crayford Ness. For the most part it can be followed by boot or boat and, in some sections, by bike. Everyone will have their own strategy for meeting its logistical challenges, but for many camping will provide some, or indeed all, of the preferred mode of accommodation. Details of all types of accommodation can be found on the EA website (www.visitthames.co.uk/places-to-stay) and on www.nationaltrail.co.uk/en_GB/trails/thames-path which also details sections of towpath suitable for cycling as well as for wheelchair users.

The EA also produce a helpful selection of publications covering everything from walking to boating the Thames, downloadable from www.visitthames.co.uk/about-the-river/publications. Several enterprising riverside farmers offer camping and B&B facilities conveniently placed for walkers and canoeists. The Thames Path is a footpath and in some areas cycling is expressly discouraged. Where possible an alternative route on quiet country lanes has been identified (and marked with a pecked line). Between Oxford and Reading National Cycle Network (NCN) Route 5 is an alternative and similarly NCN4 between Reading and Maidenhead. Thereafter the majority of the Thames Path is suitable for cyclists.

NAVIGATIONAL NOTES

The original course of the river may be navigable for small craft from below Shifford Lock to Duxford Ford, but the turning area is restricted to the width of the river. This is not part of the maintained fairway so proceed at your own risk.

- **Bablock Hythe**
Oxon. Mentioned by Matthew Arnold in *The Scholar Gypsy*, 1853, who was seen: 'In hat of antique shape, and cloak of grey, crossing the stripling Thames at Bab-lock-hithe'. A Roman stone altar, now in the Ashmolean, was dredged from the river here. There has been a ferry here since AD904, and it has been a little erratic in recent years. The area is surrounded by an unappealing estate of temporary homes.

- **Stanton Harcourt**
Oxon. PO. A superb grey stone village between the Thames and the Windrush, the waters reflecting the quiet glory of the buildings.

The grand cruciform church has fine monuments in the Harcourt Chapel. The PO can be found in the village hall and is *open Tue, Thu & Sat 09.00-12.30*.
Stanton Harcourt Manor Main Road, Witney OX29 5RJ. The Harcourts built this manor, one of the earliest unfortified manor houses in England, between 1380–1470, with a Gatehouse being added in 1540. Now only Pope's Tower, the scene of Alexander Pope's translation of the *Iliad*, and the unique Great Kitchen, survive. The kitchen is unique in England, in that smoke escaped through vents which were opened manually – there is no chimney. Not open to the public.

WALKING AND CYCLING
The prominent dome-shaped Harrowdown Hill can be approached by footpath from the river about a mile west of Newbridge. Views from the top amply repay the modest effort.

Pubs and Restaurants (pages 134-135)

🍷✕ **1 The Rose Revived Inn** Newbridge, Witney OX29 7QD (01865 300221; www.chefandbrewer.com/pubs/oxfordshire/rose-revived/hotel). Old Cotswold stone inn. Real ale. Food (including breakfast *from 07.00 (Sat-Sun 08.00)*) available *until 21.00 daily*. Dog- and family-friendly, large riverside garden. Traditional pub games and Wi-Fi. B&B. Mooring. Bar *open 11.00-23.00 (Sun 22.30)*.

🍷 **2 The Maybush** Abingdon Road, Newbridge OX29 7QD (01865 300100; www.themaybushnewbridge.co.uk). One of the first Eco-pubs in the country, following its extensive 2015 refurbishment, this pub serves real ale and food *Mon-Sat 12.00-20.00 (Fri-Sat 21.00) & Sun 12.00-18.00*. Dog-friendly, garden. Real fires. Mooring. *Open Mon-Sat 11.00-21.00 (Fri-Sat 22.00) & Sun 11.00-19.00*.

🍷✕ **3 The Plough** Eaton Road, Appleton OX13 5JR (01865 863535). Welcoming village pub, built in 1683, at the heart of the community serving real ales, real cider and food *Mon-Fri 17.00-21.00; Sat-Sun L and E*. Dog- and family-friendly, garden. Traditional pub games, real fires, sports TV and Wi-Fi. Camping. *Open daily 15.00-23.00 (Sat-Sun 12.00)*.

🍷✕ **4 The Ferryman Inn** Bablock Hythe, Northmoor, Witney OX29 5AT (01865 880028; www.theferrymaninn.co.uk). A famous pub, serving a large park homes site situated next door, dispensing real ale. Meals available *L and E when open*. Dog- and child-friendly, riverside garden. Traditional pub games and Wi-Fi. Camping. B&B. Mooring and slipway. *Open Mon and Wed 12.00-21.00; Thu and Sun 12.00-16.30 & Fri-Sat 12.00-23.00*.

🍷✕ **5 The Bear & Ragged Staff** 28 Appleton Road, Cumnor OX2 9QH (01865 862329; www.facebook.com/bearandraggedstaff). Complete with its integral fireplace and surrounded by oak beams, the bar of this large dining pub dispenses real ale and food (using *seasonal* ingredients) available *Mon-Wed L and E; Thu-Sat 12.00-22.00 (Thu 21.30) & Sun 12.00-21.00*. Dog- and family-friendly, garden. Traditional pub games and Wi-Fi. B&B. *Open Mon-Sat 11.00-23.00 (Fri-Sat 00.00) & Sun 12.00-22.30*.

🍷✕ **6 The Harcourt Arms** Main Road, Stanton Harcourt, Witney OX29 5RJ (01865 416516; www.harcourtarms.com). Handsome 16th-C hostelry with inglenook fireplaces dispensing real ale and serving food *Sun-Thu L and E (not Sun E) & Fri-Sat 12.00-21.00* (although the restaurant has more *restricted hours*). Breakfast available *daily 08.00-10.00*. Dog- and family-friendly, garden. Wi-Fi. B&B. *Open 12.00-22.00 (Sun 17.00)*.

🍷✕ **7 The Eight Bells** High Street, Eaton OX13 5PR (01865 862261). Welcoming pub and restaurant serving real ale and Thai food *Tue-Sun E*. Dog- and family-friendly, garden. Folk night *Tue*. Newspapers, real fires and Wi-Fi. *Open Tue-Sun 17.00-00.00 (Sat-Sun 12.00)*.

Tadpole Bridge

Godstow

The Thames meanders extravagantly past Farmoor Reservoir and the very pretty Pinkhill Lock, with its *picnic site*, towards Swinford. Below Eynsham Lock the entrance to the Wharf Stream can be seen on the east side, followed by the Cassington Cut, which bypassed the lower reaches of the Evenlode, when that river was navigable. Opposite are the dense woodlands of Wytham Great Wood, falling steeply down Wytham Hill to the river's edge. The Seacourt Stream leaves the Thames at Hagley Pool, and a short distance below is King's Lock. Access to the Oxford Canal can be gained via a backwater and the Duke's Cut, which join the weir stream. Pixey Mead lies to the west, its peace shattered by the incessant traffic of the Oxford bypass, which crosses the river above Godstow. On the weir stream is the old Trout Inn: overlooking the lock cut are the ruins of Godstow Abbey. By Port Meadow the river is now significantly wider, flowing between sandy banks to Binsey, where a small jetty indicates the presence of the village and its handsome thatched pub. The navigation channel below Binsey becomes comparatively narrow and tree-lined after Medley Footbridge. Soon a water crossroads is reached, with the unnavigable Bulstake Stream running off to the west, while to the east a short, narrow cut to the Oxford Canal branches off under a very low railway bridge. A smart terrace of railway houses stands beside the river, all with doors opening onto the towpath. The journey through Oxford proper begins at the notoriously low (7ft 6in) Osney Bridge, an obstacle which makes it impossible for larger Thames cruisers to penetrate upstream.

Pubs and Restaurants (pages 138-139)

1 The Talbot Inn Oxford Road, Eynsham, Witney OX29 4BT (01865 882900; www.talboteynsham.co.uk). Dating from 1776, the tenant was also once the wharfinger with responsibility for operating the weighbridge on the now unnavigable wharf stream. Today this attractive pub dispenses real ale and serves food *daily L and E*. Dog- and child-friendly, outside seating and patio. Camping. B&B. *Open Mon-Sat 12.00-22.00 (Fri-Sat 22.30) & Sun 12.00-21.00.*

2 The Trout Inn Godstow Road, Godstow, Wolvercote, Oxford OX2 8PN (01865 510930; www.thetroutoxford.co.uk). A lovely ivy-covered stone building, with a riverside terrace, built in 1138 as a hospice for Godstow Nunnery. Peacocks roam the large gardens. Real ale served and food is available *daily 12.00-21.00*. Dog- and family-friendly. *Open 12.00-23.00 (Sun 22.30).*

3 The White Hart 126 Godstow Road, Wolvercote, Oxford OX2 8PQ (01865 511978; www.whitehartwolvercote.co.uk). Once a bakery and then a blacksmith's, this friendly community-run pub serves real ales and food *Wed-Sat 17.30-21.00 (Sat 15.30) & Sun 10.30-15.00* (see Community Market below). Dogs and families welcome, garden. *Regular live music. Traditional pub games, sports TV and Wi-Fi. Open Mon-Thu 16.00-23.00 (Wed-Thu 15.30), Fri 14.00-00.00 & Sat-Sun 10.30-00.00 (Sun 20.00).* Wolvercote Community Market operates here *every Sun 10.00-12.00* selling a wide range of farm produce, while *breakfasts* and *lunches* are served in the pub.

4 The Perch Inn Binsey Lane, Binsey, Oxford OX2 0NG (01865 728891; www.the-perch.co.uk). Moor at the jetty and walk 50yds along a path to this large and handsome 800-year-old thatched pub, standing in a superb large garden with willow trees. Real ale is served in the low-ceilinged bar, where the ghost of a sailor is said to appear. Food is available *daily 12.00-21.00*. Family-friendly, garden. Wi-Fi. *Open 11.00-22.00.*

5 Wytham Stores and Tea Garden Wytham, Oxford OX2 8QA (01865 243800; www.wythamstores.co.uk). Purveying hot and cold drinks, snacks, cakes, collectables and antiques. History centre. *Open 09.00-17.00 but closed Wed and Sun.*

Swinford Toll Bridge A fine stone balustraded bridge and toll house, where a small toll is collected. It was built in 1777.

● **Eynsham**
Oxon. PO, stores, *off-licence, chemist, DIY, takeaway, garage (distant)*. Once a town of considerable importance, boasting a Benedictine Abbey founded in the 11th C. Today Eynsham has a good selection of shops in the Market Square, around the old town hall. Stores *open daily 06.00-23.00.*

Wytham Great Wood A marvellous wood of over 600 acres, owned by Oxford University, whose field station is a good example of English vernacular architecture. A haven for birds; the hobby has nested here, nightingales and warblers sing, and teal visit in winter. There is a heronry at Wytham. Private, permit required from Wytham Sawmill Office, Keeper's Hill, Oxford OX2 8QQ.

- **Godstow**
  Oxon. A cluster of buildings around the few remains of Godstow Nunnery, founded in the 12th C by the noblewoman Evida. With many royal benefactors, the nunnery soon became prosperous, owning lands in 17 counties. Henry II's mistress Rosamund Clifford was buried here c.1176. Later, Oxford scholars were banned from the buildings in 1432 for 'junketing of every sort'. Dissolution took place in 1539, and in 1645 it was destroyed by Fairfax, commander of Cromwell's New Model Army. St Leonards, a two-storey domestic chapel and part of the abbey, was later restored, but now stands roofless. The bridge and the Trout Inn make a charming setting.

- **Wytham**
  Oxon. A very pretty small village set into the side of Wytham Hill, at its best when approached from the river. Wytham Abbey, originally 16th-C, has many later additions: the whole is pleasingly irregular.

NAVIGATIONAL NOTES

1 Access to the Oxford Canal can be gained via the weir stream above King's Lock and through Duke's Cut. Care needs to be taken as the Cut is often overgrown reducing the width and air draught. Maximum dimensions on this charming rural canal are: length 70ft 0in, beam 7ft 0in, headroom 7ft 0in. The canal is described in detail in *Nicholson Waterways Guide 1: Grand Union, Oxford & the South East*.

2 Take great care at Godstow Bridge, where the arches are narrow and low.

3 Proceeding downstream below Binsey, note that the navigation channel is under the iron footbridge on the west side, by the boatyard. Access to the Oxford Canal can be made along the channel above Osney Bridge.

4 The headroom at Osney Bridge is 7ft 6in at normal levels, less when the river is in spate. Those proceeding upstream who are in any doubt regarding the headroom should consult the lock keeper. And remember, the water levels can change very quickly, so you could get stuck *upstream*.

5 The east side of the river is shallow at Port Meadow.

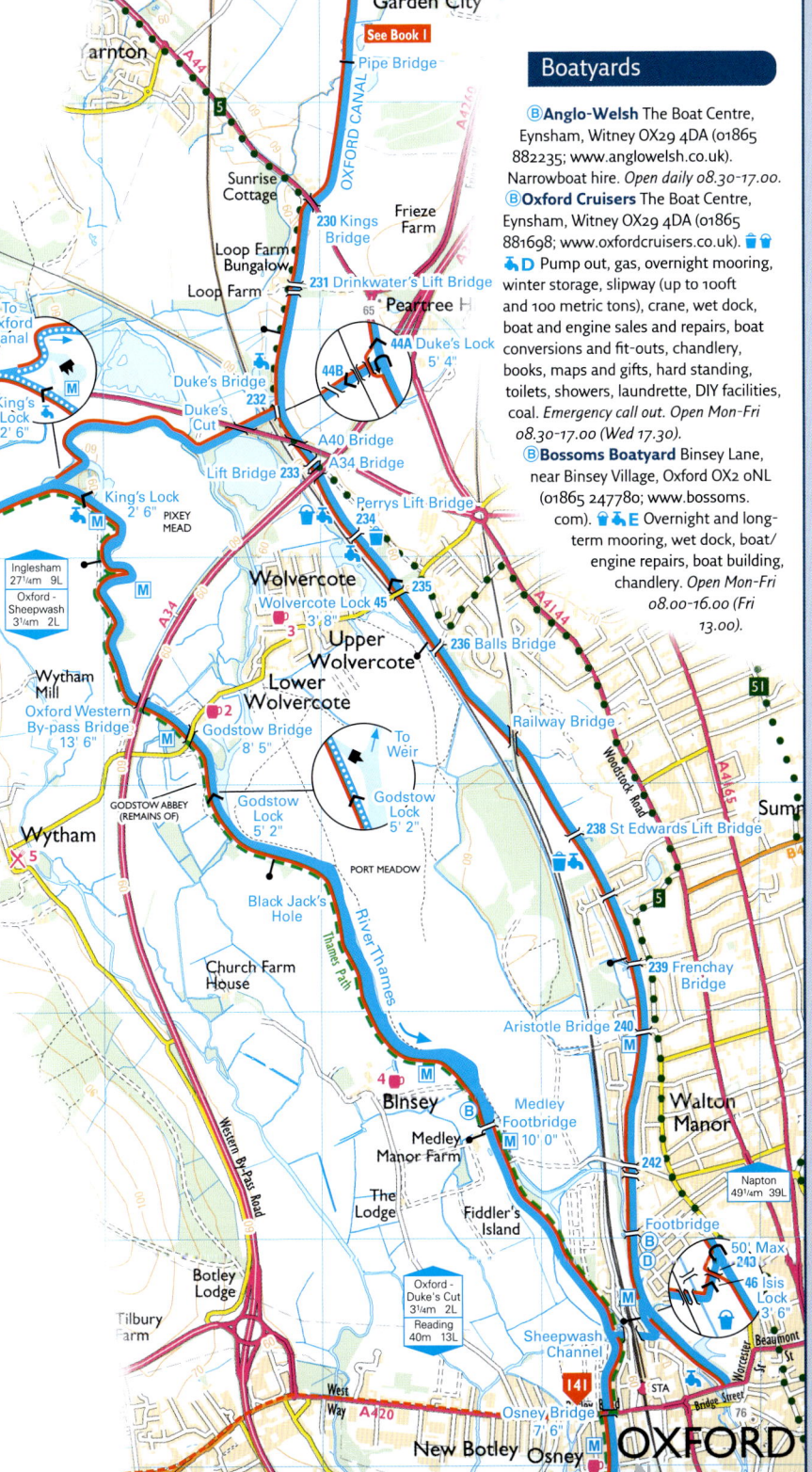

Oxford

This section, while not particularly picturesque, provides plenty of interest, in stark contrast to the water meadows above the town. Below Osney Bridge is a lovely stretch of urban waterway, with terraced houses facing the river, a handsome *pub* and a lock with a new timber boathouse – an environment much appreciated by the local workers who spend their lunch-breaks here in the summer. There are many access points to the towpath, which is well used by cyclists, joggers and walkers. Just above Osney Railway Bridge stands a touching memorial to Edgar Wilson who, on 15 June 1889, saved the lives of two boys here, at the cost of his own. Folly Bridge is always a hive of activity during the summer; Salter's trip boat base is here, along with a large riverside *pub*. Punts are available for hire and small motor and rowing boats proceed up and down. Christ Church Meadow lies to the east, and is thronged with tourists and sunbathers when the weather is fine. Below is a long row of boathouses, facing the mock Tudor of the University Rowing Club building. Downstream of Donnington Road Bridge suburbia keeps its distance and the river proceeds along a green passage to Iffley Lock, with its pretty balustraded footbridges and fine lock house, all surrounded by trees, with a white-painted *pub* nearby. There is an area of parkland to the west, on an isthmus created by the Weirs Mill Stream, followed by the functional steel of Kennington Railway Bridge. As the river dog-legs past Rose Isle pylons run parallel, but still the houses and factories, for the most part, keep away. Gradually the Oxford conurbation is left behind as the river passes through a mixture of woodland, suburbia and light industry, then curves through a maze of backwaters, used as boat club moorings, to Sandford Lock, the deepest on the river above Teddington and distinguished by the presence of large mill buildings. Below here the Thames passes through open country criss-crossed by electricity pylons. An absolutely fascinating stretch.

BOAT TRIPS
Salter Bros Folly Bridge, Oxford OX1 4LA (01865 243421; www.salterssteamers.co.uk). Established in 1858, the passenger boat services were introduced in 1888. Although now diesel powered, the boats are affectionately known as 'Salter's Steamers'. Scheduled services *mid May–mid Sep, daily* from Oxford, Abingdon, Wallingford, Reading, Henley-on-Thames, Marlow, Windsor and Staines, with some intermediate stops. These trips are heavily booked in the main holiday season, so telephone first, don't just turn up. Boats also available for party hire. Bar on board. Also punts and self-drive for hire.

- **Oxford**
Oxon. All services. The town was founded in the 10th C and has been a university city since the 13th C. Today it is a lively cosmopolitan centre of learning, tourism and industry.
Tourist Information Centre 15-16 Broad Street, Oxford OX1 3AS (01865 686430; www.experienceoxfordshire.org). Here you will find a good selection of city guides and maps, and helpful and informative staff. *Opens at 09.30 throughout the year and closes 16.00-17.00 according to the season.* It is, of course, the 39 **Colleges** which give Oxford its unique character – they can all be visited, but opening times vary, so check with the Tourist Information Centre. Those noted here are particularly representative of their periods.
Merton College Merton Street OX1 4JD. One of the earliest collegiate foundations, dating from 1264, the buildings are especially typical of the Perpendicular and Decorative periods. The chapel was begun in 1294 and Mob Quad was the first of the Oxford quadrangles. The library, mainly 14th-C, has a famous collection of rare books and manuscripts. During the Victorian era, the college was enlarged, and the Grove Buildings are by William Butterfield, with alterations in 1929 by T. Harold Hughes.
New College Holywell Street OX1 3BN. The college was founded by William of Wykeham, Bishop of Winchester, in 1379. The chapel, a noble example of early Perpendicular, was greatly restored by Sir George Scott in the 19th C. The great west window, after a cartoon by Reynolds, and Epstein's *Lazarus* are noteworthy. The 14th-C cloister and the workmanship of the wrought-iron screen, 1684, between the Garden Quad and the Garden, are outstanding memorials of their times.
Keble College Parks Road OX1 3PG. Built by William Butterfield in 1870, Keble is the only Oxford college entirely in the Victorian Gothic style. The frontage of red and grey patterned brickwork and the tracery windows display great self-confidence. The chapel, with its glass and mosaics, bricks, tiles and brass, contains Holman Hunt's *The Light of the World*.
St Catherine's College Manor Road OX1 3UJ. An important and interesting example of a new college, designed by the Danish architect, Arne Jacobsen in

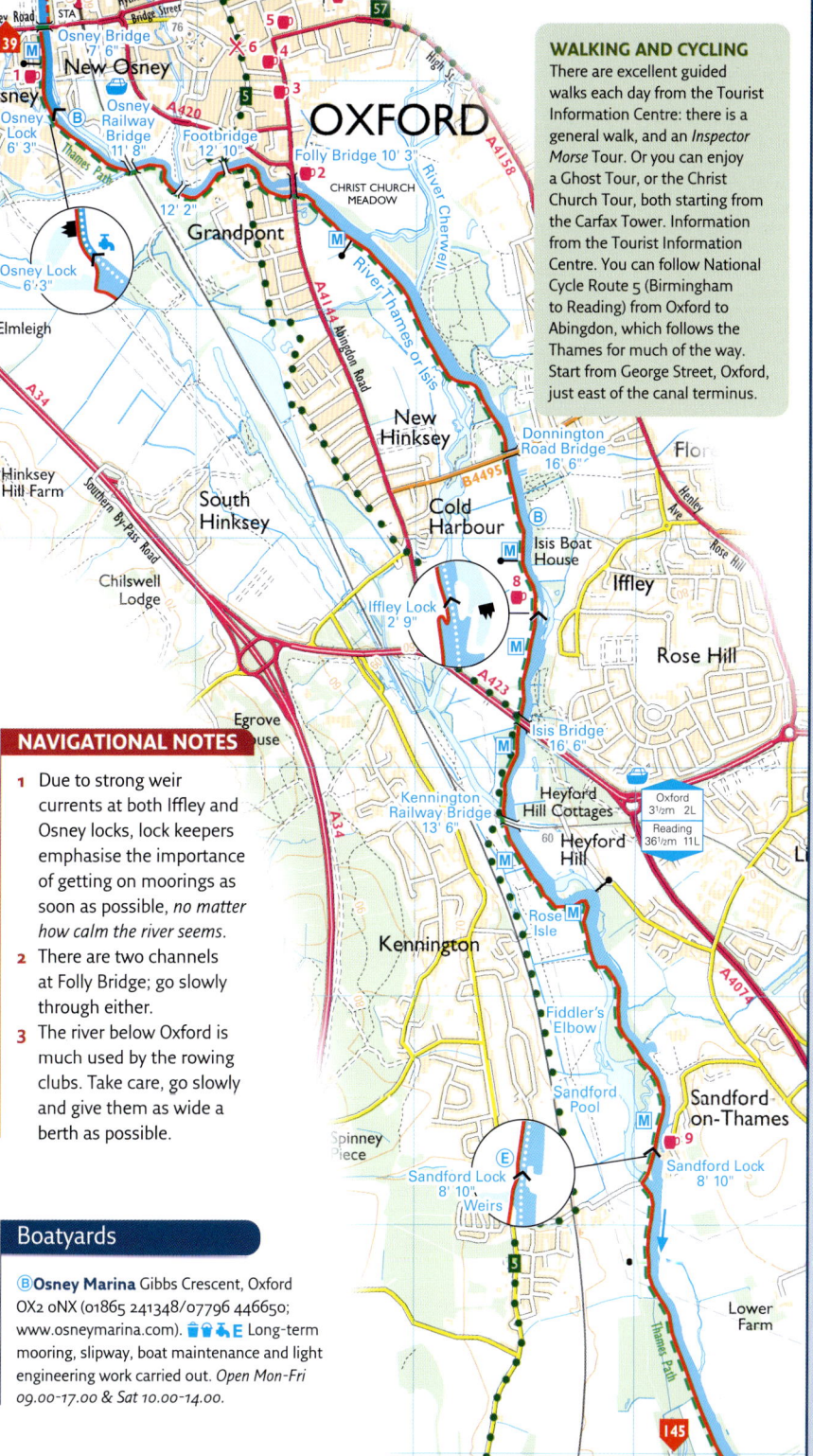

River Thames — Oxford

WALKING AND CYCLING

There are excellent guided walks each day from the Tourist Information Centre: there is a general walk, and an *Inspector Morse* Tour. Or you can enjoy a Ghost Tour, or the Christ Church Tour, both starting from the Carfax Tower. Information from the Tourist Information Centre. You can follow National Cycle Route 5 (Birmingham to Reading) from Oxford to Abingdon, which follows the Thames for much of the way. Start from George Street, Oxford, just east of the canal terminus.

NAVIGATIONAL NOTES

1. Due to strong weir currents at both Iffley and Osney locks, lock keepers emphasise the importance of getting on moorings as soon as possible, *no matter how calm the river seems*.
2. There are two channels at Folly Bridge; go slowly through either.
3. The river below Oxford is much used by the rowing clubs. Take care, go slowly and give them as wide a berth as possible.

Boatyards

B **Osney Marina** Gibbs Crescent, Oxford OX2 0NX (01865 241348/07796 446650; www.osneymarina.com). Long-term mooring, slipway, boat maintenance and light engineering work carried out. *Open Mon-Fri 09.00-17.00 & Sat 10.00-14.00.*

1964. The entrance to the college is reached through an unprepossessing car park area, but in the main quadrangle the effect is one of stark impact. The mass of glass windows with their bands of ribbed concrete stretch like concertinas on either side of the quadrangle. All is bleak but full of atmosphere. The furniture and college plate were also designed by Jacobsen.

St Anne's College Woodstock Road OX2 6HS. This college reflects some of the most exciting modern building in Oxford. The Wolfson block in the main quadrangle was designed by Howell, Killick and Partridge, 1964. With its two curving wings and square jutting windows, all of pre-cast concrete, this building is impressive and original. Facing the block is the Dining Hall by Gerald Banks, 1964, and to one side is Hartland House, mainly 1930s but with 1951 additions by Sir Giles Gilbert Scott.

Other interesting buildings include:

Radcliffe Camera Radcliffe Square. Dr Radcliffe left £40,000 for the building of this library by James Gibbs, 1739, to house his Physic library. It is a vast domed Italianate rotunda, now a Bodleian reading room, and not open to the public. The staircase and skylight can be admired through the doorway.

Sheldonian Theatre Broad Street OX1 3AZ (01865 277299; www.ox.ac.uk/sheldoniantheatre). Built by Christopher Wren in 1669 under the auspices of Gilbert Sheldon, Archbishop of Canterbury, the theatre was designed to be used for university ceremonies and degrees, which are still awarded here. For many years it also housed the workshops of the University Press. The interior, with its ceiling by Robert Streeter, is delightful. *Phone or email for opening hours. Closed when in use for university ceremonies, meetings and concerts.* Charge.

The Bodleian Old Library Catte Street OX1 3BG (01865 287400; www.bodleian.ox.ac.uk/libraries/old-library). Named after Thomas Bodley, who died in 1613 leaving a fine collection of rare manuscripts, the old Bodleian buildings, mainly 16th-C and early 17th-C, also incorporates Duke Humfrey's library, dating from the 15th C. Bodley extended Duke Humfrey's library and also financed the rebuilding of the Schools Quadrangle. Under the Copyright Act the Bodleian is entitled to claim a copy of every book published in the British Isles. It currently holds over 6½ million volumes and 160,000 manuscripts. *Open for guided tours (university ceremonies permitting) daily 10.00-16.00 (booking essential).* The tour lasts 45 mins and tickets are sold in the Divinity School. Charge. Please note that children under 14 years of age *are not permitted on the tours.* Café and shop. The Divinity School is *open Mon-Sat 09.00-17.00 (Sat 10.00) & Sun 11.00-17.00.* Charge.

Christ Church Cathedral St Aldgate's, Oxford OX1 1DP (01865 276150; www.chch.ox.ac.uk). The cathedral, with its inconspicuous entrance in Tom Quad, was originally part of the Priory of St Frideswide. It is mainly 12th-C with later additions and is typically Romanesque. The most splendid feature is the 16th-C stone-vaulted fan roof of the choir. There is medieval glass and also 19th-C glass by Burne-Jones. The Chapter House is a 13th-C masterpiece. Hidden gardens and guided tours. *Open daily 10.00-17.00.* Charge.

St Mary the Virgin The High Street, Oxford OX1 4BJ (01865 279111; www.universitychurch.ox.ac.uk). The fine 14th-C spire is a landmark. The church is typical of the Perpendicular style, apart from the magnificent Baroque porch with its twisted columns by Nicholas Stone, 1637. Tower and cemetery visits. *Open daily 09.30-17.00 (Sun 12.00).* Charge.

Ashmolean Museum Beaumont Street OX1 2PH (01865 278000; www.ashmolean.org). The oldest public museum in Britain (opened in 1683) and one of the most rewarding outside London. It has an outstanding collection of Near Eastern and European archaeology, as well as the Farrer collection of 17th- and 18th-C silver. The Herberden Coin Room has a vast display of early coins, while in the Department of Fine Art, the Michelangelo and Raphael drawings are to be admired. The museum also has the bulk of the archaeological material from the Upper Thames. *Open Tue-Sun 10.00-17.00.* Free. Café *open 10.00-16.30.*

Christ Church Gallery St Aldgate's, Oxford OX1 1DF (01865 276172; www.chch.ox.ac.uk). Built by Powell and Moya in 1968, the gallery displays Christ Church's private collection. Exceptional Renaissance drawings by Michelangelo, Leonardo da Vinci and Rubens, as well as 14th-18th-C paintings, mainly Italian. *Open Wed-Mon 11.00-17.00 (Sun 14.00). Last entry 16.30.* Charge.

Oxford University Press Museum Great Clarendon Street OX2 6DP (https://global.oup.com/uk/archives/5.html). A unique collection historic books, documents and presses extending back to 15th C, just two years after Caxton set up his first press in Westminster. Visits available *Mon-Fri* for individuals and groups *booked at least one day in advance.* Free.

Oxford University Museum of Natural History Parks Road OX1 3PW (01865 272950; www.oumnh.ox.ac.uk). The building by Deane and Woodward, 1855-60, in high Victorian Gothic was much admired by Ruskin. The interior is a forest of columns and skeletons covered by a glass roof. One great rarity is the head and claw of a dodo. Café. *Open daily 09.00-17.00.* Free.

Christ Church Meadows OX1 1DP. The meadows lie behind Christ Church and Merton and have fine views and a path leading down to the river. The path is lined with college barges (not many remaining) and boathouses. In the afternoons you can often watch the rowing eights. Enter the Meadows from St Aldates.

Oxford Botanic Garden & Arboretum Rose Lane OX1 4AZ (01865 610300; www.obga.ox.ac.uk). The oldest botanic garden in Britain, founded by Henry Lord Danvers in 1621. The garden was originally intended for the culture of medicinal plants, but today it fosters an extensive collection of rare plants for research and teaching. The gateway is by Inigo Jones. Shop, tours and picnic areas. *Open daily 10.00-18.00.* Charge.

Pubs and Restaurants (page 141)

There are many fine pubs and restaurants in Oxford. Those listed here are on or near the river, with one notable exception.

🍺 **1 The Punter** 7 South Street, Osney Island, Oxford OX2 0BE (01865 248832; www.thepunteroxford.co.uk). The site of a community-owned hydro scheme, this pub is heavily committed to real ale and serves food from an entirely vegetarian and vegan menu *Mon-Fri L and E & Sat-Sun 12.00-20.30*. Family-friendly, outside seating. Traditional pub games and Wi-Fi. *Open Sun-Thu 12.00-22.30 & Fri-Sat 12.00-23.00*.

🍺 **2 The Head of the River** Folly Bridge, Oxford OX1 4LB (01865 721600; www.headoftheriveroxford.co.uk). A three-storey pub and dining complex built in a converted grain warehouse. Real ale and bar meals *Mon-Sat 08.00-21.00 (Fri-Sat 22.00) & Sun 08.00-20.00*. Dog- and child-friendly, large terrace. Traditional pub games, sports TV and Wi-Fi. B&B. *Open daily 08.00-23.00 (Sun 22.00)*.

🍺 **3 Old Tom** 101 St Aldates, Oxford OX1 1BT (01865 243043; www.oldtomoxford.com). A unique experience that perfectly combines old world English pub with the best of Thai cuisine. Real ales. Food served *L and E*. Family-friendly, garden. Traditional pub games. *Open daily 12.00-22.30*.

🍺 **4 Saint Aldates Tavern** 108 St Aldates, Oxford OX1 1BU (01865 241185; www.staldatestavernoxford.co.uk). Not the original hostelry but there has been an inn on this site since 1397. Today's example dispenses an excellent selection of real ales and food *daily 12.00-21.00*. Dog- and family-friendly. Traditional pub games, sports TV and Wi-Fi. *Open 12.00-23.00 (Sun 22.00)*.

🍺✕ **5 The Chequers** 131 High Street, Oxford OX1 4DH (01865 727463; www.nicholsonspubs.co.uk). A 15th-C inn, with the original panelling and fireplace in the Monks bar at the front. Real ale, and meals *daily 12.00-21.00*. Dog- and family-friendly, outdoors courtyard seating. Traditional pub games, sports TV and Wi-Fi. *Open 12.00-23.00 (Sun 22.30)*.

✕ **6 Art Café** 14 Bonn Square, Oxford OX1 1LT (01865 242464; www.artcafeoxford.co.uk). Unfussy, wood décor, compact eatery exhibiting local art. Wide selection of free range, organic, gluten free and vegan foods available. Serving hot and cold meals, paninis, baguettes, wraps and salads to eat in or take away. *Open Mon-Fri 07.00-19.00, Sat 07.30-19.00 & Sun 08.00-18.00*.

🍺 **7 The Turf Tavern** Bath Place, Oxford, off Holywell Street OX1 3SU (01865 243235; www.greeneking-pubs.co.uk/pubs/oxfordshire/turf-tavern). Surprisingly secluded from the bustle of the city this pub is one of the most distinctive in Oxford. Made famous through Hardy's *Jude the Obscure*, this 13th-C tavern has become popular with both students and tourists. Real ale. Bar meals available *daily 11.00-21.00*. Dog- and family-friendly, gardens. Real fires and Wi-Fi. *Open 11.00-23.00*.

🍺 **8 The Isis Farmhouse** Haystack Corner, The Towing Path, Iffley Lock OX4 4EL (01865 243854; www.theisisfarmhouse.co.uk). Friendly licensed riverside café, with large garden, formerly the Isis Tavern. With no direct road access, the beer was once delivered from the river, and during the 19th C they received 5 shillings, or 7 shillings and 6 pence for each corpse removed from the river (it depended upon which side the body was found). Today there is real ale and food available *Thu-Sun 12.00-21.00*. Dog- and family-friendly, riverside garden. Gypsy jazz *Sun E*. Traditional pub games, newspapers and real fires. Mooring. *Open Thu-Sun 12.00-22.00*.

🍺 **9 The King's Arms** Church Road, Sandford Lock, Sandford-on-Thames OX4 4YB (01865 777095; www.chefandbrewer.com/pubs/oxfordshire/kings-arms). A fine lockside pub, with ceiling beams from old barge timbers, dispensing real ale and food *daily 11.30-21.00 (Fri-Sun 09.30)*. Dog- and family-friendly, lockside garden. Traditional pub games and Wi-Fi. *Open Mon-Thu 11.00-23.00 & Fri-Sun 09.30-23.00 (Sun 22.30)*. Home of the annual World Poohsticks Championships held in May (www.poohsticks.uk/venue) – *see page 148*.

PADDLING

Peripheral paddling opportunities abound on this section of the Thames, starting with the River Windrush at Newbridge (www.thames.me/uk/s02040.htm) followed by the Evenlode (www.charlbury.info/community/41) and – just upstream – the delightful River Cherwell (www.gopaddling.info/rivers/river-cherwell) which can take paddlers to a union with the South Oxford Canal at one of several locations north of Oxford.

The Oxford Canoe and Kayak Club Riverside Centre, Donnington Bridge Road, Cowley, Oxford OX4 4AZ (01865 328454; www.canoeoxford.org.uk) is situated on the Thames, meets *weekly Apr-Oct*, welcomes paddleboarders and has both a youth and adult section.

There is a slipway available at The Ferryman Inn (*see Pubs and Restaurants on page 136*).

Abingdon

Hills close in from the east as Radley College Boathouse is passed and the landscaped grounds of Nuneham House come into view, followed by the steeply wooded slope of Lock Wood. After Nuneham Railway Bridge the river passes the entrance to the Swift Ditch – once the main navigation channel, where one of the earliest pound locks on the Thames was built around 1620. Its remains were incorporated into an overspill weir in 1967. Above Abingdon Lock a handsome river frontage faces the open fields and sports grounds of Andersey Island, in an area noted for mute swans. The River Ock enters the Thames under a bridge (dated 1824) by the Old Anchor Inn, a mellow and welcoming building. Now the river heads for open country and enters Culham Reach, passing the wooden bridge across the Swift Ditch, standing beside the old road bridge and its more modern replacement. A sharp turn east marks the entrance to Culham Cut, overlooked by the 17th-C greystone manor.

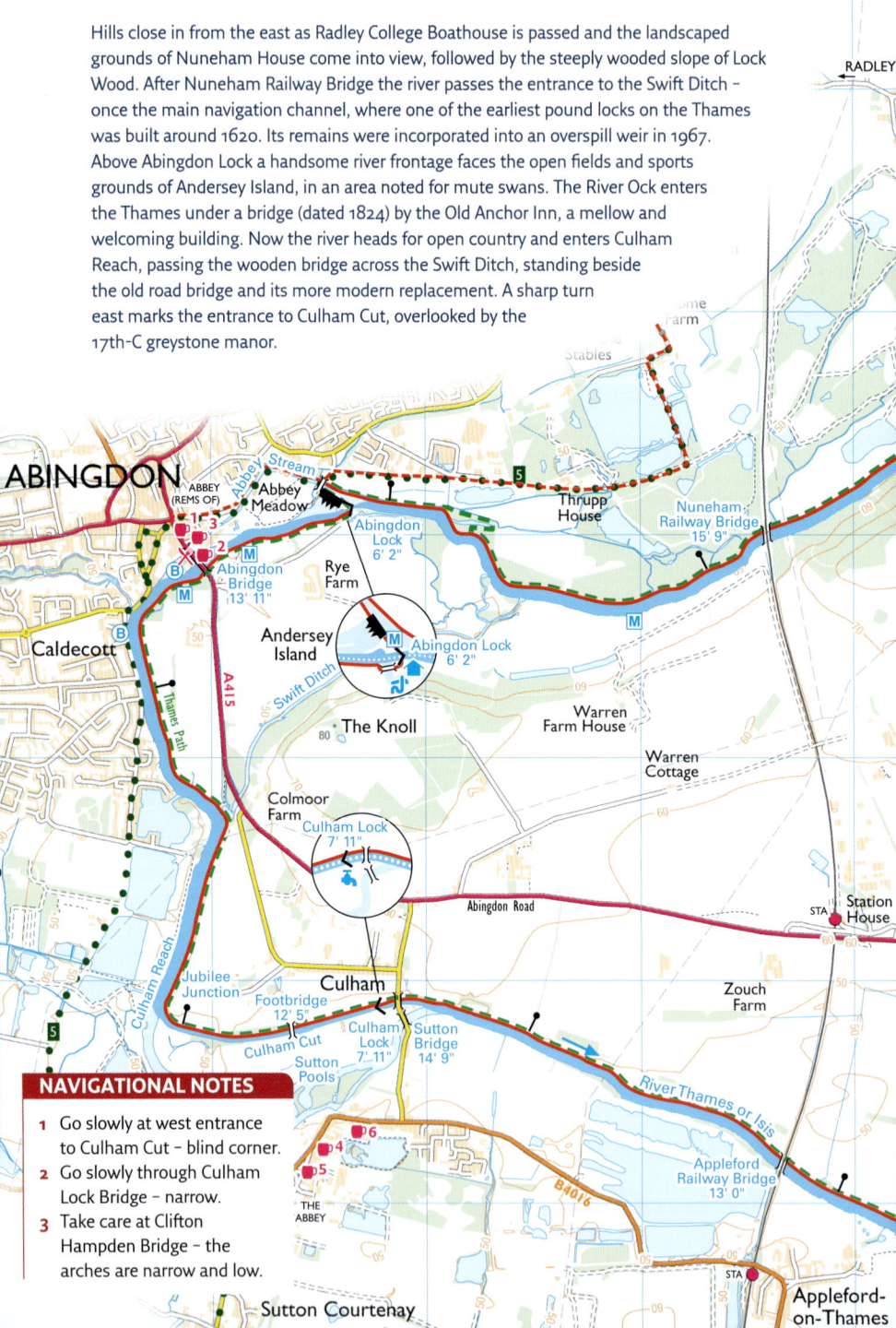

NAVIGATIONAL NOTES

1. Go slowly at west entrance to Culham Cut – blind corner.
2. Go slowly through Culham Lock Bridge – narrow.
3. Take care at Clifton Hampden Bridge – the arches are narrow and low.

River Thames — Abingdon

There is a footpath to the *pub* and village from the footbridge, with very limited *moorings* adjacent to it. Sutton Courtenay lies to the south beyond the weir stream and Sutton Pools. After Culham Lock the river resumes a more direct course, passing under a steel girder railway bridge before starting its eccentric sweep to Dorchester. The main navigation passes through Clifton Cut and the lock, below which is the entrance to the weir stream, navigable as far as the Plough at Long Wittenham. Beyond a caravan park to the east is Clifton Hampden Bridge, with the church and thatched cottages clustered on rising ground beyond – a superb setting. Burcot stands above the river to the north, which now begins to head south, passing Dorchester.

Boatyards

Ⓑ **Abingdon Bridge Marine** The Bridge, Abingdon OX14 3HX (01235 521125; www.abingdonbridgemarine.co.uk). Pump out, gas, day-hire craft, long-term mooring, slipway (20ft). *Open (during the season) 09.00-18.00.* Also incorporates:

Ⓑ **Abingdon Riverside Café** (01235 797575). *Open daily 09.00-21.00.*

BOAT TRIPS
Regular service to Oxford leaves from here, operated by Salters Steamers – *see* **Boat Trips** on page 140.

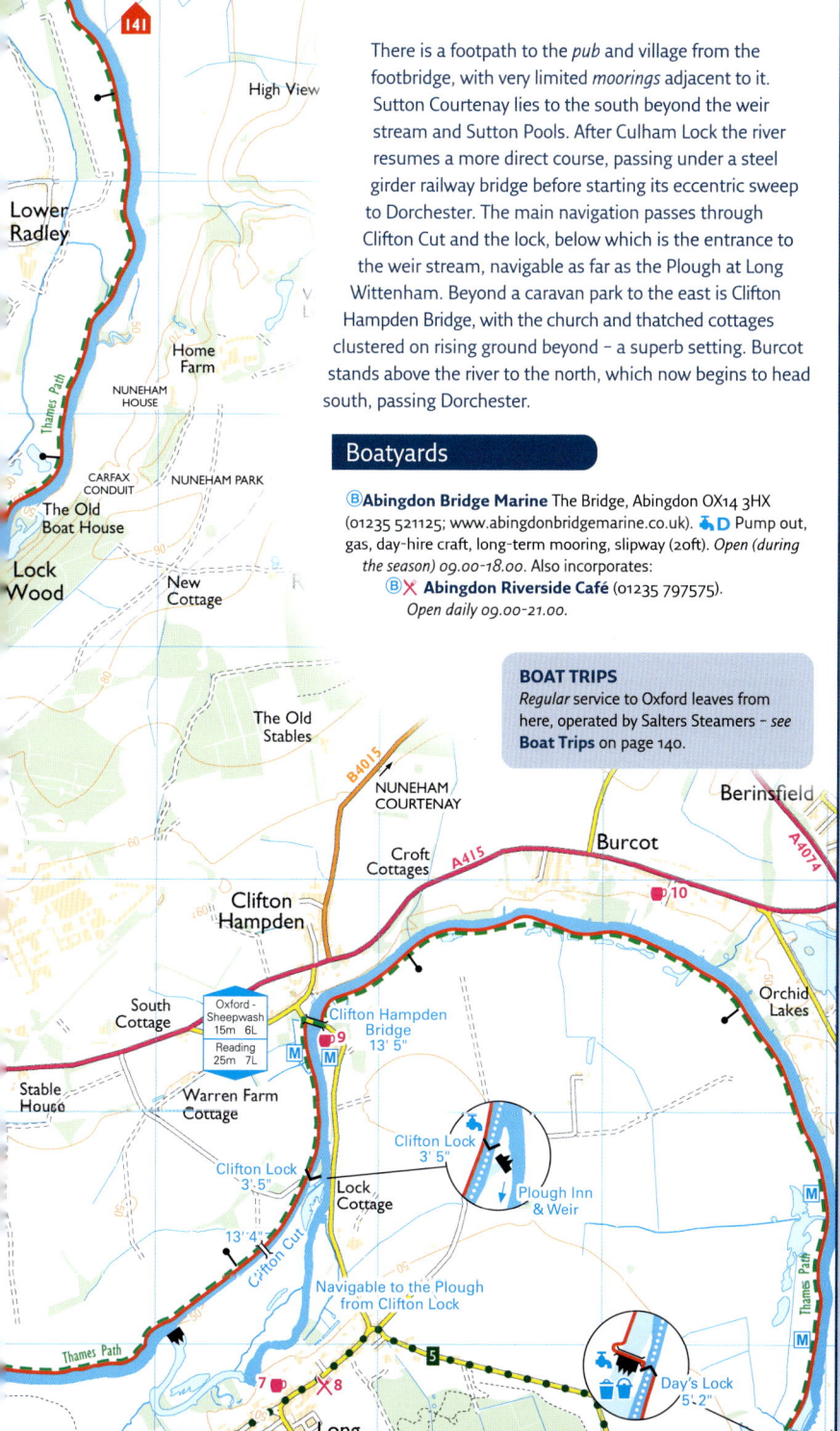

145

- **Radley**
  Oxon. Stores, station. A straggling commuter suburb.
  Radley College OX14 2HR. Founded in 1847. The college is based on Radley Hall, 1721–7, with many later additions. It is famed as a rowing school.
  Nuneham Park Nuneham Courtenay OX44 9PG. An 18th-C Palladian mansion by Leadbetter, splendidly situated in landscaped grounds (*see* Nuneham Courtenay, below) by Mason and Brown. Rousseau stayed here in 1767, and planted foreign wild flowers in the gardens. The Temple is by Athenian Stuart. Particularly noticeable from the river, standing on a wooded slope, is the Carfax Conduit, an ornamental fountain built in 1615 and once part of Oxford's water supply system. Originally situated in Carfax, it was moved here in 1786. In times of celebration wine and beer were run through it. Private, no pubic access.

- **Nuneham Courtenay**
  Oxon. An 18th-C model village of startling regularity along the main road, the result of a mass upheaval around 1760 when the 1st Earl of Harcourt required the original village site as part of his landscaped garden. Oliver Goldsmith (1730–74) wrote bitterly of this practice in *The Deserted Village* (1770):
  'The man of wealth and pride
  Takes up a space that many poor supplied'.
  However, whether the early villagers, moving from ancient clay-built cottages into far more modern houses, would have seen it that way is open to question. The site of the original village is by the estate road.

- **Abingdon**
  Oxon. All services. A busy 18th-C market town which grew up around the abbey, founded in AD695. Little of the original building now remains, except the Abbey Gate, Long Gallery and Checker, which has a 13th-C chimney, and is used as an Elizabethan-style theatre. Abbey Meadow, by the river, is a public park with a swimming pool, toilets, café and putting green. The best views of the town are from the river or the bridge, which is of medieval origin but was rebuilt in 1927. The river is dominated by the gaol, an impressive stone bastille built 1805–11 (now a leisure and sports centre) and St Helen's Church. Set among almshouses, the church has five aisles, making it broader than it is long. Long Alley Almshouses, beside the Old Anchor Inn, were built 1446–7 by the Fraternity of the Holy Cross. John Mason of Abingdon created Christ's Hospital, which has administered them since. The porches and lantern were added in 1605 and 1618. This area, around St Helen's Wharf, shows the town at its best. Each year in Abingdon, *on the Saturday closest to the summer solstice*, the people of Ock Street elect a Mayor for the day. Morris dancers perform outside each inn along the street, a custom of uncertain origin.
  Abingdon County Hall Museum Market Place, Abingdon OX14 3HG (01235 523703; www.abingdon.gov.uk/abingdon-county-hall-museum). What is recognised as one of the finest town halls in England stands in the Market Place. Built 1678–82 by Christopher Kempster, one of Wren's city masons, it is high and monumental with an open ground floor, once used as a market. *Open Tue-Sun & B Hol Mon 10.00–16.00.* Free.
  Swan Upping (www.royal.gov.uk) In the *third week of July*, the Queen's Swan Keeper, 19 other men (including representatives of the Vintners' and Dyers' Companies) and a supply of 'tea' (an intoxicating mixture of dark rum and milk) take to the river in double sculling skiffs, to ceremonially mark the swans. The men wear colourful uniforms, and 'round up' the swans, which are then checked, weighed and tagged with a stainless steel leg ring (beak-marking ceased a while ago). The count is carried out between Abingdon and Sunbury, and these days performs an important conservation role. This tradition dates from the 12th C, when swans were an important source of food. David Barber is currently (2017) her Majesty's Swan Keeper – a unique appointment. Swans on the river now number around 1200.
  Tourist Information Centre Roysse Court, Abingdon OX14 3HU (01235 522642; www.experienceoxfordshire.org/venue/abingdon-visitor-information-centre). *Open Mon-Fri 10.00–16.00.*

- **Culham**
  Oxon. A pretty village with a fine green and replica stocks.

- **Sutton Courtenay**
  Oxon. A large village, both wealthy and rewarding, built around a green. Eric Blair (George Orwell) and Henry Asquith (Prime Minister of the Liberal government, 1908–16) are buried in the churchyard here. Overlooking the weir stream is Norman Hall, a remarkably original late 12th-C manor house. The 14th-C abbey was never used as such, but as a grange.

- **Long Wittenham**
  Oxon. Access by boat along the weir stream from Clifton Lock. A fine straggling village along the original course of the river. The 13th-C church contains choir stalls from Exeter College, Oxford.
  Pendon Museum At the far end of Long Wittenham village OX14 4QD (01865 407365; www.pendonmuseum.com). A museum of miniature landscapes and transport. The main display is an ambitious recreation of the Vale of White Horse area in the 1930s, with 25 miniature trains running automatically, controlled by a computer. There are also miniature recreations of a Great Western Railway branch on Dartmoor, John Ahern's famous Madder Valley layout, and a row of shops based upon The Shambles in York. *Open daily 11.00–16.00. Last entry 15.15.* Telephone for details. Charge.

- **Clifton Hampden**
  Oxon. PO, stores. A cluster of thatched cottages away from the brick bridge (a Norman folly built in 1864). The small church on a mound is very picturesque.

River Thames Abingdon

Pubs and Restaurants (pages 144-145)

There are many pubs and eating places to be found in Abingdon.

🍺✖ **1 The Crown & Thistle** 18 Bridge Street, Abingdon OX14 3HS (01235 522556; www.crownandthistleabingdon.co.uk). Bar and restaurant in old 17th-C coaching inn, with attractive cobbled courtyard. Real ales. Meals served *Mon-Sat 08.00-22.00 (Fri-Sat 22.30) & Sun 08.00-21.00*. Dog- and child-friendly. Real fires and Wi-Fi. B&B. *Open Mon-Sat 08.00-23.00 (Fri-Sat 00.30) & Sun 08.00-22.30.*

🍺✖ **2 The Nags Head on the Thames** The Bridge, Abingdon OX14 3HX (01235 639023; www.thenagsheadonthethames.co.uk). This Grade II listed pub is situated halfway across the bridge with riverside gardens. Real ale and food available *daily 12.00-21.00 (Sun 20.00)*. Dog- and child-friendly, island garden. Traditional pub games, newspapers, real fires and Wi-Fi. *Open 12.00-23.00 (Sun 21.00).*

🍺 **3 The Broad Face** 30-32 Bridge Street, Abingdon OX14 3HR (01235 538612; www.thebroadface.com). Bright and welcoming, this pub serves real ale and food *Mon-Sat L and E & Sun 12.00-18.30*. Family-friendly, outside seating. Wi-Fi. *Open Mon-Sat 12.00-23.00 (Fri-Sat 01.00) & Sun 12.00-22.00.*

🍺 **4 The George** 4 Church Street, Sutton Courtenay OX14 4NJ (01235 848142; www.georgesuttoncourtenay.co.uk). Imposing 17th-C, Grade II listed half-timbered hostelry serving real ale and good cheer. Delicatessen in the foyer supplying food to take in, together with *regular Fri or Sat* pop-up street food vans stationed outside for similar supplies. Dog- and family-friendly, beer garden. Real fires and Wi-Fi. *Open Mon-Thu L and E & Fri-Sun 12.00-23.00 (Sun 21.30).*

🍺 **5 The Swan Foodhouse & Bar** The Green, Sutton Courtenay OX14 4AE (01235 847446; www.theswanfoodhouse.com). A quiet red-brick pub serving real ale and food made from seasonal, local produce *Tue-Sun L and E (not Sun E)*. Also breakfast *Tue-Fri 08.30-11.30*. Family-friendly, garden. *Open Tue-Fri L and E & Sat-Sun 12.00-23.00 (Sun 21.00).*

🍺✖ **6 The Fish** 4 Appleford Road, Sutton Courtenay OX14 4NQ (01235 848242; www.thefishatsuttoncourtenay.co.uk). Set in an attractive brick and timber building, this pub serves real ale and food *Tue-Sun L and E (not Sun E)*. Garden. *Open Tue-Sat L and E & Sun 12.00-17.00.*

🍺✖ **7 The Plough Inn** 24 High Street, Long Wittenham OX14 4QH (01865 407738; www.theploughinnlw.co.uk). The weir stream is navigable from Clifton Lock to this attractive pub, which serves real ale and real cider. Food is available *daily L and E (not Sun E)*. Dog- and family-friendly, riverside garden and play area. Traditional pub games, real fires and Wi-Fi. *Open 12.00-23.00 (Sun 21.00).*

✖🍷 **8 The Vine & Spice** 35 High Street, Long Wittenham OX14 4QH (01865 409900; www.thevineandspice.co.uk). Cosy, welcoming Indian bar/restaurant, bedecked with flowers in the summer. Real ale. Meals served *L and E*. Children welcome. Garden. Wi-Fi. *Open daily L and E.*

🍺✖ **9 The Barley Mow** Clifton Hampden Road, Clifton Hampden OX14 3EH (01865 407847; www.chefandbrewer.com/pubs/oxfordshire/barley-mow). Deservedly famous and superbly old-fashioned thatched pub built in 1350. It was described by Jerome K. Jerome as having 'quite a story book appearance'. Real ale and food available *11.30-21.00 (Sat-Sun 09.30)*. Family-friendly, garden. Real fires and Wi-Fi. Camping nearby. *Open daily 11.00-23.00 (Sat-Sun 09.30).*

🍺✖ **10 The Chequers** Abingdon Road, Burcot OX14 3DP (01865 407771; www.chequers-burcott.co.uk). A reasonable walk from Clifton Hampden or Dorchester to visit this handsome and totally civilised thatched pub. Real ale and food available *12.00-21.00 (Sun 20.00)*. Also breakfast served *daily 08.00-10.00*. Family-friendly, garden. Real fires. Camping nearby. *Open 12.00-23.00 (Sun 22.00).*

WALKING AND CYCLING

Abingdon Town Council publish an active travel map giving details of walking and cycling opportunities around the town – visit www.abingdon.gov.uk/shop-eat-drink/active-travel-map-of-abingdon-on-thames. There are excellent walks across the weir at Sutton Courtenay, by Sutton Pools. NCN5 provides a traffic free cycle route to Oxford via a mix of railway path, dedicated cycle routes and the towpath.

Osney Lock, Oxford

147

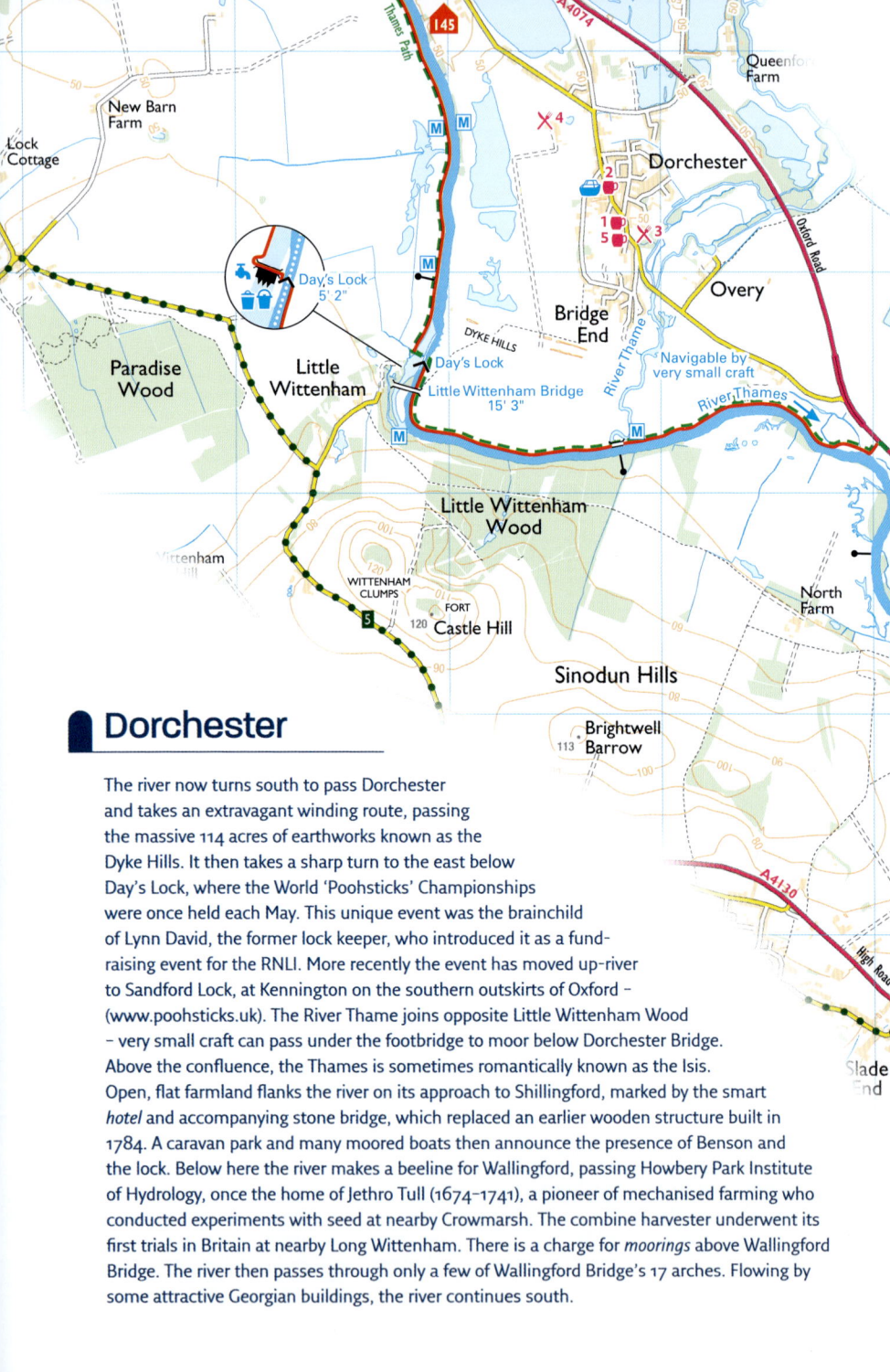

Dorchester

The river now turns south to pass Dorchester and takes an extravagant winding route, passing the massive 114 acres of earthworks known as the Dyke Hills. It then takes a sharp turn to the east below Day's Lock, where the World 'Poohsticks' Championships were once held each May. This unique event was the brainchild of Lynn David, the former lock keeper, who introduced it as a fund-raising event for the RNLI. More recently the event has moved up-river to Sandford Lock, at Kennington on the southern outskirts of Oxford – (www.poohsticks.uk). The River Thame joins opposite Little Wittenham Wood – very small craft can pass under the footbridge to moor below Dorchester Bridge. Above the confluence, the Thames is sometimes romantically known as the Isis. Open, flat farmland flanks the river on its approach to Shillingford, marked by the smart *hotel* and accompanying stone bridge, which replaced an earlier wooden structure built in 1784. A caravan park and many moored boats then announce the presence of Benson and the lock. Below here the river makes a beeline for Wallingford, passing Howbery Park Institute of Hydrology, once the home of Jethro Tull (1674–1741), a pioneer of mechanised farming who conducted experiments with seed at nearby Crowmarsh. The combine harvester underwent its first trials in Britain at nearby Long Wittenham. There is a charge for *moorings* above Wallingford Bridge. The river then passes through only a few of Wallingford Bridge's 17 arches. Flowing by some attractive Georgian buildings, the river continues south.

Boatyards

ⓑ ✕ ♀ **Benson Waterfront Leisure Park** Benson Cruiser Station, Benson OX10 6SJ (01491 838304; www.bensonwaterfront.co.uk). 🚻🚿🛒 D E Long-term mooring, winter storage, toilets, showers, shop, camping, lodges. ✕ ♀ **Waterfront Café Bar & Bistro** (01491 833732; www.waterfrontcafe.co.uk). *Open daily 08.30-21.00.*

ⓑ **Le Boat** Benson Cruiser Station, Benson OX10 6SJ (01491 824067; www.leboat.co.uk/boating-holidays/england/thames/benson). 🚻🚿🛒D Gas, pump out, boat hire. *Open Mon, Wed and Fri-Sat 09.00-17.00 & Tue and Thu 10.00-16.00.*

ⓑ **Bygone Boating Ltd** Benson Cruiser Station, Benson OX10 6SJ (07375 677823; www.bygoneboating.co.uk). Hiring a fleet of classic wooden motor cruisers. Slipway. Ferry operators – see **Boat Trips**. *Open daily 08.00-18.00.*

NAVIGATIONAL NOTES

1. Take care at the blind corner below Little Wittenham Bridge.
2. Wallingford Bridge – use the central arch.

BOAT TRIPS

Ferret operated by Bygone Boats (07375 677823; www.bensonferry.wordpress.com) runs ferry trips from the slipway at Benson Waterfront to the west side of Benson Lock *daily 09.00-17.00* dependent on weather and river conditions. Details including latest updates are available at www.facebook.com/groups/bensonferry.

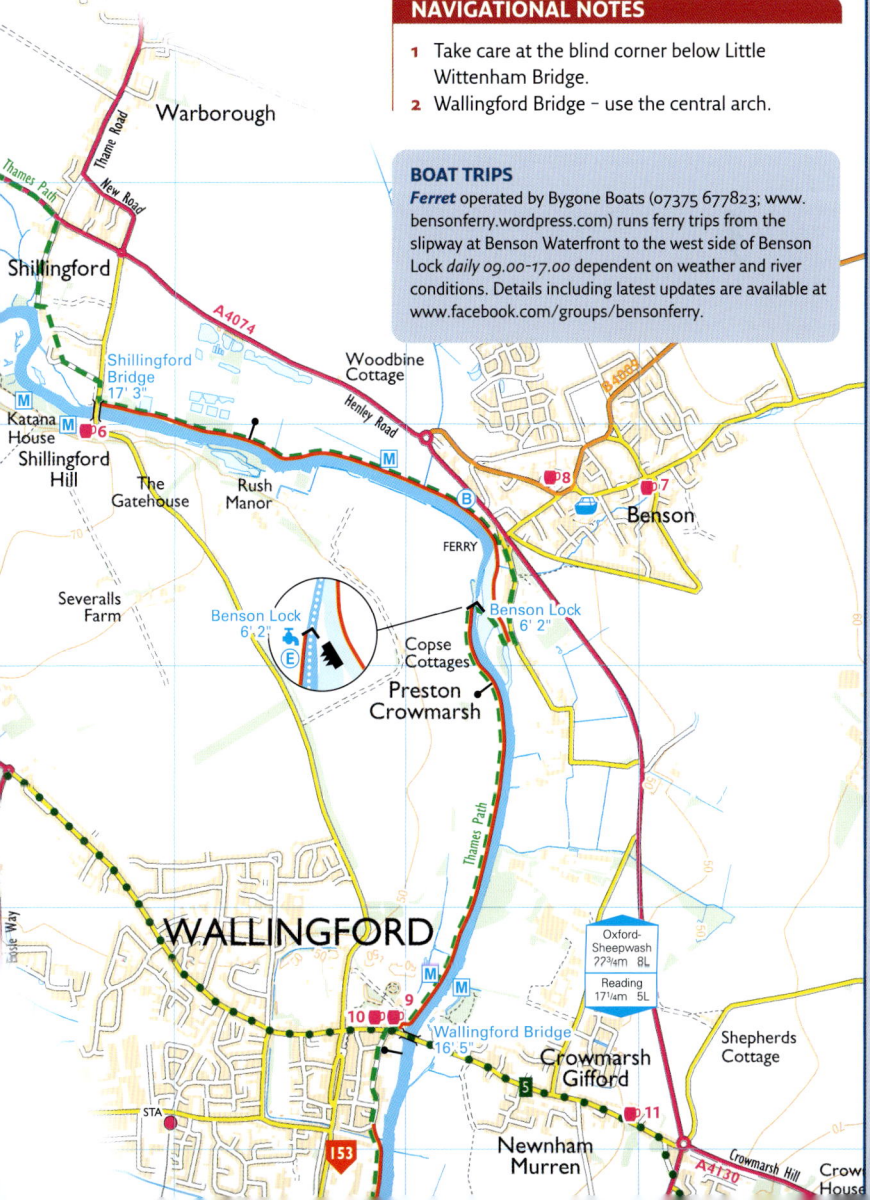

- **Little Wittenham**
Oxon. The church here is nicely situated amongst the woods.
- **Dorchester**
Oxon. Stores, farm shop, off-licence. This large village of pretty cottages and hotels was once a small Roman town sited on the River Thames, was used for the location of Midsomer Murders. It is accessible from the river by footpath over the Dyke Hills from Day's Lock. Small craft may navigate up the River Thame to Dorchester Bridge. The town is quite quiet, now it has a bypass, and today only the abbey Church of SS Peter and Paul, founded in the 7th C, reveals that this was once the cathedral city of Wessex, then Mercia. Approached through a Butterfield lych gate, the mostly decorated abbey gives little clue to the splendid size and proportion of its interior. The most important feature is the Jesse window, with stonework imitating trees. The figures seem to grow organically from the body of Jesse. Note also the tomb of Sir John Holcombe: the realism and fluidity of the effigy has inspired many modern sculptors. The Old Monastery Guest House, built c.1400 and used in the 17th C as a grammar school, now houses the Abbey Museum (see below), although most Roman finds are in the Ashmolean. Stores open *daily 07.00-21.00*. The farm shop (07956 615626; www.bishopscourtfarm.com) also includes a café, alpaca walking and moorings – *open Mon-Fri 09.00-16.00 & Sat-Sun 09.30-17.00*.
Dorchester Abbey Museum The Abbey Guest House, Dorchester OX10 7HR (01865 340007; www.dorchester-abbey.org.uk). Shop. *Open Wed-Thu and Sat-Sun 14.00-17.00*. Donations.
- **Shillingford**
Oxon. The extremely handsome triple-arched bridge and the hotel stand away from the village, a discreet residential area to the north.
- **Benson**
Oxon. PO, stores, chemist, butcher, takeaway, fish & chips, off-licence, library, garage. A friendly village with a pleasant river frontage, although it is hard to believe this was once a seat of the Kings of Mercia. The church is 13th-C. The *PO* is in the Parish Hall, *open Tue-Thu 09.30-12.30 & Wed 13.00-16.00*. The shop is *open daily 07.00-22.00*.

- **Wallingford**
Oxon. All services (station distant). One of the oldest Royal Boroughs, the town received its charter in 1155. Well-preserved banks and ditches of Saxon defences still remain. From the river the town is dominated by the unusual openwork spire of St Peter's Church (key at the TIC), built by Sir Robert Taylor in 1777. At the rear of the George Hotel is the entrance to the splendid Castle Gardens, where footpaths lead to the remains of the Norman castle built on a mound by Robert D'Oilly in 1071, held for the Empress Matilda during her fight with King Stephen for the English crown, and finally destroyed by Fairfax in 1646. The town hall, built in 1670, has a typical open ground floor. The 17-arched bridge is of medieval origins (possibly as early as 1141), and was rebuilt in 1809 when the balustrade was added. It still has a Bridge Chamberlain, appointed each year by the town council. Walk up the hill from the river and turn left to enjoy the town centre, shops and market square. Rugfest is a *summer* music festival (www.rugfest.org) held in the town while Bunkfest (http://bunkfest.co.uk) is a community family festival that takes place at the *beginning of Sep*.
Wallingford Museum Flint House, High Street, Wallingford OX10 0DB (01491 835065; www.wallingfordmuseum.org.uk). Housed in a part of a medieval hall-house. Take a walk through Saxon and Medieval Wallingford, and visit a Victorian shop. *Open Mar-Nov, Tue-Sat 14.00-17.00 (Sat 10.30) & Jun-Aug 14.00-17.00*. Charge.
The Corn Exchange Market Place, Wallingford OX10 0EG (01491 825000, www.cornexchange.org.uk). Theatre and cinema.
Cholsey and Wallingford Railway Cholsey Station, Wallingford OX10 9GQ (01491 835067; www.cholsey-wallingford-railway.com). This line opened in 1866 to link the Great Western Railway's main line with the Wycombe Extension Railway. The last British Rail service ran on 31 May 1981. Now 2½ miles of track have been purchased, and steam and diesel trains are run between Cholsey and St John's Road, Wallingford. *45 minute* round trip. Visit website for further details.
Tourist Information Centre Town Hall, Market Place, Wallingford OX10 0EG (01491 826972; www.wallingfordtowncouncil.gov.uk/visitors/town-information-centre). *Open Mon-Sat 09.30-15.30 (Sat 13.30)*.

AND BABY MAKES THREE . . .

Babies who are not yet walking can be coped with fairly easily on a boating holiday. Children between the ages of one and five are probably the most difficult to deal with, and the following points may be helpful:

1. Mum, Dad and two toddlers on a heavily locked length of canal will have problems. If you cannot gather a larger crew to help, a river such as the Thames, where the locks are operated by keepers, is ideal.
2. Ensure buoyancy aids are worn by children when they are up on deck.
3. Avoid traditional style narrowboats with a small unprotected rear deck. Thames cruisers, with an enclosed cockpit, are ideal.
4. Airing cupboards are useful for drying all the washing produced by small children.
5. Pack their favourite toys and games.
6. Allow time for plenty of stops, where children can run off their excess energy.

From the age of six, children, properly supervised, can become useful crew members.

PADDLING

AV Boats have a variety of craft for hire including canoes, kayaks and paddleboards from their two bases at Nags Head Island, The Bridge, Abingdon OX14 3HX (01235 539090; www.avboats.co.uk) and Unit 3, Benson Waterfront, Benson, Wallingford OX10 6SJ (01491 835545; www.avboats.co.uk). Moi's SUP School (07770 903860; www.moisupschool.co.uk/oxfordshire/paddleboarding-places) helpfully points you in the direction of 10 varied paddles in Oxfordshire. He operates from the Rose Revived at Newbridge – *see Pubs and Restaurants on page 136* – while equally useful is the Paddle Up round up of good launching sites on the river at www.paddleup.co.uk/blog/places-to-launch-on-river-thames.
There is a slipway at The Beetle & Wedge Boathouse – *see Pubs and Restaurants on page 152.*

Pubs and Restaurants (pages 148–149)

1 The George Hotel 25 High Street, Dorchester-on-Thames OX10 7HH (01865 340404; www.george-dorchester.co.uk). Built in 1495 as the brew-house of the nearby abbey, this comfortable galleried inn is often used for film and TV locations. Otherwise, real ale and food is available *L and E*, together with breakfast *07.00-09.00 (Sat-Sun 08.00-10.00)*. Dog- and family-friendly, garden. Real fires and Wi-Fi. B&B. *Open daily 12.00-22.30.*

2 The White Hart Hotel 26 High Street, Dorchester OX10 7HN (01865 340074; www.white-hart-hotel-dorchester.co.uk). A 16th-C coaching inn serving real ale and food *daily L and E*. Family-friendly. Real fires and Wi-Fi. B&B. *Open 12.00-23.00.*

3 Dorchester Abbey Tearooms 14A High Street, Dorchester OX10 7HR (01865 340007; www.dorchester-abbey.org.uk). Next to the abbey. Delicious biscuits, cakes and scones, all home-made and including lemon drizzle cake. Quiet, enclosed garden. Children welcome. Run by the village ladies, and all the profits go to charity. *Open Wed-Thu 15.00-17.00 & Sat-Sun 14.30-17.00.*

4 Snug Café & Farm Shop Bishop Court Farm, Wallingford OX10 7HP (01865 590390; www.bishopscourtfarm.com/snug). Local fresh seasonal delights embracing breakfast and lunches, teas, coffees, cakes and snacks. Takeaway service. Mooring. *Open Mon-Fri 09.00-16.00 & Sat-Sun 09.30-17.00.*

5 The Fleur de Lys 9 High Street, Dorchester OX10 7 HH (01865 818475; www.facebook.com/TheFleurDoT). This charming 16th-C inn is on the main street of Dorchester opposite the Abbey. The popular hostelry has a dining room, cosy bar and a large garden. Meals available *Wed-Fri E & Sat-Sun 12.00-21.00*. Real ale. Dog- and family-friendly, garden. Traditional pub games, real fires and Wi-Fi. Takeaway service. *Open Wed-Fri 17.00-22.00 (Fri 23.00) & Sat-Sun 12.00-23.00.*

6 Shillingford Bridge Hotel Shillingford Road, Shillingford Bridge OX10 8LZ (01865 858567; www.shillingfordbridgehotel.co.uk). Smart riverside hotel with excellent moorings (modest fee). Patrons may use the outdoor heated swimming and paddling pools, *closed after 19.00*. Real ale. Bar and restaurant meals available *L and E, daily*. Children welcome. Pleasant riverside garden. Wi-Fi. B&B. *Open all day.*

7 The Crown Inn at Benson 52 High Street, Benson OX10 6RP (01491 528930; www.facebook.com/TheCrownInnatBenson). Welcoming, comfortable 16th-C inn with inglenooks, log fires and a ghost. Real ale and food available *Mon-Sat L and E & Sun 12.00-20.00*. Dog- and family-friendly, garden. Real fires, sports TV and Wi-Fi. B&B. *Open Mon-Sat 07.30-23.00 Sun 08.30-22.00.*

8 The Three Horseshoes 2 Oxford Street, Benson OX10 6LX (01491 838242; www.thethreehorseshoesbenson.co.uk). Traditional 17th-C pub serving real ale with food available *L and E (not Sun E)*. Family-friendly, outside seating and play area. B&B. *Open Mon-Sat 12.00-22.30 (Fri-Sat 00.00) & Sun 12.00-22.00.*

9 The Boat House 103 High Street, Wallingford OX10 0BL (01491 834100; www.greeneking.co.uk/pubs/oxfordshire/boat-house). Lively riverside pub, with terrace and conservatory. Food available *daily 09.00-21.00*. Quiz *Mon*. Family-friendly. Sports TV and Wi-Fi. *Open 09.00-23.00 (Fri-Sat 00.00)*

10 The George Hotel 83 High Street, Wallingford OX10 0BS (01491 836665; www.peelhotels.co.uk/george-hotel). An attractive 16th-C Grade II listed inn, dispensing real ale and food *L and E*. Family-friendly, garden. Real fires, sports TV and Wi-Fi. B&B. *Open daily 11.00-23.00 & Sun 12.00-22.30.*

11 The Bell 75-79 The Street, Crowmarsh Gifford, Wallingford OX10 8EF (01491 835324; www.hungryhorse.co.uk). Large family pub serving real ale and food *daily 11.30-21.00*. Child-friendly, garden and play area. Family quiz *Wed*. Traditional pub games and Wi-Fi. *Open 11.30-23.00 (Sun 22.30).*

WALKING AND CYCLING

There are great walks from either side of Little Wittenham Bridge. To the south there are paths to the hill fort at the summit of the Sinodun Hills, returning over Round Hill. To the north you can follow the riverside path to the River Thame, turning north towards Dorchester. You then return via the Dyke Hills.

Moulsford

A broad stretch of river, pleasant but unremarkable. The buildings of Carmel College stand in wooded grounds in Mongewell Park, which fronts the Thames for a mile. North Stoke lies back from the river to the east. The islands above Brunel's lovely skewed brick arched railway bridge are supposedly haunted. Gradually the hills close in as the valley narrows towards Goring. The Beetle & Wedge Boathouse marks the site of the old ferry which once linked Moulsford and South Stoke. These villages face each other across the river, but they are now totally separate.

● **North Stoke**
Oxon. An attractive red brick village among trees. The church is pleasingly original and unrestored, with notable wall paintings.

● **Cholsey**
Oxon. PO, stores, chemist, butcher, takeaway, off-licence, station (¾ mile distant). An undistinguished village but there is a pub, a range of shops and a station nearby. The shop is *open Mon-Sat 06.00-22.00 & Sun 07.00-22.00.*

● **Moulsford**
Oxon. A roadside village with large houses by the river. The small, secluded church was rebuilt by Gilbert Scott in 1846: his fee was reputedly £64.

● **South Stoke**
Oxon. A pretty residential village among trees. St Andrew's Church is 13th-C. Access can be gained from the river opposite the Beetle & Wedge Boathouse.

ROW, ROW, ROW YOUR BOAT . . .

In the early part of the 20th C it was not uncommon for those who were lucky enough to live by the river to own a camping boat. The Thames Gig was typical of such craft, and could have been 25ft long with a 4ft beam, constructed perhaps by Hammertons of Thames Ditton. Clinker built in mahogany and propelled by two pairs of sculls, it would have two rowing thwarts, passenger seats in the stern and bows, a camping cover and, for comfort, a carpet! A crew of two could propel such a craft at 6mph over still water for considerable distances, with the added options of a small sail on a mast stepped at the bow if the wind was favourable, or a tow line to haul from the bank when the current was adverse.

Pubs and Restaurants

🍺✕ **1 The Red Lion** 39 Wallingford Road, Cholsey, Wallingford OX10 9LG (01491 599842; www.theredlioncholsey.co.uk). Friendly village local serving real ales and home-cooked food *Sat-Sun 12.00-21.00 (Sun 16.30)*. Dog- and Child-friendly, garden. Wi-Fi. *Open Tue-Thu 17.00-22.00 & Fri-Sun 12.00-23.00 (Sun 18.00).*

✕ 🍷 **2 Memories of Bengal** 12 Wallingford Road, Cholsey OX10 9LQ (01491 662777; www.memoriesofbengal.co.uk). Indian restaurant serving food *daily 17.30-22.00 (Fri-Sat 23.00) & Sun 12.00-14.30.* Vegan options. Wi-Fi. Takeaway service.

✕ 🍷 **3 Shangki-Li Peking Restaurant** 20 The Forty, Ilges Lane, Cholsey OX10 9ND (01491 651919). Popular Chinese restaurant, with a highly regarded all-you-can-eat menu, situated rather bizarrely above the local Tesco. Friendly staff and excellent service. *Open Tue-Sun 18.00-22.00 (Fri-Sun 17.00).*

🍺 **4 The Morning Star** 98 Papist Way, Cholsey OX10 9QL (01491 651413). Unpretentious village pub half a mile from the river. Real ale. Traditional pub games and sports TV. *Open Mon-Thu 13.00-23.30 (Wed 21.00) & Fri-Sun 12.00-00.00 (Sun 21.00).*

🍺✕ **5 The Beetle & Wedge Boathouse** Ferry Lane, Moulsford OX10 9JF (01491 651381; www.beetleandwedge.co.uk). A *beetle* is a mallet used to hit the *wedge* which split trees into planks for floating down river to London; a practice last recorded in 1777 but recalled in the name of this justly famous pub, where H.G. Wells stayed while writing *Mr Polly* – it features in the book as the Potwell Inn. The building is a former manor house, standing in a superb riverside situation, with a lovely garden and a jetty. Children and dogs are welcome and the large garden is a plus. Food available *Mon-Sat L and E & Sun 12.00-20.00.* B&B. *Open 11.00-23.30 (Sun 12.00).*

🍺✕ **6 The Perch & Pike** The Street, South Stoke, Reading RG8 0JS (01491 520647; www.perchandpike.co.uk). Cosy 18th-C red brick and flint pub, with low beams, open log fires, antique furniture and, perhaps, a ghost. Real ale. Food available *Wed-Sun L and E (not Sun E).* Dog- and family-friendly, garden. Newspapers, real fires, sports TV and Wi-Fi. B&B. *Open Wed-Thu L and E & Fri-Sun 12.00-23.00 (Sun 17.00).*

Boatyards

B Sheridan Marine Sheridan Boatyard, Moulsford OX10 9HU (01491 652085; www.sheridanmarine.com). Gas, long-term mooring, winter storage, crane, boat and engine sales and repairs, chandlery, books and maps and gifts, refreshments, DIY facilities. Stockist of traditional boat and engine fittings: British Seagull, Freeman Cruisers, Watermota, Nanni Diesels and others. *Open Mon-Fri 09.30-17.30 & Sat 10.00-15.00.*

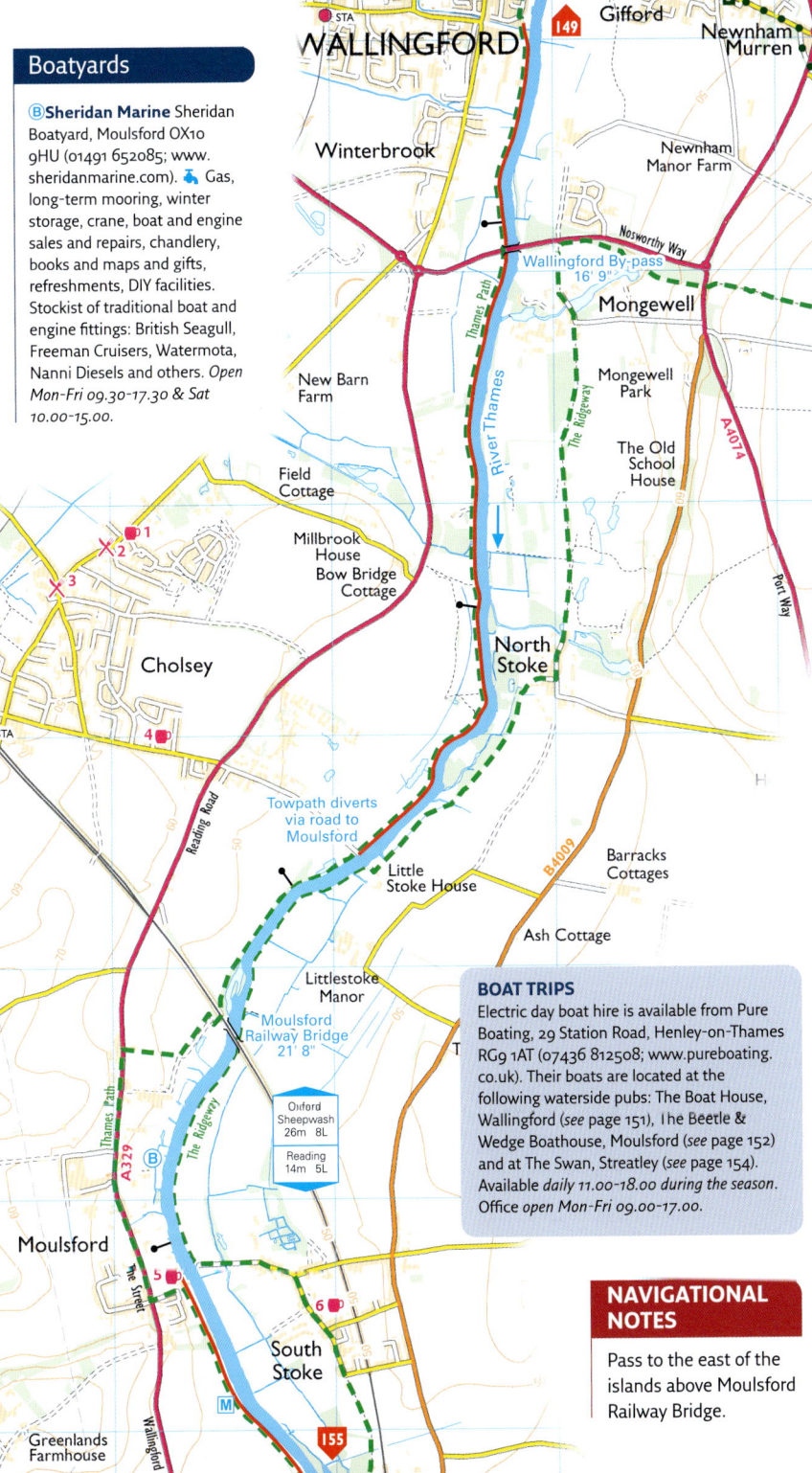

BOAT TRIPS

Electric day boat hire is available from Pure Boating, 29 Station Road, Henley-on-Thames RG9 1AT (07436 812508; www.pureboating.co.uk). Their boats are located at the following waterside pubs: The Boat House, Wallingford (see page 151), The Beetle & Wedge Boathouse, Moulsford (see page 152) and at The Swan, Streatley (see page 154). Available *daily 11.00-18.00 during the season. Office open Mon-Fri 09.00-17.00.*

NAVIGATIONAL NOTES

Pass to the east of the islands above Moulsford Railway Bridge.

Goring

Approaching Cleeve Lock the valley narrows, with Lardon Chase rising steeply to the west behind Streatley. Little of Goring can be seen from the river – boathouses, the mill and a glimpse of the church as the river enters one of its most attractive parts. In the meadows to the east of Basildon there is a picturesque group of buildings around a church, while on the east bank beech woods rise steeply from the river's edge. The brick Gatehampton Railway Bridge was built by Brunel – beyond this Basildon House stands in wooded grounds, to the west of Beale Park.

Pubs and Restaurants

1 Don Giovanni at the Leatherne Bottel Restaurant Bridle Way, Goring RG8 0HS (01491 872667; www.leathernebottel.co.uk). Riverside, above Cleeve Lock. There was a well here in Roman times which produced medicinal water. Now it is a smart riverside restaurant in idyllic surroundings, serving fresh local produce available *Tue-Sun L and E (not Sun E)*. Riverside terrace. Mooring.

2 The Swan Streatley RG8 9HR (01491 878800; www.coppaclub.co.uk/theswanatstreatley). Beautifully situated club and hotel dispensing real ale and food *daily 08.00-23.00*. Plush interiors and fine riverside gardens. Dog- and family-friendly. Traditional pub board games, newspapers, real fires and Wi-Fi. *Open Mon-Fri 07.30-23.00 (Fri 23.30) & Sat-Sun 08.00-23.30 (Sun 22.00)*.

3 Pierreponts Foodstore and Café High Street, Goring RG8 9AB (01491 874464; www.pierreponts.co.uk). Beside Goring Bridge and Lock. Highly regarded riverside establishment serving breakfast, brunch, lunch and afternoon tea. Also coffee, delicious cakes. All food is freshly cooked using local produce wherever possible. Pavement seating. Dog- and child-friendly. *Open Tue-Sun 08.30-17.00*.

4 The Miller of Mansfield High Street, Goring RG8 9AW (01491 756563; www.themillerofmansfield.com). Plush, 18th-C coaching inn serving real ale and food *L and E*, together with breakfast *daily 08.00-10.30*. Dog- and family-friendly, garden. Real fires and Wi-Fi. B&B. *Open 12.00-22.00*.

5 The Bell Inn Bell Lane, Aldworth RG8 9SE (01635 578272). Providing the only heritage pub interior in Berkshire, this gem dispenses real ales, real ciders and a selection of hot soup, filled rolls, ploughman's platters and hot puddings! Dog- and family-friendly, garden. Traditional pub games. *Open Tue-Sun 12.00-20.00*.

6 The Bull Reading Road, Streatley RG8 9JJ (01491 872392; www.bullinnpub.co.uk). Friendly 16th-C restaurant/pub at a busy crossroads. In 1895, when the Thames froze over, the pub sold water at 6d a bucket. Real ale and food available *daily 12.00-20.00*. Dog- and family-friendly, garden. Traditional pub games, newspapers, real fires, sports TV and Wi-Fi. *Open 12.00-23.00 (Sun 21.30)*.

7 The Catherine Wheel Station Road, Goring RG8 9HB (01491 872379; www.tcwgoring.co.uk). Two original rooms from this 17th-C building are still in evidence, one with its enormous inglenook fireplace. Real ale and food available *Tue-Sun L and E (not Tue L)*. Dog- and family-friendly, garden. Real fires and Wi-Fi. *Open Tue-Sat 16.00-22.00 (Fri-Sat 23.00) & Sun 12.00-21.00*.

- **Goring**
Oxon. Stores, off-licence, chemist, fish & chips, takeaways, butcher, station. One of the most important prehistoric fords across the river, linking the Icknield Way and the Ridgeway. The village is set in a splendid deep wooded valley by one of the most spectacular reaches on the river. A holiday paradise of indeterminate age, it retains many pretty brick and flint cottages. The church, of handsome proportions, is well situated by the river. Its bell, dating from 1290, is one of the oldest in England. Goring Mill stands below the bridge, an approximate replica (built 1923) of the earlier timber structure. Between Goring and Henley, the Thames passes through the Chilterns Area of Outstanding Natural Beauty, which covers 309 square miles. Stores *open daily 07.00-23.00*.

- **Streatley**
Berks. A continuation of Goring on the west bank, but its 18th-C charm is diminished by the traffic roaring through. Of note are the old malt houses converted into a village hall by W. Ravenscroft in 1898. Lardon Chase (NT) rises to the north.

- **Lower Basildon**
Berks. An attractive group of buildings surround the church in a superb riverside situation. The 13th-C church contains a portrait group of two boys drowned in 1886. Jethro Tull (1674-1741), pioneer of agricultural mechanisation, lies buried in the churchyard.
Basildon Park Lower Basildon RG8 9NR (01491 672382; www.nationaltrust.org.uk/visit/oxfordshire-buckinghamshire-berkshire/basildon-park). Built by John Carr of York for Sir Francis Sykes, who made his fortune in India, between 1776 and 1783, this is the most splendid Palladian mansion in Berkshire. Rescued from virtual dereliction in 1952 by Lord and Lady Iliffe, the building has been carefully restored. Octagon Room, Shell Room, Anglo-Indian objects in Nabob's Room, and many fine pictures and pieces of furniture. Exhibition of works by Graham Sutherland. 19th-C pleasure grounds. Waymarked walks. *Open daily 10.00-17.00*. Charge.

River Thames — Goring

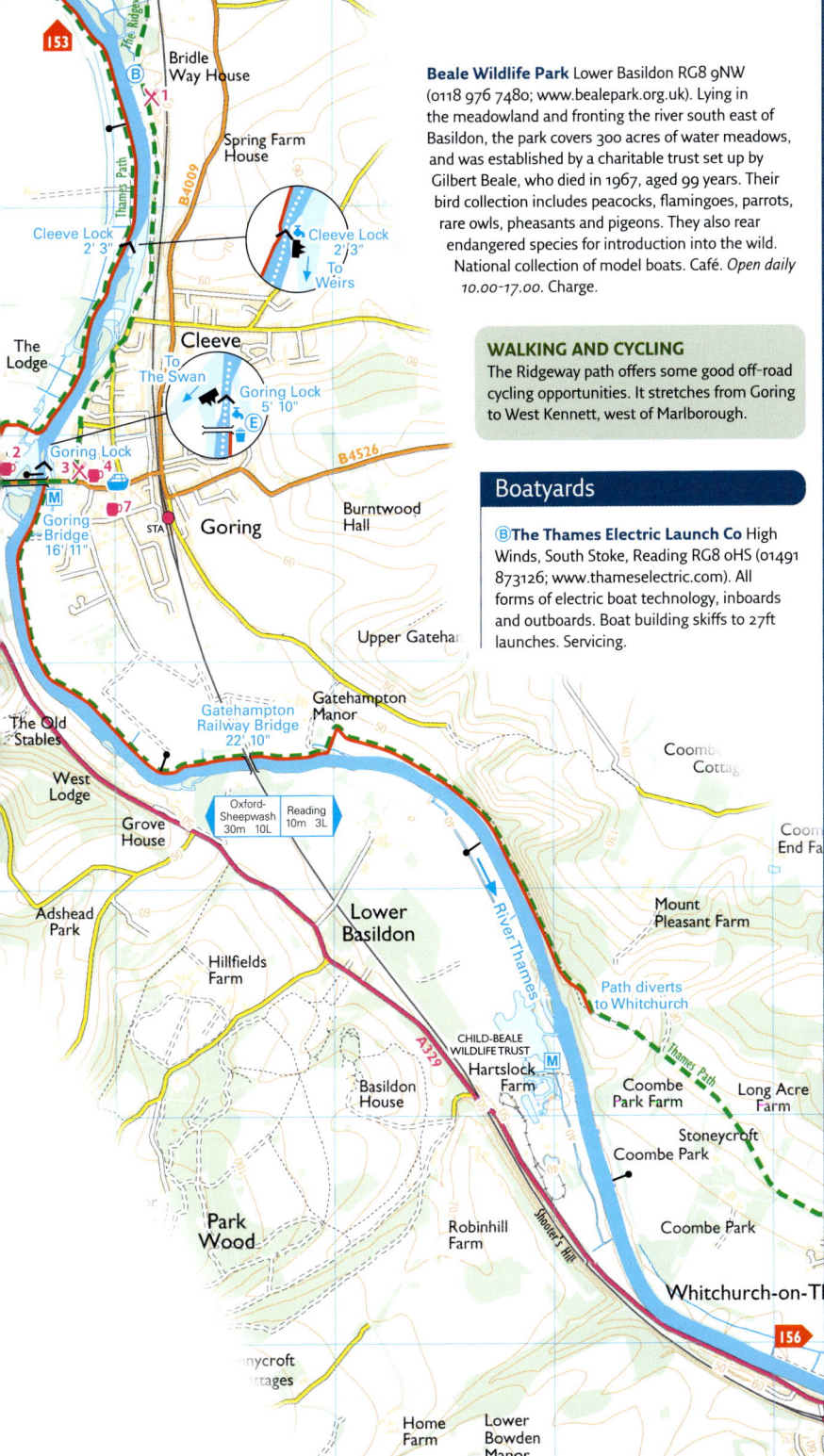

Beale Wildlife Park Lower Basildon RG8 9NW (0118 976 7480; www.bealepark.org.uk). Lying in the meadowland and fronting the river south east of Basildon, the park covers 300 acres of water meadows, and was established by a charitable trust set up by Gilbert Beale, who died in 1967, aged 99 years. Their bird collection includes peacocks, flamingoes, parrots, rare owls, pheasants and pigeons. They also rear endangered species for introduction into the wild. National collection of model boats. Café. *Open daily 10.00-17.00.* Charge.

WALKING AND CYCLING
The Ridgeway path offers some good off-road cycling opportunities. It stretches from Goring to West Kennett, west of Marlborough.

Boatyards
ⓑ The Thames Electric Launch Co High Winds, South Stoke, Reading RG8 0HS (01491 873126; www.thameselectric.com). All forms of electric boat technology, inboards and outboards. Boat building skiffs to 27ft launches. Servicing.

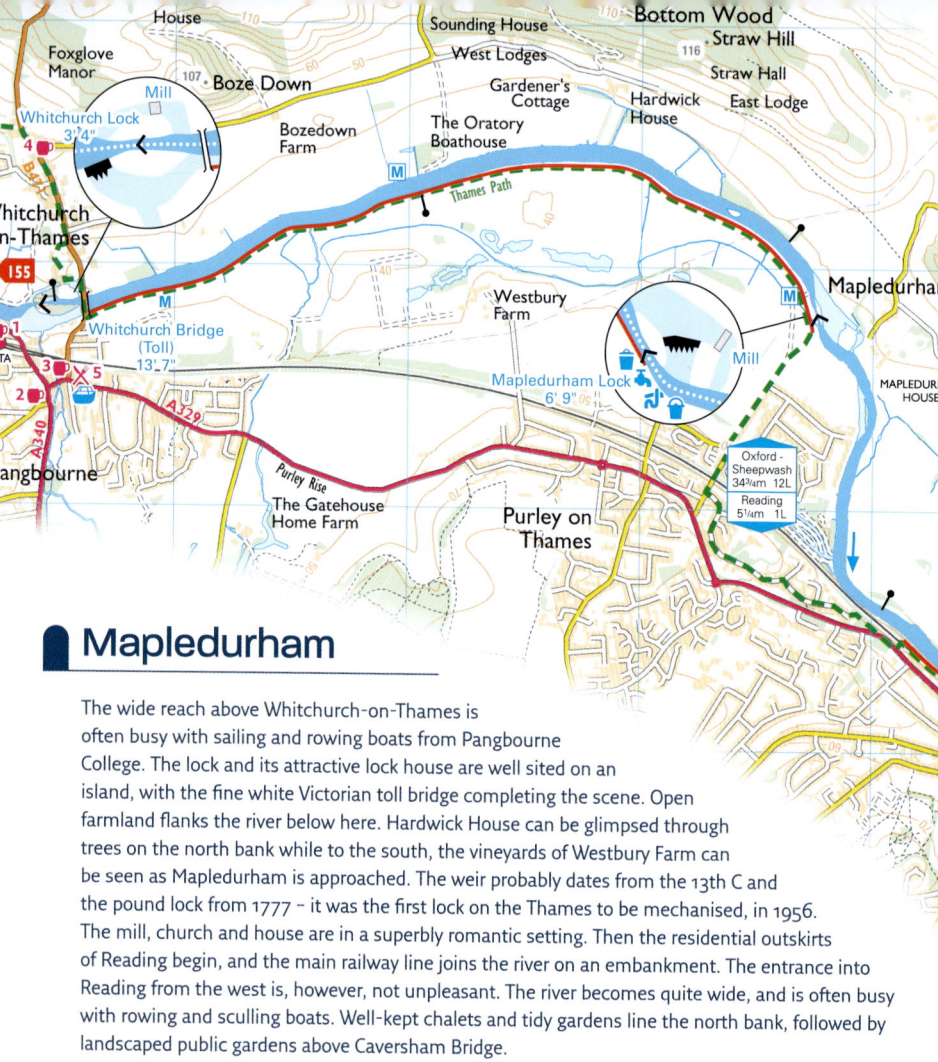

Mapledurham

The wide reach above Whitchurch-on-Thames is often busy with sailing and rowing boats from Pangbourne College. The lock and its attractive lock house are well sited on an island, with the fine white Victorian toll bridge completing the scene. Open farmland flanks the river below here. Hardwick House can be glimpsed through trees on the north bank while to the south, the vineyards of Westbury Farm can be seen as Mapledurham is approached. The weir probably dates from the 13th C and the pound lock from 1777 – it was the first lock on the Thames to be mechanised, in 1956. The mill, church and house are in a superbly romantic setting. Then the residential outskirts of Reading begin, and the main railway line joins the river on an embankment. The entrance into Reading from the west is, however, not unpleasant. The river becomes quite wide, and is often busy with rowing and sculling boats. Well-kept chalets and tidy gardens line the north bank, followed by landscaped public gardens above Caversham Bridge.

● **Pangbourne**
Berks. All services. A large, well-equipped commuter town, still preserving traces of Edwardian elegance, built at the confluence of the Thames with the Pang, which is a famous trout stream. The Nautical College, an imposing William and Mary style mansion, is by Sir John Belcher, built 1897-8. Pangbourne Meadow is now a National Trust property of 7 acres. The Scottish author of *The Wind in the Willows*, Kenneth Grahame (1859–1932), who was also Secretary to the Bank of England, lived in Church Cottage, Pangbourne, and told this story to his four-year-old son Alastair in 1904.

● **Whitchurch-on-Thames**
Oxon. Quiet and attractive with a good group of mill buildings, overlooked by the mainly Victorian church. A small toll for motor vehicles is collected at the Victorian iron bridge.

● **Mapledurham**
Oxon. A cluster of period houses and cottages stand in the water meadows close to the restored and working water mill, one of the oldest corn and grist mills on the Thames. The scene is typical of an early 19th-C landscape painting and should be visited (but *see below*).

Mapledurham House Mapledurham RG4 7TR (0118 972 3350; www.mapledurham.co.uk). Still occupied by descendants of the Blount family, who purchased the original manor in 1490 and built the present Elizabethan manor house, with grounds sweeping down to the Thames. The estate is private and there are no rights of way from the river to the village, nor any footpaths alongside the river on the north bank. In 1643 the house was sacked by the Roundheads, a year before Sir Charles Blount was killed during the siege of Oxford. Following a period of relative

Pubs and Restaurants

🍺✕ **1 The Swan** Shooters Hill, Pangbourne RG8 7DU (0118 984 4494; www.swanpangbourne.co.uk). Above the weir. Jerome K. Jerome, his two colleagues and a 'shamed looking dog' abandoned their *Three Men in a Boat* journey here (on the way back) and took the train to London. Real ale. Food available *Mon-Fri L and E*. Dog- and family-friendly, riverside beer garden. Traditional pub games, real fires and Wi-Fi. *Open daily 12.00-22.00 (Sat 23.00).*

🍺✕ **2 The Elephant Hotel** 3 Church Road, Pangbourne RG8 7AR (0118 984 2244; www.elephanthotel.co.uk). Old coaching inn with restaurant. Real ales. Bar meals and à la carte *available L and E*. Dog- and family-friendly, garden. Traditional pub games, newspapers, real fires and Wi-Fi. B&B. *Open Mon-Sat 12.00-23.00 (Sat 00.00) & Sun 12.00-22.00.*

🍺✕ **3 The George Hotel Best Western** The Square, Pangbourne RG8 7AJ (0118 984 2237; www.thegeorgehotelpangbourne.co.uk). Modernised hotel and bar serving real ale and food *Tue-Sun L and E (not Sun E)*. Dog- and family-friendly, garden. Sports TV and Wi-Fi. B&B. *Open Mon-Sat 12.00-23.00 (Fri-Sat 00.00) & Sun 12.00-22.00).*

🍺 **4 The Greyhound** High Street, Whitchurch-on-Thames RG8 7EL (0118 343 3016; www.greyhoundwhitchurchonthames.co.uk). With plenty of oak beams and wood panelling, this pub serves real ale and real cider. Pop-up street food vendors attend *Fri and Sat E & Sun 13.00-19.00*. Dog- and family-friendly, garden. Quiz *Tue*. Traditional pub games, real fires, sports TV and Wi-Fi. *Open Mon-Thu 17.00-23.00 & Fri-Sun 12.00-23.00 (Sun 22.30).*

✕ 🍷 **5 La'De Restaurant** 3-5 Reading Road, Pangbourne RG8 7LR (0118 327 9143; www.ladekitchen.com). Understated establishment featuring Mediterranean cuisine including pizzas and kebabs. Children welcome. Takeaway service. *Open daily 11.00-23.00.*

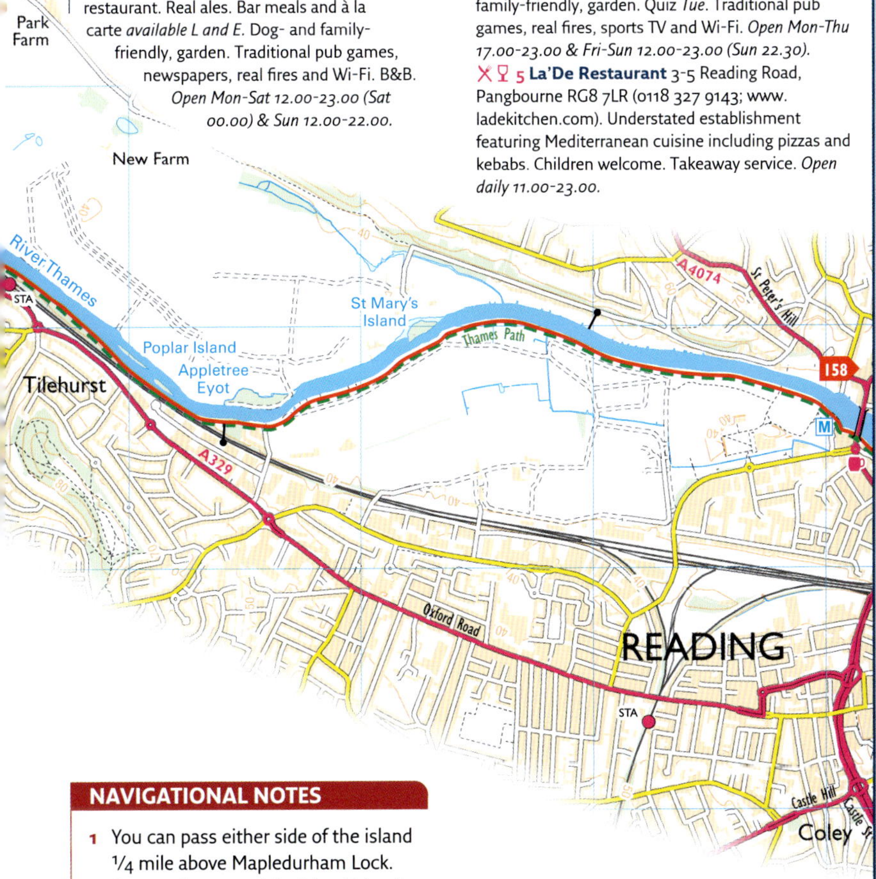

NAVIGATIONAL NOTES

1. You can pass either side of the island ¼ mile above Mapledurham Lock.
2. Pass to the east of the island ¼ mile below Mapledurham Lock.

impoverishment, the house was restored to what we see today by Michael Henry Blount (1789-1874). Mapledurham has interesting literary connections with Alexander Pope, Galsworthy's *Forsyte Saga* and Grahame's *The Wind in the Willows*. More recently it has been the setting for the film *The Eagle has Landed*, and has appeared in various television series including *Inspector Morse*. Only open for weddings and group tours.

Reading

Caversham Bridge was built in 1926. The original bridge on this site was erected in the 13th C, and at one time had a chapel on it. Fry's Island is situated between the bridges; there are two boatyards on it. Reading lies to the south, a busy modern town which does little to welcome visitors from the river. Just below Reading Bridge is Caversham Lock, on the edge of King's Meadow. A little further down, to the east and under the railway bridge, is the entrance to the Kennet & Avon Canal (*see page 107*). Beyond this junction the scenery is initially uninspiring but this all changes when Sonning Lock and Mill appear amongst the willows. The 18th-C bridge and the large white hotel beside it mark the western extremity of Sonning village, which lies back from the river. About a mile below Sonning, St Patrick's Stream (unnavigable, with the River Loddon flowing in), makes its detour around Borough Marsh. The main course of the river passes numerous islands and skirts Warren Hill, a chalk ridge, before reaching Shiplake Lock. It then passes Shiplake and weaves through a group of islands to the west of Wargrave Marsh, a low-lying area enclosed by the Hennerton Backwater (navigable only by small boats).

> **BOAT TRIPS**
> **Thames Rivercruise** Thames Side Promenade, Caversham, Reading RG4 8BD (0118 948 1088; www.thamesrivercruise.co.uk). *Caversham Lady* and other vessels available for river trips, events and private charter *all year round*. Visit website for further details.
> **Salter Bros** 206 Caversham Bridge Road, Reading RG1 8AZ (0118 957 2388; www.salterssteamers.co.uk). Scheduled *summer* service up and down river, with various stops. Open daily 09.00-17.00.

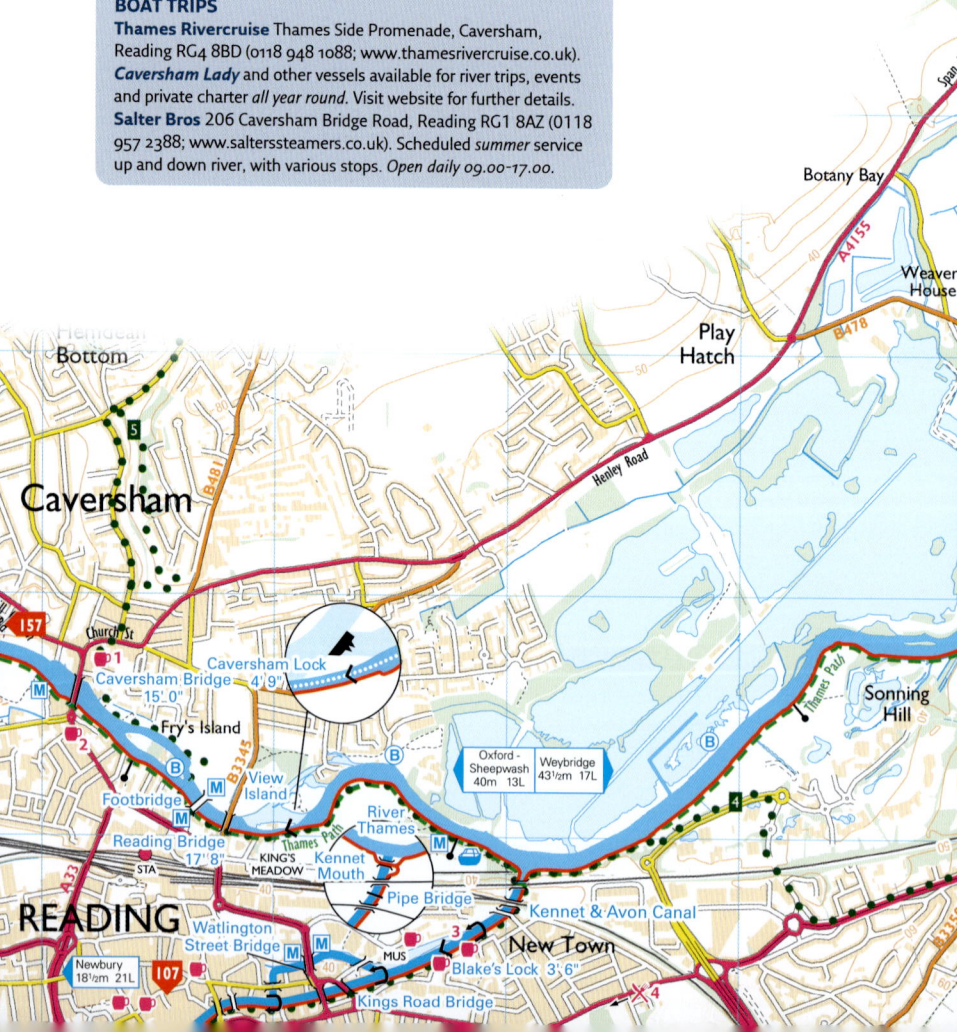

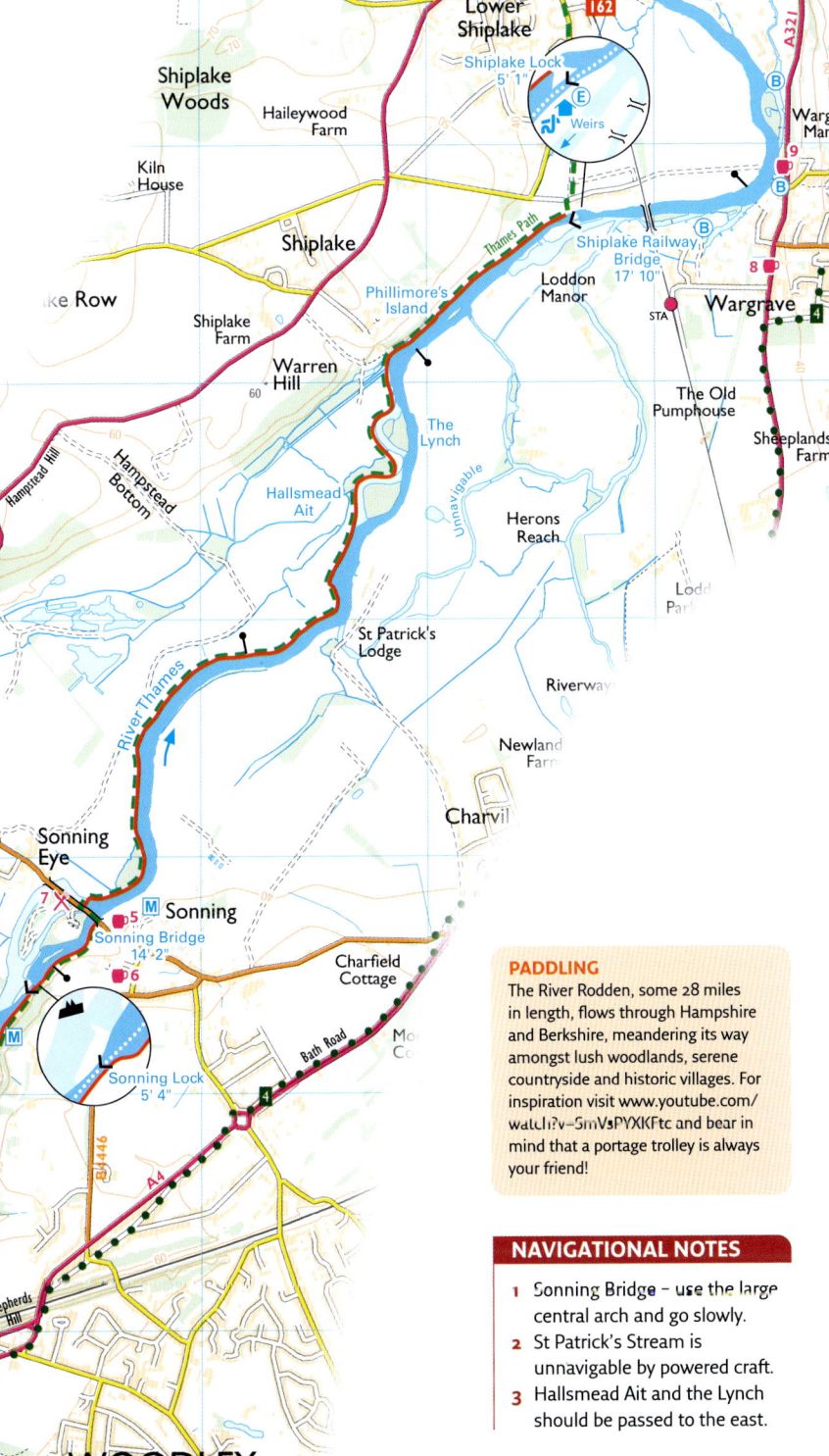

River Thames
Reading

PADDLING

The River Rodden, some 28 miles in length, flows through Hampshire and Berkshire, meandering its way amongst lush woodlands, serene countryside and historic villages. For inspiration visit www.youtube.com/watch?v=5mVsPYXKFtc and bear in mind that a portage trolley is always your friend!

NAVIGATIONAL NOTES

1. Sonning Bridge – use the large central arch and go slowly.
2. St Patrick's Stream is unnavigable by powered craft.
3. Hallsmead Ait and the Lynch should be passed to the east.

Boatyards

Ⓑ**Caversham Boat Services** Fry's Island, Thames Side, Reading RG1 8DG (0118 957 4323/07093 301319; www.cavershamboatservices.co.uk). 🚻🚿 D Pump out, hire craft, day-hire boats, long-term mooring, slipway, boat and engine repairs, gas, toilets, books, maps and gifts. *Open daily 08.30–17.30.*

ⒷBetter Boating Co Mill Green, Caversham, Reading RG4 8EX (0118 947 9536). 🚻🚿 D Pump out, crane (40 tonnes) gas, long- and short-term moorings, engine repairs, boat repairs, chandlery, toilets. *Open Mon-Fri 09.00-17.00 & Sat-Sun 10.00-16.00.*

ⒷWalker Outboards (0118 947 8641; www.walkeroutboards.co.uk) are also based here. *Open Mon-Sat 09.00-17.00 (Sat 12.00).*

Ⓑ✕ 🍽**Thames & Kennet Marina** Caversham Lakes, Henley Road, Reading RG4 6LQ (0118 948 2911; www.tingdene-marinas.co.uk). 🚻🚿🛁 D E

Pump out, gas, overnight and long-term mooring, winter storage, chandlery, telephone, toilets, showers, books and maps, boat sales, coal/logs, boat valeting, Wi-Fi, bar and café. *Open Mon-Sun 09.00-17.00 (Sun 10.00).*

Ⓑ**Val Wyatt Marine** Willow Marina, Willow Lane, Wargrave RG10 8LH (0118 940 3211; www.valwyattmarine.co.uk). 🚻🚿 Pump out, gas, overnight and long-term mooring, winter storage, slipway, boat & engine sales & repairs, chandlery, books, maps and gifts, DIY facilities, trailer boat parking, Wi-Fi. *Open Mon-Fri 09.00-17.30 & Sat-Sun 10.00-16.00.*

Ⓑ**John Bushnell** Thameside Marina, Waterman's Way, Station Road, Wargrave RG10 8HB (0118 940 2161; www.bushnells.co.uk). Long-term mooring, winter storage, dry storage, 25 tonne travel lift, boat sales and repairs, toilets, showers. *Open Mon-Fri 08.00-17.00 & Sat 10.00-16.00.*

● **Reading**
Berks. All services. A very busy town lacking a cohesive centre – it is an amalgam of university and industry with a constant stream of traffic scything through. The university buildings are uninspiring, but some of the Victorian buildings are better, and the museum houses one of the most fascinating archaeological collections in the country. (*See also page 108.*)
Abbey Ruins Fragmentary remains of the 12th-C abbey, built by Henry I, lie on the edge of Forbury Park. The Abbey was one of the largest in England and at one time comparable with Bury St Edmunds. The 13th-C gatehouse still stands. It was once the Abbey School where Jane Austen studied in 1785-7, although the structure was greatly altered by Gilbert Scott in 1869. The Church of St Lawrence near the Market Place was originally attached to the outer gate.
Gaol Forbury Road. Designed by Scott & Moffat, 1842-4 in Scottish Baronial style. Oscar Wilde (1854–1900) wrote *De Profundis* in 1897 while imprisoned here for homosexual practices (the *Ballad of Reading Gaol* was actually written in Paris in 1898).
Reading Museum The Town Hall, Blagrave Street RG1 1QH (0118 937 3400; www.readingmuseum.org.uk). Features *The Story of Reading*, tracing the town's development from a Saxon settlement on the River Kennet to the present day. Special features include a reconstructed section of the abbey and the Oracle gates entrance to the 17th-C workhouse. In the upper gallery is a full 230ft sweep of Britain's Bayeux Tapestry, Reading's faithful replica of the 11th-C original. Huntley & Palmers, the Reading biscuit makers, display a collection of 300 biscuit tins. *Open Tue-Sat 10.00-16.00 (Sat 17.00).* Donations.
Museum of English Rural Life University of Reading, Redlands Road RG1 5EX (0118 378 8660; http://merl.reading.ac.uk). The first museum in England to specialise in rural life as it was lived about 150 to 175 years ago, before the invention of the tractor. The majority of exhibits date from the period 1850–1950, and include farm equipment, beekeeping equipment, corn dollies, sewing machines and so on. *Open Tue-Sun 09.00-17.00 (Sat-Sun 10.00).* Free.
Tourist Information Centre Visit www.visit-reading.com/visitor-info/tourist-information.

● **Caversham**
Berks. All services – cinema and station in Reading (½ mile distant). A residential continuation of Reading, which is at its best by the river, where parks and gardens stretch alongside. The library in Church Street is worth a look – it is a jolly Edwardian building, built in 1907, with a central green copper clock supported by an angel.

● **Sonning**
Berks. A very pretty and meticulously preserved village. The largely 19th-C church has remarkable monuments, and some good 15th-C brasses. The most interesting house in the town is Lutyens' Deanery Gardens, built for Edward Hudson in 1901. To the west of Sonning is Holme Park – the Reading Blue Coat School; its wooded grounds drop steeply to the river. The railway passes in a spectacular cutting to the south, built by Brunel.
Stanlake Park Wine Estate Stanlake Park, Twyford RG10 0BN (0118 934 0176; www.stanlakepark.com). Book in advance for a tour and wine tasting. The shop and wine bar are *open Sun, Tue-Thu 09.00-18.00 (Thu 20.00) & Fri-Sat 21.00.*

● **Wargrave**
Berks. PO, stores, off-licence, chemist, station. A well-situated town on rising ground among trees and overlooking the Thames. The church was burnt down in 1914 by the suffragettes – some say it was because the vicar refused to take the word 'obey' out of the marriage service. The striking Woodclyffe Hall, in the High Street, was built in 1901. Henry Kingsley (1830–76), the novelist, often stayed here. East of the town is Wargrave Manor, an early 19th-C building.

The River Loddon joins St Patrick's Stream to the south west – here, in black swampy soil, the Loddon Lily (*Leucojum aestivum*) is native. Loddon Pondweed (*Potamogeton nodosus*, now a threatened species) its leaves beautifully veined, may also be found. Stores *open Sun-Fri 08.00-19.00 (Sun 13.30) & Sat 07.00-17.00.*

PADDLING

Reading Canoe Club, The Warren, Caversham, Reading RG4 7TH (www.reading-canoe.org.uk/docs/IntroductionToReadingCanoeClub.pdf) is a long-established and sociable club embracing slalom, racing and flat water. It makes basic equipment available to its members and encourages all ages.

The Wokingham Waterside Centre, Thames Valley Park Drive, Earley Road, Reading RG6 1PQ (0118 926 8280; www.wokinghamwatersidecentre.com) is a modern facility beside the river, just east of its junction with the Kennet & Avon, offering a wide range of paddling opportunities for adults, children and families, including kayak hire.

Thames Canoe Hire, Scours Lane, Tilehurst, Reading RG30 6AY (0118 941 2777; www.thamescanoehire.com) offer all the year round (subject to weather and river conditions) canoe and kayak hire and can arrange pick up/drop off with *two weeks notice*. Also ex-hire craft for sale.

Pubs and Restaurants (pages 158-159)

If you do not mind dodging the traffic, there are plenty of pubs in Reading (*see page 109 for a selection*) – those visiting from the Thames may wish to travel a couple of miles up- or downstream, where the surroundings are a little more congenial.

🍺✕ **1 The Crown** 3 Bridge Street, Caversham, Reading RG4 8AA. (0118 947 1407; www.thecrowncaversham.co.uk). Modern décor with exposed timber and brickwork, this pub serves real ale and food *daily 12.00-20.30*. Dog- and family-friendly, patio. Traditional pub games, sports TV and Wi-Fi. *Open Mon-Sat 12.00-23.00 (Fri-Sat 23.30) & Sun 12.00-22.30.*

🍺✕ **2 The Moderation** 213 Caversham Road, Reading RG1 8BB (0118 959 5577; www.themodreading.com). East meets west in the interior décor where this hostelry dispenses real ale and food *daily L and E*. Dog- and family-friendly, garden. Newspapers, sports TV and Wi-Fi. *Open 12.00-23.00 (Fri-Sat 00.00).*

🍺 **3 The Fisherman's Cottage** 224 Kennet Side, Reading RG1 3DW (07925 336269; https://thefishermanscottagepubreading.co.uk). Gastropub serving Mediterranean and Asian selections, alongside traditional pub favourites – *Tue-Sun 12.00-22.00 (Sun 19.00)* – together with real ale. Dog- and child-friendly *(until 20.00)* outside seating. *Regular* live music. Quiz *Tue*. Traditional pub games, real fires and Wi-Fi. *Open Tue-Thu 12.00-23.00 (Tue 16.00) & Fri-Sun 12.00-00.00 (Sun 22.00).*

✕ 🍷 **4 Piwnica Restaurant** 81 London Road, Reading RG1 5BY (0118 958 9908/07831 851434; www.piwnica.co.uk). Welcoming, family-run establishment offering a tasty trip through a selection of appetising Polish cooking, exploring a wide range of national dishes. Children welcome. Their website is a wee gem of a scene-setter! Takeaway service. *Open Thu-Tue 12.00-22.00.*

🍺✕ **5 The Great House Hotel** (Coppa Club) Thames Street, Sonning RG4 6UT (0118 921 9890; www.coppaclub.co.uk/thegreathousesonning). Beautifully situated riverside hotel and restaurant of great character, with fine gardens and lawns. One dining room is 700 years old; the main bar is a beamed room with a stone fireplace. Real ale and food available *daily 08.00-22.00* including breakfast. Dog- and family-friendly, massive riverside gardens. Real fires and Wi-Fi. B&B. *Open Mon-Fri 07.30-23.00 (Fri 23.30) & Sat-Sun 08.00-23.30 (Sun 22.00).*

🍺✕ **6 The Bull Inn** High Street, Sonning RG4 6UP (0118 969 3901; www.bullinnsonning.co.uk). Lovely, old half-timbered pub in a 15th-C church house covered with wisteria. There are comfy cushioned settles, massive beams and inglenook fireplaces inside, with wooden tables in a courtyard facing the church outside. Real ale and food available *Mon-Fri L and E & Sat-Sun 12.00-21.00 (Sun 20.00)* – breakfast *daily 09.00-10.30*. Dog- and family-friendly. Newspapers, real fires, sports TV and Wi-Fi. B&B. *Open 09.00-23.00 (Sun 22.00).*

✕ 🍷 **7 The Mill at Sonning** Sonning Eye, Reading RG4 6TY (0118 969 8000; www.millatsonning.com). This 17th-C flourmill has been recently converted into a bar, restaurant and theatre. The riverside Waterwheel Bar serves drinks, hot food, cakes and coffee *Tue-Sun 11.00-17.00* and the restaurant serves a wide range of food *Tue-Sat E & Sun L.*

🍺 **8 The Bull Hotel** 76/78 High Street, Wargrave RG10 8DE (0118 940 3120; www.bullwargrave.co.uk). Friendly 15th-C coaching inn. Real ale. Excellent bar and restaurant meals *L and E (not Sun E)*. Dog- and family-friendly, garden. Real fires and Wi-Fi. Look out for the 19th-C ghost of an ex-landlady. B&B. *Open Mon-Fri L and E & Sat-Sun 12.00-23.00.*

🍺✕ **9 The St George & Dragon** High Street, Wargrave RG10 8HY (0118 940 4474; www.stgeorgeanddragon.co.uk). Real ales. Food *daily 12.00-22.00 (Sun 21.00)*. Dog- and family-friendly, garden. Real fires, sports TV and Wi-Fi. *Open 11.00-23.00 (Sun 22.30).*

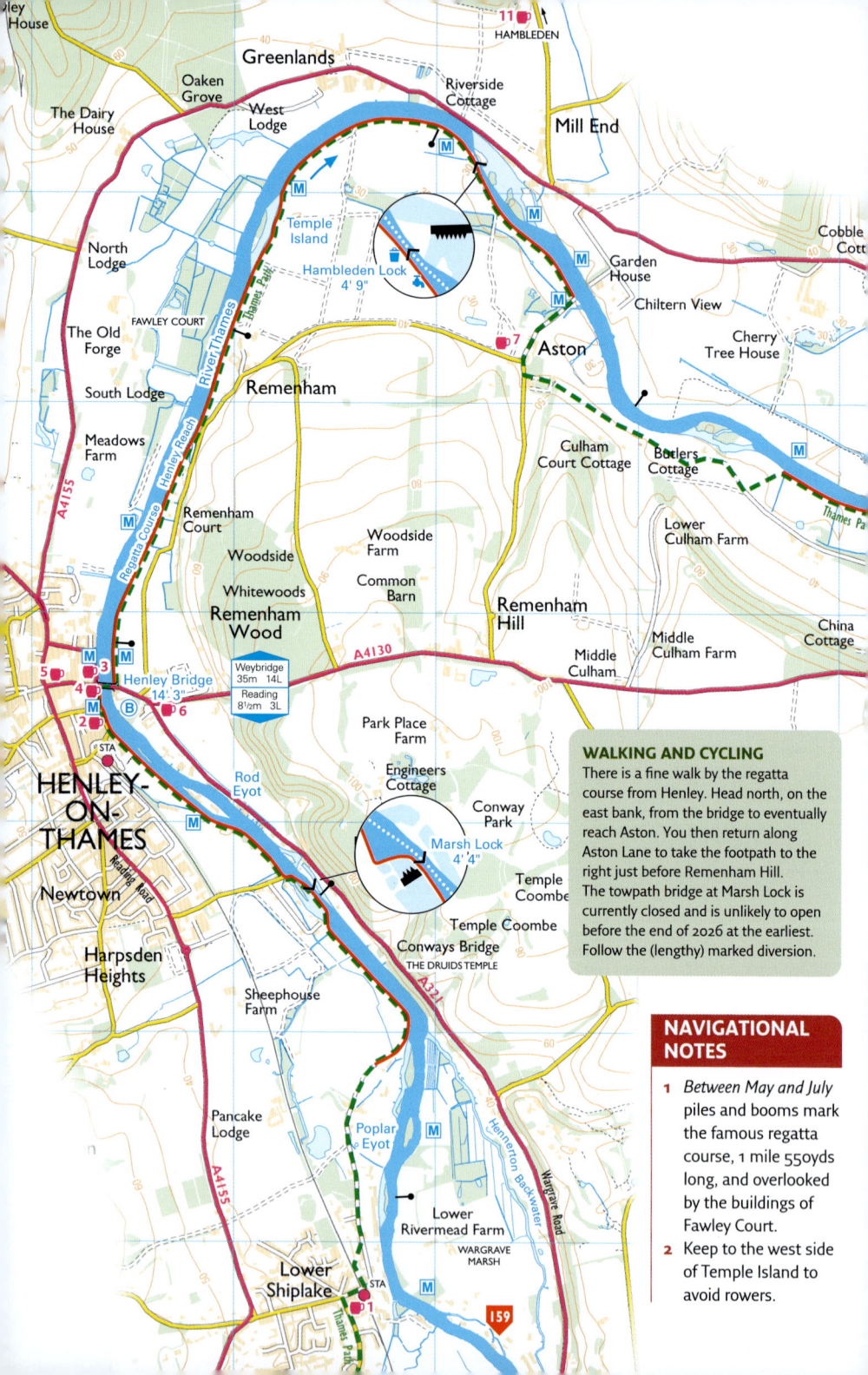

Henley-on-Thames

The Thames continues north towards Temple Combe Woods, which rise steeply to the east.

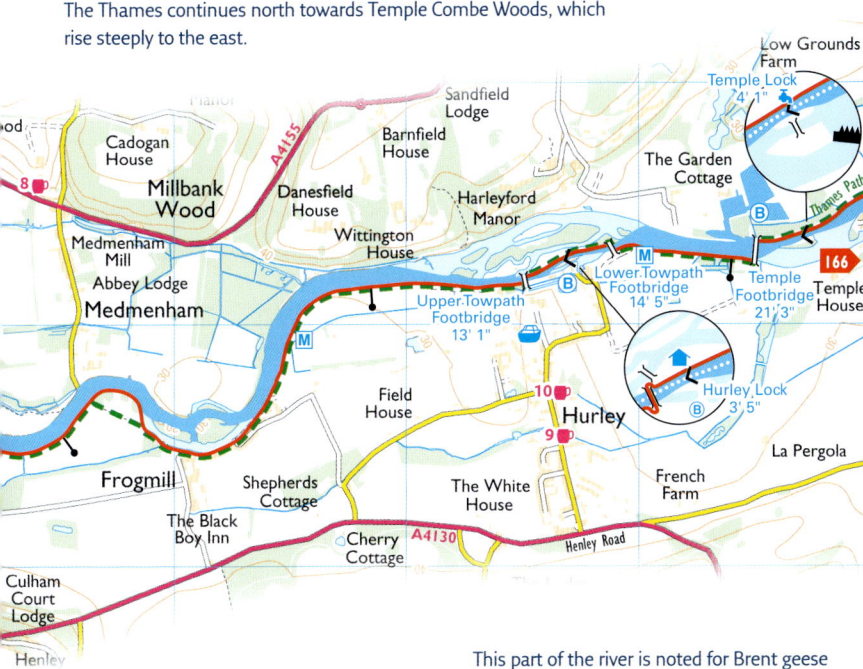

This part of the river is noted for Brent geese and some handsome wooden boathouses. To the north east of Marsh Lock is Park Place; in the grounds is part of Wren's original spire for St Bride's Church, Fleet Street. The house was once occupied by General Conway, whose daughter, Mrs Damer, sculpted the masks of Thames and Isis on Henley Bridge. The town of Henley-on-Thames lies to the west of the river, with an attractive waterfront, many moored boats and resident swans, facing the rise of Remenham Wood to the east. Below Temple Island the river passes the immaculate grounds of the Henley Management College before reaching Hambleden Lock, beautifully situated with an extensive weir (footpath over) and a fine weatherboarded mill, now converted into flats. The tiny village of Aston can be seen on a hillside to the south below the lock; the Thames then divides around thickly wooded islands and meanders past Medmenham and St Mary's Abbey. Beyond the next group of islands a large caravan site heralds the approach of Hurley, where the weir streams rush among more islands by the lock. To the north is Danesfield, a home built at the turn of the 20th C by a Manchester millionaire.

Boatyards

Ⓑ **Hobbs of Henley** Station Road, Henley RG9 1AZ (01491 572035; www.hobbsofhenley.com). ⚓ P D Day-boat hire *(Apr-Sep)* passenger boat charter and river trips, long-term mooring, winter storage, crane, outboard engine repairs. *Open daily 08.30-17.30 (17.00 Oct-Mar).*

Ⓑ **Peter Freebody's Boatyard** Thames Boat Houses, Mill Lane, Hurley SL6 5ND (01628 824382; www.peterfreebody.com). Overnight and long-term mooring, winter storage, crane, boat and engine sales and repairs, boat handling tuition. Established at Hurley since 1933 and before that at Caversham. Primarily a boat builder, this is a very famous yard, restoring and building many boats, including steam launches and electric boats. *Open Mon-Fri 08.00-16.30.*

● **Lower Shiplake**
Oxon. Butcher, station. A village of desirable commuter houses climbing up into the hills that border the river. The splendidly situated Church of SS Peter and Paul contains some medieval Belgian glass of great beauty. Tennyson married Emily Sellwood here in 1850. To the north, near the station, George Orwell lived as a boy at Roselawn, Station Road.

● **Henley-on-Thames**
Oxon. All services. A fine market town and one of the most popular resorts on the river, described by Dickens as 'the Mecca of the rowing man'. The main street runs down to the Thames from the Victorian town hall, where, from the river, the most obvious features are the 18th-C stone bridge (note the masks of Thames and Isis) and the church, a large and gloomy building. The Red Lion Hotel, near the church, has received some notable visitors, including King Charles I (1632 and 1642), the Duke of Marlborough (early 18th C), the poet William Shenstone (1750) and Johnson and Boswell (1776). The Kenton Theatre (01491 575698) in New Street is the fourth oldest in the country, being built in 1805. The first Oxford and Cambridge boat race was rowed between Hambleden and Henley on 10 June 1829 - the race is now rowed between Putney and Mortlake. The first Henley Regatta (01491 572153) was held in 1839, becoming Royal in 1851, with Prince Albert as patron. This is now held *annually in the first week of July*; the town becomes very busy indeed, and everyone seems to be on a picnic. The epitome of an English summer (when the sun shines).

River and Rowing Museum Mill Meadows, Henley-on-Thames RG9 1BF (01491 415600; www.rrm.co.uk). In a building clad with green oak and set upon columns in the water meadows just outside Henley, the museum has three galleries illustrating the river, the town of Henley, and rowing. Exhibits range from the world's oldest rowing boat to a state-of-the-art monocoque racing machine, and include a river gallery, with an aquarium of Thames fish. It also has a very fine painting of Henley by Jan Siberechts, dated 1698, showing the river busy with barges. Café, shop and library. *Open daily 10.00-16.00.* Charge.

Fawley Court Marlow Road, Henley-on-Thames RG9 3AE (01491 574917; www.fawleycourt.co.uk). The court, in a fine riverside situation, was designed by Wren and built in 1684 on the arched basement of an earlier fortified manor house. It was later to be decorated by Grinling Gibbons and classicised by James Wyatt. The grounds were laid out by 'Capability' Brown in 1770. It now owned by the Marian Fathers and has a museum founded by Father Joseph Jarzebowski, consisting of a library, various documents of the Polish monarchy, including Laksi's *Code of Laws* dating from 1506, and Polish militaria, and paintings and sculpture illustrating ancient history and the Middle Ages.

Temple Island RG9 2LY The temple was built by James Wyatt in 1771 as a vista for Fawley Court, and has a set of hand-painted wall decorations by him. It is thought to be the earliest example in England of the Etruscan style. Owned by the Mackenzie family for over 130 years, the island was sold in 1988. Visited by King Edward VII and Queen Alexandra, it is very pretty, with views down the river to Henley.

Tourist Information Centre Town Hall, Market Place, Henley-on-Thames RG9 2AQ (01491 576982; www.henleytowncouncil.gov.uk/services/information-centre). *Open Mon-Fri 09.30-16.00 (Fri 15.00) & Sat 10.00-16.00 (12.00 Nov-Mar).*

● **Hambleden**
Bucks. PO, stores. Set back from the river and surrounded by heavily wooded hills, this is one of the most attractive villages – all mellow flint and brick – in Buckinghamshire, and worth the walk up from the river. The 14th-C church and the houses round the green make it a perfect village setting, with the 17th-C Manor House in the background. The mill and mill house look good by the lock.

● **Medmenham**
Bucks. A village straggling up from the now defunct ferry into the woods behind. Medmenham Abbey (St Mary's Abbey) is a charming agglomeration of building styles:1595, 18th-C Gothic and mostly 1898. It was the house of the orgiastic Hell Fire Club, under the patronage of Sir Francis Dashwood. It was decorated in a suitably pornographic and sacrilegious style, but understandably none of this survived the 19th C.

● **Hurley**
Berks. In the old part of the village the long, dark and narrow nave of the church is all that remains of Hurley Priory (St Mary's), founded before 1087 for the Benedictine Order. Opposite the church are a 14th-C tithe barn (now a dwelling) and a dovecote. *Open Mon-Fri 08.00-16.00 & Sat-Sun 08.00-13.00 (Sun 09.30).*

Harleyford Manor Henley Road, Marlow SL7 2DX (01628 471361; www.harleyford.co.uk). On the north bank opposite Hurley. The red-brick Georgian manor was built in the late 1740s by Sir Robert Taylor for Sir William Clayton, and has been recently restored. Notable amongst visitors to The Manor have been Emperor Napoleon III, Prime Minister Disraeli and author Kenneth Grahame. The superbly landscaped grounds contain an ice house and the ruins of a Georgian temple. The whole estate is an Area of Outstanding Natural Beauty, and is now used as a leisure environment, with holiday lodges, a golf course and marina.

BOAT TRIPS

Hobbs & Sons Station Road, Henley-on-Thames RG9 1AZ (01491 572035; www.hobbsofhenley.com). Skippered vessels for private charter, including Edwardian-style motor launches. Boat hire and public cruises.
Magna Carta (07836 551912; www.magna-carta.co.uk). Luxury cruises on a hotel barge, based at Henley.

Pubs and Restaurants (pages 162-163)

🍺✕ **1 The Baskerville** Station Road, Lower Shiplake, Henley RG9 3NY (0118 940 3332; www.thebaskerville.com). Pub with a wood-panelled bar featuring a variety of rowing artefacts, dispensing real ale and food *L and E (not Sun E)*. Dog-and family-friendly, enclosed garden. Traditional pub games, real fires, sports TV and Wi-Fi. B&B. *Open daily 12.00-23.00 (Sun 22.00).*

🍺✕ **2 The Anchor Inn** 58 Friday Street, Henley RG9 1AH (01491 574753; www.theanchorhenley.co.uk). Cosy and friendly 15th-C pub, haunted by a friendly cleaning lady! Real ale. Traditional English food *L and E (not Sun E)*. Dog-friendly, garden. Real fires. *Open Mon-Thu 14.00-23.00 (Wed-Thu 12.00) & Fri-Sun 12.00-00.00 (Sun 22.00).*

🍺✕ **3 The Relais Henley** 2-4 Hart Street, by the bridge, Henley RG9 2AR (01491 523288; www.therelaishenley.com). A very auspicious and much-visited (*see* Henley-on-Thames opposite) 15th-C red brick hotel serving food *daily 07.00-22.00* (including breakfast). Bar *open 12.00-23.00.*

🍺✕ **4 The Angel on the Bridge** Thameside, Henley Bridge RG9 1BH (01491 410678; www.theangelhenley.com). Beautiful and historic 14th-C inn adjoining the bridge. Real ale. Food available *Mon-Fri L and E & Sat-Sun 11.30-21.30 (Sun 19.00)*. Dog- and family-friendly, riverside terrace. Quiz *Wed*. Traditional pub games, real fires and Wi-Fi. *Open 11.00-23.00 (Sun 22.00).*

🍺✕ **5 The Catherine Wheel Hotel** 7-15 Hart Street, Henley RG9 2AR (01491 848488; http://hotels.jdwetherspoon.com/hotels/the-catherine-wheel-hotel/). Real ales with food available *daily 07.00-23.30 (Fri 00.30)*. Family-friendly, garden. B&B. *Open 07.00-00.00 (Fri 01.00).*

🍺✕ **6 The Little Angel** Remenham Lane, Remenham RG9 2LS (01491 411008; www.thelittleangel.co.uk). A 17th-C pub serving real ale and food *L and E (not Sun E)*. Dog- and child-friendly, patio. *Open Mon-Sat 11.30-23.30 & Sun 12.00-21.00.*

🍺✕ **7 The Flower Pot Hotel** Ferry Lane, Aston, Henley RG9 3DG (01491 574721; www.brakspear.co.uk). Attractive, old-fashioned pub built about 1890. Real ale and restaurant food served *L and E (not Sun E)*. Bar menu available *12.00-21.00*. Dog- and family-friendly, patio. Traditional pub games, real fires, sports TV and Wi-Fi. B&B. *Open Tue-Sat 11.30-22.00 & Sun 11.30-19.30.*

🍺✕ **8 The Olde Dog and Badger** Henley Road, Medmenham SL7 2HE (01491 572709; www.dogandbadger.co.uk). This fine old pub dates from 1390 and has historical associations with the Hell Fire Club (*see* Medmenham opposite). Real ale and food available *Wed-Sun 12.00-21.00 (Sun 18.00)*. Outside seating. Newspapers. *Open Wed-Sat 12.00-23.00 (Wed 22.00) & Sun 12.00-20.00.*

🍺 **9 The Rising Sun** High Street, Hurley SL6 5LT (01628 825733; www.risingsunhurley.co.uk). Popular, traditional village pub with exposed beams, open fires and home-made pub food served *Tue-Sun 12.00-21.00 (Sun 20.00)*. Pizza *Mon 16.00-21.00*. Dog- and family-friendly. Garden. Quiz *Tue*. Real fires and Wi-Fi. *Open Sun-Wed 12.00-21.00 (Mon 16.00) & Thu-Sat 12.00-23.00.*

🍺✕ **10 The Olde Bell** High Street, Hurley SL6 5LX (01628 825881; www.theoldebell.co.uk). Describing itself as a modern coaching inn, this establishment serves bar meals *12.30-21.30* and offers an a la carte restaurant menu *daily, L and E*, using locally grown, seasonal produce wherever possible. Real ale. Dog- and child-friendly, garden. Traditional pub games, newspapers and Wi-Fi. *Open daily 12.00-23.00.*

🍺✕ **11 The Stag & Huntsman Hotel** Hambleden, Henley RG9 6RP (01491 571227; www.stagandhuntsman.com). Lovingly restored, traditional brick and flint pub – which has retained its old-fashioned charm – serving real ale and appetising food, with the emphasis on Estate produce featuring a large amount of game, available *L and E (not Sun E)*. Dog- and family-friendly, pretty garden. Real fires and Wi-Fi. B&B. *Open Mon-Sat 11.00-22.30 (Fri-Sat 23.30) & Sun 11.00-18.00.*

Shepperton Lock

Marlow

On the reach below Temple Lock you may well see canoeists and dinghy sailors from the National Sports Centre at Bisham Abbey, so take care. At the end of this long wide stretch is the elegant white Marlow suspension bridge, with the lock just beyond. The Marlow-Bisham bypass crosses below here, and this is followed by the Scouts Boating Centre, so once again the river is often full of small craft. Then the Thames turns to skirt the steep hills of Quarry Wood. Below the trees, at the water's edge, there are many smart chalets, a strange, grey, castellated building housing holiday flats, and Woottens Boatyard, with handsome old boathouses nearby, dated 1885. To the north the Marlow branch line hides flooded gravel workings and a sewage works. There follows an excellent and therefore popular stretch of the Thames, commencing at Bourne End, where the water is very wide and favoured for sailing. Below Cookham Bridge the river splits into four – make sure you take the clearly marked lock cut, which was opened on 1 November 1830. Formosa Island lies to the south, Hedsor Wharf to the north. Emerging from the cut you are confronted with a steep hillside thickly wooded with beech – this is Cliveden, owned by the National Trust. These woods continue to Taplow and Boulter's Lock, where a main road skirts the river on the Maidenhead side, and the bridge by the lock is usually packed with gongoozlers (on-lookers) on sunny summer days.

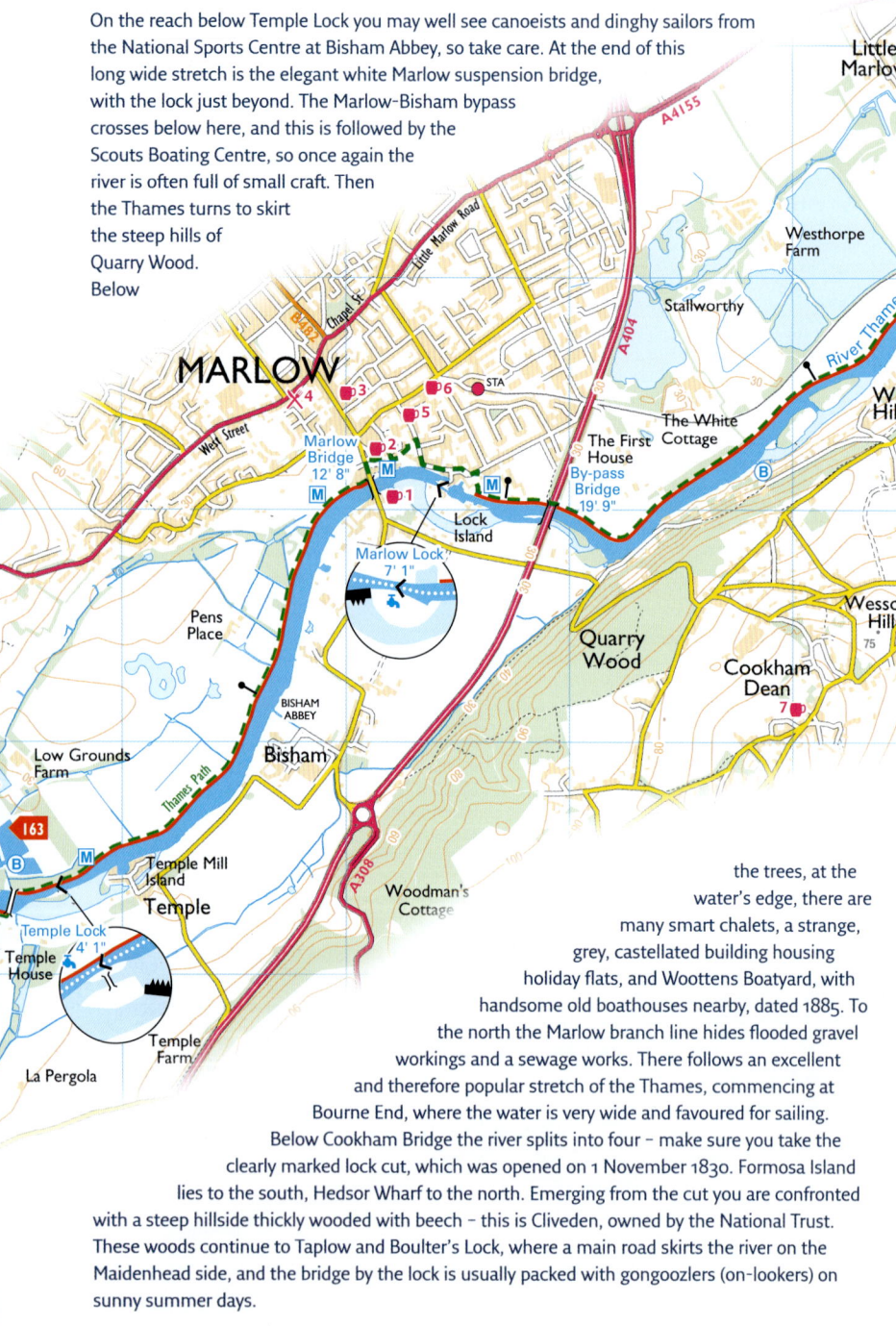

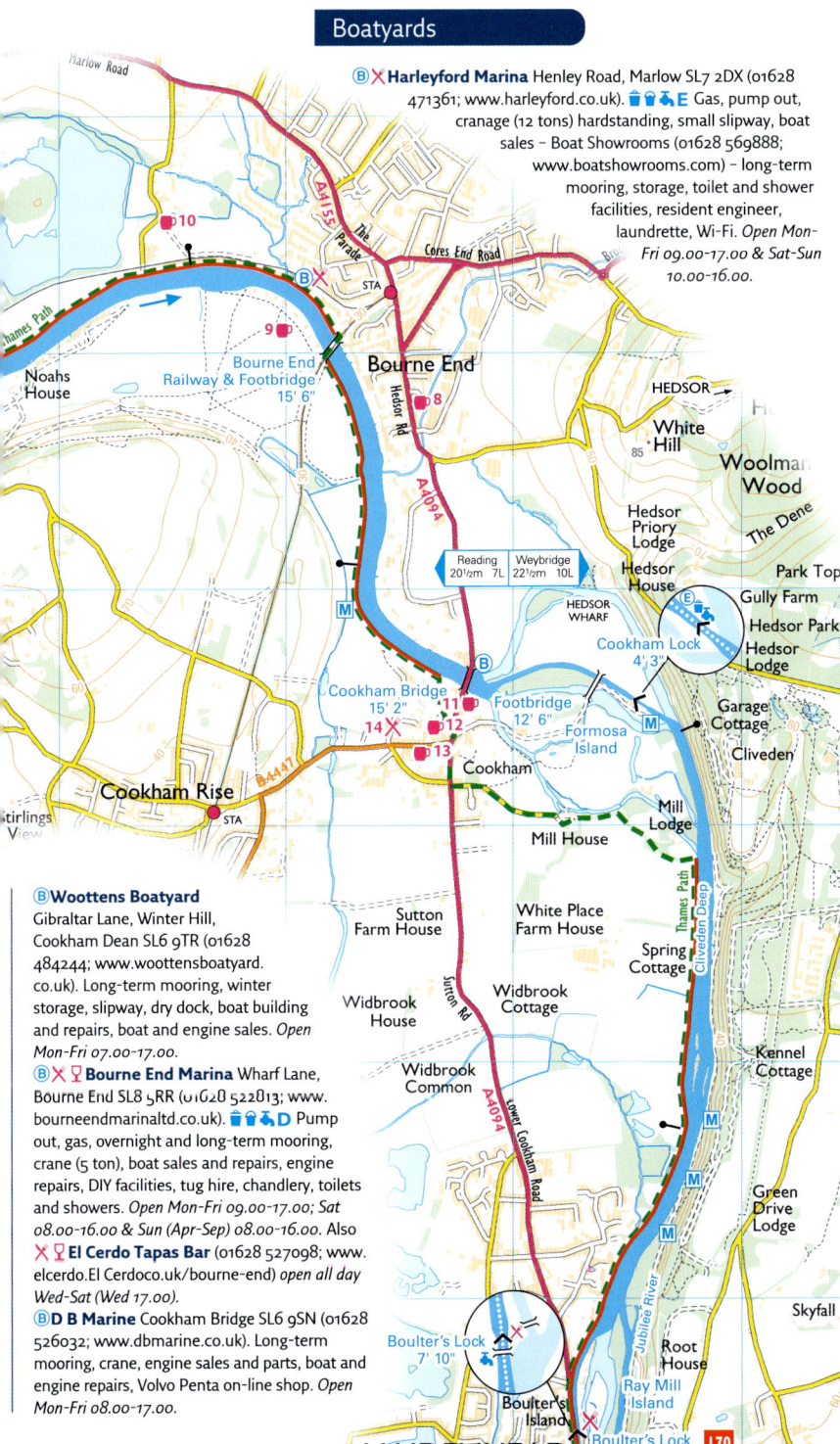

> **WALKING AND CYCLING**
> There is good riverside walking south of Marlow Bridge – turn right just before Temple Lock, and return via Lower Pound Lane. There is also a stiff walk to the top of Winter Hill, but it is worth the effort. Walk north west from Cookham across the golf course, then along Alleyns Lane to Cookham Dean. Follow the path to Quarry Wood, turn right and walk to the summit of Winter Hill for splendid views. Continue with the river to your left to return to Cookham.

Pubs and Restaurants (pages 166–167)

🍺✕ **1 The Compleat Angler Hotel** Marlow Bridge Lane, Marlow SL7 1RG (0344 879 9128; www.macdonaldhotels.co.uk/compleatangler/). A restaurant and hotel with a riverside terrace, by the famous suspension bridge. It used to be the Anglers Rest; now the name commemorates Izaak Walton's famous book, published in 1653. Food available *daily L and E* together with afternoon tea. Dog-friendly, outside seating. B&B. *Open all day.*

🍺✕ **2 The Two Brewers** St Peter Street, Marlow SL7 1NQ (01628 484140; www.pubanddining.co.uk/two-brewers-marlow). Having survived a devastating fire in 2013, this delightful riverside pub now dispenses real ale and excellent food *daily 11.00-21.00*. Dog- and family-friendly, garden. *Regular* live music. Wi-Fi. *Open 11.00-23.00 (Fri-Sat 00.00).*

🍺✕ **3 The Chequers Inn** 51-53 High Street, Marlow SL7 1BA (01628 482053; www.thechequersmarlow.co.uk). Real ale and real cider together with food *Mon-Sat L and E & Sun 12.00-20.00* available in a 16th-C inn. Breakfast served *08.00-11.30 (Sun 10.00)*. Garden and Wi-fi. B&B. *Open Mon-Sat 08.00-23.00 (Fri-Sat 00.00) & Sun 08.00-22.00.*

✕♀ **4 The Vanilla Pod** 31 West Street, Marlow SL7 2LS (01628 898101; www.thevanillapod.co.uk). Intimate French-influenced fine-dining eatery, serving seasonal dishes in T.S. Eliot's former home. *Open Tue-Sat L and E.*

🍺 ✕ **5 The Prince of Wales** 1 Mill Road, Marlow SL7 1PX (01628 482970; www.facebook.com/POWmarlow). A pub with modern décor, in lounge bar style, serving real ale and food *Mon-Sat 07.00-14.00 & Sun L*. Dog- and family-friendly, patio. Sports TV and Wi-Fi. B&B. *Open daily 12.00-23.00 (Fri-Sat 00.00).*

🍺 **6 The Marlow Donkey** Station Road, Marlow SL7 1NW (01628 482022; www.facebook.com/MarlowDonkeyPub). Victorian pub near the station – The Donkey was a famous local train, as the sign indicates. Real ale available together with food served *11.00-21.00 (Fri-Sun 10.00)*. Family-friendly, conservatory and large garden. Quiz *Thu*. Real fires, sports TV and wi-fi. *Open Mon-Thu 11.00-23.00 & Fri-Sun 10.00-00.00 (Sun 23.00).*

🍺✕ **7 The Jolly Farmer** Church Road, Cookham Dean SL6 9PD (01628 482905; www.thejollyfarmerpub.co.uk). Opposite the Norman church, this friendly pub dispenses real ale and food *Wed-Sun 12.00-21.00 (Sun 17.30)*. Dog- and family-friendly, large garden and play area. Real fires and Wi-Fi. *Open Mon 15.00-21.00 & Tue-Sun 12.00-23.00 (Sun 19.00).*

🍺✕ **8 The Walnut Tree** Hedsor Road, Bourne End SL8 5DN (01628 532417; www.walnuttreebourneend.co.uk). A 16th-C traditional pub serving real ale and food *Tue-Sun L and E (not Tue or Sun E)*. Dog-friendly, large garden. Real fires and Wi-Fi. *Open Tue-Thu L and E & Fri-Sun 12.00-22.00 (Sun 18.00).*

🍺✕ **9 The Bounty** Riverside, Cockmarsh, Bourne End SL8 5RG (01628 520056; www.facebook.com/thebounty1). Quirky, characterful pub, only accessible on foot or by boat, dispensing real ale and food *Sat-Sun 11.30-22.00*. Dog- and family-friendly, garden. Traditional pub games and real fires. *Open 12.00-23.00 but Oct-Mar weekends only, 12.00-dusk.*

🍺✕ **10 The Spade Oak** Coldmoorholme Lane, Bourne End SL8 5PS (01628 520090; www.thespadeoak.co.uk). Predominantly a food pub, serving meals *daily 12.00-22.00* and real ale. Dog-friendly, garden. Real fires, sports TV and Wi-Fi. *Open 11.00-23.00 (Sat-Sun 09.00).*

🍺✕ **11 The Ferry** Sutton Road, Cookham SL6 9SN (01628 525123; www.theferry.co.uk). Relaxed, gastro-style pub by the bridge serving real ale and food *Mon-Sat 12.00-22.00 (Sat 22.30 & Sun 12.00-21.00)*. *Open daily 11.00-23.00 (Sat-Sun 09.00).*

🍺✕ **12 Bel & The Dragon** High Street, Cookham SL6 9SQ (01628 521263; www.belandthedragon-cookham.co.uk). An attractive pub dating from 1417, serving real ale and food *Mon-Sat L and E & Sun 12.00-20.00*. Family-friendly, garden. Real fires. B&B. *Open daily 07.30-23.00.*

🍺✕ **13 The Kings Arms** High Street, Cookham SL6 9SJ (01628 530667; www.thekingsarmscookham.co.uk). Village pub, serving real ale and food *all day*. Terrace and garden with picnic tables. Real fires. *Open Mon-Sat 11.00-23.00 (Fri-Sat 00.00) & Sun 11.00-22.30.*

✕♀ **14 Malik's** Royal Exchange, High Street, Cookham SL6 9SF (01628 520085; www.maliks.co.uk). Award-winning cuisine from the Indian sub-continent served in a cosy, beamy, smart restaurant *daily L and E*. Takeaway service.

- **Bisham**
Berks. A largely Georgian village set back from the river, behind the abbey. The church is set apart from both, being superbly sited almost at the river's edge. Although rebuilt, it still has a Norman tower.
Bisham Abbey SL7 1RT. The abbey, built mainly in the 14th and 16th C, was a private house from 1540. It is now a sports centre of the Central Council of Physical Recreation, a hive of activity where young players and coaches come together under the aegis of their respective governing bodies of sport. They train in the sport of their choice, ranging from archery to weight lifting. River activities feature strongly in the training programme. *The centre is not open to casual visitors.*

- **Marlow**
Bucks. All services. A very handsome and lively Georgian town, with a wide tree-lined High Street connecting the bridge with the Market Place. A marvellous view of the weir can be had from the white suspension bridge, built by Tierny Clarke in 1831-6 and reconstructed, retaining its original width, in 1966. The town's most ancient building is the Old Parsonage, once part of a great 14th-C house and containing panelled rooms and beautifully decorated windows. West Street, at the top of the High Street, has great literary associations – Thomas Love Peacock wrote *Nightmare Abbey* at no. 47, Shelley wrote *Revolt to Islam* in Albion House, while his wife Mary Godwin created *Frankenstein* there. T. S. Eliot also lived in West Street for a while, after World War I.

- **Cookham Dean**
Berks. Large parts of Cookham Dean are owned by the National Trust. The village stands above steep beech woods by the river. Winter Hill has one of the best views over the Thames Valley, and is well worth the steep walk. Kenneth Grahame, who wrote *The Wind in the Willows*, published 1908, lived at Mayfield between 1906-10. It is thought that Quarry Wood may have been the wild wood mentioned in the story.

- **Bourne End**
Berks. PO, stores, chemist, off-licence, takeaways, bakery, butcher, library, garage, station. A riverside commuter village, famous for Bourne End Sailing Week. Cock Marsh opposite, 132 acres, is owned by the National Trust. Stores *open daily 07.00-23.00.*

- **Cookham**
Berks. PO, stores, butcher, off-licence, takeaways, chemist, bakery, greengrocer, garage, station. A pretty and busy village of pubs, antique shops, restaurants and boutiques, with bijou cottages filling the gaps in between. Cookham is famous as the home of the artist Stanley Spencer, who was born in 'Fernlea', in the High Street – the quite amazing variety of his work is splendidly exhibited in the old Wesleyan Chapel. His *Last Supper*, painted in 1920, hangs in the splendid square-towered Holy Trinity Church, built by the Normans in 1140 on the site of a Saxon building. There are fine 16th-C monuments, and the church is floodlit after dark. The bridge, an iron structure, was built in 1867. Community stores *open 06.00-22.00.*
Stanley Spencer Gallery 16 High Street, Cookham SL6 9SJ (01628 531092; www.stanleyspencer.org.uk). Opened in 1962, this is the only gallery devoted to an artist which is situated in the village of his birth, and where he attended Sunday school. Along with his paintings, there is a collection of memorabilia associated with this remarkable man. Shop. *Open daily 10.30-16.00. Last entry 16.00.* Charge.
Odds Farm Park Wooburn Common, High Wycombe HP10 0LX (01628 520188; www.oddsfarm.co.uk). The best approach is by taxi from Maidenhead. A rare breed centre, where children (and adults) can observe the animals in close proximity. Tractor rides, log play and a calendar of special events throughout the summer. *Open daily 10.00-17.30. Last entry 16.30.* Charge.

- **Hedsor**
Bucks. A priory and an over-restored church on the hill. It is worth the walk up for the splendid views over the beech woods. Hedsor House was rebuilt in 1862 in an Italianate style. Lord Boston's Folly, an 18th-C structure, faces the church from the opposite hill.
Hedsor Wharf An important shipping point for timber, paper and coal for over 500 years until the lock cut bypassed it in 1830. At the lower end of Hedsor Water there was once a lock – the original cottage still stands, a single room cut from the chalk and fronted with brick.
Cliveden Taplow, Maidenhead SL6 0JA (01628 605069; www.nationaltrust.org.uk/visit/oxfordshire-buckinghamshire-berkshire/cliveden). A most marvellous stretch of beech woods from Hedsor to Taplow surrounds the house, which was built in 1851 by Charles Barry for the Duke of Sutherland. It was the home of Nancy, Lady Astor, and was the background to many 20th-C political intrigues and scandals, ending with the Profumo affair in 1963. Fine tapestries and furniture, and a theatre which heard the first performance of *Rule Britannia*. Splendid gardens. It is now a stately home/hotel, leased from the National Trust. *Telephone or visit website for opening hours and booking arrangements.* Charge. Restaurant. Temporary moorings (charge).

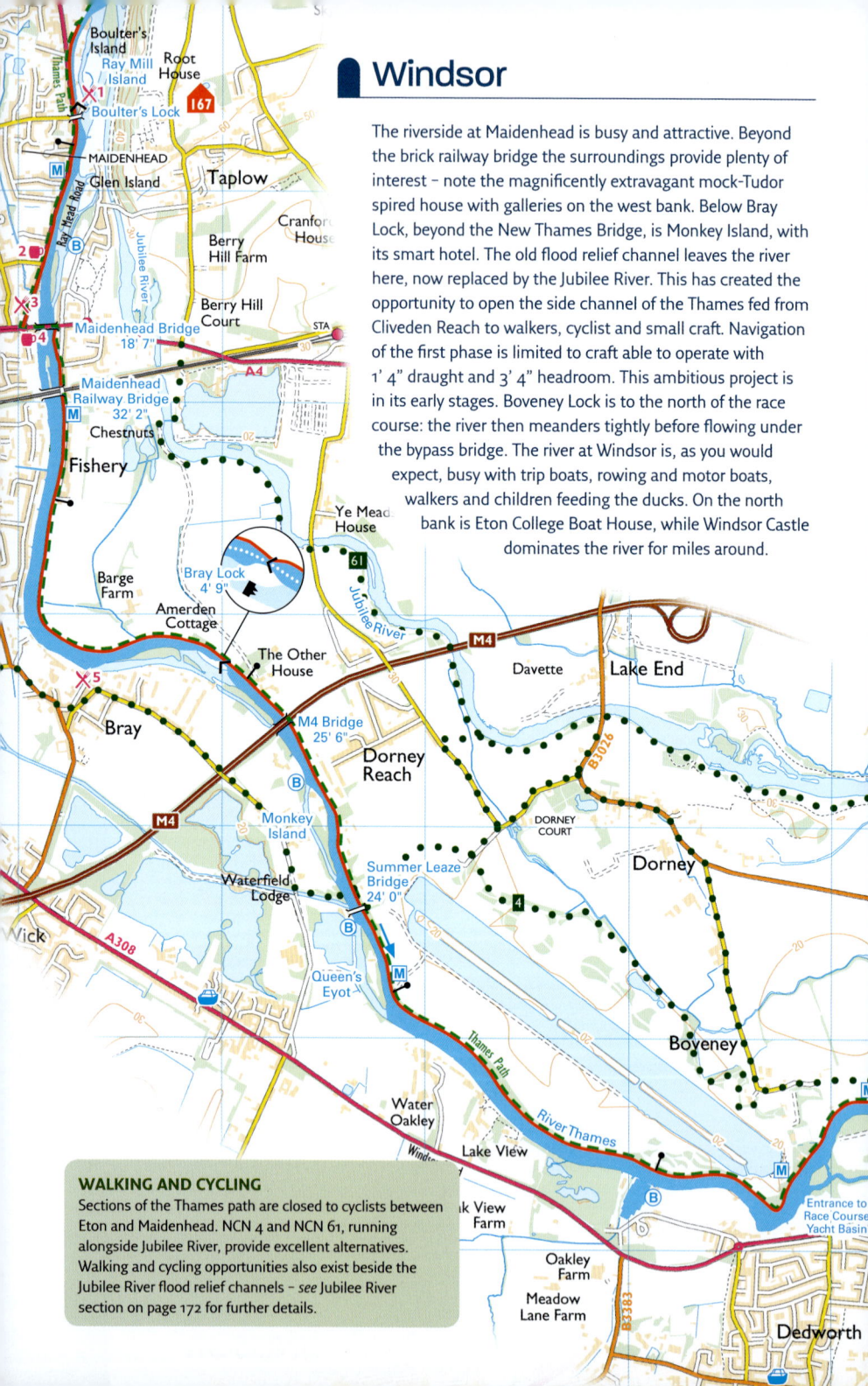

Windsor

The riverside at Maidenhead is busy and attractive. Beyond the brick railway bridge the surroundings provide plenty of interest – note the magnificently extravagant mock-Tudor spired house with galleries on the west bank. Below Bray Lock, beyond the New Thames Bridge, is Monkey Island, with its smart hotel. The old flood relief channel leaves the river here, now replaced by the Jubilee River. This has created the opportunity to open the side channel of the Thames fed from Cliveden Reach to walkers, cyclist and small craft. Navigation of the first phase is limited to craft able to operate with 1' 4" draught and 3' 4" headroom. This ambitious project is in its early stages. Boveney Lock is to the north of the race course: the river then meanders tightly before flowing under the bypass bridge. The river at Windsor is, as you would expect, busy with trip boats, rowing and motor boats, walkers and children feeding the ducks. On the north bank is Eton College Boat House, while Windsor Castle dominates the river for miles around.

WALKING AND CYCLING

Sections of the Thames path are closed to cyclists between Eton and Maidenhead. NCN 4 and NCN 61, running alongside Jubilee River, provide excellent alternatives. Walking and cycling opportunities also exist beside the Jubilee River flood relief channels – see Jubilee River section on page 172 for further details.

River Thames — Windsor

Leaving Windsor, the Thames winds around Home Park, passing the famous college, on the north bank. Turbines have been installed in the weir at Romney Lock to provide a clean energy source for Windsor Castle.

BOAT TRIPS

French Brothers The Clewer Boathouse, Clewer Court Road, Windsor SL4 5JH (01753 851900; www.frenchbrothers.co.uk). Craft available for private hire, with food and bars. Also passenger services from Windsor, Runnymede and Maidenhead. Steam launch for private charter.

Salter Bros Thames Side, Windsor SL4 1QN (01753 865832; www.salterssteamers.co.uk). A company synonymous with the Thames. Scheduled *summer* services all major locations between Oxford and Windsor.

Boatyards

Ⓑ**Bray Marina** Monkey Island Lane, Bray SL6 2EB (01628 623654; www.mdlmarinas.co.uk/marinas/mdl-bray-marina). 🚻🚿🔧P D E Gas, overnight and long-term mooring, winter storage, crane (10 ton), boat/engine sales and repairs, chandlery, toilets, showers, books, maps, DIY facilities, hard standing, Wi-Fi. ✕ 🍴 Mediterranevm Bar & Restaurant (01628 633512; www.mediterranevm.co.uk/about-us/). *Open Mon-Fri L and E & Sat-Sun 12.00-22.00 (Sun 21.00).* Marina *open 24 hours.*

Ⓑ**Windsor Marina** Maidenhead Road, Windsor SL4 5TZ (01753 853911; www.mdlmarinas.co.uk/marinas/mdl-windsor-marina). 🚻🚿🔧P D E Pump out, gas, overnight/long-term mooring, winter storage, slipway, boat sales and repairs, engine repairs, boat hoods and upholstery, telephone, toilets, showers, DIY facilities, Wi-Fi. Marina *open 24 hours.*

Ⓑ**Racecourse Marina** Maidenhead Road, Windsor SL4 5HT (01753 851501; www.tingdeneboating.com/inland-marinas-uk/racecourse). 🚻🚿🔧P D Pump out, gas, overnight and long-term mooring, winter storage, crane, boat and engine sales and repairs, small chandlery, telephone, toilets, showers, licensed club, book and maps, hard standing, yacht club, Wi-Fi. *Open daily 09.00-17.00 (Sun 10.00).*

Ⓑ**Stanley & Thomas** Tom Jones Boatyard, Romney Lock, Windsor SL4 6HU (01753 833166/07936 023698; www.tomjonesboatyard.co.uk). Long-term mooring, winter storage, crane, boat building, boat and engine sales and repairs, restoration and repairs to historic boats, painting and varnishing. *Emergency call out.*

171

- **Maidenhead**
Berks. All services. A dormitory suburb of London, close to the M4 motorway, and with much new development.
Tourist Information Centre Central Library, St Ives Road, Maidenhead SL6 1QU (01628 796502; www.windsor.gov.uk). *Open Mon-Sat 09.00-19.00 (Sat 17.00) & Sun 11.00-14.00.*
The Jubilee River (www.slough.gov.uk/downloads/file/2672/jubilee-river-information-leaflet) An imaginative solution to the ever-present threat of flooding in the Thames Valley, this newly constructed 7-mile river takes full account of environmental considerations. Built at a cost of £100 million, it passes under the main railway line from Paddington, and the M4 motorway, before rejoining the Thames near Eton College. Over 250,000 native trees have been planted – creating habitat for mandarin ducks, reed and sedge warblers, bittern, bearded tit and marsh harriers. A footpath and cycleway accompanies its course, and there are hides for birdwatchers. Boating Activity is restricted to paddling. But should a drought occur, as in 1976, this new river would be sacrificed to the more long-standing demands of the Thames, whatever the environmental cost.
Maidenhead Railway Bridge These two beautiful arches, each 123ft long, are reputedly the largest brickwork spans in the world. They were built in 1839 by Brunel.

- **Bray**
Berks. PO, stores, off-licence, takeaway. Despite commuter development, Bray still retains its village centre. The largely 13th-C church is approached via a fine brick gatehouse of 1450. Simon Alwyn, the 16th-C vicar of Bray, who changed his creed three times to hold the living under Henry VIII, Edward VI, Mary and Elizabeth I, lies buried in the churchyard. Just outside the village is the Jesus Hospital, founded in 1627.
Monkey Island On the island are the fishing lodge and pavilion of the 3rd Duke of Marlborough, built in 1744 on rubble salvaged from the Great Fire of London. The Lodge was constructed from wooden blocks, cut to look like stone and still in good condition; the nearby Temple has a fine Wedgwood-style ceiling. In one of the restaurant rooms of the Pavilion there are monkey paintings on the ceiling, completed by Andie de Clermont before 1738. The name of the island, however, is a corruption of 'Monk's Eyot'. The Pavilion became an inn around 1840, and was fashionable at the start of the 20th C when Edward VII and Queen Alexandra had afternoon tea on the lawn. It is now a hotel (01628 623400; www.monkeyislandestate.co.uk).
Down Place A pretty 18th-C riverside mansion, once the meeting place of the Kit Kat Club. Steele, Addison, Walpole and Congreve were members. Nearby is Oakley Court, a magnificent Victorian Gothic castle of 1859.
Dorney Court and Church Near Windsor SL4 6QP (01628 604638; www.dorneycourt.co.uk). A gabled and timbered Tudor manor house, built c.1440, and occupied by the Palmer family for 400 years. Restorations have not altered the original feeling of the house which contains fine furniture and paintings. The church contains a Norman font, 17th-C woodwork and a Garrard monument. It is reputedly haunted by a cavalier, a Turk and a young girl in white. *Open daily in June 12.30-16.00.* Charge. Garden, tearoom and gift shop open *daily*.

- **Boveney**
Bucks. A village scattered around a green, with Tudor buildings and a pretty flint and clapboard church.

- **Windsor**
Berks. All services. The main street curves around the castle and is full of pubs, restaurants and souvenir shops. The Church of St John the Baptist in the High Street, built 1820-2, has three galleries supported by delicate cast iron piers. The town hall was built by Wren in 1689-90 after a design by Sir Thomas Fitch. The ceiling appears to be supported by four Tuscan columns which stop two inches short: a private joke of the architect's at the expense of a doubting mayor. To the west of the town there is a fine riverside park. Theatre at the Theatre Royal (01753 853888; www.theatreroyalwindsor.co.uk).
Tourist Information Centre The Old Booking Hall, Windsor Royal Shopping, Thames Street, Windsor SL4 1PJ (01753 743900; www.windsor.gov.uk). *Open daily.*
Windsor Castle SL4 1NJ (020 7766 7304; www.rct.uk/visit/windsor-castle). The largest inhabited castle in the world, established by William the Conqueror during the 1070s, the present building was started by Henry II, 1165-79. Most succeeding monarchs have left their mark, notably Charles II, and Queen Victoria who spent over £1 million on modernisation. It has been meticulously restored following the disastrous fire of 20 November 1992 (the Queen and Duke of Edinburgh's 45th wedding anniversary!). The building falls into three sections:
Lower Ward St George's Chapel, the finest example of Perpendicular architecture in the country, containing the tombs of ten sovereigns. The Albert Memorial Chapel, originally built by Henry VII and turned into a Victorian shrine.
Middle Ward The Round Tower, with a panoramic view over twelve counties.
Upper Ward The Private Apartments and the State Apartments, containing a collection of paintings. The castle is surrounded by parks. Home Park borders on the river and contains Frogmore House, built by Wyatt in 1792 out of an earlier house, and the Royal Mausoleum. The castle precincts are *open daily* – other parts of the castle are *often open* to the public but check times. Charge.
Legoland Winkfield Road, Windsor SL4 4AY (0871 2222 001; www.legoland.co.uk). A building-brick fantasy covering over 150 acres, with 40 rides, shows and attractions, including Lego Traffic, and Miniland, built from 32 million Lego bricks. *Open early Mar-Oct, daily.* Charge. Doors close if it gets crowded!
Windsor Great Park SL4 2HT (01753 860 222; www.windsorgreatpark.co.uk). A total area of 4,800 acres between the Thames and Virginia Water. There has been a starling roost in the park for over 100 years,. and a heronry at Fort Belvedere.

- **Eton**
Berks. PO, stores, bank, chemist, takeaways, garage, station (¼ mile distant). The long and rambling High Street is a pleasant place to walk.

River Thames — Windsor

Eton College Eton High Street, Eton SL4 6DW (01753 671177; www.etoncollege.com). Founded by Henry VI in 1440 to provide education for 70 poor scholars. The buildings date from 1441 to the present day. Now 1280 boys attend. Eighteen former British prime ministers have been educated here. Short guided tours are offered on some *Wed, Fri, Sat, Sun and daily* during Eton's holidays. Pre-booking essential. Tickets available from Royal Windsor Information Centre or Eton College Gift Shop on the High Street.

Pubs and Restaurants (pages 170–171)

1 The Boathouse at Boulters Lock Boulters Lock Island, Maidenhead SL6 8PE (01628 621291; www.boathouseboulterslock.co.uk). Bar and restaurant right by the lock in the Old Ray Flour Mill, built 1726 and converted in 1950. Real ale and food available *Mon-Sat 12.00-21.00 & Sun 09.30-20.00*. Riverside patio. Sports TV and Wi-Fi. *Open Mon-Thu 10.00-22.00 & Fri-Sun 09.30-23.00 (Sun 21.00).*

2 The Thames Hotel Ray Mead Road, Maidenhead SL6 8NR (01628 628721; www.thameshotel.co.uk). Relaxed riverside hotel and restaurant, run by an Italian family. Built in the 1880s by a prosperous local boat builder – indeed at one time it had a telegraph office. Princess Frederika of Hanover, and many other distinguished guests, have stayed here. Real ale. Bar and Italian restaurant meals *Mon-Sat L and E & Sun 12.00-21.00*. Family-friendly, riverside terrace. B&B. *Open daily 11.00-23.30.*

3 Thai Orchid 2 Ray Mead Road, Maidenhead SL6 8NJ (01628 777555; www.thaiorchidmaidenhead.co.uk). A wide selection of Thai dishes served in an elegant, traditional setting. *Open Tue-Sun L and E (not Sat L)*. Takeaway service.

4 The Blue River Café Thames Riviera Hotel The Bridge, Bridge Road, Maidenhead SL6 8DW (01628 674057; www.bluerivercafe.co.uk). The Blue River Café is located inside the striking Edwardian building housing the hotel and serves modern English food *Mon-Sat 07.00-22.00 & Sun 08.00-21.30*. Family-friendly, riverside terrace. B&B. *Open Mon-Sat 07.00-00.00 & Sun 08.00-22.30.*

5 The Waterside Inn Ferry Road, Bray SL6 2AT (01628 620691; www.waterside-inn.co.uk). Smart riverside restaurant in a beautiful setting, run by Michel Roux's son Alain – considered by some to be the best restaurant in the country. Exciting menu, attentive waiters, expensive wine. *Open L and E (closed Mon, and Tue Sep-May)*. Booking essential. Children over 12 welcome. B&B. *Open L and E.*

6 Sir Christopher Wren's House Hotel 52 Thames Street, Windsor SL4 1PX (01753 442400; www.sirchristopherwren.co.uk). A Thames-side residential hotel, built by Sir Christopher Wren as a family home, with cocktail bar and restaurant overlooking the river. Restaurant serves excellent food *L and E* plus *afternoon teas*. Children welcome. Outside seating. Wi-Fi. *Open all day.*

Windsor has many fine pubs, the following are those nearest the river:

7 The Two Brewers 34 Park Street, Windsor SL4 1LB (01753 855426; www.twobrewerswindsor.co.uk). Describing itself as being 'dedicated to life, liberty, food, drink and other less serious matters', this small, cosy, wood panelled 17th Century inn dispenses real ale and food *daily (not Fri and Sat E)*. Dog-friendly but no children inside. Pavement seating. Newspapers, Real fires and Wi-Fi. *Open Mon-Sat 11.30-23.30 & Sun 12.00-22.30.*

8 The Royal Windsor Public House & Dining 9 Datchet Road, Windsor SL4 1QD (01753 980164; www.pubanddining.co.uk/royal-windsor). There was a brewery here in 1539, when the building was owned by St George's Chapel and the pub was known as The Crown. On 8 March 1834 it was reported that Mrs Bitmead, of The Royal Oak, was fined ten shillings for allowing her pig to escape, and rampage around the town. Real ale is served in the bar and food is available *daily 10.00-22.00 (Sun 11.00)*. Outside seating and real fires. *Open Mon-Sat 10.00-23.00 (Fri-Sat 00.00) & Sun 11.00-22.00.*

9 Latino Taverna 3 Church Lane, Windsor SL4 1PA (01753 857711; www.latinotaverna.co.uk/cms/index.php). Friendly, family-run Greek restaurant, set on a picturesque cobbled street in the most historic part of Windsor, serving a wide range of Greek and continental cuisine. On *Sat* evenings the first floor transforms from *weekday* relaxed Mediterranean ambience into a combination of dinner and dancing to live Greek bouzouki music! Children welcome. *Open Sun-Mon and Thu 12.00-22.00 (Sun 21.00) & Fri-Sat 12.00-22.30.*

10 The Waterman's Arms Brocas Street, Eton SL4 6BW (01753 861001; www.watermans-eton.com). The interior of this cosy, welcoming pub, dating from 1682, features rowing memorabilia and murals while the bar serves real ales and food *Mon-Fri L and E (not Mon-Wed E) & Sat-Sun 12.00-20.30 (Sun 16.45)*. Dog-friendly, patio. Quiz *Thu*. Traditional pub games, newspapers, real fires and Wi-Fi. *Open Mon-Sat 12.00-22.30 (Fri-Sat 00.00) & Sun 12.00-21.00.*

The following four pubs and restaurants are easily found in Eton High Street, straight up from the bridge:

11 The Crown and Cushion 84 High Street, Eton SL4 6AF (01753 861531; www.thecrownandcushioneton.co.uk). Friendly establishment serving traditional pub food *daily 12.00-21.00 (Sun 18.00)*. Family-friendly, garden. Newspapers, sports TV and Wi-Fi. B&B. *Open 12.00-23.00 (Sun 22.30).*

12 The Christopher Hotel 110 High Street, Eton SL4 6AN (01753 852359; www.thechristopher.co.uk). Friendly old coaching inn serving food *daily 12.00-21.00*. Dog-friendly and courtyard terrace. Newspapers, sports TV and Wi-Fi. B&B. *Open 11.00-00.00 (Sun 22.30).*

13 The George Inn 77 High Street, Eton SL4 6AF (01753 861797; www.georgeinn-eton.co.uk). Wooden floors and lighting by carriage lamps and candles, provides a warm atmosphere in what is also the Winsor & Eton Brewery shop. Real ales and food available *Mon-Fri L and E & Sat-Sun 12.00-21.00 (Sun 17.00)*. Dog- and family-friendly, garden. Quiz *Wed*. Real fires and Wi-Fi. B&B. *Open Sun-Fri 12.00-23.00 (Sun-Mon 22.00) & Sat 12.00-00.00.*

14 Côte Windsor 71 -72 High Street, by Windsor Bridge, Eton SL4 6AA (01753 868344; www.cote.co.uk/restaurant/windsor). Modern French food served in a riverside restaurant *daily 09.00-22.00 (Sun 21.30)*. Terrace seating *in summer*.

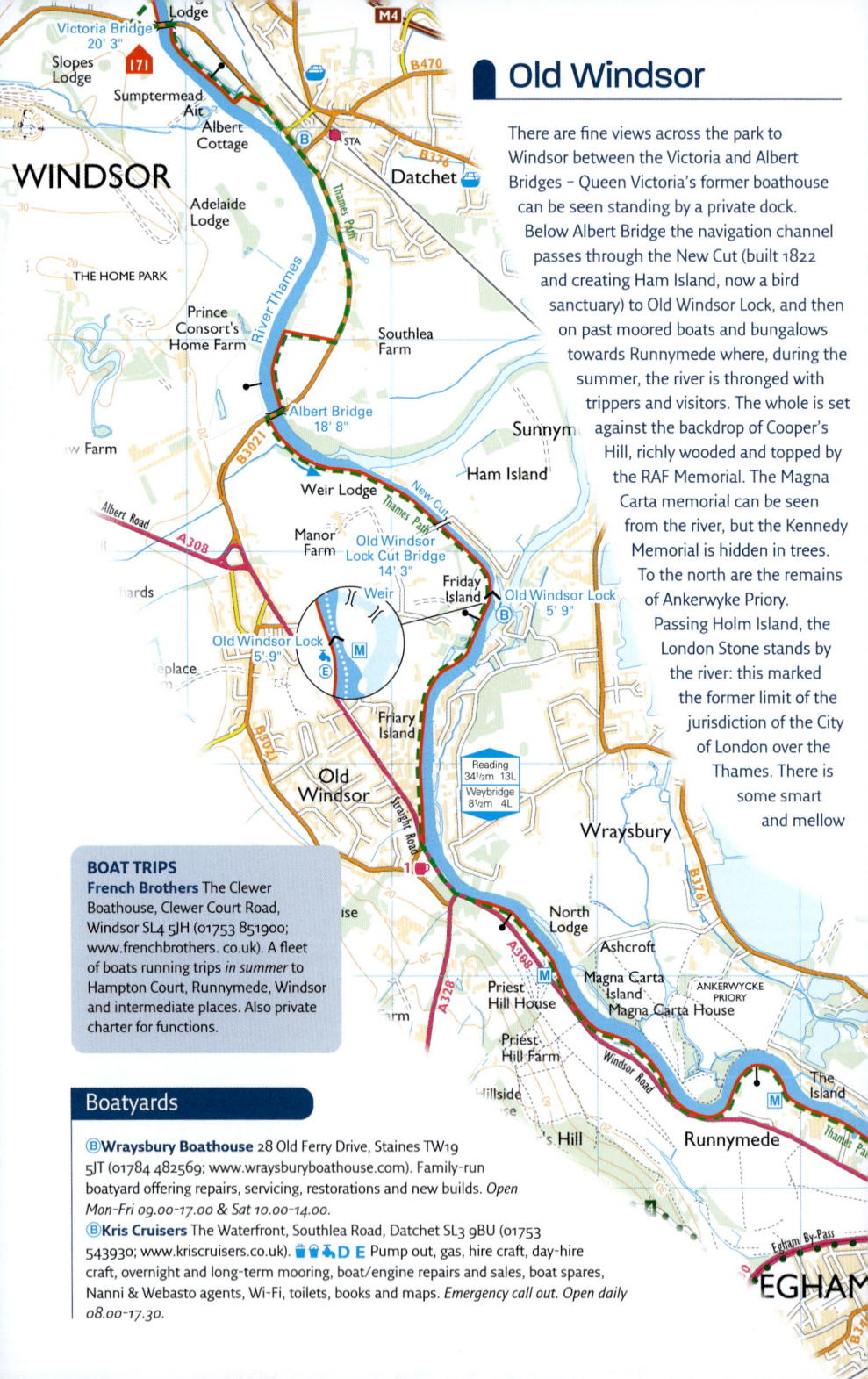

housing on the north bank above Staines Bridge, but for the most part the riverside is lined with a wonderful, and sometimes very eccentric, array of holiday chalets and bungalows, along with houseboats and moored craft of indiscriminate vintage.

- **Datchet**
  Berks. Stores, chemist, off-licence, takeaways, fish & chips, garage, station. At its best around the green, where there is still a village feeling. Stores *open daily 06.00-23.00.*

- **Old Windsor**
  Berks. PO, stores, chemist, off-licence, fish & chips, takeaways, station. A great expanse of suburban houses with no sign of the 9th-C village, built around the site of a Saxon royal palace. The 13th-C church is hidden among trees. The *PO* is ½ mile west of the Bells of Ouzeley, along the A308 Windsor Road.

- **Runnymede**
  Surrey. Beside the river on the south bank, this is a stretch of open parkland backed by the wooded slope of Cooper's Hill. The paired gatehouses, by Lutyens, introduce an area of memorials. The inspiration is the sealing of the Magna Carta in 1215. On top of the hill is the Commonwealth Air Forces Memorial. This quadrangular structure, built by Sir Edward Maufe in 1953, perfectly exploits its situation. Below are the Magna Carta Memorial and the Kennedy Memorial, the latter built on
  an acre of ground given to the American people. This is a popular venue in summer. There are excellent pleasure gardens with a *café* alongside the river.

- **Ankerwyke** Built on the site of a Benedictine nunnery is Ankerwyke Priory, a low, early 19th-C mansion surrounded by trees, among which is the Ankerwyke Yew, whose trunk is 33ft in circumference.

- **Staines-upon-Thames**
  Surrey. All services. A commuter town which has expanded hugely over the last 30 years. However, the area around the pleasantly situated church has remained virtually unchanged. Clarence Street, which culminates in Rennie's stone bridge, built 1829-32, still has the feeling of an 18th-C market town. To the north are huge reservoirs.

Pubs and Restaurants

🍺✕ **1 The Bells of Ouzeley** Straight Road, Old Windsor SL4 2SH (01753 861526; www.harvester.co.uk/restaurants/southeast/thebellsofouzeleyoldwindsor). There has been a pub on this site for about 800 years, although it nearly all came to an end during World War II, when a V1 flying bomb destroyed part of the building. Food available *daily 09.00-22.00*. Family-friendly, outside seating. Wi-Fi. *Open 09.00-22.00 (Fri-Sat 23.00).* Takeaway service.

🍺✕ **2 The Runnymede-on-Thames** Windsor Road, Egham TW20 0AG (01784 220600; www.runnymedehotel.com). Smart hotel with riverside gardens, conference facilities and the Leftbank waterfront restaurant, created by Suchà Design at a cost of £1m, and based upon an aquatic theme. Also informal restaurant, bar and conservatory. Food available *all day*. Children welcome. B&B.

🍺 **3 The Bells** 124 Church Street, Staines-upon-Thames TW18 4ZB (01784 454240; www.thebellspub.co.uk). Comfortable 18th-C pub, opposite the supposedly-haunted St Mary's Church, dispensing real ale, with food available *Mon-Thu L and E & Fri-Sun 12.00-21.00*. Dog-friendly, patio garden. Sports TV. *Open Mon-Sat 12.00-23.00 (Fri-Sat 00.00) & Sun 12.00-22.30.*

🍺✕ **4 The Slug & Lettuce** 15-18 Clarence Street, Staines-upon-Thames TW18 4SU (01784 456914; www.facebook.com/SlugandLettuceStaines). Popular chain pub, serving food *all day*, including breakfast. Family-friendly, riverside terrace. *Open Sun-Wed 10.00-23.00 (Sun 22.30) & Thu-Sat 10.00-01.00 (Thu 00.00).*

🍺✕ **5 The Swan Hotel** The Hythe, Staines-upon-Thames TW18 3JB (01784 452494; www.swanstaines.co.uk). Rambling, riverside, 18th-C hotel dispensing real ale and food *Mon-Thu L and E & Fri-Sun 12.00-21.00 (Sun 20.00)*. Dog- and family-friendly, riverside seating. Real fires and Wi-Fi. Mooring. B&B. *Open Mon-Sat 11.30-23.00 & Sun 12.00-22.30.*

> **WALKING AND CYCLING**
> There are excellent walks by the river at Runnymede, where the land is owned by the National Trust.

River Thames — Old Windsor

175

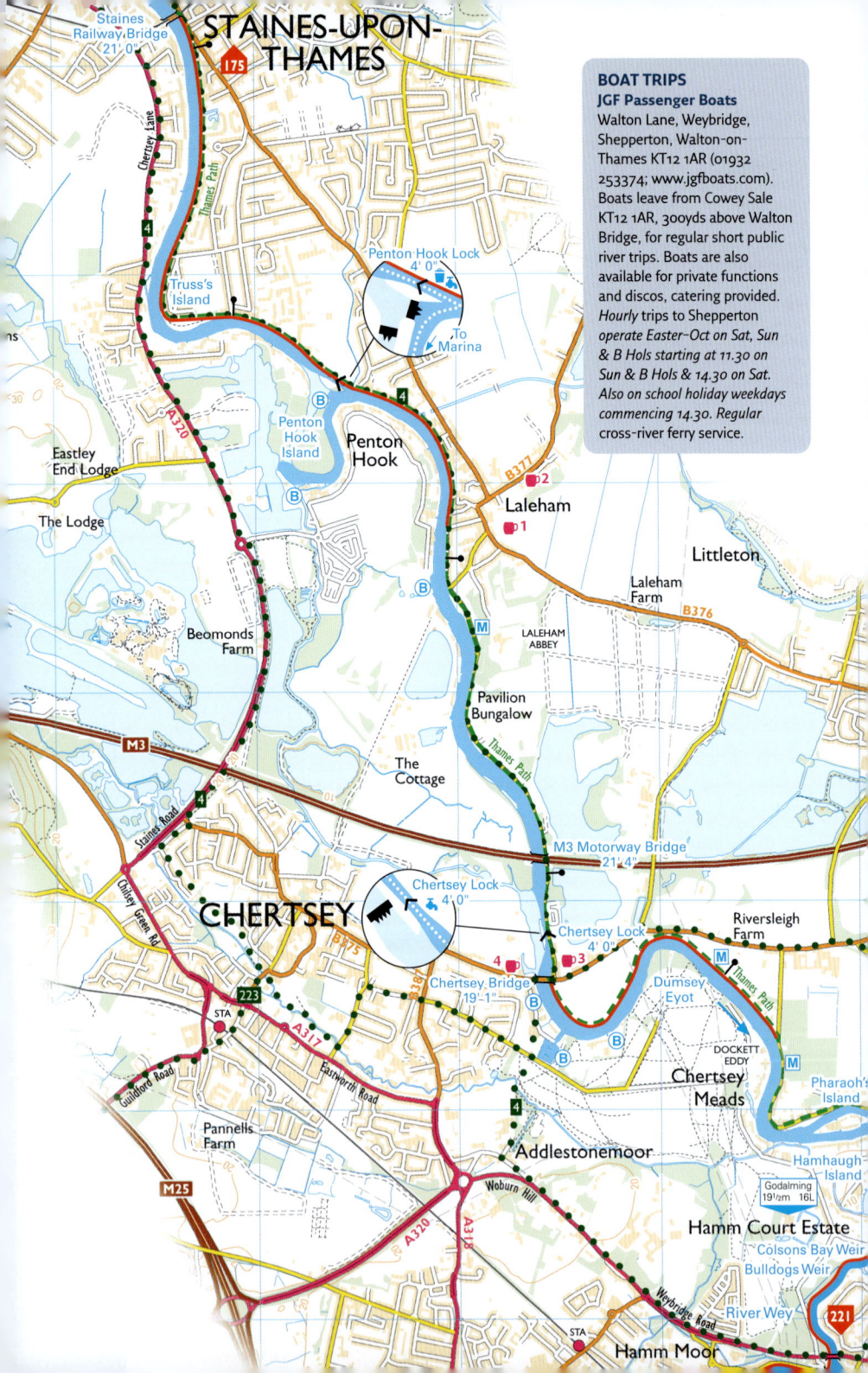

Weybridge

At Penton Hook a large marina has been established in flooded gravel pits – it is approached from below the lock. Laleham follows, and soon the bungalows disappear and Laleham Abbey and park provide a brief breathing space before Chertsey looms large. The river twists and turns on its way to Weybridge, where the River Wey (see page 219) flows in from the south joining it, and the Basingstoke Canal (see page 15) to the Thames. Desborough Cut removes two large loops from the navigable course before the river makes a direct run for Sunbury-on-Thames, leaving Walton-on-Thames to the east.

NAVIGATIONAL NOTES

1. Note that Penton Hook Marina is approached from *below* the lock.
2. The River Wey joins the Thames *below* Shepperton Lock.
3. The old course of the river north of Desborough Island is navigable, but it may be shallow in places.
4. *Nauticalia* runs a ferry service below Shepperton Lock TW17 9LQ for the National Trust (01932 244396; www.theferrypoint.com/pedestrian-ferry-to-weybridge) so walkers can enjoy this ancient crossing, noticing that 'droves of sheep will be carried at the fare of one shilling per score (shepherd to clean up afterwards)'.
5. A *24hr* transit licence is available for boaters travelling from the River Wey to the tidal Thames, which is cheaper than an Environmental Agency *day* licence.

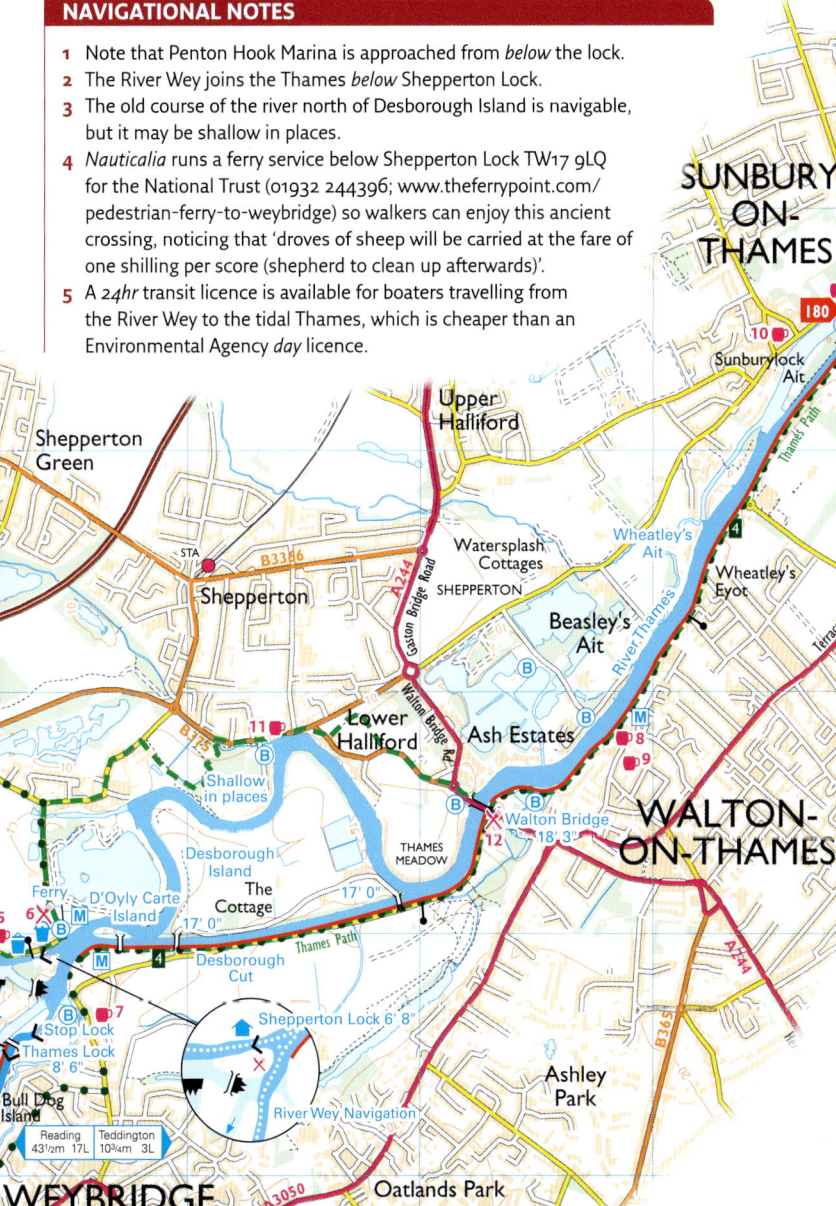

Boatyards

ⒷPenton Hook Marina Staines Lane, Chertsey KT16 8PY (01932 568681; www.mdlmarinas.co.uk/marinas/mdl-penton-hook-marina). 🚽🚿♿P D Pump out, gas, overnight and long-term mooring, winter storage, slipway, crane, boat and engine sales and repairs, chandlery, telephone, toilets, DIY facilities, hoods and covers, laundrette, brokerage, Wi-Fi. Marina open 24 hours.

ⒷChertsey Meads Marine The Meads, Chertsey KT16 8LN (01932 564699; www.chertseymeadsmarine.co.uk). ♿D E Pump out, gas, day-boat hire, overnight and long-term mooring, winter storage, slipway, crane, boat and engine repairs, DIY facilities, books and maps. Emergency call out. Open daily 09.00-18.00.

ⒷLindon Lewis Marine Shepperton Marina, Felix Lane, Shepperton, Middlesex TW17 8NS (01932 247427; www.lindonlewismarine.co.uk). 🚽♿ E Gas, overnight and long-term mooring, winter storage, slipway, boat building, boat and engine repairs, chandlery, boat and engine sales, DIY facilities, hardstanding, toilets. Café nearby. Open Mon-Sat 09.00-17.30 (Sat 17.00).

ⒷXWalton Marina Walton Bridge, Walton-on-Thames KT12 1QW (01932 226305; www.tingdeneboating.com/inland-marinas-uk/walton). 🚽🚿♿D Pump out, gas, overnight and long-term mooring, winter storage, slipway, crane, boat and engine sales and repairs, chandlery, toilets, showers, books, maps and gifts, Wi-Fi. Also The Boathouse Café (01932 550980; www.coffeeattheboathouse.com) open daily 09.00-17.00. Marina open 09.00-17.00 (Sun 10.00).

ⒷBridge Marine Thames Meadow, Shepperton TW17 8LT (01932 245126; www.bridgemarine.co.uk). 🚽♿E Gas, day hire boats, winter storage, slipway, crane, boat and engine sales and repairs, chandlery, toilets, books, maps and gifts, DIY facilities. Emergency call out. Open Mon-Sat 09.00-17.00.

ⒷShepperton Marina Felix Lane, Shepperton TW17 8NS (01932 260277; www.sheppertonmarina.com). 🚽🚿♿P D Pump out, gas, overnight and long-term mooring, winter storage, crane, boat and engine sales and repairs, chandlery, toilets, showers, books, maps and gifts, DIY facilities. Emergency call out. Open Mon-Sat 09.00-17.30 & Sun 10.00-17.00.

ⒷW Bates & Son Bridge Wharf, Chertsey KT16 8LG (01932 571141; www.bateswharf.co.uk). 🚽🚿♿ long- and short-term mooring, boat sales, chandlery, hardstanding, engineering, toilets and showers.

See also **Boatyard** entries on page 221 – Wey & Godalming Navigations.

- **Laleham**
Surrey. PO, stores, off-licence. The first impression of Laleham is one of bungalows and houseboats. The village does not exploit the river at all, and the centre lacks the riverside feeling of some other towns hereabouts. The 18th- and 19th-C church is well placed in a wooded graveyard, which contains the tomb of Matthew Arnold (1822–88, see Bablock Hythe on page 118). To the south of the town is Laleham Park. Formerly the grounds of Laleham House, built about 1805, it is now a wooded public park reaching down to the river. Stores open Mon-Sat 06.00-19.00 & Sun 07.00-14.00.
Thorpe Park Staines Road, Chertsey KT16 8PN (0871 663 1673; www.thorpepark.com). One of the country's first theme parks, constantly being upgraded. Attractions include Colossus, which hurtles through ten loops over 2800ft long at speeds of 40 mph, along with the highest log flume ride in the UK, Rumba Rapids and the Canada Creek Railway. Treats include 'Rush' – the world's largest speed swing, and 'Slammer', the ultimate free-fall. Young visitors can enjoy Mr Monkey's Banana Ride. Open daily Easter-Oct. Charge.
- **Chertsey**
Surrey. All services. From the river the first sight of Chertsey is James Paine's stone bridge, built 1780–2. Chertsey just manages to retain a feeling of the 18th C, especially around Windsor Street, which runs past the site of the abbey, once one of the greatest in England. Founded in AD666 and rebuilt in the 12th C, it was finally destroyed during the Reformation. It is thought likely that materials from the abbey were used in the construction of Hampton Court.
- **Weybridge**
Surrey. All services. A commuter town in the stockbroker belt, built around the confluence of the rivers Wey and Thames – the junction is marked by a pretty iron bridge of 1865. Weybridge represents the frontier of the suburbia that now spreads almost unbroken to London.
- **Shepperton**
Surrey. All services. Recognisable from the river by the lawns of the 19th-C manor house, Shepperton is a surprising example of village survival. The square contains a number of relatively intact 18th-C inns. The church, with its fine brick tower, was built in the 17th and 18th C, and has box pews. To the north of the church is the rectory, which has a pretty Queen Anne front. The famous film studios are to the north, near the vast Queen Mary Reservoir.
- **Walton-on-Thames**
Surrey. All services.
- **Sunbury-on-Thames**
Surrey. PO, stores, off-licence, chemists, takeaways, fish & chips, stations. Sunbury has a pleasant village feeling. Sunbury Court, the grand mansion of the town, was built in 1770 and is now a conference and holiday venue.

WALKING AND CYCLING

National Cycle Route (NCN) 4 connects Weybridge with Putney Bridge, using quiet streets and cycle paths. Follow the signs on the Thames towpath from its junction with the River Wey to pass through Kingston upon Thames and Richmond Park. This is part of the Thames Valley Cycle Route, which stretches all the way to Oxford and comprises NCN 4 to Reading and NCN 5 between Reading and Oxford. Footways (www.footways.london) is a network of quiet, enjoyable walking routes in London.

Pubs and Restaurants (pages 176–177)

🍺✗ **1 The Three Horseshoes** 25 Shepperton Road, Laleham TW18 1SE (01784 455014; www.threehorseshoeslaleham.co.uk). Having been a police station and a morgue, this is now a characterful, relaxed and comfortable pub, once patronised by the Prince Regent, Sir Arthur Sullivan and Marie Lloyd. Real ale and food available *Mon-Sat 12.00-21.00 (Fri-Sat 21.30) & Sun 12.00-20.00*. Dog- and child-friendly (*until 19.00 in bar*), garden. Newspapers and Wi-Fi. *Open Mon-Sat 10.00-22.30 (Fri-Sat 23.00) & Sun 10.00-22.00*.

🍺✗ **2 The Feathers** The Broadway, Laleham TW18 1RZ (01784 278508; www.thefeatherslaleham.com). Very much food-led, this establishment serves meals *Mon-Sat L and E & Sun 12.00-21.00*. *Sun roasts*. *Open daily 12.00-23.00*.

🍺✗ **3 The Kingfisher** Chertsey Bridge Road, Chertsey KT16 8LF (01932 579811; www.thekingfisherchertsey.co.uk). Cosy traditional pub, with low ceilings and timbered walls. Real ale. Food available *daily 12.00-21.00* – vegan options. Family-friendly, riverside patio. Wi-Fi. Camping nearby. *Open 11.00-23.00*.

🍺✗ **4 The Bridge Hotel** Chertsey Bridge Road, Chertsey KT16 8JZ (01932 565644; www.bridgehotelchertsey.co.uk). A modern hotel and pub serving real ale and food *Mon-Sat 12.00-21.00 (Fri-Sat 21.30) & Sun 12.00-20.00*. Breakfast is available *daily 07.00-10.30 (Sun 08.00)*. Dog and family-friendly, garden. Camping nearby. *Open Mon-Sat 07.00-22.30 (Fri-Sat 23.00) & Sun 07.00-22.00*.

🍺✗ **5 The Thames Court** Ferry Lane, The Towpath, Shepperton TW17 9LJ (01932 221957; www.vintageinn.co.uk/restaurants/south-east/thethamescourtshepperton). Oak beams, stone-flagged floors and exposed brick walls characterise this pub dispensing real ale and food *daily 12.00-22.00 (Sun 21.30)*. Family-friendly, garden. Newspapers and Wi-Fi. *Open 11.00-23.30 (Sun 23.00)*.

✗ **6 The Ferry Coffee Shop** The Ferry Point, Ferry Lane, Shepperton TW17 9LQ (01932 221094; www.ferrycoffeeshop.com). Friendly staff and pleasant surroundings for teas, coffees, cold drinks, hot and cold sandwiches cakes and snacks. The Weybridge Ferry goes from here (*see Navigation Note 4, page 177*) and the coffee shop is one of a number of artisan outlets in the attractive Ferry Point Courtyard. *Open daily 09.00-17.00*.

🍺 **7 The Old Crown** 83 Thames Street, Weybridge KT13 8LP (01932 842844; www.theoldcrownweybridge.co.uk). Rambling weather-boarded, traditional family-run, Grade II listed pub – by the old course of the River Wey – which has remained in the same hands since 1959. Real ales and excellent food available *daily L and Thu-Sat E*. Dog- and child-friendly (*until 21.00*), riverside garden. Wi-Fi. Moorings nearby. *Open Mon-Sat 11.00-23.00 & Sun 12.00-22.00*.

🍺✗ **8 The Swan** 50 Manor Road, Walton-on-Thames KT12 2PF (01932 225964; www.swanwalton.com). Friendly, open-plan pub – said to date from 1770 – serving real ale and food *daily 12.00-21.30 (Sun 21.00)*. Dog- and family-friendly, riverside garden. Wi-Fi. *Open 11.00-23.00 (Fri-Sat 00.00)*.

🍺 **9 The Old Manor Inn** 113 Manor Road, Walton-on-Thames KT12 2NZ (01932 221359). Real ale in a small, cosy, local's pub. Dog- and child-friendly (*until 19.30*), garden backing onto 14th-C manor house where a previous inhabitant signed Charles I's death warrant. Traditional pub games, real fires, sports TV and Wi-Fi. *Open Mon-Sat 12.00-23.00 (Fri-Sat 00.00) & Sun 12.00-22.00*.

🍺✗ **10 The Flower Pot Hotel** Thames Street, Sunbury TW16 6AA (01932 780741; www.theflowerpotsunbury.co.uk). A 17th-C pub/restaurant, which has been totally transformed into a stylish upmarket inn, with boutique accommodation. Real ale and food available *Mon-Fri L and E & Sat-Sun 08.00-22.00 (Sun 21.00)*. Breakfast from 07.00 (*Sat-Sun 08.00*). Quiz *Sun*. Terrace and real fires. B&B. *Open Mon-Fri 07.00-23.00 & Sat-Sun 08.00-23.30*.

🍺✗ **11 The Red Lion** Russell Road, Shepperton TW17 9HX (01932 244526; www.redlionshepperton.com). One of the oldest pubs in Shepperton (the first recorded licensee was in 1722) now with a more modern look, dispensing real ale and food *daily 12.00-21.00 (Sun 18.00)*. Takeaway fish & chips available *Fri E*. Also *morning* coffee and *afternoon* tea. Dog- and family-friendly, patio and riverside beer garden. Newspapers and Wi-Fi. *Open Mon-Sat 11.00-23.00 (Mon-Tue 22.00) & Sun 12.00-21.30*.

✗ **12 Wilde Brunch** Cowey Sale, Shepperton, Walton-on-Thames KT12 1QP (07912 601966; www.wildebrunch.com). Family run, serving dishes that reflect the changing seasons, using ethically sourced ingredients (but without the high prices) there is appetising food to be had here *daily 08.30-16.00*. Children welcome. Outside seating beside the river and in the park.

See also **Pubs and Restaurants** for the Wey & Godalming Navigations on page 221.

Hampton Court

Sunbury Court Island is lined with immaculate chalets and bungalows: opposite and to the east is a vast area of reservoirs and waterworks. Platt's Eyot once supported a community of engineers and craftsmen, with boatbuilding being carried out from the 1850s. Immisch built electric launches here after 1889, in a yard later taken over by Thorneycrofts. They built 170 torpedo boats here between 1938-45, but left during the 1960s. Below Platt's Eyot is Hampton, where the ferry still survives (see Boat Trips page 181). Hampton Church stands on the north bank opposite Garrick's Ait. Bushy Park stretches away to the north east of the river. Tagg's Island and Ash Island are lined with smart moored craft and eccentric houseboats, including a large Swiss chalet behind Tagg's Island. Below Hampton Bridge is Hampton Court Palace, standing close to the river, and separated from it by an extremely long red brick wall.

Further downstream, Thames Ditton Island is absolutely packed with yet more bungalows and chalets. The river then becomes very wide as it curves past Thames Ditton, flanked by the parkland of Hampton Court to the west and the housing and industry of Surbiton and Kingston upon Thames to the east.

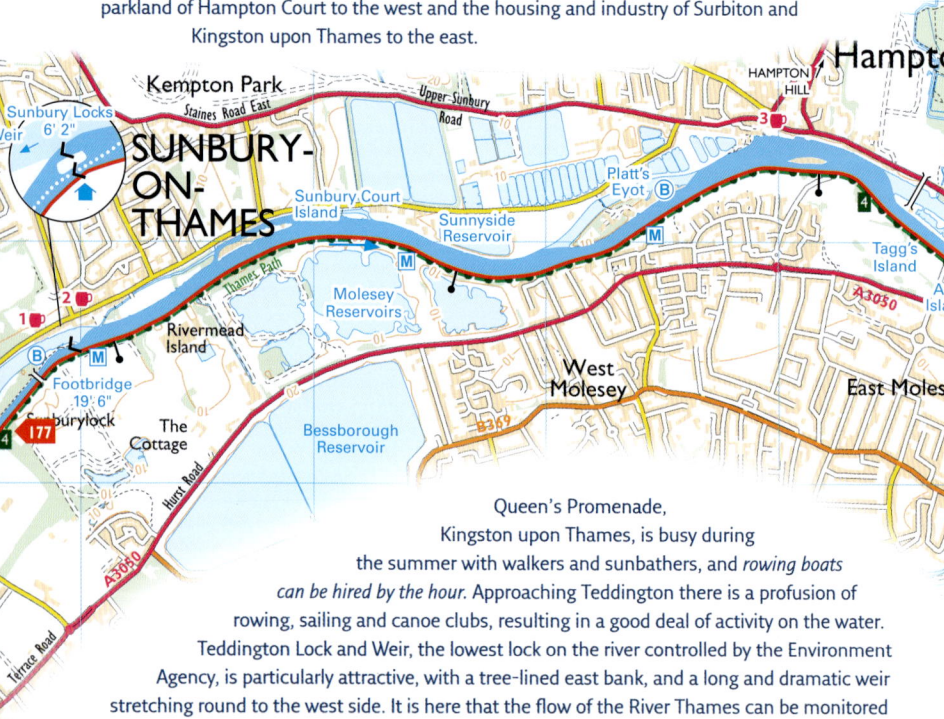

Queen's Promenade, Kingston upon Thames, is busy during the summer with walkers and sunbathers, and *rowing boats can be hired by the hour*. Approaching Teddington there is a profusion of rowing, sailing and canoe clubs, resulting in a good deal of activity on the water. Teddington Lock and Weir, the lowest lock on the river controlled by the Environment Agency, is particularly attractive, with a tree-lined east bank, and a long and dramatic weir stretching round to the west side. It is here that the flow of the River Thames can be monitored precisely (up to 15,000 million gallons per day in times of flood). On the east bank, 265yds below Teddington Lock, an obelisk marks the boundary of the jurisdiction of the Environment Agency and the Port of London Authority.

PADDLING
The Jubilee River is part of The Maidenhead, Windsor and Eton Flood Alleviation Scheme. It was built by The Environment Agency and completed in 2001 and today provides additional paddling opportunities accessed from the Thames north of Ray Mill Island at Maidenhead. See also section on the Jubilee River on page 172 and www.richardgower.com/blog/supjubileeriver.
The River Mole rises in West Sussex and flows into the Thames at Hampton Court having just joined the River Ember. Further details can be found at www.gopaddling.info/rivers/river-mole) and inspiration lies at http://www.canoedaysout.com/trip/1657.

River Thames

Hampton Court

BOAT TRIPS

Turk Launches Town End Pier, 68 High Street, Kingston upon Thames KT1 1HN (020 8546 2434; www.turks.co.uk). Operating a public service to Hampton Court, Kingston upon Thames and Richmond in *summer*. Also private charter for up to 150 people.

Hampton Ferry Thames Street, Hampton, London, TW12 2EW (020 8979 7471; www.visitrichmond.co.uk/outdoor-activities/hampton-ferry-p1584801). The oldest ferry on the Thames that has been providing a service since 1514 for passengers and (more recently) their bicycles. Operates *weekends & B Hols Apr-Oct, 10.00-18.00 & also weekdays May-Sep*. Also, an additional limited rush hour service on *weekdays Apr-Oct*. Hire boats available *Mon-Sun 10.00-16.30 in season*.

NAVIGATIONAL NOTES

1. Sunbury Locks – the mechanised lock on the south side is normally used. The hand-operated lock on the north side is used only during busy periods *in the summer.*
2. Teddington Locks (020 8940 8723). Traffic lights are in use at these locks. Please observe the red and green light signals.
3. Below Teddington the Thames becomes tidal and is under jurisdiction of the Port of London Authority (PLA). Use of a PLA mooring is by prior permission only and all enquiries should be directed in the first instance to the PLA Marine Services Department (01474 562421; marineservices@pla.co.uk).
4. The river below Teddington Lock is tidal for two hours either side of high water.
5. Those using the Skiff Lock should follow the lock keeper's instructions.
6. **Teddington to Brentford** – leave Teddington 20 minutes before high water.
7. **Teddington to Limehouse** – leave Teddington 30 minutes before high water.
   Note for both 6 & 7 Locks **must** be booked *at least 48 hours in advance* – see www.canalrivertrust.org.uk/about-us/where-we-work/london-and-south-east/boating-information/boating-facilities/locks-to-the-river-thames). *If you fail to do this, you will be left in the tideway.* Times are approximate and depend upon the speed of your boat. If in any doubt – check before you leave.

Boatyards

Ⓑ**Port Hampton Estates Limited** Platts Eyot, Lower Sunbury Road, Hampton TW12 2HF (020 8979 8116). 🚽 ⚓ Long-term mooring, crane, toilets, DIY facilities.

Ⓑ**Turk Launches** Town End Pier, 68 High Street, Kingston upon Thames KT1 1HN (020 8546 2434; www.turks.co.uk). ⚓ Pump out, long-term mooring, boat building, boat sales and repairs. *Summer* ferry to Hampton Court and Richmond. *Open daily 09.00-18.00.*

Ⓑ**Stewart Marine Harts Boatyard** Portsmouth Road, Surbiton KT6 4HJ (020 8398 2119; www.stewartmarine.co.uk). Specialist wide-beam boat builders. Moorings, chandlery and slipway, dayboat hire. *Open Mon-Fri 09.00-17.30.*

Ⓑ ✕ ♀ **TDM Marine Ltd** Thames Ditton Marina, Portsmouth Road, Surbiton KT6 5QD (020 8398 6159; www.tdmmarine.co.uk). D Gas, long-term mooring, slipway, crane, boat building, boat repairs, engine repairs, toilets, café/bar, cycle sales and repairs. *Open Tue-Sat 10.00-16.00.* Also ✕ ♀ **The Hideaway Restaurant** (020 3745 2021; www.hideaway-surbs.co.uk). *Open all day.*

● **Hampton**
Surrey. PO, stores, off-licence, chemist, takeaways, fish & chips, bakery, butcher, delicatessen, garage, stations. A lively riverside town with excellent eateries and pubs. Hampton is linked by ferry to the south bank. The church, built in 1831, is prominent on the riverside. Despite the proximity of Hampton Court, the village owes its existence to Hampton House, bought by David Garrick in 1754, and subsequently altered by Adam. By the river is Garrick's Temple, built to house Roubiliac's bust of Shakespeare. Nearby stands the large Swiss chalet which was brought over from Switzerland in 1899. Technically the shops are predominantly in Hampton Hill. There is a useful cycle repair shop – Birdie Bikes, 7 Wensleydale Road, Hampton TW12 2LP (020 8941 9397; www.birdiebikes.co.uk) *open Mon-Fri 09.00-18.00 (Wed 16.00) Sat 09.00-17.00 & Sun 10.00-15.00.* The stores are *open daily 07.00-23.00.*

Hampton Court Palace East Molesey KT8 9AU (0844 482 7777; www.hrp.org.uk). Probably the greatest secular building in England. Cardinal Wolsey, son of an Ipswich butcher, was graced by ambition and ability to such an extent that at the age of 40 he had an income of £50,000 a year. He was thus able to build the grandest private house in England. Work began in 1514. Henry VIII was offended by the unashamed ostentation of his lieutenant and in 1529, following Wolsey's downfall and his failure to secure the annulment of Henry VIII's first marriage, the king took over the house. Henry spent more on Hampton Court than on any other building, establishing it as a Royal Palace. Subsequently Wren added to it, but little work, other than repairs, has been done since. Visit the State Apartments, the Tudor Kitchen, the Wolsey Rooms, the King's & Queen's Apartments, the Georgian Rooms, the Courtyards and the Cloisters. In the formal gardens (at their best in *mid May*) are the Great Vine, planted in 1789, and the Maze where Harris, one of Jerome K. Jerome's *Three Men in a Boat,* got hopelessly lost, along with 20 followers and a keeper. *Open Wed-Fri 10.00-16.30 & Sat-Sun*

10.00-17.00 (last time slot 15.30). Closed Xmas. The gardens close at 18.00, or dusk. Charge. Teas in the grounds. River launches connect with Westminster, Richmond and Kingston upon Thames. Behind the palace is Bushy Park, enclosing 2000 acres. It is a formal design reminiscent of Versailles, and is famous for deer.

Hampton Green Hampton Court Road, Hampton, East Molesey KT8 9BS. A fine collection of 18th-C and earlier buildings surround Hampton Green, just to the north of Hampton Court Bridge. The bridge was designed by Lutyens in 1933.

● **Thames Ditton**
Surrey. PO, stores, off licence, chemist, fish & chips, takeaways, bakery, delicatessen, station. The centre of this unspoilt riverside village has managed to avoid the careless development of the surrounding area. The church here has an interesting graveyard, a lovely garden and there are several good brasses inside. Pretty whitewashed houses stand close by the suspension bridge which leads to Thames Ditton Island. Stores *open daily 07.00-22.00*.

● **Kingston upon Thames**
Surrey. All services. A Royal Borough where seven Saxon kings were crowned. The coronation stone is displayed outside the Guildhall. There is a good river frontage, centred round the stone bridge built 1825-8 by Lapidge. Away from the river the market place is the centre of the town. The Lovekyn Chapel on London Road dates largely from the Tudor period and is surrounded by many interesting 18th-C buildings. The Italianate town hall, 1838-40, is one of the most striking structures in the area. There are also the five conduit houses built by Cardinal Wolsey to supply water to Hampton Court.

● **Teddington**
Gt London. All services. R. D. Blackmore (1825-1900), author of *Lorna Doone*, lived in Teddington from 1860. The site of his home, Gomer House, is at the end of Doone Close, near the station. The riverside, viewed from the Surrey bank, is one of Teddington's most pleasing aspects. The television studios stand in Broom Road, near the weir.

Pubs and Restaurants (pages 180-181)

🍺✖ **1 The Magpie** 64 Thames Street, Sunbury TW16 6AF (01932 782024; www.magpiesunbury.com). Rambling old waterside pub serving real ale and food *daily 12.00-21.30*. Dog- and family-friendly, riverside patio. Traditional pub games, newspapers, real fires and Wi-Fi. *Open 12.00-23.00*.

🍺✖ **2 The Phoenix** 26-28 Thames Street, Sunbury TW16 6AF (01932 785358; www.thephoenixsunbury.uk). Part village local and part a food-oriented pub: real ale and meals served *Mon-Sat 12.00-20.30 (Thu-Sat 21.00) & Sun 12.00-19.00*. Dog- and family-friendly, riverside garden. Quiz *Sun*. Real fires. Mooring. *Open daily 12.00-22.00 (Thu-Sat 23.00)*.

🍺✖ **3 The Bell Inn** 8 Thames Street, Hampton TW12 2EA (020 8941 9799; www.thebellinnhampton.co.uk). A gastro pub with rural styling, this pub serves a good range of real ale and food *Wed-Fri L and E & Sat-Sun 12.00-22.00 (Sun 21.00)*. Family-friendly, garden. Quiz *Sun*. Sports TV and Wi-Fi. *Open daily 12.00-23.00*.

🍺✖ **4 The Kings Arms** 2 Lion Gate, Hampton Court Road, Molesey, East Moseley KT8 9DD (020 8016 6630; www.kingsarmshamptoncourt.com/the-six-restaurant). Elegant Georgian hotel, dating back to 1658 and built into the palace wall, dispensing real ale and food *daily 08.00-21.30 (Sun 18.00)*. Breakfast *08.00-10.30*. Garden. B&B. *Open 08.00-23.00 (Sun 22.00)*.

✖♀ **5 The Maisie Thai Restaurant** Summer Road, Thames Ditton KT7 0QQ. (020 8358 6880; www.maisie-thai.com). Serving a choice selection of Thai Cuisine's best dishes, using only choice, fresh and classic ingredients from the country, served *daily 17.00-21.00 (Sat-Sun 22.00)*.

🍺✖ **6 Ye Olde Swan Hotel** Summer Road, Thames Ditton KT7 0QQ (020 8398 1814; www.greeneking.co.uk/pubs/surrey/ye-olde-swan). Backing onto the Thames, this large pub can trace its history back to the 13th C, but now dispenses real ale and food *daily 11.00-22.00*. Dog- and family-friendly, riverside patio. Real fires and Wi-Fi. *Open 11.00-23.00*.

🍺✖ **7 The King's Head** 123 High Street, Teddington TW11 8HG (020 3166 2900; www.kingsheadteddington.com). Refurbished with snugs, three separate rooms, open fireplaces, walled patio and an open kitchen. Food available *daily 12.00-21.45 (Sun 21.00)*. Dog- and family-friendly. Traditional pub games and Wi-Fi. *Open 12.00-23.00 (Sun 22.00)*.

🍺 **8 The Swan** 22 High Street, Hampton Wick KT1 4DB (020 8977 2644; www.swanhamptonwick.co.uk). Faux timber-framed building, dating from 1905, serving real ale and food *Tue-Sat L and E & Sun 12.00-18.00*. Family-friendly, courtyard seating. Traditional pub games, real fires and sports TV. *Open Mon-Sat 12.00-23.00 (Mon 15.00) & Sun 12.00-22.30*.

🍺✖ **9 The Anglers** 3 Broom Road, Teddington TW11 9NR (020 8977 7475; www.anglers-teddington.co.uk). Pleasant riverside bar and restaurant, overlooking Teddington Lock, dispensing real ale and food *daily 10.00-21.30 (Sun 21.00)*. Dog- and family-friendly, outside seating. Board games, real fires and Wi-Fi. Mooring. *Open 10.00-23.00*.

🍺✖ **10 Tide End Cottage** 8 Ferry Road, Teddington TW11 9NN (020 8977 7762; www.greeneking-pubs.co.uk/pubs/middlesex/tide-end-cottage). Quaint little riverside pub, offering a choice of real ale and food *daily 12.00-21.00*. Dog- and family-friendly. Real fires and Wi-Fi. *Open 12.00-23.00*.

Richmond

As the river passes Eel Pie Island and enters Horse Reach, Richmond Hill can be seen rising gently from the east bank, with the large Star and Garter Home dominating the view. To the west lies Marble Hill Park, where a ferry connects this with Ham House – the last surviving ferry on the tidal Thames (see **Boat Trips** on page 185). The river is the focal point of Richmond – indeed the view of the river from Richmond Hill is dramatic and much painted and photographed. Richmond Bridge is an elegant, slightly humped, 18th-C structure – one of the prettiest bridges on the river. Beyond the railway bridge is Richmond half-tide lock, movable weir and footbridge, built in 1894. Its brightly painted arches belie its more serious function of tide control. The river curves around Old Deer Park, with Isleworth Ait to the west, and the old village and church close by the river to the north. Behind wooded banks is Syon Park, and opposite are the Royal Botanic Gardens, Kew. Immediately below the park is the entrance to the Grand Union Canal, a direct link with Birmingham (see *Nicholson Waterways Guide 1: Grand Union, Oxford & the South East*).

Boatyards

Ⓑ Hammerton Ferry Boat House Marble Hill Park/Orleans Road, Twickenham TW1 3BL (020 8892 9620, 07759 482899; www.hammertonsferry.co.uk). Rowing boat hire, short- and long-term mooring, engineering services. They also operate the ferry boat service – see **Boat Trips** on page 185. *Open daily 10.00-18.00 (Dec-Feb dusk)*.
Ⓑ AMAC Boat Repairs Phoenix Wharf, Eel Pie Island, Twickenham TW1 3DY (07940 273471; www.amacboatrepairs.co.uk). Partial and full rebuilds, slipway, dry dock, painting, tug services, surveys. *Open Mon-Fri 09.00-17.00*.
Ⓑ Eel Pie Boatyard Eel Pie Island, Twickenham TW1 3DY (020 8892 3626; www.eelpieboatyard.co.uk).
Wet dock, dry dock, craneage and a wide range of marine repairs. Specialist towing service. DIY facilities. *Open Mon-Fri 09.30-17.30*.
Ⓑ Brentford Dock Marina 2 Justin Close, Brentford Dock TW8 8QE (020 8568 5096; www.brentforddock.com/marina). Pump out, overnight and long term-mooring, boat sales, toilets, showers, Wi-Fi. *Open daily 11.00-18.00*.
Ⓑ MSO Marine Construction Dock Road, Brentford TW8 8AG (020 8560 5159; www.msomarine.co.uk). Wide range of marine services including boat building, repair and maintenance, crane, dry dock, painting and hull blacking, welding and fabrication, barge conversions. *Open Mon-Fri 07.30-17.00 & Sat 08.00-12.00*.

Pubs and Restaurants

🍺 1 **The White Swan** Riverside, Twickenham TW1 3DN (020 8744 2951; www.whiteswantwickenham.co.uk). Startlingly attractive black and white balconied pub right by the river's edge. Fine choice of real ales. Excellent bar meals *daily 12.00-21.00 (Sun 18.00)*. Quiz *Wed*. Children and dogs welcome, and there is riverside seating. *Open 11.00-23.00 (Sun-Tue 22.00)*.
🍺✗ 2 **The Barmy Arms** The Embankment, Twickenham TW1 3DU (020 8892 0863; www.greeneking.co.uk/pubs/middlesex/barmy-arms). Lively pub serving real ale, and food *12.00-21.00 (Sat-Sun 11.00)*. Dog- and child-friendly, riverside seating. Sports TV and Wi-Fi. *Open 11.00-23.00 (Sun 22.30)*.
🍺 3 **The Rose of York** Petersham Road, Richmond TW10 6UY (020 8948 5867; www.roseofyorkrichmond.com). A Samuel Smith's pub. Large, comfortable, typically English, panelled in oak, warmed by a coal fire and decorated with reproductions of paintings of the famous turn in the river by Turner and Reynolds. Good views of the Thames from the terrace and courtyard. Food served *L and E (not Sun E)*. Children welcome, garden. Wi-Fi. B&B. *Open daily 12.00-23.00 (Sun 22.30)*.
🍺 4 **The White Cross** Riverside (off Water Lane), Richmond TW9 1TH (020 8940 6844; www.thewhitecrossrichmond.com). Lively riverside pub with a terrace, serving real ale. Dogs and children *(until 21.00)* welcome. Meals available *daily 12.00-22.00 (Sun 21.00)*. Look out for the unusual fireplace. Wi-Fi. *Open 11.00-23.00 (Sun 22.00)*.
🍺 5 **The Waterman's Arms** 10-12 Water Lane, Richmond TW9 1TJ (020 3638 9160; www.watermansrichmond.co.uk). Small cosy and popular pub, in a cobbled riverside street, which was once frequented by the watermen who trudged up from the river. Meals available *Wed-Sun 12.00-23.00*. Wi-Fi. *Open Wed-Sun 12.00-23.00*.
🍺 6 **The London Apprentice** 62 Church Street, Isleworth TW7 6BG (020 8560 1915; www.greenekingpubs.co.uk). A 15th-C riverside pub with Elizabethan and Georgian interiors, decorated with prints of Hogarth's *Apprentices*. Real ale. Bar meals available *daily 12.00-21.00 (Sat 11.00)*. Dog- and child-friendly, patio. Wi-Fi. *Open Mon-Sat 12.00-23.00 (Sat 11.00) & Sun 11.00-22.30*.

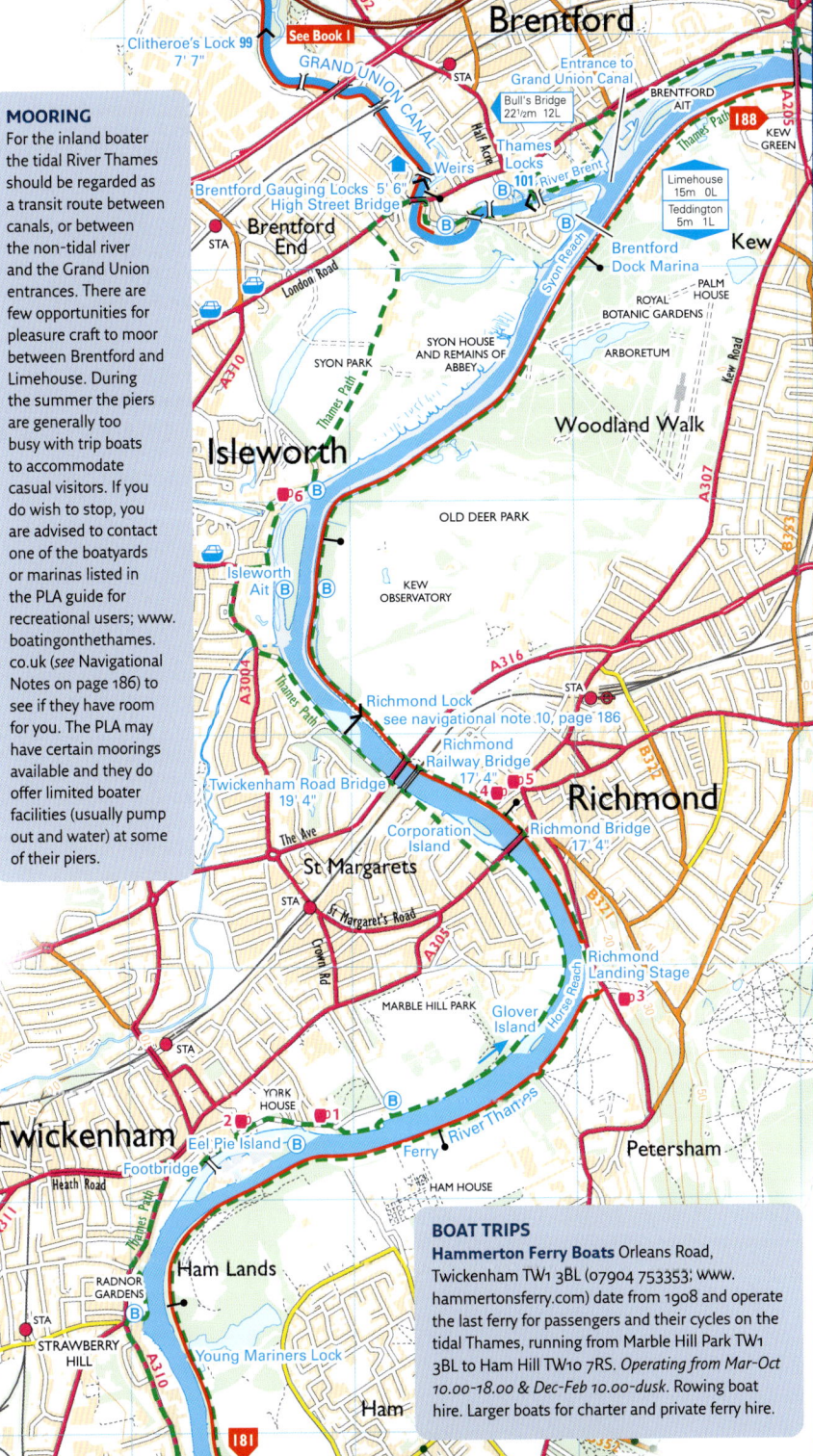

River Thames — Richmond

MOORING

For the inland boater the tidal River Thames should be regarded as a transit route between canals, or between the non-tidal river and the Grand Union entrances. There are few opportunities for pleasure craft to moor between Brentford and Limehouse. During the summer the piers are generally too busy with trip boats to accommodate casual visitors. If you do wish to stop, you are advised to contact one of the boatyards or marinas listed in the PLA guide for recreational users; www.boatingonthethames.co.uk (*see* Navigational Notes on page 186) to see if they have room for you. The PLA may have certain moorings available and they do offer limited boater facilities (usually pump out and water) at some of their piers.

BOAT TRIPS

Hammerton Ferry Boats Orleans Road, Twickenham TW1 3BL (07904 753353; www.hammertonsferry.com) date from 1908 and operate the last ferry for passengers and their cycles on the tidal Thames, running from Marble Hill Park TW1 3BL to Ham Hill TW10 7RS. *Operating from Mar-Oct 10.00-18.00 & Dec-Feb 10.00-dusk.* Rowing boat hire. Larger boats for charter and private ferry hire.

NAVIGATIONAL NOTES

1 From **Brentford** to **Limehouse** navigation on the tidal Thames is far more complex than on the upper, non-tidal, reaches. The river here is a commercial waterway first and foremost and pleasure craft must take great care. The River Thames below Teddington Lock is controlled by the Port of London Authority (PLA) who produce a selection of useful information downloadable from www.pla.co.uk/leisure-boating: the *Recreational Users Guide* is essential reading. Other general navigation queries are also covered on this website. Useful information can also be found at www.thamescruising.co.uk. While hire companies do not usually allow their craft to be taken onto the tideway, owners of pleasure boats may wish to make the passage along the Thames below Teddington Locks and between the canals at Brentford and Limehouse. With proper planning this should present no particular difficulties. However, do check with your insurance company who may have special requirements.

2 **Brentford** to **Limehouse Basin** – leave Brentford ½ *hour before high water* to gain the benefit of the ebb tide. Limehouse Basin is fitted with sector gates and the lock is open in line with the times published annually at www.canalrivertrust.org.uk/about-us/where-we-work/london-and-south-east/boating-facilities/locks-to-the-river-thames. Information is also available directly from the CRT Regional Office 0303 040 4040; enquiries.londonsoutheast@canalrivertrust.org.uk. Always telephone Limehouse Basin (020 7308 9930) and inform them of your intentions.

3 **Limehouse Basin** to **Brentford** – pass through the entrance lock at Limehouse 2½ *hours before high water* London Bridge, to gain the benefit of the flood tide. Thames Lock, Brentford is manned *for a period before, and following high water (2 hours each side if this falls within normal working hours)* and you should contact the lock keeper to pre-book passage *outside the normal working hours* (which are the same as Limehouse) on 020 8568 2779. Brentford Gauging Lock is boater operated using a Watermate key.

4 **Brentford** to **Teddington** – pass through Thames Lock, Brentford, 2 *hours before high water* to gain the benefit of the flood tide. Teddington lock keeper can be contacted on 020 8940 8723 and Richmond lock keeper can be contacted on 020 8940 0634.

5 **VHF Radio** – all vessels of 45ft (13.7 metres) or greater in length must carry a VHF radio capable of communicating with the harbourmaster at port control – channel 14. An exception is made for narrowboats over 45ft in transit between the Grand Union Canal at Brentford and the non-tidal Thames at Teddington Lock as river traffic in this area is relatively light. **This is the only passage on the tideway where such a dispensation now operates.** If no radio is available such vessels must telephone the PLA Duty Officer at London VTS (020 3260 7711) immediately before and upon completion of the transit.

6 **Warning lights** – see PLA publication *River Thames Recreational Users Guide* – details at 1. above. The short video '*Cruising through Central London*' downloadable from www.youtube.com/watch?v=CG2ZcVWvNOs is also very helpful.

7 **Draught** – the depth at the centre span of Westminster Bridge is approximately 2ft 8in at chart datum (about 4ft at mean low water springs). In practice there is usually a greater depth than this. The depth at all the other bridges is greater than at Westminster.

8 **Headroom** – on the tidal river the clearance at bridges is given as the maximum at mean high water springs – this is less than the headroom at chart datum (lowest astronomical tide). In practice this means that there will usually be more headroom than that indicated.

9 **Canals** – those who wish to navigate on the adjoining Canal and River Trust's canals will require a licence available from: Boat Licensing, PO Box 162, Leeds LS9 1AX (0303 040 4040; www.canalrivertrust.org.uk/enjoy-the-waterways/boating/buy-your-boat-licence).
Details of the inland waterways encountered at Brentford and Limehouse can be found in *Nicholson Waterways Guide 1: Grand Union, Oxford & the South East*.

10 **Richmond Lock** – (020 8940 0634). The weirs are raised from approximately 2 hours before until approximately 2 hours after high water. At all other times, the lock must be used. The lock keeper can also be contacted on VHF channel 80.

Ham House Ham Street, Ham TW10 7RS (020 8940 1950; www.nationaltrust.org.uk). A superb 17th-C riverside mansion, the exterior largely by Sir John Vavassour. The lavish Restoration interior has a collection of Stuart furniture, and is haunted by a ghostly dog. There are also formal gardens and an ice house. House *open Easter–Oct 12.00–17.00; shop, gardens and café open 11.00–18.00. Nov & early Dec house open 12.00–16.00;* shop, gardens and café *open 11.00–16.30*. Telephone for further details of opening times. Charge.

- **Twickenham**

Gt London. All services. Twickenham was one of the most elegant and desirable areas in the 18th C. The church, with its three-storey tower, dates largely from 1714. The poet Alexander Pope, 1688–1744, moved to Twickenham in 1717. Deformed at an early age by a bone disease, his most notable work was the 'Rape of the Lock', although the lock in question was associated with hair, rather than the river. Monuments to him and to his parents can be found in the church. York House, built c.1700, and now Municipal Offices, has an astonishing collection of statues in its riverside gardens.
Strawberry Hill Waldegrave Road, Twickenham TW1 4SX. The surviving glory of Twickenham is Walpole's Gothic fantasy, one of the earliest examples of the 18th-C Gothic Revival. Designed first by John Chute and Richard Bentley between 1753–63, and later by Thomas Pitt, it expresses Walpole's appreciation of Gothic forms and spirit. Strawberry Hill now houses St Mary's Training College.
Marble Hill House Richmond Road, Twickenham TW1 2NL (020 8892 5115; www.english-heritage.org.uk/visit/places/marble-hill). A restored Palladian mansion, built in 1724–9 by George II for his mistress, Henrietta Howard. Fine collection of paintings and furniture dating from the early 18th C, plus the Lazenby Bequest Chinoiserie (chinese motifs) display. *Open Apr-Oct, Wed-Sun.* House *open 10.00–17.00;* park *07.00–20.00 & café 08.00–16.00.* Free.
Eel Pie Island Twickenham. In Edwardian times the hotel on the island ran tea dances. In the 1960s it housed a noisy night club which featured popular rock groups.
Tourist Information Centre Civic Centre 44, York Street, Twickenham TW1 3BZ (020 8891 7272; www.visitrichmond.co.uk).

- **Petersham**

Surrey. PO, stores, chemist, off-licence, takeaways. But for the traffic, this would be one of the most elegant village suburbs near London. It is exceptionally rich in fine houses of the late 17th and 18th C. Captain George Vancouver, who sailed with Cook and discovered the island off the coast of Canada which is named after him, lived in River Lane and is now buried in the churchyard here. *Stores open daily 07.00–23.00.*

- **Richmond**

Surrey. All services. One of the prettiest riverside towns in the London area. Built up the side of the hill, Richmond has been able to retain its Georgian elegance and still has the feeling of an 18th-C resort. Richmond Green is the centre, both aesthetically and socially; it is surrounded by early 18th-C houses. Only the brick and terracotta theatre, built in 1899, breaks the pattern; so deliberately that it is almost refreshing. The gateway of Richmond Palace is all that remains of the Royal residence built by Henry VII, out of the earlier Palace of Shene. Behind the gate, in Old Palace Yard, is the Trumpeter's House, c.1708. At the top of Richmond Hill stands Wick House, built for Joshua Reynolds in 1772. It is from here that he painted marvellous views over the Thames.
Richmond Theatre 1 Little Green, Richmond TW9 1QJ (0844 871 7651; www.atgtickets.com). Productions from London's West End and touring companies.
Richmond Park The largest of the royal parks, created by Charles I in 1637, it covers 2358 acres. The park remained a favourite hunting ground until the 18th C. Private shooting stopped in 1904 but the hunting lodges can still be seen. White Lodge, built for George II in 1727, now houses the Royal Ballet School. Park *open 07.00 – dusk (07.30 in winter).*
Old Deer Park TW9 2RA. Kew Observatory was built here in 1729 (by William Chambers for George III) and was used by the Meteorological Office until 1981. The three obelisks nearby were used to measure London's official time.
Richmond Bridge This fine stone bridge with its five arches and parapet is one of the most handsome on the Thames, and was frequently the subject for paintings in the 18th–19th C. Built in the classical style by James Paine, 1777, it replaced the earlier horse ferry, and was a toll bridge until 1859.
Tourist Information Centre Richmond Station, The Quadrant, Richmond TW9 2NA (www.visitrichmond.co.uk). Information kiosk outside the station *open daily 10.00–15.00 (14.00 in winter).*

- **Isleworth**

Gt London. PO, stores, off-licence, fish & chips, takeaways, hardware, station. The prettiest view of this village is from the stretch of river just before Syon House. The 15th-C tower of All Saints' Church, the London Apprentice Inn and a collection of fine Georgian houses all make for a delightful setting. Vincent Van Gogh taught here and used the Thames as the subject for his first attempts at painting.
Syon Park Park Road, Brentford (020 8560 0881; www.syonpark.co.uk). Set in 55 acres of parkland, landscaped by 'Capability' Brown, Syon House is built on the site of a 15th-C convent. The present square structure with its corner turrets is largely 16th-C, although the interior was remodelled by Robert Adam in 1762. The house itself is mainly of interest on account of the magnificent neo-classical rooms by Adam. Katherine Howard was confined here before her execution in 1542 and Lady Jane Grey stayed here for the nine days preceding her death in 1554. Conservatory (1827) by Charles Fowler. The Butterfly House houses a huge variety of live butterflies and insects from all over the world. *Telephone or visit website for opening times of the house.* Gardens *open Wed-Sun 10.30–16.30.*

West London

Immediately below Brentford Dock Marina is the entrance to the Grand Union Canal, a direct link with Birmingham and places north. On the north bank opposite Kew is Strand-on-the-Green, a cluster of desirable houses and fashionable *pubs* facing the towpath.

The Oxford and Cambridge Boat Race finish is below Chiswick Bridge, the line being marked on both banks by wooden piles and the University Stone. The river is flanked by elegant houses at Hammersmith and Chiswick, but further downstream becomes grimy and industrial. There is, however, as always on the lower Thames, plenty of interest. Below the splendid Hammersmith Bridge, on the south bank, lies one of the most bizarre buildings on the whole riverside – the Harrods Depository – a cupolated building in the same terracotta as the main store. There is a small wharf in front where a light railway used to run directly into the building. Barn Elms Reservoir is now host to a variety of watersports and is ideal for fishing and birdwatching.

River Thames — West London

PADDLING
Not a watercourse to make a direct diversion for off the tidal Thames! However, the River Wandle offers interesting paddling as a separate, stand-alone expedition following arrival in the capital. Further encouragement can be found at www.canoelondon.com/kayaking-river-wandle-south-london.

MOORING
For the inland boater the tidal River Thames should be regarded as a transit route between canals, or between the non-tidal river and the Grand Union exits. There are few opportunities for pleasure craft to moor between Brentford and Limehouse, Chiswick Pier (see below) being a notable exception. During the summer the piers are generally too busy with trip boats to accommodate casual visitors. If you do wish to stop, you are advised to contact one of the boatyards or marinas listed in the PLA Leisure Guide (see Navigational Notes on page 186) to see whether they have room for you. The PLA may have certain moorings available and they do offer limited boater facilities (usually pump out and water) at some of their piers. There is *24hr* mooring in Limehouse Basin.

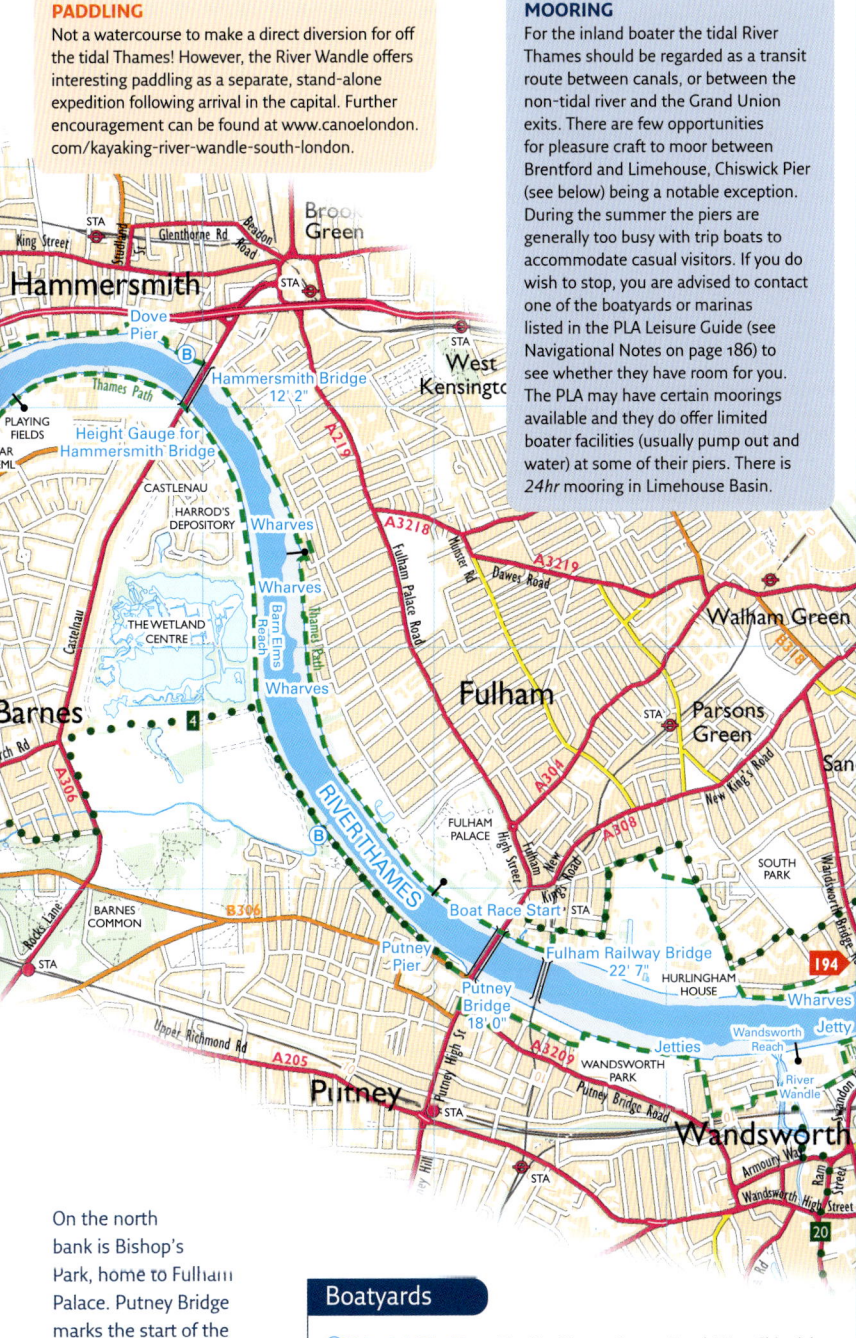

On the north bank is Bishop's Park, home to Fulham Palace. Putney Bridge marks the start of the Oxford and Cambridge Boat Race and gives way to a stretch of industry.

Boatyards

B Chiswick Pier Trust The Pier House, Corney Reach Way, Chiswick W4 2UG (020 8742 2713; www.chiswickpier.org.uk). Pump out, telephone, mooring (up to 14 days), showers, toilets, electrical hook-up. *Open Mon-Fri 11.00-15.00.*

WALKING AND CYCLING
A splendid section for walking – the path keeps to the south side throughout and Kew Gardens and Kew Palace are worth a visit. Across the river is Strand-on-the-Green, with its fine houses and pubs. There is a foot crossing on Barnes Railway Bridge, and walkers can choose which bank they follow to Hammersmith – the scenic route is on the south bank, the pubs on the north. After the fascinating walk around Barnes to Putney, the Thames towpath terminates, giving way to road as far as Putney Bridge. The course of the river can be followed through London by paths along both sides of the river (*London A-Z Street Atlases* are helpful guides).

Kew
TW9. Old Kew centres around the Green, the 18th-C houses built for members of the Court of George III, and the entrance to the Royal Botanic Gardens. The church of St Anne dates from 1714 but was greatly altered in the 19th C.
Musical Museum 399 High Street, Brentford TW8 0DU (020 8560 8108; www.musicalmuseum.co.uk). A fascinating collection of automatic, old and odd musical instruments and a concert hall complete with stage and a Wurlitzer cconsole. *Regular* events and Concerts. *Open Fri-Sun 10.00-16.00*. No small children. Charge.
London Museum of Water & Steam Green Dragon Lane, Brentford TW8 0EN (020 8568 4757; www.waterandsteam.org.uk). Huge Victorian building housing a large collection of steam pumping engines, restored to working order by volunteers. Also a collection of old traction engines, a working forge and steam railway. Tearoom. Wi-Fi. *Open Thu-Sun & B Hols 10.00-16.00*. Charge (under 5s free).
Royal Botanic Gardens Kew Road, Kew, Richmond TW9 3AE (020 8332 5655; www.kew.org). On the south bank of the Thames, opposite Brentford. (Access from the south side of the Gardens or from the Thames towpath.) One of the world's great botanic gardens, with thousands of rare outdoor and hothouse plants. Kew Palace, also worth a visit, was built in 1631 in the Dutch style. Gardens *open daily from 10.00; there are slight seasonal variations in closing times*. Telephone for current information. Charge.

Kew Bridge Opened by Edward VII in 1903 and officially called the King Edward VII Bridge. A fine stone structure designed by Sir John Wolfe Barry and Cuthbert Brereton, it replaced the earlier granite bridge of 1789.
Kew Railway Bridge When it was opened in 1869 this five-span lattice girder bridge, designed by W. R. Galbraith, was part of the London and South Western Railway extension.

Chiswick
W4. Chiswick stretches between Kew Bridge and Hammersmith Terrace and provides some of the most picturesque scenery on the London stretch of the Thames. Georgian houses extend along Strand-on-the-Green and again at Chiswick Mall. Between these points, running down to the riverside, originally stood three 18th-C mansions: of the three, only Chiswick House remains. The site of Grove House has been built over, and Duke's Meadows, part of the grounds of Chiswick House, is now a recreation ground. Chiswick Cemetery backs on to St Nicholas Church where Lord Burlington and William Kent are buried.
Chiswick Bridge W4. Built in 1933, designed by Sir Herbert Baker and opened to the public by the Prince of Wales, this bridge has the longest concrete arch of any bridge on the Thames. The centre span measures 150ft.
Chiswick House and Gardens Burlington Lane, Chiswick W4 2RP (020 3141 3350; www.chiswickhouseandgardens.org.uk). Lovely Palladian villa built in the grand manner by 3rd Earl of Burlington 1725-30, modelled on Palladio's Villa

Blackfriars Bridge with St Paul's Cathedral behind

Capra at Vicenza. Café and shop. Gardens (free) *open daily 07.00-dusk*; house and kitchen garden *open Apr-Sep* (garden *Oct*) *Thu-Sun 11.00-16.00*. Charge.

- **Mortlake**
SW14. In the 17th C Mortlake was famous for its tapestry workshop, established by James I and staffed by Flemish weavers. Some of the Mortlake Tapestries can still be seen in the Victoria and Albert Museum. The riverside here is picturesque along Thames Bank where there is a fine collection of 18th-C houses. Mortlake also marks the end of the Oxford and Cambridge Boat Race at Chiswick Bridge (although the first race took place at Henley in 1829).
Barnes Railway Bridge SW13. This light and elegant iron bridge by Locke was opened in 1849 to connect with the Richmond line. Similar in design to Richmond Railway Bridge.
Oxford v Cambridge Boat Race On a *Saturday afternoon in March or April* this famous annual event is held over a 4-mile course from Putney to Mortlake. Get to the riverside early for a good view.

- **North Bank**
Hammersmith Terrace W6. A terrace of 17 identical houses on the river bank, built c.1750. The late Sir Alan Herbert, historian of the Thames, lived in the Terrace.
Upper Mall W6. Separated from Lower Mall by Furnivall Gardens, Upper Mall boasts some fine 18th-C buildings including the Dove Inn, originally a coffee house. William Morris lived in Kelmscott House between 1878 and 1896.
Lower Mall W6. Bustling in the summer months with rowers from the number of boathouses and rowing clubs which have been established here for over a century. Lower Mall is home to the Rutland and Blue Anchor pubs, and a number of pretty 18th-C cottages.
Hammersmith Bridge W6. The first suspension bridge in London. The original, built 1824 by William T. Clarke, was replaced in 1883 by the present splendid construction by Sir Joseph Bazalgette.
Fulham SW6. In the 18th and 19th C Fulham was the 'great fruit and kitchen garden north of the Thames', a place of market and nursery gardens, attracting the more prosperous Londoners in search of purer air. Today little is left of the fertile village and the area has become quite built-up. Fulham has, however, remained an attractive area, nowadays better known for its abundance of restaurants and bars. Also home to two of London's most famous football clubs, Fulham and Chelsea. Bishop's Park and Hurlingham House can be seen from the river.
Fulham Palace SW6. The palace lies behind the long avenues of Bishop's Park, with grounds stretching to the river. The site was first acquired by Bishop Waldhere in AD704 and continued as a residence of the Bishops of London until 1973. A fascinating mixture of architectural styles, from the Tudor courtyard with its mellow red brick to the restrained elegance of the Georgian east front.
Putney Bridge W6. The wooden toll bridge of 1729 was replaced by the present bridge designed by Sir Joseph Bazalgette in 1884. Putney Bridge marks the start of the Oxford and Cambridge Boat Race.
Fulham Railway Bridge SW6. This trellis girder iron bridge was part of the Metropolitan extension to the District Railway. Designed by William Jacomb, it was opened in 1889 and connects with a footbridge running parallel to it. Part of the London Transport underground system.
Hurlingham House Ranelagh Gardens SW6. This is the only large 18th-C residence still surviving in Fulham. The house has a fine river front with Corinthian columns and is now the centre of the Hurlingham Club. Members play tennis, golf, polo and croquet in the grounds.

- **South Bank**
Barnes Terrace SW13. The delightful village of Barnes lies behind the attractive ironwork façade of Barnes Terrace. The terrace was, and still is, a fashionable place to live, with former residents including Sheridan and Gustav Holst.
Castelnau SW13. Barnes is rich in Victorian houses and some of the most interesting are

to be seen in Castelnau. Remarkably standardised, they are largely semi-detached and typical of early Victorian villa architecture with their arched windows.

Barn Elms SW13. Formerly the manor house of Barnes, the estate was later leased to Sir Francis Walsingham, Secretary of State to Elizabeth I. Today, all that remains of the former layout is part of the ornamental pond and the ice house. The Reservoir at Barn Elms now plays host to a variety of watersports, plus fishing and birdwatching.

Putney SW15. The Embankment is picturesque. The London Rowing Club and Westminster School have their boathouses here and the eights and sculls can be seen practising most afternoons.

BOAT TRIPS
One of the best ways to understand the layout of a large, water-bound city is to take a boat trip and London is no exception to this rule. There is a large number to choose from, although most originate from Westminster Pier. Broadly speaking the options available encompass a selection of down-river trips as far as the Thames Barrier (and the Visitor Centre) and a range of up-river trips, which can reach as far as Hampton Court. The latter takes a full day. There are also evening dinner and dance cruises. Go to the pier (without your boat) to compare the plethora of options and make a choice, or visit www.riverthames.co.uk. A further option is to combine travel on the Docklands Light Railway (DLR) with a river trip for which both individual and family Rail and River Rover tickets are available. For further details contact the DLR (0343 222 1234; www.tfl.gov.uk/modes/dlr) or City Cruises (020 7740 0400; www.cityexperiences.com/uk/city-cruises/).

Limehouse Basin

Central London

The short stretch of intrusive industry, sprawling along the south bank, is soon relieved at Battersea by the splendid St Mary's Church opposite Lots Road Power Station and Chelsea Harbour. Albert Bridge, restored in 1991, is a remarkable sight when illuminated at night by over 4000 bulbs. From here on the River Thames curves through the heart of the capital, and has been London's lifeline for 2000 years. Indeed it was instrumental in the Roman settlement which created London as an international port. Once used as the local bypass, being cheaper and safer than travel by road, it has carried Viking longships, Roman galleys, Elizabethan barges and Victorian steamers. One of the best ways to see London is still from the Thames. The buildings and sights lining its twisting, turning path are as varied as London itself. It is fascinating by day and magical by night.

> **WALKING AND CYCLING**
> There is an excellent series of walks leaflets – entitled *Walk This Way* – produced by the Cross River Partnership and promoting all aspects of the South Bank of the River Thames downloadable at www.crossriverpartnership.org/news/walk-this-way. For quiet, enjoyable walks in London, taking in plenty of green spaces, visit www.footways.london. You can pick up a free copy of their map from the Capital's mainline railway stations or download it onto your smartphone at www.footways.london/digital-map.

- **North Bank**
Wandsworth Bridge SW6. In 1938 the 19th-C bridge was replaced with the existing structure by E. P. Wheeler, now painted a distinctive bright blue.
Chelsea Harbour SW11. A modern development dominated by the Belvedere tower block. The golden ball on its roof slides up and down with the level of the river. The development contains offices, restaurants, a luxury hotel, smart shops, apartments and the marina. Chelsea Wharf, just along the bank, has been transformed from old warehouses into modern business units.
Battersea Railway Bridge SW11. The West London Extension Railway, of which this bridge was a part, was opened in 1863 to connect the south of England directly with the north. Because it did not end at a London terminus, it became a target for bombing during World War II.
Lots Road Power Station SW11. This huge and dominating structure was built in 1904 to provide electricity for the new underground railway.
Battersea Bridge SW11. The original Battersea Bridge, 1772, a picturesque wooden structure by Henry Holland, has been portrayed in paintings by Whistler and Turner. The replacement iron structure, opened in 1890, was designed by Sir Joseph Bazalgette.
All Saints Church SW3. Chelsea Embankment. Rebuilt in 1964 after severe bomb damage during the war. Contains two 13th-C chapels, one restored by Sir Thomas More 1528, a Jacobean altar table and one of the best series of monuments in a London parish church. Henry VIII married Jane Seymour here before their state wedding in 1536.
Cheyne Walk SW3. Cheyne Walk, with its houseboats and its row of delightful riverside Queen Anne houses, has been home to Lloyd George, Hilaire Belloc, George Eliot, Isambard Kingdom Brunel, Turner and Whistler.
Carlyle's House 24 Cheyne Row SW3 5HL (020 7352 7087; www.nationaltrust.org.uk/carlyles-house). Once the haunt of writers such as Dickens and Tennyson, and the home of Thomas and Jane Carlyle 1834-81. Telephone for opening times. Charge.
Albert Bridge SW3. A delightful suspension bridge connecting Chelsea and Battersea, built by Ordish 1871-3. The bridge was strengthened in 1973 by a huge solid support under the main span. Illuminated by over 4,000 bulbs, the bridge is particularly beautiful at night.
Chelsea Embankment SW3. Chelsea Embankment, stretching between Albert Bridge and Chelsea Bridge, was built in 1871. The embankment is bordered on the north bank by the grounds of the Chelsea Royal Hospital where the Chelsea Flower Show is held annually in *May*. Norman Shaw's famous Old Swan House stands at No. 17 Chelsea Embankment.
Tate Britain Millbank SW1P 4RG (020 7887 8888; www.tate.org.uk/visit/tate-britain). Founded in 1897 by Sir Henry Tate, the sugar magnate and by Sidney HJ Smith. Following the opening of Tate Modern, the Millbank gallery has redefined its role, concentrating on British art over the last 500 years. Five thematic displays portray historic and modern works in an imaginative and often disturbing way which, whilst adding an element of surprise, successfully demonstrates continuity over the centuries. The Clore Gallery houses the works of Turner and Constable and special displays depicting major artists range from Blake to Hockney.
Open daily 10.00-18.00. Free (except for special exhibitions).

Millbank Tower Millbank SW1. The traditional balance of the river bank has been overturned by this 387ft-high office building by Ronald Ward and Partners, 1963.

Victoria Tower Gardens Abingdon Street SW1. A sculpture of Rodin's Burghers of Calais, 1895, stands close to the river and near the entrance to the gardens is a monument to Mrs Emmeline Pankhurst and Dame Christabel Pankhurst, champions of the women's suffragette movement in the early 1900s. Emmeline Pankhurst is reputedly the last person to have been incarcerated in the cell at the bottom of Big Ben (1902).

Houses of Parliament Parliament Square SW1A 0AA (www.parliament.uk). Originally the Palace of Westminster, and a principal royal palace until 1512. Became known as parliament or 'place to speak' in 1550. Westminster Hall, one of the few remaining parts of the original royal palace, has an impressive hammerbeam roof. The present Victorian-Gothic building was designed in 1847 by Sir Charles Barry and Augustus Pugin specifically to house Parliament and has 1100 rooms, 100 staircases and over 2 miles of passages. The Houses of Parliament and Big Ben – the bell clock housed in the adjoining St Stephen's Tower – make up London's most famous landmark.

Westminster Abbey 20 Dean's Yard SW1P 3PA (020 7222 5152; www.westminster-abbey.org). Original church by Edward the Confessor 1065. Rebuilding commenced in 1245 by Henry III who was largely influenced by the new French cathedrals. Completed by Henry Yevele and others 1376-1506 (towers incomplete and finished by Hawksmoor 1734). Henry VII Chapel added 1503; fine Perpendicular with wonderful fan vaulting. The Abbey contains the Coronation Chair, and many tombs and memorials of the Kings and Queens of England. *Open Mon-Fri 09.30-15.30 (last entry) & Sat 09.00-15.00 (last entry). Sun open* for services. Charge.

Victoria Embankment WC2R. The Embankment was created by Joseph Bazalgette in 1868, reclaiming 37 acres of mud from the Thames banks, making the river narrower and the water faster flowing, thereby ending the skating era on the once-frozen waters. The building of the Embankment provided a wall against flooding, a riverside walk, a new west-east sewerage system and part of the District Line Railway. It was completed in 1870, Bazalgette was knighted, and his bust incorporated into the parapet by Hungerford Bridge.

Cleopatra's Needle WC2R. Victoria Embankment SW1. A 60ft-high ancient Egyptian granite obelisk, presented to Britain by the Viceroy of Egypt, Mohammed Ali, in 1819 and brought to London by sea in 1878. When it was erected various articles were buried beneath it for posterity – the morning's newspapers, a razor, coins, four Bibles in different languages and photographs of '12 of the best-looking Englishwomen of the day'. The bronze sphinxes were added (facing the wrong way) in 1882.

Somerset House Strand WC2R 1LA (020 7845 4600; www.somersethouse.org.uk). Built in 1776 by Sir William

River Thames — Central London

Chambers on the site of Protector Somerset's house, this magnificent building with its arches, terrace, and river entrances decorated with lions and Tuscan columns, was intended to compete with the splendour of Adam's Adelphi. Once occupied by the General Register Office whose records of birth and death go back to 1836, it now houses the permanent collections and special exhibitions of The Courtauld Gallery, and the Embankment Galleries. Special events and outdoor concerts and film shows are held *regularly*. Somerset House is now partially comprised of a series of open spaces, shops, cafés and restaurants adjoining the Thames, so *opening times vary*.

The Temple EC4. The name derives from the Order of Knights Templar who occupied the site from 1160–1308. In the 17th C the Temple was leased to the benchers of the Inner and Middle Temple, two Inns of Court. These inns, together with Lincoln's Inn and Gray's Inn, hold the ancient and exclusive privilege of providing advocates in the courts of England and Wales. A visit should be made on foot, as only a few of the Temple buildings are visible from the river. On the Embankment, Sir Joseph Bazalgette's arch and stairs mark the 19th-C access to the Temple from the river.

City of London A thriving and commercial centre, stretching between Blackfriars Bridge and London Bridge, which has within its square mile such famous institutions as the Bank of England, the Stock Exchange, the Royal Courts of Justice and the Guildhall.

Mermaid Theatre 2 Puddle Dock, Blackfriars EC4V 3DB (020 7236 1919; www.the-mermaid.co.uk). The original theatre, the first in the City since the 16th C, was opened in a converted warehouse in 1959 following energetic campaigning by Lord Bernard Miles. It was rebuilt on a new site and re-opened in 1981.

Fishmongers' Hall EC4. Built in the grand classical manner in 1831–4 by Henry Roberts to replace the original hall which was burnt down in the Great Fire of 1666. The Fishmongers' Company administers the annual Doggett's Coat and Badge Race for Thames Watermen. This race, the oldest annually contested sporting event and the longest rowing race in the world (1 furlong short of 5 miles), was introduced in 1715. Doggett, an Irish comedian and staunch Hanoverian, who used the services of the watermen to ferry him to and from the theatres, decided to mark the anniversary of the accession of George I to the throne by instituting an annual race for watermen. The race is from London Bridge to Cadogan Pier, Chelsea, and is usually held at the *end of July*. The victor is presented with a red coat, breeches and cap, and a silver arm badge bearing the words 'The Gift of the late Thomas Doggett'.

Monument EC4. A 17th-C hollow fluted column by Wren, built to commemorate the Great Fire of London. It marked the northern end of the original London Bridge and stands at 202ft, a foot in height for every foot in distance from where the fire started in Pudding Lane. Gives a magnificent view over the city.

Old Billingsgate Market Lower Thames Street EC3. The yellow-brick Victorian building with arcaded ground floor was built by Sir Horace Jones, 1875, although the first reference to a market at Billingsgate was made in AD870. A free fish market was established by statute in 1699, but until the 18th C coal, corn and provisions were also sold. The fish-porters wore leather

hats with flat tops and wide brims, formerly known as bobbing hats. Bobbing was the charge made by the porter to carry fish from the wholesaler to the retailer. These hats enabled the porter to carry about a hundredweight of fish on his head. The market moved down river to new premises on the Isle of Dogs in 1982.
The Custom House Lower Thames Street EC3. A custom house has stood beside Billingsgate since AD870. The present building is by Laing, 1813-17, but the river façade was rebuilt by Smirke in 1825. Badly bombed in the war, the building has been restored.
Tower of London Tower Hill EC3N 4AB (0330 320 6000; www.hrp.org.uk/TowerOfLondon). Although greatly restored and altered over the centuries, the Tower of London is probably the most important work of military architecture in Britain and has been used as a palace, a fortress and a prison since William the Conqueror built the White Tower in 1078. Café and shop. *Open daily 09.00-17.30 (Sun-Mon 10.00). Last admission 15.30.* Charge.
Tower Bridge SE1 2UP (020 7403 3761; www.towerbridge.org.uk). This spectacular bridge was built by Sir John Wolfe Barry in 1894 and the old hydraulic lifting mechanism was originally powered by steam. Exhibition, Victorian engine room and walkways with fantastic views. Shop. *Open daily 09.30-17.00 (last admission).* Charge.
● **South Bank**
Wandsworth SW18. Until the 19th C Wandsworth was a village oasis on the River Wandle – a good fishing river – and was noted for a local silk and hat industry. The course of the Wandle can still be traced near the Church of All Saints. The Surrey Iron Railway, whose wagons were drawn by horses, ran alongside the river. Past residents include Defoe, Thackeray and Voltaire, but today little remains to point to the past.
Battersea SW11. Many of the old riverside warehouses are now gone and tall tower blocks dominate.
St Mary's Church Church Road *SW11*. The church is one of the few relics of Battersea's 18th-C village. Built in 1775 by Joseph Dixon, it is strangely Dutch in character.
Battersea Park SW11 4NJ (www.batterseapark.org). The park was laid out by Sir James Pennethorne as a public garden and opened by Queen Victoria in 1858. Re-designed in the 1950s for the Festival of Britain, there is a boating lake, a deer park, an Alpine showhouse, herb garden and greenhouse, a children's zoo and sculptures by Moore, Hepworth and Epstein. The London Peace Pagoda which stands close to the river was built in 1985 by monks and nuns of the Japanese Buddhist order Nipponzan Myohoji.
Battersea Power Station SW8 4BU (www.batterseapowerstation.co.uk). This vast oblong of brick with its four chimneys was designed by Sir Giles Gilbert Scott, 1932-4. Redundant as a power station since 1980, it has now been developed to give an imaginative mix of retail and residential with its own tube station and pier.
Albert Embankment SE1. Designed as a broad footwalk by Sir Joseph Bazalgette, 1867, the Embankment stretches between Vauxhall and Westminster Bridges. The upper Embankment was once the site of the 18th-C Vauxhall Gardens, whose Chinese pavilions and walks were the envy of Europe.
Lambeth Palace Lambeth Palace Road SE1 7JU (020 7898 1200; www.archbishopofcanterbury.org/lambeth-palace/visit-lambeth-palace). The London residence of the Archbishop of Canterbury since 1197. Remarkable Tudor gatehouse, fine medieval crypt. A 14th-C Hall with a splendid roof and portraits of archbishops on its walls. The Guard Room, which houses the library, was rebuilt in medieval style in 1633. For details of pre-bookable tours visit www.facebook.com/visitlampal.
London County Hall Belvedere Road SE1 7PB. Designed by Ralph Knott in 1911, this was once the imposing headquarters of the Greater London Council. Today it houses various attractions and events such as Agatha Christie's Witness for the Prosecution. Tickets are available by visiting www.witnesscountyhall.com/venue.
London Eye Jubilee Gardens SE1 7PB (0871 781 3000; www.londoneye.com). A gigantic ferris wheel offering a bird's eye view over London. O*pening times vary according to season.* Contact for details.
Shell Centre SE1. Part of the area known as the South Bank, the Shell Centre was designed by Sir Howard Robertson in 1962, and is of greyish white concrete with monotonous little square windows. The central 351ft-high skyscraper rises like a huge grey mountain.
South Bank Centre SE1 8XX (020 3879 9555; www.southbankcentre.co.uk). Royal Festival Hall, the Queen Elizabeth Hall, the Purcell Room, the National Theatre, the National Film Theatre, the Hayward Gallery and the Museum of the Moving Image make up the complex which originated with the Festival of Britain in 1951. The Festival Hall, completed in 1951 and built by Sir Robert Matthew and Sir Leonard Martin, seats 3400. The Queen Elizabeth Hall by Hubert Bennett, 1967, is much smaller and intended for recitals.
The Shard SE1 (www.the-shard.com). A 72-storey skyscraper in Southwark designed by Renzo Piano. At 1,016ft it is the tallest building in the UK. Construction commenced in March 2009 and it was completed in November 2012. It has a viewing gallery and an open observation deck 801ft above the Thames and its concrete core is clad with steel and glass. Majoring on energy efficiency, its office complex houses 32 companies, together with 10 apartments, three restaurants and a hotel.
Upper Ground SE1. The decrepit warehouses that used to line the south bank have been demolished, and replaced by the impressive London Weekend Television building and Gabriel's Wharf – South Bank's answer to Covent Garden.
Bankside SE1. In the 16th C the Rose Theatre, the Swan and the Globe were all situated around Bankside, and until the 19th C the area was the site of playhouses and amusement gardens. Today the area has been developed and almost all is changing apart from the few remaining 17th- and 18th-C houses and the Anchor pub, an historic tavern with strong smuggling connections. A Tudor theatre has been

reconstructed near the site of the original Globe Theatre as part of the International Shakespeare Globe Centre, and the Shakespeare Globe Museum illustrates the theatre of the age (*see* below).
Shakespeare Globe Theatre 21 New Globe Walk, Bankside SE1 9DT (020 7401 9919; www.shakespearesglobe.com). Converted 18th-C warehouse on the site of a 16th-C bear-baiting ring and the Hope Playhouse. Guided tours available. Box office *open Mon-Fri 11.00-18.00 & Sat-Sun 10.00-18.00 (Sun 17.00).* ✗♿ Swan Bar & Restaurant *open daily 12.00-20.45 (Sun 11.30).*
Tate Modern Bankside SE1 9TG (020 7887 8888; www.tate.org.uk/visit/tate-modern). The Tate Gallery's international collection of 20th-C art is housed within the former Bankside Power Station, designed in 1935 by Sir Giles Gilbert Scott. Displays are themed and stylistic and historical parallels are drawn between works from different periods to challenge the viewers perception of non-representational art. Genres range from Surrealism and New Reaslism through to Pop Art and Minimal Art. Striking views from the top floor – both of the sculptures inside the building and out over the Thames. Café and shop. *Open daily 10.00-18.00. Last admissions 45 mins before closing.* Free. A boat service connects the two Tate Galleries – www.tate.org.uk/visit/tate-boat – and also stops at the London Eye. Charge.
Southwark Cathedral London Bridge SE1 9DA (020 7367 6700; www.southwark.anglican.org). Built by Augustinian Canons but destroyed by fire in 1206 and greatly restored. The tower was built c.1520 and the nave, by Blomfield, 1894-7. In the Middle Ages the cathedral was part of the Augustinian Priory of St Mary Overie. Despite its 19th-C additions, it is still one of the most impressive Gothic buildings in London. Exhibitions, refectory and shop. *Open Mon-Sat 09.00-18.00 & Sun 08.30-17.00.* Donations.

- **Bridges**
See www.pla.co.uk/Safety/Thames-Bridges-Heights for navigational detail on the following bridges:
Chelsea Bridge SW3. The original bridge designed by Thomas Page, 1858, was rebuilt as a suspension bridge in 1934 by Rendel, Palmer and Tritton.
Victoria Railway Bridge SW1. When it was opened in 1859, this was the widest railway bridge in the world – 132ft wide and 900ft long – and it provided 10 separate accesses to Victoria Station.
Vauxhall Bridge SW1. James Walker's Regent's Bridge which opened in 1816 was the first iron bridge to span the Thames in London. The present structure, designed by Sir Alexander Binnie, was opened in 1906. The bronze figures alongside the bridge represent Agriculture, Architecture, Engineering, Learning, the Fine Arts and Astronomy.
Lambeth Bridge SW1Y. Originally the site of a horse ferry, the first bridge was built here in 1861, designed by P. W. Barlow. This was replaced in 1932 by the present steel-arch bridge designed by George Humphreys and Sir Reginald Blomfield.

Westminster Bridge SW1Y. Built in 1750, Westminster Bridge was the second bridge to be built across the Thames in central London. The present bridge, by Thomas Page, replaced the old stone one in 1862.
Charing Cross Railway Bridge SE1. Also known as Hungerford Bridge, it has replaced the original suspension bridge which was demolished in 1864. A separate walkway and cycleway run alongside to Waterloo Station with excellent views of the City.
Waterloo Bridge SE1. John Rennie's early 19th-C bridge, a beautiful design of Greek columns and nine elliptical arches, was replaced in 1945 by Sir Giles Gilbert Scott's concrete bridge, faced with Portland stone.
Millennium Bridge EC4. Constructed in 1999 and, in conjunction with the new walkway on the upstream side of Hungerford Bridge, forms part of the City's Cross River Partnership initiative to provide an integrated transport and regeneration strategy for Thames side in central London.
Southwark Bridge EC4. Southwark Bridge was built in 1814 and was the largest bridge ever built of cast iron. Replaced 1912-21 by the present five-span steel bridge of Mott and Hay, with Sir Ernest George as architect. Southwark Causeway, the steps on the south side, were used by Wren when he travelled across the river to supervise work on St Paul's.
Cannon Street Railway Bridge EC3. Built in 1866 as part of the extension of the South Eastern Railway, the bridge's engineers were J. Hawkshaw and J. W. Barry. A prominent structure on account of the 19th-C train shed jutting out to the side of the bridge.
London Bridge EC3. Until 1749 London Bridge was the only bridge to span the Thames in London. The first recorded wooden bridge was Saxon, but it is possible that a Roman structure may have existed here. In 1176 the wooden bridge was replaced by a stone structure, with houses, shops and a church built upon it, similar in appearance to the Ponte Vecchio in Florence. The heads of traitors were displayed on the spikes of the fortified gates at either end. In 1831 this bridge was demolished and a new bridge, by John Rennie, replaced it. A granite bridge with five arches, this soon became too narrow to meet the demands of modern traffic and because of structural faults could not be widened. A new bridge, constructed under the direction of the City Engineer, was opened to traffic in 1973. Built out of concrete, it has a flat-arched profile in three spans carried on slender piers. The McCulloch Corporation of Arizona paid £2,460,000 for the facing materials of Rennie's bridge, which has been reconstructed spanning Lake Havasu.
Blackfriars Bridge SE1. Blackfriars Bridge was built in 1760. It cost £230,000 and was mainly paid for by fines which had accumulated from men refusing the post of Sheriff. Replaced by the present structure in 1860. Note the pulpits, a reminder of the religious significance of its name.
Blackfriars Railway Bridge SE1. Built in 1886 for the London, Chatham and Dover Railway, this elegant iron bridge, with its high parapet and decorative coat of arms at each end, can best be seen from the road bridge.

River Thames — East London

WALKING AND CYCLING

Tower Hamlets produces an excellent series of walks leaflets covering the docks and river within the borough and highlighting much of the history of the area. Available by visiting www.towerhamlets.gov.uk/lgnl/leisure_and_culture/walking/walks/walks.aspx. Visit www.mycanarywharf.com for details specific to Canary Wharf.

New uses have been devised for these huge areas of dereliction, ranging from the City Airport to the Canary Wharf development. New housing and new industry have been drafted in, often with scant regard for established communities and cultures. In converting redundant warehouses the value of these solid symbols of a previous prosperity and optimism has at least been recognised.

St Katharine Docks 50 St Katharine's Way, St Katharine's & Wapping E1W 1LA (020 7264 5312; www.skdocks.co.uk). St Katharine Docks was the first of the docks to be rejuvenated. Built on 23 acres in 1828, from a design by Thomas Telford, the original docks were closed down in 1968. Five years later an £80 million building scheme was begun which included the Tower Thistle Hotel and the World Trade Centre. The magnificent warehouses have been restored and now house shops, apartments, offices, restaurants, a yacht club and marina. Visiting cruisers nestle alongside resident yachts and barges. Marina *open daily 09.00-17.00*.

Tobacco Dock Pennington Street E1. Designed by Terry Farrell in 1989, this 19th-C former warehouse has been converted into a shopping and leisure complex. Development work was carried out using original suppliers of materials wherever possible.

Butler's Wharf SE1 (www.conranandpartners.com/projects/butlers-wharf). Transformed from narrow alleys, where Oliver Twist's Bill Sikes met his end, into a smart restaurant, shopping and office complex including the Conran restaurants and the Butler's Wharf Chop House.

Marine Policing Unit 98-102 Wapping High St, Wapping, London E1W 2NE (020 7230 1212; www.thamespolicemuseum.org.uk/museum.html). At Wapping, on the north bank of the river just downstream from St Katharine Docks, can be seen the HQ of the Metropolitan Police's Marine Policing Unit with its impressive fleet of high-speed vessels and state-of-art workshop built out over the river. Visits to their fascinating museum are by prior appointment only – *see* website.

Cherry Garden Pier SE16. Where ships sound their signal if they want Tower Bridge to be raised. Turner sat here to paint *The Fighting Temeraire* as she was being towed to be broken up.

Rotherhithe Tunnel SE16. Built 1904-8 by Sir Maurice Fitzmarice, the tunnel is still used as a thoroughfare between Rotherhithe and Stepney. The top of the tunnel is 48ft below the high-water mark to allow for large ships passing above.

YHA London Thameside 20 Salter Road SE16 5PR (0345 371 9756; www.yha.org.uk/hostel/yha-london-thameside). This prominent landmark on the south bank of the river is a luxurious youth hostel catering for families, groups and individual travellers.

Limehouse Basin E14. This used to be called the Regent's Canal Dock, and forms part of the Grand Union Canal system, which was opened in 1820 to allow barges to trade between London and Birmingham. The Limehouse Cut also provides access to the River Lea.

Royal Naval Victualling Yard Grove Street SE8. Founded in 1513 as the Royal Dock for Henry VIII's navy, the yard became the principal naval dockyard in the kingdom, rivalling Woolwich. Sir Francis Drake was knighted here after his world voyage on the *Golden Hind*, and it was from this yard that Captain Cook's *Discovery* set sail.

Docklands Stretching from Tower Pier to Beckton is London's Docklands. The area has undergone massive change from a thriving, commercial port through closure to regeneration. The London Docklands Development Corporation (LDDC) was set up in 1981 to create a new city for the 21st C incorporating riverside apartments, shops, restaurants and offices.

Canary Wharf Tower One Canada Square, Canary Wharf E14. Designed by Cesar Pelli, 1988-90, this 800ft building is the tallest in the UK. Clad in stainless steel and topped with a pyramid, the 50-storey building boasts a magnificent lobby finished in Italian and Guatemalan marble. Thirty-two passenger lifts operate from the lobby and are the fastest in the country. Canary Wharf itself is full of elegant architecture, stately streets, well-planted squares and outdoor spaces.

Isle of Dogs E14. Until the industrialisation of the early 19th C, the Isle of Dogs was mainly pastureland and marshes. Windmills stood by the river. By 1799 the Port of London had become so overcrowded that Parliament authorised the building of a new dock on the Isle of Dogs, under the auspices of the West India Company. Built by William Jessop, the two West India Docks were opened in 1802. In 1870 the South Dock was added. It was built on the site of the City Canal which had connected Limehouse Reach and Blackwall Reach between 1805 and 1829. The Millwall Docks, the most southern, were completed in 1864. The West India Docks are also the site of Billingsgate Fish Market, which was moved here from its old site near London Bridge in 1982.

Island Gardens Saunders Ness Road E14. This small park at the south tip of the Isle of Dogs was opened in 1895 to commemorate the spot which Wren considered had the best view of Greenwich Palace across the water.

Greenwich Tunnel E14. The Blackwall Tunnel, opened in 1897, was designed as a road traffic tunnel. In 1902 it was decided to build a pedestrian subway to link Greenwich with the Isle of Dogs. There was opposition from the watermen and lightermen who, rightly, feared for their jobs. The southern entrance to the footway is in Cutty Sark Gardens, Greenwich, and the northern entrance is in Island Gardens, Isle of Dogs.

Greenwich SE10. Once a small fishing village, the historic town of Greenwich marks the eastern approach to London. Its royal and naval past is illustrated by the magnificent riverside grouping of the Queen's House, the Royal Naval College, the National Maritime Museum and the Old Royal Observatory. From the Observatory the views are magnificent, spanning Docklands and the City right through to Westminster. Museums, bookshops, antique shops, and a street market *open daily 10.00-17.30* make for a bustling village atmosphere away from the industrialisation of the Docklands area.

River Thames

East London

Cutty Sark King William Walk SE10 9HT (020 8858 4422; www.rmg.co.uk/cutty-sark). One of the great 19th-C tea and wool sailing clippers, stands in dry dock. Phoenix-like she has risen from near total destruction by fire in 2007 and is once again open to visitors *daily 10.00-17.00. Café. Charge.*

Greenwich Park Blackheath Gate, Charlton Way, Greenwich SE10 8QY (0300 061 2381; www.royalparks.org.uk/parks/greenwich-park). The park, laid out for Charles II by the French royal landscape gardener André Le Nôtre, commands a magnificent view of the Royal Naval College and of the river. It contains 13 acres of woodland and deer park, a bird sanctuary and archaeological sites. Crooms Hill lies to the west of the park, lined with a wealth of 17th-,18th- and 19th-C houses, the oldest being at the southern end near Blackheath. Greenwich Theatre stands at the foot of the hill. *Open daily 06.00-21.00. Closes earlier in winter. Free.*

National Maritime Museum Park Row, Greenwich SE10 9NF (020 8858 4422; www.rmg.co.uk/national-maritime-museum). At the heart of the Greenwich World Heritage Site, comprising three sites: the Maritime Galleries, the Royal Observatory and the Queen's House. The Maritime Galleries cover the country's encounters with the world at sea from the 16th to the early 20th centuries. The original observatory, still standing, was built by Wren for Flamsteed, first Astronomer Royal, in the 17th C. Astronomical instruments and exhibits relating to the history of astronomy, planetarium shows and the time ball which provided the first public time signal in 1833 still operates. Home to the Meridian Line, interactive science stations and the largest refracting telescope in the UK. The Queen's House is a delightful white house in the Palladian style, built for Queen Anne of Denmark by Inigo Jones, 1618. It showcases the museums's fine-art collection. *Open daily, 10.00-17.00. Free.*

Old Royal Naval College King William Walk, Greenwich SE10 9NN (020 8269 4799; www.ornc.org). Mary II commissioned Wren to rebuild the palace as a hospital for aged and disabled seamen. Designed in the Baroque style, it was completed in 1705. The Painted Hall, or Dining Hall, has a swirling Baroque ceiling by Thornhill, one of the finest of its period. The neo-classical chapel dates from 1789. In 1873 the hospital became the Royal Naval College to provide for the higher education of naval officers. *Open daily 10.00-17.00. Free.*

Execution Dock SE16. At the entrance to Blackwall Tunnel. This is where, until the late 19th-C, the bodies of convicted pirates were hung in iron cages until three tides had washed over them.

O2 Arena Peninsula Square SE10 0DX (020 8463 2000; www.theo2.co.uk). Once the Millennium Dome, now home to concerts, sports, cinema, exhibitions, special events, bars and restaurants. The structure is enormous: it is as high as Nelson's Column and the Eiffel Tower would fit inside it, lying on its side! *Open daily 10.00-23.00.*

Blackwall Tunnel SE16. Built in 1897 by Sir Alexander Binnie. There are now two tunnels; the second opened in 1967. One is for northbound traffic, the other for southbound.

Thames Barrier 1 Unity Way, Woolwich SE18 5NJ (020 8305 4188; www.gov.uk/the-thames-barrier). The Barrier is best seen from the river. As you round the bend, the steel fins rise up from the water. Completed in 1982, it is the world's largest movable flood barrier and is designed to swing up from the river bed and create a stainless steel barrage to stem periodically dangerous high tides. Each gate weighs 3000 tonnes and is the equivalent of a five-storey building in height. The structures housing the machines which operate the gates seem to have been inspired by the sails of Sydney Opera House. Blackwall Reach, on the way to the Barrier, was where, in 1606, Captain John Smith and the Virginia Settlers left on their journey to found the first permanent colony in America.

LONDON RIVER SERVICES

Since Roman times the importance of the Thames has been recognised as a highway for both commerce and passenger carrying alike, with ferries and their attendant piers developing where necessary. In the latter half of the 20th C there was a move away from the river to buses, tubes and taxis, the river piers largely reduced to serving pleasure traffic. However, as part of the Thames 2000 initiative and funded by the Millennium Commission, five new piers were built at strategic points along the river: Blackfriars, Tate Britain, Waterloo, Westminster and the Tower of London. Forming part of an integrated transport strategy for the Thames, new vessels, services and upgraded piers have meant new links along and across the Thames. A series of central London fast ferry services operate alongside shuttle services to Greenwich, and pleasure and sightseeing cruises. Visit the Transport for London website www.tfl.gov.uk/modes/river/ for further details. To ease your wider-ranging travel challenges around the city, download the Citymapper app: www.citymapper.com/london. Describing itself as the 'Ultimate Transport App', it does not lie!

WEY & ARUN JUNCTION CANAL AND ARUN NAVIGATION

ARUN NAVIGATION
MAXIMUM DIMENSIONS
Length: 68' 3"
Beam: 11' 9"
Draught: 3' 2"

MILEAGE
PALLINGHAM: Junction with the River Arun to:
Lee Farm Lock: 1½ miles
Lordings (or Orfold) Lock: 3 miles
NEWBRIDGE: Junction with the Wey & Arun Junction Canal: 4½ miles
Locks: 5 (including Orfold Flood Gates and counting Pallingham Staircase as two)

WEY & ARUN JUNCTION CANAL
MAXIMUM DIMENSIONS
Length: 68' 6"
Beam: 12' 2"
Draught: 3' 2" (deeper on the top pound)

Where WACT have built or rebuilt a lock from scratch (Loxwood, Southland, Gennets Bridge):
Length: 72' 2"
Beam: 14' 5"

In some cases, where WACT have restored a lock (Brewhurst, Devil's Hole):
Length: 72' 2"
Beam: 12' 2"

MILEAGE
NEWBRIDGE: Junction with the Arun Navigation to:
Loxwood: 6¼ miles
Compasses Bridge: 12½ miles
Run Common: 15½ miles

GUN'S MOUTH: Junction with the Wey & Godalming Navigations: 18½ miles
Locks: 24 (23 as built)

WEY & ARUN CANAL TRUST (WACT)
Canal Centre, The Wharf, High Street, Loxwood, Billingshurst, West Sussex, RH14 0RD 01403 753999 (beside the Onslow Arms public house)
canalcentre@weyandarun.co.uk
www.weyandarun.co.uk

General Note: With a waterway that closed almost 150 years ago it would be surprising, indeed, if all the bridges, locks and associated infrastructure remained intact. It many cases structures marked on the map are no longer extant so it is the site of such features that has been recorded, hopefully to be replaced in the course of future restoration. Pretty well all the first 1½ miles of the navigation, from Stonebridge heading south, now lie under housing, roads and gardens and therefore the locks and bridges marked along this stretch are shown to give an idea of the approximate position of the originals. The route for its replacement has yet to be finalised.

Paddling: Category 1. *However, paddlers should apply to WACT for a permit to use the Loxwood (and only navigable) section (charge). A licence to paddle is included in Paddle UK membership but members should call at the Canal Centre if they arrive during opening hours (see WACT website).*

Just as Goole – a town that came into being largely as result of the arrival of that great Yorkshire waterway, the Aire and Calder Navigation – is often cited as having 'been born under Victoria and died with her,' so the Wey & Arun Junction Canal could similarly be viewed as 'being born under Napoleon and dying with him.'

Officially opening on 28th September 1816, it was already apparent by 1821 (Napoleon having died on 5th May of the same year) that the expected stream of laden barges surging across the Surrey and Sussex countryside was never going to materialise, despite efforts to improve the waterway (especially the Arun Navigation) over the intervening five years.

Often described as 'London's Lost Route to the Sea' this is a navigation whose raison d'etre was as much military as it was a waterway to promote local trade in the face of unreliable road transport and burgeoning national canal mania. As a strategic waterway, ultimately linking the massive naval dockyards of Chatham and Portsmouth, there was much to recommend it as (to quote Paul Vine from his excellent treatise on the navigation carrying the same title) 'the military adventures of the first Napoleon resulted in events which made patent the many risks to which British shipping was exposed when sailing up the English Channel.'

However, this drawn out conflict was something of a double-edged sword: on the one hand it doubtless tipped the balance in favour of construction while, on the other, materials and the cost of labour escalated in price as a result of the drawn out hostilities. It also staggered under the weight of a more global view, again propounded by Mr Vine, namely that 'no canals constructed after 1793 were ever to reap excessive profits'. Nevertheless, Josias Jessop (son of William Jessop) was commissioned to make a survey and reported that a revised route through Sidney Wood (the first, some 1½ miles shorter, bisected Alford village) would cost an estimated £86,132 but carried the advantage of a longer summit pound. Five miles long, this section now had double the water storage capacity.

Meanwhile, Lord Egremont of the nearby Petworth Estate, in his redrafted canal prospectus (which appeared in the Times on 17th October 1811) drew attention to the fact that the navigation would open up a 90-mile direct connection between the metropolis and Littlehampton: only 16 miles from Spithead and 22 miles from Portsmouth (a route that became more secure with the opening of the Portsmouth & Arundel Canal in 1823).

He expected Sussex corn, flour and timber to be carried into London, while he noted that the 10,000 tons of coal consumed annually by the good people of Guildford and Godalming would be considerably reduced in price. Apart, of course, from the obvious military hardware, he envisage that Portland stone, groceries, chalk, lime, ironware, slate, timber, manure, firewood, culm, bark and 'other articles' would also go to make up the cargoes. Likewise he was at pains to point out that the inland route from London Bridge to Portsmouth was 116 miles, 100 miles shorter than the coastal voyage.

In the event the waterway – which although in the planning stages for six years, was actually constructed in a record three years – saw its best year in 1824 with the carriage of 3,650 tons, rather than the hoped for 55,000 tons.

The chief problem was the never-to-be-solved difficulty of securing consistently reliable back loads, in conjunction with the somewhat limited (for a broad canal) tonnages carried when loaded. Forty tons was the maximum weight that a barge could convey end-to-end, although unreliable water depth often limited this to a more realistic 20-30 tons.

After the annual shareholders meeting in 1866, the management committee recommended that the company should be wound up, much to the chagrin of the barge-masters of Arundel and Littlehampton. Despite buying up all available shares, there was little that they could do to reverse the substantial operating deficit and stem the navigation's decline – in the face of neglect and the inevitable railway competition – into abandonment in 1871.

WALKING AND CYCLING

The restoration to navigation of the Wey & Arun Canal is an ambitious, on-going waterways project set in a surprisingly rural location. Access for walkers and, to a limited extent cyclists, precedes the arrival of end-to-end navigation by a considerable margin, which does carry some restrictions and limitations, although these are not necessarily too onerous.

The route plotted in this guide, known as the Wey-South Path, dates from the early 1970s and is way-marked throughout by small silver roundels with blue or black lettering. It does not always follow the towpath but, where the public right of access has been extinguished and not reinstated, makes use of public footpaths, bridleways and quiet, minor roads. It aims to keep as close to the line of the navigation as is practical and, as restoration proceeds, will doubtless be modified to embrace new sections of towpath.

Anyone following the course of this waterway would be well advised to read this guide in conjunction with The Wey-South Path, published by W&A Enterprises Ltd and obtainable from the WACT – details on page 202. Also included in this volume are 12, very worthwhile, circular walks based around the path. It cannot be stressed too strongly that, with the abandonment of the navigation in 1871, significant tracts of the Wey & Arun Canal now run through private land to which there is **no public access**. Therefore, to stray off the designated footpaths and bridleways, is to **jeopardise future restoration** and the painstaking efforts already put into re-establishing rights of navigation and access.

Amberley

The River Arun wanders contentedly, as though without a care in the world, through flat open marshy countryside, creating valuable habitats rich with flora and fauna. These open vistas, punctuated by a wide diversity of living creatures, are flanked by the South Downs: elevated ground that perfectly frames the serenity of the scene. South of Pulborough the two major roads diverge and continue their progress to the coast, giving this soft yielding slough a wide berth, to the lasting benefit of all those who wish to enjoy its peace and tranquillity.

- **Amberley**
West Sussex. PO, stores. Well known for its proliferation of thatched cottages and as a producer of limestone. The village has also acted as a magnet to the literati over the years, numbering Arnold Bennett, John Cowper Powys and Arthur Rackham (to mention but a few) amongst its many visitors. The artist, Edward Stott, spend the last 29 years of his life here.
Amberley Castle Amberley, Arundel BN18 9LT (01798 831992; www.amberleycastle.co.uk). A 12th-C fortified manor house with high curtain walls and towers at each corner, a medieval gateway, and a hall. It was used as a fortress by the bishops of Chichester. The walls, gateway and two of the towers remain in what is now a Grade I listed building sympathetically restored as a high-class hotel.
Amberley Pottery Church Street, Amberley, Arundel BN18 9ND (01798 831876; www.amberleypottery.co.uk). Makers of country pottery for the table and general domestic use, together with 'one-off' commissions. *Open Thu-Sun 11.00-15.00.*
Amberley Museum New Barn Road, Amberley BN18 9LT (01798 831370; www.amberleymuseum.co.uk). Set in a 36-acre site, this museum is dedicated to the industrial heritage of the South East. Exhibits include a narrow-gauge railway and classic bus service (both providing free, nostalgic travel around the site), Connected Earth Telecommunications Hall, Milne Electricity Hall, Printing Workshop, working displays of traditional craft skills and much more. Café and picnic areas. *Open Mar-Oct, Wed-Sun 10.00-17.00 & B Hols. Daily during school Hols. Allow ½ a day for your visit.* Charge.

- **Houghton Bridge**
West Sussex. Station. Small village presiding over an attractive River Arun crossing, situated in the South Downs National Park. Reputed to have been a stopping-off point for Charles, fleeing his defeat at the Battle of Worcester.
Weald & Downland Living Museum Town Lane, Singleton PO18 0EU (01243 811363; www.wealddown.co.uk). Depicting 950 years of rural life in the South East through its unrivalled collection of rescued buildings, re-erected in a beautiful 40-acre setting within the South Downs National Park. Re-created work places and work spaces jostle harmoniously with historic gardens, farm buildings, restored homes and working craftsmen. *Regular children's events. Café. Open Mar-Oct daily 10.00-17.00 & Nov-Feb 10.00-16.00.* Charge.
Tourist Information Centre Arundel Museum, River Road, Arundel BN18 9PA (01903 885866; www.visitarundel.co.uk and www.sussexbythesea.com). *Open daily 09.00-18.00.*

Pubs and Restaurants

1 The George & Dragon Turnpike Road, Houghton, Arundel BN18 9LW (01798 831559; www.thegeorgeanddragonhoughton.co.uk). Reputed to be one of the three oldest pubs in Sussex (parts date from 13th C), this welcoming hostelry serves real ale and food *Mon L & Wed-Sun L ad E (not Sun E)*. Garden with breathtaking views over the Sussex Downs; children and dogs welcome. Real fires. *Open Mon L & Wed-Sun 12.00-23.00 (Sun 17.00).*

2 The Bridge Inn Houghton Bridge, Amberley BN18 9LR (01798 831619; www.bridgeinnamberley.com). Locally-sourced, home-cooked food and real ale combine in a warm welcome in this Grade II listed pub that serves food *Wed-Thu L and E & Fri-Sun 12.00-20.30 (Sun 16.00).* Patio and beer garden; children and dogs welcome. Real fires and Wi-Fi. *Open Wed-Sun 12.00-23.00 (Sun 17.00).* Also *open B Hols 12.00-17.00; food served 12.00-15.00.*

3 Riverside South Downs Houghton Bridge, Amberley BN18 9LP (01798 831066; www.riversidesouthdowns.com). Breakfast, lunch, pizzas, baguettes, cream teas and homemade cakes sum up the appetising fayre available at this riverside gem. *Open daily 09.00-16.30.* Boat and bike hire.

4 The Sportsman Inn Rackham Road, Amberley BN18 9NR (01798 831787; www.thesportsmansussex.co.uk). Binoculars are available to watch the wildlife in this 17th-C pub, close to the Amberley Wild Brooks, together with a wide range of real ales and food *Mon-Fri L and Thu-Sat E.* Dog- and child-friendly; garden. Real fires and Wi-Fi. B&B. *Open daily 10.00-22.00.*

5 Amberley Castle Hotel Church Street, Amberley BN18 9LT (01798 831992; www.amberleycastle.co.uk). Luxury hotel in a 900-year-old castle, resplendent behind its 60ft curtain wall and portcullis (which remains open!), serving up-market meals *L and E daily.* Tennis courts and 18-hole putting green. Garden. B&B.

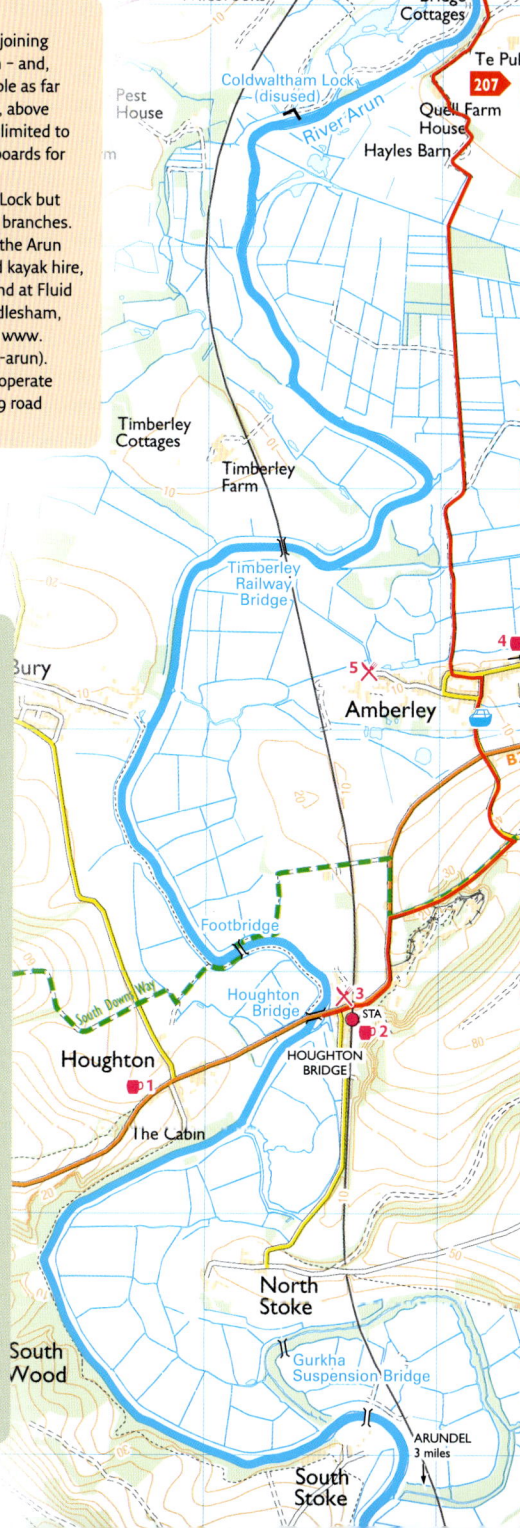

PADDLING

The River Arun is a tidal navigation – joining the English Channel at Littlehampton – and, on a spring tide, the effect is noticeable as far as Pallingham Farm Bridge. However, above Pulborough navigation is realistically limited to dinghies, canoes, kayaks and paddleboards for all but the most intrepid. The river is paddle-able upstream of Pallingham Lock but can be obstructed by fallen trees and branches. At times of high rainfall the whole of the Arun Valley is prone to flooding. Canoe and kayak hire, together with instruction, can be found at Fluid Adventures, Unit 1A, Keynor Farm, Sidlesham, Chichester PO20 7LL (01243 942777; www.fluidadventures.co.uk/contact/#river-arun). They are open *daily 09.00-17.00* and operate from Pulborough RH20 2BJ at the A29 road bridge crossing the River Arun.

BOAT TRIPS

Boats for hire from Riverside South Downs – *see page 204.*

WALKING AND CYCLING

For the walker the Wey-South Path is, for the most part level and relatively easy going, although it can be muddy after heavy rain and during the winter months. In places, particularly between Haybarn Bridge and Newbridge, the canal and the River Arun are only separated by the width of the towpath, so care should be taken when conditions are slippery. The Wey-South is passable by mountain bike, although it is not a bridleway throughout and it is therefore doubtful if this was ever envisaged when the path was established! However, it is only for the intrepid cyclist as sections of the path become eroded and there are numerous gates, stiles and fences to be negotiated.

The Wey-South Path links with the South Downs Way, the West Sussex Literary Trail and the Monarch's Way at Houghton Bridge, while Amberley railway station is conveniently close to the Path's finishing point.

It is quite feasible to follow paths south along the remainder of the Arun, via Arundel, to its meeting with the sea at Littlehampton. *See* OS Explorer map 121 (Arundel & Pulborough). Bikes and eBikes can be hired from Riverside South Downs – *see page 204.*

Pulborough

Pulborough lies to the north of a large open tract of farm- and marsh-land through which the meandering River Arun grows ever more dominant as it picks its way doggedly towards the South Downs and, ultimately, its union with the sea at Littlehampton. With its well-connected railway it makes one of two convenient starting points for exploring the navigation, the start of which is located at Pallingham, a little under two miles to the north west. Sadly, the double entrance lock – where the canal leaves the Arun – is inaccessible as it is badly overgrown and hidden in a private garden. Although the Wey-South Path is obliged to throw one of its most extravagant deviations at this point (owing to the constraints of private ownership) both the waterway and the river, that it follows so studiously, are never far away as all three settle snugly into some delightfully harmonious countryside. Whilst man's efforts to bridge the tidal river have culminated in the lovely 14th-C Greatham Bridge downstream of Pulborough, they are rivalled (trumped, some might say) by the similarly aged Stopham Bridge, its central arch raised for navigation during 'improvements' in July 1822, at a cost of £286.

- **Adversane**
West Sussex. Known as Hadfoldsham until the mid-19th C, this hamlet is built astride a slight kink in the Roman Stane Street. A row of cottages opposite the old forge, beside the Blacksmith's Arms, were converted from a former malt warehouse, which probably utilised the original road alignment for its foundations. Originally owned by Allen Bros – maltsters from Horsham – the warehouse was used to store malt smuggled from the Continent during the Napoleonic Wars and there was reputed to be a connecting passage from its cellars to the pub opposite.

Pubs and Restaurants

1 The Labouring Man Old London Road, Coldwaltham RH20 1LF (01798 872215; www.labouringman.com/en-GB). Village local dispensing real ale and food *L and E (not Sun E)*. Dogs welcome, garden. Traditional pub games, newspapers, real fires and Wi-Fi. B&B. *Open Mon-Fri L and E & Sat-Sun 12.00-23.00 (Sun 22.00).*

2 The White Hart Stopham Bridge, Stopham RH20 1DS (01798 874903; www.thewhitehartpulborough.com). In a splendid position, overlooking the ancient Stopham bridge, this fine riverside pub serves real ales and food *Mon-Fri L and E (not Sun E)*. Dog- and family-friendly. Gardens alongside the river bank. Real fires. *Open daily 12.00-22.00 (Sun 18.00).*

3 River Moon 18 Swan Court, Pulborough RH20 1RJ (01798 874141; www.rivermoon.co.uk). Freshly-prepared, authentic Thai cuisine served *daily L and E*. Children welcome. Takeaway service.

4 Macklin's 3 Lower Street, Pulborough RH20 2BH (07930 988666; www.facebook.com/macklinsatheroundabout). Spacious micropub run by friendly, enthusiastic staff serving real ales. Dog-friendly. *Open Tue-Sat 16.00-23.00 (Sat 14.00) & Sun 14.00-20.00.*

5 The Chequers Hotel Old Rectory Lane, Pulborough RH20 1AD (01798 872486; www.chequershotelpulborough.co.uk). Dating from 16th C, this hotel and restaurant offers relaxed dining with superb views over the Arun Wild Brooks and South Downs beyond. Wi-Fi. B&B.

6 The Rising Sun The Street, Nutbourne, Pulborough RH20 2HE (01798 812191; www.therisingsunnutbourne.co.uk). Fine old stone building with flag-floored bar and a cosy restaurant serving real ale and food *daily L and E (not Sun E)*. Dog-friendly, superb garden. Traditional pub games, real fires and Wi-Fi. *Open Sun-Thu L and E (not Sun E) & Fri-Sat 11.00-23.00.*

7 The White Horse Mare Hill Road, Pulborough RH20 2DY (01798 872189; www.whitehorsepulborough.com). This 15th-C pub, overlooking the Pulborough Brooks Wildlife Nature Reserve, serves real ales and food *daily L and E (not Sun E)*. Dog- and child-friendly. Garden. Wi-Fi. *Open L and E (not Sun E).*

8 So India Stane Street, Codmore Hill, Pulborough RH20 1BG (01798 874748; www.soindia.co.uk). Boasting authentic cuisine from the Grand Moghuls, this establishment is *open daily L and E* and offers a takeaway service.

9 The Swan Inn Lower Street, Fittleworth RH20 1EN (01798 865154; www.swaninnfittleworth.com). A coaching inn since 1382 and the venue for past meetings of the Ancient Order of Froth Blowers (founded in 1924 – *see* p208), this welcoming hostelry serves real ale and food *L and E*. It was also a regular haunt of the composer, Edward Elgar. Children and dogs welcome, garden. Real fires and B&B. Awaiting new management so *opening times to be confirmed – see website*.

- **Coldwaltham**
West Sussex. Easily missed – as the arrow-straight Roman Stane Street whisks travellers rapidly past – the village hosts the charming 13th-C St Giles Church, flanked by one of the county's oldest yew trees (believed to be 3000 years old). Of somewhat younger origins are the attractive, 13th-C Greatham Bridge and the route of the former 1¾ mile, southern extension of the Arun Navigation, including the 375yd tunnel under Hardham Hill. Both are in the immediate vicinity of the village and a ½ mile section of the abandoned towpath is utilised by the Wey-South Path.

Nymans House and Gardens Staplefield Lane, Handcross RH17 6EB (01444 405250; www.nationaltrust.org.uk/nymans). World-famous garden and semi-derelict house, partially destroyed by fire in 1947, this was the home of the artistic Messel family. Anne Messel was the mother of Lord Snowdon and a founder of the Victorian Society. Shop, café and bookshop. Garden, woods and plant centre, etc. *Open daily 10.00-17.00 (Fri 20.30). House open daily Mar-Oct, 11.00-15.00. (Closed Xmas & Boxing Day).* Charge.

> **WALKING AND CYCLING**
> From Pulborough railway station (where there is plenty of parking – charge) follow the path heading north east out of the car park, alongside the railway, until it meets the unclassified road. Turn left over the railway bridge along Coombelands Lane and, after ¾ mile, where the road bears sharply to the right, you will have joined the route of the Wey-South Path. Left takes you down to the River Arun at Stopham Bridges, while following the road north past the horse gallops takes you to Pallingham Quay Farm and the start of the Arun Navigation where it leaves the river. Make sure you follow the way-marked Path left down the farm driveway in Pickhurst, some 100yds before the second road junction on the right.

Parham House & Gardens Parham Park, Pulborough RH20 4HS (01903 742021; www.parhaminsussex.co.uk). Simon Jenkins, journalist and former chairman of the National Trust, placed Parham in his Top Twenty of 'England's Thousand Best Homes' perfectly capturing its essence when he said "Nothing at Parham is superfluous, nothing unloved. It is a house of magic." Amongst its gems are the Long Gallery, the Great Hall, the Walled Gardens and the Pleasure Grounds. Plant, garden and gift shop, and a restaurant. *Open Apr-Sep, Wed-Fri, Sun & B Hols (although events occasionally preclude Sun opening) 12.00-17.00 (house 14.00).* House and garden tours available. Charge.

● **Petworth**
West Sussex. PO, stores, off-licence, chemist, hardware, delicatessen, bakery, takeaway, library. A settlement made rich from cloth weaving in the Middle Ages. Petworth House was the home of the 3rd Earl of Egremont, principal investor and driving force behind the Wey & Arun Junction Canal. Today Petworth is a centre for antiques with more than 30 outlets at the last count. Shop *open daily 07.00-22.00.*

Coultershaw Heritage Site and Beam Pump Petworth GU28 0JE (01798 667244; www.coultershaw.co.uk). Centuries of water power: everything from an 18th-C water pump to a 21st-C water turbine housed in historic buildings set around the mill pond. Telephone for details of *opening times.*

Petworth Cottage Museum – Mrs Cummings's Cottage 346 High Street, Petworth GU28 0AU (01798 342100; www.petworthcottagemuseum.co.uk). The museum is a Leconfield Estate worker's cottage restored and furnished as it might have been in about 1910. There is also has a rare collection of Petworth Goss China. *Open Apr-Oct, Tue-Sat & B Hol Mon, 14.00-16.30.* Charge.

Petworth House & Park Church Street, Petworth GU28 9LR (01798 342207; www.nationaltrust.org.uk/petworth-house-and-park). 17th-C, Grade I mansion set in 700 acres of parkland designed by Capability Brown, housing the finest art collection in the National Trust's care. Later alterations were to the design of Anthony Salvin. Shop and café. *Open daily 10.00-17.00 (house 11.00).* The park is *open 08.00-dusk daily.* Charge.

● **Pulborough**
West Sussex. All services. Originally a fording point for the Roman Stane Street, running between Chichester and London, the village became an important resting place for cattle drovers taking sheep and cattle from the Downs into the Capital's Smithfield Market, a bridge having been built in Saxon times. There is evidence of a Motte and Bailey castle to the west of the village (today, virtually a small town) whilst the 12 hour, Le Mans-style lawn mower endurance race holds a more contemporary claim to fame. It is held in July and runs *from 20.00-08.00* with the winner covering some 330 miles... over 390 laps or so!

St Mary's Church 2 London Road, Pulborough RH20 1AP (01798 875773; www.stmaryspulborough.org.uk). 13th-C church with 15th-C extensions built in the Perpendicular style. There is a Norman font and the lancet windows and piscina date from the original construction. *Open Mon-Fri 14.00-16.00.*

Pulborough Brooks Nature Reserve Uppertons Barn Visitor Centre, Wiggonholt, Pulborough RH20 2EL (01798 875851; www.rspb.org.uk/days-out/reserves/pulborough-brooks). RSPB-managed SSSI on the Arun flood plain offering a wide diversity of habitats including wetlands, woodland and heathland, Pulborough Brooks is a haven for a great range of wildlife. Café and shop. *Open daily 10.00-16.00.* Charge.

South Downs Light Railway Pulborough Garden Centre, Stopham Road, Pulborough RH20 1DS (07518 753784; www.south-downs-railway.com). 10¼" gauge steam railway running for almost a mile around the garden centre. Great fun for children and adults of all ages! *Open Mar-Sep weekends and B Hols & Wed during school holidays.* Trains run *every 15 mins 11.00-12.30 & 13.30-15.30.* Also special *seasonal* events. Charge.

Tourist Information Centre Arundel Museum, River Road, Arundel BN18 9PA (01907 885866; www.arundelmuseum.org/tourist-information). *Open daily 09.00-18.00.*

ANCIENT ORDER OF FROTH BLOWERS

The Ancient Order of Froth Blowers was a whimsical, charitable organisation formed in 1924 in the bar of The Swan Inn, Fittleworth (*see* page 190) "to foster the noble Art and gentle and healthy Pastime of froth blowing amongst Gentlemen of leisure and ex-Soldiers." It was created by Bert Temple, a silk-merchant and ex-soldier, with the initial intention of raising £100 for the children's charities of the notable London surgeon, Sir Alfred Fripp.
Membership was five shillings (25p) with each member receiving a pair of silver and blue cuff-links, plus a membership booklet and card entitling them to 'blow froth off any member's beer and occasionally off non-members' beer provided they are not looking or are of a peaceful disposition'. Their motto was 'Lubrication in Moderation'.
By 1929 the membership stood at 700,000 and had raised over £100,000 (equal to £5.5m at today's values) for hospital cots, funding holidays and outings for thousands of needy children.
A quote from the articles of membership describes them as 'a sociable and law-abiding fraternity of absorptive Britons who sedately consume and quietly enjoy with commendable regularity and frequention the truly British malted beverage as did their forbears and as Britons ever will, and be damned to all pussyfoot hornswogglers from overseas and including low brows, teetotalers and MPs and not excluding nosey parkers, mock religious busy bodies and suburban fool hens all of which are structurally solid bone from the chin up'.
The Temperance movement, believing alcohol to be the chief cause of the "wee waifs'" suffering, found their popularity upsetting and the order came to a natural end soon after the death of Bert Temple in 1931.

Newbridge

At Haybarn Bridge (redundant from Bar Lane, Keighley on the Leeds & Liverpool Canal) the navigation is re-joined and the towpath is now followed for the next four miles. The turf-sided Orfold Flood Lock (the lower gates restored) and adjacent Bridge (subjects of one of WACT's earlier restorations) are both interesting features but the pièce de résistance lies in Lordings Aqueduct, Lock and the restored waterwheel, designed to lift water from the river and into the canal: a unique structure on the British inland waterways system. It's hard to conceive that the meandering stream that still dogs the canal, first on its west bank and then (after the Aqueduct) on its eastern perimeter, was initially navigated by barges to a junction with the canal at Newbridge. This capricious water course – suffering drought in summer and flooding in winter – was very much the Achilles heel of the navigation in its early days. Between Newbridge and Loves Bridge are structures dating from the very early days of WACT activity. Rowner Lock (used briefly in 1982) and its accommodation bridge was the scene of their first working party on 28th March 1971 and this section was used as a pilot for the ensuing restoration project. Northlands Bridge was constructed for the Trust in 1979/80.

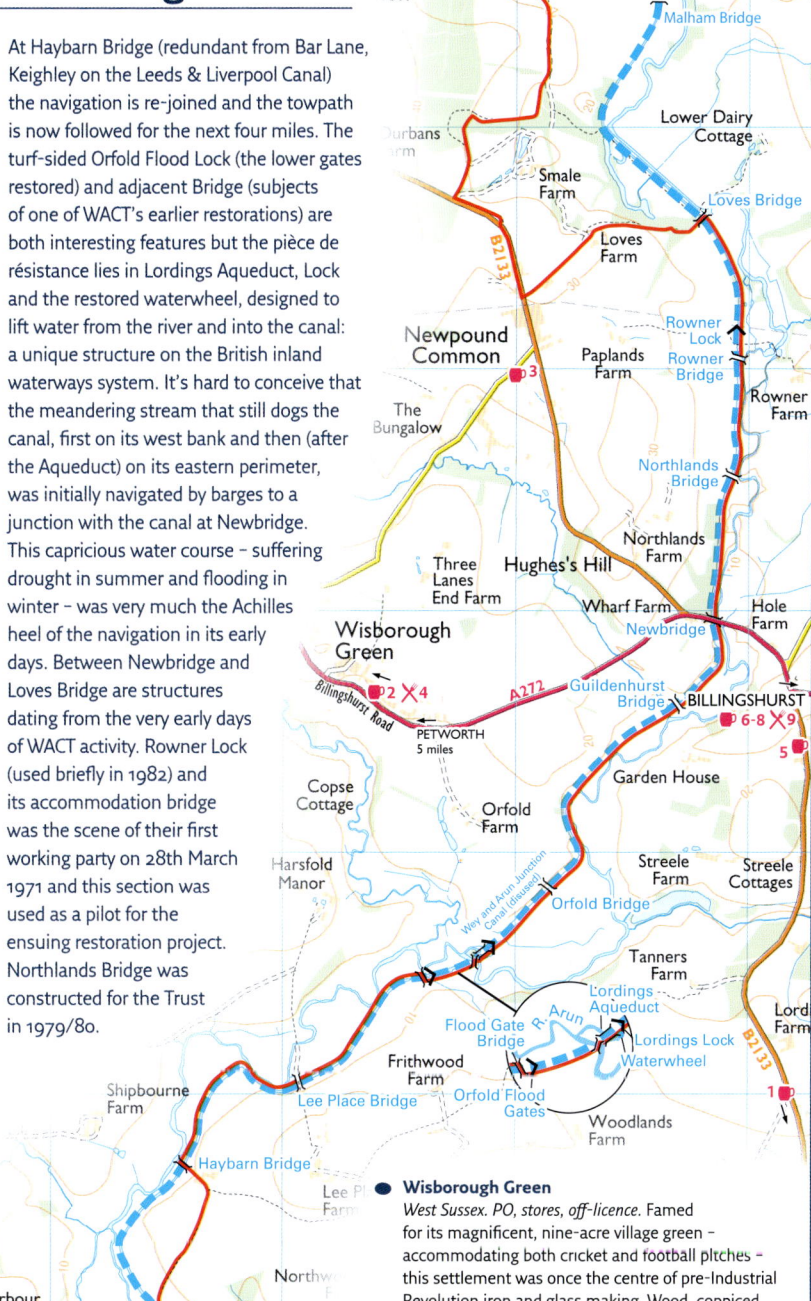

- **Wisborough Green**
  West Sussex. PO, stores, off-licence. Famed for its magnificent, nine-acre village green – accommodating both cricket and football pitches – this settlement was once the centre of pre-Industrial Revolution iron and glass making. Wood, coppiced from local forests, provided the fuel in the form of charcoal until the practice was finally outlawed. An annual, charity balloon festival takes place in September putting the green to further good use.

● **Billingshurst**
West Sussex. PO, stores, chemist, baker, butcher, hardware, fish & chips, takeaways, off-licence, library, station. A crossroads village heralding the meeting of the Roman Stane Street with the old Wealden Highway. St Mary's Church dates from the very early 13th C with extensive work carried out in 15th- and 16th C. Stores *open daily 06.00-22.00 (Sun 07.00)*.
Fishers Farm Park Newpound Lane, Wisborough Green RH14 0EG (01403 700063; www.fishersfarmpark.co.uk). Family attraction with horse and tractor rides, animal encounters, indoor soft play, adventure playground and café. Also holiday cottages and film nights. *Open daily 10.00-17.00*. Charge.
Horsham Museum & Art Gallery 9 Causeway, Horsham RH12 1HE (01403 254959; www.horshammuseum.org). With more than 26 galleries covering subjects from local trades to fashion, and pre-history to the poet Percy B. Shelley, this museum staggers under the accolade of the 'Victoria & Albert in miniature'. Also changing exhibitions of contemporary art. *Open Tue-Sat 10.00-16.00*. Free.

Pubs and Restaurants (page 209)

🍺✕ **1 The Blacksmiths Arms** Stane Street, Adversane RH14 9JH (01403 588470; www.1010restaurant.uk). Modern internal décor, real ales and food available *Mon-Sat L and E & Sun 12.00-20.00*. Regular live music, real fires and a garden. *Open Mon-Sat 12.00-22.00 (Sat 23.00) & Sun 12.00-21.00*.

🍺✕ **2 The Cricketers Arms** Durbans Road, Wisborough Green RH14 0DG (01403 700369; www.facebook.com/Wisborough). Overlooking the village green, and home to the British Lawnmower Racing Association (see Pulborough page 192) this pub serves real ales and food *L and E*. Traditional pub games and real fires. *Open 12.00-23.00*.

🍺 **3 The Bat & Ball** Newpound Common, Wisborough Green RH14 0EH (01403 700313; www.haywards-batandball.co.uk). Sledges, skis, and some rather novel chandeliers decorate this hostelry, which dispenses real ale and excellent food *daily 12.00-21.00 (Sun 18.00)*. Family-friendly, garden. Wi-Fi. Camping. *Open 12.00-23.00 (Sun 20.00)*.

✕ **4 The Old Mill Café** Billingshurst Road, Wisborough Green RH14 0DY (01403 700094; www.justbillingshurst.co.uk/directory/old-mill-cafe). *Open Wed-Sun 09.00-14.30 (Sat-Sun 15.30)* this friendly establishment serves breakfasts, light lunches and afternoon teas. Also coffee, panini, omelettes, sandwiches and cakes. Outside seating.

🍺 **5 The Lime Burners** Newbridge, Billingshurst RH14 9JA (01403 782311; www.limeburnersbillingshurst.co.uk). Originally sited beside the canal at Newbridge, this traditional country pub still serves real ales and food *L and E* from its new location. Newspapers and B&B. Camping (with toilets, showers and hot water). *Open Tue-Sun L and E*.

🍺 **6 The Kings Head** 40 High Street, Billingshurst RH14 9NY (01403 782012; www.facebook.com/thekingsheadbillingshurst). Town-centre pub dating from 18th C, serving real ales and food *L and E*. Sun roasts. Dog- and family-friendly; outside seating. Real fires, sports TV and Wi-Fi. *Open Mon-Sat 11.00-23.00 (Fri-Sat 00.00) & Sun 12.00-23.00*.

🍺✕ **7 The Six Bells** 76 High Street, Billingshurst RH14 9QS (01403 782124). Timber-framed, Grade II listed, 16th-C coaching inn serving real ales and excellent food *daily 12.00-20.00 (Sun 17.00)*. Quiz Thu. Dog- and family-friendly; enclosed garden. Traditional pub games, real fires and Wi-Fi. *Open Mon-Sat 12.00-22.30 (Fri-Sat 00.00) & Sun 12.00-21.00*.

🍺 **8 The Kings Arms** 80 High Street, Billingshurst RH14 9QS (01403 782072; www.kingsarmsbillingshurst.wordpress.com). Friendly, two-bar, town-centre pub serving real ales and food *L and E*. Sun roasts. Dogs and children welcome, large garden. Traditional pub games and live music Fri. *Open Sun-Thu 11.00-23.00 & Fri-Sat 12.00-00.00*.

✕ **9 Truffles** 8 The Maltings, High Street, Billingshurst RH14 9JL (01403 785429; www.trufflesbakery.co.uk). Welcoming bakery-cum-café serving tasty food from breakfast through 'til tea in generous portions. Family-friendly. *Open Mon-Sat 07.30-15.00*.

WALKING AND CYCLING

Resist the temptation to follow the bank of the canal, rather than the somewhat lengthy detour imposed by the Wey-South Path at this point. Taking the direct route risks jeopardising relationships, built up by WACT with local landowners over many years, and can seriously hinder long-term restoration. Instead, enjoy the elevated views from the Path, seeing the Arun Valley from a different perspective.
Take care when negotiating the busy B2133 on the outskirts of Newpound and look for a path that leads off the apex of the bend, between the chevrons, approximately 150yds after the footpath finishes. This is the start of a path running along the field boundary, separated from the road by the hedge-line.
At Malham Farm it is possible to take a short diversion eastwards to view Malham Lock, restored in 1996, and then continue north to Bignor Bridge before heading west to re-join the main Path. There is **no right of way** along the canal between Loves Bridge and Malham Lock.

Loxwood

There is plenty to see once the towpath (which extends along the entire restored section of the waterway) is regained at Drungewick Lane Bridge: an aqueduct, six operational locks and numerous accommodation bridges, not to mention the re-instated B2133 crossing in Loxwood. Beyond Gennets Bridge Lock, close to the Sussex-Surrey border, the Sidney Wood Lock Flight 8-16 begins in earnest. Although Locks 9-16 are still derelict (and in some cases virtually non-existent) the stretch of towpath through Sidney Wood is as magical as any length of waterway in the country, rivalling the Chesterfield west of Turnerwood and the Thames & Severn – where it challenges the Cotswold scarp above Brimscombe Port – to name but two.

- **Alfold**
  Surrey. PO, stores. In the late Middle Ages Alfold is recorded as being a part of Shalford Manor, whilst the nearby Sidney Wood was a source of charcoal for glassmaking until the early 17th C, when it was redeployed into the local gunpowder industry. A few hundred yards to the south of the Grade II* listed shop there is a driveway, complete with a diminutive steel turntable, thus ensuring that a parked car enters and leaves the property in a forward facing direction!
  St Nicholas Church Rosemary Lane, Alfold GU6 8EU (01403 753821). Focus of an attractive, village-centre grouping, this Grade I listed building with its broach spire and Jacobean pulpit is of 12th-C origins with 13th- and 15th-C additions and Victorian alterations.
- **Ifold**
  West Sussex. Stores. Curious maze of housing that, devoid of its own church, cannot bear the appellation 'village'. During the 1930s the Ifold Estate was sold off as plots for holiday and weekend homes. Mains water arrived with the coronation, in 1953.
- **Loxwood**
  West Sussex. Butcher. Centre of an excellent network of paths and bridleways criss-crossing the Low Weald, linking the coast to London in much the same way as did the construction of the Wey & Arun. In the mid-19th C the village was also home to the Society of Dependants, widely known as 'Cokelers': a Christian sect founded by John Sirgood. They opened a co-operative store in Loxwood with members investing and working in the business. This is extemporised in a verse from the Dependants' hymn book:
  > Christ's Combination Stores for me
  > Where I can be so well supplied,
  > Where I can one with brethren be,
  > Where competition is defied.
- **Plaistow**
  West Sussex. Stores, off-licence. Picture post card, Sussex village with its centre an attractive grouping of Victorian church and primary school, spacious green, pub and stores.
- **Rudgwick**
  West Sussex. PO, stores, chemist, off-licence. Rich in timber-framed buildings, and lying close to the Surrey border, Rudgwick holds an important place in the history of palaeontology. The species *Polacanthus rudgwickensis* is named after a specimen discovered in the old Brickworks in 1985, excavated by Morris Zdzalek (works engineer) and Sylvia Standing, both keen archaeologists. The dinosaur was a heavily armoured herbivore, about 13ft long, who lived around 125 million years ago. Stores *open daily 07.00-22.00.*
  Southwater Cycles Bonnington Farm, Drungewick Lane, Loxwood RH14 0RS (01403 701002/07714 247522; www.southwatercycles.com). Sales, service, hire, parts and accessories. Their hire fleet includes a wide range of bicycles, child trailers, trailer bikes and luggage trailers. Booking advisable. Camping nearby. *Service by appointment only.*

> **PADDLING**
> The Wey & Arun Canal Trust publish helpful guidance to paddlers at www.weyarun.org.uk/backdrop/files/WACT%20Canoeing%20leaflet%202021%20press.pdf mentioning the annual flotilla based in Pulborough. Further downstream, and indeed further afield across Hampshire and West Sussex, Go Paddling introduces the paddler to an exciting range of additional opportunities: www.gopaddling.info/places-to-paddle-in-hampshire-and-west-sussex.

Wey & Arun Canal Trust trip boat at Loxwood

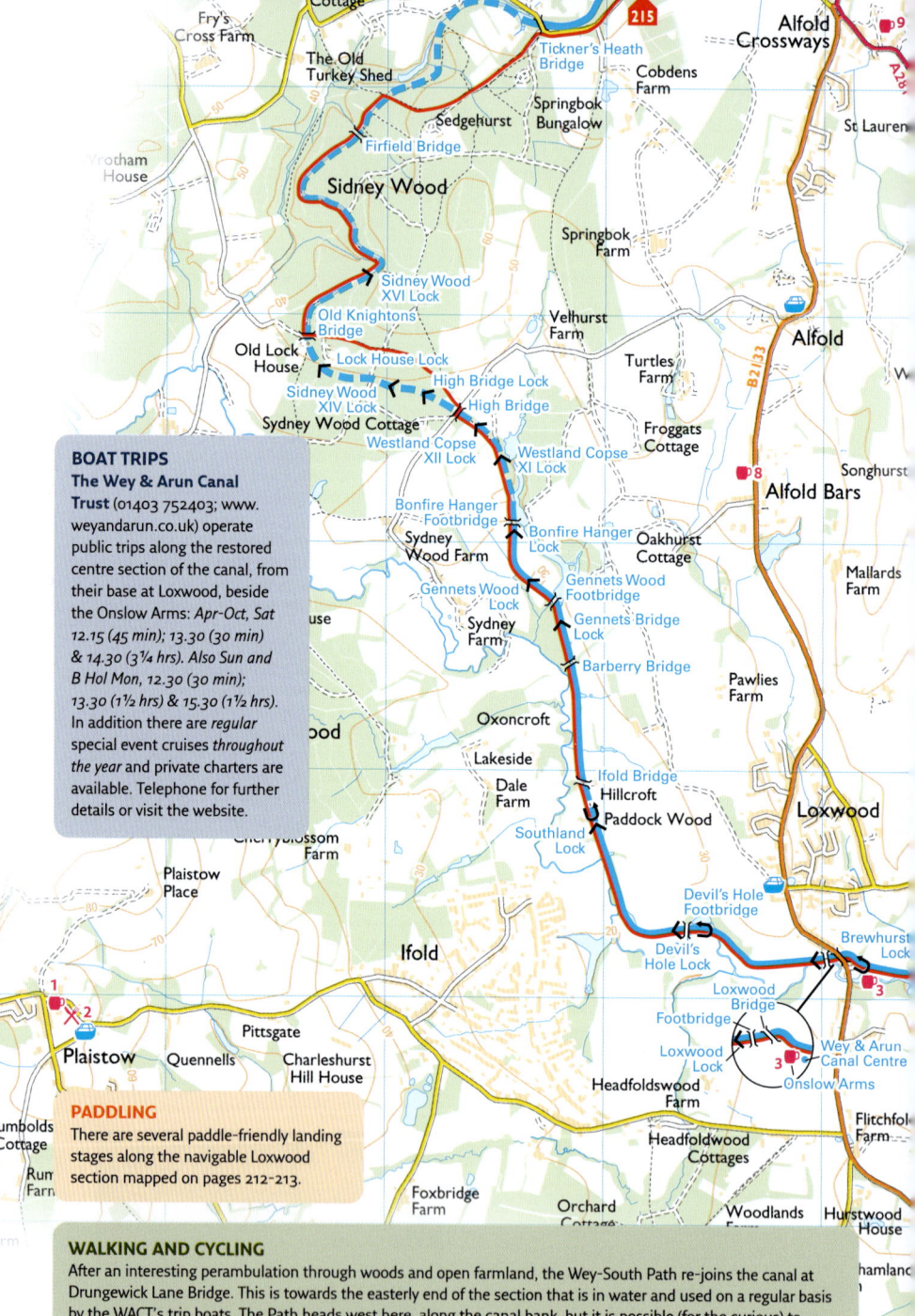

BOAT TRIPS
The Wey & Arun Canal
Trust (01403 752403; www.weyandarun.co.uk) operate public trips along the restored centre section of the canal, from their base at Loxwood, beside the Onslow Arms: Apr-Oct, Sat 12.15 (45 min); 13.30 (30 min) & 14.30 (3¼ hrs). Also Sun and B Hol Mon, 12.30 (30 min); 13.30 (1½ hrs) & 15.30 (1½ hrs). In addition there are *regular special event cruises throughout the year* and private charters are available. Telephone for further details or visit the website.

PADDLING
There are several paddle-friendly landing stages along the navigable Loxwood section mapped on pages 212-213.

WALKING AND CYCLING
After an interesting perambulation through woods and open farmland, the Wey-South Path re-joins the canal at Drungewick Lane Bridge. This is towards the easterly end of the section that is in water and used on a regular basis by the WACT's trip boats. The Path heads west here, along the canal bank, but it is possible (for the curious) to follow a permissive path east to Drungewick Lock which is currently the limit of both navigation and walking. For cycle hire – and all things to do with bicycles – see Southwater Cycles on page 211.

Pubs and Restaurants

🍺 **1 Olde Sun Inn** Plaistow, Billingshurst RH14 0PX (01403 871313). Quiet, friendly village local with exposed beams serving real ale and food *daily L and E*. Garden and real fires. *Open Mon-Fri E, Sat L and E & Sun 13.00-16.00*.

✗ **2 Corner Kitchen** Plaistow Stores, Plaistow RH14 0PX (01403 871236; www.facebook.com/cornerkitchenplaistow). Small village café and coffee shop serving light meals, snacks, homemade cakes and freshly ground coffee. *Open Mon-Sat 07.00-17.00 (Sat 08.00) & Sun 09.00-13.00*.

🍺 **3 The Onslow Arms** High Street, Loxwood RH14 0RD (01403 752022; www.onslowarmsloxwood.com). Friendly, welcoming pub that is very much a focus for the Wey & Arun Canal, the excellent information centre being in its car park. Real ales and a range of appetising food are served *daily L and E*. Dog- and family-friendly, garden and play area. Real fires and Wi-Fi. *Open Mon-Sat 12.00-22.00 (Fri-Sat 23.00) & Sun 12.00-20.00*.

🍺✗ **4 The Blue Ship** Opposite Okehurst Road North, The Haven RH14 9BS (01403 822709; www.theblueship.co.uk). Dating from the 16th C, this pub has four separate rooms retaining many of its original features and now serves real ale and highly-regarded food *Fri E; Sat L and E & Sun L*. Dog- and family-friendly, garden. Traditional pub games and real fires. Camping. *Open Fri E; Sat L and E & Sun L*.

🍺 **5 The Fox Inn** Guildford Road, Rudgwick, Bucks Green RH12 3JP (01403 822386; www.foxinn.co.uk). This low-beamed, 16th-C hostelry serves a mix of traditional English pub fayre alongside Chinese dishes *Mon-Fri L and E; Sat 12.00-21.30 & Sun 12.00-19.30*. Real ale. Children and dogs welcome, garden. Real fires and Wi-Fi. *Occasional live music and quizzes. Open 12.00-23.00 (Sun 22.30)*.

✗ **6 The Milk Churn** Kiln House, The Brickworks, 4 Lynwick Street, Rudgwick RH12 3DH (01403 823980; www.bookhamharrison.co.uk/the-milk-churn). Real coffee (and its variants), teas, toasties, soup, ploughman's, sandwiches, filled rolls, homemade cakes and milk shakes. *Open Mon-Fri 08.30-16.00 & Sat-Sun 10.00-16.00*.

🍺✗ **7 The Kings Head** Church Street, Rudgwick RH12 3EB (01403 822200; www.kingsheadrudgwick.co.uk). Situated opposite the Norman church, this friendly village pub serves real ales and homemade food *Wed-Fri L and E & Sat-Sun all day*. Dog- and family-friendly, garden. Traditional pub games and real fires. *Open Wed-Fri L and E & Sat-Sun 12.00-21.00 (Sun 19.00)*.

🍺✗ **8 The Sir Richard Tichborne** Loxwood Road, Alfold Bars RH14 0QS (01403 751873; www.thetichborne.co.uk). With its origins in Medieval times, the present pub was established in 1873, losing nothing of its original rural, rustic charm in the process. Excellent food, sourced from local produce, is available *12.00-21.00 (Sun 16.00)* together with real ales. Dogs and children welcome, garden. Real fires and Wi-Fi. *Open daily 12.00-22.00 (Sun 18.00)*.

🍺✗ **9 The Barn at Alfold** Horsham Road, Alfold Crossways GU6 8HF (01403 752288). Dating from 1590, and built round a generously-beamed barn, this restaurant-cum-bar majors on a wide range of superb food sourced from locally produced ingredients. Fish a speciality (though from Billingsgate!). Drinkers, while welcome, may be banished to the garden *during busy meal times: Tue-Sun L and E (not Sun E). Open Tue-Sun L and E (not Sun E)*.

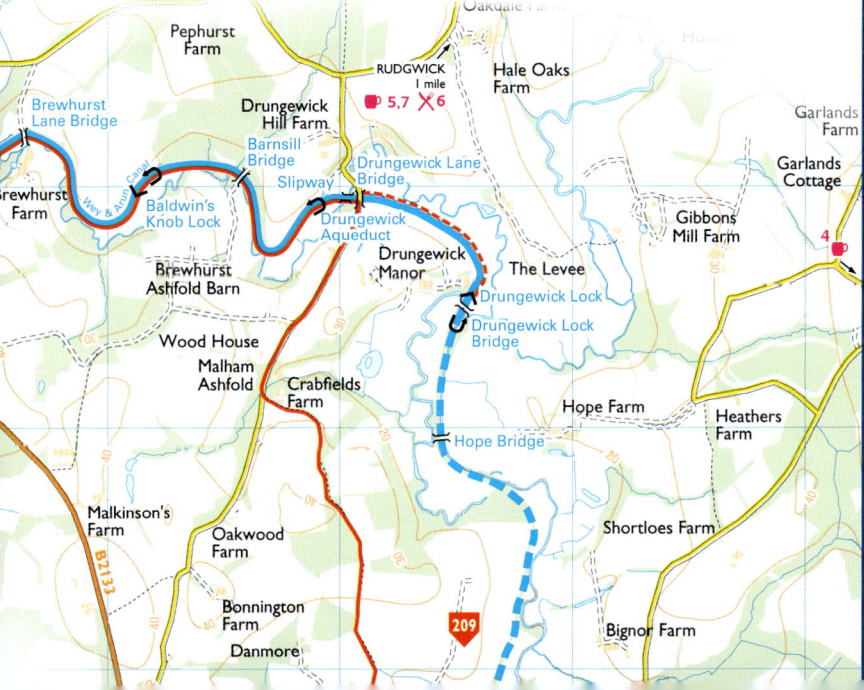

Dunsfold

Compasses Bridge, beside Dunsfold Aerodrome, is one of WACT's major triumphs. Relegated to a causeway, as part of the Canadian Army's record-breaking construction of this wartime airfield, the new – and very high profile – structure was built to a strict time scale and specification, and demonstrates just how effective (and efficient) volunteer organisations within the field of canal restoration can be. Whilst the Wey-South Path takes a second wander into the not unattractive Surrey countryside the waterway, once past Fast Bridge, begins to establish a purposeful course northwards towards its junction with the River Wey. Although a 'fully paid up member' of the Home Counties, somewhat surprisingly, Surrey is regarded as the English county with the highest percentage of its area covered by woodland: something that anyone following the course of this delightful waterway can hardly fail to be aware of.

- **Alfold Crossways**
Surrey. *Stores, off-licence, garage.* A largely residential settlement a mile or so north of Alfold. The *shop* is in the garage and is *open daily 06.00-22.00*.
- **Cranleigh**
Surrey. *PO, stores, chemists, fishmonger, delicatessen, off-licence, hardware, DIY store, library, garage.* Rapidly expanding dormitory village: the self-proclaimed largest in England. This is another Wealden settlement, originally founded on iron making fuelled by charcoal from forest coppice and later important for brick manufacture from the London clays. The origin of the name relates to cranes, as depicted in the Parish Council's civic coat of arms, which were once prevalent in the area.
Cranleigh Arts Centre 1 High Street, Cranleigh GU6 8AS (01483 278000; www.cranleighartscentre.org). Films comedy and theatre in this lively arts centre. Art Tea House *open as per Centre opening times* and licensed bar *open 45 min before and during most events*. Wi-Fi. *Open Tue-Sat 10.00-16.30 (Sat 09.00).*
Cranleigh Leisure Centre Village Way, Cranleigh GU6 8AF (01483 274400; www.everyoneactive.com/centre/cranleigh-leisure-centre). Workout classes, swimming, indoor cycling, gym, crèche, soft play and café. *Open Mon-Fri 06.30-22.00 (21.00) & Sat-Sun 08.00-19.00 (Sun 20.00).* Charge.

- **Dunsfold**
Surrey. *PO, stores, off-licence.* One of the many settlements in the area with the suffix 'fold' attached to its name denoting the practice of cattle containment in what would otherwise, in Medieval times, have been a heavily wooded area. More recently, after much of the forest had been denuded through construction and shipbuilding demand, sheep would be folded (fenced in) on crop residues, or as part of a controlled grazing regime, fattening store lambs on root crops. The shop is a focus for lively and friendly community engagement and is *open Mon-Sat 07.00-18.00 & Sun 08.00-12.30. PO open Mon-Fri 08.30-17.00 (Wed 13.30).*
Dunsfold Aerodrome Built by the Canadian Army in 1942, in a record-breaking six months, the airfield was initially a World War II bomber base for the Royal Canadian Air Force, before being handed over to the RAF. With the termination of hostilities, it played an important part in the Berlin Airlift before being leased, until 2002, by Hawker Siddeley, who later became part of BAe Systems. The Harrier vertical take-off fighter was developed and assembled here, together with other significant post-war military aircraft. Its present owners have made several unsuccessful bids to develop the site as an eco-town although there are also on-going, contested plans to realise both its housing and full aviation potential.
St Mary & All Saints Church Dunsfold GU8 4LT (www.dunsfoldchurch.co.uk). Reputed to house the oldest pews in the country, this Grade I listed building was described by William Morris as "The most beautiful country church in all England".

Pubs and Restaurants

- **1 The Sun Inn** The Common, Dunsfold GU8 4LE (01483 200242; www.suninndunsfold.co.uk). Elegant 18th-C, Grade II listed hostelry overlooking the common, serving real ale and food *Tue-Sun L and E (not Sun E).* Dog- and family-friendly; outside seating. Real fires, traditional pub games, newspapers and Wi-Fi. *Open Mon 16.00-22.00 & Tue-Sun 12.00-23.00 (Sun 19.00).*
- **2 The Three Compasses** Dunsfold Road, Alfold GU6 8HY (01483 275729; www.thethreecompassesalfold.co.uk). 400-year-old pub, with exposed beams and an inglenook, serving real ales and food *Tue-Sat L and E & Sun 12.00-15.00.* Children's play area. Dogs welcome and traditional pub games. *Open Mon-Fri 12.00-23.00 (Mon 14.00) & Sat-Sun 11.00-23.00 (Sun 21.00).*

Wey & Arun Junction Canal and Arun Navigation

3 The Three Horseshoes
4 High Street, Cranleigh GU6 8AE (01483 276978; www.threehorseshoescranleigh.co.uk). With an appealing tile hung frontage this pub, dispensing real ale and food *Mon-Fri L and E (not Mon L) & Sat-Sun 12.00-21.00 (Sun 16.00)* boasts exposed beams and an inglenook fireplace. Family- and dog-friendly, garden. Traditional pub games and Wi-Fi. *Open daily 12.00-23.00 (Mon 15.30).*

4 The White Hart Hotel
Ewhurst Road, Cranleigh GU6 7AE (01483 275566; www.facebook.com/thewhitehartcranleigh). Family-run pub, serving real ale and food *Tue-Fri L and E; Sat 12.00-21.30 & Sun 12.00-18.00*. Courtyard garden. Dogs and families welcome. Traditional pub games and Wi-Fi. B&B. *Open Mon-Thu 15.00-23.00 & Fri-Sun 12.00-00.00 (Sun 22.30).*

WALKING AND CYCLING
This is the third section of the Wey-South Path that is obliged to deviate significantly from the route of the navigation – the second within the Surrey boundaries. Again the walker (and cyclist) is rewarded by interesting countryside but care must be taken to focus on the map to avoid taking a wrong turning. On no account attempt to follow the perceived line of the original towpath as in many cases it is totally obliterated and **you would be trespassing** to the detriment of the on-going restoration of the canal.

5 The Curry Inn 84
214-216 High Street, Cranleigh GU6 8RL (01483 273992; www.curryinn84.co.uk). Welcoming, family run restaurant, exploring the cuisine of South Asia using carefully sourced ingredients, together with classic cooking techniques. Children welcome. *Open daily L and E (not Fri L).* Takeaway service.

6 The Richard Onslow
113-117 High St, Cranleigh GU6 8AU (01483 274922; www.therichardonslow.co.uk). Two bar, food-orientated pub serving real ale and meals *Mon-Sat L and E & Sun 12.00-21.00*. Bar *open Mon-Sat 12.00-23.00 (Fri-Sat 00.00) & Sun 12.00-22.30*. Garden and Wi-Fi. Children's toys, colouring books and high chairs provided. B&B. *Open Mon-Sat 12.00-23.00 (Fri-Sat 00.00) & Sun 12.00-22.30.*

Dunsfold

Shalford

At Run Common, once the site of one of the many wharfs associated with road crossings along this waterway, the path deviates away from the navigation for a final time, picking up the abandoned railway track. In places this follows a route through high, shady cuttings, most welcome if the day's walking has been in hot sunshine. Traces of the canal bed can be glimpsed to the east until the sprawl of housing finally obliterates the original alignment. At Gosden Aqueduct – within sight of Tannery Lane Bridge – where the waterway originally crossed Cranleigh Waters, contact is again made with the navigation before it wanders off, heading for the River Wey at Gun's Mouth. It is intended that the new course of the canal will be in the bed of Cranleigh Waters, passing beneath the busy A281 through Stonebridge, and thence making a connection directly with the river via an existing cut, which is to be dredged and widened. One delightful surprise, confronting anyone enjoying this northern section, is to stumble into the restored Bramley & Wonersh railway station complete with platforms, a shelter with timetables, a gradient post and the original station signs.

- **Shamley Green**
Surrey. *PO, stores, off-licence*. Situated in the Surrey Hills Area of Outstanding Natural Beauty (AONB), the village is reputed to have the highest cat population density in the United Kingdom.

- **Bramley**
Surrey. *PO, stores, butcher, greengrocer, fish & chips, takeaway, off-licence, library, garage*. There is evidence of Iron Age occupation close to the village but the Middle Ages would have seen its real establishment. The arrival of the Guildford – Arundel turnpike road in 18th C heralded substantial expansion, as did the coming of the canal and railway during the following century. Gertrude Jekyll spent her formative years at Bramley House, whilst the row of elegant shop fronts, on the west side of the High Street, owe their origins to William Lawn Head who converted several houses to become Head's Stores. There are a *PO, stores and off-licence* in neighbouring Wonersh.

- **Shalford**
Surrey. *PO, stores, chemist, takeaways, off licence, station*. Stretched out along the River Wey, made navigable to Godalming in 1763, Shalford was well placed to develop its gunpowder manufacture, its tanning and brickmaking industries, together with brewing and timber export. Gradually, throughout the 19th C, common land was built upon and the present day village was established around the green. Many of the houses lining the A281 to the north were timber-framed in origin and, once rendered – often with the addition of an extra storey – took on a fashionable Georgian mantle during the 18th C. Stores open Mon-Sat 06.30-20.30 (Sat 07.00) & Sun 08.00-18.00.
Chilworth Manor Halfpenny Lane, Chilworth GU4 8NN (www.chilworthmanor.net). Comprised of the 17th-C Randyll Wing (built by gunpowder miller Vincent Randyll and his son Morgan) and the later Marlborough Wing – a more sophisticated construction, employing red brick in an elegant

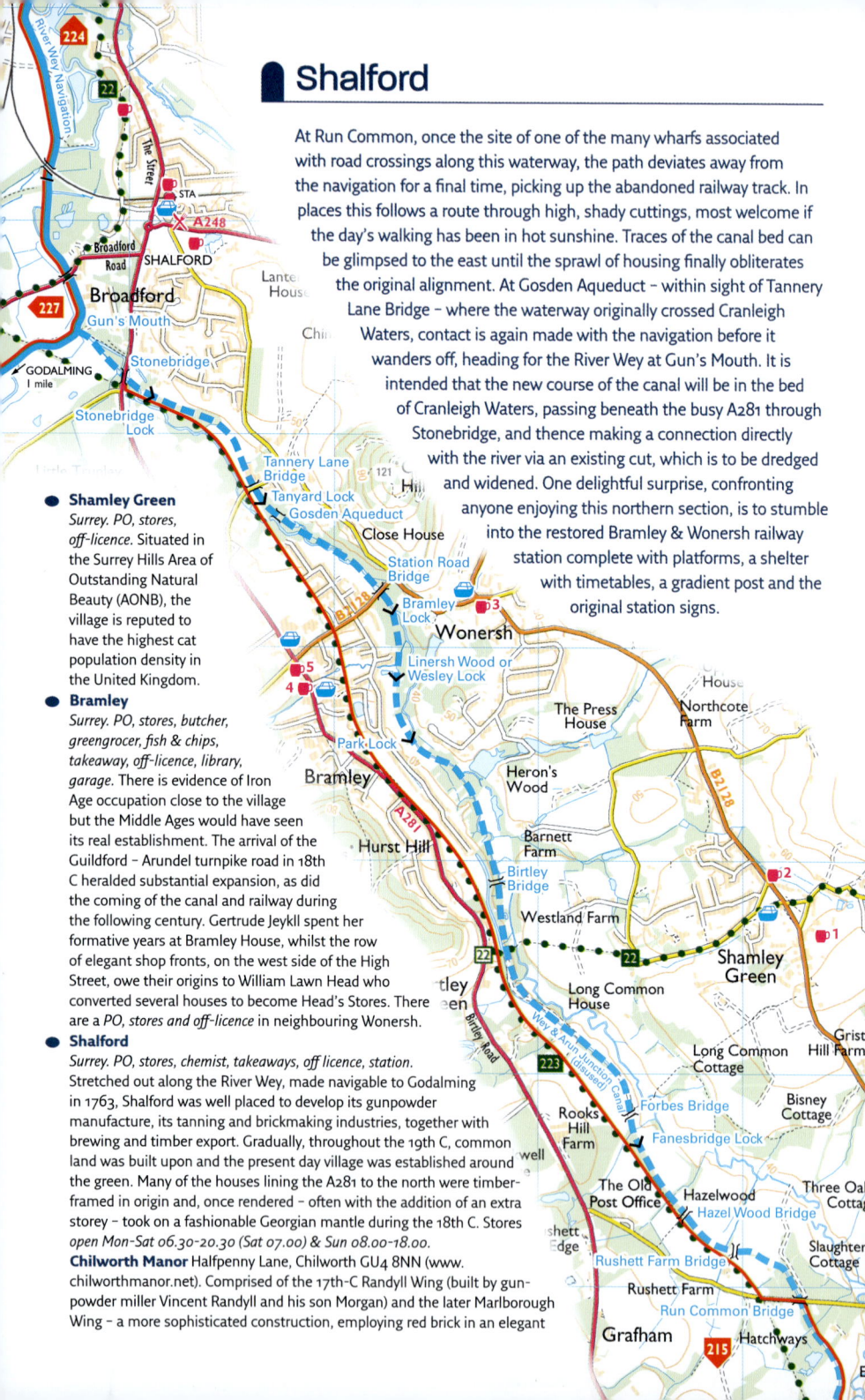

façade, decorative stucco and Ionic pilasters. Sarah, Duchess of Marlborough purchased the property in 1725 (at a time when she was at loggerheads with Sir John Vanbrugh, over his designs and costs for work at Blenheim Palace) and added the eponymous wing, rather than demolish Randyll's work and begin again. She employed the same philosophy in the walled garden, adding terraces to the original layout, running up the hill in four tiers towards St Martha's Hill and surrounded on three sides by stone walls. Today the house stands in 40 acres of parkland and a vineyard is under development.

Leith Hill Place Leith Hill Lane, Near Coldharbour Village, Dorking RH5 6LY (01306 711685; www.nationaltrust.org.uk/leith-hill-place). Childhood home of one Britain's greatest composers, Ralph Vaughan Williams. Opened to the public for the first time in 2013, this is a house in transition: a refreshingly informal place where you can sit on the furniture, play the piano or take an audio tour of the top floor to enjoy the Vaughan Williams display. Colour-coded trails. Tearoom. *Open 11.00-15.00 weekends Apr-Oct & Fri in season*. Telephone for further details. Charge.

Leith Hill Tower Leith Hill Lane, Near Coldharbour Village, Dorking RH5 6LX (01306 712711; www.nationaltrust.org.uk/leith-hill). Built by local landowner Richard Hull in 1765 – a man who wanted to see and be seen – his love of the tower led him to be buried underneath. Rising to 1029ft above the countryside, it is possible to see (with the aid of the installed telescope) the southern clock face of Big Ben to the north and the English Channel through the Shoreham Gap to the south. *Open 11.00-15.00 on weekends and B Hols & Fri throughout school summer holidays*. Charge.

Shalford Mill Shalford GU4 8BS (01483 561389; www.nationaltrust.org.uk/visit/surrey/shalford-mill). A mix of atmosphere and intrigue, mingles with the smell of tallow and old timbers, stirred up by evocative graffitied lime-washed walls and ancient hessian sacks. Into the mix blend the romantic story of the eccentric activities of the Ferguson Gang, in their successful attempt to save the mill from demolition, whilst drawing attention to the creeping urbanisation of the countryside during the 1930s. No expedition to the Mill is complete without a parallel visit to: www.surreyculturallives.org/items/show/1. *Open Apr-Oct, Wed & Sun 11.00-17.00*. Charge.

Winkworth Arboretum Hascombe Road, Godalming GU8 4AD (01483 208477; www.nationaltrust.org.uk/visit/surrey/winkworth-arboretum). The Arboretum exhibits spectacular collections of azaleas, rhododendron and holly hugging slopes leading down to landscaped lakes. The trees were planted from 1938 onwards by Dr Wilfrid Fox. You can visit the boathouse viewpoints and the wetlands, picnic in the Badgers Bowl glade or marvel at the unique chainsaw sculptures. Also colour-coded trails. Tearoom. *Open daily 10.00-17.00 (tearoom 16.00) (dusk in winter)*. Charge.

Pubs and Restaurants

1 The Bricklayers Arms The Green, Shamley Green, Guildford GU5 0UA (01483 898377; www.bricklayersarmspub.co.uk). This cosy Georgian pub, with sofas round the fire in *winter*, serves real ale and food *Tue-Sun L and E (not Sun E)*. Dogs- and children welcome, garden. Traditional pub games, real fires and Wi-Fi. *Open Tue-Thu L and E & Fri-Sun 11.30-22.30 (Sun 17.00)*.

2 The Red Lion The Green, Shamley Green GU5 0UB (01483 664161; www.redlionshamleygreen.com). The outside seating is a good place from which to view a *Sunday summer's* game of cricket, whilst indoors real ale is dispensed together with food *L and E (not Sun E in winter)*. Dog- and family friendly, garden. Real fires and Wi-Fi. *Open daily 12.00-22.00*.

3 The Grantley Arms The Street, Wonersh GU5 0PE (01483 893351; www.thegrantleyarms.co.uk). Describing itself as a traditional, yet contemporary pub with a laid back attitude, this hostelry serves (predominantly local) real ales and restaurant meals *daily 12.00-21.30 (Fri-Sat 22.00)*. Child- and dog-friendly, terrace. Real fires, sports TV and Wi-Fi. *Open daily 11.00-23.00 (Sun 22.30)*.

4 The Wheatsheaf High Street, Bramley GU5 0HB (01483 892722; www.wheatsheaf-bramley.co.uk). Traditional, family-run, village inn serving real ales and food *Mon-Fri 15.00-19.00 (Sat 12.00) & Sun 12.30-16.00*. Dogs and children welcome, garden. Sports TV, traditional pub games, real fires and Wi-Fi. B&B. *Open Mon-Fri 15.00-22.00 & Sat-Sun 12.00-23.00 (Sun 20.00)*.

5 The Jolly Farmer High Street, Bramley GU5 0HB 01483 893355; www.jollyfarmer.co.uk). Cosy, welcoming hostelry where the philosophy is simple: 'keep it fresh, keep it local.' Real ale (and real cider in *summer*) is available together with excellent food *Wed-Sun L and E (not Sun E)*. Also a selection of interesting continental lagers. Outside seating; dog- and family-friendly. Wi-Fi and B&B. *Open 11.00-23.00 (Sun 12.00)*.

See also Wey & Godalming Navigations for **Pubs and Restaurants** in the Shalford area – page 228.

WALKING AND CYCLING

This section of the Wey-South Path is almost entirely along the abandoned track bed of the former Horsham & Guildford Direct Railway – opened in 1865 and closed almost exactly 100 years later – which was taken over by the London, Brighton & South Coast Railway Company even before full completion of the route. The going for walker and cyclist alike is very easy.

Coxes Mill and Coxes Lock, Weybridge (see page 221)

WEY & GODALMING NAVIGATIONS

MAXIMUM DIMENSIONS
Length: 71' 6"
Beam: 13' 10"
Draught: 3' to Guildford
2' 6" above Guildford
Headroom: 7' to Guildford
6' to Godalming (at normal levels)

MILEAGES
THAMES LOCK (junction with River Thames) to:
Woodham Junction: 3 miles
Cartbridge: 9 miles
Guildford: 15 miles
Gun's Mouth: 17¼ miles
Godalming: 19½ miles

Locks: 16 (including Worsfold and Walsham Flood Gates)

Navigation Authority:
The National Trust
River Wey Navigations
Dapdune Wharf
Wharf Road
Guildford GU1 4RR
Visitor Services Manager: 01483 561389
riverwey@nationaltrust.org.uk
www.nationaltrust.org.uk/visit/surrey/river-wey-and-godalming-navigations-and-dapdune-wharf

Paddling: Category 1–2. *This is a river navigation which can be challenging in flood conditions. A licence to paddle is included in Paddle UK membership.*

Annual or visitor's licences are issued at Dapdune Wharf, or at Thames Lock. A copy of *Information for Boat Users* is supplied with each licence and can also be downloaded at www.nationaltrust.org.uk/river-wey-godalming-navigations-and-dapdune-wharf. It is essential reading for all those navigating this waterway.

The speed limit is 4 knots – in practice, slower. Watch your wash. Use only the correct Wey Navigation lock handle, available from Thames Lock, the NT Navigation Office or Guildford and Farncombe Boat Houses. When leaving locks, exit gates should be left open, but with all the paddles *down*.

As a river navigation, the Wey is subject to flooding, increasing the speed of the current and pull of the weirs. Under certain conditions, locks may be padlocked and craft should moor up in a sheltered place and seek advice. Water points on this navigation can be difficult to identify as they are not standard. The towpath side of the navigation is available for mooring.

Boats have used the River Wey since medieval times, but the present navigation dates from the 17th C. In 1651 authorisation was given to make the river navigable for 15 miles from Weybridge to Guildford. This involved the building of 12 locks and 10 miles of artificial cut. This early navigation had the usual battles with mill owners, but gradually trade developed, predominantly local and agricultural in character. More unusual were the extensive Farnham Potteries, who shipped their wares to London along the Wey. In 1763 the Godalming Navigation was opened, adding another four miles to the waterway, and by the end of the 18th C considerable barge traffic was using the river. This was greatly increased by the building of the Basingstoke Canal in 1796, and the Wey & Arun Junction Canal in 1816; the latter offered a direct route from London to Portsmouth and the south coast. This canal closed in 1871, but trade continued to thrive on the Wey and as late as 1960 barges were still carrying timber to Guildford. Grain traffic to Coxes Mill continued until 1968, with a brief revival in the early 1980s. There is now no commercial carrying on the navigation. In 1964 the Wey Navigation was given to the National Trust by Harry Stevens, its last private owner. In 1968 the Godalming Navigation Commissioners passed their section to Guildford Corporation, who in turn passed it on to the National Trust. It remains an artery of peace and tranquillity amidst the noise and bustle of Surrey, and will amply repay a visit.

Weybridge

The River Wey Navigation joins the Thames below Shepperton Lock where the correct channel is clearly signposted. Just around the corner is the Pound Gate used only when the water level is low or when a deep draughted vessel is passing through. Thames Lock is in an attractive wooded setting beside a smart new apartment conversion, and the keeper here is available to advise you. An informative display can be seen in the stable by the lock. Just above, beyond the weirs, smart houses and gardens line the east bank; the west is wooded. There is a sharp westward turn (*see Navigational Notes*) followed immediately by Weybridge Town Lock, where Addlestone Road flanks the navigation on its way to Ham Moor. Note the towline roller on the corner, installed to allow towed craft to negotiate the bend. Just below the railway bridge at Coxes Mill, the *water point* is hidden behind the wall of the old stable block. The large mill pond to the west is owned and managed as a wildlife habitat. Beyond Parvis Bridge the towpath skirts the old grist mill (NT), where all kinds of cattle and poultry food were produced. At New Haw Lock there's a *supermarket, takeaway and gas* is available at the tool hire depot. Much of New Haw consists of 20th-C Georgian-style commuter housing. Moored craft line the east bank above New Haw Lock (with its pretty lock cottage) as the cut makes a beeline for Byfleet, cowering under the massive concrete structures and earth embankments of the M25 motorway – there is no longer any peace to be had here. The Basingstoke Canal (*see* page 15) leaves the Wey Navigation in the midst of a flurry of bridges. Beyond Parvis Bridge, where rowing boats can be hired *during the summer months* (01932 355311; www.weydays.co.uk) the Wey Navigation becomes more rural.

NAVIGATIONAL NOTES

1 Thames Lock (01932 843106). Attended. Licences, free *Information for Boat Users*, plus visitor passes. Lock handles (windlasses) for sale or hire. All those wishing to enter the lock should consult the lock keeper. Craft with draught deeper than 1ft 9in coming up from the Thames should advise the lock keeper – who may then use the pound gate to increase the water level before they enter the lock. *Open 09.00-13.00 and 14.00-18.30 or sunset*. Boats need to be at the lock at least *15 minutes* before closing time.

2 Weybridge Old Bridge – the navigation channel is clearly marked, and is the most westerly bridge-hole (furthest right) when coming upstream. The lock is immediately above the bridge and there is a winding hole below the lock.

● **Weybridge**
Surrey. All services. A commuter town in the stockbroker belt, built around the confluence of the rivers Wey and Thames – the junction is marked by a pretty iron bridge dated 1865. Weybridge represents the frontier of the suburbia which now spreads almost unbroken to London. Behind the town lie the remains of Brooklands (*see* below).
Coxes Mill *Surrey.* Overlooking Coxes Lock is a magnificent group of mostly 19th-C mill buildings, partly brick, partly concrete and partly weather-board, the best industrial architecture on the river.
Brooklands Museum Brooklands Drive, Weybridge KT13 0SL (01932 857281; www.brooklandsmuseum.com). Assembled within what remains of the Brooklands race track, the world's first purpose-built motor racing circuit, constructed by wealthy landowner Hugh Locke King in 1907. Its heyday was in the 1920s and 30s, when records were being set by the likes of Malcolm Campbell and John Cobb, driving vehicles with evocative names, such as the Delage, Bentley and Bugatti. It became very fashionable, and was known as the Ascot of Motorsport. It was also an aerodrome and an aircraft factory, and it was here that A. V. Roe made the first flight in a British aeroplane. The Sopwith Pup and Camel were developed here, and later the Hawker Hurricane and the Vickers Wellington were built here – the only Wellington that saw war time service, salvaged in 1985 from Loch Ness and restored, is on display. The outbreak of war in 1939 brought an end to racing, and aircraft production ceased in 1987. Now you can walk on part of the legendary circuit, and see historic racing cars and aircraft, including a *Concorde*, in the museum. The clubhouse is a listed building. You can also visit the Raleigh Cycle Exhibition, a reminder that cycle races were also held at Brooklands. Special events are staged throughout the year. *Open 10.00-17.00 (16.00 winter). Closed Xmas*. Charge.

● **West Byfleet**
Surrey. PO, stores, chemist, takeaways, butcher, baker, bank, fish & chips, library, garage, station. Although buried by modern commuter housing, parts of the old village can be found. The church with its bellcote is mostly late 13th-C, and the 17th-C brick manor house is an elegant delight.

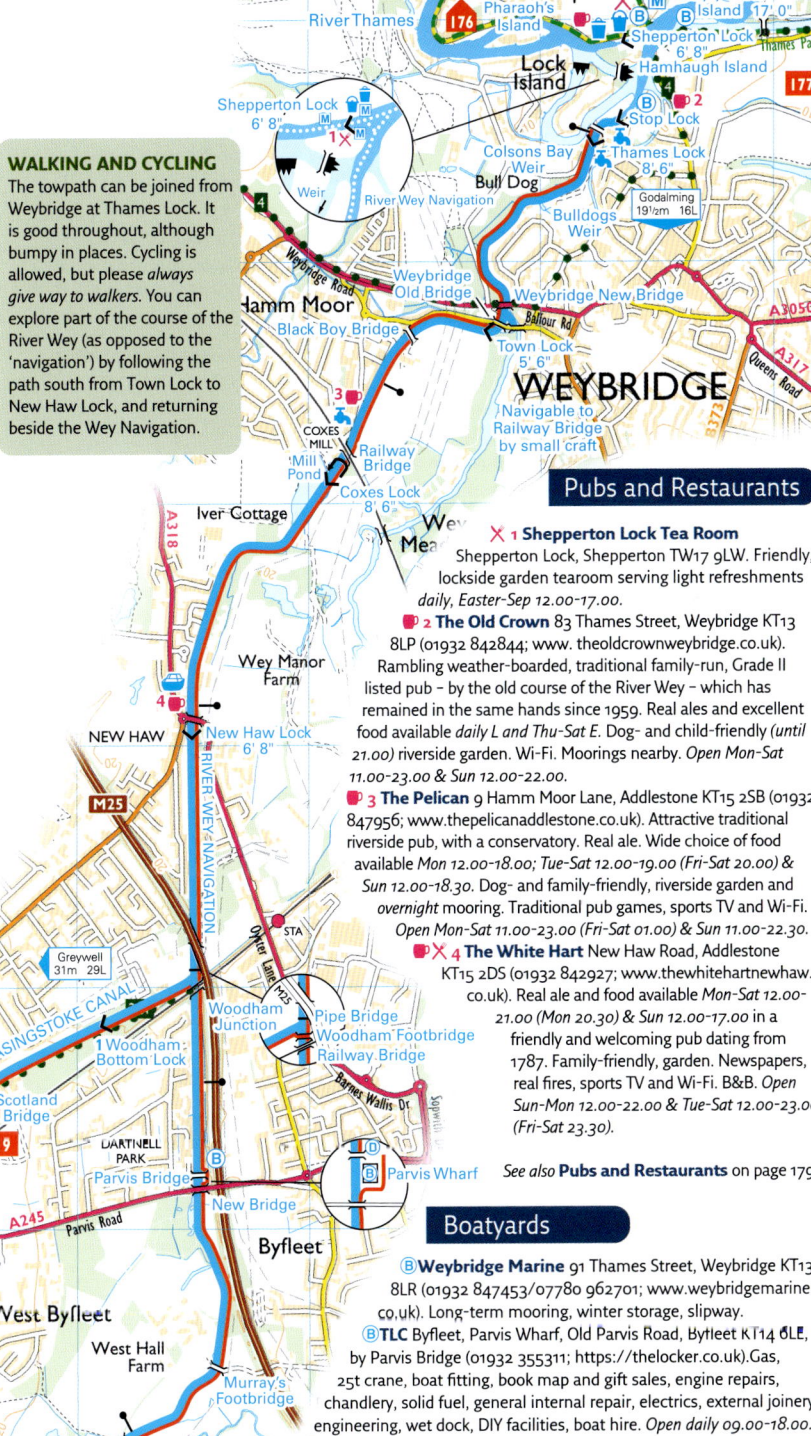

WALKING AND CYCLING
The towpath can be joined from Weybridge at Thames Lock. It is good throughout, although bumpy in places. Cycling is allowed, but please *always give way to walkers*. You can explore part of the course of the River Wey (as opposed to the 'navigation') by following the path south from Town Lock to New Haw Lock, and returning beside the Wey Navigation.

Pubs and Restaurants

1 Shepperton Lock Tea Room Shepperton Lock, Shepperton TW17 9LW. Friendly, lockside garden tearoom serving light refreshments daily, *Easter-Sep 12.00-17.00.*

2 The Old Crown 83 Thames Street, Weybridge KT13 8LP (01932 842844; www.theoldcrownweybridge.co.uk). Rambling weather-boarded, traditional family-run, Grade II listed pub – by the old course of the River Wey – which has remained in the same hands since 1959. Real ales and excellent food available *daily L and Thu-Sat E.* Dog- and child-friendly (*until 21.00*) riverside garden. Wi-Fi. Moorings nearby. *Open Mon-Sat 11.00-23.00 & Sun 12.00-22.00.*

3 The Pelican 9 Hamm Moor Lane, Addlestone KT15 2SB (01932 847956; www.thepelicanaddlestone.co.uk). Attractive traditional riverside pub, with a conservatory. Real ale. Wide choice of food available *Mon 12.00-18.00; Tue-Sat 12.00-19.00 (Fri-Sat 20.00) & Sun 12.00-18.30.* Dog- and family-friendly, riverside garden and *overnight* mooring. Traditional pub games, sports TV and Wi-Fi. *Open Mon-Sat 11.00-23.00 (Fri-Sat 01.00) & Sun 11.00-22.30.*

4 The White Hart New Haw Road, Addlestone KT15 2DS (01932 842927; www.thewhitehartnewhaw. co.uk). Real ale and food available *Mon-Sat 12.00-21.00 (Mon 20.30) & Sun 12.00-17.00* in a friendly and welcoming pub dating from 1787. Family-friendly, garden. Newspapers, real fires, sports TV and Wi-Fi. B&B. *Open Sun-Mon 12.00-22.00 & Tue-Sat 12.00-23.00 (Fri-Sat 23.30).*

See also **Pubs and Restaurants** on page 179.

Boatyards

Ⓑ **Weybridge Marine** 91 Thames Street, Weybridge KT13 8LR (01932 847453/07780 962701; www.weybridgemarine.co.uk). Long-term mooring, winter storage, slipway.

Ⓑ **TLC** Byfleet, Parvis Wharf, Old Parvis Road, Byfleet KT14 6LE, by Parvis Bridge (01932 355311; https://thelocker.co.uk). Gas, 25t crane, boat fitting, local map and gift sales, engine repairs, chandlery, solid fuel, general internal repair, electrics, external joinery, engineering, wet dock, DIY facilities, boat hire. *Open daily 09.00-18.00.*

Ⓑ **Byfleet Boat Club** 4 Old Parvis Road, West Byfleet KT14 6LE (01932 340828/07599 200508; www.byfleetboatclub.com). Rowing boat and pedalo hire *Sat-Sun & B Hols, Easter-Sep.* Charge. *Open daily 09.00-18.00.*

Pyrford

The popular Anchor pub is close to the bridge at Pyrford, with Pyrford Marina opposite; just beyond is Pyrford Lock and many colourful moored craft. The old sanitary station still retains a manual water pump which you can use only for rinsing (it is NOT drinking water). The navigation then passes Pyrford Place, with its lovely old Elizabethan summerhouse with a pagoda roof, beside a charming little riverside terrace. Except in times of flood you may pass uninterrupted through Walsham Flood Gates, the last remaining turf-sided lock on the navigation, with old style vertical paddles, overlooked by the quaintly business-like lock cottage. The large weir is to the east. The river then becomes wider and strewn with lily pads, before it splits to form a trio of islands at Newark, where the remains of Newark Priory can be seen at the water's edge. The lock cut continues to Newark Lock – above here the river winds towards Papercourt Lock, arguably the prettiest on the river, with its stepped weir and charming garden. Factories and offices line the south bank as the navigation passes under High Bridge and approaches Cart Bridge, to the west of Send. It is, surprisingly, quite peaceful – a relief considering the boundless activity all around. The restored National Trust Workshop is by the lock, often with a few sturdy barges moored opposite. Then once again the Wey resumes its rural course, passing Triggs Lock, with another attractive lock cottage, this one dating from 1770. At one time it had a blacksmith's shop attached, and to the north there used to be a small wharf. William Stevens became lock keeper here in 1812 – it was one of his descendants, Harry Stevens, who was to give the navigation to the National Trust in 1964.

- **Pyrford Village**
  Surrey. Surrounded by water meadows and trees, Pyrford remains a 'real' village. Brick cottages overlook the church, an almost intact Norman building 'built of puddingstone, dressed with clunch'; such a thing is rare in the Home Counties and is thus an even greater pleasure. The north porch is half-timbered and dates from the 16th C. Inside are wall paintings depicting scenes from the flagellation and the Passion, *c.*1200: the pulpit is 17th-C. There are many attractive 18th-C houses.
  The Summerhouse of Pyrford Place Canalside above Walsham Footbridge. Built at the end of the 17th C. The estate was inherited by Francis Egerton, who became Lord Chancellor. His son, Thomas Egerton had a secretary, John Donne, who wooed Anne More, a lonely heiress, in this summerhouse. They later married and lived at Pyrford Place. *Strictly private - NO landing.*
  Royal Horticultural Society Gardens Wisley Lane, Wisley GU23 6QB (01483 224234; www.rhs.org.uk/gardens/wisley). By footpath south east of Pigeon House Bridge to Ockham Mill, then north east towards Wisley, or by footpath from Pyrford Lock. A 200-acre botanic garden acquired by the RHS in 1904 and famous for its trials and improvements of new varieties. Notable collections of old-fashioned and new roses, rhododendrons, camellias, heathers and rock garden plants. Walled garden with tender perennial shrubs and climbers, Country Garden, Temperate Glasshouse and Garden of the Senses. *Open daily 10.00-18.00 (Sat-Sun 09.00). Charge.*
  Newark Priory Near Pyrford Green. The tall broken flint of this 12th-C Augustinian priory stand in a meadow at the river's edge, an enticing and romantic ruin. Unfortunately there is no right of navigation up to the walls.

- **Send**
  Surrey. PO, stores, off-licence, takeaway. The church lies close to the River Wey and well to the south west of the main centre. Although nicely sited amongst trees and 18th-C houses, the village looks at its best from the river. Stores *open daily 06.00-22.00 (Sun 07.00).*

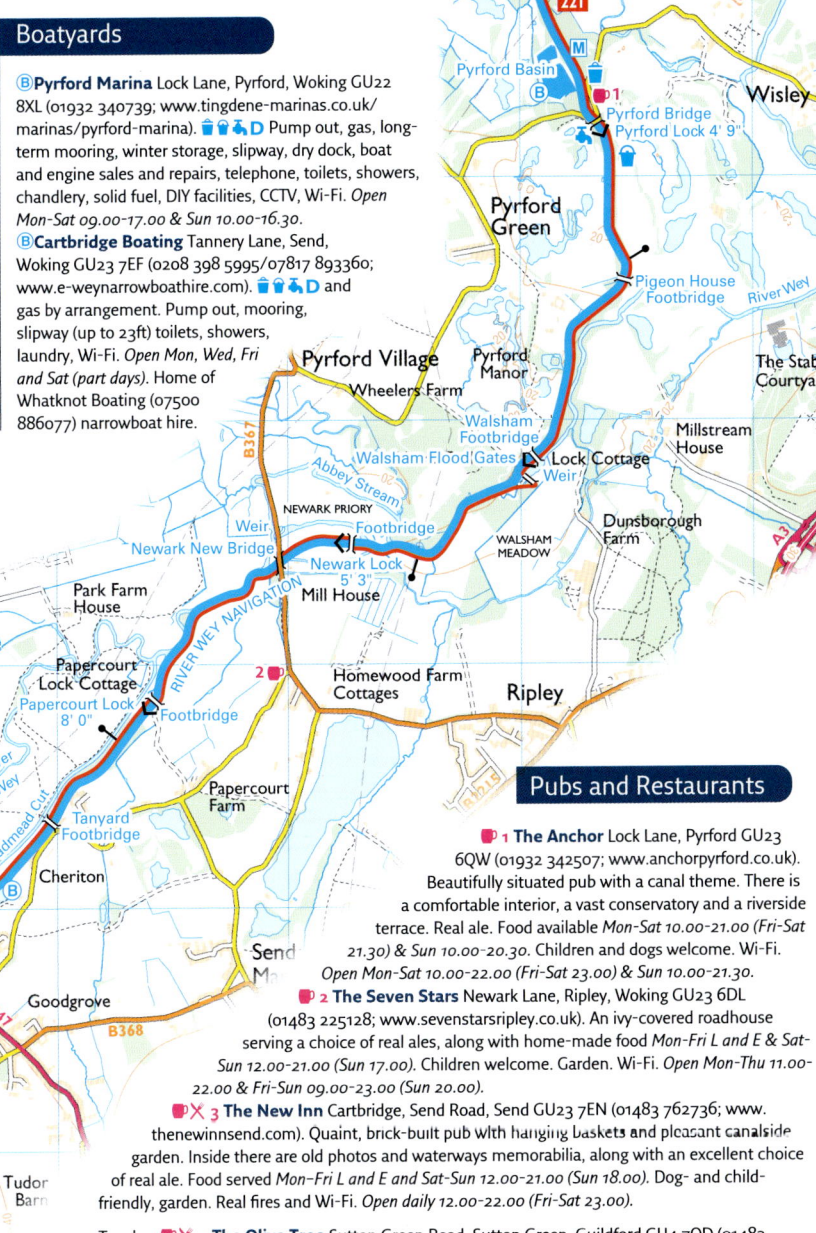

Boatyards

ⓑ **Pyrford Marina** Lock Lane, Pyrford, Woking GU22 8XL (01932 340739; www.tingdene-marinas.co.uk/marinas/pyrford-marina). 🛒🚻♿D Pump out, gas, long-term mooring, winter storage, slipway, dry dock, boat and engine sales and repairs, telephone, toilets, showers, chandlery, solid fuel, DIY facilities, CCTV, Wi-Fi. *Open Mon-Sat 09.00-17.00 & Sun 10.00-16.30.*

ⓑ **Cartbridge Boating** Tannery Lane, Send, Woking GU23 7EF (0208 398 5995/07817 893360; www.e-weynarrowboathire.com). 🛒🚻♿D and gas by arrangement. Pump out, mooring, slipway (up to 23ft) toilets, showers, laundry, Wi-Fi. *Open Mon, Wed, Fri and Sat (part days).* Home of Whatknot Boating (07500 886077) narrowboat hire.

Pubs and Restaurants

🍺 1 **The Anchor** Lock Lane, Pyrford GU23 6QW (01932 342507; www.anchorpyrford.co.uk). Beautifully situated pub with a canal theme. There is a comfortable interior, a vast conservatory and a riverside terrace. Real ale. Food available *Mon-Sat 10.00-21.00 (Fri-Sat 21.30) & Sun 10.00-20.30.* Children and dogs welcome. Wi-Fi. *Open Mon-Sat 10.00-22.00 (Fri-Sat 23.00) & Sun 10.00-21.30.*

🍺 2 **The Seven Stars** Newark Lane, Ripley, Woking GU23 6DL (01483 225128; www.sevenstarsripley.co.uk). An ivy-covered roadhouse serving a choice of real ales, along with home-made food *Mon-Fri L and E & Sat-Sun 12.00-21.00 (Sun 17.00).* Children welcome. Garden. Wi-Fi. *Open Mon-Thu 11.00-22.00 & Fri-Sun 09.00-23.00 (Sun 20.00).*

🍺✕ 3 **The New Inn** Cartbridge, Send Road, Send GU23 7EN (01483 762736; www.thenewinnsend.com). Quaint, brick-built pub with hanging baskets and pleasant canalside garden. Inside there are old photos and waterways memorabilia, along with an excellent choice of real ale. Food served *Mon-Fri L and E and Sat-Sun 12.00-21.00 (Sun 18.00).* Dog- and child-friendly, garden. Real fires and Wi-Fi. *Open daily 12.00-22.00 (Fri-Sat 23.00).*

Try also: 🍺✕ 4 **The Olive Tree** Sutton Green Road, Sutton Green, Guildford GU4 7QD (01483 729999; www.theolivetreesuttongreen.co.uk).

NAVIGATIONAL NOTES

1. All the locks on this section are unattended.
2. Walsham and Worsfold Flood Gates are normally left open, except in times of flood. When closed the chamber should be used as a normal lock, unless flood boards instruct otherwise.
3. Be wary of the cross current below Papercourt Lock.
4. For up to date information on river conditions visit: www.riverweyconditionsnt.wordpress.com.

Guildford

The navigation now begins to sweep around Sutton Place, and comes very close to the A3, with its constant rumble of traffic. Care should be exercised at Broadoak Bridge (note the towline roller on the corner) and Bower's Lock (*see* below). The run to Stoke Lock is tree-lined, but it is now very clear that Guildford is being approached and the scene is becoming increasingly urban. A few willows overhang by Stoke Bridge, but soon all is back gardens, roads and factories. The scene gradually improves and, at Dapdune Wharf, the National Trust has established a visitor centre, with a fine restored Wey barge amongst other exhibits. At Walnut Footbridge the Odeon Cinema is riverside. At Onslow Bridge the change of scene is completed: the town turns to face the water – and what a jolly scene it is – with riverside walks, a handsome mill, the theatre, pubs and restaurants, all overlooked by the castle. Note especially the rare treadwheel crane standing on what was the old Guildford Town Wharf: from here the Wey Navigation becomes the Godalming Navigation and leaves Guildford in an ideal setting, with parkland to the east and pleasant private gardens glimpsed over high walls to the west. A footbridge marks the site of the old St Catherine's Ferry on the Pilgrims' Way, and a small stream spills into the river here below a pretty grotto, where those who pass are 'treading the path trod by Geoffrey Chaucer's Canterbury Pilgrims in the reign of King Edward the Third'. Just beyond is St Catherine's Sands, a favourite haunt of the local children during warm school holidays. The old Guildford Boat House is a charming Victorian building.

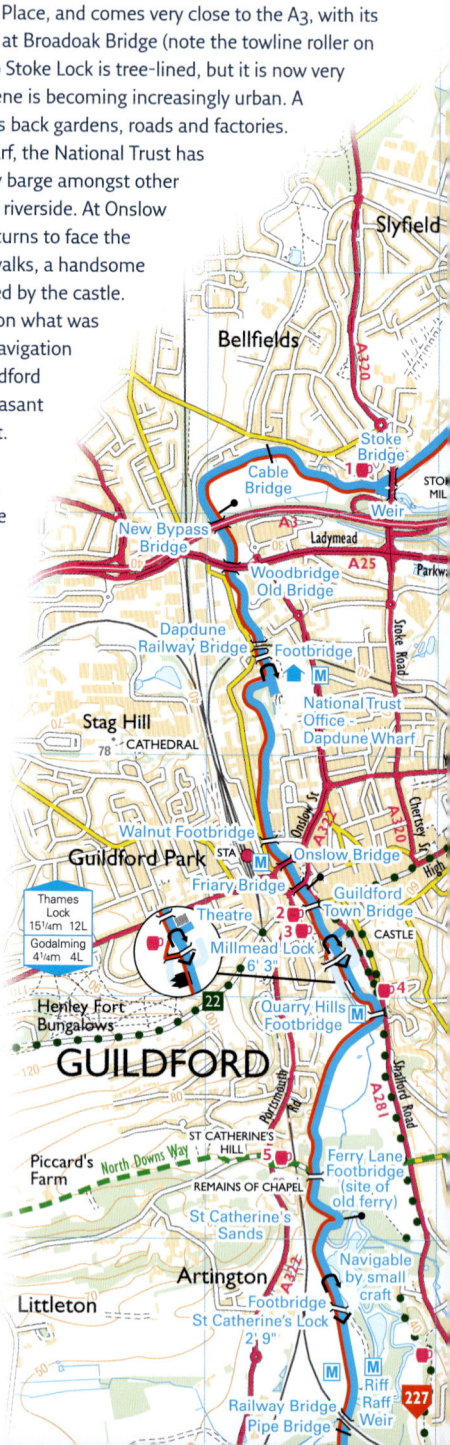

NAVIGATIONAL NOTES

1. At Broadoak Bridge pass through the arch closest to the towing path.
2. When approached from downstream Bower's Lock is to the left before the footbridge. When locking down, take the sharp blind turn to the right with care.
3. Keep clear of the weir above St Catherine's Lock.

WALKING AND CYCLING

There are excellent short walks through the Riverside Park and Shalford Meadows (*see* page 226). The North Downs Way, which stretches 141 miles between Farnham and Dover, crosses the navigation by The Old Ferry Footbridge. *See also* Wey & Arun Junction Canal page 202.

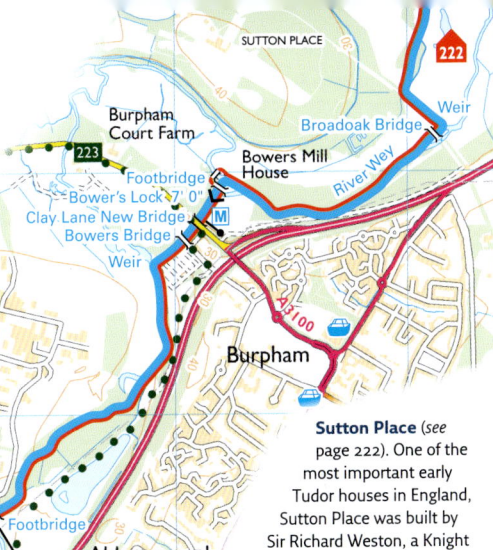

Wey & Godalming Navigations

Guildford

Sutton Place (see page 222). One of the most important early Tudor houses in England, Sutton Place was built by Sir Richard Weston, a Knight of Bath, Gentleman of the Privy Chamber and Under Treasurer of England. It is a brick house, with terracotta ornamentation, built originally around a square; one side was demolished in 1786 leaving the plan more open. The house is an interesting mixture of Renaissance and English styles, and was once owned by the late Paul Getty. Private.

● **Guildford**
Surrey. All services. The town is built on the steep sides of the Wey valley and so its centre is very compact, overlooked on the west by the bulk of the cathedral, and on the east by the castle ruins, where the public gardens contain a life-size statue of Alice stepping through the looking glass, celebrating the town's association with Lewis Carroll (see page 226). The castle grounds continue as Castle Cliffe Gardens: 'The Chestnuts', where the author once lived, is close by. The best parts of the town are around the traffic-free cobbled High Street, which leads steeply down to the river, where there are interesting mill and wharf buildings, including the last tread wheel operated crane in existence. The High Street is rich with good buildings of all periods; facing each other at the top, the Baroque splendour of the 17th-C Guildhall and the 18th-C simplicity of Holy Trinity Church demonstrate this rich diversity. The University of Surrey has been developed on the slopes of the cathedral hill; the buildings show a better feeling for architecture than many other modern universities. The strength of Guildford as a cultural centre is shown by the modern Yvonne Arnaud Theatre, standing on an attractive riverside site, surrounded by trees but still in the town centre, and the number of festivals held here throughout the summer. Guildford seems to have been by tradition a popular and self-contained town, and this feeling still survives.

Pubs and Restaurants

There are lots of pubs, restaurants and tearooms to choose from in Guildford. The following are all close to the navigation.

● **1 The Row Barge** 7 Riverside, Guildford GU1 1LW (01403 958488; www.therowbargeguildford.com). Beside Stoke Bridge. This live rugby and sports pub has a pleasant garden and moorings, close to the Guildford Waterside Centre. Real ale is served together with food Mon and Fri-Sat 12.00-19.00; Tue-Thu 12.00-19.00 (Thu 21.00) & Sun 12.00-17.00. Live music Sat. Dog- and child-friendly (until 21.00), garden. Traditional pub games, real fires, sports TV, newspapers and Wi-Fi. Open 12.00-00.00 (Fri-Sat 01.00).

● **2 The White House** 8 High Street, Guildford GU2 4AJ (01483 302006; www.whitehouseguildford.co.uk). A smart pub in an attractive riverside building, with a shady terrace by the water and the largest pub garden in Guildford. Real ale. Meals served daily 12.00-22.00 (Sun 19.00). Children and dogs welcome. Wi-Fi. Open Mon-Sat 11.00-23.00 & Sun 12.00-22.00.

● **3 The Britannia** 9 Millmead, Guildford GU2 4BE (01483 572160; www.britanniaguildford.co.uk). Overlooking the lock, this is a handsome red brick pub. Real ale. Food served 12.00-21.00 (Sun 19.00). Dog- and child-friendly (until 21.00), outside seating. Traditional pub games, real fires and Wi-Fi. Open daily 12.00-22.00 (Thu-Sat 23.00).

● ✕ **4 The Weyside** Shalford Road, Millbrook, Guildford GU1 3XJ (01483 568024; www.theweyside.co.uk). Large riverside pub with a garden, conservatory and terrace. Real ale and food available daily 12.00-21.30. Dog- and child-friendly, garden. Wi-Fi. Open 11.00-00.00.

● ✕ **5 Ye Olde Ship Inn** Portsmouth Road, Guildford GU2 4EB (01483 575731; www.yeoldeshipinn.pub). Up the old Pilgrims' Way, this friendly pub serves real ale and interesting food cooked using a wood-burning oven available Tue-Thu L and E & Fri-Sun 12.00-21.00 (Sun 19.00). Dog- and child-friendly (until 21.00), garden. Real fires and Wi-Fi. Open Tue L and E; Wed-Sat 12.00-23.00 (Fri-Sat 11.00) & Sun 11.00-21.00.

225

Riverside Park Nature Reserve Guildford GU1 1QE (www.guildford.gov.uk/riverside). By Stoke Lock. A natural 75-acre countryside park, consisting of four main habitats – meadow, wetland, open water and woodland – containing oak, ash and chestnut, an assortment of reeds, sedges and grassland, with bluebells and red campions in the spring. Newts, frogs and toads, dragonflies and damselflies can be found near the lake, along with grass snakes (which are harmless), all managed with conservation in mind. Picnic tables.

Guildford Cathedral Stag Hill, Guildford GU2 7UP (01483 444751; www.guildford-cathedral.org.uk). The brick mass of the cathedral overlooks the town – it is an uncompromising and unsubtle thing, the last fling of the Gothic revival. Designed by Edward Maufe in 1932, it was only completed in 1961, and sadly reveals its period all too clearly. From the outside it is a mixture of cinema, power station and church; the inside is a complete contrast – a wealth of detail, and delicate use of shape and form, far more genuinely Gothic in feeling. Interesting furniture, fittings, glass and statuary. Café and shop. *Open Mon-Fri 08.30-18.30 (Tue 07.30 and Wed & Sat 18.00) & Sun 07.30-19.00.* Donations.

Guildford House Gallery 155 High Street, Guildford GU1 3AJ (01483 444751; www.guildford.gov.uk/article/17187). The building dates from 1660, and contains fine decorative plasterwork, and a fine carved staircase. Permanent and visiting exhibitions. Craft shop. *Open Tue-Sat 10.00-16.30. Free.*

Guildford Castle Castle Street, Guildford GU1 3UQ. The huge motte dates from the 11th C, topped by a tower keep c.1170. It remains an imposing ruin.

Guildford Museum Castle Arch, Quarry Street, Guildford GU1 3SX (01483 444751; www.guildford.gov.uk/article/21724). Prehistoric, Roman and Saxon exhibits along with displays of Victorian life. Space is also devoted to Lewis Carroll. *Open Wed-Sat 12.00-16.30. Free.*

The Undercroft 72 High Street, Guildford GU1 3HE (01483 444751). A vaulted medieval basement 13 x 19ft with a rib-vaulted ceiling, dating from the 13th C, with an exhibition illustrating life in medieval Guildford. *Open May-Sep, Wed and Sun 14.00-16.00.* Free.

Lewis Carroll's Grave You can find the grave of this Victorian author, who was born Charles Lutwidge Dodgson in Daresbury (*see* Guide 5), near the chapel in the Mount Cemetery GU2 4JB which is to the south west of Onslow Bridge. Visit www.guildford.gov.uk/themountcemetery and www.lewiscarrollsociety.org.uk for further details.

Guided Walks Contact the TIC (*below*). Topics include Historic and Unknown Guildford, plus Ghosts and Legends, and Lewis Carroll. *May-Sep Sun, Mon and Wed 14.30 and Thu 19.30.*

Shalford Meadows East of St Catherine's Sands. There are rich plant communities in this riverside water-meadow.

Dapdune Wharf Visitor Centre Wharf Road, Guildford GU1 4RR (01483 561389; www.nationaltrust.org.uk/visit/surrey/river-wey-and-godalming-navigations-and-dapdune-wharf). Towpath access is via the footbridge beside the railway bridge. This was once the barge building centre of the River Wey Navigation, and has been tastefully restored with a stable, smithy, barge building shed and old cottages. Displays tell the story of the people who lived and worked here. Some handsome restored craft can be seen outside, including the barge *Reliance*, built 1931-2, one of 11 Wey barges built here by the Stevens family. It traded between the Wey and London Docks until it hit Cannon Street Bridge, in London, and sank. It languished on the mud flats at Leigh-on-Sea in Essex, to be later salvaged and returned to Dapdune for restoration. Bookshop and tearoom. *Open Mar-Oct 11.00-17.00.* Charge.

Tourist Information Centre 155 High Street, Guildford GU1 3AJ (01483 444333; www.guildford.gov.uk/article/25590). *Open Tue-Sat 10.00-16.30.*

Boatyards

ⓑ**Farncombe Boat House** Catteshall Lock, Godalming GU7 1NH (01483 421306; www.farncombeboats.co.uk). 🚽 D Pump out, gas, narrowboat hire, day-boat hire, rowing boats, long-term mooring, boat building, boat and engine sales and repairs, toilets, books and maps.

WALKING AND CYCLING
Stretches of the towpath approaching Godalming consist of very soft sand, which is not very kind to bicycles! Be warned. You can explore a section of the Wey & Arun Junction Canal on foot by following the path south east from Broadford Bridge and then returning across Bramley Common to the Godalming Navigation, where you cross Unstead Bridge and head north along the towpath. *See also* Wey & Arun Junction Canal - **Walking and Cycling** - page 203.

PADDLING
The National Trust, as owner and operator of this waterway, provides useful information to paddlers at www.nationaltrust.org.uk/visit/surrey/river-wey-and-godalming-navigations-and-dapdune-wharf/river-wey-information-for-canoeists, while www.gopaddling.info/rivers/river-wey offers further helpful insight.

Godalming

The river passes Shalford through flat meadow land, and by former riverside mills above the low Broadford Bridge. There are craft moored here and at Gun's Mouth, the entrance to the unnavigable Wey & Arun Junction Canal (see page 202). A fine wooded stretch below Unstead Lock ends abruptly, an indication that the main roads are closer than you might think. The gardens of very smart residences line the Farncombe bank as the river approaches Catteshall Lock, the highest on the river and the furthest south on the linked navigable system. There are good *moorings* at Lammas Lands on the towpath side above here, and it is only a short walk to Town Bridge, the usual head of navigation and the end of the Godalming Navigation. Those who left the Thames to journey to Godalming will be sad their voyage is over, as the Wey Navigations provide a priceless rural lung, and one of the few local refuges from the stress of Surrey. Their preservation is of the highest priority.

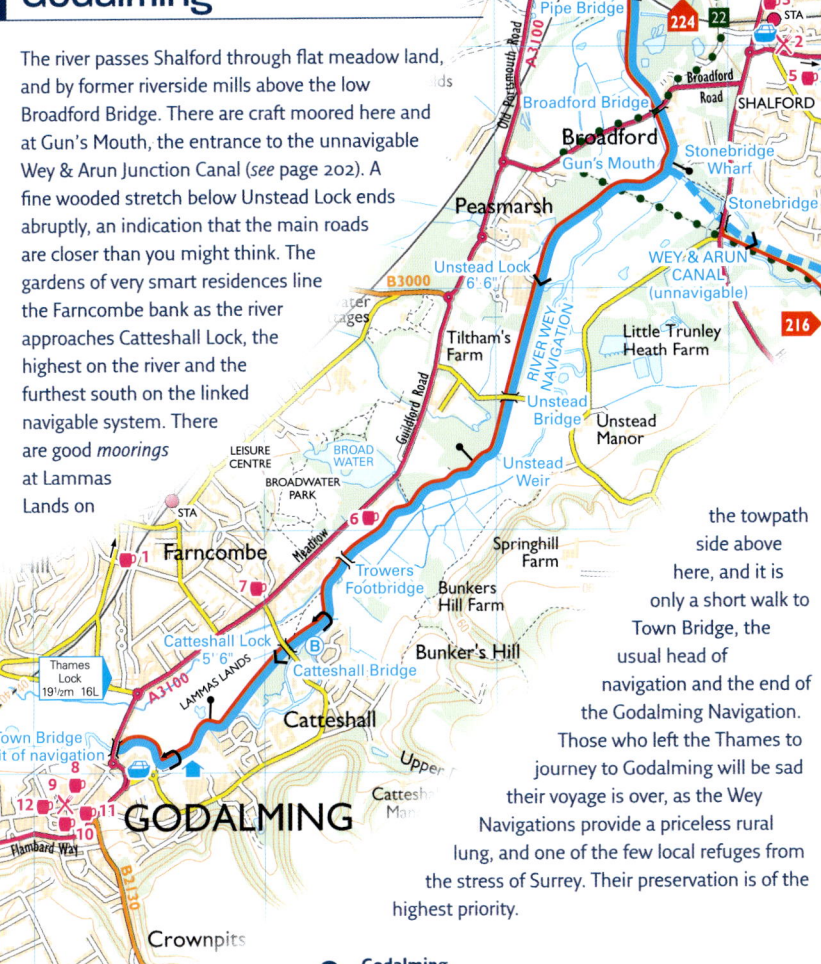

● Godalming
Surrey. All services. The head of navigation is near the heavy stone bridge to the north east of the town centre. By tradition a cloth-making town, Godalming has developed in a haphazard way over the years, but its busy streets have plenty to offer. At its centre, The Town Hall, known as 'the Pepperpot', was built in 1814 by John Perry, a local man. It is a modestly handsome building with an open ground floor, and is ideally situated. The area around it was the first in the world to benefit from electric street lighting. The church of St Peter and St Paul, with its rare and tall leaded 13th-C spire, gives the town a dramatic skyline.

NAVIGATIONAL NOTES

1 Broadford Bridge is low, with only 6ft 4in maximum headroom.
2 In Godalming, at the last winding hole, navigators are advised to wind with their bows to the towpath side of the navigation.
3 Small, shallow draught craft may be able to pass under Town Bridge to reach Boarden Bridge – but note that it is beyond the navigable limit, and there is a weir just above the railway bridge.

Pubs and Restaurants (page 227)

🍺 **1 The Cricketers** 37 Nightingale Road, Farncombe, Godalming GU7 2HU (01483 424860; www.facebook.com/cricketers.farncombe). Once the home of the first English cricket captain to tour Australia, this Victorian pub now dispenses real ale and serves food (including a homemade pie *of the day*) *L and E* (*not Sun E*). Dog- and child-friendly, garden. Newspapers, real fires, sports TV and Wi-Fi. *Open Mon-Sat 12.00-23.00 (Fri-Sat 23.30) & Sun 12.00-22.00.*

✕ **2 The Snooty Fox** 3-5 Kings Road, Shalford GU4 8JU (01483 303038; www.thesnootyfox.uk). Bistro-style coffee shop serving seasonal dishes, breakfast, baguettes, burgers, soup, jacket potatoes, tea and freshly ground coffee. Children's menu. *Open daily 07.00-16.00 (Sat-Sun 08.00).*

🍺✕ **3 The Queen Victoria** Station Row, Shalford GU4 8BY (01483 893030; www.thequeenvic.pub). First opened as a beer house in 1850, becoming a pub in 1864, this pub now serves real ale and food *Wed-Sun L and E (not Sun E)*. Dog- and child-friendly, patio garden. Real fires and Wi-Fi. *Open Mon-Sat 12.00-23.00 (Fri-Sat 00.00) & Sun 12.00-22.00.*

🍺✕ **4 The Seahorse** 52-54 The Street, Shalford GU4 8BU (01483 514351; www.theseahorseguildford.co.uk). Although built as a pub in the early 18th C, the Seahorse came close to playing an entirely different role in 1940. With the immanent threat of invasion, it found itself on the GHQ Stopline: a ring of defences designed to slow down a German advance on London. Today things are far more sedate and this hostelry now serves real ale and food *Mon-Sat 12.00-22.00 (Fri-Sat 22.30) & Sun 12.00-21.00*. Dog- and family-friendly, garden. Real fires and Wi-Fi. *Open daily 11.00-23.00 (Sun 22.30).*

🍺✕ **5 The Percy Arms** 75 Dorking Road, Chilworth GU4 8NP (01483 561765; www.thepercyarms.net). South African owned and themed pub, serving British cuisine with a South African twist *daily L and E* from several extensive menus. Real ale. Dog- and family-friendly, garden. Summer barbecues. Take away and butchery. Wi-Fi. B&B. *Open 08.00-22.00 (Sat-Sun 09.00).*

🍺✕ **6 The Ragged Robin** Guildford Road, Farncombe GU7 3UX (01483 427134; www.boutiquehotelier.com/the-ragged-robin-godalming-surrey). Riverside hotel with garden currently undergoing extensive renovation. Visit the website for details of its *re-opening* as a gastro-pub with rooms *in 2025*.

🍺 **7 The Mead Row** 77 Meadrow, Farncombe GU7 3JG (01483 425642; www.facebook.com/leathernbottle). Small locals' pub serving real ale and, until food is available, you may order a local takeaway and the pub will provide a plate and cutlery! Dog- and child-friendly, garden. Newspapers, real fires, sports TV and Wi-Fi. *Open 15.00-23.00 (Fri-Sun 12.00).*

🍺✕ **8 The King's Arms & Royal Hotel** 22-25 High Street, Godalming GU7 1EB (01483 421545; www.kingsarmsandroyal.co.uk). Traditional coaching inn which was visited by Peter the Great in 1698. Real ale. Food served *Mon-Thu L and E & Fri-Sun 12.00-20.30*. Brunch is available *Mon-Sun 07.00-12.00* and afternoon tea (booking essential) *daily 14.00-18.00*. Dog- and family-friendly, garden. Wi-Fi. B&B. *Open Mon-Sat 10.00-23.00 & Sun 12.00-22.00.*

✕ **9 Piazza Firenze** 28 High Street, Godalming GU7 1DZ (01483 418675; www.piazzafirenze.com). Friendly, welcoming establishment serving delicious, authentic Italian food from a reasonably priced menu. Attentive staff. Child-friendly. *Open Mon-Sat 11.00-23.00 & Sun 12.00-22.30.*

🍺 **10 The Volunteer** 5 Wharf Street, Godalming GU7 1NN (01483 419643). Having recently led a somewhat chequered career, this single-roomed community pub is now back in business serving real ale. Dog- and family-friendly. Sports TV and Wi-Fi. *Open Mon-Thu 16.00-23.00 (Thu 00.00) & Fri-Sun 12.00-00.00 (Sun 22.00).*

🍺✕ **11 The Sun Inn** 1 Wharf Street, Godalming GU7 1NN (01483 415505). Popular pub majoring on sports TV and live *weekend* music. Traditional, home-made pub meals are served *Tue-Thu L and E (not Tue L) & Fri-Sun 12.00-18.00 (Sun 16.00)*. Real ale. Dog- and child-friendly (*until 21.00*) outside seating. Traditional pub games, real fires, newspapers, sports TV and Wi-Fi. B&B. *Open Mon-Thu 11.00-23.00 (Thu 00.00) Fri-Sat 11.00-01.00 & Sun 12.00-23.00.*

🍺 **12 The Jack Phillips** 48-56 High Street, Godalming GU7 1DY (01483 521750; www.jdwetherspoon.com/pubs/the-jack-phillips-godalming). A modern building but with hints of an Art Deco saloon aboard an ocean-going liner, this pub is named after a heroic wireless operator who went down with the Titanic. Now dispensing a wide range of inexpensive real ales and food *daily 08.00-23.00*. Family-friendly, outside seating. Wi-Fi. *Open Mon-Thu 08.00-23.00 (Thu 0.00) & Fri-Sun 08.00-01.00 (Sun 00.00).*

See also Wey & Arun Junction Canal - **Pubs and Restaurants** - page 217.

PADDLING

The National Trust provides detailed trail information along the river at www.nationaltrust.org.uk/visit/surrey/river-wey-and-godalming-navigations-and-dapdune-wharf/guildford-to-st-catherines-lock-canoe-trail while there is canoe and kayak hire, together with comprehensive instruction, to be found at Fluid Adventures, Unit 1A, Keynor Farm, Sidlesham, Chichester PO20 7LL (01243 942777; www.fluidadventures.co.uk/contact/#river-wey). They are open *daily 09.00-17.00* and operate from the National Trust base at Dapdune Wharf, Guildford GU1 4RR. For a comprehensive range of paddleboarding instruction (and hire) based at Godalming, visit Roar Outdoor (07983 570764/07834 910510; www.roaroutdoor.co.uk) while further insight into paddling the River Wey is available at www.paddlecrawl.co.uk/river-wey.html.

INDEX

A la Ronde 52
Abbey Ruins 108
Abingdon 80, 127, 130, 144-147
Adam, Robert 71
Adversane 206
Afold 211
Afold Crossways 214
Albert Bridge 174, 193
Albert Embankment 196
Aldermaston 104, 105
Aldermaston House 104
Aldermaston Wharf 104
Aldershot 17, 24, 26
Aldershot Military Museum 27
Alfred Jewel 37
All Cannings 85, 86
All Saints Church, Chelsea 193
Allington 86
Alton Barnes 86
Alton Priors Church 85
Amberley 204
Amberley Castle 204
Amberley Working Museum & Heritage Centre 204
Ankerwyke Priory 175
Appleton 134
Army Catering Corps 26
Army Medical Services Museum 26
Arun Navigation 202-216
Ash Vale 24, 26
Ash Wharf Bridge 24
Ashmolean Museum 142
Aston 155
Austen, Jane 160
Avington 96
Avoncliff 78
Avoncliff Aqueduct 73
Avon Gorge 58, 60
Avonmouth 58, 60
Avonmouth Dock 61
Avon Valley 71, 74, 76
Avon Valley Railway 67
Avon Walkway 63
Ayshford Court and Chapel 45

Bablock Hythe 136
Baldwin, Thomas 71
Bampton 132
Bampton in the Bush 133
Bankside 196
Barcombe 122-125
Barley Mow Bridge 28
Barn Elms 192
Barn Elms Reservoir 199
Barnes Railway Bridge 191
Barnes Terrace 191

Barnfield Theatre 55
Basildon 154, 155
Basildon Park 154
Basingstoke Canal 17-31, 177, 203, 220
Basingstoke Canal Authority 25
Basingstoke Canal Museum 26
Bath 59, 66, 69, 71, 84
Bath Abbey 71
Bathampton 69, 72
Bathford Church 69, 73
Bathpool 34, 35
Bathpool Swing Bridge 34
Battersea Park 196
Battersea Power Station 192
Battersea Railway Bridge 193
Battle of Newbury, The 100
Battle of Roundway Down 84
Battle of Sedgemoor 38
Bay of Fundy 60
Beale Park 154, 155
Begum Shah Jehan 18
Benson 150
Berkshire Downs 108
Bicton Park Botanical Gardens 52
Billingshurst 210
Binsey 137
Bisham Abbey 166, 169
Bishop Cannings Church 85
Bishop's Park 179
Bitton 66
Blackfriars Bridge 197
Blackfriars Railway Bridge 197
Blackwater Valley Road 24
Blake Museum 38
Bloomers Hole Footbridge 130
Boehill Bridge 45
Borough Marsh 158
Boulter's Lock 168
Bourne End 169
Boveney Lock 170, 172
Bradford Basin 76
Bradford on Avon 76, 78
Bradford on Avon Lock 79
Bradford Upper Wharf 78
Bramley 216
Bray Lock 170, 172
Brentford Dock Marine 188
Brewhouse Theatre and Arts Centre 36
Bridgwater & Taunton Canal 32-40
Bridgwater 38-40

Bridgwater Docks 40
Brimslade Farm 90
Bristol & Taunton Canal Navigation 32
Bristol 32, 34, 45, 58, 59, 62-66, 69
Bristol Cathedral 64
Bristol Industrial Museum 64
Bristol Zoo Gardens 64
Broadford Bridge 227
Broadoak Bridge 224
Brooklands Museum 20, 220
Brookwood 22
Brookwood Bottom Lock 22
Brookwood Cemetery 22
Brookwood Lye 22
Bruce Trust 92
Bruce Tunnel 90, 91
Brunel, I.K. 50-52, 62, 152, 154
Buckland 133
Buckland Bridge 45
Buckland House 133
Bull's Lock 102
Bulstake Stream 137
Burbage Wharf 90, 91
Burghfield Bridge 106
Burslecombe 41, 45
Buscot Lock 104, 130
Buscot Wharf 130, 131
Bushy Park 180
Butler's Wharf 200
Byfleet 220

Caen Hill 59, 76, 82
Caen Hill Lock 85
Campbell, Malcolm 18
Canary Wharf 199, 200
Cannon Street Railway Bridge 197
Carlyle's House 193
Cart Bridge 206
Cassington Cut 137
Castlenau 191
Catteshall Lock 227
Caversham 160
Caversham Bridge 156, 158
Central London 193-197
Chambers, W.I. 18
Chard Canal 34, 35
Charing Cross Railway Bridge 197
Chelsea Bridge 197
Chelsea Embankment 193
Chelsea Harbour 193
Chequers Bridge 28
Cherry Garden Pier 200
Chertsey 177, 178

Cheyne Walk 193
Chiltern Hills 108
Chilworth Manor 216
Chimney 132
Chiswick 190
Chiswick Bridge 188, 190
Chiswick House 190
Chobham Road Bridge 18
Cholsey 152
Christ Church Cathedral 142
Christ Church Gallery 142
Christ Church Meadow 140, 142
City Museum & Art Gallery 64
City of London 195
Claverton 73
Claverton Manor 73
Claverton Pumping Station 73
Cleeve Lock 154
Cleopatra's Needle 194
Cleveland House 69
Clifton Cut 145
Clifton Hampden Bridge 145, 146
Clifton Suspension Bridge Visitor Centre 64
Cliveden 166, 169
Cockle Sand 50
Cody, Samuel 24, 26
Coldwaltham 207
Collumpton 41
Colt Hill Bridge 30
Colthorp Bridge 102
Compasses Bridge 214
Cookham 169
Cookham Bridge 166
Cookham Dean 169
Cooper's Hill 174, 175
Copse Lock 96
Cornwall 50
Cotswolds 126, 130
Coultershaw Heritage Site & Beam Pump 208
County Lock 106
Coxes Mill 220
Cranleigh 214
Cranleigh Arts Centre 214
Creech St Michael 32, 34, 35
Crofton 90, 91
Crofton Pumping Station 100
Crookham 28-29
Crowmarsh 148
Crownhill Bridge 42
Culham Cut 144
Culham Lock 145
Cumber Lake 104
Cutty Sark 201

Dapdune Wharf 224, 226
Datchet 175
Dawlish 50
Day's Lock 148
Deepcut 22, 24
Denford Mill 96
Desborough Cut 177
Design Museum 200
Devizes 59, 76, 80, 82, 84
Devon Wildlife Trust 55
Docklands 200
Donnington Road Bridge 140
Dorchester 145, 148-151
Dorchester Abbey Museum 150
Dorchester Bridge 148
Dorney Court and Church 172
Douai Abbey and School 103
Double Bridge 28
Double Locks 49
Down Place 172
Drewett Lock 96
Drungewick Lock 212
Dudley Weatherley Jubilee Bridge 41
Duke's Cut 137
Dundas Aqueduct 73, 74
Dunmill Lock 96
Dunsfold 214
Dunsfold Aerodrome 214
Dyke Hill 148

East London 198-200
East Manley Farm 42
Easton-in-Gordano 61
Eaton Hastings 131
Eel Pie Island 184, 187
Eelmoor Bridge 24
Eelmoor Flash 24
Elmbridge Museum 18
Ermine Street 126
Eton 173
Eton College 171, 173
Eugenie, Empress 26
Exeter 32, 34, 45, 48-50, 54-56
Exeter Cathedral 55
Exeter Picture House 56
Exeter Quay 56
Exeter Ship Canal 32, 48-57
Exminster 52
Exminster Marshes 52, 54
Exmouth 48, 52
Exton 52
Eynsham Lock 137

Faringdon House 132
Farmoor Reservoir 137
Farnborough 24, 26
Farnborough Airport 26
Farncombe Bank 227
Farnham Potteries 219

Father Thames 128
Fawley Court 164
Fenacre 45
Firepool Lock 32, 34
Fishers Farm Park 210
Fishmongers' Hall 195
Fleet 28
Floating Harbour 64
Fobney Lock 106
Fobney Meadow 106
Folly Bridge 140
Folly Farm 105
Formosa Island 166
Fosse Way 126
Freshford 74
Frimley Green 22
Frost Fairs 127
Froxfield 92, 93, 94
Fry's Island 158
Fulham Palace 189, 191
Fulham Railway Bridge 191

Garrick's Ait 180
Gatehampton Railway Bridge 154
Georgian House 64
Gloucester & Sharpness Canal 60, 130
Godalming 227
Godalming Navigation 219, 227
Godstow 137, 138
Godston Abbey 137
Goring 152, 154, 155
Gosden Aqueduct 216
Grafton Lock 128
Grand Union Canal 184, 188
Grand Western Canal 41-47
Great Bedwyn 91, 92, 94
Great Bottom Flash 24
Greatham Bridge 206
Great Stink, The 127
Great Tithe Barn 78
Greenway Bridge 43
Greenwich 200
Greenwich Park 201
Greenwich Tunnel 200
Greywell 30-31
Greywell Tunnel 17, 26, 30
Greywell Village 30
Guildford 224, 225
Guildford Castle 226
Guildford Cathedral 226
Guildford House Gallery 226
Guildford Museum 226
Guildford Town Wharf 208
Gun's Mouth 227

Ha'penny Bridge 128
Halberton 45, 46

Halberton Village 43
Ham House 184, 187
Ham Island 174
Ham Moor 220
Hambleden Lock 155, 164
Hammersmith Bridge 188, 191
Hammersmith Terrace 191
Hampton 182
Hampton Bridge 180
Hampton Church 180
Hampton Court 180-183
Hampton Court Palace 182
Hampton Green 183
Hamsey 122
Hamstead Lock 96
Hamstead Park 96, 100
Hanham Lock 66
Hardwick House 156
Harleyford Manor 164
Harmsworth, A.J. 17
Heale's Lock 102
Hedsor 169
Hedsor Wharf 166
Henley-on-Thames 127, 163-165
Hermitage Bridge 22
Hexagon 109
High Bridge 106
Hilperton 76, 78
Hinton Waldrist and Longworth 134
Hocktide Ceremonies 94
Holburne Museum 71
Holcombe Rogus 46
Hole Footbridge 128
Holm Island 175
Holy Trinity Church 78
Home Park 171
Hopkins, Gerard Manley 42
Hore, John 58
Horsell Common 18
Horsham Museum & Art Gallery 210
Horton Bridge 85
Houghton Bridge 204
Houses of Parliament 194
Hungerford 92-94, 96
Huntworth 32, 38
Hurley 155, 164
Hurlingham House 191

Icknield Way 126
Ifold 211
Imax Theatre 64
Inglesham 128, 130
Inglesham Round House 130
Inland Waterways Assocation 17
Isfield 122
Isleworth Ait 184

Isle of Dogs 200
Isleworth 187

Jane Austen Centre 72
Jessop, William 41, 59, 110
Jubilee River, The 172

Kelmscott 131
Kelmscott Manor 131
Kelston Park 66, 69
Kennedy Memorial 174
Kennet & Avon Canal 17, 32, 34, 41, 58-109, 158
Kennet & Avon Canal Trust 78, 84
Kennington Railway Bridge 140
Kenton 52
Kew 190
Kew Bridge 190
Kew Railway Bridge 190
Keynsham 66, 67
Keynsham Lock 66
Killerton House 56
Kiln Bridge 22
King, Hugh Locke 18
King John's Castle 21
King's Arms 49
King's Lock 137
King's Meadow 158
Kingston 170
Kingston upon Thames 183
Kintbury 96, 97
Knaphill 22
Knightshayes Court 44

Lady's Bridge 88
Laffan's Plain 26
Lakeside Park 26
Laleham 177, 178
Laleham Abbey 177
Lambeth Bridge 197
Lammas Lands 227
Lansdown Hill 84
Lapwing 52
Lardon Chase 154
Latton 80, 81
Lechlade-on-Thames 128-131
Leith Hill Place 217
Leith Hill Tower 217
Lewes 110, 111, 116-121
Lewis Carroll's Grave 226
Limehouse Basin 200
Limpley Stoke 58, 73
Little Bedwyn 92, 94
Little Faringdon Mill 130
Little Wittenham Wood 148, 150
Living Rainforest 100
Lock Inn Cottage 78

St Nicholas Church 100
St Nicholas Church, Afold 211
St Nicholas School 100
St Patrick's Stream 158, 161
St Peter's Church, Ash 26
St Peter's Church, Oxon 150
St Peter and St Paul Church, Godalming 227
Saltford 67
Saltford Lock 66
Saltford Mead 66
Sampford Peverell 45, 46
Sandford Lock 140
Sapperton Tunnel 130
Savernake Forest 90
Saxon Church of St Lawrence 78
Seend Cleeve 80, 81
Seend Top Lock 80
Sells Green 80, 81
Semington 78, 80
Semington Locks 80
Send 222
Severn Estuary 60
Shakespeare Globe Museum 197
Shalford 216, 217
Shalford Meadows 226
Shalford Mill 217
Shamley Green 216
Sheldonian Theatre 142
Shelley's Walk 130
Shepperton 178
Shifford Lock 134
Shillingford 148, 150
Shiplake 164
Shiplake Lock 158
Shirehampton Park 60
Somerset 80
Somerset Brick and Tile Museum 40
Somerset Cricket Museum 36
Somerset House 194
Somerset Space Walk 33, 37
Somersetshire Coal Canal 74
Sonning 160
Sonning Lock 158
Sonning Village 158
South Bank Art Centre 196
South Downs Light Railway 208
South Stoke 152
Southampton 17
Southwark Bridge 197
Southwark Cathedral 197
Spring Lake 24
Staines-upon-Thames 175
Staines Bridge 175
Standard's Lock 28

Standlake 134
Stanlake Park Wine Estate 160
Stanley Spencer Gallery 169
Stanton Harcourt 136
Stanton St Bernard 86
Star and Garter Home 184
Starcross 50-52
SS Great Britain 65
Stoke Bridge 224
Stoke Lock 224
Stopham Bridge 206
Strawberry Hill 187
Streatley 154
Stroundwater Canal 130
Sulhamstead 104, 105
Sulhamstead Lock 104
Sunbury-on-Thames 177, 179
Sunbury Court Island 180
Surbiton 180
Surrey & Hampshire Canal Society 17
Sutton Courtenay 145, 146
Sutton Place 225
Swan Hotel 132
Swan Upping 146
Swift Ditch 127, 144
Swindon 80
Swineford 66, 67
Sydney Gardens 69
Syon Park 184, 187

Tacchi-Morris Museum 36
Tadpole 132, 133
Tadpole Bridge 132
Tagg's Island 170
Taplow 164
Tate Britain 193
Tate Modern 197
Taunton 34-36, 41
Taunton Road Bridge 38
Teddington 140, 178, 183
Teddington Lock and Weir 180
Temple Combe Woods 155
Temple Island 155, 164
Temple Lock 166
Temple, The 195
Thames & Severn Canal 128, 130
Thames Conservancy 106
Thames Ditton 180, 183
Thames Flood Barrier 201
Thames Lock 219, 220
Thames Path 128
Thatcham 102, 103
Theale 105, 106
Theale Swing Bridge 104
Thorne St Margaret 41

Tidcombe Bridge 42
Tidcombe Hall 42
Tiverton 41-45
Tiverton Castle 44
Tiverton Museum of Mid Devon Life 44
Tiverton Road Bridge 42, 45
Topsham 48-50, 54-56
Topsham Ferry 55
Tottenham House 90
Totterdown Basin 63
Tower Bridge 198
Tower of London 196
Town Bridge 227
Triggs Lock 222
Tull, Jethro 148
Turf Lock 49, 50
Twickenham 187
Tyle Mill 104, 105

Uckfield 123
Ufton Green 105
Ufton Swing Bridge 108
Undercroft, The 226
University Botanic Gardens 142
Unstead Lock 227
Up Nateley 17, 30
Upper Thames 130

Vale of Pewsey 88
Vauxhall Bridge 197
Victoria Art Gallery 72
Victoria Bridge 174
Victoria Embankment 194
Victoria Tower Gardens 193

Wadworth 84
Wales 60
Wallingford Bridge 148, 150
Wallingford Museum 150
Walsham Flood Gates 222
Walton-on-Thames 177, 178
Wandsworth 196
Wandsworth Bridge 193
Wargrave 160
Wargrave Marsh 158
Warleigh Manor 73
Warren Hill 158
Waterloo Bridge 197
Watermill Theatre & Restaurant 100
Watershed 65
Watling Street 126
Waytown Tunnel 45
Weald & Downland Open Air Museum 204
Weirs Mill Stream 140
West Byfleet 18
West Country 60
West London 188-191

West Mills 98
Westbury Farm 156
Westleigh 45, 46
Westminster Abbey 194
Westminster Bridge 197
Westonzoyland Pumping Station Museum of Steam Power and Land Drainage 40
Wey & Arun Canal Trust 212
Wey & Arun Junction Canal 202-216, 220
Wey & Goldaming Navigations 219-227
Wey Navigation 219, 220, 222-225
Weybridge 177-179, 220-221
Weybridge Town Lock 220
Wey-South Path 203, 205
Wharf Stream 137
Wharfenden Lake 24
Whipcott 45
Whitchurch-on-Thames 156
Widmead Lock 102
Wilcot 88
Wilton 90, 91
Wilton Windmill 91
Wiltshire & Berkshire Canal 80, 81
Wiltshire Heritage Museum 84
Wiltshire Wolds 82
Windsor 170-173
Windsor Castle 171, 172
Woking 17, 18, 22
Woking, Aldershot & Basingstoke Canal 17
Winkworth Arboretum 217
Woodborough Hill 85, 88
Woodclyffe Hall 160
Woodham 18
Woodham Junction 18, 24
Woodham Top Lock 18
Woolhampton 103
Woolhampton Park 103
Woolwich Green Lake 104
Wootton Rivers 85, 90, 91
Wootton Top Lock 90
World of Country Life 52
Wren, Christopher 155, 183
Wyke House 76, 79
Wytham Abbey 138
Wytham Great Wood 137
Wytham Hill 137, 138

Youngman, Pip 37

Loddon Lily (*Leucojum aestivum*) 161
Loddon Pondweed (*Potamogeton nodosus*) 161
London 17, 127, 128
London Bridge 197
London Eye 196
London Museum of Water & Steam 190
London Stone 175
Long Wittenham 146, 148
Lordings Aqueduct 209
Lots Road Power Station 193
Lowdwells 41, 42
Lowdwells Lock 45
Lower Basildon 154
Lower Foxhangers 82
Loxwood 211
Lutyens' Deanery Gardens 160
Lympstone 50, 52

Magna Carta Memorial 174, 175
Maidenhead 170, 172
Maidenhead Railway Bridge 172
Manley Bridge 42
Mapledurham 156, 157
Mapledurham House 156
Marble Hill Park 184, 187
Marlow 166-169
Marlow Suspension Bridge 166
Marsh Lane Bridge 63, 82
Marsh Lock 155
Maunsel Canal Centre 37
Medley Footbridge 137
Medmenham 155, 164
Mermaid Theatre 195
Microwood Museum 72
Millbank Tower 193
Millennium Bridge 197
Mongewell Park 152
Monkey Island 170, 172
Monument 195
Monument Bridge 18
Morris, William 130, 131
Mortlake 191
Moulsford 152, 153
Mud Dock 63
Museum of Costume 72
Museum of English Rural Life 109, 160
Musical Museum 190
Mytchett 24-27
Mytchett Lake 24, 26

National Maritime Museum 201
Nature Discovery Centre 102
Netham Lock 63
New Basingstoke Canal 17
Newbridge, Oxon 134, 135, 136
Newbridge, W.Sussex 209
New Cut 174
New Haw 220
New Mill 88, 89
New Thames Bridge 170
New Victoria Theatre 18
Newark Lock 222
Newark Priory 222
Newbridge 134, 135, 136
Newbury 17, 58, 96, 98-102
Newbury Lock 98
Newick 122
Nightingale, Florence 26
North Newton 36, 37
North Stoke 152
North Warnborough 30, 31
Northcott Theatre 56
Northmoor 134
Nuneham House 144
Nuneham Park 146
Nymans House 207

O2 Arena 201
Odiham 30, 31
Odiham Castle 30, 31
Offham 121
Okehampton 50
Old Billingsgate Market 195
Old Bodleian 142
Old Deer Park 184, 187
Old Monkey March Lock 102
Old Royal Naval College 201
Old Windsor 174
Onslow Bridge 224
Orfold Flood Lock 209
Osney Bridge 137, 140
Oxford 140-143
Oxford Canal 137
Oxford University Press Museum 142
Oxford v Cambridge Boat Race 188, 189, 191

Palace of Westminster 127
Pangbourne 156
Papercourt Lock 222
Parham House 208
Parvis Bridge 220
Pendon Museum 146
Penton Hook 177
Peters Tower 50
Petersham 187
Petworth 208
Petworth Cottage Museum 208
Petworth House 208
Pewsey 88, 89, 94
Phoenix Arts Centre 56
Piddinghoe 112-115
Pierce, Ruth 84

Pilgrims' Way 224
Pill 60, 61
Pinkerton, John 17
Pinkhill Lock 137
Pixey Mead 137
Plaistow 211
Platt's Eyot 180
Plumpton 121
Pondtail Bridges 28
Portishead 60
Portishead Dock 61
Portsmouth 17, 219
Postal and Courier Services 26
Postal Museum 72
Powderham 50-53
Powderham Castle 50, 52
Princes Hall 27
Pulborough 206, 208
Pulborough Brooks Nature Reserve 208
Pulteney Bridge 16, 71
Putney 192
Putney Bridge 189, 191
Pyestock Hill 28
Pyrford 222
Pyrford Lock 222
Pyrford Marina 222
Pyrford Place 222
Pyrford Village 222

Quarry Wood 166
Queen's Avenue Bridge 24, 27
Queen's House 201
Queen's Promenade 180

Radcott Lock 1132
Radley 146
Reading 58, 59, 98, 105-109, 156, 158-161
Reading Bridge 158
Reading Museum 108, 160
Reading Road South Bridge 28
Redcliffe Bascule Bridge 63
Redshank 52
Reed warbler 52
Remenham Wood 155
Rennie, John 32, 41, 58, 59, 74, 76, 78, 88
Richmond 184-187
Richmond Bridge 184, 187
Richmond half-tide Lock 184
Richmond Hill 184
Richmond Park 187
Richmond Theatre 187
River Avon 60, 69, 130
River Biss 76
River Dunn 92, 93
River Exe 45, 48
River Kennet 93, 96, 104, 108
River Loddon 158, 161

River Museum 109
River Parrett 32, 34, 38
River Thames 126-200
River Tone 32, 34, 36
River Wey 177, 219
River Wey Navigation 18, 220
Riverside Park 226
Riverside Valley Park 56
Rochdale Canal 69
Rock Bridge 43
Roe, A.V. 18
Roman Baths Museum 72
Rose Isle 140
Royal Albert Memorial Museum & Art Gallery 56
Royal Botanic Gardens, Kew 184, 190
Royal Corps of Transport 26
Royal Crescent 72
Royal Horticultural Society's Garden 222
Royal Logistic Corps Museum 26
Royal Observatory 201
Royal Photographic Society 72
Royal Pioneer Corps 26
Rudgwick 211
Run Common 216
Runnymeade 174, 175
Rushey Lock 132

St Catherine's Ferry 224
St Catherine's Sands 224
St George's Bristol 64
St James Church 36
St John's 22
St John's Bridge 130
St John's Church, Devizes 84
St John's Lock, River Thames 128
St John's Locks, Basingstoke Canal 22
St Katherine Dock 200
St Mary & All Saints Church, Dunsfold 214
St Mary Magdalene Church 36
St Mary Redcliffe 65
St Mary's Abbey 155
St Mary's Church, Barley Mow Bridge 28
St Mary's Church, Battersea 193
St Mary's Church, Bridgwater 39
St Mary's Church, Devizes 84
St Mary's Church, Pulborough 208
St Mary's Church, SW11 196
St Michael's Abbey 26